# GREAT DESTINY

THE RT. HON. SIR WINSTON CHURCHILL
K.G., O.M., C.H.

# GREAT
# DESTINY

*Sixty years of the memorable events in the
life of the man of the century recounted
in his own incomparable words*

Edited by F. W. Heath

G. P. PUTNAM'S SONS
NEW YORK

© 1962, 1965 BY ODHAMS PRESS LIMITED, LONDON

FIRST AMERICAN EDITION, 1965

Library of Congress Catalog
Card Number: 65-14193

# ACKNOWLEDGMENTS

Selections from the following works are used by permission of Charles Scribner's Sons: AMID THESE STORMS (Copyright 1932 Charles Scribner's Sons; renewal copyright © 1960 Winston S. Churchill); MY EARLY LIFE (published originally as A ROVING COMMISSION) (Copyright 1930 Charles Scribner's Sons; renewal copyright © 1958 Winston Churchill); MARLBOROUGH, HIS LIFE AND TIMES, Volumes 1, 2, 3, 4, 5 and 6 (Copyright 1933, 1934, 1935, 1936, 1937, 1938 Charles Scribner's Sons; renewal copyright © 1961, 1962 Winston S. Churchill); THE WORLD CRISIS (in 4 volumes) (Copyright 1923, 1927 Charles Scribner's Sons; renewal copyright 1951, 1955 Winston S. Churchill); THE UNKNOWN WAR; *The Eastern Front* (Copyright 1931 Charles Scribner's Sons; renewal copyright © 1959 Winston S. Churchill); THE AFTERMATH (Copyright 1929 Charles Scribner's Sons; renewal copyright © 1957 Winston S. Churchill).

Selections from the following works are used by permission of G. P. Putnam's Sons: GREAT CONTEMPORARIES (Copyright 1937, 1939 by Winston S. Churchill); STEP BY STEP (Copyright 1939 by Winston S. Churchill); BLOOD, SWEAT, AND TEARS (Copyright 1941 by Winston S. Churchill).

Selections from the following works are used by permission of Cassell and Co. Ltd., London: THE UNRELENTING STRUGGLE (Copyright 1942 by Cassell & Co. Ltd., London); THE END OF THE BEGINNING (Copyright 1943 by Cassell & Co. Ltd., London); ONWARDS TO VICTORY (Copyright 1944 by Cassell & Co. Ltd., London).

THE SINEWS OF PEACE was published in the United States by Houghton Mifflin Company.

# CONTENTS

CONTENTS

# THE VOICE OF COURAGE

# ILLUSTRATIONS

#### PHOTOGRAPHS

Nos. 1, 2, 15, 16, 20, 21: *Paul Popper Limited*, London.
Nos. 3, 4, 5, 6, 7, 8, 9, 13, 14, 19, 23: *Radio Times Hulton
Picture Library*, London. Nos. 10, 12, 18: *Keystone Press
Agency*, New York. Nos. 17, 22: *London Daily Express*.

# INTRODUCTION

THIS book consists of extracts from all Sir Winston Churchill's books, with the exception of the six volumes of *The Second World War* and *A History of the English-speaking Peoples*, together with some of his most famous speeches, either in full or condensed, since so many of these are historic and have passed into our language.

The plan and purpose of the book has been to select such passages of varying length as will show the high quality of Sir Winston Churchill's prose and, at the same time, to present the history of his life, activities and achievements as he himself has recorded them.

No other statesman in this or any other country has ever written such complete, authoritative and intensely personal accounts not only of his own life and career but of the history of his country in peace and war over so long a period of time. As the holder of many high offices of state in the First World War, and as the most famous of all our Prime Ministers in the Second, he produced long personal histories which have become classics and permanent and indispensable source books for all military historians and students of war.

Destiny had indeed played its decisive part in Sir Winston Churchill's chequered career when he became Prime Minister in 1940, for the whole of his life, with its successes, failures, frustrations and humiliations, had been one long preparation for the holding of a supreme position of power and influence and for the execution of a tremendous task. The great hour of national danger and the many grave crises so soon to follow were, under Providence, matched by a great man of superb and incomparable genius and of unconquerable courage.

As an author Sir Winston Churchill's writings are, within their own sphere, unique, for with two exceptions they are all based upon his personal experiences. They cover a period of nearly sixty years, ranging as they do from his despatches as a war correspondent in his early twenties to the six volumes of his history of the Second World War completed in his late seventies.

Sir Winston Churchill wrote that "the history of the human race is war" and Clausewitz, the famous German military historian, declared that, "War is the prolongation of politics by other means." In essence and implication both statements have a terrible significance; but looking back over the long world history of human conflicts it is impossible to deny the broad truth of both.

The whole of Sir Winston Churchill's life and career was devoted to politics and war. His intense interest as a child in collecting and playing with toy soldiers persuaded his father, Lord Randolph Churchill, that the Army was obviously his son's career, and, after a struggle, he passed into Sandhurst at a third attempt. This book, therefore, is almost entirely an anthology of politics and war. The books that still stand the test of time are all devoted to these two main subjects with the exception, of course, of *My Early Life* which is accepted as one of the best autobiographies in the language. But even this autobiography provides much intimate information about war and politics.

In order to follow the development of Sir Winston Churchill's work as a military historian and as a biographer—for it is in these two spheres of authorship that he achieved enduring fame—it is necessary to remember how much he owed to his experiences as a war correspondent at a very early age. It was these experiences that enabled him to write *The Story of the Malakand Field Force*, a brilliant account of the campaign under General Sir Bindon Blood against the rebellion of the tribe of the Mamunds on the North West Frontier of India. This was the first book to reveal Sir Winston Churchill's great gifts as a military historian. This was followed by *The River War*, a very personal account of Lord Kitchener's campaign against the Mahdi and the re-conquest of the Sudan. This book contains the account of Sir Winston Churchill's own part in the Battle of Omdurman as leader of a troop of the 21st Lancers. *The River War* was highly praised and further established his reputation as a military historian. It remains the best book written on the Sudan campaign.

He had not long to wait for another war, this time in South Africa. In this war the authorities intervened and would not allow him the privilege he had previously enjoyed of serving as an officer and also acting as a war correspondent. He dealt with this problem by obtaining a roving commission with the South African Light

Horse. By this means he knew much of what was happening, as his books *London to Ladysmith via Pretoria* and *Ian Hamilton's March* (based upon his despatches to the *Morning Post*) clearly show. By a strange coincidence the Boer War gave him world-wide recognition as the result of his capture by and escape from the Boers, and of this experience he wrote an exciting and unforgettable account. After the end of the Boer War he entered politics as Conservative member for Oldham and later joined the Liberal Party for a time. The wars were over until 1914.

During this period of peace he wrote the life of his father, *Lord Randolph Churchill*, now generally acclaimed as one of the best of political biographies. It was written out of deep affection for, and intense loyalty to, his father. Perhaps because of this, which clearly inspired the excellence of this writing, some critics have said that Sir Winston Churchill never produced a better book. But to others this praise may seem excessive.

Peace prompted no other major work, but the First World War did so: the production of *The World Crisis*, *The Aftermath* and *The Eastern Front*, from which more extracts are taken in this anthology than from any other books. His personal record of the First World War read in conjunction with his personal record of the Second have secured for Sir Winston Churchill an unassailable position among the greatest of all military historians.

This high assessment is also based upon *Marlborough, His Life and Times*, written during the author's years out of office from 1929-1939. They have been described as the "years of his political wilderness". He was excluded from the Conservative government of the time because of certain personal political animosities and also because of his disagreements with the government on the contentious subjects of India, re-armament and appeasement. During this difficult and bitter period of his life Sir Winston Churchill wrote the four volumes of the life of his great ancestor, John Churchill, first Duke of Marlborough. No one was better placed and fitted to write this biography of a great man whose career and achievements were wholly concerned with politics and war. In spite of certain criticisms to the effect that the author took too loyal and partisan a view of the Duke of Marlborough in describing some of his activities and general be-

13

haviour which were questionable, the biography will remain the standard work on its subject.

In this period of partial political eclipse he continued in the House of Commons to attack the Government in a ruthless and fearless manner from his famous seat below the gangway. He had then time to engage in journalism, of which craft he was always a master. Some of the articles he then wrote in various newspapers and periodicals were later published in such books as *Thoughts and Adventures, Great Contemporaries* and *Step by Step*. The last of these has become historical, for in it are recorded his trenchant warnings, which fell upon deaf ears, of the dangers of German re-armament, and his frightening forecasts of the coming of another world war which in due course proved to be only too true. Such is destiny that in a very short time he became once again First Lord of the Admiralty, and then Prime Minister, to "ride the whirlwind and direct the storm" of the Second World War.

F. W. HEATH

# EARLY YEARS

# MY EARLY LIFE

*This famous autobiography covers the first twenty-five years of the author's life. It shows, as the author says, "the point of view appropriate to my years, whether as a child, a schoolboy, a cadet, a subaltern, a war correspondent, or a youthful politician". The book was first published in 1930 and contains brief accounts of some military campaigns on which he had already written books thirty years before. Extracts from these books will be found under their titles.*

IT WAS at "The Little Lodge"[1] I was first menaced with Education. The approach of a sinister figure described as "the Governess" was announced. Her arrival was fixed for a certain day. In order to prepare for this day Mrs. Everest[2] produced a book called *Reading without Tears*. It certainly did not justify its title in my case. I was made aware that before the Governess arrived I must be able to read without tears. We toiled each day. My nurse pointed with a pen at the different letters. I thought it all very tiresome. Our preparations were by no means completed when the fateful hour struck and the Governess was due to arrive. I did what so many oppressed peoples have done in similar circumstances: I took to the woods. I hid in the extensive shrubberies—forests they seemed—which surrounded "The Little Lodge". Hours passed before I was retrieved and handed over to "the Governess". We continued to toil every day, not only at letters but at words, and also at what was much worse, figures. Letters after all had only got to be known, and when they stood together in a certain way one recognized their formation and that it meant a certain sound or word which one uttered when pressed sufficiently. But the figures were tied into all sorts of tangles and did things to one another which it was extremely difficult to forecast with complete accuracy. You had to say what

[1] The home of Lord Randolph Churchill in Dublin when he acted as Secretary to his father, the Duke of Marlborough, the Viceroy.
[2] His nurse.

they did each time they were tied up together, and the Governess apparently attached enormous importance to the answer being exact. If it was not right it was wrong. It was not any use being "nearly right". In some cases these figures got into debt with one another: you had to borrow one or carry one, and afterwards you had to pay back the one you had borrowed. These complications cast a steadily gathering shadow over my daily life. They took one away from all the interesting things one wanted to do in the nursery or in the garden. They made increasing inroads upon one's leisure. One could hardly get time to do any of the things one wanted to do. They became a general worry and preoccupation. More especially was this true when we descended into a dismal bog called "sums". There appeared to be no limit to these. When one sum was done, there was always another. Just as soon as I managed to tackle a particular class of these afflictions, some other much more variegated type was thrust upon me.

My mother took no part in these impositions, but she gave me to understand that she approved of them and she sided with the Governess almost always. My picture of her in Ireland is in a riding habit, fitting like a skin and often beautifully spotted with mud. She and my father hunted continually on their large horses; and sometimes there were great scares because one or the other did not come back for many hours after they were expected.

My mother always seemed to me a fairy princess: a radiant being possessed of limitless riches and power. She shone for me like the Evening Star. I loved her dearly—but at a distance.

Mr. Gladstone was a very dangerous man who went about rousing people up, lashing them into fury so that they voted against the Conservatives and turned my grandfather out of his place as Lord-Lieutenant of Ireland. He liked this place much less than his old office of Lord President of the Council, which he had held in Lord Beaconsfield's previous Government. When he was Lord-Lieutenant he had to spend all his money on giving entertainments to the Irish in Dublin; and my grandmother had also got up a great subscription called "The Famine Fund". However, it was borne in upon me that the Irish were a very ungrateful people: they did not say so much as "Thank you" for the entertainments, nor even for

"The Famine Fund". The Duke would much rather have stayed in England where he could live in his own home at Blenheim and regularly attend the Cabinet. But he always did whatever Lord Beaconsfield told him to do. Lord Beaconsfield was the great enemy of Mr. Gladstone, and everybody called him "Dizzy". However, this time "Dizzy" had been thoroughly beaten by Mr. Gladstone, so we were all flung out into Opposition and the country began to be ruined very rapidly. Everyone said it was "going to the dogs". And then on top of all this Lord Beaconsfield got very ill. He had a long illness; and as he was also very old, it killed him. I followed his illness from day to day with great anxiety, because everyone said what a loss he would be to his country and how no one else could stop Mr. Gladstone from working his wicked will upon us all. I was always sure Lord Beaconsfield was going to die, and at last the day came when all the people I saw went about with very sad faces because, as they said, a great and splendid statesman, who loved our country and defied the Russians, had died of a broken heart because of the ingratitude with which he had been treated by the Radicals.

I have already described the dreaded apparition in my world of "the Governess". But now a much worse peril began to threaten. I was to go to school. I was now seven years old, and I was what grown-up people in their offhand way called "a troublesome boy". It appeared that I was to go away from home for many weeks at a stretch in order to do lessons under masters. The term had already begun, but still I should have to stay seven weeks before I could come home for Christmas. Although much that I had heard about school had made a distinctly disagreeable impression on my mind, an impression, I may add, thoroughly borne out by the actual experience, I was also excited and agitated by this great change in my life. I thought in spite of the lessons, it would be fun living with so many other boys, and that we should make friends together and have great adventures. Also I was told that "school days were the happiest time in one's life". Several grown-up people added that in their day, when they were young, schools were very rough: there was bullying, they didn't get enough to eat, they had "to break the ice in their pitchers" each morning (a thing I have never seen done in my life). But now it was all changed. School life nowadays was one long treat. All the boys enjoyed it. Some of my cousins who were a little older had been quite sorry—I was told—to come home for the holidays. Cross-examined, the cousins did not confirm this; they only grinned. Anyhow I was perfectly helpless. Irresistible tides drew me swiftly forward. I was no more consulted about leaving home than I had been about coming into the world.

The school my parents had selected for my education was one of the most fashionable and expensive in the country. It modelled itself upon Eton and aimed at being preparatory for that public school above all others. It was supposed to be the very last thing in schools. Only ten boys in a class; electric light (then a wonder); a swimming pond; spacious football and cricket grounds; two or three school treats, or "expeditions" as they were called, every term; the masters all M.A.s in gowns and mortar-boards; a chapel of its own; no hampers allowed; everything provided by the authorities. It was a dark November afternoon when we arrived at this establishment. We had tea with the headmaster, with whom my mother conversed in the most easy manner. I was preoccupied with the fear of spilling my cup and so making "a bad start". I was also miserable at the idea of being left alone among all these strangers in this great, fierce, formidable place. After all I was only seven, and I had been so happy in my nursery with all my toys. I had such wonderful toys: a real steam engine, a magic lantern, and a collection of soldiers already nearly a thousand strong. Now it was to be all lessons. Seven or eight hours of lessons every day except half-holidays, and football or cricket in addition.

When the last sound of my mother's departing wheels had died away, the headmaster invited me to hand over any money I had in my possession. I produced my three half-crowns, which were duly entered in a book, and I was told that from time to time there would be a "shop" at the school with all sorts of things which one would like to have, and that I could choose what I liked up to the limit of the seven and sixpence. Then we quitted the headmaster's parlour and the comfortable private side of the house, and entered the more bleak apartments reserved for the instruction and accommodation of the pupils. I was taken into a Form Room and told to sit at a desk. All the other boys were out of doors, and I was alone with the Form Master. He produced a thin greeny-brown covered book filled with words in different types of print.

"You have never done any Latin before, have you?" he said.

"No, sir."

"This is a Latin grammar." He opened it at a well-thumbed page. "You must learn this," he said, pointing to a number of words in a frame of lines. "I will come back in half an hour and see what you know."

Behold me then on a gloomy evening, with an aching heart, seated in front of the First Declension.

| Mensa | a table |
|-------|---------|
| Mensa | O table |
| Mensam | a table |
| Mensae | of a table |
| Mensae | to or for a table |
| Mensa | by, with or from a table |

What on earth did it mean? Where was the sense in it? It seemed absolute rigmarole to me. However, there was one thing I could always do: I could learn by heart. And I thereupon proceeded, as far as my private sorrows would allow, to memorize the acrostic-looking task which had been set me.

In due course the master returned.

"Have you learnt it?" he asked.

"I think I can *say* it, sir," I replied; and I gabbled it off.

He seemed so satisfied with this that I was emboldened to ask a question.

"What does it mean, sir?"

"It means what it says. Mensa, a table. Mensa is a noun of the First Declension. There are five Declensions. You have learnt the singular of the First Declension."

"But," I repeated, "what does it mean?"

"Mensa means a table," he answered.

"Then why does mensa also mean O table," I inquired, "and what does O table mean?"

"Mensa, O table, is the vocative case," he replied.

21

"But why O table?" I persisted in genuine curiosity.

"O table—you would use that in addressing a table, in invoking a table." And then seeing he was not carrying me with him, "You would use it in speaking to a table."

"But I never do," I blurted out in honest amazement.

"If you are impertinent, you will be punished, and punished, let me tell you, very severely," was his conclusive rejoinder.

Such was my first introduction to the classics from which, I have been told, many of our cleverest men have derived so much solace and profit.

The Form Master's observations about punishment were by no means without their warrant at St. James's School. Flogging with the birch in accordance with the Eton fashion was a great feature in its curriculum. But I am sure no Eton boy, and certainly no Harrow boy of my day, ever received such a cruel flogging as this headmaster was accustomed to inflict upon the little boys who were in his care and power. They exceeded in severity anything that would be tolerated in any of the Reformatories under the Home Office. My reading in later life has supplied me with some possible explanations of his temperament. Two or three times a month the whole school was marshalled in the Library, and one or more delinquents were haled off to an adjoining apartment by the two head boys, and there flogged until they bled freely, while the rest sat quaking, listening to their screams. This form of correction was strongly reinforced by frequent religious services of a somewhat High Church character in the chapel.

How I hated this school, and what a life of anxiety I lived there for more than two years. I made very little progress at my lessons, and none at all at games. I counted the days and the hours to the end of every term, when I should return home from this hateful servitude and range my soldiers in line of battle on the nursery floor. The greatest pleasure I had in those days was reading. When I was nine and a half my father gave me *Treasure Island*, and I remember the delight with which I devoured it. My teachers saw me at once backward and precocious, reading books beyond my years and yet at the bottom of the Form. They were offended. They had large resources of compulsion at their disposal, but I was stubborn. Where my reason, imagination or interest were not engaged, I would not or I could not learn. In all the twelve years I was at school no one ever succeeded in making me write a Latin verse or learn any Greek except the alphabet. I do not at all excuse myself for this foolish neglect of opportunities procured at so much expense by my parents and brought so forcibly to my attention by my preceptors. Perhaps if I had been introduced to the ancients through their history and customs, instead of through their grammar and syntax, I might have had a better record.

I fell into a low state of health at St. James's School, and finally after a serious illness my parents took me away. Our family doctor, the celebrated Robson Roose, then practised at Brighton; and as I was now supposed to be very delicate, it was thought desirable that I should be under his constant care. I was accordingly, in 1883, transferred to a school at Brighton kept by two ladies. This was a smaller school than the one I had left. It was also cheaper and less pretentious. But there was an element of kindness and of sympathy which I had found conspicuously lacking in my first experiences. Here I remained for three years; and though I very nearly died from an attack of double pneumonia, I got gradually much stronger in that bracing air and gentle surroundings. At this school I was allowed to learn things which interested me: French, history, lots of poetry by heart, and above all riding and swimming. The impression of those years makes a pleasant picture in my mind, in strong contrast to my earlier schoolday memories.

I had scarcely passed my twelfth birthday when I entered the inhospitable regions of examinations, through which for the next seven years I was destined to journey. These examinations were a great trial to me. The subjects which were dearest to the examiners were almost invariably those I fancied least. I would have liked to have been examined in history, poetry and writing essays. The examiners, on the other hand, were partial to Latin and mathematics. And their will prevailed. Moreover, the questions which they asked on both these subjects were almost invariably those to which I was unable to suggest a satisfactory answer. I should have liked to be asked to say what I knew. They always tried to ask what I did not know. When I would have willingly displayed my knowledge, they sought to expose my ignorance. This sort of treatment had only one result: I did not do well in examinations.

This was especially true of my Entrance Examination to Harrow. The headmaster, Mr. Welldon, however, took a broad-minded view of my Latin prose: he showed discernment in judging my general ability. This was the more remarkable, because I was found unable to answer a single question in the Latin paper. I wrote my name at the top of the page. I wrote down the number of the question "I". After much reflection I put a bracket round it thus "(I)". But thereafter I could not think of anything connected with it that was either relevant or true. Incidentally there arrived from nowhere in particular a blot and several smudges. I gazed for two whole hours at this sad spectacle: and then merciful ushers collected my piece of foolscap with all the others and carried it up to the headmaster's table. It was from these slender indications of scholarship that Mr. Welldon drew the conclusion that I was worthy to pass into Harrow. It is very much to his credit. It showed that he was a man capable of looking beneath the surface of things: a man not dependent upon paper manifestations. I have always had the greatest regard for him.

In consequence of his decision, I was in due course placed in the third, or lowest, division of the Fourth, or bottom, Form. The names of the new boys were printed in the School List in alphabetical order; and as my correct name, Spencer-Churchill, began with an "S", I gained no more advantage from the alphabet than from the wider sphere of letters. I was in fact only two from the bottom of the whole school; and these two, I regret to say, disappeared almost immediately through illness or some other cause.

The Harrow custom of calling the roll is different from that of Eton. At Eton the boys stand in a cluster and lift their hats when their names are called. At Harrow they file past a master in the schoolyard and answer one by one. My position was therefore revealed in its somewhat invidious humility. It was the year 1887. Lord Randolph Churchill had only just resigned his position as Leader of the House of Commons and Chancellor of the Exchequer, and he still towered in the forefront of politics. In consequence large numbers of visitors of both sexes used to wait on the school steps, in order to see me march by; and I frequently heard the irreverent comment, "Why, he's last of all!"

I continued in this unpretentious situation for nearly a year. However, by being so long in the lowest form I gained an immense advantage over the cleverer boys. They all went on to learn Latin and Greek and splendid things like that. But I was taught English. We were considered such dunces that we could learn only English. Mr. Somervell—a most delightful man, to whom my debt is great—was charged with the duty of teaching the stupidest boys the most disregarded thing—namely, to write mere English. He knew how to do it. He taught it as no one else has ever taught it. Not only did we learn English parsing thoroughly, but we also practised continually English analysis. Mr. Somervell had a system of his own. He took a fairly long sentence and broke it up into its components by means of black, red, blue and green inks. Subject, verb, object: Relative Clauses, Conditional Clauses, Conjunctive and Disjunctive Clauses! Each had its colour and its bracket. It was a kind of drill. We did it almost daily. As I remained in the Third Fourth ($\beta$) three times as long as anyone else, I had three times as much of it. I learned it thoroughly. Thus I got into my bones the essential structure of the ordinary British sentence—which is a noble thing. And when in after years my schoolfellows who had won prizes and distinction for writing such beautiful Latin poetry and pithy Greek epigrams had to come down again to common English, to earn their living or make their way, I did not feel myself at any disadvantage. Naturally I am biased in favour of boys learning English. I would make them all learn English: and then I would let the clever ones learn Latin as an honour, and Greek as a treat. But the only thing I would whip them for is not knowing English. I would whip them hard for that.

I first went to Harrow in the summer term. The school possessed the biggest swimming-bath I had ever seen. It was more like the bend of a river than a bath, and it had two bridges across it. Thither we used to repair for hours at a time, and bask between our dips, eating enormous buns, on the hot asphalt margin. Naturally it was a good joke to come up behind some naked friend, or even enemy, and push him in. I made quite a habit of this with boys of my own size or less. One day when I had been no more than a month in the school, I saw a boy standing in a meditative posture wrapped in a towel on the very brink. He was no bigger than I was, so I thought him fair game. Coming stealthily behind, I pushed him in, holding on to his towel out of humanity, so that it should not get wet. I was startled to see a furious face emerge from the foam, and a being evidently of enormous strength making its way by fierce strokes to the shore. I fled; but in vain. Swift as the wind my pursuer overtook me, seized me in a ferocious grip and hurled me into the deepest part of the pool. I soon scrambled out on the other side, and found myself surrounded by an agitated crowd of younger boys. "You're in for it," they said. "Do you know what you have done? It's Amery; he's in the Sixth Form. He is Head of his House; he is champion at Gym; he has got his football colours." They continued to recount his many titles to fame and reverence, and to dilate upon the awful retribution that would fall upon me. I was convulsed not only with terror, but with the guilt of sacrilege. How could I tell his rank when he was in a bath-towel and so small? I determined to apologize immediately. I approached the potentate in lively trepidation. "I am very sorry," I said. "I mistook you for a Fourth Form boy. You are so small." He did not seem at all placated by this; so I added in a most brilliant recovery, "My father, who is a great man, is also small." At this he laughed, and after some general remarks about my "cheek" and how I had better be careful in the future, signified that the incident was closed.

I have been fortunate to see a good deal more of him, in times when three years' difference in age is not so important as it is at school. We were afterwards to be Cabinet colleagues for a good many years.

It was thought incongruous that while I apparently stagnated in the lowest form, I should gain a prize open to the whole school for reciting to the headmaster twelve hundred lines of Macaulay's "Lays of Ancient Rome" without making a single mistake. I also succeeded in passing the preliminary examination for the Army while still almost at the bottom of the school. This examination seemed to have called forth a very special effort on my part, for many boys far above me in the school failed in it. I also had a piece of good luck. We knew that among other questions we should be asked to draw from memory a map of some country or other. The night before by way of final preparation I put the names of all the maps in the atlas into a hat and drew out New Zealand. I applied my good memory to the geography of that Dominion. Sure enough the first question in the paper was: "Draw a map of New Zealand". This was what is called at Monte Carlo an *en plein*, and I ought to have been paid thirty-five times my stake. However, I certainly got paid very high marks for my paper.

I was now embarked on a military career. This orientation was entirely due to my collection of soldiers. I had ultimately nearly fifteen hundred. They were all of one size, all British, and organized as an infantry division with a cavalry brigade. My brother Jack commanded the hostile army. But by a Treaty for the Limitation of Armaments he was only allowed to have coloured troops; and they were not allowed to have artillery. Very important! I could muster myself only eighteen field-guns—besides fortress pieces. But all the other services were complete—except one. It is what every army is always short of—transport. My father's old friend, Sir Henry Drummond Wolff, admiring my array, noticed this deficiency and provided a fund from which it was to some extent supplied.

The day came when my father himself paid a formal visit of inspection. All the troops were arranged in the correct formation of attack. He spent twenty minutes studying the scene—which was really impressive—with a keen eye and captivating smile. At the end he asked me if I would like to go into the Army. I thought it would be splendid to command an army, so I said "Yes" at once: and immediately I was taken at my word. For years I thought my father with his experience and flair had discerned in me the qualities of military genius. But I was told later that he had only come to the conclusion that I was not clever enough to go to the Bar. However that may be, the toy soldiers turned the current of my life. Henceforward all my education was directed to passing into Sandhurst, and afterwards to the technical details of the profession of arms. Anything else I had to pick up for myself.

I spent nearly four and a half years at Harrow, of which three were in the Army class. To this I was admitted in consequence of having passed the preliminary examination. It consisted of boys of the middle and higher forms of the school and of very different ages, all of whom were being prepared either for the Sandhurst or the Woolwich examination. We were withdrawn from the ordinary movement of the school from form to form. In consequence I got no promotion or very little, and remained quite low down upon the School List, though working alongside of boys nearly all in the Fifth Form. Officially I never got out of the Lower School, so I never had the privilege of having a fag of my own. When in the passage of time I became what was called "a three-yearer", I ceased to have to fag myself, and as I was older than other boys of my standing, I was appointed in my House to the position of Head of the Fags. This was my first responsible office, and the duties, which were honorary, consisted in keeping the roster of all the fags, making out the list of their duties and dates and placing copies of these lists in the rooms of the monitors, football and cricket champions and other members of our aristocracy. I discharged these functions for upwards of a year, and on the whole I was resigned to my lot.

Meanwhile I found an admirable method of learning my Latin translations. I was always very slow at using a dictionary: it was just like using a telephone directory. It is easy to open it more or less at the right letter, but then you have to turn backwards and forwards and peer up and down the columns and very often find yourself three or four pages the wrong side of the word you want. In short, I found it most laborious, while to other boys it seemed no trouble. But now I formed an alliance with a boy in the Sixth Form. He was very clever and could read Latin as easily as English. Caesar, Ovid, Virgil, Horace and even Martial's epigrams were all the same to him. My daily task was perhaps ten or fifteen lines. This would ordinarily have taken me an hour or an hour and a half to decipher, and then it would probably have been wrong. But my friend could in five minutes construe it for me word by word, and once I had seen it exposed, I remembered it firmly. My Sixth-Form friend for his part was almost as much troubled by the English essays he had to write for the headmaster as I was by these Latin crossword puzzles. We agreed together that he should tell me my Latin translations and that I should do his essays. The arrangement worked admirably. The Latin master seemed quite satisfied with my work, and I had more time to myself in the mornings. On the other hand once a week or so I had to compose the essays of my Sixth-Form friend. I used to walk up and down the room dictating—just as I do now—

and he sat in the corner and wrote it down in long-hand. For several months no difficulty arose; but once we were nearly caught out. One of these essays was thought to have merit. It was "sent up" to the headmaster, who summoned my friend, commended him on his work and proceeded to discuss the topic with him in a lively spirit. "I was interested in this point you make here. You might, I think, have gone even further. Tell me exactly what you had in your mind." Mr. Welldon in spite of very chilling responses continued in this way for some time, to the deep consternation of my confederate. However, the headmaster, not wishing to turn an occasion of praise into one of cavilling, finally let him go with the remark "You seem to be better at written than at oral work". He came back to me like a man who has had a very narrow squeak, and I was most careful ever afterwards to keep to the beaten track in essay-writing.

I will here make some general observations about Latin which probably have their application to Greek as well. In a sensible language like English important words are connected and related to one another by other little words. The Romans in that stern antiquity considered such a method weak and unworthy. Nothing would satisfy them but that the structure of every word should be reacted on by its neighbours in accordance with elaborate rules to meet the different conditions in which it might be used. There is no doubt that this method both sounds and looks more impressive than our own. The sentence fits together like a piece of polished machinery. Every phrase can be tensely charged with meaning. It must have been very laborious even if you were brought up to it; but no doubt it gave the Romans, and the Greeks, too, a fine and easy way of establishing their posthumous fame. They were the first comers in the fields of thought and literature. When they arrived at fairly obvious reflections upon life and love, upon war, fate or manners, they coined them into the slogans or epigrams for which their language was so well adapted, and thus preserved the patent rights for all time. Hence their reputation. Nobody ever told me this at school. I have thought it all out in later life.

But even as a schoolboy I questioned the aptness of the Classics for the prime structure of our education. So they told me how Mr.

Gladstone read Homer for fun, which I thought served him right; and that it would be a great pleasure to me in after life. When I seemed incredulous, they added that Classics would be a help in writing or speaking English. They then pointed out the number of our modern words which are derived from the Latin or Greek. Apparently one could use these words much better, if one knew the exact source from which they had sprung. I was fain to admit a practical value. But now even this has been swept away. The foreigners and the Scotch have joined together to introduce a pronunciation of Latin which divorces it finally from the English tongue. They tell us to pronounce "audience" "owdience"; and "civil" "keyweel". They have distorted one of my most serviceable and impressive quotations into the ridiculous booby "Wainy, Weedy, Weeky". Punishment should be reserved for those who have spread this evil.

It took me three tries to pass into Sandhurst. There were five subjects, of which Mathematics, Latin and English were obligatory, and I chose in addition French and Chemistry. In this hand I held only a pair of Kings—English and Chemistry. Nothing less than three would open the jackpot. I had to find another useful card. Latin I could not learn. I had a rooted prejudice which seemed to close my mind against it. Two thousand marks were given for Latin. I might perhaps get four hundred! French was interesting but rather tricky, and difficult to learn in England. So there remained only Mathematics. After the first examination was over, when one surveyed the battlefield, it was evident that the war could not be won without another army being brought into the line. Mathematics was the only resource available. I turned to them—I turned on them—in desperation. All my life from time to time I have had to get up disagreeable subjects at short notice, but I consider my triumph, moral and technical, was in learning Mathematics in six months. At the first of these three ordeals I got no more than 500 marks out of 2,500 for Mathematics. At the second I got nearly 2,000. I owe this achievement not only to my own "back-to-the-wall" resolution—for which no credit is too great; but to the very kindly interest taken in my case by a much respected Harrow master, Mr. C. H. P. Mayo. He convinced me that Mathematics was not a hopeless bog of nonsense, and that there were meanings and rhythms behind the comical hieroglyphics; and that I was not incapable of catching glimpses of some of these.

Of course what I call Mathematics is only what the Civil Service Commissioners expected you to know to pass a very rudimentary examination. I suppose that to those who enjoy this peculiar gift, Senior Wranglers and the like, the waters in which I swam must seem only a duck-puddle compared to the Atlantic Ocean. Nevertheless, when I plunged in, I was soon out of my depth. When I look back upon those care-laden months, their prominent features rise from the abyss of memory. Of course I had progressed far beyond Vulgar Fractions and the Decimal System. We were arrived in an "Alice-in-Wonderland" world, at the portals of which stood "A Quadratic Equation". This with a strange grimace pointed the way to the Theory of Indices, which again handed on the intruder to the full rigours of the Binomial Theorem. Further dim chambers lighted by sullen, sulphurous fires were reputed to contain a dragon called the "Differential Calculus". But this monster was beyond the bounds appointed by the Civil Service Commissioners who regulated this stage of Pilgrim's heavy journey. We turned aside, not indeed to the uplands of the Delectable Mountains, but into a strange corridor of things like anagrams and acrostics called Sines, Cosines and Tangents. Apparently they were very important, especially when multiplied by each other, or by themselves! They had also this merit—you could learn many of their evolutions off by heart. There was a question in my third and last Examination about these Cosines and Tangents in a highly square-rooted condition which must have been decisive upon the whole of my after life. It was a problem. But luckily I had seen its ugly face only a few days before and recognized it at first sight.

The Unionist Government had been beaten, though only by forty, in the Summer Election of 1892 and Mr. Gladstone had taken office with the help of the Irish Nationalists. The new Parliament, having met to change the Administration, was in accordance with the wise and happy practice of those days prorogued for a six months' holiday. The Session of 1893 and the inevitable reopening of the Home Rule struggle were eagerly and anxiously awaited. Naturally our household had not been much grieved at the defeat of what my father had described as "a government and party which for five years have boycotted and slandered me". In fact our whole family with its many powerful branches and all his friends looked forward to the new situation with lively hope. It was thought that he would in Opposition swiftly regain the ascendancy in Parliament and in his party which had been destroyed by his resignation six years before.

No one cherished these hopes more ardently than I. Although in the past little had been said in my hearing, one could not grow up in my father's house, and still less among his mother and sisters, without understanding that there had been a great political disaster. Dignity and reticence upon this subject were invariably preserved before strangers, children and servants. Only once do I remember my father having breathed a word of complaint about his fortunes to me, and that for a passing moment. Only once did he lift his visor in my sight. This was at our house at Newmarket in the autumn of 1892. He had reproved me for startling him by firing off a double-barrelled gun at a rabbit which had appeared on the lawn beneath his windows. He had been very angry and disturbed. Understanding at once that I was distressed, he took occasion to reassure me. I then had one of the three or four long intimate conversations with him which are all I can boast. He explained how old people were not always very considerate towards young people, that they were absorbed in their own affairs and might well speak roughly in sudden annoyance. He said he was glad I liked shooting, and that he had arranged for me to shoot on 1 September (this was the end of August) such partridges as our small property contained. Then he proceeded to talk to me in the most wonderful and captivating manner about school and going into the Army and the grown-up life which lay beyond. I listened spellbound to this sudden complete departure from his usual reserve, amazed at his intimate comprehension of all my affairs. Then at the end he said, "Do remember things do not always go right with me. My every action is misjudged and every word distorted. . . . So make some allowances."

I became an absorbed spectator of Mr. Gladstone's last great Parliamentary battle. Indeed it far outweighed in my mind the

Blenheim, Winston Churchill's birthplace (30 November, 1874).
(*Below*) The green writing room with the Battle of Blenheim tapestry

Winston, aged seven

In 1889, with his mother
and brother Jack

dreaded examination—the last shot—which impended in August. As time wore on I could not help feeling that my father's speeches were not as good as they used to be. There were some brilliant successes: yet on the whole he seemed to be hardly holding his own. I hoped of course that I should grow up in time to come to his aid. I knew that he would have received such a suggestion with unaffected amusement; but I thought of Austen Chamberlain who was allowed to fight at his father's side, and Herbert Gladstone who had helped the Grand Old Man to cut down the oak trees and went everywhere with him, and I dreamed of days to come when Tory Democracy would dismiss the "Old Gang" with one hand and defeat the Radicals with the other.

During this year [1893] I met at my father's house many of the leading figures of the Parliamentary conflict, and was often at luncheon or dinner when across his table not only colleagues, but opponents, amicably interchanged opinions on the burning topics of the hour. It was then that I first met Mr. Balfour, Mr. Chamberlain, Mr. Edward Carson, and also Lord Rosebery, Mr. Asquith, Mr. John Morley and other fascinating ministerial figures. It seemed a very great world in which these men lived; a world where high rules reigned and every trifle in public conduct counted: a duelling-ground where although the business might be ruthless, and the weapons loaded with ball, there was ceremonious personal courtesy and mutual respect. But of course I saw this social side only when my father had either intimate friends or persons of high political consequence as his guests. I have heard that on neutral ground he was incredibly fierce, and affronted people by saying the most blunt or even savage things. Certainly those who did not know him well approached him with caution or heavily armed.

So soon as I was convalescent[1] I began to go to the House of Commons and listen to the great debates. I even managed to squeeze into the Distinguished Strangers' Gallery when Mr. Gladstone wound up the second reading of the Home Rule Bill. Well do I remember the scene and some of its incidents. The Grand Old Man looked like a great white eagle at once fierce and splendid. His sentences rolled forth majestically and everyone hung upon his lips and gestures, eager to cheer or deride. He was at the climax of a

---

[1] He had been seriously injured in a fall from a fir tree.

tremendous passage about how the Liberal Party had always carried every cause it had espoused to victory. He made a slip. "And there is no cause," he exclaimed (Home Rule), "for which the Liberal Party has suffered so much or *descended so low*." How the Tories leapt and roared with delight! But Mr. Gladstone, shaking his right hand with fingers spread claw-like, quelled the tumult and resumed, "But we have risen again. . . ."

I was also a witness of his celebrated tribute to Mr. Chamberlain on his son Austen's maiden speech. "I will not enter upon any elaborate eulogy of that speech. I will endeavour to sum up in a few words what I desire to say of it. It was a speech which must have been dear and refreshing to a father's heart." From where I crouched on the floor of the Gallery peering through the balustrade I could see the effect these words instantaneously produced on Mr. Chamberlain. He was hit as if a bullet had struck him. His pale almost sallow countenance turned pink with emotion he could not, or did not care to, restrain. He half rose and made a little bow, and then hunched himself up with lowered head. There does not seem to be much in these words, however well chosen, when they are written down. It was the way the thing was done that swept aside for a moment the irreparable enmities of years.

My brother and I were sent this summer by our parents for a so-called walking-tour in Switzerland, with a tutor. I need hardly say we travelled by train so far as the money lasted. The tutor and I climbed mountains. We climbed the Wetterhorn and Monte Rosa. The spectacle of the sunrise striking the peaks of the Bernese Oberland is a marvel of light and colour unsurpassed in my experience. I longed to climb the Matterhorn, but this was not only too expensive but held by the tutor to be too dangerous. All this prudence, however, might easily have been upset by an incident which happened to me in the lake of Lausanne. I record this incident that it may be a warning to others. I went for a row with another boy a little younger than myself. When we were more than a mile from the shore, we decided to have a swim, pulled off our clothes, jumped into the water and swam about in great delight. When we had had enough, the boat was perhaps one hundred yards away. A breeze had begun to stir the waters. The boat had a small red awning over its stern seats. This awning acted as a sail by catching the breeze. As we swam towards the boat, it drifted farther off. After this had happened several times we had perhaps halved the distance. But meanwhile the breeze was freshening and we both, especially my companion, began to be tired. Up to this point no idea of danger had crossed my mind. The sun played upon the sparkling blue waters; the wonderful panorama of mountains and valleys, the gay hotels and villas still smiled. But now I saw Death as near as I believe I have ever seen him. He was swimming in the water at our side, whispering from time to time in the rising wind which continued to carry the boat away from us at about the same speed we could swim. No help was near. Unaided we could never reach the shore. I was not only an easy, but a fast swimmer, having represented my House at Harrow, when our team defeated all comers. I now swam for life. Twice I reached within a yard of the boat and each time a gust carried it just beyond my reach; but by a supreme effort I caught hold of its side in the nick of time before a still stronger gust bulged the red awning again. I scrambled in, and rowed back for my companion who, though tired, had not apparently realized the dull yellow glare of mortal peril that had so suddenly played around us. I said nothing to the tutor about this serious experience, but I have never forgotten it; and perhaps some of my readers will remember it too.

My stay at the Royal Military College formed an intermediate period in my life. It brought to a close nearly twelve years of school. Thirty-six terms each of many weeks (interspersed with all-too-short holidays) during the whole of which I had enjoyed few gleams of success, in which I had hardly ever been asked to learn anything which seemed of the slightest use or interest, or allowed to play any game which was amusing. In retrospect these years form not only the least agreeable, but the only barren and unhappy period of my life. I was happy as a child with my toys in my nursery. I have been happier every year since I became a man. But this interlude of school makes a sombre grey patch upon the chart of my journey. It was an unending spell of worries that did not then seem petty, and of toil uncheered by fruition; a time of discomfort, restriction and purposeless monotony.

This train of thought must not lead me to exaggerate the character of my school days. Actually no doubt they were buoyed up by the laughter and high spirits of youth. Harrow was a very good school, and a high standard of personal service prevailed among its masters. Most of the boys were very happy, and many found in its classrooms and upon its playing-fields the greatest distinction they have ever known in life. I can only record the fact that, no doubt through my own shortcomings, I was an exception. I would far rather have been apprenticed as a bricklayer's mate, or run errands as a messenger boy, or helped my father to dress the front windows of a grocer's shop. It would have been real; it would have been natural; it would have taught me more; and I should have done it much better. Also I should have got to know my father, which would have been a joy to me.

Certainly the prolonged education indispensable to the progress of Society is not natural to mankind. It cuts against the grain. A boy would like to follow his father in pursuit of food or prey. He would like to be doing serviceable things so far as his utmost strength allowed. He would like to be earning wages however small to help to keep up the home. He would like to have some leisure of his own to use or misuse as he pleased. He would ask little more than the right to work or starve. And then perhaps in the evenings a real love of learning would come to those who were worthy—and why try to stuff it into those who are not?—and knowledge and thought would open the "magic casements" of the mind.

I was on the whole considerably discouraged by my school days. Except in Fencing, in which I had won the Public School Championship, I had achieved no distinction. All my contemporaries and even younger boys seemed in every way better adapted to the conditions of our little world. They were far better both at the games and at the lessons. It is not pleasant to feel oneself so completely outclassed and left behind at the very beginning of the race. I had been surprised on taking leave of Mr. Welldon to hear him predict, with a confidence for which I could see no foundation, that I should be able to make my way all right. I have always been very grateful to him for this.

I am all for the public schools but I do not want to go there again.

I enjoyed the riding-school [at Sandhurst] thoroughly, and got on—and off—as well as most. My father arranged in my holidays, or vacations as it was now proper to call them, for me to go through an additional course of riding-school at Knightsbridge Barracks with the Royal Horse Guards. I bit the tan there on numerous occasions. Afterwards when I joined my regiment I had another full five months' course, and taking them altogether, I think I was pretty well trained to sit and manage a horse. This is one of the most important things in the world.

Horses were the greatest of my pleasures at Sandhurst. I and the group in which I moved spent all our money on hiring horses from the very excellent local livery stables. We ran up bills on the strength of our future commissions. We organized point-to-points and even a steeplechase in the park of a friendly grandee, and bucketed gaily about the countryside. And here I say to parents, and especially to wealthy parents, "Don't give your son money. As far as you can afford it, give him horses." No one ever came to grief—except honourable grief—through riding horses. No hour of life is lost that is spent in the saddle. Young men have often been ruined through owning horses, · or through backing horses, but never through riding them; unless of course they break their necks, which, taken at a gallop, is a very good death to die.

I can see my father now in a somewhat different light from the days when I wrote his biography. I have long passed the age at which he died. I understand only too plainly the fatal character of his act of resignation. He was "the daring pilot in extremity". That was his hour. But conditions changed with the Unionist victory of 1886. Quiet times were required and political repose. Lord Salisbury represented to the nation what it needed and desired. He settled down heavily to a long steady reign. Naturally he was glad to have the whole power in his own hands, instead of dividing it with a restless rival, entrenched in the leadership of the House of Commons and the control of the public purse. It is never possible for a man to recover his lost position. He may recover another position in the fifties or sixties, but not the one he lost in the thirties or forties. To hold the leadership of a party or nation with dignity and authority require that the leader's qualities and message shall meet not only the need but the mood of both.

Moreover from the moment Lord Randolph Churchill became Chancellor of the Exchequer responsible in large measure for the affairs of the nation, he ceased in vital matters to be a Tory. He adopted with increasing zest the Gladstonian outlook, with the single exception of Irish Home Rule; and in all social and labour questions he was far beyond what the Whig or middle-class Liberal of that epoch could have tolerated. Even on Ireland his convictions were unusually independent. The Conservative Party would not have relished any of this. Indeed I think if he had lived to keep his health, it is more than likely that he would have resisted the South African War to an extent that would have exposed him to odium with the very working-class elements of whose goodwill he was so proud. His only real card of re-entry would have been to forestall Mr. Chamberlain's Protection campaign. Everything that I know suggests to me that he would far more likely have been one of its chief opponents. He was not the man to take his decisions from party caucuses. When he was faction-fighting he fought to win, seizing anything that came along. But when responsible, his contribution to public affairs was faithful and original. He never sat down to play a cold, calculated game. He said what he thought. It was better so.

Mr. Gladstone's reputation as an orator depends less upon his published speeches than upon the effect they produced at the time upon the audience. Lord Randolph Churchill's place in our political history is measured not by his words and actions, but by the impression which his personality made upon his contemporaries. This was intense, and had circumstances continued favourable, might well have manifested itself in decisive episodes. He embodied that force, caprice and charm which so often springs from genius.

Now that I have been reading over all the letters which he wrote to me laboriously with his own hand after the fashion of those days, I feel that I did not at the time appreciate how much he thought and cared for me. More than ever do I regret that we did not live long enough in company to know each other. I used to go to see Lord Rosebery in the later years of his life because, apart from the respect I bore this distinguished man, I loved to hear him talk about my father. I had a feeling of getting nearer to my father when I

talked with his intimate and illustrious friend. The last time I saw
Lord Rosebery I said how much I would have liked to roll back the
years, and talk about things with my father on even terms. The
aged statesman said in a wonderful way: "Ah! he'd have understood."

In my last term at Sandhurst—if the reader will permit a digression
—my indignation was excited by the Purity Campaign of Mrs.
Ormiston Chant. This lady was a member of the London County
Council and in the summer of 1894 she started an active movement
to purge our music-halls. Her attention was particularly directed
to the promenade of the Empire Theatre. This large space behind
the dress circle was frequently crowded during the evening performances, and especially on Saturdays, with young people of both
sexes, who not only conversed together during the performance and
its intervals, but also from time to time refreshed themselves with
alcoholic liquors. Mrs. Ormiston Chant and her friends made a
number of allegations affecting both the sobriety and the morals of
these merrymakers; and she endeavoured to procure the closing of
the promenade and above all of the bars which abutted on it. It
seemed that the majority of the English public viewed these matters
in a different light. Their cause was championed by the *Daily
Telegraph*, in those days our leading popular newspaper. In a series
of powerful articles headed "Prudes on the Prowl" the *Daily
Telegraph* inaugurated a wide and spirited correspondence to which
persons were wont to contribute above such pseudonyms as "Mother
of Five", "Gentleman and Christian", "Live and Let Live", "John
Bull" and so forth.

In this cause I was keenly anxious to strike a blow. I noticed one
day in the *Daily Telegraph* that a gentleman—whose name escapes
me—proposed to found a League of Citizens to resist and counter
the intolerance of Mrs. Chant and her backers. This was to be
called "The Entertainments Protection League". The League proposed to form committees and an executive, to take offices and
enrol members, to collect subscriptions, to hold public meetings,
and to issue literature in support of its views. I immediately volunteered my services. I wrote to the pious Founder at the address
which he had given, expressing my cordial agreement with his aims

and my readiness to co-operate in every lawful way. In due course I received an answer on impressively headed notepaper informing me that my support was welcomed, and inviting my attendance at the first meeting of the Executive Committee, which was to be held on the following Wednesday at six o'clock in a London hotel.

Wednesday was a half-holiday, and well-conducted cadets could obtain leave to go to London simply by asking for it. I occupied the three days' interval in composing a speech which I thought I might be called upon to deliver to a crowded executive of stern-faced citizens, about to unfurl that flag of British freedom for which "Hampden died on the battlefield and Sidney on the scaffold". As I had never attempted to speak in public before, it was a serious undertaking. I wrote and re-wrote my speech three or four times over, and committed it in all its perfection to my memory.

It was a serious constitutional argument upon the inherent rights of British subjects; upon the dangers of State interference with the social habits of law-abiding persons; and upon the many evil consequences which inevitably follow upon repression not supported by healthy public opinion. It did not overstate the case, nor was it blind to facts. It sought to persuade by moderation and good humour, and to convince by logic tempered with common sense. There was even in its closing phases an appeal for a patient mood towards our misguided opponents. Was there not always more error than malice in human affairs? This task completed I awaited eagerly and at the same time nervously the momentous occasion.

As soon as our morning tasks were done I gobbled a hasty luncheon, changed into plain clothes (we were taught to abhor the word "mufti", and such abominable expressions as "civvies" were in those days unknown) and hastened to the railway station, where I caught a very slow train to London. I must mention that this was for me a time of straitened finance; in fact the cost of the return railway ticket left me with only a few shillings in my pocket, and it was more than a fortnight before my next monthly allowance of £10 was due.

I whiled away the journey by rehearsing the points and passages on which I principally relied. I drove in a hansom cab from Waterloo to Leicester Square, near which the hotel appointed for the meeting of the Executive was situated. I was surprised and a little disconcerted at the dingy and even squalid appearance of these back streets and still more at the hotel when my cab eventually drew up before it. However, I said to myself, they are probably quite right to avoid the fashionable quarters. If this movement is to prosper it must be based upon the people's will; it must respond to those simple instincts which all classes have in common. It must not be compromised by association with gilded youth or smart society. To the porter I said: "I have come to attend the meeting of the Entertainments Protection League announced to be held this day in your hotel."

The porter looked rather puzzled, and then said: "I think there's a gentleman in the smoking-room about that." Into the smoking-room, a small dark apartment, I was accordingly shown, and there I met face to face the Founder of the new body. He was alone. I was upset; but concealing my depression under the fast-vanishing rays of hope, I asked: "When do we go up to the meeting?" He too seemed embarrassed. "I have written to several people, but they have none of them turned up, so there's only you and me. We can draw up the Constitution ourselves, if you like." I said: "But you wrote to me on the headed paper of the League." "Well," he said, "that only cost 5s. It's always a good thing to have a printed heading on your notepaper in starting these sort of things. It encourages people to come forward. You see it encouraged you!" He paused as if chilled by my reserve, then added: "It's very difficult to get people to do anything in England now. They take everything lying down. I do not know what's happened to the country; they seem to have no spirit left."

Nothing was to be gained by carrying the matter further and less than nothing by getting angry with the Founder of the League. So I bade him a restrained but decisive farewell, and walked out into the street with a magnificent oration surging within my bosom and only half a crown in my pocket.

I passed out of Sandhurst into the world. It opened like Aladdin's cave. From the beginning of 1895 down to the present time of writing I have never had time to turn round. I could count almost on my fingers the days when I have had nothing to do. An endless moving picture in which one was an actor. On the whole Great

Fun! But the years 1895 to 1900 which are the staple of this story exceed in vividness, variety and exertion anything I have known—except of course the opening months of the Great War.

When I look back upon them I cannot but return my sincere thanks to the high gods for the gift of existence. All the days were good and each day better than the other. Ups and downs, risks and journeys, but always the sense of motion, and the illusion of hope. Come on now all you young men, all over the world. You are needed more than ever now to fill the gap of a generation shorn by the war. You have not an hour to lose. You must take your places in life's fighting line. Twenty to twenty-five! These are the years! Don't be content with things as they are. "The earth is yours and the fulness thereof." Enter upon your inheritance, accept your responsibilities. Raise the glorious flags again, advance them upon the new enemies, who constantly gather upon the front of the human army, and have only to be assaulted to be overthrown. Don't take No for an answer. Never submit to failure. Do not be fobbed off with mere personal success or acceptance. You will make all kinds of mistakes; but as long as you are generous and true, and also fierce, you cannot hurt the world or even seriously distress her. She was made to be wooed and won by youth. She has lived and thrived only by repeated subjugations.

My father died on 24 January [1895] in the early morning. Summoned from a neighbouring house where I was sleeping, I ran in the darkness across Grosvenor Square, then lapped in snow. His end was quite painless. Indeed he had long been in stupor. All my dreams of comradeship with him, of entering Parliament at his side and in his support, were ended. There remained for me only to pursue his aims and vindicate his memory.

I was now in the main the master of my fortunes. My mother was always at hand to help and advise; but I was now in my twenty-first year and she never sought to exercise parental control. Indeed she soon became an ardent ally, furthering my plans and guarding my interests with all her influence and boundless energy. She was still at forty young, beautiful and fascinating. We worked together on even terms, more like brother and sister than mother and son. At least so it seemed to me. And so it continued to the end.

[In 1895] Mrs. Everest died. As soon as I heard she was seriously ill I travelled up to London to see her. She lived with her sister's family in North London. She knew she was in danger, but her only anxiety was for me. There had been a heavy shower of rain. My jacket was wet. When she felt it with her hands she was greatly alarmed for fear I should catch cold. The jacket had to be taken off and thoroughly dried before she was calm again. Her only desire was to see my brother Jack, and this unhappily could not be arranged. I set out for London to get a good specialist, and the two doctors consulted together upon the case, which was one of peritonitis. I had to return to Aldershot by the midnight train for a very early morning parade. As soon as it was over, I returned to her bedside. She still knew me, but she gradually became unconscious. Death came very easily to her. She had lived such an innocent and loving life of service to others and held such a simple faith that she had no fears at all, and did not seem to mind very much. She had been my dearest and most intimate friend during the whole of the twenty years I had lived. I now telegraphed to the clergyman with whom she had served nearly a quarter of a century before. He had a long memory for faithful service. We met at the graveside.

When I think of the fate of poor old women, so many of whom have no one to look after them and nothing to live on at the end of their lives, I am glad to have had a hand in all that structure of pensions and insurance which no other country can rival and which is especially a help to them.

At the beginning of November, 1895, we sailed for New York, and journeyed thence to Havana.

The minds of this generation, exhausted, brutalized, mutilated and bored by war, may not understand the delicious yet tremulous sensations with which a young British officer bred in the long peace approached for the first time an actual theatre of operations.[1] When first in the dim light of early morning I saw the shores of Cuba rise and define themselves from dark-blue horizons, I felt as if I sailed with Long John Silver and first gazed on Treasure Island. Here was a place where real things were going on. Here was a scene of vital action. Here was a place where anything might happen. Here was

[1] The guerrilla war between the Spaniards and the Cuban rebels in 1895.

43

a place where something would certainly happen. Here I might leave my bones. These musings were dispersed by the advance of breakfast, and lost in the hurry of disembarkation.

Behold next morning a distinct sensation in the life of a young officer! It is still dark, but the sky is paling. We are on our horses, in uniform; our revolvers are loaded. In the dusk and half-light, long files of armed and laden men are shuffling off towards the enemy. He may be very near; perhaps he is waiting for us a mile away. We cannot tell; we know nothing of the qualities either of our friends or foes. We have nothing to do with their quarrels. Except in personal self-defence we can take no part in their combats. But we feel it is a great moment in our lives—in fact, one of the best we have ever experienced. We think that something is going to happen; we hope devoutly that something will happen; yet at the same time we do not want to be hurt or killed. What is it then that we do want? It is that lure of youth—adventure, and adventure for adventure's sake. You might call it tomfoolery. To travel thousands of miles with money one could ill afford, and get up at four o'clock in the morning in the hope of getting into a scrape in the company of perfect strangers, is certainly hardly a rational proceeding. Yet we knew there were very few subalterns in the British Army who would not have given a month's pay to sit in our saddles.

However, nothing happened.

At two o'clock the *siesta* was over. Bustle arose in the silent midday bivouac. At three in the afternoon we were once more on the way, and marched four hours at a speed of certainly not less than $2\frac{3}{4}$ miles an hour. As dusk was falling we reached our camping ground for the night. The column had covered eighteen or nineteen miles, and the infantry did not seem in the least fatigued. These tough Spanish peasants, sons of the soil, could jog along with heavy loads over mere tracks with an admirable persistence. The prolonged midday halt was like a second night's rest to them.

I have no doubt that the Romans planned the time-table of their days far better than we do. They rose before the sun at all seasons. Except in war time we never see the dawn. Sometimes we see sunset. The message of the sunset is sadness; the message of the dawn is hope. The rest and the spell of sleep in the middle of the day refresh the human frame far more than a long night. We were not made by Nature to work, or even to play, from eight o'clock in the morning till midnight. We throw a strain upon our system which is unfair and improvident. For every purpose of business or pleasure, mental or physical, we ought to break our days and our marches into two. When I was at the Admiralty in the War, I found I could add nearly two hours to my working effort by going to bed for an hour after luncheon.

Following this routine, we marched for several days, through wonderful country, without a sign or sound or sight of war. Meanwhile we got quite friendly with our Spanish hosts; and speaking execrable French in common, though from different angles, we managed to acquire some understanding of their views. The Chief of the Staff, Lieutenant-Colonel Benzo, for instance, on one occasion referred to the war "which we are fighting to preserve the integrity of our country". I was struck by this. I had not, no doubt owing to my restricted education, quite realized that these other nations had the same sort of feeling about their possessions as we in England had always been brought up to have about ours. They felt about Cuba, it seemed, just as we felt about Ireland. This impressed me much. I thought it rather cheek that these foreigners should have just the same views and use the same sort of language about their country and their colonies as if they were British. However, I accepted the fact and put it in my mental larder. Hitherto I had (secretly) sympathized with the rebels, or at least with the rebellion; but now I began to see how unhappy the Spanish were at the idea of having their beautiful "Pearl of the Antilles" torn away from them, and I began to feel sorry for them.

On this day when we halted for breakfast every man sat by his horse and ate what he had in his pocket. I had been provided with half a skinny chicken. I was engaged in gnawing the drumstick when suddenly, close at hand, almost in our faces it seemed, a ragged volley rang out from the edge of the forest. The horse immediately behind me—not my horse—gave a bound. There was excitement and commotion. A party of soldiers rushed to the place whence the volley had been fired, and of course found nothing except a few empty cartridge cases. Meanwhile I had been meditating upon the wounded horse. It was a chestnut. The bullet had struck between his ribs, the blood dripped on the ground, and there was a circle of dark red on his bright chestnut coat about a foot wide. He hung his head, but did not fall. Evidently, however, he was going to die, for his saddle and bridle were soon taken off him. As I watched these proceedings I could not help reflecting that the bullet which had struck the chestnut had certainly passed within a foot of my head. So at any rate I had been "under fire". That was something. Nevertheless, I began to take a more thoughtful view of our enterprise than I had hitherto done.

*In the spring of 1896 the author's regiment—the 4th Hussars —was at Hounslow Barracks waiting to sail for India. At Hounslow he enjoyed "the only idle spell I have ever had".*

I sustained one disturbing experience at Deepdene.[1] I was invited, and it was a great honour for a second lieutenant, to join a weekend party given to the Prince of Wales. Colonel Brabazon was also among the guests. I realized that I must be upon my best behaviour: punctual, subdued, reserved, in short display all the qualities with which I am least endowed. I ought to have caught a six o'clock train to Dorking; but I decided to travel by the 7.15 instead. This was running things very fine, but it was not until my journey was half completed that I realized that I should be almost certainly late for dinner. The train was due to arrive at 8.18, and then there would be ten minutes' drive from the station. So I proceeded, much to the concern of the gentleman who shared my carriage, to dress in the train between the stations. The train was horribly slow and seemed to lose a few minutes at each stop. Of course it stopped at every station. It was twenty to nine before I reached Dorking. I nipped out of the carriage to find a servant on the platform evidently disturbed. I jumped into the brougham and saw by the speed at which the two horses were being urged that a serious crisis awaited me at my destination. However, I thought, "I will slip in and take my

[1] Deepdene near Dorking was the home of Lord William Beresford, brother of the famous admiral, Lord Charles Beresford.

46

place almost unnoticed at the table, and make my apologies afterwards."

When I arrived at Deepdene, I found the entire company assembled in the drawing-room. The party it seemed without me would be only thirteen. The prejudice of the Royal Family of those days against sitting down thirteen is well known. The Prince had refused point-blank to go in, and would not allow any rearrangement of two tables to be made. He had, as was his custom, been punctual to the minute at half-past eight. It was now twelve minutes to nine. There, in this large room, stood this select and distinguished company in the worst of tempers, and there on the other hand was I, a young boy asked as a special favour and compliment. Of course I had a perfectly good explanation. Oddly enough, it was one that I have had to use on more than one occasion since. I had not started soon enough! I put it aside. I stammered a few words of apology, and advanced to make my bow. "Don't they teach you to be punctual in your regiment, Winston?" said the Prince in his most severe tone, and then looked acidly at Colonel Brabazon, who glowered. It was an awful moment! We went in to dinner two by two and sat down an unexceptionable fourteen. After about a quarter of an hour the Prince, who was a naturally and genuinely kind-hearted man, put me at my ease again by some gracious chaffing remark.

I do think unpunctuality is a vile habit, and all my life I have tried to break myself of it. "I have never been able," said Mr. Welldon to me some years later, "to understand the point of view of persons who make a practice of being ten minutes late for each of a series of appointments throughout the day." I entirely agree with this dictum. The only straightforward course is to cut one or two of the appointments altogether and so catch up. But very few men have the strength of mind to do this. It is better that one notability should be turned away expostulating from the doorstep, than that nine just deputations should each fume for ten minutes in a stuffy ante-room.

The time was now come for us to embark for the East. We sailed from Southampton in a trooper carrying about 1,200 men, and after a voyage of twenty-three days cast anchor in Bombay

Harbour and pulled up the curtain on what might well have been a different planet.

It may be imagined how our whole shipful of officers and men were delighted after being cooped up for nearly a month to see the palms and palaces of Bombay lying about us in a wide crescent. We gazed at them over the bulwarks across the shining and surf-ribbed waters. Everyone wanted to go on shore at once and see what India was like. The delays and formalities of disembarkation which oppress the ordinary traveller are multiplied for those who travel at the royal expense. However, at about three o'clock in the afternoon orders were issued that we were to land at eight o'clock when it would be cool; and in the meantime a proportion of officers might go ashore independently. A shoal of tiny boats had been lying around us all day long, rising and falling with the swell. We eagerly summoned some of these. It took about a quarter of an hour to reach the quays of the Sassoon Dock. Glad I was to be there; for the lively motion of the skiff to which I and two friends had committed ourselves was fast becoming our main pre-occupation. We came alongside of a great stone wall with dripping steps and iron rings for hand-holds. The boat rose and fell four or five feet with the surges. I put out my hand and grasped at a ring; but before I could get my feet on the steps the boat swung away, giving my right shoulder a sharp and peculiar wrench. I scrambled up all right, made a few remarks of a general character, mostly beginning with the earlier letters of the alphabet, hugged my shoulder and soon thought no more about it.

Let me counsel my younger readers to beware of dislocated shoulders. In this, as in so many other things, it is the first step that counts. Quite an exceptional strain is required to tear the capsule which holds the shoulder joint together; but once the deed is done, a terrible liability remains. Although my shoulder did not actually go out, I had sustained an injury which was to last me my life, which was to cripple me at polo, to prevent me from ever playing tennis, and to be a grave embarrassment in moments of peril, violence and effort. Since then, at irregular intervals my shoulder has dislocated on the most unexpected pretexts; sleeping with my arm under the pillow, taking a book from the library shelves, slipping on a staircase, swimming, etc. Once it very nearly went out through a too expansive gesture in the House of Commons, and·I thought how astonished the members would have been to see the speaker to whom they were listening, suddenly for no reason throw himself upon the floor in an instinctive effort to take the strain and leverage off the displaced arm bone.

This accident was a serious piece of bad luck. However, you never can tell whether bad luck may not after all turn out to be good luck. Perhaps if in the charge of Omdurman I had been able to use a sword, instead of having to adopt a modern weapon like a Mauser pistol, my story might not have got so far as the telling. One must never forget when misfortunes come that it is quite possible they are saving one from something much worse; or that when you make some great mistake, it may very easily serve you better than the best-advised decision. Life is a whole, and luck is a whole, and no part of them can be separated from the rest.

I resolved to read history, philosophy, economics, and things like that; and I wrote to my mother asking for such books as I had heard of on these topics. She responded with alacrity, and every month the mail brought me a substantial package of what I thought were standard works. In history I decided to begin with Gibbon. Some one had told me that my father had read Gibbon with delight; that he knew whole pages of it by heart, and that it had greatly affected his style of speech and writing. So without more ado I set out upon the eight volumes of Dean Milman's edition of Gibbon's *Decline and Fall of the Roman Empire*. I was immediately dominated both by the story and the style. All through the long glistening middle hours of the Indian day, from when we quitted stables till the evening shadows proclaimed the hour of Polo, I devoured Gibbon. I rode triumphantly through it from end to end and enjoyed it all. I scribbled all my opinions on the margins of the pages, and very soon found myself a vehement partisan of the author against the disparagements of his pompous-pious editor. I was not even estranged by his naughty footnotes. On the other hand the Dean's apologies and disclaimers roused my ire. So pleased was I with *The Decline and Fall* that I began at once to read Gibbon's Autobiography, which luckily was bound up in the same edition. When I read his reference to his old nurse: "If there be any, as I trust there are some, who rejoice that I live, to that dear and excellent woman their gratitude is due," I thought of Mrs. Everest; and it shall be her epitaph.

From Gibbon I went to Macaulay. I had learnt *The Lays of Ancient Rome* by heart, and loved them; and of course I knew he had written a history; but I had never read a page of it. I now embarked on that splendid romance, and I voyaged with full sail in a strong wind. I remembered then that Mrs. Everest's brother-in-law, the old prison warder, had possessed a copy of Macaulay's History, purchased in supplements and bound together, and that he used to speak of it with reverence. I accepted all Macaulay wrote as gospel, and I was grieved to read his harsh judgments upon the Great Duke of Marlborough. There was no one at hand to tell me that this historian with his captivating style and devastating self-confidence was the prince of literary rogues, who always preferred the tale to the truth, and smirched or glorified great men and garbled documents according as they affected his drama. I cannot forgive him for imposing on my confidence and on the simple faith of my old friend the warder. Still I must admit an immense debt upon the other side.

From November to May I read for four or five hours every day history and philosophy. Plato's Republic—it appeared he was for all practical purposes the same as Socrates; the Politics of Aristotle, edited by Mr. Welldon himself; Schopenhauer on Pessimism; Malthus on Population; Darwin's Origin of Species: all interspersed with other books of lesser standing. It was a curious education. First because I approached it with an empty, hungry mind, and with fairly strong jaws; and what I got I bit; secondly, because I had no one to tell me: "This is discredited", "You should read the answer to that by so and so; the two together will give you the gist of the argument", "There is a much better book on that subject", and so forth. I now began for the first time to envy those young cubs at the university who had fine scholars to tell them what was what; professors who had devoted their lives to mastering and focusing ideas in every branch of learning; who were eager to distribute the treasures they had gathered before they were over-taken by the night. But now I pity undergraduates, when I see what frivolous lives many of them lead in the midst of precious fleeting opportunity. After all, a man's Life must be nailed to a cross either of Thought or Action. Without work there is no play.

When I am in the Socratic mood and planning *my* Republic, I make drastic changes in the education of the sons of well-to-do citizens. When they are sixteen or seventeen they begin to learn a craft and to do healthy manual labour, with plenty of poetry, songs, dancing, drill and gymnastics in their spare time. They can thus let off their steam on something useful. It is only when they are really thirsty for knowledge, longing to hear about things, that I would let them go to the University. It would be a favour, a coveted privilege, only to be given to those who had either proved their worth in factory or field or whose qualities and zeal were preeminent. However, this would upset a lot of things; it would cause commotion and bring me perhaps in the end a hemlock draught.

My various readings during the next two years led me to ask myself questions about religion. Hitherto I had dutifully accepted everything I had been told. Even in the holidays I always had to go once a week to church, and at Harrow there were three services every Sunday, besides morning and evening prayers throughout the week. All this was very good. I accumulated in those years so fine a surplus in the Bank of Observance that I have been drawing confidently upon it ever since. Weddings, christenings, and funerals have brought in a steady annual income, and I have never made too close inquiries about the state of my account. It might well even be that I should find an overdraft. But now in these bright days of youth my attendances were well ahead of the Sundays. In the Army too there were regular church parades, and sometimes I marched the Roman Catholics to church, and sometimes the Protestants. Religious toleration in the British Army had spread until it overlapped the regions of indifference. No one was ever hampered or prejudiced on account of his religion. Everyone had the regulation facilities for its observance. In India the deities of a hundred creeds were placed by respectful routine in the Imperial Pantheon. In the regiment we sometimes used to argue questions like "Whether we should live again in another world after this was over?" "Whether we have ever lived before?" "Whether we remember and meet each other after Death or merely start again like the

Buddhists?" "Whether some high intelligence is looking after the world or whether things are just drifting on anyhow?" There was general agreement that if you tried your best to live an honourable life and did your duty and were faithful to friends and not unkind to the weak and poor, it did not matter much what you believed or disbelieved. All would come out right. This is what would nowadays I suppose be called "The Religion of Healthy-Mindedness".

Some of the senior officers also dwelt upon the value of the Christian religion to women ("It helps to keep them straight"); and also generally to the lower orders ("Nothing can give them a good time here, but it makes them more contented to think they will get one hereafter"). Christianity, it appeared, had also a disciplinary value, especially when presented through the Church of England. It made people want to be respectable, to keep up appearances, and so saved lots of scandals. From this standpoint ceremonies and ritual ceased to be of importance. They were merely the same idea translated into different languages to suit different races and temperaments. Too much religion of any kind, however, was a bad thing. Among natives especially, fanaticism was highly dangerous and roused them to murder, mutiny or rebellion. Such is, I think, a fair gauging of the climate of opinion in which I dwelt.

I began to read a number of books which challenged the whole religious education I had received at Harrow. The first of these books was *The Martyrdom of Man* by Winwood Reade. This was Colonel Brabazon's great book. He had read it many times over and regarded it as a sort of Bible. It is in fact a concise and well-written universal history of mankind, dealing in harsh terms with the mysteries of all religions and leading to the depressing conclusion that we simply go out like candles. I was much startled and indeed offended by what I read. But then I found that Gibbon evidently held the same view; and finally Mr. Lecky, in his *Rise and Influence of Rationalism* and *History of European Morals*, both of which I read this winter, established in my mind a predominantly secular view. For a time I was indignant at having been told so many untruths, as I then regarded them, by the schoolmasters and clergy who had guided my youth. Of course if I had been at a University my difficulties might have been resolved by the eminent professors and divines who are gathered there. At any rate, they would have shown me equally convincing books putting the opposite point of view. As it was I passed through a violent and aggressive anti-religious phase which, had it lasted, might easily have made me a nuisance. My poise was restored during the next few years by frequent contact with danger. I found that whatever I might think and argue, I did not hesitate to ask for special protection when about to come under the fire of the enemy: nor to feel sincerely grateful when I got home safe to tea. I even asked for lesser things than not to be killed too soon, and nearly always in these years, and indeed throughout my life, I got what I wanted. This practice seemed perfectly natural, and just as strong and real as the reasoning process which contradicted it so sharply. Moreover the practice was comforting and the reasoning led nowhere. I therefore acted in accordance with my feelings without troubling to square such conduct with the conclusions of thought.

It is a good thing for an uneducated man to read books of quotations. Bartlett's *Familiar Quotations* is an admirable work, and I studied it intently. The quotations when engraved upon the memory give you good thoughts. They also make you anxious to read the authors and look for more. In this or some other similar book I came across a French saying which seemed singularly apposite. "*Le cœur a ses raisons, que la raison ne connaît pas.*" It seemed to me that it would be very foolish to discard the reasons of the heart for those of the head. Indeed I could not see why I should not enjoy them both. I did not worry about the inconsistency of thinking one way and believing the other. It seemed good to let the mind explore so far as it could the paths of thought and logic, and also good to pray for help and succour, and be thankful when they came. I could not feel that the Supreme Creator who gave us our minds as well as our souls would be offended if they did not always run smoothly together in double harness. After all, He must have foreseen this from the beginning and of course He would understand it all.

Accordingly I have always been surprised to see some of our bishops and clergy making such heavy weather about reconciling the Bible story with modern scientific and historical knowledge. Why do they want to reconcile them? If you are the recipient of a message which cheers your heart and fortifies your soul, which promises you reunion with those you have loved in a world of larger opportunity and wider sympathies, why should you worry about the shape or colour of the travel-stained envelope; whether it is duly stamped, whether the date on the postmark is right or wrong? These matters may be puzzling, but they are certainly not important. What is important is the message and the benefits to you of receiving it. Close reasoning can conduct one to the precise conclusion that miracles are impossible: that "it is much more likely that human testimony should err, than that the laws of nature should be violated"; and at the same time one may rejoice to read how Christ turned the water into wine in Cana of Galilee or walked on the lake or rose from the dead. The human brain cannot comprehend infinity, but the discovery of mathematics enables it to be handled quite easily. The idea that nothing is true except what we comprehend is silly, and that ideas which our minds cannot reconcile are mutually destructive, sillier still. Certainly nothing could be more repulsive both to our minds and feelings than the spectacle of thousands of millions of universes—for that is what they say it comes to now—all knocking about together for ever without any rational or good purpose behind them. I therefore adopted quite early in life a system of believing whatever I wanted to believe, while at the same time leaving reason to pursue unfettered whatever paths she was capable of treading.

*The following extracts describe the author's personal experiences during the charge of the 21st Lancers in the Battle of Omdurman. He gives a further description in "The River War".*

I propose to describe exactly what happened to me: what I saw and what I felt. I recalled it to my mind so frequently after the event that the impression is as clear and vivid as it was a quarter of a century ago. The troop I commanded was, when we wheeled into line, the second from the right of the regiment. I was riding a handy, sure-footed, grey Arab polo pony. Before we wheeled and began to gallop, the officers had been marching with drawn swords. On account of my shoulder I had always decided that if I were involved in hand-to-hand fighting, I must use a pistol and not a sword. I had purchased in London a Mauser automatic pistol, then the newest and the latest design. I had practised carefully with this during our march and journey up the river. This then was the weapon with which I determined to fight. I had first of all to return my sword into its scabbard, which is not the easiest thing to do at a gallop. I had then to draw my pistol from its wooden holster and bring it to full cock. This dual operation took an appreciable time, and until it was finished, apart from a few glances to my left to see what effect the fire was producing, I did not look up at the general scene.

Then I saw immediately before me, and now only half the length of a polo ground away, the row of crouching blue figures firing frantically, wreathed in white smoke. On my right and left my neighbouring troop leaders made a good line. Immediately behind was a long dancing row of lances couched for the charge. We were going at a fast but steady gallop. There was too much trampling and rifle fire to hear any bullets. After this glance to the right and left and at my troop, I looked again towards the enemy. The scene appeared to be suddenly transformed. The blue-black men were still firing, but behind them there now came into view a depression like a shallow sunken road. This was crowded and crammed with men rising up from the ground where they had hidden. Bright flags appeared as if by magic, and I saw arriving from nowhere Emirs on horseback among and around the mass of the enemy. The Dervishes appeared to be ten or twelve deep at the thickest, a great grey mass gleaming with steel, filling the dry watercourse. In the same twinkling of an eye I saw also that our right overlapped their left, that my troop would just strike the edge of their array, and that the troop on my right would charge into air. My subaltern comrade on the right, Wormald of the 7th Hussars, could see the situation too; and we both increased our speed to the very fastest gallop and curved inwards like the horns of the moon. One really had not time to be frightened or to think of anything else but these particularly necessary actions which I have described. They completely occupied mind and senses.

The collision was now very near. I saw immediately before me, not ten yards away, the two blue men who lay in my path. They were perhaps a couple of yards apart. I rode at the interval between them. They both fired. I passed through the smoke conscious that I was unhurt. The trooper immediately behind me was killed at this place and at this moment, whether by these shots or not I do not know. I checked my pony as the ground began to fall away beneath his feet. The clever animal dropped like a cat four or five feet down on to the sandy bed of the watercourse, and in this sandy bed I found myself surrounded by what seemed to be dozens of men. They were not thickly packed enough at this point for me to experience any actual collision with them. Whereas Grenfell's troop next but one on my left was brought to a complete standstill and suffered very heavy losses, we seemed to push our way through as one has sometimes seen mounted policemen break up a crowd. In less time than it takes to relate, my pony had scrambled up the other side of the ditch. I looked round.

Once again I was on the hard, crisp desert, my horse at a trot. I had the impression of scattered Dervishes running to and fro in all directions. Straight before me a man threw himself on the ground. The reader must remember that I had been trained as a cavalry soldier to believe that if ever cavalry broke into a mass of infantry, the latter would be at their mercy. My first idea therefore was that the man was terrified. But simultaneously I saw the gleam of his curved sword as he drew it back for a ham-stringing cut. I had room and time enough to turn my pony out of his reach, and leaning over on the offside I fired two shots into him at about three yards. As I straightened myself in the saddle, I saw before me another figure with uplifted sword. I raised my pistol and fired. So close were we that the pistol itself actually struck him. Man and sword disappeared below and behind me. On my left, ten yards away, was an Arab horseman in a bright-coloured tunic and steel helmet, with chain-mail hangings. I fired at him. He turned aside. I pulled my horse into a walk and looked around again.

In one respect a cavalry charge is very like ordinary life. So long as you are all right, firmly in your saddle, your horse in hand, and well armed, lots of enemies will give you a wide berth. But as soon as you have lost a stirrup, have a rein cut, have dropped your weapon, are wounded, or your horse is wounded, then is the moment when from all quarters enemies rush upon you. Such was the fate of not a few of my comrades in the troops immediately on my left. Brought to an actual standstill in the enemy's mass, clutched at from every side, stabbed at and hacked at by spear and sword, they were dragged from their horses and cut to pieces by the infuriated foe. But this I did not at the time see or understand. My impressions continued to be sanguine. I thought we were masters of the situation, riding the enemy down, scattering them and killing them. I pulled my horse up and looked about me. There was a mass of Dervishes about forty or fifty yards away on my left. They were huddling and clumping themselves together, rallying for mutual protection. They seemed wild with excitement, dancing about on their feet, shaking their spears up and down. The whole scene seemed to flicker. I have an impression, but it is too fleeting to define, of brown-clad Lancers mixed up here and there with this surging mob. The scattered individuals in my immediate neighbourhood made no attempt to molest me. Where was my troop? Where were the other troops of the squadron? Within a hundred yards of me I could not see a single officer or man. I looked back at the Dervish mass. I saw two or three riflemen crouching and aiming their rifles at me from the fringe of it. Then for the first time that morning I experienced a sudden sensation of fear. I felt myself absolutely alone. I thought these riflemen would hit me and the rest devour me like wolves. What a fool I was to loiter like this in the midst of the enemy! I crouched over the saddle, spurred my horse into a gallop and drew clear of the *mêlée*. Two or three hundred yards away I found my troop already faced about and partly formed up.

The other three troops of the squadron were re-forming close by. Suddenly in the midst of the troop up sprang a Dervish. How he got there I do not know. He must have leaped out of some scrub or hole. All the troopers turned upon him thrusting with their lances: but he darted to and fro causing for the moment a frantic commotion. Wounded several times, he staggered towards me raising his spear. I shot him at less than a yard. He fell on the sand, and lay there dead. How easy to kill a man! But I did not worry about it. I found that I had fired the whole magazine of my Mauser pistol, so I put in a new clip of ten cartridges before thinking of anything else.

I was still prepossessed with the idea that we had inflicted great slaughter on the enemy and had scarcely suffered at all ourselves.

Three or four men were missing from my troop. Six men and nine or ten horses were bleeding from spear-thrusts or sword cuts. We all expected to be ordered immediately to charge back again. The men were ready, though they all looked serious. Several asked to be allowed to throw away their lances and draw their swords. I asked my second sergeant if he had enjoyed himself. His answer was: "Well, I don't exactly say I enjoyed it, Sir; but I think I'll get more used to it next time." At this the whole troop laughed.

But now from the direction of the enemy there came a succession of grisly apparitions; horses spouting blood, struggling on three legs, men staggering on foot, men bleeding from terrible wounds, fish-hook spears stuck right through them, arms and faces cut to pieces, bowels protruding, men gasping, crying, collapsing, expiring. Our first task was to succour these; and meanwhile the blood of our leaders cooled. They remembered for the first time that we had carbines. Everything was still in great confusion. But trumpets were sounded and orders shouted, and we all moved off at a trot towards the flank of the enemy. Arrived at a position from which we could enfilade and rake the watercourse, two squadrons were dismounted and in a few minutes with their fire at three hundred yards compelled the Dervishes to retreat. We therefore remained in possession of the field. Within twenty minutes of the time when we had first wheeled into line and begun our charge, we were halted and breakfasting in the very watercourse that had so very nearly proved our undoing. There one could see the futility of the much vaunted *Arme Blanche*. The Dervishes had carried off their wounded, and the corpses of thirty or forty enemy were all that could be counted on the ground. Among these lay the bodies of over twenty Lancers, so hacked and mutilated as to be mostly unrecognizable. In all out of 310 officers and men the regiment had lost in the space of about two or three minutes five officers and sixty-five men killed and wounded, and 120 horses—nearly a quarter of its strength.

Such were my fortunes in this celebrated episode. It is very rarely that cavalry and infantry, while still both unshaken, are intermingled as the result of an actual collision. Either the infantry keep their heads and shoot the cavalry down, or they break into confusion and are cut down or speared as they run. But the two or three thousand Dervishes who faced the 21st Lancers in the watercourse at Omdur-

man were not in the least shaken by the stress of battle or afraid of
cavalry. Their fire was not good enough to stop the charge, but
they had no doubt faced horsemen many a time in the wars with
Abyssinia. They were familiar with the ordeal of the charge. It was
the kind of fighting they thoroughly understood. Moreover, the
fight was with equal weapons, for the British too fought with sword
and lance as in the days of old.[1]

I was most anxious not to be a burden upon my mother in any
way; and amid the movements and excitements of the campaigns
and polo tournaments I reflected seriously upon the financial aspects
of my military life. My allowance of £500 a year was not sufficient
to meet the expenses of polo and the Hussars. I watched the remorseless piling up year by year of deficits which, although not large—as
deficits go—were deficits none the less. I now saw that the only
profession I had been taught would never yield me even enough
money to avoid getting into debt, let alone to dispense with my
allowance and become completely independent as I desired. To
have given the most valuable years of one's education to reach a
position of earning about 14s. a day out of which to keep up two
horses and most costly uniforms seemed hardly in retrospect to have
been a very judicious proceeding. To go on soldiering even for a
few more years would plainly land me and all connected with me
in increasing difficulties. On the other hand the two books I had
already written and my war correspondence with the *Daily Telegraph*
had already brought in about five times as much as the Queen had
paid me for three years of assiduous and sometimes dangerous work.
Her Majesty was so stinted by Parliament that she was not able to
pay me even a living wage. I therefore resolved with many regrets
to quit her service betimes. The series of letters I had written for
the *Morning Post* about the battle of Omdurman, although unsigned,
had produced above £300. Living at home with my mother my
expenses would be small, and I hoped to make from my new book
about the Sudan Campaign, which I had decided to call *The
River War*, enough to keep me in pocket money for at least
two years.

[1] The famous charge of the 21st Lancers at Omdurman, in which the author commanded a troop.

Besides this I had in contemplation a contract with the *Pioneer* to write them weekly letters from London at a payment of £3 apiece. I have improved upon this figure in later life; but at this time I reflected that it nearly equalled the pay I was receiving as a subaltern officer.

I therefore planned the sequence of the year 1899 as follows: To return to India and win the Polo Tournament: to send in my papers and leave the army: to relieve my mother from paying my allowance: to write my new book and the letters to the *Pioneer*: and to look out for a chance of entering Parliament. These plans as will be seen were in the main carried out. In fact from this year until the year 1919, when I inherited unexpectedly a valuable property under the will of my long dead great-grandmother Frances Anne, Marchioness of Londonderry, I was entirely dependent upon my own exertions. During all these twenty years I maintained myself, and later on my family, without ever lacking anything necessary to health or enjoyment. I am proud of this, and I commend my example to my son, indeed to all my children.

In the spring of 1899 I became conscious of the fact that there was another Winston Churchill who also wrote books; apparently he wrote novels, and very good novels too, which achieved an enormous circulation in the United States. I received from many quarters congratulations on my skill as a writer of fiction. I thought at first these were due to a belated appreciation of the merits of *Savrola*. Gradually I realized that there was "another Richmond in the field", luckily on the other side of the Atlantic. I proceeded to indite my transatlantic double a letter which with his answer is perhaps a literary curiosity.

LONDON,
*7 June*, 1899.

Mr. Winston Churchill presents his compliments to Mr. Winston Churchill, and begs to draw his attention to a matter which concerns them both. He has learnt from the press notices that Mr. Winston Churchill proposes to bring out another novel, entitled *Richard Carvel*, which is certain to have a considerable sale both in England and America. Mr. Winston Churchill is also the author of a novel now being published in serial form in

*Macmillan's Magazine,* and for which he anticipates some sale both in England and America. He also proposes to publish on 1 October another military chronicle on the Sudan War. He has no doubt that Mr. Winston Churchill will recognize from this letter—if indeed by no other means—that there is grave danger of his works being mistaken for those of Mr. Winston Churchill. He feels sure that Mr. Winston Churchill desires this as little as he does himself. In future to avoid mistakes as far as possible, Mr. Winston Churchill has decided to sign all published articles, stories, or other work, "Winston Spencer Churchill", and not "Winston Churchill" as formerly. He trusts that this arrangement will commend itself to Mr. Winston Churchill, and he ventures to suggest, with a view to preventing further confusion which may arise out of this extraordinary coincidence, that both Mr. Winston Churchill and Mr. Winston Churchill should insert a short note in their respective publications explaining to the public which are the works of Mr. Winston Churchill and which those of Mr. Winston Churchill. The text of this note might form a subject for future discussion if Mr. Winston Churchill agrees with Mr. Winston Churchill's proposition. He takes this occasion of complimenting Mr. Winston Churchill upon the style and success of his works, which are always brought to his notice whether in magazine or book form, and he trusts that Mr. Winston Churchill has derived equal pleasure from any work of his that may have attracted his attention.

WINDSOR, VERMONT,
21 *June,* 1899.

Mr. Winston Churchill is extremely grateful to Mr. Winston Churchill for bringing forward a subject which has given Mr. Winston Churchill much anxiety. Mr. Winston Churchill appreciates the courtesy of Mr. Winston Churchill in adopting the name of "Winston Spencer Churchill" in his books, articles, etc. Mr. Winston Churchill makes haste to add that, had he possessed any other names, he would certainly have adopted one of them. The writings of Mr. Winston Spencer Churchill (henceforth so called) have been brought to Mr. Winston Churchill's notice since the publication of his first story in the

*Century.* It did not seem then to Mr. Winston Churchill that the works of Mr. Winston Spencer Churchill would conflict in any way with his own attempts at fiction.

The proposal of Mr. Winston Spencer Churchill to affix a note to the separate writings of Mr. Winston Spencer Churchill and Mr. Winston Churchill, the text of which is to be agreed on between them,—is quite acceptable to Mr. Winston Churchill. If Mr. Winston Spencer Churchill will do him the favour of drawing up this note, there is little doubt that Mr. Winston Churchill will acquiesce in its particulars.

Mr. Winston Churchill, moreover, is about to ask the opinion of his friends and of his publishers as to the advisability of inserting the words "The American", after his name on the title-page of his books. Should this seem wise to them, he will request his publishers to make the change in future editions.

Mr. Winston Churchill will take the liberty of sending Mr. Winston Churchill copies of the two novels he has written. He has a high admiration for the works of Mr. Winston Spencer Churchill and is looking forward with pleasure to reading *Savrola.*

All was settled amicably, and by degrees the reading public accommodated themselves to the fact that there had arrived at the same moment two different persons of the same name who would from henceforward minister copiously to their literary, or if need be their political requirements. When a year later I visited Boston, Mr. Winston Churchill was the first to welcome me. He entertained me at a very gay banquet of young men, and we made each other complimentary speeches. Some confusion, however, persisted; all my mails were sent to his address and the bill for the dinner came in to me. I need not say that both these errors were speedily redressed.

*In 1899 the author contested Oldham as a Conservative candidate. He was defeated. In the following year he was elected by the small margin of 230 votes*

One day I was asked to go to the House of Commons by a Mr. Robert Ascroft, Conservative member for Oldham. He took me down to the smoking-room and opened to me an important project. Oldham is a two-member constituency, and at this time the Conservatives held both seats. Ascroft the senior member had a strong position, as he was not only supported by the Conservative electors, but was also the tried and trusted solicitor for the Oldham Cotton Operatives Trade Unions. It appeared that his colleague had been for some time ailing, and Mr. Ascroft was on the look-out for someone to run in double harness with him. He evidently thought I should do. He made some sensible remarks. "Young people," he said, "very often do not have as much money as older ones." I knew nothing to enable me to contradict this painful fact. He seemed to think, however, that all obstacles could be surmounted, and I agreed to come down at an early date and address a meeting at Oldham under his auspices.

Some weeks passed—and the newspapers reported Mr. Ascroft's sudden death. It seemed strange that he, so strong and busy, seeming perfectly well, should flash away like this, while the colleague whose health had caused him so much anxiety survived. Robert Ascroft was greatly respected by the Oldham working folk. They made a subscription of more than £2,000, the bulk collected in very small sums, to set up a statue to him as "The Workers' Friend". They stipulated—and I thought it characteristic of these Lancashire operatives—that the money was not to go to anything useful; no beds at a hospital, no extensions to a library, no fountain even, just a memorial. They did not want to give a present to themselves.

The vacancy now had to be filled, and they immediately pitched on me. I had been, it was said, virtually selected by the late honoured member. My name was already on the hoardings to address a meeting. Add to this my father's memory, and the case was complete. I received straight away without ever suing, or asking, or appearing before any committee, a formal invitation to contest the seat. At the Conservative Central Office the "Skipper" seemed quite content with the local decision, but he urged that advantage should be taken of the by-election to vacate both seats at the same time. In his view the government was not at that moment in a good position to win Lancashire by-elections. They did not want to have a second vacancy at Oldham in a few months' time. Lord Salisbury could afford to be indifferent to the loss of a couple of seats. Better to lose them both now and have done with Oldham till the general election, when they could win them back. The significance of this attitude was not lost upon me. But in those days any political fight in any circumstances seemed to me better than no fight at all. I therefore unfurled my standard and advanced into the battle.

The fight was long and hard. I defended the virtues of the government, the existing system of society, the Established Church and the unity of the Empire. "Never before," I declared, "were there so many people in England, and never before had they had so much to eat." I spoke of the vigour and the strength of Britain, of the liberation of the Sudan and of the need to keep out the foreign goods made by prison labour. Mr. Mawdsley followed suit. Our opponents deplored the misery of the working masses, the squalor of the slums, the glaring contrast between riches and poverty, and in particular, indeed above all, the iniquities of the Clerical Tithes Bill. The contest would have been most uneven, but for the uncanny gift which the Lancashire working folk possess of balancing up the pros and cons of those who seek their votes. They apply all sorts of correctives to the obvious inequalities of the game. I delivered harangues from morning till night, and Mr. Mawdsley continued steadily to repeat his slogan that the Liberals were undoubtedly more hypocritical than the Tories.

Halfway through the election all my principal supporters besought me to throw over the Clerical Tithes Bill. As I was ignorant of the needs which had inspired it and detached from the passions which it aroused, the temptation to discard it was very great. I yielded to the temptation. Amid the enthusiastic cheers of my supporters I announced that, if returned, I would not vote for the measure. This was a frightful mistake. It is not the slightest use defending governments or parties unless you defend the very worst thing about which they are attacked. At the moment I made my declaration the most vehement debates were taking place upon this Bill. At Westminster the government were taunted with the fact that their own chosen candidate could not face a Lancashire electorate upon the issue, and at Oldham the other side, stimulated by my admission, redoubled their attacks upon the Bill. Live and learn! I think I may say without

As a schoolboy at Harrow in 1889

With the 4th Hussars, Bangalore, South India, 1896

conceit that I was in those days a pretty good candidate. At any rate we had real enthusiasm on our side, and it rejoiced my heart to see these masses of working people who ardently, and for no material advantage, asserted their pride in our Empire and their love for the ancient traditions of the realm. However, when the votes were counted we were well beaten. In a poll of about 23,000 votes—then as big as was known in England—I was 1,300 behind and Mr. Mawdsley about thirty lower.

Then came the recriminations which always follow every kind of defeat. Everyone threw the blame on me. I have noticed that they nearly always do. I suppose it is because they think I shall be able to bear it best. The high Tories and the Carlton Club said "Serve him right for standing with a Socialist. No man of any principle would have done such a thing!" Mr. Balfour, then Leader of the House of Commons, on hearing that I had declared against his Clerical Tithes Bill, said in the Lobby, quite justifiably I must admit, "I thought he was a young man of promise, but it appears he is a young man of promises". Party newspapers wrote leading articles to say what a mistake it was to entrust the fighting of great working-class constituencies to young and inexperienced candidates, and everyone then made haste to pass away from a dismal incident. I returned to London with those feelings of deflation which a bottle of champagne or even soda-water represents when it has been half emptied and left uncorked for a night.

★    ★    ★

I received the warmest of welcomes on returning home.[1] Oldham almost without distinction of party accorded me a triumph. I entered the town in state in a procession of ten landaus, and drove through streets crowded with enthusiastic operatives and mill-girls. I described my escape[2] to a tremendous meeting in the Theatre Royal. As our forces had now occupied the Witbank Colliery district, and those who had aided me were safe under British protection, I was free for the first time to tell the whole story.

This harmony was inevitably to be marred. The Conservative leaders determined to appeal to the country before the enthusiasm

[1] From South Africa in 1900.
[2] From the Boers. See p. 187 et seq.

of victory died down. They had already been in office for five years. A general election must come in eighteen months, and the opportunity was too good to be thrown away. Indeed they could not have carried out the policy of annexing the Boer Republics and of suppressing all opposition by force of arms without parley, except in a new Parliament and with a new majority. Early in September therefore Parliament was dissolved. We had the same kind of election as occurred in a far more violent form after the Great War in December 1918. All the Liberals, even those who had most loyally supported the war measures, including some who had lost their sons, were lapped in a general condemnation as "Pro-Boers". Mr. Chamberlain uttered the slogan, "Every seat lost to the government is a seat gained to the Boers" and Conservatives generally followed in his wake. The Liberal and Radical masses, however, believing in the lull of the war that the fighting was over, rallied stubbornly to their party organizations. The election was well contested all over the country. The Conservatives in those days had a large permanent majority of the English electorate. The prevailing wave of opinion was with them, and Lord Salisbury and his colleagues were returned with a scarcely diminished majority of 134 over all opponents, including the 80 Irish Nationalists. His majority in the main island was overwhelming.

I stood in the van of this victory. In those days our wise and prudent law spread a general election over nearly six weeks. Instead of all the electors voting blindly on one day, and only learning next morning what they had done, national issues were really fought out. A rough but earnest and searching national discussion took place in which leading men on both sides played a part. The electorate of a constituency was not unmanageable in numbers. A candidate could address all his supporters who wished to hear him. A great speech by an eminent personage would often turn a constituency or even a city. Speeches of well-known and experienced statesmen were fully reported in all the newspapers and studied by wide political classes. Thus by a process of rugged argument the national decision was reached in measured steps.

In those days of hammer and anvil politics, the earliest election results were awaited with intense interest. Oldham was almost the first constituency to poll. I fought on the platform that the war was just and necessary, that the Liberals had been wrong to oppose it, and in many ways had hampered its conduct; that it must be fought to an indisputable conclusion, and that thereafter there should be a generous settlement. I had a new colleague at my side, Mr. C. B. Crisp, a City of London merchant. Mr. Mawdsley was no more. He was a very heavy man. He had taken a bath in a china vessel which had broken under his weight, inflicting injuries to which he eventually succumbed. My opponents, Mr. Emmott and Mr. Runciman, had both adopted in the main Lord Rosebery's attitude towards the war; that is to say, they supported the country in the conflict, but alleged gross incompetence in its conduct by the Conservative Party. The Liberals, it appeared, would have made quite a different set of mistakes. As a second string, they suggested that the Liberals would have shown such tact in their diplomacy that war might possibly have been avoided altogether, and all its objects—like making President Kruger give way—have been achieved without shedding blood. All this of course rested on mere assertion. I rejoined that however the negotiations had been conducted, they had broken down because the Boers invaded British territory; and that however ill the war had been waged, we had now repulsed the invaders and taken both their capitals. The Conservative Party throughout the country also argued that this was a special election on the sole national issue of the justice of the war and to win a complete victory; and that ordinary class, sectarian, and party differences ought to be set aside by patriotic men. This at the time was my sincere belief.

Mr. Chamberlain himself came to speak for me. There was more enthusiasm over him at this moment than after the Great War for Mr. Lloyd George and Sir Douglas Haig combined. There was at the same time a tremendous opposition; but antagonism had not wholly excluded admiration from their breasts. We drove to our great meeting together in an open carriage. Our friends had filled the theatre; our opponents thronged its approaches. At the door of the theatre our carriage was jammed tight for some minutes in an immense hostile crowd, all groaning and booing at the tops of their voices, and grinning with the excitement of seeing a famous fellow-citizen whom it was their right and duty to oppose. I watched my honoured guest with close attention. He loved the roar of the multitude, and with my father could always say "I have never feared the English democracy." The blood mantled in his cheek, and his eye as it caught mine twinkled with pure enjoyment. I must explain that in those days we had a real political democracy led by a hierarchy of statesmen, and not a fluid mass distracted by newspapers. There was a structure in which statesmen, electors and the press all played their part. Inside the meeting we were all surprised at Mr. Chamberlain's restraint. His soft purring voice and reasoned incisive sentences, for most of which he had a careful note, made a remarkable impression. He spoke for over an hour; but what pleased the audience most was that, having made a mistake in some fact or figure to the prejudice of his opponents, he went back and corrected it, observing that he must not be unfair. All this was before the liquefaction of the British political system had set in.

When we came to count the votes, of which there were nearly thirty thousand, it was evident that the Liberals and Labourists formed the stronger party in Oldham. Mr. Emmott headed the poll. However, it appeared that about two hundred Liberals who had voted for him had given their second votes to me out of personal goodwill and war feeling. So I turned Mr. Runciman out of the second place and was elected to the House of Commons by the modest margin of 230 votes. I walked with my friends through the tumult to the Conservative Club. There I found already awaiting me the glowing congratulations of Lord Salisbury. The old Prime Minister must have been listening at the telephone, or very near it, for the result. Then from every part of the country flowed in a stream of joyous and laudatory messages. Henceforward I became a "star turn" at the election. I was sought for from every part of the country. I had to speak in London the next night, and Mr. Chamberlain demanded the two following nights in the Birmingham area. I was on my way to fulfil these engagements, when my train was boarded by a messenger from Mr. Balfour informing me that he wished me to cancel my London engagement, to come back at once to Manchester and speak with him that afternoon, and to wind up the campaign in Stockport that night. I obeyed.

Mr. Balfour was addressing a considerable gathering when I arrived. The whole meeting rose and shouted at my entry. With his great air the Leader of the House of Commons presented me to the audience. After this I never addressed any but the greatest meetings. Five or six thousand electors—all men—brimming with interest, thoroughly acquainted with the main objects, crowded into the finest halls, with venerated pillars of the party and many-a-year members of Parliament sitting as supporters on the platform! Such henceforward in that election and indeed for nearly a generation were my experiences. I spent two days with Mr. Chamberlain at Highbury. He passed the whole of one of them in bed resting; but after I had been carried around in a special train to three meetings in the Midland area, he received me at supper in his most gleaming mood with a bottle of '34 port. For three weeks I had what seemed to me a triumphal progress through the country. The party managers selected the critical seats, and quite a lot of victories followed in my train. I was twenty-six. Was it wonderful that I should have thought I had arrived? But luckily life is not so easy as all that: otherwise we should get to the end too quickly.

There seemed, however, to be still two important steps to be taken. The first was to gather sufficient money to enable me to concentrate my attention upon politics without having to do any other work. The sales of *The River War* and of my two books of war correspondence from South Africa, together with the ten months' salary amounting to £2,500 from the *Morning Post*, had left me in possession of more than £4,000. An opportunity of increasing this reserve was now at hand. I had planned to lecture all the autumn and winter at home and in America. The English tour began as soon as the election was over. Having already spoken every night for five weeks, I had now to undergo two and a half months of similar labours interrupted only by the week's voyage across the ocean. The lectures in England were successful. Lord Wolseley presided over the first, and the greatest personages in the three kingdoms on both sides of politics took the chair as I moved from one city to another. All the largest halls were crowded with friendly audiences to whom, aided by a magic lantern, I unfolded my adventures and escape, all set in the general framework of the war. I hardly ever earned less than £100 a night, and often much more. At the Philharmonic Hall in Liverpool I gathered over £300. Altogether in the month of November I banked safely over

£4,500, having toured little more than half of Great Britain.

Parliament was to meet in the opening days of December, and I longed to take my seat in the House of Commons. I had, however, instead to cross the Atlantic to fulfil my engagements. A different atmosphere prevailed in the United States. I was surprised to find that many of these amiable and hospitable Americans who spoke the same language and seemed in essentials very like ourselves, were not nearly so excited about the South African War as we were at home. Moreover a great many of them thought the Boers were in the right; and the Irish everywhere showed themselves actively hostile. The audiences varied from place to place. At Baltimore only a few hundreds assembled in a hall which would have held five thousand. At Boston, on the other hand, an enormous pro-British demonstration was staged, and even the approaches to the Fremont Hall were thronged. The platform here was composed of three hundred Americans in red uniforms belonging to an Anglo-American Society, and the aspect of the meeting was magnificent. In Chicago I encountered vociferous opposition. However, when I made a few jokes against myself, and paid a sincere tribute to the courage and humanity of the Boers, they were placated. On the whole I found it easy to make friends with American audiences. They were cool and critical, but also urbane and good-natured.

Throughout my journeyings I received the help of eminent Americans. Mr. Bourke Cockran, Mr. Chauncey Depew, and other leading politicians presided, and my opening lecture in New York was under the auspices of no less a personage than "Mark Twain" himself. I was thrilled by this famous companion of my youth. He was now very old and snow-white, and combined with a noble air a most delightful style of conversation. Of course we argued about the war. After some interchanges I found myself beaten back to the citadel "My country right or wrong". "Ah," said the old gentleman, "When the poor country is fighting for its life, I agree. But this was not your case". I think, however, I did not displease him; for he was good enough at my request to sign every one of the thirty volumes of his works for my benefit; and in the first volume he inscribed the following maxim intended, I daresay, to convey a gentle admonition: "To do good is noble; to teach others to do good is nobler, and no trouble."

70

All this quiet tolerance changed when we crossed the Canadian border. Here again were present the enthusiastic throngs to which I had so easily accustomed myself at home. Alas, I could only spend ten days in these inspiring scenes. In the middle of January I returned home and resumed my tour of our cities. I visited every one of them. When I spoke in the Ulster Hall, the venerable Lord Dufferin introduced me. No one could turn a compliment so well as he. I can hear him now saying with his old-fashioned pronunciation, "And this young man—at an age when many of his contemporaries have hardly left their studies—has seen more active service than half the general *orficers* in Europe." I had not thought of this before. It was good.

When my tour came to an end in the middle of February, I was exhausted. For more than five months I had spoken for an hour or more almost every night except Sundays, and often twice a day, and had travelled without ceasing, usually by night, rarely sleeping twice in the same bed. And this had followed a year of marching and fighting with rarely a roof or a bed at all. But the results were substantial. I had in my possession nearly £10,000. I was entirely independent and had no need to worry about the future, or for many years to work at anything but politics. I sent my £10,000 to my father's old friend, Sir Ernest Cassel, with the instruction "Feed my sheep". He fed the sheep with great prudence. They did not multiply fast, but they fattened steadily, and none of them ever died. Indeed from year to year they had a few lambs; but these were not numerous enough for me to live upon. I had every year to eat a sheep or two as well, so gradually my flock grew smaller, until in a few years it was almost entirely devoured. Nevertheless, while it lasted, I had no care.

I found myself in marked reaction from the dominant views of the Conservative Party. I was all for fighting the war, which had now flared up again in a desultory manner, to a victorious conclusion; and for that purpose I would have used far larger numbers, and also have organized troops of a higher quality than were actually employed. I would also have used Indian troops. At the same time I admired the dauntless resistance of the Boers, resented the abuse with which they were covered and hoped for an honourable peace which should bind these brave men and their leaders to us for ever. I thought farm-burning a hateful folly; I protested against the execution of Commandant Scheepers; I perhaps played some part behind the scenes in averting the execution of Commandant Kruitzinger. My divergences extended to a wider sphere. When the Secretary of State for War said, "It is by accident that we have become a military nation. We must endeavour to remain one," I was offended. I thought we should finish the war by force and generosity, and then make haste to return to paths of peace, retrenchment and reform.

Although I enjoyed the privilege of meeting in pleasant circles most of the Conservative leaders, and was always treated with extraordinary kindness and good-nature by Mr. Balfour; although I often saw Mr. Chamberlain and heard him discuss affairs with the greatest freedom, I drifted steadily to the left. I found that Rosebery, Asquith and Grey and above all John Morley seemed to understand my point of view far better than my own chiefs. I was fascinated by the intellectual stature of these men and their broad and inspiring outlook upon public affairs, untrammelled as it was by the practical burden of events.

The reader must remember that not having been to a University, I had not been through any of those processes of youthful discussion by which opinion may be formed or reformed in happy irresponsibility. I was already a well-known public character. I—at least—attached great importance to everything I said, and certainly it was often widely published. I became anxious to make the Conservative Party follow Liberal courses. I was in revolt against "jingoism". I had a sentimental view about the Boers. I found myself differing from both parties in various ways, and I was so untutored as to suppose that all I had to do was to think out what was right and express it fearlessly. I thought that loyalty in this outweighed all other loyalties. I did not understand the importance of party discipline and unity, and the sacrifices of opinion which may lawfully be made in their cause.

Events were soon to arise in the fiscal sphere which were to plunge me into new struggles and absorb my thoughts and energies at least until September, 1908, when I married and lived happily ever afterwards.

# MY AFRICAN JOURNEY

*A collection of letters describing the lighter side of a journey in North-East Africa. Most of them were first published in the Strand Magazine, and in book form in 1908.*

THE MANNER of killing a rhinoceros in the open is crudely simple. It is thought well usually to select the neighbourhood of a good tree, *where one can be found*, as the centre of the encounter. If no tree is available, you walk up as near as possible to him from any side except the windward, and then shoot him in the head or the heart. If you hit a vital spot, as sometimes happens, he falls. If you hit him anywhere else, he charges blindly and furiously in your direction, and you shoot him again, or not, as the case may be.

Bearing all this carefully in mind, we started out to do battle with Behemoth. We had advanced perhaps two hundred yards towards him, when a cry from one of the natives arrested us. We looked sharply to the right. There, not a hundred and fifty paces distant, under the shade of a few small trees, stood two other monsters. In a few more steps we should have tainted their wind and brought them up with a rush; and suppose this had happened, when perhaps we were already compromised with our first friend, and had him wounded and furious on our hands! Luckily warned in time, to creep back to the shoulder of the hill, to skirt its crest, and to emerge a hundred and twenty yards from this new objective was the work of a few minutes. We hurriedly agreed to kill one first before touching the other. At such a range it is easy to hit so great a target; but the bull's-eye is small. I fired. The thud of a bullet which strikes with an impact of a ton and a quarter, tearing through hide and muscle and bone with the hideous energy of cordite, came back distinctly. The large rhinoceros started, stumbled, turned directly towards the sound and the blow, and then bore straight down upon us in a peculiar trot, nearly as fast as a horse's gallop, with an activity surprising in so huge a beast.

73

Great is the moral effect of a foe who advances. Everybody fired. Still the ponderous brute came on, as if he were invulnerable; as if he were an engine, or some great steam barge impervious to bullets, insensible to pain or fear. Thirty seconds more, and he will close. An impalpable curtain seems to roll itself up in the mind, revealing a mental picture, strangely lighted, yet very still, where objects have new values, and where a patch of white grass in the foreground, four or five yards away, seems to possess astonishing significance. It is there that the last two shots that yet remain before the resources of civilization are exhausted must be fired. There is time to reflect with some detachment that, after all, we were the aggressors; we it is who have forced the conflict by an unprovoked assault with murderous intent upon a peaceful herbivore; that if there is such a thing as right and wrong between man and beast—and who shall say there is not?—right is plainly on his side; there is time for this before I perceive that, stunned and dazed by the frightful concussions of modern firearms, he has swerved sharp to the right, and is now moving across our front, broadside on, at the same swift trot. More firing, and as I reload someone says he is down, and I fire instead at his smaller companion, already some distance off upon the plain. But one rhinoceros hunt is like another, except in its details, and I will not occupy the reader with the account of this new pursuit and death. Suffice it to say that, in all the elements of neurotic experience, such an encounter seems to me fully equal to half an hour's brisk skirmish at six or seven hundred yards—and with an important addition. In war there is a cause, there is duty, there is the hope of glory, for who can tell what may not be won before night? But here at the end is only a hide, a horn, and a carcase, over which the vultures have already begun to wheel.

*    *    *

Nothing causes the East African colonist more genuine concern than that his guest should not have been provided with a lion. How to find, and, having found, to kill, a lion is the unvarying theme of conversation; and every place and every journey is judged by a simple standard—"lions or no lions". At the Thika camp, then, several gentlemen, accomplished in this important sport, have come together with ponies, rifles, Somalis, and all the other accessories.

Some zebras and kongoni have been killed and left lying in likely looking places to attract the lions; and at 4 a.m., rain or shine, we are to go and look for them.

First find the lion, lured to a kill, driven from a reed-bed, or kicked up incontinently by the way. Once viewed he must never be lost sight of for a moment. Mounted on ponies of more or less approved fidelity, three or four daring Britons or Somalis gallop after him, as in India they ride the pig—that is to say, neck or nothing—across rocks, holes, tussocks, nullahs, through high grass, thorn scrub, undergrowth, turning him, shepherding him, heading him this way and that until he is brought to bay. For his part the lion is no seeker of quarrels; he is often described in accents of contempt. His object throughout is to save his skin. If, being unarmed, you meet six or seven lions unexpectedly, all you need do—according to my information—is to speak to them sternly and they will slink away, while you throw a few stones at them to hurry them up. All the highest authorities recommend this.

But when pursued from place to place, chased hither and thither by the wheeling horsemen, the naturally mild disposition of the lion becomes embittered. First he begins to growl and roar at his enemies, in order to terrify them, and make them leave him in peace. Then he darts little short charges at them. Finally, when every attempt at peaceful persuasion has failed, he pulls up abruptly and offers battle. Once he has done this, he will run no more. He means to fight, and to fight to the death. He means to charge home; and when a lion, maddened with the agony of a bullet-wound, distressed by long and hard pursuit, or, most of all, a lioness in defence of her cubs, is definitely committed to the charge, death is the only possible conclusion. Broken limbs, broken jaws, a body raked from end to end, lungs pierced through and through, entrails torn and protruding—none of these count. It must be death—instant and utter—for the lion, or down goes the man, mauled by septic claws and fetid teeth, crushed and crunched, and poisoned afterwards to make doubly sure. Such are the habits of this cowardly and wicked animal.

It is at the stage when the lion has been determinedly "bayed" that the sportsman from London is usually introduced upon the scene. He has, we may imagine, followed the riders as fast as the inequalities of the ground, his own want of training, and the burden of a heavy rifle will allow him. He arrives at the spot where the lion is cornered in much the same manner as the matador enters the arena, the others standing aside deferentially, ready to aid him or divert the lion. If his bullet kills, he is, no doubt, justly proud. If it only wounds, the lion charges the nearest horseman. For forty yards the charge of a lion is swifter than the gallop of a racehorse. The riders, therefore, usually avoid waiting within that distance. But sometimes they do not; or sometimes the lion sees the man who has shot him; or sometimes all sorts of things happen which make good stories—afterwards.

★     ★     ★

At Nyoro station nearly nine hundred natives were at work cutting timber for the railway, which is entirely dependent on wood fuel. The contractor in charge, a young English gentleman, who was described to me as being a model employer of native labour in government contracts, had taken the trouble to cut a path through the forest across a loop of the line in order that I might see what it was like inside. Through this leafy tunnel, about a mile and a half long, we all accordingly dived. There was nothing sinister in the aspect of this forest, for all its density and confusion. The great giants towered up magnificently to a hundred and fifty feet. Then came the ordinary forest trees, much more thickly clustered. Below this again was a layer of scrub and bushes; and under, around, and among the whole flowed a vast sea of convolvulus-looking creeper. Through all this four-fold veil the sunlight struggled down every twenty yards or so in gleaming chequers of green and gold.

On the way the method of fuel-cutting is explained. So far as the labourer is concerned, it is an elaborate system of piece-work, very accurately and fairly adjusted, and, as is so often the case where the white employer takes personal care of his men, there appeared to be no difficulty in finding any number of natives. But they are a plaguey company. Few will stay for more than a month or two, however satisfied they may be with their work and its rewards; and just as they begin to get skilful, off they go to their villages to cultivate their gardens and their families, promising to come back another year, or after the harvest, or at some other remote and indefinite date. And meanwhile the railway must have its fuel every day and day after day, with the remorseless monotony of the industrial machine.

But what a way to cut fuel! A floating population of clumsy barbarians pecking at the trees with native choppers more like a toy hoe than an axe, and carrying their loads when completed a quarter of a mile on their heads to the wood-stack, while the forest laughs at the feebleness of man. I made a calculation. Each of the nine hundred natives employed costs on the whole £6 a year. The price of a steam tree-felling plant, with a mile of mono-rail tram complete, is about £500. The interest and sinking fund on this capital outlay represent the wages of four natives, to which must be added the salary of a competent white engineer, equal to the wage of forty natives, and the working expenses and depreciation roughly estimated at the wage of twenty natives more; in all the wage of sixty-five natives. Such a plant, able to cut trees six feet in diameter through in four or five minutes, to cut timber as well as fuel, to saw it into the proper lengths for every purpose with the utmost rapidity, and to transport it by whole truck-loads when sawn to the railway siding, would accomplish a week's work of the sixty-five natives it replaced in a single day, and effect a sevenfold multiplication of power. It is no good trying to lay hold of Tropical Africa with naked fingers. Civilization must be armed with machinery if she is to subdue these wild regions to her authority. Iron roads, not jogging porters; tireless engines, not weary men; cheap power, not cheap labour; steam and skill, not sweat and fumbling: there lies the only way to tame the jungle—more jungles than one.

\* \* \*

The Ripon Falls are, for their own sake, well worth a visit. The Nile springs out of the Victoria Nyanza, a vast body of water nearly as wide as the Thames at Westminster Bridge, and this imposing river rushes down a stairway of rock from fifteen to twenty feet deep, in smooth, swirling slopes of green water. It would be perfectly easy to harness the whole river and let the Nile begin its long and beneficent journey to the sea by leaping through a turbine.[1]

[1] This imaginative conception became a reality when Her Majesty Queen Elizabeth II opened the Owen Falls Dam on 29 April, 1954.

It is possible that nowhere else in the world could so enormous a mass of water be held up by so little masonry. Two or three short dams from island to island across the falls would enable, at an inconceivably small cost, the whole level of the Victoria Nyanza— over an expanse of 150,000 square miles—to be gradually raised six or seven feet; would greatly increase the available water-power; would deepen the water in Kavirondo Bay, so as to admit steamers of much larger draught; and, finally, would enable the lake to be maintained at a uniform level, so that immense areas of swampy foreshore, now submerged, now again exposed, according to the rainfalls, would be converted either into clear water or dry land, to the benefit of man and the incalculable destruction of mosquitoes.

*     *     *

Fancy mistaking a hippopotamus—almost the largest surviving mammal in the world—for a water lily. Yet nothing is more easy. The whole river is dotted with floating lilies detached from any root and drifting along contentedly with the current. It is the habit of the hippo to loll in the water showing only his eyes and the tips of his ears, and perhaps now and again a glimpse of his nose, and thus concealed his silhouette is, at three hundred yards, almost indistinguishable from the floating vegetation. I thought they also looked like giant cats peeping. So soon, however, as they saw us coming round a corner and heard the throbbing of the propeller, they would raise their whole heads out of the water to have a look, and then immediately dive to the bottom in disgust. Our practice was then to shut off steam and drift silently down upon them. In this way one arrives in the middle of the herd, and when curiosity or want of air compels them to come up again there is a chance of a shot. One great fellow came up to breathe within five yards of the boat, and the look of astonishment, of alarm, of indignation, in his large, expressive eyes—as with one vast snort he plunged below— was comical to see. These creatures are not easy to kill. They bob up in the most unexpected quarters, and are down again in a second. One does not like to run the risk of merely wounding them, and the target presented is small and vanishing. I shot one who sank with a harsh sort of scream and thud of striking bullet. We waited about a long time for him to float up to the surface, but in vain.

# OFF TO THE WARS

# THE STORY OF THE
# MALAKAND FIELD FORCE

*First published in 1898, this book is based on letters written*
*for the "Daily Telegraph" when the author was acting for*
*that newspaper as a war correspondent and as an officer*
*attached to the famous Force commanded by Major-General*
*Sir Bindon Blood. The operations of the Force were excep-*
*tional in the long history of the wars against the powerful*
*tribes of the North-West Frontier of India.*
*The book is regarded as classic on the campaign, and revealed*
*at a very early age the author's remarkable gifts not only as a*
*correspondent but as a military historian.*

THE INHABITANTS of these wild but wealthy valleys are of many tribes, but of similar character and condition. The abundant crops which a warm sun and copious rains raise from a fertile soil support a numerous population in a state of warlike leisure. Except at the times of sowing and of harvest, a continual state of feud and strife prevails throughout the land. Tribe wars with tribe. The people of one valley fight with those of the next. To the quarrels of communities are added the combats of individuals. Khan assails khan, each supported by his retainers. Every tribesman has a blood feud with his neighbour. Every man's hand is against the other, and all against the stranger.

Nor are these struggles conducted with the weapons which usually belong to the races of such development. To the ferocity of the Zulu are added the craft of the Redskin and the marksmanship of the Boer. The world is presented with that grim spectacle, "the strength of civilization without its mercy". At a thousand yards the traveller falls wounded by the well-aimed bullet of a breech-loading rifle. His assailant, approaching, hacks him to death with the ferocity of a South-Sea Islander. The weapons of the nineteenth century are in the hands of the savages of the Stone Age.

Every influence, every motive, that provokes the spirit of murder among men, impels these mountaineers to deeds of treachery and violence. The strong aboriginal propensity to kill, inherent in all human beings, has in these valleys been preserved in unexampled strength and vigour. That religion, which above all others was founded and propagated by the sword—the tenets and principles of which are instinct with incentives to slaughter and which in three continents has produced fighting breeds of men—stimulates a wild and merciless fanaticism. The love of plunder, always a characteristic of hill tribes, is fostered by the spectacle of opulence and luxury which, to their eyes, the cities and plains of the south display. A code of honour not less punctilious than that of old Spain is supported by vendettas as implacable as those of Corsica.

The tale that I have to tell [of the Malakand Field Force] is one of frontier war. Neither the importance of the issues, nor the numbers of the combatants, are on a European scale. The fate of empires does not hang on the result. Yet the narrative may not be without interest, or material for reflection. In the quarrels of civilized nations, great armies, many thousands strong, collide. Brigades and battalions are hurried forward, and come perhaps within some fire zone, swept by concentrated batteries, or massed musketry. Hundreds or thousands fall killed and wounded. The survivors struggle on blindly, dazed and dumfounded, to the nearest cover. Fresh troops are continuously poured on from behind. At length one side or the other gives way. In all this tumult, this wholesale slaughter, the individual and his feelings are utterly lost. Only the army has a tale to tell. With events on such a scale, the hopes and fears, the strength and weakness, of man are alike indistinguishable. Amid the din and dust little but destruction can be discerned. But on the frontier, in the clear light of morning, when the mountain side is dotted with smoke puffs, and every ridge sparkles with bright sword blades, the spectator may observe and accurately appreciate all grades of human courage—the wild fanaticism of the *Ghazi*, the composed fatalism of the Sikh, the stubbornness of the British soldier, and the jaunty daring of his officers. He may remark occasions of devotion and self-sacrifice, of cool cynicism and stern resolve. He may participate in moments of wild enthusiasm, or of

82

savage anger and dismay. The skill of the general, the quality of the troops, the eternal principles of the art of war, will be as clearly displayed as on historic fields. Only the scale of the statistics is reduced.

A single glass of champagne imparts a feeling of exhilaration. The nerves are braced, the imagination is agreeably stirred, the wits become more nimble. A bottle produces a contrary effect. Excess causes a comatose insensibility. So it is with war, and the quality of both is best discovered by sipping.

The rumours of coming war grew stronger and stronger. The bazaars of India, like the London coffee-houses of the last century, are always full of marvellous tales—the invention of fertile brains. A single unimportant fact is exaggerated, and distorted, till it becomes unrecognizable. From it, a thousand wild, illogical, and fantastic conclusions are drawn. These again are circulated as facts. So the game goes on. But amid all this falsehood, and idle report, there often lies important information. The bazaar stories not only indicate the state of native opinion, but not infrequently contain the germ of truth. In Eastern lands, news travels by strange channels, and often with unaccountable rapidity. As July [1897] advanced the bazaar at Malakand became full of tales of the Mad Fakir. His miracles passed from mouth to mouth, with suitable additions.

A great day for Islam was at hand. A mighty man had arisen to lead them. The English would be swept away. By the time of the new moon, not one would remain. The Great Fakir had mighty armies concealed among the mountains. When the moment came these would sally forth—horse, foot and artillery—and destroy the infidel. It was even stated that the Mullah had ordered that no one should go near a certain hill, lest the heavenly hosts should be prematurely revealed. So ran the talk. But among all these frothy fabrications there lay a solemn warning.

Though the British military and political officers were compelled to take official notice of the reports received with reference to the tribal gathering, and to make arrangements for the safety of their posts, they privately scouted the idea that any serious events were impending.

On the afternoon of 26 July [1897] the subalterns and younger officers of the Malakand garrison proceeded to Khàr to play polo. Thither also came Lieutenant Rattray, riding over from Chakdara fort. The game was a good one, and the tribesmen of the neighbouring village watched it as usual in little groups, with a keen interest. Nothing in their demeanour betrayed their thoughts or intentions. The young soldiers saw nothing, knew nothing, and had they known would have cared less. There would be no rising. If there was, so much the better. They were ready for it. The game ended and the officers cantered back to their camps and posts.

It was then that a strange incident occurred—an incident eminently characteristic of the frontier tribes. As the *syces* were putting the rugs and clothing on the polo ponies, and loitering about the ground after the game, the watching natives drew near, and advised them to be off home at once, for that there was going to be a fight. They knew, these Pathans, what was coming. The wave of fanaticism was sweeping down the valley. It would carry them away. They were powerless to resist. Like one who feels a fit coming on, they waited. Nor did they care very much. When the Mad Fakir arrived, they would fight and kill the infidels. In the meantime there was no necessity to deprive them of their ponies. And so with motives, partly callous, partly sportsmanlike, and not without some faint suspicion of chivalry, they warned the native grooms, and these taking the hint reached the camp in safety.

Late on this same afternoon Major Deane reported to Brigadier-General Meiklejohn, who commanded the Malakand garrison, that matters had assumed a very grave aspect; that a great armed gathering had collected around the Mad Mullah's standard, and that an attack was probable. He advised that the Guides should be called up to reinforce the brigade. A telegram was immediately despatched to Mardan ordering them to march without delay. At 8.30 Lieutenant P. Eliott-Lockhart, who was the senior officer then with the regiment, received the order. At 1.30 a.m. they began their now famous march.

Suddenly in the stillness of the night a bugle-call sounded on the parade ground of the "crater" camp. Everyone sprang up. It was the "Assembly". For a moment there was silence while the officers seized their swords and belts and hurriedly fastened them on. Several thinking that it was merely the warning for the movable column to fall in, waited to light their cigarettes. Then from many quarters the loud explosion of musketry burst forth, a sound which for six days and nights was to know no intermission.

The attack on the Malakand and the great frontier war had begun. The noise of firing echoed among the hills. Its echoes are ringing still. One valley caught the waves of sound and passed them to the next, till the whole wide mountain region rocked with the confusion of the tumult. Slender wires and long-drawn cables carried the vibrations to the far-off countries of the West. Distant populations on the continent of Europe thought that in them they detected the dull, discordant tones of decline and fall. Families in English homes feared that the detonations marked the death of those they loved—sons, brothers or husbands. Diplomatists looked wise, economists anxious, stupid people mysterious and knowledgeable. All turned to have the noise stopped. But that was a task which could not be accomplished until thousands of lives had been sacrificed and millions of money spent.

In the attack on the Malakand camp, all the elements of danger and disorder were displayed. The surprise, the darkness, the confused and broken nature of the ground; the unknown numbers of the enemy; their merciless ferocity; every appalling circumstance was present. But there were men who were equal to the occasion. As soon as the alarm sounded, Lieutenant-Colonel McRae of the 45th Sikhs, a holder of the Gold Medal of the Royal Humane Society and of long experience in Afghanistan and on the Indian frontier, ran to the Quarter Guard, and collecting seven or eight men, sent them under command of Major Taylor, of the same regiment, down the Buddhist road to try and check the enemy's advance. Hurriedly assembling another dozen men, and leaving the Adjutant, Lieutenant Barff, with directions to bring on more, he ran with his little party after Taylor in the direction of the entrance gorge of the Kotal camp. Two roads give access to the Malakand camp, from the plain of Khàr. At one point the Buddhist road, the higher of the two, passes through a narrow defile and turns a sharp corner. Here, if anywhere, the enemy might be held or at least delayed until the troops got under arms. Overtaking Major Taylor, Colonel McRae led the party, which then amounted to perhaps twenty men, swiftly down the road. It was a race on which the lives of hundreds depended. If the enemy could turn the corner, nothing could check their rush, and the few men who tried to oppose them would be cut to pieces. The Sikhs arrived first, but by a very little. As they turned the corner they met the mass of the enemy, nearly a thousand strong, armed chiefly with swords and knives, creeping silently and stealthily up the gorge, in the hope and assurance, of rushing the camp and massacring every soul in it. The whole road was crowded with the wild figures. McRae opened fire at once. Volley after volley was poured into the dense mass, at deadly range. At length the Sikhs fired independently. This checked the enemy, who shouted and yelled in fury at being thus stopped. The small party of soldiers then fell back, pace by pace, firing incessantly, and took up a position in a cutting about fifty yards behind the corner. Their flanks were protected on the left by high rocks, and on the right by boulders and rough ground, over which in the darkness it was impossible to move. The road was about five yards wide. As fast as the tribesmen turned the corner they were shot down. It was a strong position.

Meanwhile the enemy rushed to the attack with wild courage and reckless fury. Careless of life, they charged the slender line of defence. Twice they broke through and penetrated the enclosure. They were met by men as bold as they. The fighting became desperate. The general himself hurried from point to point, animating the soldiers and joining in the defence with sword and revolver. As soon as the enemy broke into the commissariat lines they rushed into the huts and sheds eager for plunder and victims.

Lieutenant Manley, the Brigade Commissariat Officer, stuck stubbornly to his post, and with Sergeant Harrington endeavoured to hold the hut in which he lived. The savage tribesmen burst in the door and crowded into the room. What followed reads like a romance.

The officer opened fire at once with his revolver. He was instantly cut down and hacked to pieces. In the struggle the lamp was smashed. The room became pitch dark. The sergeant, knocking down his assailants, got free for a moment and stood against the wall motionless. Having killed Manley, the tribesmen now began to search for the sergeant, feeling with their hands along the wall and groping

in the darkness. At last, finding no one, they concluded he had
escaped, and hurried out to look for others. Sergeant Harrington
remained in the hut till it was retaken some hours later, and so
saved his life.

Another vigorous attack was made upon the Quarter Guard.
Lieutenant Watling, who met it with his company of sappers,
transfixed a *Ghazi* with his sword, but such was the fury of the
fanatic that as he fell dead he cut at the officer and wounded him
severely. The company were driven back. The Quarter Guard was
captured, and with it the reserve ammunition of the sappers.
Lieutenant Watling was carried in by his men, and, as soon as he
reached the dressing station, reported the loss of this important post.

Brigadier-General Meiklejohn at once ordered a party of the
24th to retake it from the enemy. Few men could be spared from
the line of defence. At length a small but devoted band collected.
It consisted of Captain Holland, Lieutenant Climo, Lieutenant
Manley, R.E., the general's orderly, a Sepoy of the 45th Sikhs, two
or three sappers and three men of the 24th; in all about a dozen.

The general placed himself at their head. The officers drew their
revolvers. The men were instructed to use the bayonet only. Then
they advanced. The ground is by nature broken and confused to an
extraordinary degree. Great rocks, undulations and trees, rendered
all movements difficult. Frequent tents, sheds and other buildings
increased the intricacies. Amidst such surroundings were the enemy,
numerous and well armed. The twelve men charged. The tribesmen
advanced to meet them. The officers shot down man after man
with their pistols. The soldiers bayoneted others. The enemy drew
off discomfited, but half the party were killed or wounded.

As the night wore on, the attack of the enemy became so vigorous,
that the brigadier decided to call for a reinforcement of a hundred
men from the garrison of the fort. This work stood high on a hill,
and was impregnable to an enemy unprovided with field guns.
Lieutenant Rawlins volunteered to try and reach it with the order.
Accompanied by three orderlies, he started. He had to make his
way through much broken ground infested by the enemy. One
man sprang at him and struck him on the wrist with a sword,
but the subaltern, firing his revolver, shot him dead, reached the

fort in safety, and brought back the sorely-needed reinforcement.

It was thought that the enemy would make a final effort to capture the enclosure before dawn, that being the hour which Afghan tribesmen usually select. But they had lost heavily, and at about 3.30 a.m. began to carry away their dead and wounded. The firing did not, however, lessen until 4.15 a.m., when the sharpshooters withdrew to the heights, and the fusillade dwindled to "sniping" at long range.

The first night of the defence of the Malakand camp was over. The enemy, with all the advantages of surprise, position and great numbers, had failed to overcome the slender garrison. Everywhere they had been repulsed with slaughter. But the British losses had been severe.

The telegraph had carried the news of the events of the night to all parts of the world. In England those returning from Goodwood Races read the first details of the fighting on the posters of the evening papers. At Simla, the Government of India awoke to find themselves confronted with another heavy task. Other messages recalled all officers to their regiments, and summoned reinforcements to the scene by road and rail. In the small hours of the 27th, the officers of the 11th Bengal Lancers at Nowshera were aroused by a frantic telegraph operator, who was astounded by the news his machine was clicking out. This man in his shirt sleeves, with a wild eye, and holding an unloaded revolver by the muzzle, ran round waking everyone. The whole country was up. The Malakand garrison was being overwhelmed by thousands of tribesmen. All the troops were to march at once. He brandished copies of the wires he had received. In a few moments official instructions arrived. The 11th Bengal Lancers, the 38th Dogras and the 35th Sikhs started at dawn. No. 1 and No. 7 British Mountain Batteries were also ordered up. The Guides Cavalry had already arrived. Their infantry under Lieutenant Lockhart reached the Kotal at 7.30 p.m. on the 27th, having, in spite of the intense heat and choking dust, covered thirty-two miles in seventeen and a half hours. This wonderful feat was accomplished without impairing the efficiency of the soldiers, who were sent into the picket line, and became engaged as soon as they arrived. An officer who commanded the Dargai post told me that, as they passed the guard there, they shouldered arms with parade precision, as if to show that twenty-six miles under the hottest sun in the world would not take the polish off the Corps of Guides. Then they breasted the long ascent to the top of the pass, encouraged by the sound of the firing, which grew louder at every step.

Help in plenty was thus approaching as fast as eager men could march, but meanwhile the garrison had to face the danger as best they could alone. As the 31st Punjaub Infantry, who had been the last to leave the north camp, were arriving at the Kotal, about one thousand tribesmen descended in broad daylight and with the greatest boldness, and threatened their left flank. They drove in two pickets of the 24th, and pressed forward vigorously. Lieutenant Climo with two companies advanced up the hill to meet them, supported by the fire of two guns of the Mountain Battery. A bayonet charge was completely successful. The officers were close enough to make effective use of their revolvers. Nine bodies of the enemy were left on the ground, and a standard was captured. The tribesmen then drew off, and the garrison prepared for the attack, which they knew would come with the dark.

As the evening drew on the enemy were observed assembling in ever-increasing numbers. Great crowds of them could be seen streaming along the Chakdara road, and thickly dotting the hills with spots of white. They all wore white as yet. The news had not reached Buner, and the sombre-clad warriors of Ambeyla were still absent. The glare of the flames from the north camp was soon to summon them to the attack of their ancient enemies. The spectacle as night fell was strange, ominous, but not unpicturesque. Gay banners of every colour, shape and device, waved from the surrounding hills. The sunset caught the flashing of sword-blades behind the spurs and ridges. The numerous figures of the enemy moved busily about preparing for the attack. A dropping fire from the sharp-shooters added an appropriate accompaniment. In the middle, at the bottom of the cup, was the "crater" camp and the main enclosure with the smoke of the evening meal rising in the air. The troops moved to their stations, and, as the shadows grew, the firing swelled into a loud, incessant roar.

Lieutenant Ford was dangerously wounded in the shoulder. The bullet cut the artery, and he was bleeding to death when Surgeon-Lieutenant J. H. Hugo came to his aid. The fire was too hot to allow of lights being used. There was no cover of any sort. It was at the bottom of the cup. Nevertheless the surgeon struck a match at the peril of his life and examined the wound. The match went out amid a splutter of bullets, which kicked up the dust all around, but by its uncertain light he saw the nature of the injury. The officer had already fainted from the loss of blood. The doctor seized the artery, and, as no other ligature was forthcoming, he remained under fire for three hours holding a man's life, between his finger and thumb. When at length it seemed that the enemy had broken into the camp he picked up the still unconscious officer in his arms, and, without relaxing his hold, bore him to a place of safety. His arm was for many hours paralysed with cramp from the effects of the exertion of compressing the artery.

I think there are few, whatever may be their views or interests, who will not applaud this splendid act of devotion. The profession of medicine, and surgery, must always rank as the most noble that men can adopt. The spectacle of a doctor in action among soldiers, in equal danger and with equal courage, saving life where all others are taking it, allaying pain where all others are causing it, is one which must always seem glorious, whether to God or man. It is impossible to imagine any situation from which a human being might better leave this world, and embark on the hazards of the Unknown.

The command of this powerful force [for the relief of Chakdara] was entrusted to Brigadier-General Sir Bindon Blood, K.C.B., who was granted the local rank of Major-General.

Thirty-seven years of soldiering, of war in many lands, of sport of every kind, have steeled alike muscle and nerve. Sir Bindon Blood, himself, till warned by the march of time, a keen polo player, is one of those few officers of high rank in the army who recognize the advantages to soldiers of that splendid game. He has pursued all kinds of wild animals in varied jungles, has killed many pigs with the spear and shot every species of Indian game, including thirty tigers to his own rifle.

It would not be fitting for me, a subaltern of horse, to offer any criticism, though eulogistic, on the commander under whom I have had the honour to serve in the field. I shall content myself with saying that the general is one of that type of soldiers and administrators, which the responsibilities and dangers of an empire produce, a type which has not been, perhaps, possessed by any nation except the British, since the days when the Senate and the Roman people sent their proconsuls to all parts of the world.

Sir Bindon Blood had with his staff ascended the Castle Rock, to superintend the operations generally. From this position the whole field was visible. On every side, and from every rock, the white figures of the enemy could be seen in full flight. The way was open. The passage was forced. Chakdara was saved. A great and brilliant success had been obtained. A thrill of exultation convulsed everyone. In that moment the general, who watched the triumphant issue of his plans, must have experienced as fine an emotion as is given to man on earth. In that moment, we may imagine that the weary years of routine, the long ascent of the lower grades of the service, the frequent subordination to incompetence, the fatigues and dangers of five campaigns, received their compensation. Perhaps, such is the contrariness of circumstances, there was no time for the enjoyment of these reflections. The victory had been gained. It remained to profit by it. The enemy would be compelled to retire across the plain. There at last was the chance of the cavalry. The four squadrons were hurried to the scene.

The 11th Bengal Lancers, forming line across the plain, began a merciless pursuit up the valley. The Guides pushed on to seize the Amàndara Pass and relieve Chakdara. All among the rice fields and the rocks, the strong horsemen hunted the flying enemy. No quarter was asked or given, and every tribesman caught was speared or cut down at once. Their bodies lay thickly strewn about the fields, spotting with black and white patches the bright green of the rice crop. It was a terrible lesson and one which the inhabitants of Swat and Bajaur will never forget. Since then their terror of Lancers has been extraordinary. A few sowars have frequently been sufficient to drive a hundred of these valiant savages in disorder to the hills, or prevent them descending into the plain for hours.

Meanwhile the infantry had been advancing swiftly. The 45th Sikhs stormed the fortified village of Batkhela near the Amàndara Pass, which the enemy held desperately. Lieutenant-Colonel McRae, who had been relieved from the command of the regiment by the arrival of Colonel Sawyer, was the first man to enter the village. Eighty of the enemy were bayoneted in Batkhela alone. It was a terrible reckoning.

I am anxious to finish with this scene of carnage. The spectator, who may gaze unmoved on the bloodshed of the battle, must avert his eyes from the horrors of the pursuit unless, indeed, joining in it himself, he flings all scruples to the winds and, carried away by the impetus of the moment, indulges to the full those deep-seated instincts of savagery, over which civilization has but cast a veil of doubtful thickness.

The morning of the 30th [August] brought no cessation of the fighting [at Chakdara], but the enemy, disheartened by their losses of the previous night, did not attack until 7 p.m. At that hour they advanced and made a fresh effort. They were again repulsed. Perhaps the reader is tired of the long recital of the monotonous succession of assaults and repulses. What must the garrison have been by the reality? Until this day—when they snatched a few hours' sleep—they had been continually fighting and watching for ninety-six hours. Like men in a leaking ship, who toil at the pumps ceaselessly and find their fatigues increasing and the ship sinking hour by hour, they cast anxious, weary eyes in the direction whence help might be expected. But none came. And there are worse deaths than by drowning.

Men fell asleep at the loopholes and at the service of the field gun. Even during the progress of the attacks, insulted nature asserted itself, and the soldiers drifted away from the roar of the musketry, and the savage figures of the enemy, to the peaceful unconsciousness of utter exhaustion. The officers, haggard but tireless, aroused them frequently.

At other times the brave Sepoys would despair. The fort was ringed with the enemy. The Malakand, too, was assailed. Perhaps it was the same elsewhere. The whole British Raj seemed passing away in a single cataclysm. The officers encouraged them. The

92

Government of the Queen-Empress would never desert them. If they could hold out, they would be relieved. If not, they would be avenged. Trust in the young white men who led them, and perhaps some dim half-idolatrous faith in a mysterious Sovereign across the seas, whose soldiers they were, and who would surely protect them, restored their fainting strength.

During the whole time of the siege the difficulty of maintaining signalling communication with the Malakand was extreme. But for the heroism of the signallers, it would have been insuperable. One man in particular, Sepoy Prem Singh, used every day at the risk of his life to come out through a porthole of the tower, establish his heliograph, and, under a terrible fire from short range, flash urgent messages to the main force. The extreme danger, the delicacy of the operation of obtaining connection with a helio, the time consumed, the composure required, these things combined to make the action as brave as any. Early on Saturday morning a supply of water was sent to the guard of the signal tower. It was the last they got until 4.30 on Monday afternoon.

When the attack on the fort [at Chakdara] began, the enemy numbered perhaps 1,500 men. Since then they had been increasing every day, until on the 1st and 2nd, they are estimated to have been between twelve thousand and fourteen thousand strong. Matters now began to assume a still graver aspect. At five o'clock on the evening of the 31st a renewed attack was made in tremendous force on the east side of the fort. But it was beaten back with great loss by the Maxims and the field gun. All night long the firing continued, and Sunday morning displayed the enemy in far larger numbers than hitherto. They now captured the Civil Hospital, a detached building, the walls of which they loopholed, and from which they maintained a galling fire. They also occupied the ridge, leading to the signal tower, thus cutting off all communication with its guard. No water reached those unfortunate men that day. The weather was intensely hot. The fire from the ridge made all interior communication difficult and dangerous. The enemy appeared armed to a great extent with Martini-Henry rifles and Sniders, and their musketry was most harassing. The party in the tower kept sending by signal, pressing requests for water, which could not be supplied. The situation became critical.

93

Still the garrison displayed a determined aspect, and though the tribesmen occupied the ridge, the Civil Hospital and an adjoining nullah, none set foot within the defences.

At length the last day of the struggle came. At daybreak the enemy in tremendous numbers came on to the assault, as if resolute to take the place at any cost. They carried scaling ladders and bundles of grass. The firing became intense. In spite of the cover of the garrison several men were killed and wounded by the hail of bullets which was directed against the fort, and which splashed and scarred the walls in every direction.

Then suddenly, as matters were approaching a crisis, the cavalry of the relieving column appeared over the Amàndara ridge. The strong horsemen mercilessly pursued and cut down all who opposed them. When they reached the Bridgehead on the side of the river remote from the fort, the enemy began to turn and run. The garrison had held out stubbornly and desperately throughout the siege. Now that relief was at hand, Lieutenant Rattray flung open the gate, and followed by half a dozen men charged the Civil Hospital. Captain Baker and Lieutenant Wheatley followed with a few more. The hospital was recaptured. The enemy occupying it, some thirty in number, were bayoneted. It was a finish in style. Returning, the sallying party found the cavalry—the 11th Bengal Lancers—checked by a *sungar* full of tribesmen. This they charged in flank, killing most of its occupants, and driving the rest after their comrades in rout and ruin. The last man to leave the *sungar* shot Lieutenant Rattray in the neck, but that officer, as distinguished for physical prowess, as for military conduct, cut him down. This ended the fighting. It is not possible to think of a more fitting conclusion.

It is a significant fact, that, though the cavalry horses were exposed to the enemy's fire the whole time, hardly any were killed or wounded. The tribesmen, feeling sure that the place was theirs, and hoping that these fine beasts would fall into their hands alive, had abstained from shooting them.

It is no exaggeration to say, that perhaps half the tribesmen who attacked the Malakand had thought that the soldiers there were the only troops that the Sirkar [the government] possessed. "Kill these," they had said, "and all is done." What did they know of the distant regiments which the telegraph wires were drawing, from far down in the south of India? Little did they realize they had set the world humming; that military officers were hurrying seven thousand miles by sea and land from England, to the camps among the mountains; that long trains were carrying ammunition, material and supplies from distant depots to the front; that astute financiers were considering in what degree their action had affected the ratio between silver and gold, or that sharp politicians were wondering how the outbreak in Swat might be made to influence the impending bye-elections. These ignorant tribesmen had no conception of the sensitiveness of modern civilization, which thrills and quivers in every part of its vast and complex system at the slightest touch.

They saw only the forts and camps on the Malakand Pass and the swinging bridge across the river.

While the people of Lower Swat, deserted by the Mad Mullah, and confronted with the two brigades, were completely humbled and subdued, the Upper Swatis, encouraged by their priests, and, as they believed, safe behind their "gate", assumed a much more independent air. They sent to inquire what terms the government would offer, and said they would consider the matter. Their contumacious attitude induced the political officers to recommend the movement of troops, through their country, to impress them with the determination and power of the Sirkar.

The expedition into the Upper Swat Valley was accordingly sanctioned, and Sir Bindon Blood began making the necessary preparations for the advance. The prospects of further fighting were eagerly welcomed by the troops, and especially by those who had arrived too late for the relief of Chakdara, and had had thus far only long and dusty marches to perform. There was much speculation and excitement as to what units would be selected, everyone asserting that his regiment was sure to go; that it was their turn; and that if they were not taken it would be a great shame.

An incident now ensued, which, though it afforded an opportunity for a splendid act of courage, yet involved an unnecessary loss of life, and must be called disastrous. As the cavalry got clear of the broken ground, the leading horsemen saw the tribesmen swiftly running towards the hills, about a mile distant. Carried away by the excitement of the pursuit, and despising the enemy for their slight resistance, they dashed impetuously forward in the hope of catching them before they could reach the hills.

Lieutenant-Colonel Adams, on entering the plain, saw at once that if he could seize a small clump of trees near a cemetery, he would be able to bring effective dismounted fire to bear on the retreating tribesmen. He therefore collected as many men as possible, and with Lieutenant Maclean, and Lord Fincastle, the *Times* correspondent, rode in the direction of these points. Meanwhile Captain Palmer, who commanded the leading squadron, and Lieutenant Greaves of the Lancashire Fusiliers, who was acting war correspondent of *The Times of India*, galloped across the rice fields after the enemy. The squadron, unable to keep up, straggled out in a long string, in the swampy ground.

At the foot of the hills the ground was firmer, and reaching this, the two officers recklessly dashed in among the enemy. It is the spirit that loses the Empire many lives, but has gained it many battles. But the tribesmen, who had been outmanoeuvred rather than outfought, turned savagely on their pursuers. The whole scene was witnessed by the troops on the ridge. Captain Palmer cut down a standard-bearer. Another man attacked him. Raising his arm for a fresh stroke, his wrist was smashed by a bullet. Another killed his horse. Lieutenant Greaves, shot through the body, fell at the same moment to the ground. The enemy closed around and began hacking him, as he lay, with their swords. Captain Palmer tried to draw his revolver. At this moment two sowars got clear of the swampy rice fields, and at once galloped, shouting, to the rescue, cutting and slashing at the tribesmen. All would have been cut to pieces or shot down. The hillside was covered with the enemy. The wounded officers lay at the foot. They were surrounded. Seeing this Lieutenant-Colonel Adams and Lord Fincastle, with Lieutenant Maclean and two or three sowars, dashed to their assistance. At their charge the tribesmen fell back a little way and opened a heavy fire. Lord Fincastle's horse was immediately shot and he fell to the ground. Rising, he endeavoured to lift the wounded Greaves on to Colonel Adams' saddle, but at this instant a second bullet struck that unfortunate officer, killing him instantly. Colonel Adams was slightly, and Lieutenant Maclean mortally, wounded while giving assistance, and all the horses but two were shot. In spite of the terrible fire, the body of Lieutenant Greaves and the other two wounded officers were rescued and carried to the little clump of trees.

For this gallant feat of arms both the surviving officers, Colonel Adams and Lord Fincastle, were recommended for, and received, the Victoria Cross. It was also officially announced that Lieutenant Maclean would have received it, had he not been killed. There are many, especially on the frontier, where he was known as a fine soldier and a good sportsman, who think that the accident of death should not have been allowed to interfere with the reward of valour.

The extremes of fortune, which befell Lord Fincastle and Lieutenant Greaves, may well claim a moment's consideration. Neither officer was employed officially with the Force. Both had travelled up at their own expense, evading and overcoming all obstacles in an endeavour to see something of war. Knights of the sword and pen, they had nothing to offer but their lives, no troops to lead, no duties to perform, no watchful commanding officer to report their conduct. They played for high stakes, and Fortune, never so capricious as on the field of battle, dealt to the one the greatest honour that a soldier can hope for, as some think, the greatest in the gift of the Crown, and to the other Death.

We camped with the 2nd Brigade on the night of the 6th [September], and next morning, while the stars were still shining, resumed the march. Five miles from Sarai the road dwindles to a mule track, and henceforward is not fit for wheeled traffic. In spite of this, the 10th Field Battery had succeeded in getting their guns along it, and had brought them safely to Panjkora. But soldiers will accomplish a good deal to get nearer the enemy. The scenery before the gorge of the river is reached is gloomy, but grand. Great cliffs tower up precipitously on the further bank and the path is cut in the face of the rock. The river, which flows swiftly by, plunges into a narrow cleft about a mile below the bridge, and disappears among the mountains. It abounds in fish, but is rapid and dangerous, and, while the troops were encamped near it, two gunners lost their lives by falling in, and being carried down. Indeed, watching the dead bodies of several camels being swept along, swirled around, and buffeted against the rocks, it was not hard to understand these accidents.

At length the bridge is reached. It is a frail structure, supported on wire ropes. At each end are gates, flanked by little mud towers. The battery was established on a knoll to the right, and the long muzzles of the guns peered through stone embrasures at the opposite hills. It was round the bases of these hills that much hard fighting took place in the Chitral campaign. About half a mile beyond the bridge, I was shown the place where the Guides had been so hard pressed, and for a whole night had had to stand at bay, their colonel killed, the bridge broken, and the river in flood, against the tribesmen in overwhelming numbers.

The field telegraph stopped at the bridgehead, and a small tent with a half-dozen military operators marked the breaking of the slender thread that connected us, across thousands of miles of sea and land, with London. Henceforward a line of signal stations with their flickering helios would be the only links. We were at the end of the wire. I have often stood at the other and watched the tape machine click off the news as it arrives; the movements of the troops; the prospects of action; the fighting; the casualties. How different are the scenes. The club on an autumn evening—its members grouped anxiously around, discussing, wondering, asserting; the noise of the traffic outside; the cigarette smoke and electric lights within. And, only an hour away along the wire, the field, with the bright sunlight shining on the swirling muddy waters; the black forbidding rocks; the white tents of the brigade a mile up the valley; the long streak of vivid green rice crop by the river; and in the foreground the brown-clad armed men. I can never doubt which is the right end to be at. It is better to be making the news than taking it; to be an actor rather than a critic.

The service camp of an Anglo-Indian brigade is arranged on regular principles. The infantry and guns are extended in the form of a square. The animals and cavalry are placed inside. In the middle is the camp of the headquarters staff, with the tent of the brigadier facing that of the general commanding the division. All around the perimeter a parapet is built, varying in height according to the proximity, and activity, of the enemy. This parapet, not only affords cover from random shots, but also makes a line for the men to form on in case of a sudden attack. Behind it the infantry lie down to sleep, a section of each company, as an inlying picket, dressed and accoutred. Their rifles are often laid along the low wall with the bayonets ready fixed. If cavalry have to be used in holding part of the defences, their lances can be arranged in the same way. Sentries every twenty-five yards surrounded the camp with a line of watchers.

To view the scene by moonlight is alone an experience, which would repay much travelling. The fires have sunk to red, glowing specks. The bayonets glisten in a regular line of blue-white points. The silence of weariness is broken by the incessant and uneasy shuffling of the animals and the occasional neighing of the horses. All the valley is plunged in gloom and the mountains rise high and black around. Far up their sides, the twinkling watch-fires of the tribesmen can be seen. Overhead is the starry sky, bathed in the pale radiance of the moon. It is a spectacle that may inspire the philosopher no less than the artist. The camp is full of subdued noises. Here is no place for reflection, for quiet or solemn thought. The day may have been an exciting one. The morrow may bring an action. Some may be killed, but in war-time life is only lived in the present. It is sufficient to be tired and to have time to rest, and the camp, if all the various items that compose it can be said to have a personality, shrugs its shoulders and, regarding the past without regret, contemplates the future without alarm.

Everyone has read of the sufferings of the British troops in having to campaign in the hot weather during the Indian Mutiny. September in these valleys is as hot as it is easy to imagine or elegant to describe, and the exposure to the sun tells severely on the British battalions as the hospital returns show. Of course, since Mutiny days, many salutary changes have been made in the dress and equipment of the soldier. The small cap with its insufficient puggaree is replaced by the pith helmet, the shade of which is increased by a long quilted covering. The high stock and thick, tight uniforms are gone, and a cool and comfortable khaki kit has been substituted. A spine protector covers the back, and in other ways, rational improvements have been effected. But the sun remains unchanged, and all precautions only minimize, without preventing the evils. Slowly the hours pass away. The heat is intense. The air glitters over the scorched plain, as over the funnel of an engine. The wind blows with a fierce warmth, and instead of bringing relief, raises only whirling dust devils, which scatter the shelters and half-choke their occupants. The water is tepid, and fails to quench the thirst. At last the shadows begin to lengthen, as the sun sinks towards the western mountains. Everyone revives. Even the animals seem to share the general feeling of relief. The camp turns out to see the sunset and enjoy the twilight. The feelings of savage hatred against the orb of day fade from our minds, and we strive to forget that he will be ready at five o'clock next morning to begin the torment over again.

The funerals of the British officers and men, killed the day before, took place at noon. Everyone who could, attended; but all the pomp of military obsequies was omitted, and there were no Union Jacks to cover the bodies, nor were volleys fired over the graves, lest the wounded should be disturbed. Somewhere in the camp— exactly where, is now purposely forgotten—the remains of those who had lost, in fighting for their country, all that men can be sure of, were silently interred. No monument marked the spot. The only assurance that it should be undisturbed is that it remains unknown. Nevertheless, the funerals were impressive. To some the game of war brings prizes, honour, advancement, or experience; to some the consciousness of duty well discharged; and to others— spectators, perhaps—the pleasure of the play and the knowledge of men and things. But here were those who had drawn the evil numbers—who had lost their all, to gain only a soldier's grave. Looking at these shapeless forms, coffined in a regulation blanket, the pride of race, the pomp of empire, the glory of war appeared but the faint and unsubstantial fabric of a dream; and I could not help realizing with Burke: "What shadows we are and what shadows we pursue."

It is no disparagement but rather to the honour of men, that they should be prepared to back with their lives, causes which claim their sympathy. It is indeed to such men that human advancement has been due. I do not allude to this matter, to raise hostile feelings against the Afghan tribesmen or their ruler, but only to explain the difficulties encountered in the Màmund Valley by the 2nd Brigade of the Malakand Field Force: to explain how it was that defenders of obscure villages were numbered by thousands, and why the weapons of poverty-stricken agriculturists were excellent Martini-Henry rifles.

The Màmunds themselves were now genuinely anxious for peace. Their valley was in our hands; their villages and crops were at our mercy; but their allies, who suffered none of these things, were eager to continue the struggle. They had captured most of the rifles of the dead soldiers on the 16th, and they had no intention of giving them up. On the other hand, it was obvious that the British Raj could not afford to be defied in this matter. We had insisted on the rifles being surrendered, and that expensive factor, imperial prestige, demanded that we should prosecute operations till we got them, no matter what the cost might be. The rifles were worth little. The men and officers we lost were worth a great deal. It was unsound economics, but imperialism and economics clash as often as honesty and self-interest. We were therefore committed to the policy of throwing good money after bad, in order to keep up our credit; as a man who cannot pay his tradesmen, sends them fresh orders in lieu of settlement. Under these unsatisfactory conditions the negotiations opened. They did not, however, interfere with the military situation, and the troops continued to forage daily in the valley, and the tribesmen to fire nightly into the camp.

At the end of the week a message from the Queen, expressing sympathy with the sufferings of the wounded, and satisfaction at the conduct of the troops, was published in Brigade orders. It caused the most lively pleasure to all, but particularly to the native soldiers, who heard with pride and exultation, that their deeds and dangers were not unnoticed by that august Sovereign, before whom they know all their princes bow, and to whom the Sirkar itself is but a servant. The cynic and the socialist may sneer after their kind; yet the patriot, who examines with anxious care those forces which tend to the cohesion or disruption of great communities, will observe how much the influence of a loyal sentiment promotes the solidarity of the empire.

I could not help thinking that polo has had a good deal to do with strengthening the good relations of the Indian princes and the British officers. It may seem strange to speak of polo as an imperial factor, but it would not be the first time in history that national games have played a part in high politics. Polo has been the common ground, on which English and Indian gentlemen have met on equal terms, and it is to that meeting that much mutual esteem and respect is due. Besides this, polo has been the salvation of the subaltern in India, and the young officer no longer, as heretofore, has a "centre piece" of brandy on his table night and day. The pony and polo stick have drawn him from his bungalow and mess-room, to play a game which must improve his nerve, his judgment and his temper. The author of the *Indian Polity* asserts that the day will come when British and native officers will serve together in ordinary seniority, and on the same footing. From what I know of the British officer, I do not myself believe that this is possible, but if it should ever come to pass, the way will have been prepared on the polo ground.

I pause to consider for a moment the conditions, and circumstances, by which the pursuit of a military career differs from all others. In political life, in art, in engineering, the man with talents who behaves with wisdom may steadily improve his position in the world. If he makes no mistakes he will probably achieve success. But the soldier is more dependent upon external influences. The only way he can hope to rise above the others is by risking his life in frequent campaigns. All his fortunes, whatever they may be, all his position and weight in the world, all his accumulated capital, as it were, must be staked afresh each time he goes into action. He may have seen twenty engagements, and be covered with decorations and medals. He may be marked as a rising soldier. And yet each time he comes under fire his chances of being killed are as great as, and perhaps greater than, those of the youngest subaltern, whose luck is fresh. The statesman, who has put his power to the test, and made a great miscalculation, may yet retrieve his fortunes. But the indiscriminating bullet settles everything.

I would that it were in my power to convey to the reader, who has not had the fortune to live with troops on service, some just appreciation of the compensations of war. The healthy, open-air life, the vivid incidents, the excitement, not only of realization but of anticipation, the generous and cheery friendships, the chances of distinction which are open to all, invest life with keener interests, and rarer pleasures. The uncertainty and importance of the present reduce the past and future to comparative insignificance, and clear the mind of minor worries. And when all is over, memories remain, which few men do not hold precious. As to the hardships, these though severe may be endured. Ascetics and recluses have in their endeavours to look beyond the grave suffered worse things. Nor will the soldier in the pursuit of fame and the enjoyment of the pleasures of war be exposed to greater discomforts than Diogenes in his tub, or the Trappists in their monastery. Besides all this, his chances of learning about the next world are infinitely greater. And yet, when all has been said, we are confronted with a mournful but stubborn fact. In this contrary life, so prosaic is the mind of man, so material his soul, so poor his spirit, that there is no one who has been six months on active service, who is not delighted to get safe home again, to the comfortable monotonies of peace.

The cheeriness and patience of the wounded men exceeds belief. Perhaps it is due to a realization of the proximity in which they have stood to death; perhaps partly to that feeling of relief, with which a man turns for a spell from war to peace. In any case it is remarkable. A poor fellow—a private in the Buffs—was hit at Zagai, and had his arm amputated at the shoulder. I expressed my sympathy, and he replied, philosophically: "You can't make omelettes without breaking eggs", and after a pause added, with much satisfaction, "The regiment did well that day." He came of a fighting stock, but I could not help speculating on the possible future which awaited him. Discharge from the service as medically unfit, some miserable pension insufficient to command any pleasures but those of drink, a loafer's life, and a pauper's grave. Perhaps the regiment—the officers, that is to say—would succeed in getting him work, and would from their own resources supplement his pension. But what a wretched and discreditable system is that, by which the richest nation in the world neglects the soldiers who have served it

103

well, and which leaves to newspaper philanthropy, to local institutions, and to private charity, a burden which ought to be proudly borne by the State.

It may seem difficult to believe that fifty bullets could fall in a camp, only one hundred yards square—crowded with animals and men—without any other result than to hit a single mule in the tail. Such was, however, the fact. This shows of what value a little active service is to the soldier. The first time he is under fire he imagines himself to be in great danger. He thinks that every bullet is going to hit him, and that every shot is aimed at him. Assuredly he will be killed in a moment. If he goes through this ordeal once or twice he begins to get some idea of the odds in his favour. He has heard lots of bullets and they have not hurt him. He will get home safely to his tea this evening just as he did the last time. He becomes a very much more effective fighting machine.

From a military point of view the perpetual frontier wars in one corner or other of the Empire are of the greatest value. This fact may one day be proved, should our soldiers ever be brought into contact with some peace-trained conscript army in anything like equal numbers.

Though the firing produced very little effect on the troops—most of whom had been through the experience several times before—it was a severe trial to the wounded, whose nerves, shattered by pain and weakness, were unable to bear the strain. The surgeon in charge—Major Tyrrell—told me that the poor fellows quivered at every shot as if in anticipation of a blow. A bullet in the leg will make a brave man a coward. A blow on the head will make a wise man a fool. Indeed I have read that a sufficiency of absinthe can make a good man a knave. The triumph of mind over matter does not seem to be quite complete as yet.

I saw a strange thing happen, while the firing was going on, which may amuse those who take an interest in the habits and development of animals. Just in front of my tent, which was open, was a clear space, occupied by a flock of goats and sheep. The brilliant moonlight made everything plainly visible. Every time a bullet whistled over them or struck the ground near, they ducked and bobbed in evident terror. An officer, who also noticed this, told me it was the first time they had been under fire; and I have been wondering ever since whether this explains their fear or makes it more inexplicable.

The duties of the civil officers, in a campaign, are twofold: firstly, to negotiate, and secondly, to collect information. It would seem that for the first of these duties they are indispensable. The difficult language and peculiar characters of the tribesmen are the study of a lifetime. A knowledge of the local conditions, of the power and influence of the khans, or other rulers of the people; of the general history and traditions of the country, is a task which must be entirely specialized. Rough and ready methods are excellent while the tribes resist, but something more is required when they are anxious to submit. Men are needed who understand the whole question, and all the details of the quarrel, between the natives and the government, and who can in some measure appreciate both points of view. I do not believe that such are to be found in the army. The military profession is alone sufficient to engross the attention of the most able and accomplished man.

Respecting the second duty, it is difficult to believe that the collection of information as to the numbers and intentions of the enemy would not be better and more appropriately carried out by the Intelligence Department and the cavalry. Civil officers should not be expected to understand what kind of military information a general requires. It is not their business.

On one point, however, I have no doubts. The political officers must be under the control of the general directing the operations. There must be no *"Imperium in imperio"*. In a Field Force one man only can command—and all in it must be under his authority. Differences, creating difficulties and leading to disasters, will arise whenever the political officers are empowered to make arrangements with the tribesmen, without consulting and sometimes without even informing the man on whose decisions the success of the war and the lives of the soldiers directly depend.

The necessity for having the officers in the same dress as the men was apparent to all who watched the operations. The conspicuous figure which a British officer in his helmet presented, in contrast to the native soldiers in their turbans, drew a well-aimed fire in his direction. Of course, in British regiments, the difference is not nearly so marked. Nevertheless, at close quarters the keen-eyed tribesmen always made an especial mark of the officers, distinguishing them chiefly, I think, by the fact that they do not carry rifles. The following story may show how evident this was.

When the Buffs were marching down to Panjkòra, they passed the Royal West Kent coming up to relieve them at Inàyat Kila. A private in the up-going regiment asked a friend in the Buffs what it was like at the front. "Oh," replied the latter, "you'll be all right so long as you don't go near no officers, nor no white stones." Whether the advice was taken is not recorded, but it was certainly sound, for three days later—on 30 September—in those companies of the Royal West Kent Regiment that were engaged in the village of Agrah, eight out of eleven officers were hit or grazed by bullets.

The fatigues experienced by troops in mountain warfare are so great that every effort has to be made to lighten the soldier's load. At the same time the more ammunition he carries on his person the better. Mules laden with cartridge-boxes are very likely to be shot, and fall into the hands of the enemy. In this manner over six thousand rounds were lost on 16 September by the two companies of Sikhs.

The thick leather belts, pouches, and valise equipment of British infantry are unnecessarily heavy. I have heard many officers suggest having them made of web. The argument against this is that the web wears out. That objection could be met by having a large supply of these equipments at the base for issue as soon as the old were unfit for use. It is cheaper to wear out belts than soldiers.

Great efforts should be made to give the soldier a piece of chocolate, a small sausage, or something portable and nutritious to carry with him to the field. In a war of long marches, of uncertain fortunes, of retirements often delayed and always pressed, there have been many occasions when regiments and companies have unexpectedly had to stop out all night without food. It is well to remember that the stomach governs the world.

The courage of the soldier is not really contempt for physical evils and indifference to danger. It is a more or less successful attempt to simulate these habits of mind. Most men aspire to be good actors in the play. There are a few who are so perfect that they do not seem to be actors at all. This is the ideal after which the rest are striving. It is one very rarely attained.

Three principal influences combine to assist men in their attempts: preparation, vanity and sentiment. The first includes all the force of discipline and training. The soldier has for years contemplated the possibility of being under fire. He has wondered vaguely what kind of an experience it would be. He has seen many who have gone through it and returned safely. His curiosity is excited. Presently comes the occasion. By road and railway he approaches daily nearer to the scene. His mind becomes familiar with the prospect. His comrades are in the same situation. Habit, behind which force of circumstances is concealed, makes him conform. At length the hour arrives. He observes the darting puffs of smoke in the distance. He listens to the sounds that are in the air. Perhaps he hears something strike with a thud and sees a soldier near him collapse like a shot pheasant. He realizes that it may be his turn next. Fear grips him by the throat.

Then vanity, the vice which promotes so many virtues, asserts itself. He looks at his comrades and they at him. So far he has shown no sign of weakness. He thinks, they are thinking him brave. The dearly longed-for reputation glitters before his eyes. He executes the orders he receives.

But something else is needed to make a hero. Some other influence must help him through the harder trials and more severe ordeals, which may befall him. It is sentiment which makes the difference in the end. Those who doubt should stroll to the camp fire one night and listen to the soldiers' songs. Every one clings to something that he thinks is high and noble, or that raises him above the rest of the world in the hour of need. Perhaps he remembers that he is sprung from an ancient stock, and of a race that has always known how to die; or more probably it is something smaller and more intimate; the regiment, whatever it is called—"The Gordons", "The Buffs", "The Queen's"—and so nursing the name—only the unofficial name of an infantry battalion after all—he accomplishes great things and maintains the honour and the Empire of the British people.

Looking on the story of the great frontier war; at all that has been told, and all that others may tell, there must be many who today will only deplore the losses of brave soldiers, and hard-earned money. But those, who from some future age shall, by the steady light of history, dispassionately review the whole situation, its causes, results and occasion, may find other reflections, as serious perhaps, but less mournful. The year 1897, in the annals of the British people, was marked by a declaration to the whole world of their faith in the higher destinies of their race. If a strong man, when the wine sparkles at the feast and the lights are bright, boasts of his prowess, it is well he should have an opportunity of showing in the cold and grey of the morning that he is no idle braggart. And unborn arbiters, with a wider knowledge, and more developed brains, may trace in recent events the influence of that mysterious Power which, directing the progress of our species and regulating the rise and fall of empires, has afforded that opportunity to a people of whom at least it may be said that they have added to the happiness, the learning and the liberties of mankind.

# THE RIVER WAR

*The success of "The River War" when it was first pub-
lished in 1899 established the author's reputation as a military
historian for it at once became, and has always remained, the
best personal account ever written of the reconquest of the
Sudan. The book describes in exact detail the operations
directed by Lord Kitchener of Khartoum from 1896 to
1899 during the rebellion of the Mahdi against the British.
The author was attached to the 21st Lancers, and he gives in
this book his first remarkable description of the famous charge
of that regiment at Omdurman in which he fought as the
leader of a troop. This battle was the final one of the campaign
which restored the basin of the Upper Nile to Anglo-
Egyptian administration.*

THE REAL Sudan, known to the statesman and the explorer, lies
far to the south—moist, undulating, and exuberant. But there is
another Sudan, which some mistake for the true, whose solitudes
oppress the Nile from the Egyptian frontier to Omdurman. This
is the Sudan of the soldier. Destitute of wealth or future, it is rich
in history. The names of its squalid villages are familiar to distant
and enlightened peoples. The barrenness of its scenery has been
drawn by skilful pen and pencil. Its ample deserts have tasted the
blood of brave men. Its hot, black rocks have witnessed famous
tragedies. It is the scene of the war.

This great tract, which may conveniently be called "The Military
Sudan", stretches with apparent indefiniteness over the face of the
continent. Level plains of smooth sand—a little rosier than buff, a
little paler than salmon—are interrupted only by occasional peaks of
rock—black, stark, and shapeless. Rainless storms dance tirelessly
over the hot, crisp surface of the ground. The fine sand, driven by
the wind, gathers into deep drifts, and silts among the dark rocks
of the hills, exactly as snow hangs about an Alpine summit; only it
is a fiery snow, such as might fall in hell. The earth burns with the

quenchless thirst of ages, and in the steel-blue sky scarcely a cloud obstructs the unrelenting triumph of the sun.

Through the desert flows the river—a thread of blue silk drawn across an enormous brown drugget; and even this thread is brown for half the year.

In the account of the River War the Nile is naturally supreme. It is the great melody that recurs throughout the whole opera. The general purposing military operations, the statesman who would decide upon grave policies, and the reader desirous of studying the course and results of either, must think of the Nile. It is the life of the lands through which it flows. It is the cause of the war: the means by which we fight; the end at which we aim. Imagination should paint the river through every page in the story. It glitters between the palm-trees during the actions. It is the explanation of nearly every military movement. By its banks the armies camp at night. Backed or flanked on its unfordable stream they offer or accept battle by day. To its brink, morning and evening, long lines of camels, horses, mules, and slaughter cattle hurry eagerly. Emir and Dervish, officer and soldier, friend and foe, kneel alike to this god of ancient Egypt and draw each day their daily water in goatskin or canteen. Without the river none would have started. Without it none might have continued. Without it none could ever have returned.

All who journey on the Nile, whether in commerce or war, will pay their tribute of respect and gratitude; for the great river has befriended all races and every age. Through all the centuries it has performed the annual miracle of its flood. Every year when the rains fall and the mountain snows of Central Africa begin to melt, the head-streams become torrents and the great lakes are filled to the brim. A vast expanse of low, swampy lands, crossed by secondary channels and flooded for many miles, regulates the flow, and by a sponge-like action prevents the excess of one year from causing the deficiency of the next. Far away in Egypt, prince, priest, and peasant look southwards with anxious attention for the fluctuating yet certain rise. Gradually the flood begins. The Bahr-el-Ghazal from a channel of stagnant pools and marshes becomes a broad and navigable stream. The Sobat and the Atbara from dry watercourses with occasional pools, in which the fish and crocodiles are crowded, turn to rushing rivers. But all this is remote from Egypt. After its confluence with the Atbara no drop of water reaches the Nile, and it flows for seven hundred miles through the sands or rushes in cataracts among the rocks of the Nubian desert. Nevertheless, in spite of the tremendous diminution in volume caused by the dryness of the earth and air and the heat of the sun—all of which drink greedily—the river below Assuan is sufficiently great to supply nine millions of people with as much water as their utmost science and energies can draw, and yet to pour into the Mediterranean a low-water surplus current of 61,500 cubic feet per second. Nor is its water its only gift. As the Nile rises its complexion is changed. The clear blue river becomes thick and red, laden with the magic mud that can raise cities from the desert sand and make the wilderness a garden. The geographer may still in the arrogance of science describe the Nile as "a great, steady-flowing river, fed by the rains of the tropics, controlled by the existence of a vast head reservoir and several areas of repose, and annually flooded by the accession of a great body of water with which its eastern tributaries are flushed"; but all who have drunk deeply of its soft yet fateful waters —fateful, since they give both life and death—will understand why the old Egyptians worshipped the river, nor will they even in modern days easily dissociate from their minds a feeling of mystic reverence.

From 1819 to 1883 Egypt ruled the Sudan. Her rule was not kindly, wise, or profitable. Its aim was to exploit, not to improve the local population. The miseries of the people were aggravated rather than lessened: but they were concealed. For the rough injustice of the sword there were substituted the intricacies of corruption and bribery. Violence and plunder were more hideous, since they were cloaked with legality and armed with authority. The land was undeveloped and poor. It barely sustained its inhabitants. The additional burden of a considerable foreign garrison and a crowd of rapacious officials increased the severity of the economic conditions. Scarcity was frequent. Famines were periodical. Corrupt and incapable Governors-General succeeded each other at Khartoum with bewildering rapidity. The constant changes, while they prevented the continuity of any wise policy, did not interrupt the misrule. With hardly any exceptions, the Pashas were consistent in oppression. The success of their administration was measured by the Ministries in Egypt by the amount of money they could extort from the natives; among the officials in the Sudan, by the number of useless offices they could create. There were a few bright examples of honest men, but these, by contrast, only increased the discontents.

The authority of a tyrannical government was supported by the presence of a worthless army. Nearly forty thousand men were distributed among eight main and numerous minor garrisons. Isolated in a roadless country by enormous distances and natural obstacles, and living in the midst of large savage populations of fanatical character and warlike habits, whose exasperation was yearly growing with their miseries, the Viceregal forces might depend for their safety only on the skill of their officers, the excellence of their discipline, and the superiority of their weapons. But the Egyptian officers were at that time distinguished for nothing but their public incapacity and private misbehaviour. The evil reputation of the Sudan and its climate deterred the more educated or more wealthy from serving in such distant regions, and none went south who could avoid it. The army which the Khedives maintained in the Delta was, judged by European standards, only a rabble. It was badly trained, rarely paid, and very cowardly; and the scum of the army of the Delta was the cream of the army of the Sudan. The officers remained for long periods, many all their lives, in the obscurity of the remote provinces. Some had been sent there in disgrace, others in disfavour. Some had been forced to serve out of Egypt by extreme poverty, others were drawn to the Sudan by the hopes of gratifying peculiar tastes. The majority had harems of the women of the country, which were limited only by the amount of money they could lay their hands on by any method. Many were hopeless and habitual drunkards. Nearly all were dishonest. All were indolent and incapable.

\* \* \*

The names of two men of character and fame are for ever connected with the actual outburst. One was an English general, the other an Arab priest; yet, in spite of the great gulf and vivid contrast between their conditions, they resembled each other in many respects. Both were earnest and enthusiastic men of keen sympathies and passionate emotions. Both were powerfully swayed by religious fervour. Both exerted great personal influence on all who came in contact with them. Both were reformers. The Arab was an African reproduction of the Englishman; the Englishman a superior and civilized development of the Arab. In the end they fought to the death, but for an important part of their lives their influence on the fortunes of the Sudan was exerted in the same direction. Mohammed Ahmed, "The Mahdi", will be discussed in his own place. Charles Gordon needs little introduction. Long before this tale begins his reputation was European, and the fame of the "Ever-victorious Army" had spread far beyond the Great Wall of China.

The misgovernment of the Egyptians and the misery of the Sudanese reached their greatest extreme in the seventh decade of the present century. From such a situation there seemed to be no issue other than by force of arms. The Arab tribes lacked no provocation. Yet they were destitute of two moral forces essential to all rebellions. The first was the knowledge that better things existed. The second was a spirit of combination. General Gordon showed them the first. The Mahdi provided the second.

It is impossible to study any part of Charles Gordon's career without being drawn to all the rest. As his wild and varied fortunes lead him from Sebastopol to Pekin, from Gravesend to South Africa, from Mauritius to the Sudan, the reader follows fascinated. Every scene is strange, terrible, or dramatic. Yet, remarkable as are the scenes, the actor is the more extraordinary; a type without comparison in modern times and with few likenesses in history. Rare and precious is the truly disinterested man. Potentates of many lands and different degree—the Emperor of China, the King of the Belgians, the Premier of Cape Colony, the Khedive of Egypt—competed to secure his services. The importance of his offices varied no less than their nature. One day he was a subaltern of sappers; on another he commanded the Chinese army; the next he directed an orphanage; or was Governor-General of the Sudan, with supreme powers of life and death and peace and war; or served as private secretary to Lord Ripon. But in whatever capacity he laboured he

113

was true to his reputation. Whether he is portrayed bitterly criticizing to Graham the tactics of the assault on the Redan; or pulling the head of Lar Wang from under his bedstead and waving it in paroxysms of indignation before the astonished eyes of Sir Halliday Macartney; or riding alone into the camp of the rebel Suliman and receiving the respectful salutes of those who had meant to kill him; or telling the Khedive Ismail that he "must have the whole Sudan to govern"; or reducing his salary to half the regulation amount because "he thought it was too much"; or ruling a country as large as Europe; or collecting facts for Lord Ripon's rhetorical efforts— we perceive a man careless alike of the frowns of men or the smiles of women, of life or comfort, wealth or fame.

It was a pity that one, thus gloriously free from the ordinary restraining influences of human society, should have found in his own character so little mental ballast. His moods were capricious and uncertain, his passions violent, his impulses sudden and inconsistent. The mortal enemy of the morning had become a trusted ally before the night. The friend he loved today he loathed tomorrow. Scheme after scheme formed in his fertile brain, and jostled confusingly together. All in succession were pressed with enthusiasm. All at times were rejected with disdain. A temperament naturally neurotic had been aggravated by an acquired habit of smoking; and the General carried this to so great an extreme that he was rarely seen without a cigarette. His virtues are famous among men; his daring and resource might turn the tide of war; his energy would have animated a whole people; his achievements are upon record; but it must also be set down that few more uncertain and impracticable forces than Gordon have ever been introduced into administration and diplomacy.

Towards the end of 1879 Gordon left the Sudan. With short intervals he had spent five busy years in its provinces. His energy had stirred the country, He had struck at the root of the slave trade, he had attacked the system of slavery, and, as slavery was the greatest institution in the land, he had undermined the whole social system. Indignation had stimulated his activity to an extraordinary degree. In a climate usually fatal to Europeans he discharged the work of five officers. Careless of his methods, he bought slaves himself, drilled them, and with the soldiers thus formed pounced on the caravans of the hunters. Traversing the country on a fleet dromedary —on which in a single year he is said to have covered 3,840 miles— he scattered justice and freedom among the astonished natives. He fed the infirm, protected the weak, executed the wicked. To some he gave actual help, to many freedom, to all new hopes and aspirations. Nor were the tribes ungrateful. The fiercest savages and cannibals respected the life of the strange white man. The women blessed him. He could ride unarmed and alone where a brigade of soldiers dared not venture. But he was, as he knew himself, the herald of the storm. Oppressed yet ferocious races had learned that they had rights; the misery of the Sudanese was lessened, but their knowledge had increased. The whole population was unsettled, and the wheels of change began slowly to revolve; nor did they stop until they had accomplished an enormous revolution.

The part played by the second force is more obscure. Few facts are so encouraging to the student of human development as the desire, which most men and all communities manifest at all times, to associate with their actions at least the appearance of moral right. However distorted may be their conceptions of virtue, however feeble their efforts to attain even to their own ideals, it is a pleasing feature and a hopeful augury that they should *wish* to be justified. No community embarks on a great enterprise without fortifying itself with the belief that from some points of view its motives are lofty and disinterested. It is an involuntary tribute, the humble tribute of imperfect beings, to the eternal temples of Truth and Beauty. The sufferings of a people or a class may be intolerable, but before they will take up arms and risk their lives some unselfish and impersonal spirit must animate them. In countries where there is education and mental activity or refinement, this high motive is found in the pride of glorious traditions or in a keen sympathy with surrounding misery. Ignorance deprives savage nations of such incentives. Yet in the marvellous economy of nature this very ignorance is a source of greater strength. It affords them the mighty stimulus of fanaticism. The French Communists might plead that they upheld the rights of man. The desert tribes proclaimed that they fought for the glory of God. But although the force of fanatical passion is far greater than that exerted by any philosophical belief, its sanction is just the same. It gives men something which they think is sublime to fight for, and this serves them as an excuse for wars which it is desirable to begin for totally different reasons. Fanaticism is not a cause of war. It is the means which helps savage peoples to fight. It is the spirit which enables them to combine— the great common object before which all personal or tribal disputes become insignificant. What the horn is to the rhinoceros, what the sting is to the wasp, the Mohammedan faith was to the Arabs of the Sudan—a faculty of offence or defence.

★ ★ ★

The reasons which forced the peoples of the Sudan to revolt were as strong as the defence which their oppressors could offer was feeble. Looking at the question from a purely political standpoint, we may say that upon the whole there exists no record of a better case for rebellion than presented itself to the Sudanese. Their country was being ruined; their property was plundered; their women were ravished; their liberties were curtailed; even their lives were threatened. Aliens ruled the inhabitants; the few oppressed the many; brave men were harried by cowards; the weak compelled the strong. Here were sufficient reasons. Since any armed movement against an established government can be justified only by success, strength is an important revolutionary virtue. It was a virtue that the Arabs might boast. They were indeed far stronger than they, their persecutors, or the outside world had yet learned. All were soon to be enlightened.

The storm gathered and the waters rose. Three great waves impelled the living tide against the tottering house founded on the desert sand. The Arab suffered acutely from poverty, misgovernment, and oppression. Infuriated, he looked up and perceived that the cause of all his miseries was a weak and cowardly foreigner, a despicable "Turk". The antagonism of races increased the hatred sprung from social evils. The moment was at hand. Then, and not till then, the third wave came—the wave of fanaticism, which, catching up and surmounting the other waves, covered all the flood with its white foam, and, bearing on with the momentum of the waters, beat in thunder against the weak house so that it fell; and great was the fall thereof.

116

All great movements, every vigorous impulse that a community may feel, become perverted and distorted as time passes, and the atmosphere of the earth seems fatal to the noble aspirations of its peoples. A wide humanitarian sympathy in a nation easily degenerates into hysteria. A military spirit tends towards brutality. Liberty leads to licence, restraint to tyranny. The pride of race is distended to blustering arrogance. The fear of God produces bigotry and superstition. There appears no exception to the mournful rule, and the best efforts of men, however glorious their early results, have dismal endings, like plants which shoot and bud and put forth beautiful flowers, and then grow rank and coarse and are withered by the winter. It is only when we reflect that the decay gives birth to fresh life, and that new enthusiasms spring up to take the places of those that die, as the acorn is nourished by the dead leaves of the oak, the hope strengthens that the rise and fall of men and their movements are only the changing foliage of the ever-growing tree of life, while underneath a greater evolution goes on continually.

The movement which Mohammed Ahmed created did not escape the common fate of human enterprise; nor was it long before the warm generous blood of a patriotic and religious revolt congealed into the dark clot of a military empire. With the expulsion or destruction of the foreign officials, soldiers, and traders, the racial element began to subside. The reason for its existence was removed. With the increasing disorders the social agitation dwindled; for communism pre-supposes wealth, and the wealth of the Sudan was greatly diminished. There remained only the fanatical fury which the belief in the divine mission of the Mahdi had excited; and as the necessity for a leader passed away, the belief in his sanctity grew weaker. But meanwhile a new force was making itself felt on the character of the revolt. The triumph no less than the plunder which had rewarded the Mahdi's victories had called into existence a military spirit distinct from the warlike passions of the tribesmen— the spirit of the professional soldier.

The siege of Khartoum was carried on while this new influence was taking the place of the original forces of revolt. There was a period when a neutral point was obtained and the Mahdist power languished. But the invasion of the Eastern Sudan by the British troops in the spring and the necessary advance of the relieving columns in the winter of 1884 revived the patriotic element. The tribes who had made a great effort to free themselves from foreign domination saw in the operations of Sir Gerald Graham and Lord Wolseley an attempt to bring them again under the yoke. The impulse which was given to the Mahdi's cause was sufficient to raise a fierce opposition to the invading forces. The delay in the despatch of the relief expedition had sealed the fate of Khartoum, and the fall of the town established the supremacy of the military spirit on which the Dervish Empire was afterwards founded.

★    ★    ★

The long and glorious defence of the town of Khartoum will always fascinate attention. That one man, a European among Africans, a Christian among Mohammedans, should by his genius have inspired the efforts of seven thousand soldiers of inferior race, and by his courage have sustained the hearts of thirty thousand inhabitants of notorious timidity, and with such materials and encumbrances have offered a vigorous resistance to the increasing attacks of an enemy who, though cruel, would yet accept surrender, during a period of 317 days, is an event perhaps without parallel in history. But it may safely be predicted that no one will ever write an account which will compare in interest or in detail with that set forth by the man himself in the famous *Journals at Khartoum*.

The brief account has delighted thousands of readers in Europe and America. Perhaps it is because he is careless of the sympathy of men that Charles Gordon so readily wins it. Before the first of the six parts into which the Journals were divided is finished, the reader has been won. Henceforth he sees the world through Gordon's eyes. With him he scoffs at the diplomatists; despises the government; becomes impatient—unreasonably, perhaps—with a certain Major Kitchener in the Intelligence Branch, whose information miscarried or was not despatched; is wearied by the impracticable Shaiggia Irregulars; takes interest in the turkey-cock and his harem of four wives; laughs at the "black sluts" seeing their faces for the first time in the mirror. With him he trembles for the fate of the "poor little beast", the *Husseinyeh*, when she drifts stern foremost on the shoal, "a penny steamer under cannon fire"; day after day he gazes through the General's powerful telescope from the palace roof down

118

the long brown reaches of the river towards the rocks of the Shabluka Gorge, and longs for some sign of the relieving steamers; and when the end of the account is reached, no man of British birth can read the last words, "Now mark this, if the Expeditionary Force—and I ask for no more than two hundred men—does not come within ten days, *the town may fall*; and I have done my best for the honour of our country. Goodbye", without being thrilled with vain regrets and futile resolutions. And then the account stops short. Nor will the silence ever be broken. The sixth instalment of the Journals was despatched on 14 December; and when it is finished the reader, separated suddenly from the pleasant companionship, experiences a feeling of loss and annoyance. Imagination, long supported, is brushed aside by stern reality. Henceforward Gordon's perils were unrecorded.

After 10 September, 1884, when General Gordon sent Colonel Stewart and Messrs. Power and Herbin down the river in the ill-fated *Abbas* steamer, he was altogether alone. Many men have bowed to the weight of responsibility. Gordon's responsibility was undivided. There was no one to whom he could talk as an equal. There was no one to whom he could—as to a trusty subordinate—reveal his doubts. To some minds the exercise of power is pleasant, but few sensations are more painful than responsibility without control. The General could not supervise the defence. The officers robbed the soldiers of their rations. The sentries slumbered at their posts. The townspeople bewailed their misfortunes, and all ranks and classes intrigued with the enemy in the hope of securing safety when the town should fall. Frequent efforts were made to stir up the inhabitants or sap their confidence. Spies of all kinds pervaded the town. The Egyptian Pashas, despairing, meditated treason. Once an attempt was made to fire the magazine. Once no less than eighty thousand *ardebs*[1] of grain was stolen from the arsenal. From time to time the restless and ceaseless activity of the commander might discover some plot and arrest the conspirators; or, checking some account, might detect some robbery; but he was fully aware that what he found out was scarcely a tithe of what he could not hope to know. The Egyptian officers were untrustworthy. Yet he had to

[1] Five and a half bushels.

trust them. The inhabitants were thoroughly broken by war, and many were disloyal. He had to feed and inspirit them. The town itself was scarcely defensible. It must be defended to the end. From the flat roof of his palace his telescope commanded a view of the forts and lines. Here he would spend the greater part of each day, scrutinizing the defences and surrounding country with his powerful glass. When he observed that the sentries on the forts had left their posts, he would send over to have them flogged and their superiors punished. When his "penny steamers" engaged the Dervish batteries he would watch, "on tenterhooks", a combat which might be fatal to the defence, but which, since he could not direct it, must be left to officers by turns timid and reckless: and in the dark hours of the night he could not even watch.

To the military anxieties was added every kind of worry which may weary a man's soul. The women clamoured for bread. The townsfolk heaped reproaches upon him. The quarrel with the British Government had cut him very deeply. The belief that he was abandoned and discredited, that history would make light of his efforts, would perhaps never know of them, filled his mind with a sense of wrong and injustice which preyed upon his spirits. The miseries of the townsfolk wrung his noble, generous heart. The utter loneliness depressed him. And over all lay the shadow of uncertainty. To the very end the possibility that "all might be well" mocked him with false hopes. The first light of any morning might reveal the longed-for steamers of relief and the uniforms of British soldiers. He was denied even the numbing anaesthetic of despair.

Yet he was sustained by two great moral and mental stimulants: his honour as a man, his faith as a Christian. The first had put all courses which he did not think right once and for all out of the question, and so allayed many doubts and prevented many vain regrets. But the second was the real source of his strength. He was sure that beyond this hazardous existence, with all its wrongs and inequalities, another life awaited him—a life which, if he had been faithful and true here upon earth, would afford him greater faculties for good and wider opportunities for their use.

\*     \*     \*

The moment was ripe. The night of 25 January arrived.

The band played as usual in the evening. Gradually the shadows fell and it became dark. The hungry inhabitants betook themselves to bed. The anxious but indomitable commander knew that the crisis impended, and knew also that he was powerless to avert it. Perhaps he slept, satisfied that he had done his duty; and in the silence of the night the savage enemy crawled stealthily towards the town. The weary and disheartened sentinels, weakened by famine and tired of war, maintained a doubtful vigilance along the ramparts. The subsiding waters of the river had left a bare gap between the White Nile and the wall. Perhaps there was treachery besides. On a sudden the loud explosion of musketry broke the stillness of the night and the slumbers of the people; and with a continual shouting thousands of Dervishes swarmed through the unprotected space and entered Khartoum.

One mob of assailants made their way to the palace. Gordon came out to meet them. The whole courtyard was filled with wild, harlequin figures and sharp, glittering blades. He attempted a parley. "Where is your master, the Mahdi?" He knew his influence over native races. Perhaps he hoped to save the lives of some of the inhabitants. Perhaps in that supreme moment imagination flashed another picture before his eyes; and he saw himself confronted with the false prophet of a false religion, confronted with the European prisoners who had "denied their Lord", offered the choice of death or the Koran; saw himself facing that savage circle with a fanaticism equal to, and a courage greater than, their own; marching in all the pride of faith "and with retorted scorn" to a martyr's death.

It was not to be. Mad with the joy of victory and religious frenzy, they rushed upon him and, while he disdained even to fire his revolver, stabbed him in many places. The body fell down the steps and lay—a twisted heap—at the foot. There it was decapitated. The head was carried to the Mahdi. The trunk was stabbed again and again by the infuriated creatures, till nothing but a shapeless bundle of torn flesh and bloody rags remained of what had been a great and famous man and the envoy of Her Britannic Majesty. The blood soaked into the ground, and left a dark stain which was not immediately effaced.

After the fall of Khartoum and the retreat of the British armies

121

the Mahdi became the absolute master of the Sudan. Whatever pleasures he desired he could command, and, following the example of the founder of the Mohammedan faith, he indulged in what would seem to Western minds gross excesses. He established an extensive harem for his own peculiar use, and immured therein the fairest captives of the war. The conduct of the ruler was imitated by his subjects. The presence of women increased the vanity of the warriors: and it was not very long before the patched smock which had vaunted the holy poverty of the rebels developed into the gaudy *jibba* of the conquerors. Since the unhealthy situation of Khartoum amid swamps and marshes did not commend itself to the now luxurious Arabs, the Mahdi began to build on the western bank of the White Nile a new capital, which, from the detached fort which had stood there in Egyptian days, was called Omdurman. Among the first buildings which he set his subjects to construct were a mosque for the services of religion, an arsenal for the storage of military material, and a house for himself. But while he was thus entering at once upon the enjoyments of supreme power and unbridled lust, the God whom he had served, not unfaithfully, and who had given him whatever he had asked, required of Mohammed Ahmed his soul; and so all that he had won by his brains and bravery became of no more account to him.

Kitchener came to Egypt and set his feet firmly on the high road to fortune. He came to Egypt when she was plunged in misery and shame, when hopeless ruin seemed already the only outcome of the public disasters, and when even greater misfortunes impended. He remained to see her prosperous and powerful; to restore empire to her people, peace to her empire, honour to her army; and among those clear-minded men of action by whom the marvellous work of regeneration has been accomplished, Herbert Kitchener will certainly occupy the second place. Lord Wolseley on his arrival soon found employment for the active officer who could speak Arabic. He served through the campaign of 1882 as a major. He joined the new army which was formed at the conclusion of the war, as one of the original twenty-six officers. In the Nile expedition of 1885 Arabic again led him to the front, and in the service of the Intelligence Department he found ample opportunity for his daring and energy.

His efforts to communicate with Gordon in Khartoum did not, however, meet with much success, and the Journals bristle with so many sarcastic comments that their editor has been at pains to explain in his preface that there was really no cause for complaint. Major Kitchener, however, gave satisfaction to his superiors in Cairo, if not to the exacting General at Khartoum, and in 1886 he was appointed Governor of Suakin. This post, always one of responsibility and danger, did not satisfy Kitchener, whose ambition was now taking definite form. Eager for more responsibility and more danger, he harried and raided the surrounding tribes; he restricted and almost destroyed the slender trade which was again springing up, and in consequence of his measures the neighbourhood of Suakin was soon in even greater ferment than usual. This culminated at the end of 1887 in the reappearance and advance of Osman Digna. The movements of the Dervishes were, however, uncertain. The defences of the town had been greatly strengthened and improved by the skill and activity of its new Governor. Osman Digna retreated. The "friendlies" were incited to follow, and Kitchener, although he had been instructed not to employ British officers or Egyptian regulars in offensive operations, went out in support. At Handub on the morning of 17 January, 1888, the friendlies attacked the camp of Osman Digna. They were at first successful; but while they dispersed to plunder the enemy rallied and, returning, drove them back with loss. Kitchener arrived on the field with the support, to find a defeat instead of a victory awaiting him. He bravely endeavoured to cover the retreat of the friendlies, and in so doing was severely—as it first seemed dangerously—wounded in the jaw. The loss among the friendlies and the support amounted to twenty men killed and two British officers and twenty-eight men wounded. The Governor returned in great pain and some discomfiture to Suakin. In spite of his wound and his reverse he was impatient to renew the conflict, but this was definitely forbidden by the British Government. Colonel Kitchener's military conduct was praised, but his policy was prevented.

The cholera spread steadily southward up the river, claiming successive victims in each camp. In the second week of July [1896] it reached the new camp at Kosheh, whence all possible precautions

123

to exclude it had proved vain. The epidemic was at first of a virulent form. As is usual, when it had expended its destructive energy, the recoveries became more frequent. But of the first thousand cases between Assuan and Suarda nearly eight hundred proved fatal. Nor were the lives thus lost to be altogether measured by the number. To all, the time was one of trial, almost of terror. The violence of the battle may be cheaply braved, but the insidious attacks of disease appal the boldest. Death moved continually about the ranks of the army—not the death they had been trained to meet unflinchingly, the death in high enthusiasm and the pride of life, with all the world to weep or cheer; but a silent, unnoticed, almost ignominious summons, scarcely less sudden and far more painful than the bullet or the sword-cut. The Egyptians, in spite of their fatalistic creed, manifested profound depression. The English soldiers were moody and ill-tempered. Even the light-hearted Sudanese lost their spirits; their merry grins were seen no longer; their laughter and their drums were stilled. Only the British officers preserved a stony cheerfulness, and ceaselessly endeavoured by energy and example to sustain the courage of their men. Yet they suffered most of all. Their education had developed their imaginations; and imagination, elsewhere a priceless gift, is amid such circumstances a dangerous burden.

It was, indeed, a time of sore trouble. To find the servant dead in the camp kitchen; to catch a hurried glimpse of blanketed shapes hustled quickly to the desert on a stretcher; to hold the lantern over the grave into which a friend or comrade—alive and well six hours before—was hastily lowered, even though it was still night; and through it all to work incessantly at pressure in the solid, roaring heat, with a mind ever on the watch for the earliest of the fatal symptoms and a thirst that could only be quenched by drinking of the deadly and contaminated Nile: all these things combined to produce an experience which those who endured are unwilling to remember, but unlikely to forget. One by one some of the best of the field army and the communication staff were stricken down. Gallant Fenwick, of whom they used to say that he was "twice a V.C. without a gazette"; Polwhele, the railway subaltern, whose strange knowledge of the Egyptian soldiers had won their stranger love; Trask, an heroic doctor, indifferent alike to pestilence or bullets; Mr. Vallom, the chief superintendent of engines at Halfa; Farmer, a young officer already on his fourth campaign; Mr. Nicholson, the London engineer; long, quaint, kind-hearted "Roddy" Owen—all filled graves in Halfa cemetery or at the foot of Firket mountain. At length the epidemic was stamped out, and by the middle of August it had practically ceased to be a serious danger. But the necessity of enforcing quarantine and other precautions had hampered movement up and down the line of communications, and so delayed the progress of the preparations for an advance.

\* \* \*

It often happens that in prosperous public enterprises the applause of the nation and the rewards of the sovereign are bestowed on those whose offices are splendid and whose duties have been dramatic. Others whose labours were no less difficult, responsible, and vital to success are unnoticed. If this be true of men, it is also true of things. In a tale of war the reader's mind is filled with the fighting. The battle—with its vivid scenes, its moving incidents, its plain and tremendous results—excites imagination and commands attention. The eye is fixed on the fighting brigades as they move amid the smoke; on the swarming figures of the enemy; on the General, serene and determined, mounted in the middle of his Staff. The long trailing line of communications is unnoticed. The fierce glory that plays on red, triumphant bayonets dazzles the observer; nor does he care to look behind to where, along a thousand miles of rail, road, and river, the convoys are crawling to the front in uninterrupted succession. Victory is the beautiful, bright-coloured flower. Transport is the stem without which it could never have blossomed. Yet even the military student, in his zeal to master the fascinating combinations of the actual conflict, often forgets the far more intricate complications of supply.

It cannot be denied that a battle, the climax to which all military operations tend, is an event which is not controlled by strategy or organization. The scheme may be well planned, the troops well fed, the ammunition plentiful, and the enemy entangled, famished, or numerically inferior. The glorious uncertainties of the field can yet reverse everything. The human element—in defiance of experience and probability—may produce a wholly irrational result, and a starving, out-manoeuvred army win food, safety, and honour by their bravery. But such considerations apply with greater force to wars where both sides are equal in equipment and discipline. In savage warfare in a flat country the power of modern machinery is such that flesh and blood can scarcely prevail, and the chances of battle are reduced to a minimum. Fighting the Dervishes was primarily a matter of transport. The Khalifa was conquered on the railway.

The first spadeful of sand of the Desert Railway was turned on the first day of 1897.

It is scarcely within the power of words to describe the savage desolation of the regions into which the line and its constructors plunged. A smooth ocean of bright-coloured sand spread far and wide to distant horizons. The tropical sun beat with senseless perseverance upon the level surface until it could scarcely be touched with a naked hand, and the filmy air glittered and shimmered as over a furnace. Here and there huge masses of crumbling rock rose from the plain, like islands of cinders in a sea of fire. Alone in this vast expanse stood Railhead—a canvas town of 2,500 inhabitants, complete with station, stores, post office, telegraph office, and canteen, and only connected with the living world of men and ideas by two parallel iron streaks, three feet six inches apart, growing dim and narrower in a long perspective until they were twisted and blurred by the mirage and vanished in the indefinite distance.

Every morning in the remote nothingness there appeared a black speck growing larger and clearer, until with a whistle and a welcome clatter, amid the aching silence of ages, the "material" train arrived, carrying its own water and 2,500 yards of rails, sleepers and accessories. At noon came another speck, developing in a similar manner into a supply train also carrying its own water, food and water for the half-battalion of the escort and the two thousand artificers and platelayers, and the letters, newspapers, sausages, jam, whisky, soda-water, and cigarettes which enable the Briton to conquer the world without discomfort. And presently the empty trains would depart, reversing the process of their arrival, and vanishing gradually along

126

a line which appeared at last to turn up into the air and run at a tangent into an unreal world.

The life of the strange and lonely town was characterized by a machine-like regularity, born perhaps of the iron road from which it derived its nourishment. Daily at three o'clock in the morning the "camp-engine" started with the "bank parties". With the dawn the "material" train arrived, the platelaying gangs swarmed over it like clusters of flies, and were carried to the extreme limit of the track. Every man knew his task, and knew, too, that he would return to camp when it was finished, and not before. Forthwith they set busily to work without the necessity of an order. A hundred yards of material was unloaded. The sleepers were arranged in a long succession. The rails were spiked to every alternate sleeper, and then the great eighty-ton engine moved cautiously forward along the unballasted track, like an elephant trying a doubtful bridge. The operation was repeated continually through the hours of the burning day. Behind the train there followed other gangs of platelayers, who completed the spiking and ballasting process; and when the sun sank beneath the sands of the western horizon, and the engine pushed the empty trucks and the weary men home to the Railhead camp, it came back over a finished and permanent line. There was a brief interval while the camp-fires twinkled in the waste, while the officers and men chatted over their evening meal, and then the darkness and silence of the desert was unbroken till morning brought the glare and toil of another long day.

The first military necessity of the war was to place the bulk of the Egyptian army at Akasha. In ordinary circumstances this would not have been a serious commissariat problem. The frontier reserves of food were calculated to meet such an emergency. But in 1895 the crops in Egypt had been much below the average. At the beginning of 1896 there was a great scarcity of grain. When the order for the advance was issued, the frontier grain stores were nearly exhausted. The new crops could not be garnered until the end of April. Thus while the world regarded Egypt as a vast granary, her soldiers were obliged to purchase four thousand tons of *doura* and one thousand tons of barley from India and Russia on which to begin the campaign.

The chief item of a soldier's diet in most armies is bread. In several of our wars the health, and consequently the efficiency, of the troops has been impaired by bad bread or by the too frequent substitution of hard biscuit. For more than a year the army up the river ate twenty tons of flour daily, and it is easy to imagine how bitter amid ordinary circumstances would have been the battle between the commissariat officers, whose duty it was to insist on proper quality, and the contractors—often, I fear, meriting the epithet "rascally"—intent only upon profit. But in the well-managed Egyptian Service no such difficulties arose. The War Department had in 1892 converted one of Ismail Pasha's gun factories near Cairo into a victualling-yard. Here were set up their own mills for grinding flour, machinery for manufacturing biscuit to the extent of sixty thousand rations daily, and even for making soap. Three great advantages sprang from this wise arrangement. Firstly, the good quality of the supply was assured. Complaints about bread and biscuit were practically unknown, and the soap—since the soldier, in contrast to the mixture of rubble and grease with which the contractors had formerly furnished him, could actually wash himself and his clothes with it—was greatly prized. Secondly, all risk of contractors failing to deliver in time was avoided. Lastly, the funds resulting from the economy had been utilized to form a useful corps of one hundred and fifty bakers. And thus, although the purchase of foreign grain added to the expense, the beginning of the war found the commissariat of the Egyptian Army in a thoroughly efficient state.

The line continued to grow rapidly, and as it grew the difficulties of supply decreased. The weight was shifted from the backs of the camels and the bottoms of the sailing-boats to the trucks of the iron road. The strong hands of steam were directed to the prosecution of the war, and the swiftness of the train replaced the toilsome plodding of the caravan. The advance of the Dervishes towards Berber checked the progress of the railway. Military precautions were imperative. Construction was delayed by the passage of the 1st British Brigade from Cairo to the front, and by the consequently increased volume of daily supplies. By 10 March, however, the line was completed to Bashtinab. On 5 May it had reached Abadia. On

128

3 July the whole railway from Wady Halfa to the Atbara was finished, and the southern terminus was established in the great entrenched camp at the confluence of the rivers. The question of supply was then settled once and for all. In less than a week stores sufficient for three months were poured along the line, and the exhausting labours of the commissariat officers ended. Their relief and achievement were merged in the greater triumph of the Railway Staff. The director and his subalterns had laboured long, and their efforts were crowned with complete success. On the day that the first troop train steamed into the fortified camp at the confluence of the Nile and the Atbara rivers the doom of the Dervishes was sealed. It had now become possible with convenience and speed to send into the heart of the Sudan great armies independent of the season of the year and of the resources of the country; to supply them not only with abundant food and ammunition, but with all the varied paraphernalia of scientific war; and to support their action on land by a powerful flotilla of gunboats, which could dominate the river and command the banks, and could at any moment make their way past Khartoum even to Sennar, Fashoda, or Sobat. Though the battle was not yet fought, the victory was won. The Khalifa, his capital, and his army were now within the Sirdar's reach. It remained only to pluck the fruit in the most convenient hour, with the least trouble and at the smallest cost.

\*     \*     \*

The news of the fall of Dongola created a panic in Omdurman. Great numbers of Arabs, believing that the Khalifa's power was about to collapse, fled from the city. All business was at a standstill. For several days there were no executions. Abdullah himself kept his house, and thus doubtfully concealed his vexation and alarm from his subjects. On the fifth day, however, having recovered his own confidence, he proceeded to the mosque, and after the morning prayer ascended his small wooden pulpit and addressed the assembled worshippers. After admitting the retreat of the Dervishes under Wad Bishara, he enlarged on the losses the "Turks" had sustained and described their miserable condition. He deplored the fact that certain of the Jehadia had surrendered, and reminded his listeners with a grim satisfaction of the horrible tortures which it was the practice of the English and Egyptians to inflict upon their captives. He bewailed the lack of faith in God which had allowed even the meanest of the Ansar to abandon the Jehad against the infidel, and he condemned the lack of piety which disgraced the age. But he proclaimed his confidence in the loyalty of his subjects and his enjoyment of the favour of God and the counsels of the late Mahdi; and having by his oratory raised the fanatical multitude to a high pitch of excitement, he thus concluded his long harangue: "It is true that our chiefs have retired from Dongola. Yet they are not defeated. Only they that disobeyed me have perished. I instructed the faithful to refrain from fighting and return to Metemma. It was by my command that they have done what they have done. For the angel of the Lord and the spirit of the Mahdi have warned me in a vision that the souls of the accursed Egyptians and of the miserable English shall leave their bodies between Dongola and Omdurman, at some spot which their bones shall whiten. Thus shall the infidels be conquered." Then, drawing his sword, he cried with a loud voice: "*Ed din mansur!* The religion is victorious! Islam shall triumph!" Whereupon the worshippers, who to the number of twenty thousand filled the great quadrangle—although they could not all hear his voice—saw his sword flashing in the sunlight, and with one accord imitated him, waving their swords and spears, and raising a mighty shout of fury and defiance. When the tumult had subsided, the Khalifa announced that those who did not wish to remain faithful might go where they liked, but that he for his part would remain, knowing that God would vindicate the faith. Public confidence was thus restored.

Major-General Sir Archibald Hunter was from many points of view the most imposing figure in the Egyptian army. He had served through the Nile Expedition of 1884-5, with some distinction, in the Khedive's service. Thenceforward his rise was rapid, even for an Egyptian officer, and in ten years he passed through all the grades from Captain to Major-General. His promotion was not, however, undeserved. Foremost in every action, twice wounded—once at the head of his brigade—always distinguished for valour and conduct, Hunter won the admiration of his comrades and superiors. During the River War he became, in spite of his hard severity, the darling of the Egyptian Army. All the personal popularity which great success might have brought to the Sirdar focused itself on his daring, good-humoured subordinate, and it was to Hunter that the soldiers looked whenever there was fighting to be done. The force now placed under his command for the attack upon Abu Hamed amounted to about 3,600 men. Until that place was taken all other operations were delayed. The Sirdar awaited the issue at Merawi.

The troops composing the "flying column" concentrated at Kassingar, a small village a few miles above Merawi, on the right (or Abu Hamed) bank of the Nile. General Hunter began his march on 29 July. The total distance from Kassingar to Abu Hamed is 146 miles. The greatest secrecy had been observed in the preparation of the force, but it was known that as soon as the column actually started the news would be carried to the enemy. Speed was therefore essential; for if the Dervish garrison in Abu Hamed were reinforced from Berber, the flying column might not be strong enough to take the village. On the other hand, the great heat and the certainty that the troops would have to fight an action at the end of the march imposed opposite considerations on the commander. To avoid the sun, the greater part of the distance was covered at night. Yet the advantage thus gained was to some extent neutralized by the difficulty of marching over such broken ground in the darkness.

Throughout the whole length of the course of the Nile there is no more miserable wilderness than the Monassir Desert. The stream of the river is broken and its channel obstructed by a great confusion of boulders, between and among which the water rushes in dangerous cataracts. The sandy waste approaches the very brim, and only a few palm-trees, or here and there a squalid mud hamlet, reveal the existence of life. The line of advance lay along the river; but no road relieved the labour of the march. Sometimes trailing across a broad stretch of white sand, in which the soldiers sank to their ankles, and which filled their boots with a rasping grit; sometimes winding over a pass or through a gorge of sharp-cut rocks, which, even in the moonlight, felt hot with the heat of the previous day—always in a long, jerky, and interrupted procession of men and camels, often in single file—the column toiled painfully like the serpent to whom it was said: "On thy belly shalt thou go, and dust shalt thou eat."

131

The astonishing news of the fall of Berber reached General Hunter on 2 September. He immediately telegraphed to Merawi. Sir Herbert Kitchener was confronted with a momentous question: should Berber be occupied or not? It may at first seem that there could be little doubt about the matter. The objective of the expedition was Omdurman. The occupation of Berber by an Egyptian garrison would settle at once the difficulties near Suakin. The town was believed to be on the clear waterway to the Dervish capital. The moral effect of its capture upon the riverain tribes and throughout the Sudan would be enormous. Berber was, in fact, the most important strategic point on the whole line of advance. This great prize and advantage was now to be had for the asking.

The opposite considerations were, however, tremendous. Abu Hamed marked a definite stage in the advance. As long as Merawi and the other posts in Dongola were strongly held, the line from Abu Hamed to Debba was capable of easy defence. Abu Hamed could soon be made impregnable to Dervish attack. The forces in Dongola could be quickly concentrated on any threatened point. At this moment in the campaign it was possible to stop and wait with perfect safety. In the meantime the Khalifa would steadily weaken and the railway might steadily grow. When the line reached the angle of the river, it would be time to continue the systematic and cautious advance. Until then prudence and reason counselled delay. To occupy Berber was to risk much. Mahmud, with a large and victorious army, lay at Metemma. Osman Digna, with two thousand men, held Adarama almost within striking distance. The railway still lagged in the desert. The Dongola garrisons must be weakened to provide a force for Berber. The Dervishes had the advantage of occupying the interior of the angle which the Nile forms at Abu Hamed. The troops in Berber would have to draw their supplies by a long and slender line of camel communication, winding along all the way from Merawi, and exposed, as a glance at the map will show, throughout its whole length to attack. More than all this: to advance to Berber must inevitably force the development of the whole war. The force in the town would certainly have its communications threatened, would probably have to fight for its very existence. The occupation of Berber would involve sooner or later a general action; not a fight like Firket, Hafir, or Abu

132

Hamed, with the advantage of numbers on the side of the Egyptian troops, but an even battle. For such a struggle British troops were necessary. At this time it seemed most unlikely that they would be granted. But if Berber was occupied, the war, until the arrival of British troops, would cease to be so largely a matter of calculation, and must pass almost entirely into the sphere of chance. The whole situation was premature and unforeseen. The Sirdar had already won success. To halt was to halt in safety; to go on was to go on at hazard. Most of the officers who had served long in the Egyptian Army understood the question. They waited the decision in suspense.

The Sirdar and the Consul-General unhesitatingly faced the responsibility together. On 3 September General Hunter received orders to occupy Berber. He started at once with three hundred and fifty men of the IXth Sudanese on board the gunboats *Tamai*, *Zafir*, *Naser* and *Fateh*. Shortly after daybreak on the 5th the Egyptian flag was hoisted over the town. Having disembarked the infantry detachment, the flotilla steamed south to try to harass the retreating Emir. They succeeded; for on the next day they caught him, moving along the bank in considerable disorder, and, opening a heavy fire, soon drove the mixed crowd of fugitives, horse and foot, away from the river into the desert. The gunboats then returned to Berber, towing a dozen captured grain-boats. Meanwhile the Sirdar had started for the front himself. Riding swiftly with a small escort across the desert from Merawi, he crossed the Nile at the Baggara Cataract and reached Berber on 10 September. Having inspected the immediate arrangements for defence, he withdrew to Abu Hamed, and there busily prepared to meet the developments which he well knew might follow at once, and must follow in the course of a few months.

The effect of the occupation of Berber upon the tribes around Suakin was decisive, and the whole country between these towns became at once tranquil and loyal. Osman Digna's influence was destroyed. The friendly villages were no longer raided. The Governor of the town became in reality, as well as in name, the Governor of the Red Sea Littoral. The route from Suakin to Berber was opened; and a Camel Corps patrol, several small caravans of traders, and a

133

party of war correspondents—who might boast that they were the first Europeans to make the journey for thirteen years—passed safely along it.

In the evening of Thursday, 7 April, 1898, the army at Umdabia paraded for the attack on Mahmud's *zeriba*. The camp lay in the scrub which grows by the banks of the Atbara, as by those of the Nile, and in order to profit by the open, level ground the four infantry brigades moved by parallel routes into the desert, and then formed facing south-east in column of brigade squares, the British brigade leading. The mounted forces, with four batteries of artillery, waited in camp until two o'clock the next morning, and did not break their march. The distance from the river bank to the open plain was perhaps a mile and a half, and the whole infantry force had cleared the scrub by six o'clock. The sun was setting, and the red glow, brightening the sandy hillocks, made the western horizon indefinite, so that it was hard to tell where the desert ended and the sky began. A few gazelle, intercepted on their way to the water by the unexpected movement of troops, trotted slowly away in the distance—white spots on the rosy-brown of the sand—and on the great plain twelve thousand infantry, conscious of their strength and eager to encounter the enemy, were beautifully arranged in four solid masses. Then the march began. The actual distance from the camp to the Dervish position was scarcely seven miles, but the circle necessary to avoid the bushes and the gradual bends of the river added perhaps another five to the length of the road. The pace of the advance was slow, and the troops had not gone far when the sun sank and, with hardly an interval of twilight, darkness enveloped everything. In the stillness of the night the brigades moved steadily forward, and only the regular scrunching of the hard sand betrayed the advance of an overwhelming force upon their enemies.

No operation of a war is more critical than a night-march. Over and over again in every country frightful disaster has overtaken the rash or daring force that has attempted it. In the gloom the shape and aspect of the ground are altered. Places well known by daylight appear strange and unrecognizable. The smallest obstacle impedes the column, which can only crawl sluggishly forward with continual checks and halts. The effect of the gloom upon the nerves of the soldiers is not less than on the features of the country. Each man tries to walk quietly, and hence all are listening for the slightest sound. Every eye seeks to pierce the darkness. Every sense in the body is raised to a pitch of expectancy. In such hours doubts and fears come unbidden to the brain, and the marching men wonder anxiously whether all will be well with the army, and whether they themselves will survive the event. And if suddenly out of the black silence there burst the jagged glare of rifles and the crash of a volley followed by the yell of an attacking foe, the steadiest troops may be thrown into confusion, and a panic, once afoot, stops only with the destruction or dispersal of the whole force. Nevertheless, so paramount is the necessity of attacking at dawn, with all the day to finish the fight, that the night-march is a frequent operation.

It was still dark, and the haze that shrouded the Dervish camp was broken only by the glare of the watch-fires. The silence was profound. It seemed impossible to believe that more than twenty-five thousand men were ready to join battle at scarcely the distance of half a mile. Yet the advance had not been unperceived, and the Arabs knew that their terrible antagonists crouched on the ridge waiting for the morning. For a while the suspense was prolonged. At last, after what seemed to many an interminable period, the uniform blackness of the horizon was broken by the first glimmer of the dawn. Gradually the light grew stronger until, as a theatre curtain is pulled up, the darkness rolled away, the vague outlines in the haze became definite, and the whole scene was revealed.

The British and Egyptian army lay along the low ridge in the form of a great bow—the British brigade on the left, MacDonald in the centre, Maxwell curving forward on the right. The whole crest of the swell of ground was crowned with a bristle of bayonets and the tiny figures of thousands of men sitting or lying down and gazing curiously before them, Behind them, in a solid square, was the transport, guarded by Lewis's brigade. The leading squadrons of the cavalry were forming leisurely towards the left flank. The four batteries and a rocket detachment, moving between the infantry, ranged themselves on two convenient positions about a hundred yards in front of the line of battalions. All was ready. Yet everything was very quiet, and in the stillness of the dawn it almost seemed that Nature held her breath.

*     *     *

At twenty minutes to eight the Sirdar ordered his bugles to sound the general advance. The call was repeated by all the brigades, and the clear notes rang out above the noise of the artillery. The superior officers—with the exception of Hunter, Maxwell, and MacDonald —dismounted and placed themselves at the head of their commands. The whole mass of the infantry, numbering nearly eleven thousand men, immediately began to move forward upon the *zeriba*. The scene as this great force crested the ridge and advanced down the slope was magnificent and tremendous. Large solid columns of men, preceded by a long double line, with the sunlight flashing on their bayonets and displaying their ensigns, marched to the assault in regular and precise array. The pipes of the Highlanders, the bands of the Sudanese, and the drums and fifes of the English regiments added a wild and thrilling accompaniment. As soon as the advance masked the batteries, the guns were run forward with the firing line, in order effectually to support the attack. The deployed battalions opened a ceaseless and crushing fire on the entrenchment, and as the necessity of firing delayed the advance of the attacking columns, the pace did not exceed a slow march.

The Dervishes remained silent until the troops were within three hundred yards. Then the smoke-puffs spurted out all along the stockades, and a sharp fusillade began, gradually and continually growing in intensity until the assaulting troops were exposed to a furious and effective fire. From two hundred and fifty yards up to the position losses began to occur. The whole entrenchment was rimmed with flame and smoke, amid which the active figures of the Dervish riflemen were momentarily visible, and behind the filmy curtain solid masses of swordsmen and spearmen appeared. The fortunate interposition of a small knoll in some degree protected the advance of the Lincoln Regiment, but in both Highland battalions soldiers began to drop. The whole air was full of a strange chirping whistle. The hard pebbly sand was everywhere dashed up into dust-spurts. Numerous explosive bullets, fired by the Arabs, made queer startling reports. The roar of the rifles drowned even the noise of the artillery. All the deployed battalions began to suffer. But they and the assaulting columns, regardless of the fire, bore down on the *zeriba* in all the majesty of war—an avalanche of men, stern, unflinching, utterly irresistible.

Yet, although the Dervishes were unable to make head against the attack, they disdained to run. Many hundreds held their ground, firing their rifles valiantly till the end. Others charged with spear and sword. The greater part retired in skirmishing order, jumping over the numerous pits, walking across the open spaces, and repeatedly turning round to shoot. The XIth Sudanese encountered the most severe resistance after the defences were penetrated. As their three deployed companies pressed on through the enclosure, they were confronted by a small inner *zeriba* stubbornly defended by the Emir Mahmud's personal bodyguard. These poured a sudden volley into the centre company at close range, and so deadly was the effect that nearly all the company were shot, falling to the ground still in their ranks, so that a British officer passing at a little distance was provoked to inquire "what they were doing lying down". Notwithstanding this severe check the regiment, gallantly led by their colonel and supported by the Xth Sudanese, rushed this last defence and slew its last defenders. Mahmud was himself captured. Having duly inspected his defences and made his dispositions, he had sheltered in a specially constructed casemate. Thence he was now ignominiously dragged, and, on his being recognized, the intervention of a British officer alone saved him from the fury of the excited Sudanese.

Still the advance continued, and it seemed to those who took part in it more like a horrible nightmare than a waking reality. Captains and subalterns collected whatever men they could, heedless of corps or nationality, and strove to control and direct their fire. *Jibba*-clad figures sprang out of the ground, fired or charged, and were destroyed at every step. And onwards over their bodies—over pits choked with dead and dying, among heaps of mangled camels and donkeys, among decapitated or eviscerated trunks, the ghastly results of the shell fire; women and little children killed by the bombardment or praying in wild terror for mercy; blacks chained in their trenches, slaughtered in their chains—always onwards marched the conquerors, with bayonets running blood; clothes, hands, and faces all besmeared; the foul stench of a month's accumulated filth in their nostrils, and the savage whistle of random bullets in their ears.

But at about twenty minutes past eight the whole force, with the Seaforth Highlanders well forward on the left, arrived at the bank of the Atbara, having marched completely through the position, and shot or bayoneted all in their path. Hundreds of Dervishes were still visible retiring across the dry bed of the river, and making for the scrub on the opposite bank. The leading companies of the Seaforth Highlanders and Lincolns, with such odd parties of Camerons as had been carried on with the attack, opened a murderous fire on these fugitives. Since they would not run their loss was heavy, and it was a strange sight—the last vivid impression of the day—to watch them struggling through the deep sand, with the dust knocked up into clouds by the bullets which struck all round them. Very few escaped, and the bodies of the killed lay thickly dotting the river-bed with heaps of dirty-white. Then at 8.25 the "Ceasefire" sounded, and the battle of the Atbara ended.

The actual pursuit was abortive. Colonel Lewis, with his two battalions, followed a line of advance which led south of the *zeriba*, and just before reaching the river bank found and fired upon a few Dervishes retreating through the scrub. All the cavalry and the Camel Corps crossed the Atbara and plunged into the bush on the further side. But so dense and tangled was the country that after three miles of peril and perplexity they abandoned the attempt, and the routed Arabs fled unmolested. The Baggara horse had ridden off during the action, headed by the prudent Osman Digna—whose position in the *zeriba* was conveniently suited to such a manoeuvre —and under that careful leadership suffered little loss. The rest of the army was, however, destroyed or dispersed. The fugitives fled up the Atbara river, leaving many wounded to die in the scrub, all along their line of retreat. Of the powerful force of twelve thousand fighting men which Mahmud had gathered at Metemma, scarcely four thousand reached Gedaref in safety. These survivors were added to the army of Ahmed Fedil, and thus prevented from spreading their evil tidings among the populace at Omdurman. Osman Digna, Wad Bishara, and other important Emirs whose devotion and discretion were undoubted, alone returned to the capital.

Several hundred prisoners were taken. They were mostly negroes —for the Arabs refused to surrender, and fought to the last or tried to escape. The captive blacks, who fight with equal willingness on either side, were content to be enlisted in the Sudanese regiments; so that many of those who served the Khalifa on the Atbara helped to destroy him at Omdurman. The most notable prisoner was the Emir Mahmud—a tall, strong Arab, about thirty years old. Immediately after his capture he was dragged before the Sirdar. "Why," inquired the General, "have you come into my country to burn and kill?" "I have to obey my orders, and so have you," retorted the captive sullenly, yet not without a certain dignity. To other questions he returned curt or evasive answers, and volunteered the opinion that all this slaughter would be avenged at Omdurman. He was removed in custody—a fine specimen of proud brutality, worthy perhaps of some better fate than to linger indefinitely in the jail at Rosetta.

With the cool of the evening the army left its bed of torment on the ridge and returned to Umdabia. The homeward march was a severe trial; the troops were exhausted; the ground was broken; the guides, less careful or less fortunate than on the previous night, lost their way. The columns were encumbered with wounded, most of whom were already in a high state of fever, and whose sufferings were painful to witness. It was not until after midnight that the camp was reached. The infantry had been continuously under arms —marching, fighting, or sweltering in the sun—for thirty hours, and most of them had hardly closed their eyes for two days. Officers and soldiers—British, Sudanese, and Egyptian—struggled into their bivouacs, and fell asleep, very weary but victorious.

★   ★   ★

All through the early months of the summer the preparations for the final advance were steadily proceeding. A second British brigade was ordered to the Sudan. A new battery of howitzer artillery—the 37th—firing enormous shells charged with lyddite, was dispatched from England. Two large forty-pounder guns were sent from

Cairo. Another British Maxim battery of four guns was formed in Cairo from men of the Royal Irish Fusiliers. Three new screw gunboats of the largest size and most formidable pattern had been passed over the indefatigable railway in sections, and were now launched on the clear waterway south of the Atbara encampment; and last, but not least, the 21st Lancers were ordered up the Nile. [The author led a troop in this regiment during the final advance to Omdurman.] Events now began to move rapidly. Within three weeks of the arrival of the reinforcements the climax of the war was over; within five weeks the British troops were returning home. There was no delay at the Atbara encampment. Even before the whole of the second brigade had arrived, some of its battalions were being dispatched to Wad Hamed, the new point of concentration. This place was a few miles north of Shabluka, and only fifty-eight miles from Omdurman. It was evident, therefore, that the decisive moment of the three years' war approached. The Staff, the British infantry, one squadron, the guns, and the stores were carried south in steamers and barges. The Egyptian division marched to Wad Hamed by brigades. The horses of the batteries, the transport animals of the British division (about 1,400 in number), the chargers of the officers, some cattle, and most of the war correspondents were sent along the left bank of the river escorted by two squadrons of the 21st Lancers and two Maxim guns.

While the army were to move along the west bank of the river —the Omdurman side—a force of Arab irregulars, formed from the friendly tribes, would march along the east bank and clear it of any Dervishes. All the debris which the Egyptian advance had broken off the Dervish Empire was thus to be hurled against that falling State. Eager for plunder, anxious to be on the winning side, Sheiks and Emirs from every tribe in the Military Sudan had hurried, with what following the years of war had left them, to Wad Hamed. On 26 August the force of irregulars numbered about 2,500 men, principally Jaalin survivors, but also comprising bands and individuals of Bisharin; of Hadendoa from Suakin; of Shukria, the camel-breeders; of Batahin, who had suffered a bloody diminution at the Khalifa's hands; of Shaiggia, Gordon's vexatious allies; and lastly some Gemilab Arabs under a reputed son of Zubehr Pasha. The command of the whole motley force was given to Major Stuart-Wortley, Lieutenant Wood accompanying him as Staff Officer; and the position of these officers among the cowed and untrustworthy Arabs was one of considerable peril.

The whole army broke camp at Royan on 28 August at four o'clock in the afternoon, and marched to Wady el Abid, six miles further south. We now moved on a broad front, which could immediately be converted into a fighting formation. This was the first time that it had been possible to see the whole force—infantry, cavalry, and guns—on the march at once. In the clear air the amazing detail of the picture was striking. There were six brigades of infantry, composed of twenty-four battalions; yet every battalion showed that it was made up of tiny figures, all perfectly defined on the plain. A Sudanese brigade had been sent on to hold the ground with pickets until the troops had constructed a *zeriba*. But a single Dervish horseman managed to evade these and, just as the light faded, rode up to the Warwickshire Regiment and flung his broad-bladed spear in token of defiance. So great was the astonishment which this unexpected apparition created that the bold man actually made good his escape uninjured.

The spectacle of the moving army—the grand army of the Nile —as it advanced towards its goal was especially wonderful in the clear air of the early morning; a long row of great brown masses of infantry and artillery, with a fringe of cavalry dotting the plain for miles in front, with the Camel Corps—chocolate-coloured men on cream-coloured camels—stretching into the desert on the right, and the white gunboats stealing silently up the river on the left, scrutinizing the banks with their guns; while far in rear the transport trailed away into the mirage, and far in front the field-glass disclosed the enemy's patrols. Day after day and hour after hour the advance was maintained. Arrived at the camping-ground, the *zeriba* had to be built; and this involved a long afternoon of fatigue. In the evening, when the dusty, tired-out squadrons returned, the troopers attended to their horses, and so went to sleep in peace. It was then that the dusty, tired-out infantry provided sentries and pickets, who in a ceaseless succession paced the *zeriba* and guarded its occupants.

The position of the next camp was a strong one, on a high swell of open ground which afforded a clear field of fire in every direction. Everyone that night lay down to sleep with a feeling of keen expectancy. One way or the other all doubts would be settled the next day. The cavalry would ride over the Kerreri Hills, if they were not occupied by the enemy, and right up to the walls of Omdurman. If the Dervishes had any army—if there was to be any battle—we should know within a few hours. The telegrams which were dispatched that evening were the last to reach England before the event. During the night heavy rain fell, and all the country was drenched. The telegraph-wire had been laid along the ground, as there had been no time to pole it. The sand when dry is a sufficient insulator, but when wet its non-conductivity is destroyed. Hence all communications ceased, and those at home who had husbands, sons, brothers, or friends in the Expeditionary Force were left in an uncertainty as great as that in which we slept—and far more painful.

It was known that the Khalifa had succeeded in concentrating at Omdurman an army of more than sixty thousand men. He remembered that all the former victories over the Egyptians had been won by the Dervishes attacking. He knew that in all the recent defeats they had stood on the defensive. He therefore determined not to oppose the advance at the Shabluka or on the march thence to Omdurman. All was to be staked on the issue of a great battle on the plains of Kerreri. The Mahdi's prophecy was propitious. The strength of the Dervish army seemed overwhelming. When the "Turks" arrived, they should be driven into the river. Accordingly the Khalifa had only watched the advance of the Expeditionary Force from Wad Hamed with a patrol of cavalry about two hundred strong. On the 30th he was informed that the enemy drew near, and on the 31st he assembled his bodyguard and regular army, with the exception of the men needed for the river batteries, on the Omdurman parade ground. He harangued the leaders, and remained encamped with his troops during the night. The next day all the male population of the city were compelled to join the army in the field, and only the gunners and garrisons on the river-face remained within. In spite, however, of his utmost vigilance, nearly six thousand men deserted during the nights of 31 August and

1 September. This and the detachments in the forts reduced the force actually engaged in the battle to fifty-two thousand men. The host that now advanced towards the British and Egyptian cavalry was perhaps four thousand stronger.

\*     \*     \*

The Anglo-Egyptian army had not formed a quadrilateral camp, as on other nights, but had lain down to rest in the formation for attack they had assumed in the afternoon. Every fifty yards behind the thorn-bushes were double sentries. Every hundred yards a patrol with an officer was to be met. Fifty yards in rear of this line lay the battalions, the men in all their ranks, armed and accoutred, but sprawled into every conceivable attitude which utter weariness could suggest or dictate. The enemy, twice as strong as the Expeditionary Force, were within five miles. They had advanced that day with confidence and determination. But it seemed impossible to believe that they would attack by daylight across the open ground. Two explanations of their advance and halt presented themselves. Either they had offered battle in a position where they could not themselves be attacked until four o'clock in the afternoon, and hoped that the Sirdar's army, even though victorious, would have to fight a rearguard action in the darkness to the river; or they intended to make a night attack. It was not likely that an experienced commander would accept battle at so late an hour in the day. If the Dervishes were anxious to attack, so much the worse for them. But the army would remain strictly on the defensive—at any rate, until there was plenty of daylight. The alternative remained—a night attack.

Here lay the great peril which threatened the expedition. What was to be done with the troops during the hours of darkness? In the daytime they recked little of their enemy. But at night, when four hundred yards was the extreme range at which their fire could be opened, it was a matter of grave doubt whether the front could be kept and the attack repelled. The consequences of the line being penetrated in the darkness were appalling to think of. The sudden appearance of crowds of figures swarming to the attack through the gloom; the wild outburst of musketry and artillery all along the *zeriba*; the crowds still coming on in spite of the bullets; the fire

143

getting uncontrolled, and then a great bunching and crumpling of some part of the front, and mad confusion, in which a multitude of fierce swordsmen would surge through the gap, cutting and slashing at every living thing; in which transport animals would stampede and rush wildly in all directions, upsetting every formation and destroying all attempts to restore order; in which regiments and brigades would shift for themselves and fire savagely on all sides, slaying alike friend and foe; and out of which only a few thousand, perhaps only a few hundred, demoralized men would escape in barges and steamers to tell the tale of ruin and defeat.

The picture—true or false—flamed before the eyes of all the leaders that night; but, whatever their thoughts may have been, their tactics were bold. Whatever advice was given, whatever opinions were expressed, the responsibility was Sir Herbert Kitchener's. Upon his shoulders lay the burden, and the decision that was taken must be attributed solely to him. He might have formed the army into a solid mass of men and animals, arranged the infantry four deep all round the perimeter, and dug as big a ditch or built as high a *zeriba* as time allowed. He might have filled the numerous houses with the infantry, making them join the buildings with hasty entrenchments, and so enclose a little space in which to squeeze cavalry, transport, and guns. Instead he formed his army in a long thin curve, resting on the river and enclosing a wide area of ground, about which baggage and animals were scattered in open order and luxurious accommodation. His line was but two deep; and only two companies per battalion and one Egyptian brigade (Collinson's) were in reserve. He thus obtained the greatest possible development of fire, and waited, prepared if necessary to stake everything on the arms of precision, but hoping with fervour that he would not be compelled to gamble by night.

The night was, however, undisturbed; and the moonlit camp, with its anxious generals, its weary soldiers, its fearful machinery of destruction, all strewn along the bank of the great river, remained plunged in silence, as if brooding over the chances of the morrow and the failures of the past. And hardly four miles away another army—twice as numerous, equally confident, equally brave—were waiting impatiently for the final settlement of the long quarrel.

144

It was not the British and Egyptian army that began the battle. If there was one arm in which the Arabs were beyond all comparison inferior to their adversaries, it was in guns. Yet it was with this arm that they opened their attack. In the middle of the Dervish line now marching in frontal assault were two puffs of smoke. About fifty yards short of the thorn fence two red clouds of sand and dust sprang up, where the projectiles had struck. It looked like a challenge. It was immediately answered. Great clouds of smoke appeared all along the front of the British and Sudanese brigades. One after another four batteries opened on the enemy at a range of about three thousand yards. The sound of the cannonade rolled up to us on the ridge, and was re-echoed by the hills. Above the heads of the moving masses shells began to burst, dotting the air with smoke-balls and the ground with bodies. But a nearer tragedy impended. The "White Flags" were nearly over the crest. In another minute they would become visible to the batteries. Did they realize what would come to meet them? They were in a dense mass, two thousand eight hundred yards from the 32nd Field Battery and the gunboats. The ranges were known. It was a matter of machinery. The more distant slaughter passed unnoticed, as the mind was fascinated by the approaching horror. In a few seconds swift destruction would rush on these brave men. They topped the crest and drew out into full view of the whole army. Their white banners made them conspicuous above all. As they saw the camp of their enemies, they discharged their rifles with a great roar of musketry and quickened their pace. For a moment the white flags advanced in regular order, and the whole division crossed the crest and were exposed. Forthwith the gunboats, the 32nd British Field Battery, and other guns from the zeriba opened on them. About twenty shells struck them in the first minute. Some burst high in the air, others exactly in their faces. Others, again, plunged into the sand and, exploding, dashed clouds of red dust, splinters, and bullets amid their ranks. The white banners toppled over in all directions. Yet they rose again immediately, as other men pressed forward to die for the Mahdi's sacred cause and in the defence of the successor of the True Prophet. It was a terrible sight, for as yet they had not hurt us at all, and it seemed an unfair advantage to strike thus cruelly when they could not reply.

145

The Khalifa's plan of attack appears to have been complex and ingenious. It was, however, based on an extraordinary miscalculation of the power of modern weapons; with the exception of this cardinal error, it is not necessary to criticize it. He first ordered about fifteen thousand men, drawn chiefly from the army of Osman Sheikh-ed-Din and placed under the command of Osman Azrak, to deliver a frontal attack. He himself waited with an equal force near Surgham Hill to watch the result. If it succeeded, he would move forward with his bodyguard, the flower of the Arab army, and complete the victory. If it failed, there was yet another chance. The Dervishes who were first launched against the *zeriba*, although very brave men, were not by any means his best or most reliable troops. Their destruction might be a heavy loss, but it would not end the struggle. While the attack was proceeding, the valiant left, consisting of the rest of the army of Osman Sheikh-ed-Din, might move unnoticed to the northern flank and curve round on to the front of the *zeriba* held by the Egyptian brigade. Ali-Wad-Helu was meanwhile to march to the Kerreri Hills, and remain out of range and, if possible, out of sight among them. Should the frontal and flank attacks be unhappily repulsed, the "enemies of God", exulting in their easy victory over the faithful, would leave their strong place and march to the capture and sack of the city. Then, while they were yet dispersed on the plain, with no *zeriba* to protect them, the chosen warriors of the True Religion would abandon all concealment, and hasten in their thousands to the utter destruction of the accursed—the Khalifa with fifteen thousand falling upon them from behind Surgham; Ali-Wad-Helu and all that remained of Osman's army assailing them from Kerreri. Attacked at once from the north and south, and encompassed on every side, the infidels would abandon hope and order, and Kitchener might share the fate of Hicks and Gordon.

While these things were passing on the northern flank, the frontal attack was in progress. The debris of the "White Flags" joined the centre, and the whole fourteen thousand pressed forward against the *zeriba*, spreading out by degrees and abandoning their dense formations, and gradually slowing down. At about eight hundred yards from the British division the advance ceased, and they could make no headway. Opposite the Sudanese, who were armed only with the Martini-Henry rifle, the assailants came within three hundred yards; and one brave old man, carrying a flag, fell at one hundred and fifty paces from the shelter trench. But the result was conclusive all along the line. The attack was shattered. The leader, clad in his new *jibba* of many colours, rode on steadfastly towards the inexorable firing line, until, pierced by several bullets, he fell lifeless. Such was the end of that stubborn warrior of many fights —wicked Osman Azrak, faithful unto death. The surviving Dervishes lay down on the ground. Unable to advance, they were unwilling to retire; and their riflemen, taking advantage of the folds of the plain, opened and maintained an unequal combat. By eight o'clock it was evident that the whole attack had failed. The loss of the enemy was more than two thousand killed, and perhaps as many wounded.

\* \* \*

As the 21st Lancers left the ridge, the fire of the Arab riflemen on the hill ceased. We advanced at a walk in mass for about three hundred yards. The scattered parties of Dervishes fell back and melted away, and only one straggling line of men in dark blue waited motionless a quarter of a mile to the left front. They were scarcely a hundred strong. The regiment formed into line of squadron columns, and continued at a walk until within three hundred yards of this small body of Dervishes. The firing behind the ridges had stopped. There was complete silence, intensified by the recent tumult. Far beyond the thin blue row of Dervishes the fugitives were visible streaming into Omdurman. And should these few devoted men impede a regiment? Yet it were wiser to examine their position from the other flank before slipping a squadron at them. The heads of the squadrons wheeled slowly to the left, and the Lancers, breaking into a trot, began to cross the Dervish front in column of troops. Thereupon and with one accord the blue-clad men dropped on their knees, and there burst out a loud, crackling fire of musketry. It was hardly possible to miss such a target at such a range. Horses and men fell at once. The only course was plain and welcome to all. The Colonel, nearer than his regiment, already saw what lay behind the skirmishers. He ordered "Right

147

wheel into line" to be sounded. The trumpet jerked out a shrill note, heard faintly above the trampling of the horses and the noise of the rifles. On the instant all the sixteen troops swung round and locked up into a long galloping line, and the 21st Lancers were committed to their first charge in war.

Two hundred and fifty yards away the dark-blue men were firing madly in a thin film of light-blue smoke. Their bullets struck the hard gravel into the air, and the troopers, to shield their faces from the stinging dust, bowed their helmets forward, like the Cuirassiers at Waterloo. The pace was fast and the distance short. Yet, before it was half covered, the whole aspect of the affair changed. A deep crease in the ground—a dry watercourse, a *khor*—appeared where all had seemed smooth, level plain; and from it there sprang, with the suddenness of a pantomime effect and a high-pitched yell, a dense white mass of men nearly as long as our front and about twelve deep. A score of horsemen and a dozen bright flags rose as if by magic from the earth. Eager warriors sprang forward to anticipate the shock. The rest stood firm to meet it. The Lancers acknowledged the apparition only by an increase of pace. Each man wanted sufficient momentum to drive through such a solid line. The flank troops, seeing that they overlapped, curved inwards like the horns of a moon. But the whole event was a matter of seconds. The riflemen, firing bravely to the last, were swept head over heels into the *khor*, and jumping down with them, at full gallop and in the closest order, the British squadrons struck the fierce brigade with one loud furious shout. The collision was prodigious. Nearly thirty Lancers, men and horses, and at least two hundred Arabs were overthrown. The shock was stunning to both sides, and for perhaps ten wonderful seconds no man heeded his enemy. Terrified horses wedged in the crowd, bruised and shaken men, sprawling in heaps, struggled, dazed and stupid, to their feet, panted, and looked about them. Several fallen Lancers had even time to remount. Meanwhile the impetus of the cavalry carried them on. As a rider tears through a bullfinch, the officers forced their way through the press; and as an iron rake might be drawn through a heap of shingle, so the regiment followed. They shattered the Dervish array, and, their pace reduced to a walk, scrambled out of the *khor* on the further side, leaving a score of troopers behind them, and dragging on with the charge more than a thousand Arabs. Then, and not till then, the killing began; and thereafter each man saw the world along his lance, under his guard, or through the back-sight of his pistol; and each had his own strange tale to tell.

Stubborn and unshaken infantry hardly ever meet stubborn and unshaken cavalry. Either the infantry run away and are cut down in flight, or they keep their heads and destroy nearly all the horsemen by their musketry. On this occasion two living walls had actually crashed together. The Dervishes fought manfully. They tried to hamstring the horses. They fired their rifles, pressing the muzzles into the very bodies of their opponents. They cut reins and stirrup-leathers. They flung their throwing-spears with great dexterity. They tried every device of cool, determined men practised in war and familiar with cavalry; and, besides, they swung sharp, heavy swords which bit deep. The hand-to-hand fighting on the further side of the *khor* lasted for perhaps one minute. Then the horses got into their stride again, the pace increased, and the Lancers drew out from among their antagonists. Within two minutes of the collision every living man was clear of the Dervish mass. All who had fallen were cut at with swords till they stopped quivering, but no artistic mutilations were attempted.

Two hundred yards away the regiment halted, rallied, faced about, and in less than five minutes were reformed and ready for a second charge. The men were anxious to cut their way back through their enemies. We were alone together—the cavalry regiment and the Dervish brigade. The ridge hung like a curtain between us and the army. The general battle was forgotten, as it was unseen. This was a private quarrel. The other might have been a massacre; but here the fight was fair, for we too fought with sword and spear. Indeed the advantage of ground and numbers lay with them. All prepared to settle the debate at once and for ever. But some realization of the cost of our wild ride began to come to those who were responsible. Riderless horses galloped across the plain. Men, clinging to their saddles, lurched helplessly about, covered with blood from perhaps a dozen wounds. Horses, streaming from tremendous gashes, limped and staggered with their riders. In 120 seconds five officers, 65 men, and 119 horses out of fewer than 400 had been killed or wounded.

The Dervish line, broken by the charge, began to re-form at once. They closed up, shook themselves together, and prepared with constancy and courage for another shock. But on military considerations it was desirable to turn them out of the *khor* first and thus deprive them of their vantage-ground. The regiment again drawn up, three squadrons in line and the fourth in column, now wheeled to the right, and, galloping round the Dervish flank, dismounted and opened a heavy fire with their magazine carbines. Under the pressure of this fire the enemy changed front to meet the new attack, so that both sides were formed at right angles to their original lines. When the Dervish change of front was completed, they began to advance against the dismounted men. But the fire was accurate, and there can be little doubt that the moral effect of the charge had been very great, and that these brave enemies were no longer unshaken. Be this as it may, the fact remains that they retreated swiftly, though in good order, towards the ridge of Surgham Hill, where the Khalifa's Black Flag still waved, and the 21st Lancers remained in possession of the ground—and of their dead.

Such is the true and literal account of the charge; but the reader may care to consider a few incidents. Colonel Martin, busy with the direction of his regiment, drew neither sword nor revolver, and rode through the press unarmed and uninjured. Major Crole Wyndham had his horse shot under him by a Dervish who pressed the muzzle of his rifle into its hide before firing. From out of the middle of that savage crowd the officer fought his way on foot and escaped in safety. Lieutenant Molyneux fell in the *khor* into the midst of the enemy. In the confusion he disentangled himself from his horse, drew his revolver, and jumped out of the hollow before the Dervishes recovered from the impact of the charge. Then they attacked him. He fired at the nearest, and at the moment of firing was slashed across the right wrist by another. The pistol fell from his nerveless hand, and, being wounded, dismounted, and disarmed, he turned in the hopes of regaining, by following the line of the charge, his squadron, which was just getting clear. Hard upon his track came the enemy, eager to make an end. Beset on all sides, and thus hotly pursued, the wounded officer perceived a single Lancer riding across his path. He called on him for help. Whereupon the trooper, Private Byrne, although already severely wounded by a bullet which had penetrated his right arm, replied without a moment's hesitation and in a cheery voice, "All right, sir!" and turning, rode at four Dervishes, who were about to kill his officer. His wound, which had partly paralysed his arm, prevented him from grasping his sword, and at the first ineffectual blow it fell from his hand, and he received another wound from a spear in the chest. But his solitary charge had checked the pursuing Dervishes. Lieutenant Molyneux regained his squadron alive, and the trooper, seeing that his object was attained, galloped away, reeling in his saddle. Arrived at his troop, his desperate condition was noticed and he was told to fall out. But this he refused to do, urging that he was entitled to remain on duty and have "another go at them". At length he was compelled to leave the field, fainting from loss of blood.

Lieutenant Nesham had an even more extraordinary escape than Molyneux. He had scrambled out of the *khor* when, as his horse was nearly stopping, an Arab seized his bridle. He struck at the man with his sword, but did not prevent him cutting his off-rein. The officer's bridle-hand, unexpectedly released, flew out, and, as it did so, a swordsman at a single stroke nearly severed it from his body. Then they cut at him from all sides. One blow sheared through his helmet and grazed his head. Another inflicted a deep wound in his right leg. A third, intercepted by his shoulder-chains, paralysed his right arm. Two more, missing him narrowly, cut right through the cantel of the saddle and into the horse's back. The wounded subaltern—he was the youngest of all—reeled. A man on either side seized his legs to pull him to the ground; but the long spurs stuck into the horse's flanks, and the maddened animal, throwing up its head and springing forward, broke away from the crowd of foes, and carried the rider—bleeding, fainting, but still alive—to safety among the rallying squadrons. Lieutenant Nesham's experience was that of the men who were killed, only that he escaped to describe it.

★　　★　　★

The three brigades advancing drove the Khalifa's Dervishes back into the desert. Along a mile of front an intense and destructive fire flared and crackled. The 32nd British Field Battery on the extreme left was drawn by its hardy mules at full gallop into action. The Maxim guns pulsated feverishly. Two were even dragged by the enterprise of a subaltern to the very summit of Surgham, and from this elevated position intervened with bloody effect. Thus the long line moved forward in irresistible strength. In the centre, under the red Egyptian flag, careless of the bullets which that conspicuous emblem drew, and which inflicted some loss among those around him, rode the Sirdar, stern and sullen, equally unmoved by fear or enthusiasm. A mile away to the rear the gunboats, irritated that the fight was passing beyond their reach, steamed restlessly up and down, like caged Polar bears seeking what they might devour. Before that terrible line the Khalifa's division began to break up. The whole ground was strewn with dead and wounded, among whose bodies the soldiers picked their steps with the customary Sudan precautions. Surviving thousands struggled away towards Omdurman and swelled the broad stream of fugitives upon whose flank the 21st Lancers already hung vengefully. Yakub and the defenders of the Black Flag disdained to fly, and perished where they stood, beneath the holy ensign, so that when their conquerors reached the spot the dark folds of the banner waved only over the dead.

While all this was taking place—for events were moving at speed—the 1st British Brigade were still doubling across the rear of Maxwell and Lewis to fill the gap between the latter and MacDonald. As they had wheeled round, the regiments gained on each other according to their proximity to the pivot flank. The brigade assumed a formation which may be described as an echelon of columns of route, with the Lincolns, who were actually the pivot regiment, leading. By the time that the right of Lewis's brigade was reached and the British had begun to deploy, it was evident that the Khalifa's attack was broken and that his force was in full retreat. In the near foreground the Arab dead lay thick. Crowds of fugitives were trooping off in the distance. The Black Flag alone waved defiantly over the corpses of its defenders. In the front of the brigade the fight was over. But those who looked away to the right saw a different spectacle. What appeared to be an entirely new army was coming down from the Kerreri Hills. While the soldiers looked and wondered, fresh orders arrived. A mounted officer galloped up. There was a report that terrible events were happening in the dust and smoke to the northward. The spearmen had closed with MacDonald's brigade; were crumpling his line from the flank; had already broken it. Such were the rumours. The orders were more precise. The nearest regiment—the Lincolnshire—was to hurry to MacDonald's threatened flank to meet the attack. The rest of the brigade was to change front half right, and remain in support. The Lincolnshires, breathless but elated, forthwith started off again at the double. They began to traverse the rear of MacDonald's brigade, dimly conscious of rapid movements by its battalions, and to the sound of tremendous independent firing, which did not, however, prevent them from hearing the venomous hiss of bullets.

Had the Khalifa's attack been simultaneous with that which was now developed, the position of MacDonald's brigade must have been almost hopeless. In the actual event it was one of extreme peril. The attack in his front was weakening every minute, but the far more formidable attack on his right rear grew stronger and nearer in inverse ratio. Both attacks must be met. The moment was critical; the danger near. All depended on MacDonald, and that officer, who by valour and conduct in war had won his way from the rank of a private soldier to the command of a brigade, was equal to the emergency.

The three Sudanese battalions were now confronted with the whole fury of the Dervish attack from Kerreri. The bravery of the blacks was no less conspicuous than the wildness of their musketry. They evinced an extraordinary excitement—firing their rifles without any attempt to sight or aim, and only anxious to pull the trigger, re-load, and pull it again. In vain the British officers strove to calm their impulsive soldiers. In vain they called upon them by name, or, taking their rifles from them, adjusted the sights themselves. The independent firing was utterly beyond control. Soon the ammunition began to be exhausted, and the soldiers turned round clamouring for more cartridges, which their officers doled out to them by twos and threes in the hopes of steadying them. It was useless. They fired them all off and clamoured for more. Meanwhile, although suffering fearfully from the close and accurate fire of the three artillery batteries and eight Maxim guns, and to a less extent from the random firing of the Sudanese, the Dervishes drew nearer in thousands, and it seemed certain that there would be an actual collision. The valiant blacks prepared themselves with delight to meet the shock, notwithstanding the overwhelming numbers of the enemy. Scarcely three rounds per man remained throughout the brigade. The batteries opened a rapid fire of case-shot. Still the Dervishes advanced, and the survivors of their first wave of assault were scarcely one hundred yards away. Behind them both green flags pressed forward over enormous masses of armed humanity, rolling on as they now believed to victory.

At this moment the Lincoln Regiment began to come up. As soon as the leading company cleared the right of MacDonald's brigade, they formed line, and opened an independent fire obliquely across the front of the Sudanese. Groups of Dervishes in twos and threes were then within one hundred yards. The great masses were within three hundred yards. The independent firing lasted two minutes, during which the whole regiment deployed. Its effect was to clear away the leading groups of Arabs. The deployment having been accomplished with the loss of a dozen men, including Colonel Sloggett, who fell shot through the breast while attending to the wounded, section volleys were ordered. With excellent discipline the independent firing was instantly stopped, and the battalion began with machine-like regularity to carry out the principles of modern musketry, for which their training had efficiently prepared them and their rifles were admirably suited. They fired on an average sixty rounds per man, and finally repulsed the attack.

After the failure of the attack from Kerreri the whole Anglo-Egyptian army advanced westward, in a line of bayonets and artillery nearly two miles long, and drove the Dervishes before them into the desert, so that they could by no means rally or re-form. The Egyptian cavalry, who had returned along the river, formed line on the right of the infantry in readiness to pursue. At half-past eleven Sir H. Kitchener shut up his glasses, and, remarking that he thought the enemy had been given "a good dusting", gave the order for the brigades to resume their interrupted march on Omdurman—a movement which was possible, now that the forces in the plain were beaten. The brigadiers thereupon stopped the firing, massed their commands in convenient formations, and turned again towards the south and the city. The Lincolnshire Regiment remained detached as a rearguard.

Meanwhile the great Dervish army, who had advanced at sunrise in hope and courage, fled in utter rout, pursued by the Egyptian cavalry, harried by the 21st Lancers, and leaving more than nine thousand warriors dead and even greater numbers wounded behind them.

Thus ended the battle of Omdurman—the most signal triumph ever gained by the arms of science over barbarians. Within the space of five hours the strongest and best-armed savage army yet arrayed against a modern European Power had been destroyed and dispersed, with hardly any difficulty, comparatively small risk, and insignificant loss to the victors.

When the Khalifa Abdullah saw that the last army that remained to him was broken, that all his attacks had failed, and that thousands of his bravest warriors were slain, he rode from the field of battle in haste, and, regaining the city, proceeded like a brave and stubborn soldier to make preparations for its defence, and, like a prudent man, to arrange for his own flight should further resistance be impossible. He ordered his great war-drum to be beaten and the *ombya* to be blown, and for the last time those dismal notes boomed through the streets of Omdurman. They were not heeded. The Arabs had had enough fighting. They recognized that all was lost. Besides, to return to the city was difficult and dangerous.

The charge of the 21st Lancers had been costly, but it was not ineffective. The consequent retirement of the Dervish brigade protecting the extreme right exposed their line of retreat. The cavalry were resolved to take full advantage of the position they had paid so much to gain, and while the second attack was at its height we were already trotting over the plain towards the long lines of fugitives who streamed across it. With the experience of the past hour in our minds, and with the great numbers of the enemy in our front, it seemed to many that a bloody day lay before us. But we had not gone far when individual Dervishes began to walk towards the advancing squadrons, throwing down their weapons, holding up their hands, and imploring mercy.

As soon as it was apparent that the surrender of individuals was accepted, the Dervishes began to come in and lay down their arms —at first by twos and threes, then by dozens, and finally by scores. Meanwhile those who were still intent on flight made a wide detour to avoid the cavalry, and streamed past our front at a mile's distance in uninterrupted succession. The disarming and escorting of the prisoners delayed our advance, and many thousands of Dervishes escaped from the field. But the position of the cavalry and the pressure they exerted shouldered the routed army out into the desert, so that retiring they missed the city of Omdurman altogether, and, disregarding the Khalifa's summons to defend it and the orders of their Emirs, continued their flight to the south. To harry and annoy the fugitives a few troops were dismounted with carbines, and a constant fire was made on such as did not attempt to come in and surrender. Yet the crowds continued to run the gauntlet, and at least twenty thousand men made good their escape. Many of these were still vicious, and replied to our fire with bullets, fortunately at very long range. It would have been madness for three hundred Lancers to gallop in among such masses, and we had to be content with the results of the carbine fire.

★   ★   ★

The Sirdar, attended by his whole Staff, with the Black Flag of the Khalifa carried behind him and accompanied by the band of the XIth Sudanese, rode in front of the XIVth battalion. The regiments were soon enveloped by the numberless houses of the suburbs and divided by the twisting streets; but the whole brigade pressed forward on a broad front. Behind followed the rest of the army—battalion after battalion, brigade after brigade—until all, swallowed up by the maze of mud houses, were filling the open spaces and blocking and choking the streets and alleys with solid masses of armed men, who marched or pushed their way up to the great wall.

For two miles the progress through the suburbs continued, and the General, hurrying on with his Staff, soon found himself, with the band, the Maxims, and the artillery, at the foot of the great wall. Several hundred Dervishes had gathered for its defence; but the fact that no *banquette* had been made on which they could stand to fire prevented their resistance from being effective. Within the wall the scenes were more terrible than in the suburbs. The effects of the bombardment were evident on every side. Women and children lay frightfully mangled in the roadway. At one place a whole family had been crushed by a projectile. Dead Dervishes, already in the fierce heat beginning to decompose, dotted the ground. The houses were crammed with wounded. Hundreds of decaying carcases of animals filled the air with a sickening smell. Here, as without the wall, the anxious inhabitants renewed their protestations of loyalty and welcome; and interpreters, riding down the narrow alleys, proclaimed the merciful conditions of the con-querors and called on the people to lay down their arms. Great piles of surrendered weapons rose in the streets, guarded by Sudanese soldiers. Many Arabs sought clemency; but there were others who disdained it; and the whirring of the Maxims, the crashes of the volleys, and a continual dropping fire attested that there was fighting in all parts of the city into which the columns had penetrated. All Dervishes who did not immediately surrender were shot or bayoneted, and bullets whistled at random along or across the streets. But while women crowded round his horse, while sullen men fired carefully from houses, while beaten warriors cast their spears on the ground and others, still resisting, were dispatched in corners, the Sirdar rode steadily onward through the confusion, the stench, and the danger, until he reached the Mahdi's Tomb.

At the mosque two fanatics charged the Sudanese escort, and each killed or badly wounded a soldier before he was shot. The day was now far spent, and it was dusk when the prison was reached. The General was the first to enter that foul and gloomy den. Charles Neufeld and some thirty heavily shackled prisoners were released. Neufeld, who was placed on a pony, seemed nearly mad with delight, and talked and gesticulated with queer animation. "Thirteen years," he said to his rescuer, "have I waited for this day." From the prison, as it was now dark, the Sirdar rode to the great square in front of the mosque, in which his headquarters were established, and where both British brigades were already bivouacking. The rest of the army settled down along the roadways through the suburbs, and only Maxwell's brigade remained in the city to complete the establishment of law and order—a business which was fortunately hidden by the shades of night.

It was not for some hours after he had left the field of battle that Abdullah realized that his army had not obeyed his summons, but were continuing their retreat, and that only a few hundred Dervishes remained for the defence of the city. He seems, if we judge from the accounts of his personal servant, an Abyssinian boy, to have faced the disasters that had overtaken him with singular composure. He rested until two o'clock, when he ate some food. Thereafter he repaired to the Tomb, and in that ruined shrine, amid the wreckage of the shell-fire, the defeated sovereign appealed to the spirit of Mohammed Ahmed to help him in his sore distress. It was the last prayer ever offered over the Mahdi's grave. The celestial counsels seem to have been in accord with the dictates of common sense, and at four o'clock the Khalifa, hearing that the Sirdar was already entering the city, and that the English cavalry were on the parade ground to the west, mounted a small donkey, and, accompanied by his principal wife, a Greek nun as a hostage, and a few attendants, rode leisurely off towards the south. Eight miles from Omdurman a score of swift camels awaited him, and on these he soon reached the main body of his routed army. Here he found many disheartened friends; but the fact that, in this evil plight, he found any friends at all must be recorded in his favour and in that of his subjects. When he arrived he had no escort—was, indeed, unarmed. The fugitives had good reason to be savage. Their leaders had led them only to their ruin. To cut the throat of this one man who was the cause of all their sufferings was as easy as they would have thought it innocent. Yet none assailed him. The tyrant, the oppressor, the scourge of the Sudan, the hypocrite, the abominated Khalifa; the embodiment, as he has been depicted to European eyes, of all the vices; the object, as he was believed in England, of his people's bitter hatred, found safety and welcome among his flying soldiers. The surviving Emirs hurried to his side. Many had gone down on the fatal plain. Osman Azrak, the valiant Bishara, Yakub, and scores whose strange names have not obscured these pages, but who were, nevertheless, great men of war, lay staring up at the stars. Yet those

158

who remained never wavered in their allegiance. Ali-Wad-Helu whose leg had been shattered by a shell splinter, was senseless with pain; but the Sheikh-ed-Din, the astute Osman Digna, Ibrahim Khalil, who withstood the charge of the 21st Lancers, and others of less note rallied to the side of the appointed successor of Mohammed Ahmed, and did not, even in this extremity, abandon his cause. And so all hurried on through the gathering darkness, a confused and miserable multitude—dejected warriors still preserving their trashy rifles, and wounded men hobbling pitifully along; camels and donkeys laden with household goods; women crying, panting, dragging little children; all in thousands—nearly thirty thousand altogether; with little food and less water to sustain them; the desert before them, the gunboats on the Nile, and behind the rumours of pursuit and a broad trail of dead and dying to mark the path of flight.

★　　★　　★

We may say with certainty that the French Government did not intend a small expedition, at great peril to itself, to seize and hold an obscure swamp on the Upper Nile. [The ensuing pages describe the "Fashoda incident" of 1898.] What part the Abyssinians were expected to play, what services had been rendered them and what inducements they were offered, what attitude was to be adopted to the Khalifa, what use was to be made of the local tribes: all this is veiled in the mystery of intrigue. It is well known that for several years France, at some cost to herself and at a greater cost to Italy, had courted the friendship of Abyssinia, and that the weapons by which the Italians were defeated at Adowa had been mainly supplied through French channels. A small quick-firing gun of continental manufacture and of recent make which was found in the possession of the Khalifa seems to point to the existence or contemplation of similar relations with the Dervishes. But how far these operations were designed to assist the Marchand Mission is known only to those who initiated them, and to a few others who have so far kept their own counsel.

The undisputed facts are few. Towards the end of 1896 a French expedition was dispatched from the Atlantic into the heart of Africa under the command of Major Marchand. The re-occupation of Dongola was then practically complete, and the British Government were earnestly considering the desirability of a further advance. In the beginning of 1897 a British expedition, under Colonel Macdonald, and comprising a dozen carefully selected officers, set out from England to Uganda, landed at Mombasa, and struck inland. The misfortunes which fell upon this enterprise are beyond the scope of this account, and I shall not dwell upon the local jealousies and disputes which marred it. It is sufficient to observe that Colonel Macdonald was provided with Sudanese troops who were practically in a state of mutiny and actually mutinied two days after he assumed command. The officers were compelled to fight for their lives. Several were killed. A year was consumed in suppressing the mutiny and the revolt which arose out of it. If the object of the expedition was to reach the Upper Nile, it was soon obviously unattainable, and the government were glad to employ the officers in making geographical surveys.

On 7 September, five days after the battle and capture of Omdurman, the *Tewfikia*, a small Dervish steamer—one of those formerly used by General Gordon—came drifting and paddling down the river. Her Arab crew soon perceived by the Egyptian flags which were hoisted on the principal buildings, and by the battered condition of the Mahdi's Tomb, that all was not well in the city; and then, drifting a little further, they found themselves surrounded by the white gunboats of the "Turks", and so incontinently surrendered. The story they told their captors was a strange one. They had left Omdurman a month earlier, in company with the steamer *Safia*, carrying a force of five hundred men, with the Khalifa's orders to go up the White Nile and collect grain. For some time all had been well; but on approaching the old government station of Fashoda they had been fired on by black troops commanded by white officers under a strange flag—and fired on with such effect that they had lost some forty men killed and wounded. Doubting who these formidable enemies might be, the foraging expedition had turned back, and the Emir in command, having disembarked and formed a camp at a place on the east bank called Reng, had sent the *Tewfikia* back to ask the Khalifa for instructions and reinforcements. The story was carried to the Sirdar and ran like wildfire through the camp. Many officers made their way to the river, where the steamer lay, to test for themselves the truth of the report. The woodwork of the hull was marked with many newly made holes, and cutting into these with their penknives the officers extracted bullets—not the roughly cast leaden balls, the bits of telegraph wire, or old iron which savages use, but the conical nickel-covered bullets of small-bore rifles such as are fired by civilized forces alone. Here was positive proof. A European Power was on the Upper Nile: which? Some said it was the Belgians from the Congo; some that an Italian expedition had arrived; others thought that the strangers were French; others, again, believed in the Foreign Office—it was a British expedition, after all. The Arab crew were cross-examined as to the flag they had seen. Their replies were inconclusive. It had bright colours, they declared; but what those colours were and what their arrangement might be they could not tell; they were poor men, and God was very great.

Curiosity found no comfort but in patience or speculation. The camp for the most part received the news with a shrug. After their easy victory the soldiers walked delicately. They knew that they belonged to the most powerful force that had ever penetrated the heart of Africa. If there was to be more war, the government had but to give the word, and the Grand Army of the Nile would do by these newcomers as they had done by the Dervishes.

On 8 September the Sirdar started up the White Nile for Fashoda with five steamers, the XIth and XIIIth Battalions of Sudanese, two companies of the Cameron Highlanders, Peake's battery of artillery, and four Maxim guns. Three days later he arrived at Reng, and there found, as the crew of the *Tewfikia* had declared, some five hundred Dervishes encamped on the bank, and the *Safia* steamer moored to it. These stupid fellows had the temerity to open fire on the vessels. Whereat the *Sultan*, steaming towards their *dêm*, replied with a fierce shell fire which soon put them to flight. The *Safia*, being under steam, made some attempt to escape—whither, it is impossible to say—and Commander Keppel by a well-directed shell in her boilers blew her up, much to the disgust of the Sirdar, who wanted to add her to his flotilla.

A few miles' further progress brought the gunboats to their destination, and they made fast to the bank near the old government buildings of the town. Major Marchand's party consisted of eight French officers or non-commissioned officers, and one hundred and twenty black soldiers drawn from the Niger district. They possessed three steel boats fitted for sail or oars, and a small steam launch, the *Faidherbe*, which latter had, however, been sent south for reinforcements. They had six months' supplies of provisions for the French officers, and about three months' rations for the men; but they had no artillery, and were in great want of small-arm ammunition. Their position was indeed precarious. The little force was stranded, without communications of any sort, and with no means of either withstanding an attack or of making a retreat. They had fired away most of their cartridges at the Dervish foraging party, and were daily expecting a renewed attack. Indeed, it was with consternation that they had heard of the approach of the flotilla. The natives had carried the news swiftly up the river that the Dervishes were coming back with five steamers, and for three nights the French had been sleeplessly awaiting the assault of a powerful enemy.

Their joy and relief at the arrival of a European force were undisguised. The Sirdar and his officers on their part were thrilled with admiration at the wonderful achievements of this small band of heroic men. Two years had passed since they left the Atlantic coast. For four months they had been absolutely lost from human ken. They had fought with savages; they had struggled with fever; they had climbed mountains and pierced the most gloomy forests. Five days and five nights they had stood up to their necks in swamp and water. A fifth of their number had perished; yet at last they had carried out their mission and, arriving at Fashoda on 10 July, had planted the tricolour upon the Upper Nile.

Moved by such reflections the British officers disembarked. Major Marchand, with a guard of honour, came to meet the General. They shook hands warmly. "I congratulate you," said the Sirdar, "on all you have accomplished." "No," replied the Frenchman, pointing to his troops; "it is not I, but these soldiers who have done it." And Kitchener, telling the story afterwards, remarked, "Then I knew he was a gentleman."

Into the diplomatic discussions that followed, it is not necessary to plunge. The Sirdar politely ignored the French flag, and, without interfering with the Marchand Expedition and the fort it occupied, hoisted the British and Egyptian colours with all due ceremony, amid musical honours and the salutes of the gunboats. A garrison was established at Fashoda, consisting of the XIth Sudanese, four guns of Peake's battery, and two Maxims, the whole under the command of Colonel Jackson, who was appointed military and civil commandant of the Fashoda district.

\* \* \*

I do not attempt to describe the international negotiations and discussions that followed the receipt of the news in Europe, but it is pleasing to remember that a great crisis found England united. The determination of the Government was approved by the loyalty of the Opposition, supported by the calm resolve of the people, and armed with the efficiency of the fleet. At first indeed, while the Sirdar was still steaming southward, wonder and suspense filled all minds; but when suspense ended in the certainty that eight French adventurers were in occupation of Fashoda and claimed a territory twice as large as France, it gave place to a deep and bitter anger. There is no Power in Europe which the average Englishman regards with less animosity than France. Nevertheless, on this matter all were agreed. They should go. They should evacuate Fashoda, or else all the might, majesty, dominion, and power of everything that could by any stretch of the imagination be called "British" should be employed to make them go.

When the final triumph, long expected, came in all its completeness it was hailed with a shout of exultation, and the people of Great Britain, moved far beyond their wont, sat themselves down to give thanks to their God, their government, and their general. Suddenly, on the chorus of their rejoicing there broke a discordant note. They were confronted with the fact that a "friendly Power" had, unprovoked, endeavoured to rob them of the fruits of their victories. They now realized that while they had been devoting themselves to great military operations, in broad daylight and the eye of the world, and prosecuting an enterprise on which they had set their hearts, other operations—covert and deceitful—had been in progress in the heart of the Dark Continent, designed solely for the mischievous and spiteful object of depriving them of the produce

163

of their labours. And they firmly set their faces against such behaviour.

First af all, Great Britain was determined to have Fashoda or fight; and as soon as this was made clear, the French were willing to give way. Fashoda was a miserable swamp, of no particular value to them. Marchand, Lord Salisbury's "explorer in difficulties upon the Upper Nile", was admitted by the French Minister to be merely an "emissary of civilization". It was not worth their while to embark on the hazards and convulsions of a mighty war for either swamp or emissary. Besides, the plot had failed. Guy Fawkes, true to his oath and his orders, had indeed reached the vault; but the other conspirators were less devoted. The Abyssinians had held aloof. The negro tribes gazed with wonder on the strangers, but had no intention of fighting for them. The pride and barbarism of the Khalifa rejected all overtures and disdained to discriminate between the various breeds of the accursed "Turks". Finally, the victory of Omdurman and its forerunner—the Desert Railway—had revolutionized the whole situation in the Nile valley. After some weeks of tension, the French Government consented to withdraw their expedition from the region of the Upper Nile.

Meanwhile events were passing at Fashoda. The town, the site of which had been carefully selected by the old Egyptian Government, is situated on the left bank of the river, on a gentle slope of ground which rises about four feet above the level of the Nile at full flood. During the rainy season, which lasts from the end of June until the end of October, the surrounding country is one vast swamp, and Fashoda itself becomes an island.

On this dismal island, far from civilization, health, or comfort, the Marchand Mission and the Egyptian garrison lived in polite antagonism for nearly three months. The French fort stood at the northern end. The Egyptian camp lay outside the ruins of the town. Civilities were constantly exchanged between the forces, and the British officers repaid the welcome gifts of fresh vegetables by newspapers and other conveniences. The Senegalese riflemen were smart and well-conducted soldiers, and the blacks of the Sudanese battalion soon imitated their officers in reciprocating courtesies. A feeling of mutual respect sprang up between Colonel Jackson and Major Marchand. The dashing commandant of the XIth Sudanese, whose Egyptian medals bear no fewer than fourteen clasps, was filled with a generous admiration for the French explorer. Realizing the difficulties, he appreciated the magnificence of the achievement; and as he spoke excellent French a good and almost cordial understanding was established, and no serious disagreement occurred. But, notwithstanding the polite relations, the greatest vigilance was exercised by both sides, and whatever civilities were exchanged were of a formal nature.

Then it became known that the French Government had ordered the evacuation of Fashoda. Some weeks were spent in making preparations for the journey, but at length the day of departure arrived. At 8.20 on the morning of 11 December the French lowered their flag with salute and flourish of bugle. The British officers, who remained in their own camp and did not obtrude themselves, were distant but interested spectators. On the flag ceasing to fly, a *sous-officier* rushed up to the flagstaff and hurled it to the ground, shaking his fists and tearing his hair in a bitterness and vexation from which it is impossible to withhold sympathy, in view of what these men had suffered uselessly and what they had done. The French then embarked, and at 9.30 steamed southward, the *Faidherbe* towing one oblong steel barge and one old steel boat, the other three boats sailing, all full of men. As the little flotilla passed the Egyptian camp a guard of honour of the XIth Sudanese saluted them and the band struck up their national anthem. The French acknowledged the compliment by dipping their flag, and in return the British and Egyptian flags were also lowered. The boats then continued their journey until they had rounded the bend of the river, when they came to land, and, honour being duly satisfied, Marchand and his officers returned to breakfast with Colonel Jackson. The meeting was very friendly. Jackson and Germain exchanged most elaborate compliments, and the commandant, in the name of the XIth Sudanese, presented the expedition with the banner of the Emir who had attacked them, which had been captured at Reng. Marchand shook hands all round, and the British officers bade their gallant opponents a final farewell.

Once again the eight Frenchmen, who had come so far and accomplished so much, set out upon their travels, to make a safe though tedious journey through Abyssinia to the coast, and thence home to the country they had served faithfully and well, and which was not unmindful of their services.

★ ★ ★

It remains to discuss the settlement made between the conquerors of the Sudan. Great Britain and Egypt had moved hand in hand up the great river, sharing, though unequally, the cost of the war in men and money. The prize belonged to both. The direct annexation of the Sudan by Great Britain would have been an injustice to Egypt. Moreover, the claim of the conquerors to Fashoda and other territories rested solely on the former rights of Egypt. On the other hand, if the Sudan became Egyptian again, it must wear the fetters of that imprisoned country. The Capitulations would apply to the Upper Nile regions, as to the Delta. Mixed Tribunals, Ottoman Suzerainty, and other vexatious burdens would be added to the difficulties of Sudan administration. To free the new country from the curse of internationalism was a paramount object. The Sudan Agreement by Great Britain and Egypt, published on 7 March, 1899, achieves this. Like most of the best work done in Egypt by the British Agency, the Agreement was slipped through without attracting much notice. Under its authority a State has been created in the Nile Valley which is neither British nor Ottoman, nor anything else so far known to the law of Europe. International jurists are confronted with an entirely new political status. A diplomatic "Fourth Dimension" has been discovered. Great Britain and Egypt rule the country together. The allied conquerors have become the joint-possessors. "What does this Sudan Agreement mean?" the Austrian Consul-General asked Lord Cromer; and the British Agent, whom twenty-two years' acquaintance with Egyptian affairs had accustomed to anomalies, replied, "It means simply this"; and handed him the inexplicable document, under which the conquered country may some day march to Peace and Plenty.

By the operations on the Blue Nile the whole of the regions bordering on the Niles were cleared of hostile forces, dotted with military posts, and brought back to Egyptian authority. The Khalifa, however, still remained in Kordofan. After he had made good his escape from the battlefield of Omdurman, Abdullah had hurried in the direction of El Obeid, moving by the wells of Shat and Zeregia, which at that season of the year were full of water after the rains. At Abu Sherai, having shaken off the pursuit of the friendlies, he halted, encamped, and busily set to work to reorganize his shattered forces.

As soon as the Sirdar, who had returned from England, received the news of the success at Rosaires he determined to make an attempt to capture the Khalifa; and on 29 December sent for Colonel Kitchener, to whom as the senior available officer he had decided to entrust this honourable enterprise. The colonel was directed to take a small mixed force into Kordofan and to reconnoitre the enemy's position. If possible, he was to attack and capture Abdullah, whose followers were believed not to exceed one thousand ill-armed men.

Camel transport was drawn from the Atbara and from the Blue Nile. The troops were conveyed by steamer to Duem, and concentrated there during the first week in 1899. The camels were collected at Kawa, and, although several of the convoys had to march as much as four hundred miles, the whole number had arrived by 10 January.

The prime difficulty of the operation was the want of water. The Khalifa's position was nearly 125 miles from the river. The intervening country is, in the wet season, dotted with shallow lakes, but by January these are reduced to mud puddles and only occasional pools remain. All the water needed by the men, horses, and mules of the column must therefore be carried. The camels must go thirsty until one of the rare pools—the likely places for which were known to the native guides—might be found. Now, the capacity of a camel for endurance without drinking is famous; but it has its limits. If he start having filled himself with water, he can march for five days without refreshment. If he then have another long drink, he can continue for five days more. But this strains his power to the extreme; he suffers acutely during the journey, and probably dies at its end. In war, however, the miseries of animals cannot be considered; their capacity for work alone concerns the commander. It was thought that, partly by the water carried in skins, partly by the drying-up pools, and partly by the camel's power of endurance, it might be just possible for a force of about 1,200 men to strike out 125 miles into the desert, to have three days to do their business in, and to come back to the Nile. This operation, which has been called the Shirkela Reconnaissance, occupied the Kordofan Field Force.

The column—numbering 1,604 officers and men and 1,624 camels and other beasts of burden—started from Kohi at 3 p.m. on 23 January, having sent on a small advanced party to the wells of Gedid twelve hours before. The country through which their route lay was of barren and miserable aspect. They had embarked on a sandy ocean with waves of thorny scrub and withered grass. From the occasional rocky ridges, which allowed a more extended view, this sterile jungle could be seen stretching indefinitely on all sides. Ten miles from the river all vestiges of animal life disappeared. The land was a desert; not the open desert of the Northern Sudan, but one vast unprofitable thicket, whose interlacing thorn bushes, unable to yield the slightest nourishment to living creatures, could yet obstruct their path.

Through this the straggling column, headed in the daylight by the red Egyptian flag and at night by a lantern on a pole, wound its weary way, the advanced guard cutting a path with axes and marking the track with strips of calico, the rearguard driving on the laggard camels and picking up the numerous loads which were cast. Three long marches brought them on the 25th to Gedid. The first detachment had already arrived and had opened up the wells. None gave much water; all emitted a foul stench, and one was occupied by a poisonous serpent eight feet long—the sole inhabitant. The camels were sent to drink at the pool seven miles away, and it was hoped that some of the water-skins could be refilled; but, after all, the green slime was thought unfit for human consumption, and they had to come back empty.

The march was resumed on the 26th. The trees were now larger; the scrub became a forest; the sandy soil changed to a dark red colour; but otherwise the character of the country was unaltered. The column rested at Abu Rokba. A few starving inhabitants who occupied the huts pointed out the grave of the Khalifa's father and the little straw house in which Abdullah was wont to pray during his visits. Lately, they said, he had retired from Aigaila to Shirkela, but even from this latter place he had made frequent pilgrimages.

At the end of the next march, which was made by day, the guides, whose memories had been refreshed by flogging, discovered a large pool of good water, and all drank deeply in thankful joy. A small but strong *zeriba* was built near this precious pool, and the reserve food and a few sick men were left with a small garrison under an Egyptian officer. The column resumed their journey. On the 29th they reached Aigaila, and here, with feelings of astonishment scarcely less than Robinson Crusoe experienced at seeing the footprint in the sand, they came upon the Khalifa's abandoned camp. A wide space had been cleared of bush, and the trees, stripped of their smaller branches, presented an uncanny appearance. Beyond stood the encampment—a great multitude of yellow spear-grass dwellings, perfectly clean, neatly arranged in streets and squares, and stretching for miles. The aspect of this strange deserted town, rising, silent as a cemetery, out of the awful scrub, chilled everyone who saw it. Its size might indeed concern their leader. At the very lowest computation it had contained twenty thousand people. How many of these were fighting men? Certainly not fewer than eight or nine thousand. Yet the expedition had been sent on the assumption that there were scarcely one thousand warriors with the Khalifa!

The news was startling. The small force were 125 miles from their base; behind them lay an almost waterless country, and in front was a powerful enemy. An informal council of war was held. The Sirdar had distinctly ordered that, whatever happened, there was to be no waiting; the troops were either to attack or retire. Colonel Kitchener decided to retire. The decision having been taken, the next step was to get beyond the enemy's reach as quickly as possible, and the force began their retreat on the same night. The homeward march was not less long and trying than the advance, and neither hopes of distinction nor glamour of excitement cheered the weary soldiers. As they toiled gloomily back towards the Nile, the horror of the accursed land grew upon all. Hideous spectacles of human misery were added to the desolation of the hot, thorny scrub and stinking pools of mud. The starving inhabitants had been lured from their holes and corners by the outward passage of the troops, and hoped to snatch some food from the field of battle. Disappointed, they now approached the camps at night in twos and threes, making piteous entreaties for any kind of nourishment. Their appeals were perforce unregarded; not an ounce of spare food remained.

Towards the end of the journey the camels, terribly strained by their privation of water, began to die, and it was evident that the force would have no time to spare. One young camel, though not apparently exhausted, refused to proceed, and even when a fire was lighted round him remained stubborn and motionless; so that, after being terribly scorched, he had to be shot. Others fell and died all along the route. Their deaths brought some relief to the starving inhabitants. For as each animal was left behind, the officers, looking back, might see first one, then another furtive figure emerge from the bush and pounce on the body like a vulture; and in many cases before life was extinct the famished natives were devouring the flesh.

On 5 February the column reached Kohi, and the Kordofan Field Force, having overcome many difficulties and suffered many hardships, was broken up, unsuccessful through no fault of its commander, its officers, or its men.

*   *   *

For nearly a year no further operations were undertaken against the Khalifa, and he remained all through the spring and summer of 1899 supreme in Kordofan, reorganizing his adherents and plundering the country—a chronic danger to the new government, a curse to the local inhabitants, and a most serious element of unrest. The barren and almost waterless regions into which he had withdrawn presented very difficult obstacles to any military expedition, and although powerful forces were still concentrated at Khartoum, the dry season and the uncertain whereabouts of the enemy prevented action. But towards the end of August trustworthy information was received by the Intelligence Department, through the agency of friendly tribesmen, that the Khalifa, with all his army, was encamped at Jebel Gedir—that same mountain in Southern Kordofan to which nearly twenty years before he and the Mahdi had retreated after the flight from Abba Island. Here among old memories which his presence revived he became at once a centre of fanaticism. Night

170

after night he slept upon the Mahdi's stone; and day after day tales of his dreams were carried by secret emissaries not only throughout the Western Sudan, but into the Ghezira and even to Khartoum. And now, his position being definite and his action highly dangerous, it was decided to move against him.

* * *

The River War is over. In its varied course, which extended over fourteen years and involved the untimely destruction of perhaps three hundred thousand lives, many extremes and contrasts have been displayed. There have been battles which were massacres, and others that were mere parades. There have been occasions of shocking cowardice and surprising heroism, of plans conceived in haste and emergency, of schemes laid with slow deliberation, of wild extravagance, and cruel waste, of economies scarcely less barbarous, of wisdom and incompetence. But the result is at length achieved, and the flags of England and Egypt wave unchallenged over the valley of the Nile.

# LONDON TO LADYSMITH

## VIA PRETORIA

*This book is, in the main, a collection of letters written for the "Morning Post" when the author acted as a war correspondent for that newspaper. It was first published in 1900 and is, in his own words, "a personal record of my adventures and impressions during the first five months of the African War", and an account of the operations by Sir Redvers Buller for the relief of Ladysmith. The book contains the first account of the author's historic capture by, and escape from, the Boers. Concerning the ethics of this escape there was sharp controversy for some time.*

WE LEFT London amid rumours of all kinds. The Metropolis was shrouded in a fog of credulous uncertainty, broken only by the sinister gleam of the placarded lie or the croak of the newsman. Terrible disasters had occurred and had been contradicted; great battles were raging—unconfirmed; and beneath all this froth the tide of war was really flowing, and no man could shut his eyes to grave possibilities. Then the ship sailed, and all was silence—a heaving silence. But Madeira was scarcely four days' journey. There we should find the answers to many questions. At Madeira, however, we learned nothing, but nothing, though satisfactory, is very hard to understand. Why did they declare war if they had nothing up their sleeves? Why are they wasting time now? Such were the questions. Then we sailed again, and again silence shut down, this time, however, on a more even keel.

Speculation arises out of ignorance. Many and various are the predictions as to what will be the state of the game when we shall have come to anchor in Table Bay. Forecasts range from the capture of Pretoria by Sir George White and the confinement of President Kruger in the deepest level beneath the Johannesburg Exchange, on the one hand, to the surrender of Cape Town to the Boers, the proclamation of Mr. Schreiner as King of South Africa, and a fall of two points in Rand Mines on the other. Between these wild extremes all shades of opinion are represented. Only one possibility is unanimously excluded—an inconclusive peace. There are on board officers who travelled this road eighteen years ago with Lord Roberts, and reached Cape Town only to return by the next boat. But no one anticipates such a result this time.

News at last! This morning we sighted a sail—a large homeward-bound steamer, spreading her canvas to catch the trades, and with who should say what tidings on board. We crowded the decks, and from every point of view telescopes, field glasses, and cameras were directed towards the stranger. She passed us at scarcely two hundred yards, and as she did so her crew and company, giving three hearty cheers, displayed a long blackboard, on which was written in white paint: "Boers defeated; three battles; Penn Symons killed." There was a little gasp of excitement. Everyone stepped back from the bulwarks. Those who had not seen ran eagerly up to ask what had happened. A dozen groups were formed, a hum of conversation arose, and meanwhile the vessels separated—for the pace of each was swift—and in a few moments the homeward bound lay far in our wake.

What does it mean—this scrap of intelligence which tells so much and leaves so much untold? Tomorrow night we shall know all. This at least is certain: there has been fierce fighting in Natal, and, under Heaven, we have held our own: perhaps more. "Boers defeated." Let us thank God for that. The brave garrisons have repelled the invaders. The luck has turned at last. The crisis is over, and the army now on the seas may move with measured strides to effect a final settlement that is both wise and just. In that short message eighteen years of heartburnings are healed. The abandoned colonist, the shamed soldier, the "cowardly Englishman", the white flag, the "How about Majuba?"—all gone for ever. At last—"the Boers defeated." Hurrah! Hurrah! Hurrah!

So Sir Penn Symons is killed! Well, no one would have laid down his life more gladly in such a cause. Twenty years ago the merest chance saved him from the massacre at Isandhlwana, and Death promoted him in an afternoon from subaltern to senior captain.

Thenceforward his rise was rapid. He commanded the First Division of the Tirah Expeditionary Force among the mountains with prudent skill. His brigades had no misfortunes: his rearguards came safely into camp. In the spring of 1898, when the army lay around Fort Jumrood, looking forward to a fresh campaign, I used often to meet him. Everyone talked of Symons, of his energy, of his jokes, of his enthusiasm. It was Symons who had built a racecourse on the stony plain; who had organized the Jumrood Spring Meeting; who won the principal event himself, to the delight of the private soldiers, with whom he was intensely popular; who, moreover, was to be first and foremost if the war with the tribes broke out again; and who was entrusted with much of the negotiations with their *jirgas*. Dinner with Symons in the mud tower of Jumrood Fort was an experience. The memory of many tales of sport and war remains. At the end the General would drink the old Peninsular toasts: "Our Men", "Our Women", "Our Religion", "Our Swords", "Ourselves", "Sweethearts and Wives", and "Absent Friends"—one for every night in the week. The night when I dined the toast was "Our Men". May the State in her necessities find others like him!

★   ★   ★

I had an opportunity of gaining some impressions of the general aspect of the coasts of Pondoland and Natal. These beautiful countries stretch down to the ocean in smooth slopes of the richest verdure, broken only at intervals by lofty bluffs crowned with forests. The many rivulets to which the pasture owes its life and the land its richness glide to the shore through deep-set creeks and chines, or plunge over the cliffs in cascades which the strong winds scatter into clouds of spray.

These are regions of possibility, and as we drove along before our now friendly wind I could not but speculate on the future. Here are wide tracts of fertile soil watered by abundant rains. The temperate sun warms the life within the soil. The cooling breeze refreshes the inhabitant. The delicious climate stimulates the vigour of the European. The highway of the sea awaits the produce of his labour. All Nature smiles, and here at last is a land where white men may rule and prosper. As yet only the indolent Kaffir enjoys its bounty, and, according to the antiquated philosophy of Liberalism, it is to such that it should for ever belong. But while Englishmen choke and fester in crowded cities, while thousands of babies are born every month who are never to have a fair chance in life, there will be those who will dream another dream of a brave system of State-aided—almost State-compelled—emigration, a scheme of old age pensions that shall anticipate old age, and by preventing paupers terminate itself; a system that shall remove the excess of the old land to provide the deficiency of the new, and shall offer even to the most unfortunate citizen of the Empire fresh air and open opportunity. And as I pondered on all these things, the face of the country seemed changed. Thriving ports and townships rose up along the shore, and, upon the hillsides, inland towers, spires, and tall chimneys attested the wealth and industry of men. Here in front of us was New Brighton; the long shelving ledge of rock was a sea-wall already made, rows of stately buildings covered the grassy slopes; the shipping of many nations lay in the roadstead; above the whole scene waved The Flag, and in the foreground on the sandy beach the great-grandchildren of the crossing-sweeper and the sandwich man sported by the waves that beat by the Southern Pole, or sang aloud for joy in the beauty of their home and the pride of their race. And then with a lurch—for the motion was still considerable—I came back from the land of dreams to reality and the hideous fact that Natal is invaded and assailed by the Boer.

The farm stood in a sheltered angle of the hill at no great distance from its summit. It was a good-sized house, with stone walls and a corrugated-iron roof. A few sheds and outhouses surrounded it, four or five blue gums afforded a little shade from the sun and a little relief to the grassy smoothness of the landscape. Two women met us at the door, one the wife, the other, I think, the sister of our host. Neither was young, but their smiling faces showed the invigorating effects of this delicious air. "These are anxious times," said the older; "we hear the cannonading every morning at breakfast. What will come of it all?" Over a most excellent luncheon we discussed many things with these kind people, and spoke of how the nation was this time resolved to make an end of the long quarrel with the Boers, so that there should be no more uncertainty and alarm among loyal subjects of the Queen. "We have always known," said the farmer, "that it must end in war, and I cannot say I am sorry it has come at last. But it falls heavily on us. I am the only man for twenty miles who has not left his farm. Of course we are defenceless here. Any day the Dutchmen may come. They wouldn't kill us, but they would burn or plunder everything, and it's all I've got in the world. Fifteen years have I worked at this place, and I said to myself we may as well stay and face it out, whatever happens." Indeed, it was an anxious time for such a man. He had bought the ground, built the house, reclaimed waste tracts, enriched the land with corn and cattle, sunk all his capital in the enterprise, and backed it with the best energies of his life. Now everything might be wrecked in an hour by a wandering Boer patrol. And this was happening to a loyal and law-abiding British subject more than a hundred miles within the frontiers of Her Majesty's dominions! Now I felt the bitter need for soldiers—thousands of soldiers—so that such a man as this might be assured. With what pride and joy could one have said: "Work on, the fruits of your industry are safe. Under the strong arm of the imperial government your home shall be secure, and if perchance you suffer in the disputes of the Empire the public wealth shall restore your private losses." But when I recalled the scanty force which alone kept the field, and stood between the enemy and the rest of Natal, I knew the first would be an empty boast, and, remembering what had happened on other occasions, I thought the second might prove a barren promise.

Their artillery is inferior in numbers, but in nothing else, to ours. Yesterday I visited Colenso in the armoured train. In one of the deserted British-built redoubts I found two boxes of shrapnel shells and charges. The Boers had not troubled to touch them. Their guns were of a later pattern, and fired powder and shell made up together like a great rifle cartridge. The combination, made for the first time in the history of war, of heavy artillery and swarms of mounted infantry is formidable and effective. The enduring courage and confident spirit of the enemy must also excite surprise. In short, we have grossly underrated their fighting powers. Most people in England—I, among them—thought that the Boer ultimatum was an act of despair, that the Dutch would make one fight for their honour, and, once defeated, would accept the inevitable. All I have heard and whatever I have seen out here contradict these false ideas. Anger, hatred, and the consciousness of military power impelled the Boers to war. They would rather have fought at their own time —a year or two later—when their preparations were still further advanced, and when the British were, perhaps, involved in other quarters. But, after all, the moment was ripe. Nearly everything was ready, and the whole people sprang to arms with alacrity, firmly believing that they would drive the British into the sea. To that opinion they still adhere. I do not myself share it; but it cannot be denied that it seems less absurd today than it did before a shot had been fired.

★　　★　　★

Seeing the engine escaping the Boers increased their fire, and the troops, hitherto somewhat protected by the iron trucks, began to suffer. The major of volunteers fell, shot through the thigh. Here and there men dropped on the ground, several screamed—this is very rare in war—and cried for help. About a quarter of the force was very soon killed or wounded. The shells which pursued the retreating soldiers scattered them all along the track. Order and control vanished. The engine, increasing its pace, drew out from the thin crowd of fugitives and was soon in safety. The infantry continued to run down the line in the direction of the houses, and, in spite of their disorder, I honestly consider that they were capable of making a further resistance when some shelter should be reached. But at this moment one of those miserable incidents—much too frequent in this war—occurred.

A private soldier who was wounded, in direct disobedience of the positive orders that no surrender was to be made, took it on himself to wave a pocket-handkerchief. The Boers immediately ceased firing, and with equal daring and humanity a dozen horsemen galloped from the hills into the scattered fugitives, scarcely any of whom had seen the white flag, and several of whom were still firing, and called loudly on them to surrender. Most of the soldiers, uncertain what to do, then halted, gave up their arms, and became prisoners of war. Those further away from the horsemen continued to run and were shot or hunted down in twos and threes, and some made good their escape.

For my part I found myself on the engine when the obstruction was at last passed and remained there jammed in the cab next to the man with the shattered arm. In this way I travelled some five hundred yards, and passed through the fugitives, noticing particularly a young officer, Lieutenant Frankland, who with a happy, confident smile on his face was endeavouring to rally his men. When I approached the houses where we had resolved to make a stand, I jumped on to the line to collect the men as they arrived, for scarcely had the locomotive left me than I found myself alone in a shallow cutting and none of our soldiers, who had all surrendered on the way, to be seen. Then suddenly there appeared on the line at the end of the cutting two men not in uniform. "Platelayers," I said to myself, and then, with a surge of realization, "Boers." My mind retains a momentary impression of these tall figures, full of animated movement, clad in dark flapping clothes, with slouch, storm-driven hats, poising on their rifles hardly a hundred yards away. I turned and ran between the rails of the track, and the only thought I achieved was this, "Boer marksmanship." Two bullets passed, both within a foot, one on either side. I flung myself against the banks of the cutting. But they gave no cover. Another glance at the figures; one was now kneeling to aim. Again I darted forward. Movement seemed the only chance. Again two soft kisses sucked in the air, but nothing struck me. This could not endure. I must get out of the cutting—that damnable corridor. I scrambled up the bank. The earth sprang up beside me, and something touched my hand, but outside the cutting was a tiny depression. I crouched in this, struggling to get my wind. On the other side of the railway a horseman galloped up, shouting to me and waving his hand. He was scarcely forty yards off. With a rifle I could have killed him easily. I knew nothing of white flags, and the bullets had made me savage. I reached down for my Mauser pistol. "This one at least," I said, and indeed it was a certainty; but alas! I had left the weapon in the cab of the engine in order to be free to work at the wreckage. What then? There was a wire fence between me and the horseman. Should I continue to fly? The idea of another shot at such a short range decided me. Death stood before me, grim sullen Death without his light-hearted companion, Chance. So I held up my hand and, like Mr. Jorrocks's foxes, cried "Capivy". Then I was herded with the

178

other prisoners in a miserable group, and about the same time I noticed that my hand was bleeding, and it began to pour with rain. Two days before, I had written to an officer in high command at home, whose friendship I have the honour to enjoy: "There has been a great deal too much surrendering in this war, and I hope people who do so will not be encouraged." Fate had intervened, yet though her tone was full of irony she seemed to say, as I think Ruskin once said, "It matters very little whether your judgments of people are true or untrue, and very much whether they are kind or unkind," and repeating that I will make an end.

*　　*　　*

The position of a prisoner of war is painful and humiliating. A man tries his best to kill another, and finding that he cannot succeed asks his enemy for mercy. The laws of war demand that this should be accorded, but it is impossible not to feel a sense of humbling obligation to the captor from whose hand we take our lives. All military pride, all independence of spirit must be put aside. These may be carried to the grave, but not into captivity. We must prepare ourselves to submit, to obey, to endure. Certain things—sufficient food and water and protection during good behaviour—the victor must supply or be a savage, but beyond these all else is favour. Favours must be accepted from those with whom we have a long and bitter quarrel, from those who feel fiercely that we seek to do them cruel injustice. The dog who has been whipped must be thankful for the bone that is flung to him.

When the prisoners captured after the destruction of the armoured train had been disarmed and collected in a group we found that there were fifty-six unwounded or slightly wounded men, besides the more serious cases lying on the scene of the fight. The Boers crowded round, looking curiously at their prize, and we ate a little chocolate that by good fortune—for we had had no breakfast—was in our pockets, and sat down on the muddy ground to think. The rain streamed down from a dark leaden sky, and the coats of the horses steamed in the damp. "*Voorwärts,*" said a voice, and, forming in a miserable procession, two wretched officers, a bare-headed, tattered correspondent, four sailors with straw hats and H.M.S. *Tartar* in gold letters on the ribbons—ill-timed jauntiness—some fifty soldiers

179

and volunteers, and two or three railwaymen, we started, surrounded by the active Boer horsemen.

"You need not walk fast," said a Boer in excellent English; "take your time." Then another, seeing me hatless in the downpour, threw me a soldier's cap—one of the Irish Fusilier caps, taken, probably, near Ladysmith. So they were not cruel men, these enemy. That was a great surprise to me, for I had read much of the literature of this land of lies, and fully expected every hardship and indignity. At length we reached the guns which had played on us for so many minutes—two strangely long barrels sitting very low on carriages of four wheels, like a break in which horses are exercised. They looked offensively modern, and I wondered why our Army had not got field artillery with fixed ammunition and eight thousand yards range. Some officers and men of the Staats Artillerie, dressed in a drab uniform with blue facings, approached us. The commander, Adjutant Roos—as he introduced himself—made a polite salute. He regretted the unfortunate circumstances of our meeting; he complimented the officers on their defence—of course, it was hopeless from the first; he trusted his fire had not annoyed us; we should, he thought, understand the necessity for them to continue; above all he wanted to know how the engine had been able to get away, and how the line could have been cleared of wreckage under his guns. In fact, he behaved as a good professional soldier should, and his manner impressed me.

Our captors conducted us to a rough tent which had been set up in a hollow in one of the hills, and which we concluded was General Joubert's headquarters. Here we were formed in a line, and soon surrounded by a bearded crowd of Boers cloaked in mackintosh. I explained that I was a Special Correspondent, and asked to see General Joubert. But in the throng it was impossible to tell who were the superiors. My credentials were taken from me by a man who said he was a Field Cornet, and who promised that they should be laid before the General forthwith. Meanwhile we waited in the rain, and the Boers questioned us. My certificate as a correspondent bore a name better known than liked in the Transvaal. Moreover, some of the private soldiers had been talking. "You are the son of Lord Randolph Churchill?" said a Scottish Boer, abruptly. I did not deny the fact. Immediately there was much talking, and all crowded round me, looking and pointing, while I heard my name repeated on every side. "I am a newspaper correspondent," I said, "and you ought not to hold me prisoner." The Scottish Boer laughed. "Oh," he said, "we do not catch lords' sons every day." Whereat they all chuckled, and began to explain that I should be allowed to play football at Pretoria.

All this time I was expecting to be brought before General Joubert, from whom I had some hopes I should obtain assurances that my character as a press correspondent would be respected. But suddenly a mounted man rode up and ordered the prisoners to march away towards Colenso. The escort, twenty horsemen, closed round us. I addressed their leader, and demanded either that I should be taken before the General, or that my credentials should be given back. But the so-called Field Cornet was not to be seen. The only response was, "*Voorwärts*," and as it seemed useless, undignified, and even dangerous to discuss the matter further with these people, I turned and marched off with the rest.

We were put into a corrugated-iron shed near the station, the floors of which were four inches deep with torn railway forms and account books. Here we flung ourselves down exhausted, and what with the shame, the disappointment, the excitement of the morning, the misery of the present, and physical weakness, it seemed that love of life was gone, and I thought almost with envy of a soldier I had seen during the fight lying quite still on the embankment, secure in the calm philosophy of death from "the slings and arrows of outrageous fortune".

After the Boers had lit two fires they opened one of the doors of the shed and told us we might come forth and dry ourselves. A newly slaughtered ox lay on the ground, and strips of his flesh were given to us. These we toasted on sticks over the fire and ate greedily, though since the animal had been alive five minutes before one felt a kind of cannibal. Other Boers not of our escort who were occupying Colenso came to look at us. With two of these who were brothers, English by race, Afrikanders by birth, Boers by choice, I had some conversation. The war, they said, was going well. Of course, it was a great matter to face the power and might of the

British Empire, still they were resolved. They would drive the English out of South Africa for ever, or else fight to the last man.

I could not sleep. Vexation of spirit, a cold night, and wet clothes withheld sweet oblivion. The rights and wrongs of the quarrel, the fortunes and chances of the war, forced themselves on the mind. What men they were, these Boers! I thought of them as I had seen them in the morning riding forward through the rain— thousands of independent riflemen, thinking for themselves, possessed of beautiful weapons, led with skill, living as they rode without commissariat or transport or ammunition column, moving like the wind, and supported by iron constitutions and a stern, hard Old Testament God who should surely smite the Amalekites hip and thigh. And then, above the rain storm that beat loudly on the corrugated iron, I heard the sound of a chaunt. The Boers were singing their evening psalm, and the menacing notes—more full of indignant war than love and mercy—struck a chill into my heart, so that I thought after all that the war was unjust, that the Boers were better men than we, that Heaven was against us, that Ladysmith, Mafeking, and Kimberley would fall, that the Estcourt garrison would perish, that foreign powers would intervene, that we should lose South Africa, and that that would be the beginning of the end. So for the time I despaired of the Empire, nor was it till the morning sun—all the brighter after the rain storms, all the warmer after the chills—struck in through the windows that things reassumed their true colours and proportions.

It was about eleven o'clock when we reached Elandslaagte Station. A train awaited the prisoners. There were six or seven closed vans for the men and a first-class carriage for the officers. Into a compartment of this we were speedily bundled. Two Boers with rifles sat themselves between us, and the doors were locked. I was desperately hungry, and asked for both food and water. "Plenty is coming," they said, so we waited patiently, and sure enough, in a few minutes a railway official came along the platform, opened the door, and thrust before us in generous profusion two tins of preserved mutton, two tins of preserved fish, four or five loaves, half a dozen pots of jam, and a large can of tea. As far as I could see the soldiers fared no worse. The reader will believe that we did not stand on ceremony, but fell to at once and made the first satisfying meal for three days. While we ate a great crowd of Boers gathered around the train and peered curiously in at the windows. One of them was a doctor, who, noticing that my hand was bound up, inquired whether I were wounded. The cut caused by the splinter of bullet was insignificant, but since it was ragged and had received no attention for two days it had begun to fester. I therefore showed him my hand, and he immediately bustled off to get bandages and hot water and what not, with which, amid the approving grins of the rough fellows who thronged the platform, he soon bound me up very correctly.

What is the true and original root of Dutch aversion to British rule? It is not Slagters Nek, nor Broomplatz, nor Majuba, nor the Jameson Raid. Those incidents only fostered its growth. It is the abiding fear and hatred of the movement that seeks to place the native on a level with the white man. British government is associated in the Boer farmer's mind with violent social revolution. Black is to be proclaimed the same as white. The servant is to be raised against the master; the Kaffir is to be declared the brother of the European, to be constituted his legal equal, to be armed with political rights. The dominant race is to be deprived of their superiority; nor is a tigress robbed of her cubs more furious than is the Boer at this prospect.

It was, as nearly as I can remember, midday when the trainload of prisoners reached Pretoria. We pulled up in a sort of siding with an earth platform on the right side which opened into the streets of the town. The day was fine, and the sun shone brightly. There was a considerable crowd of people to receive us; ugly women with bright parasols, loafers and ragamuffins, fat burghers too heavy to ride at the front, and a long line of untidy, white-helmeted policemen—"zarps" as they were called—who looked like brokendown constabulary. Someone opened—unlocked, that is, the point—the door of the railway carriage and told us to come out; and out we came—a very ragged and tattered group of officers—and waited under the sun blaze and the gloating of many eyes. About a dozen cameras were clicking busily, establishing an imperishable record of our shame. Then they loosed the men and bade them form in rank. The soldiers came out of the dark vans, in which they had been confined, with some eagerness, and began at once to chirp and joke, which seemed to me most ill-timed good humour. We waited altogether for about twenty minutes. Now for the first time since my capture I hated the enemy. The simple, valiant burghers at the front, fighting bravely as they had been told "for their farms", claimed respect, if not sympathy. But here in Pretoria all was petty and contemptible. Slimy, sleek officials of all nationalities—the red-faced, snub-nosed Hollander, the oily Portuguese half-caste—thrust or wormed their way through the crowd to look. I seemed to smell corruption in the air. Here were the creatures who had fattened on the spoils. There in the field were the heroes who won them. Tammany Hall was defended by the Ironsides.

★    ★    ★

Although there were no legitimate grounds of complaint against the treatment of British regular officers while prisoners of war, the days I passed at Pretoria were the most monotonous and among the most miserable of my life. Early in the sultry mornings, for the heat at this season of the year was great, the soldier servants—prisoners like ourselves—would bring us a cup of coffee, and sitting up in bed we began to smoke the cigarettes and cigars of another idle, aimless day. Breakfast was at nine: a nasty uncomfortable meal. The room was stuffy, and there are more enlivening spectacles than seventy British officers caught by Dutch farmers and penned together in confinement. Then came the long morning, to be killed somehow by reading, chess, or cards—and perpetual cigarettes. Luncheon at one: the same as breakfast, only more so; and then a longer afternoon to follow a long morning. Often some of the officers used to play rounders in the small yard which we had for exercise. But the rest walked moodily up and down, or lounged over the railing and returned the stares of the occasional passers-by. Later would come the *Volksstem*—permitted by special indulgence —with its budget of lies.

Sometimes we got a little fillip of excitement. One evening, as I was leaning over the railings, more than forty yards from the

184

nearest sentry, a short man with a red moustache walked quickly down the street, followed by two collie dogs. As he passed, but without altering his pace in the slightest, or even looking towards me, he said quite distinctly: "Methuen beat the Boers to hell at Belmont." That night the air seemed cooler and the courtyard larger. Already we imagined the Republics collapsing and the bayonets of the Queen's Guards in the streets of Pretoria. Next day I talked to the War Secretary. I had made a large map upon the wall and followed the course of the war as far as possible by making squares of red and green paper to represent the various columns. I said: "What about Methuen? He has beaten you at Belmont. Now he should be across the Modder. In a few days he will relieve Kimberley." De Souza shrugged his shoulders. "Who can tell?" he replied; "but," he put his finger on the map, "there stands old Piet Cronje in a position called Scholz Nek, and we don't think Methuen will ever get past him." The event justified his words, and the battle which we call Magersfontein (and ought to call "Maasfontayne") the Boers call Scholz Nek.

No sooner had I reached Pretoria than I demanded my release from the government, on the grounds that I was a press correspondent and a non-combatant. So many people have found it difficult to reconcile this position with the accounts which have been published of what transpired during the defence of the armoured train, that I am compelled to explain. Besides the soldiers of the Dublin Fusiliers and Durban Light Infantry who had been captured, there were also eight or ten civilians, including a fireman, a telegraphist, and several men of the breakdown gang. Now it seems to me that according to international practice and the customs of war, the Transvaal Government were perfectly justified in regarding all persons connected with a military train as actual combatants; indeed, the fact that they were not soldiers was, if anything, an aggravation of their case. But the Boers were at that time overstocked with prisoners whom they had to feed and guard, and they therefore announced that the civilians would be released as soon as their identity was established, and only the military retained as prisoners.

In my case, however, an exception was to be made, and General

Joubert, who had read the gushing accounts of my conduct which appeared in the Natal newspapers, directed that since I had taken part in the fighting I was to be treated as a combatant officer.

Now, as it happened, I had confined myself strictly to the business of clearing the line, which was entrusted to me, and although I do not pretend that I considered the matter in its legal aspect at the time, the fact remains that I did not give a shot, nor was I armed when captured. I therefore claimed to be included in the same category as the civilian railway officials and men of the breakdown gang, whose declared duty it was to clear the line, pointing out that though my action might differ in degree from theirs, it was of precisely the same character, and that if they were regarded as non-combatants I had a right to be considered a non-combatant too.

To this effect I wrote two letters, one to the Secretary of War and one to General Joubert; but, needless to say, I did not indulge in much hope of the result, for I was firmly convinced that the Boer authorities regarded me as a kind of hostage, who would make a pleasing addition to the collection of prisoners they were forming against a change of fortune. I therefore continued to search for a path of escape; and indeed it was just as well that I did so, for I never received any answer to either of my applications while I was a prisoner, although I have since heard that one arrived by a curious coincidence the very day *after* I had departed.

While I was looking about for means, and awaiting an opportunity to break out of the Model Schools, I made every preparation to make a graceful exit when the moment should arrive. I gave full instructions to my friends as to what was to be done with my clothes and the effects I had accumulated during my stay; I paid my account to date with the storekeeper; cashed a cheque on him for 20*l.*; changed some of the notes I had always concealed on my person since my capture into gold; and lastly, that there might be no unnecessary unpleasantness, I wrote the following letter to the Secretary of State:

STATES MODEL SCHOOLS PRISON,
*10 December, 1899.*

Sir,—I have the honour to inform you that as I do not consider that your government have any right to detain me as a military prisoner, I have decided to escape from your custody. I have every confidence in the arrangements I have made with my friends outside, and I do not therefore expect to have another opportunity of seeing you. I therefore take this occasion to observe that I consider your treatment of prisoners is correct and humane, and that I see no grounds for complaint. When I return to the British lines I will make a public statement to this effect. I have also to thank you personally for your civility to me, and to express the hope that we may meet again at Pretoria before very long, and under different circumstances. Regretting that I am unable to bid you a more ceremonious or a personal farewell,

I have the honour to be, Sir,

Your most obedient servant,

WINSTON CHURCHILL.

To Mr. de Souza,
    Secretary of War, South African Republic.

I arranged that this letter, which I took great pleasure in writing, should be left on my bed, and discovered so soon as my flight was known.

It only remained now to find a hat. Luckily for me Mr. Adrian Hofmeyr, a Dutch clergyman and pastor of Zeerust, had ventured before the war to express opinions contrary to those which the Boers thought befitting for a Dutchman to hold. They had therefore seized him on the outbreak of hostilities, and after much ill-treatment and many indignities on the western border, brought him to the States Schools. He knew most of the officials, and could, I think, easily have obtained his liberty had he pretended to be in sympathy with the Republics. He was, however, a true man, and after the clergyman of the Church of England, who was rather a poor creature, omitted to read the prayer for the Queen one Sunday, it was to Hofmeyr's evening services alone that most of the officers would go. I borrowed his hat.

\*       \*       \*

Before I had been an hour in captivity I resolved to escape. Many plans suggested themselves, were examined, and rejected. For a month I thought of nothing else. But the peril and difficulty restrained action. I think that it was the report of the British defeat at Stormberg that clinched the matter.

187

I do not pretend that impatience at being locked up was not the foundation of my determination; but I should never have screwed up my courage to make the attempt without the earnest desire to do something, however small, to help the British cause. Of course, I am a man of peace. I did not then contemplate becoming an officer of Irregular Horse. But swords are not the only weapons in the world. Something may be done with a pen. So I determined to take all hazards; and, indeed, the affair was one of very great danger and difficulty.

The States Model Schools stand in the midst of a quadrangle, and are surrounded on two sides by an iron grille and on two by a corrugated iron fence about ten feet high. These boundaries offered little obstacle to anyone who possessed the activity of youth, but the fact that they were guarded on the inside by sentries, fifty yards apart, armed with rifle and revolver, made them a wellnigh insuperable barrier. No walls are so hard to pierce as living walls. I thought of the penetrating power of gold, and the sentries were sounded. They were incorruptible. I seek not to deprive them of the credit, but the truth is that the bribery market in the Transvaal has been spoiled by the millionaires. I could not afford with my slender resources to insult them heavily enough. So nothing remained but to break out in spite of them. With another officer I formed a scheme.

After anxious reflection and continual watching, it was discovered that when the sentries near the offices walked about on their beats they were at certain moments unable to see the top of a few yards of the wall. The electric lights in the middle of the quadrangle brilliantly lighted the whole place but cut off the sentries beyond them from looking at the eastern wall, for from behind the lights all seemed darkness by contrast. The first thing was therefore to pass the two sentries near the offices. It was necessary to hit off the exact moment when both their backs should be turned together. After the wall was scaled we should be in the garden of the villa next door. There our plan came to an end. Everything after this was vague and uncertain. How to get out of the garden, how to pass unnoticed through the streets, how to evade the patrols that surrounded the town, and above all how to cover the two hundred and eighty miles to the Portuguese frontiers, were questions which would arise at a later stage. All attempts to communicate with friends outside had failed. We cherished the hope that with chocolate, a little Kaffir knowledge, and a great deal of luck, we might march the distance in a fortnight, buying mealies at the native kraals and lying hidden by day. But it did not look a very promising prospect.

We determined to try on the night of 11 December, making up our minds quite suddenly in the morning, for these things are best done on the spur of the moment. I passed the afternoon in positive terror. Nothing, since my schooldays, has ever disturbed me so much as this. There is something appalling in the idea of stealing secretly off in the night like a guilty thief. The fear of detection has a pang of its own. Besides, we knew quite well that on occasion, even on excuse, the sentries would fire. Fifteen yards is a short range. And beyond the immediate danger lay a prospect of severe hardship and suffering, only faint hopes of success, and the probability at the best of five months in Pretoria Jail.

The afternoon dragged tediously away. I tried to read Mr. Lecky's *History Of England*, but for the first time in my life that wise writer wearied me. I played chess and was hopelessly beaten. At last it grew dark. At seven o'clock the bell for dinner rang and the officers trooped off. Now was the time. But the sentries gave us no chance. They did not walk about. One of them stood exactly opposite the only practicable part of the wall. We waited for two hours, but the attempt was plainly impossible, and so with a most unsatisfactory feeling of relief to bed.

Tuesday, the 12th! Another day of fear, but fear crystallizing more and more into desperation. Anything was better than further suspense. Night came again. Again the dinner bell sounded. Choosing my opportunity I strolled across the quadrangle and secreted myself in one of the offices. Through a chink I watched the sentries. For half an hour they remained stolid and obstructive. Then all of a sudden one turned and walked up to his comrade and they began to talk. Their backs were turned. Now or never. I darted out of my hiding place and ran to the wall, seized the top with my hands and drew myself up. Twice I let myself down again in sickly hesitation, and then with a third resolve scrambled up. The top was flat. Lying on it I had one parting glimpse of the sentries, still talking, still with their backs turned; but, I repeat, fifteen yards away. Then I lowered myself silently down into the adjoining garden and crouched among the shrubs. I was free. The first step had been taken, and it was irrevocable.

It now remained to await the arrival of my comrade. The bushes of the garden gave a good deal of cover, and in the moonlight their shadows lay black on the ground. Twenty yards away was the house, and I had not been five minutes in hiding before I perceived that it was full of people; the windows revealed brightly lighted rooms, and within I could see figures moving about. This was a fresh complication. We had always thought the house unoccupied. Presently—how long afterwards I do not know, for the ordinary measures of time, hours, minutes, and seconds, are quite meaningless on such occasions—a man came out of the door and walked across the garden in my direction. Scarcely ten yards away he stopped and stood still, looking steadily towards me. I cannot describe the surge of panic which nearly overwhelmed me. I must be discovered. I dared not stir an inch. My heart beat so violently that I felt sick. But amid a tumult of emotion, reason, seated firmly on her throne, whispered, "Trust to the dark background." I remained absolutely motionless. For a long time the man and I remained opposite each other, and every instant I expected him to spring forward. A vague idea crossed my mind that I might silence him. "Hush, I am a detective. We expect that an officer will break out here tonight. I am waiting to catch him." Reason—scornful this time—replied: "Surely a Transvaal detective would speak Dutch. Trust to the shadow." So I trusted, and after a spell another man came out of the house, lighted a cigar, and both he and the other walked off together. No sooner had they turned than a cat pursued by a dog rushed into the bushes and collided with me. The startled animal uttered a "miaow" of alarm and darted back again, making a horrible rustling. Both men stopped at once. But it was only the cat, as they doubtless observed, and they passed out of the garden gate into the town.

I looked at my watch. An hour had passed since I climbed the wall. Where was my comrade? Suddenly I heard a voice from within the quadrangle say, quite loud, "All up." I crawled back to the wall. Two officers were walking up and down the other side jabbering Latin words, laughing and talking all manner of nonsense—amid which I caught my name. I risked a cough. One of the officers immediately began to chatter alone. The other said slowly and clearly, ". . . cannot get out. The sentry suspects. It's all up. Can you get back again?" But now all my fears fell from me at once. To go back was impossible. I could not hope to climb the wall unnoticed. Fate pointed onwards. Besides, I said to myself, "Of course, I shall be recaptured, but I will at least have a run for my money." I said to the officers, "I shall go on alone."

Now I was in the right mood for these undertakings—that is to say that, thinking failure almost certain, no odds against success affected me. All risks were less than the certainty. The gate which led into the road was only a few yards from another sentry. I said to myself, "*Toujours de l'audace*," put my hat on my head, strode into the middle of the garden, walked past the windows of the house without any attempt at concealment, and so went through the gate and turned to the left. I passed the sentry at less than five yards. Most of them knew me by sight. Whether he looked at me or not I do not know, for I never turned my head. But after walking a hundred yards and hearing no challenge, I knew that the second obstacle had been surmounted. I was at large in Pretoria.

I walked on leisurely through the night humming a tune and choosing the middle of the road. The streets were full of Burghers, but they paid no attention to me. Gradually I reached the suburbs, and on a little bridge I sat down to reflect and consider. I was in the heart of the enemy's country. I knew no one to whom I could apply for succour. Nearly three hundred miles stretched between me and Delagoa Bay. My escape must be known at dawn. Pursuit would be immediate. Yet all exits were barred. The town was picketed, the country was patrolled, the trains were searched, the line was guarded. I had 75*l*. in my pocket and four slabs of chocolate, but the compass and the map which might have guided me, the opium tablets and meat lozenges which should have sustained me, were in my friend's pockets in the States Model Schools. Worst of all, I could not speak a word of Dutch or Kaffir, and how was I to get food or direction?

But when hope had departed, fear had gone as well. I formed a plan. I would find the Delagoa Bay Railway. Without map or compass I must follow that in spite of the pickets. I looked at the stars. Orion shone brightly. Scarcely a year ago he had guided me when lost in the desert to the banks of the Nile. He had given me water. Now he should lead to freedom. I could not endure the want of either.

*     *     *

After walking south for half a mile, I struck the railroad. Was it the line to Delagoa Bay or the Pietersburg branch? If it were the former it should run east. But so far as I could see this line ran northwards. Still, it might be only winding its way out among the hills. I resolved to follow it. The night was delicious. A cool breeze fanned my face and a wild feeling of exhilaration took hold of me. At any rate, I was free, if only for an hour. That was something. The fascination of the adventure grew. Unless the stars in their courses fought for me I could not escape. Where, then, was the need of caution? I marched briskly along the line. Here and there the lights of a picket fire gleamed. Every bridge had its watchers. But I passed them all, making very short detours at the dangerous places, and really taking scarcely any precautions. Perhaps that was the reason I succeeded.

As I walked I extended my plan. I could not march three hundred miles to the frontier. I would board a train in motion and hide under the seats, on the roof, on the couplings—anywhere. What train should I take? The first, of course. After walking for two hours I perceived the signal lights of a station. I left the line, and, circling round it, hid in the ditch by the track about two hundred yards beyond it. I argued that the train would stop at the station and that it would not have got up too much speed by the time it reached me. An hour passed. I began to grow impatient. Suddenly I heard the whistle and the approaching rattle. Then the great yellow head-lights of the engine flashed into view. The train waited five minutes at the station and started again with much noise and steaming. I crouched by the track. I rehearsed the act in my mind. I must wait until the engine had passed, otherwise I should be seen. Then I must make a dash for the carriages.

The train started slowly, but gathered speed sooner than I had expected. The flaring lights drew swiftly near. The rattle grew into a roar. The dark mass hung for a second above me. The engine driver silhouetted against his furnace glow, the black profile of the engine, the clouds of steam rushed past. Then I hurled myself on the trucks, clutched at something, missed, clutched again, missed again, grasped some sort of hand-hold, was swung off my feet—my toes bumping on the line, and with a struggle seated myself on the couplings of the fifth truck from the front of the train. It was a goods train, and the trucks were full of sacks, soft sacks covered with coal dust. I crawled on top and burrowed in among them. In five minutes I was completely buried. The sacks were warm and comfortable. Perhaps the engine driver had seen me rush up to the train and would give the alarm at the next station: on the other hand, perhaps not. Where was the train going to? Where would it be unloaded? Would it be searched? Was it on the Delagoa Bay line? What should I do in the morning? Ah, never mind that. Sufficient for the day was the luck thereof. Fresh plans for fresh contingencies. I resolved to sleep, nor can I imagine a more pleasing lullaby than the clatter of the train that carries you at twenty miles an hour away from the enemy's capital.

How long I slept I do not know, but I woke up suddenly with all feelings of exhilaration gone, and only the consciousness of oppressive difficulties heavy on me. I must leave the train before daybreak, so that I could drink at a pool and find some hiding-place while it was still dark. Another night I would board another train. I crawled from my cosy hiding-place among the sacks and sat again on the couplings. The train was running at a fair speed, but I felt it was time to leave it. I took hold of the iron handle at the back of the truck, pulled strongly with my left hand, and sprang. My feet struck the ground in two gigantic strides, and the next instant I was sprawling in the ditch, considerably shaken but unhurt. The train, my faithful ally of the night, hurried on its journey.

It was still dark. I was in the middle of a wide valley, surrounded by low hills, and carpeted with high grass drenched in dew. I searched for water in the nearest gully, and soon found a clear pool. I was very thirsty, but long after I had quenched my thirst I continued to drink, that I might have sufficient for the whole day.

Presently the dawn began to break, and the sky to the east grew yellow and red. I saw with relief that the railway ran steadily towards the sunrise. I had taken the right line, after all.

Having drunk my fill, I set out for the hills, among which I hoped to find some hiding-place, and as it became broad daylight I entered a small grove of trees which grew on the side of a deep ravine. Here I resolved to wait till dusk. I had one consolation: no one in the world knew where I was—I did not know myself. It was now four o'clock. Fourteen hours lay between me and the night. My impatience to proceed, while I was still strong, doubled their length. At first it was terribly cold, but by degrees the sun gained power, and by ten o'clock the heat was oppressive. My sole companion was a gigantic vulture, who manifested an extravagant interest in my condition, and made hideous and ominous gurglings from time to time. From my lofty position I commanded a view of the whole valley. A little tin-roofed town lay three miles to the westward. Scattered farmsteads, each with a clump of trees, relieved the monotony of the undulating ground. At the foot of the hill stood a Kaffir kraal, and the figures of its inhabitants dotted the patches of cultivation or surrounded the droves of goats and cows which fed on the pasture. The railway ran through the middle of the valley, and I could watch the passage of the various trains. I counted four passing each way, and from this I drew the conclusion that the same number would run by night. I marked a steep gradient up which they climbed very slowly, and determined at nightfall to make another attempt to board one of these. During the day I ate one slab of chocolate, which, with the heat, produced a violent thirst. The pool was hardly half a mile away, but I dared not leave the shelter of the little wood, for I could see the figures of white men riding or walking occasionally across the valley, and once a Boer came and fired two shots at birds close to my hiding-place. But no one discovered me.

The elation and the excitement of the previous night had burnt away, and a chilling reaction followed. I was very hungry, for I had had no dinner before starting, and chocolate, though it sustains, does not satisfy. I had scarcely slept, but yet my heart beat so fiercely and I was so nervous and perplexed about the future that I could not rest. I thought of all the chances that lay against me; I dreaded and detested more than words can express the prospect of being caught and dragged back to Pretoria. I do not mean that I would rather have died than have been retaken, but I have often feared death for much less. I found no comfort in any of the philosophical ideas which some men parade in their hours of ease and strength and safety. They seemed only fair-weather friends. I realized with awful force that no exercise of my own feeble wit and strength could save me from my enemies, and that without the assistance of that High Power which interferes in the eternal sequence of causes and effects more often than we are always prone to admit, I could never succeed. I prayed long and earnestly for help and guidance. My prayer, as it seems to me, was swiftly and wonderfully answered.

The long day reached its close at last. The western clouds flushed into fire; the shadows of the hills stretched out across the valley. A ponderous Boer wagon, with its long team, crawled slowly along the track towards the town. The Kaffirs collected their herds and drew around their kraal. The daylight died, and soon it was quite dark. Then, and not till then, I set forth. I hurried to the railway line, pausing on my way to drink at a stream of sweet, cold water. I waited for some time at the top of the steep gradient in the hope of catching a train. But none came, and I gradually guessed, and I have since found that I guessed right, that the train I had already travelled in was the only one that ran at night. At last I resolved to walk on, and make, at any rate, twenty miles of my journey. I walked for about six hours. How far I travelled I do not know, but I do not think that it was very many miles in the direct line. Every bridge was guarded by armed men; every few miles were gangers' huts; at intervals there were stations with villages clustering round them. All the veldt was bathed in the bright rays of the full moon, and to avoid these dangerous places I had to make wide circuits and often to creep along the ground. Leaving the railroad I fell into bogs and swamps, and brushed through high grass dripping with dew, so that I was drenched to the waist. I had been able to take little exercise during my month's imprisonment, and I was soon tired out with walking, as well as from want of food and sleep. I felt very miserable when I looked around and saw here and there the lights of houses, and thought of the warmth and comfort within them, but knew that they only meant danger to me. After six or seven hours of walking I thought it unwise to go further lest I should exhaust myself, so I lay down in a ditch to sleep. I was nearly at the end of my tether. Nevertheless, by the will of God, I was enabled to sustain myself during the next few days, obtaining food at great risk here and there, resting in concealment by day and walking only at night. On the fifth day I was beyond Middelburg, so far as I could tell, for I dared not inquire nor as yet approach the stations near enough to read the names. In a secure hiding-place I waited for a suitable train, knowing that there is a through service between Middelburg and Lourenço Marques.

Meanwhile there had been excitement in the States Model Schools, temporarily converted into a military prison. Early on Wednesday morning—barely twelve hours after I had escaped—my absence was discovered—I think by Dr. Gunning. The alarm was given. Telegrams with my description at great length were dispatched along all the railways. Three thousand photographs were printed. A warrant was issued for my immediate arrest. Every train was strictly searched. Everyone was on the watch. The storekeeper, who knew my face well, was hurried off to Komati Poort to examine all and sundry people "with red hair" travelling towards the frontier. The newspapers made so much of the affair that my humble fortunes and my whereabouts were discussed in long columns of print, and even in the crash of the war I became to the Boers a topic all to myself. The rumours in part amused me. It was certain, said the *Standard and Diggers' News*, that I had escaped disguised as a woman. The next day I was reported captured at Komati Poort dressed as a Transvaal policeman. There was great delight at this, which was only changed to doubt when other telegrams said that I had been arrested at Brugsbank, at Middelburg, and at Bronkerspruit. But the captives proved to be harmless people after all. Finally it was agreed that I had never left Pretoria. I had—it appeared—changed clothes with a waiter, and was now in hiding at the house of some British sympathizer in the capital. On the strength of this all the houses of suspected persons were searched from top to bottom, and these unfortunate people were, I fear, put to a great deal of inconvenience. A special commission was also appointed to investigate "stringently" (a most hateful adverb in such a connexion) the causes "which had rendered it possible for the War Correspondent of the *Morning Post* to escape".

The *Volksstem* noticed as a significant fact that I had recently become a subscriber to the State Library, and had selected Mill's essay *On Liberty*. It apparently desired to gravely deprecate prisoners having access to such inflammatory literature. The idea will, perhaps, amuse those who have read the work in question.

I find it very difficult, in the face of the extraordinary efforts which were made to recapture me, to believe that the Transvaal Government seriously contemplated my release *before* they knew I had escaped them. Yet a telegram was swiftly dispatched from Pretoria to all the newspapers, setting forth the terms of a most admirable letter, in which General Joubert explained the grounds which prompted him generously to restore my liberty. I am inclined to think that the Boers hate being beaten even in the smallest things, and always fight on the win, tie, or wrangle principle; but in my case I rejoice I am not beholden to them, and have not thus been disqualified from fighting.

All these things may provoke a smile of indifference, perhaps even of triumph, after the danger is past; but during the days when I was lying up in holes and corners, waiting for a good chance to board a train, the causes that had led to them preyed more than I knew on my nerves. To be an outcast, to be hunted, to lie under a warrant for arrest, to fear every man, to have imprisonment—not necessarily military confinement either—hanging overhead, to fly the light, to doubt the shadows—all these things ate into my soul and have left an impression that will not perhaps be easily effaced.

On the sixth day the chance I had patiently waited for came. I found a convenient train duly labelled to Lourenço Marques standing in a siding. I withdrew to a suitable spot for boarding it—for I dared not make the attempt in the station—and, filling a bottle with water to drink on the way, I prepared for the last stage of my journey.

The truck in which I ensconced myself was laden with great sacks of some soft merchandise, and I found among them holes and crevices by means of which I managed to work my way to the inmost recess. The hard floor was littered with gritty coal dust, and made a most uncomfortable bed. The heat was almost stifling. I was resolved, however, that nothing should lure or compel me from my hiding-place until I reached Portuguese territory. I expected the journey to take thirty-six hours; it dragged out into two and a half days. I hardly dared sleep for fear of snoring.

I dreaded lest the trucks should be searched at Komati Poort, and my anxiety as the train approached this neighbourhood was very great. To prolong it we were shunted on to a siding for eighteen hours either at Komati Poort or the station beyond it. Once indeed they began to search my truck, and I heard the tarpaulin rustle as they pulled at it, but luckily they did not search deep enough, so that, providentially protected, I reached Delagoa Bay at last, and crawled forth from my place of refuge and of punishment, weary, dirty, hungry, but free once more.

Thereafter everything smiled. I found my way to the British Consul, Mr. Ross, who at first mistook me for a fireman off one of the ships in the harbour, but soon welcomed me with enthusiasm. I bought clothes, I washed, I sat down to dinner with a real table-cloth and real glasses; and fortune, determined not to overlook the smallest detail, had arranged that the steamer *Induna* should leave that very night for Durban. As soon as the news of my arrival spread about the town, I received many offers of assistance from the English residents, and lest any of the Boer agents with whom Lourenço Marques is infested should attempt to recapture me in neutral territory, nearly a dozen gentlemen escorted me to the steamer armed with revolvers. It is from the cabin of this little vessel, as she coasts along the sandy shores of Africa, that I write the concluding lines of this letter, and the reader who may persevere through this hurried account will perhaps understand why I write them with a feeling of triumph, and better than triumph, a feeling of pure joy.

The voyage of the *Induna* from Delagoa Bay to Durban was speedy and prosperous, and on the afternoon of the 23rd we approached our port, and saw the bold headland that shields it rising above the horizon to the southward. An hour's steaming brought us to the roads. More than twenty great transports and supply vessels lay at anchor, while three others, crowded from end to end with soldiery, circled impatiently as they waited for pilots to take them into the harbour. Our small vessel was not long in reaching the jetty, and I perceived that a very considerable crowd had gathered to receive us. But it was not until I stepped on shore that

I realized that I was myself the object of this honourable welcome. I will not chronicle the details of what followed. It is sufficient to say that many hundreds of the people of Durban took occasion to express their joy at my tiny pinch of triumph over the Boers, and that their enthusiasm was another sincere demonstration of their devotion to the imperial cause, and their resolve to carry the war to an indisputable conclusion.

I received then and have since been receiving a great number of telegrams and messages from all kinds of people and from all countries of the earth. One gentleman invited me to shoot with him in Central Asia. Another favoured me with a poem which he had written in my honour, and desired me to have it set to music and published. A third—an American—wanted me to plan a raid into Transvaal territory along the Delagoa Bay line to arm the prisoners and seize the President. Five Liberal electors of the borough of Oldham wrote to say that they would give me their votes on a future occasion "irrespective of politics". Young ladies sent me woollen comforters. Old ladies forwarded their photographs; and hundreds of people wrote kind letters, many of which in the stir of events I have not yet been able to answer.

The correspondence varied vastly in tone as well as in character, and I cannot help quoting a couple of telegrams as specimens. The first was from a worthy gentleman who, besides being a substantial farmer, is also a member of the Natal Parliament. He wrote: "My heartiest congratulations on your wonderful and glorious deeds, which will send such a thrill of pride and enthusiasm through Great Britain and the United States of America, that the Anglo-Saxon race will be irresistible."

The intention of the other, although his message was shorter, was equally plain.

"London, 30 December.—Best friends here hope you won't go making further ass of yourself.—M'NEILL."

This shows, I think, how widely human judgment may differ even in regard to ascertained facts.

Perhaps the tide of war has really begun to turn. Perhaps 1900 is to mark the beginning of a century of good luck and good sense in

British policy in Africa. When I was a prisoner at Pretoria the Boers showed me a large green pamphlet Mr. Reitz had written. It was intended to be an account of the Dutch grounds of quarrel with the English, and was called "A Century of Wrong". Much was distortion and exaggeration, but a considerable part dealt with acknowledged facts. Wrong in plenty there has been on both sides, but latterly more on theirs than on ours; and the result is war— bitter, bloody war tearing the land in twain; dividing brother from brother, friend from friend, and opening a terrible chasm between the two white races who must live side by side as long as South Africa stands above the ocean, and by whose friendly co-operation alone it can enjoy the fullest measure of prosperity. "A century of wrong!" British ignorance of South Africa, Boer ignorance of civilization, British intolerance, Boer brutality, British interference, Boer independence, clash, clash, clash, all along the line! And then fanatical truth-scorning missionaries, experimental philanthropists, high-handed jingo administrators, colonial ministers who disliked all colonies on the glorious principles of theoretic liberalism, bad generals thinking of their own reputations, not of their country's success, and a series of miserable events recalled sufficiently well by their names—Slagter's Nek, Kimberley, Moshesh, Majuba, Jameson, all these arousing first resentment, then loathing, then contempt, and, finally, a Great Desire, crystallizing into a Great Conspiracy for a United Dutch South Africa, free from the flag that has else-where been regarded as the flag of freedom. And so inevitably to war—war with peculiar sadness and horror, in which the line of cleavage springs between all sorts of well-meaning people that used to know one another in friendship; but war which, whatever its fortunes, certainly sweeps the past into obscurity. We have done with "a century of wrong". God send us now "a century of right".

*    *    *

The vast amount of baggage this army takes with it on the march hampers its movements and utterly precludes all possibility of sur-prising the enemy. I have never before seen even officers accom-modated with tents on service, though both the Indian frontier and the Sudan lie under a hotter sun than South Africa. But here today, within striking distance of a mobile enemy whom we wish to circumvent, every private soldier has canvas shelter, and the other arrangements are on an equally elaborate scale. The consequence is that roads are crowded, drifts are blocked, marching troops are delayed, and all rapidity of movement is out of the question. Meanwhile, the enemy completes the fortification of his positions, and the cost of capturing them rises. It is a poor economy to let a soldier live well for three days at the price of killing him on the fourth.

★   ★   ★

It is the remarkable characteristic of strong races, as of honourable men, to keep their tempers in the face of disappointment, and never to lose a just sense of proportion; and it is, moreover, the duty of every citizen in times of trouble to do or say or even to think nothing that can weaken or discourage the energies of the State. Sir Redvers Buller's army has met with another serious check in the attempt to relieve Ladysmith. We have approached, tested, and assailed the Boer positions beyond the Tugela, fighting more or less continuously for five days, and the result is that we find they cannot be pierced from the direction of Trichardt's Drift any more than at Colenso. With the loss of more than two thousand men out of a small army, we find it necessary to recross the river and seek for some other line of attack; and meanwhile the long and brave resistance of Ladysmith must be drawing to a close. Indeed, it is the opinion of many good judges that further efforts to relieve the town will only be attended with further loss. As to this I do not pronounce, but I am certain of one thing—that further efforts must be made, without regard to the loss of life which will attend them.

I have seen and heard a good deal of what has passed here. I have often been blamed for the freedom with which I have written of other operations and criticized their commanders. I respectfully submit that I am as venomous an amateur strategist as exists at this time. It is very easy—and much more easy than profitable—when freed from all responsibility to make daring suggestions and express decided opinions. I assert that I would not hesitate to criticize mercilessly if I was not myself sobered by the full appreciation of the extraordinary difficulties which the relief of Ladysmith presents; and if there be anyone who has any confidence in my desire to write

201

the truth I appeal to him to be patient and calm, to recognize that perhaps the task before Sir Redvers Buller and his subordinates is an actual impossibility, that if these generals are not capable men—among the best that our times produce—it is difficult to know where and how others may be obtained, and finally to brutally face the fact that Sir George White and his heroic garrison may be forced to become the prisoners of the Boers, remembering always that nothing that happens, either victory or defeat, in northern Natal can affect the ultimate result of the war. In a word, let no one despair of the Empire because a few thousand soldiers are killed, wounded, or captured.

★   ★   ★

It was therefore decided to attack Spion Kop by night, rush the Boer trenches with the bayonet, entrench as far as possible before dawn, hold on during the day, drag guns up at night, and thus dominate the Boer lines. There is, of course, no possible doubt that Spion Kop is the key of the whole position, and the reader has only to remember that the mountain divides, commands, and enfilades the enemy's lines, to appreciate this fact. The questions to be proved were whether the troops could hold out during the day, and whether the place could be converted into a fort proof against shell fire and armed with guns during the following night. Fate has now decided both.

Morning broke, and with it the attack. The enemy, realizing the vital importance of the position, concentrated every man and gun at his disposal for its recapture. A fierce and furious shell fire was opened forthwith on the summit, causing immediate and continual loss. General Woodgate was wounded, and the command devolved on a regimental officer, who, at half-past six, applied for reinforcements in a letter which scarcely displayed that composure and determination necessary in such a bloody debate.

Sir Redvers Buller then took the extreme step of appointing Major Thorneycroft—already only a local lieutenant-colonel—local Brigadier-General commanding on the summit of Spion Kop. The Imperial Light Infantry, the Middlesex Regiment, and a little later the Somersets, from General Talbot Coke's Brigade, were ordered to reinforce the defence, but General Coke was directed to remain below the summit of the hill, so that the fight might still be conducted by the best fighting man.

The Boers followed, and accompanied their shells by a vigorous rifle attack on the hill, and about half-past eight the position became most critical. The troops were driven almost entirely off the main plateau and the Boers succeeded in reoccupying some of their trenches. A frightful disaster was narrowly averted. About twenty men in one of the captured trenches abandoned their resistance, threw up their hands, and called out that they would surrender. Colonel Thorneycroft, whose great stature made him everywhere conspicuous, and who was from dawn till dusk in the first firing line, rushed to the spot. The Boers advancing to take the prisoners —as at Nicholson's Nek—were scarcely thirty yards away. Thorneycroft shouted to the Boer leader: "You may go to hell. I command on this hill and allow no surrender. Go on with your firing." Which later they did with terrible effect, killing many. The survivors, with the rest of the firing line, fled two hundred yards, were rallied by their indomitable commander, and, being reinforced by two brave companies of the Middlesex Regiment, charged back, recovering all lost ground, and the position was maintained until nightfall. No words in these days of extravagant expression can do justice to the glorious endurance which the English regiments—for they were all English—displayed throughout the long dragging hours of hell fire. Between three and four o'clock the shells were falling on the hill from both sides, as I counted, at the rate of seven a minute, and the strange discharges of the Maxim shell guns—the "pom-poms" as these terrible engines are called for want of a correct name—lacerated the hillsides with dotted chains of smoke and dust. A thick and continual stream of wounded flowed rearwards. A village of ambulance wagons grew up at the foot of the mountain. The dead and injured, smashed and broken by the shells, littered the summit till it was a bloody, reeking shambles. Thirst tormented the soldiers, for though water was at hand the fight was too close and furious to give even a moment's breathing space. But nothing could weaken the stubborn vigour of the defence. The Dorset Regiment—the last of Talbot Coke's Brigade—was ordered to support the struggling troops. The gallant Lyttelton of his own accord sent the Scottish

Rifles and the 3rd King's Royal Rifles from Potgieter's to aid them. But though their splendid attack did not help the main action; though the British artillery, unable to find or reach the enemy's guns, could only tear up the ground in impotent fury; though the shell fire and rifle fire never ceased for an instant—the magnificent infantry maintained the defence, and night closed in with the British still in possession of the hill.

I had seen some service and Captain Brooke has been through more fighting than any other officer of late years. We were so profoundly impressed by the spectacle and situation that we resolved to go and tell Sir Charles Warren what we had seen. The fight had been so close that no proper reports had been sent to the General, so he listened with great patience and attention. One thing was quite clear—unless good and efficient cover could be made during the night, and unless guns could be dragged to the summit of the hill t﹒match the Boer artillery, the infantry could not, perhaps would not, endure another day. The human machine will not stand certain strains for long.

The questions were, could guns be brought up the hill; and, if so, could the troops maintain themselves? The artillery officers had examined the track. They said, "No," and that even if they could reach the top of the hill they would only be shot out of action. Two long-range naval 12-pounders, much heavier than the field-guns, had arrived. The naval lieutenant in charge said he could go anywhere, or would have a try any way. He was quite sure that if he could get on the top of the hill he would knock out the Boer guns or be knocked out by them, and that was what he wanted to find out. I do not believe that the attempt would have succeeded, or that the guns could have been in position by daylight, but the contrast in spirit was very refreshing.

I found Colonel Thorneycroft at the top of the mountain. Every-one seemed to know, even in the confusion, where he was. He was sitting on the ground surrounded by the remnants of the regiment he had raised, who had fought for him like lions and followed him like dogs. I explained the situation as I had been told and as I thought. Naval guns were prepared to try, sappers and working parties were already on the road with thousands of sandbags. What did he think? But the decision had already been taken. He had never received any messages from the General, had not had time to write any. Messages had been sent him, he had wanted to send others himself. The fight had been too hot, too close, too interlaced for him to attend to anything but to support this company, clear those rocks, or line that trench. So, having heard nothing and expecting no guns, he had decided to retire. As he put it tersely: "Better six good battalions safely down the hill than a mop up in the morning." Then we came home, drawing down our rearguard after us very slowly and carefully, and as the ground grew more level the regiments began to form again into their old solid blocks.

Such was the fifth of the series of actions called the Battle of Spion Kop. It is an event which the British people may regard with feelings of equal pride and sadness. It redounds to the honour of the soldiers, though not greatly to that of the generals. But when all that will be written about this has been written, and all the bitter words have been said by the people who never do anything themselves, the wise and just citizen will remember that these same generals are, after all, brave, capable, noble English gentlemen, trying their best to carry through a task which may prove to be impossible, and is certainly the hardest ever set to men.

I will only relate one other incident—a miserable one. The day before the attack on Spion Kop I had chanced to ride across the pontoon bridge. I heard my name called, and saw the cheery face of a boy I had known at Harrow—a smart, clean-looking young gentleman—quite the rough material for Irregular Horse. He had just arrived and pushed his way to the front; hoped, so he said, "to get a job". This morning they told me that an unauthorised Press correspondent had been found among the killed on the summit. At least they thought at first it was a Press correspondent, for no one seemed to know him. A man had been found leaning forward on his rifle, dead. A broken pair of field glasses, shattered by the same shell that had killed their owner, bore the name "M'Corquodale". The name and the face flew together in my mind. It was the last joined subaltern of Thorneycroft's Mounted Infantry—joined in the evening, shot at dawn.

Poor gallant young Englishman! He had soon "got his job". The great sacrifice had been required of the Queen's latest recruit.

*     *     *

It is a solemn Sunday, and the camp, with its white tents looking snug and peaceful in the sunlight, holds its breath that the beating of its heart may not be heard. On such a day as this the services of religion would appeal with passionate force to thousands. I attended a church parade this morning. What a chance this was for a man of great soul who feared God! On every side were drawn up deep masses of soldiery, rank behind rank—perhaps, in all, five thousand. In the hollow square stood the General, the man on whom every-thing depended. All around were men who within the week had been face to face with Death, and were going to face him again in a few hours. Life seemed very precarious, in spite of the sunlit land-scape. What was it all for? What was the good of human effort? How should it befall a man who died in a quarrel he did not under-stand? All the anxious questionings of weak spirits. It was one of those occasions when a fine preacher might have given comfort and strength where both were sorely needed, and have printed on many minds a permanent impression. The bridegroom Opportunity had come. But the Church had her lamp untrimmed. A chaplain with a raucous voice discoursed on the details of "The siege and surrender of Jericho". The soldiers froze into apathy, and after a while the formal perfunctory service reached its welcome conclusion.

As I marched home an officer said to me: "Why is it, when the Church spends so much on missionary work among heathens, she does not take the trouble to send good men to preach in time of war? The medical profession is represented by some of its greatest exponents. Why are men's wounded souls left to the care of a village practitioner?" Nor could I answer; but I remembered the venerable figure and noble character of Father Brindle in the River War, and wondered whether Rome was again seizing the opportu-nity which Canterbury disdained—the opportunity of telling the glad tidings to soldiers about to die.

*     *     *

The terrible power of the Mauser rifle was displayed. As the charging companies met the storm of bullets they were swept away. Officers and men fell by scores on the narrow ridge. Though assailed in front and flank by the hideous whispering Death, the survivors hurried obstinately onward, until their own artillery were forced to cease firing, and it seemed that, in spite of bullets, flesh and blood would prevail. But at the last supreme moment the weakness of the attack was shown. The Inniskillings had almost reached their goal. They were too few to effect their purpose; and when the Boers saw that the attack had withered they shot all the straighter, and several of the boldest leapt out from their trenches and, running forward to meet the soldiers, discharged their magazines at the closest range. It was a frantic scene of blood and fury.

Thus confronted, the Irish perished rather than retire. A few men indeed ran back down the slope to the nearest cover, and there savagely turned to bay, but the greater part of the front line was shot down. Other companies, some from the Connaught Rangers, some headed by the brave Colonel Sitwell, from the Dublin Fusiliers, advanced to renew—it was already too late to support—the attack, and as the light faded another fierce and bloody assault was delivered and was repulsed. Yet the Irish soldiers would not leave the hill, and, persuaded at length that they could not advance further, they lay down on the ground they had won, and began to build walls and shelters, from behind which they opened a revengeful fire on the exulting Boers. In the two attacks both colonels, three majors, twenty officers, and six hundred men had fallen out of an engaged force of scarcely one thousand two hundred. Then darkness pulled down the curtain, and the tragedy came to an end for the day.[1]

★    ★    ★

At last the time came for the cavalry to cross the bridge, and as we filed on to the floating roadway we were amused to see a large fingerpost at the entrance, on which the engineers had neatly painted, "To Ladysmith". The brigade passed over the neck between Railway and Inniskilling Hills, and we massed in a suitable place on the descending slopes beyond. We looked at the country before us, and saw that it was good. Here at last was ground cavalry could work on at some speed. Ladysmith was still hidden by the

[1] The Battle of Pieters.

207

remaining ridges, but we thought that somehow, and with a little
luck, we might have a look at it before night.

Under Bulwana the wagons of the Boers and several hundred
horsemen could be seen hurrying away. It was clearly our business
to try to intercept them unless they had made good covering dispositions. Patrols were sent out in all directions, and a squadron of
Thorneycroft's Mounted Infantry proceeded to Pieters Station,
where a complete train of about twenty trucks had been abandoned
by the enemy. While this reconnaissance was going on I climbed
up Inniskilling Hill to examine the trenches. It was occupied by the
East Surrey Regiment, and the soldiers were very eager to do the
honours. They had several things to show: "Come along here, sir;
there's a bloke here without a head; took clean off, sir"; and were
mightily disappointed that I would not let them remove the blanket
which covered the grisly shape.

The trench was cut deep in the ground, and, unlike our trenches,
there was scarcely any parapet. A few great stones had been laid in
front, but evidently the Boer believed in getting well into the
ground. The bottom was knee deep in cartridge cases, and every few
yards there was an enormous heap of Mauser ammunition, thousands
of rounds, all fastened neatly, five at a time, in clips. A large proportion were covered with bright green slime, which the soldiers
declared was poison, but which on analysis may prove to be wax,
used to preserve the bullets.

The Boers, however, were not so guiltless of other charges.
A field officer of the East Surreys, recognizing me, came up and
showed me an expansive bullet of a particularly cruel pattern. The
tip had been cut off, exposing the soft core, and four slits were
scored down the side. Whole boxes of this ammunition had been
found. An officer who had been making calculations told me that
the proportion of illegal bullets was nearly one in five. I should not
myself have thought it was so large, but certainly the improper
bullets were very numerous. I have a specimen of this particular
kind by me as I write, and I am informed by people who shoot big
game that it is the most severe bullet of its kind yet invented. Five
other sorts have been collected by the medical officers, who have
also tried to classify the wounds they respectively produce.

I cannot be accused of having written unfairly about the enemy;

indeed, I have only cared to write what I thought was the truth about everybody. I have tried to do justice to the patriotic virtues of the Boers, and it is now necessary to observe that the character of these people reveals, in stress, a dark and spiteful underside. A man—I use the word in its fullest sense—does not wish to lacerate his foe, however earnestly he may desire his life.

\* \* \*

When I rejoined the South African Light Horse the Irregular Brigade had begun to advance again. Major Gough's Composite Regiment had scouted the distant ridge and found it unoccupied. Now Dundonald moved his whole command thither, and with his staff climbed to the top. But to our disappointment Ladysmith was not to be seen. Two or three other ridges hung like curtains before us. The afternoon had passed, and it was already after six o'clock. The Boer artillery was still firing, and it seemed rash to attempt to reconnoitre further when the ground was broken and the light fading.

The order was given to retire and the movement had actually begun when a messenger came back from Gough with the news that the last ridge between us and the town was unoccupied by the enemy, that he could see Ladysmith, and that there was, for the moment, a clear run in. Dundonald immediately determined to go on himself into the town with the two squadrons who were scouting in front, and to send the rest of the brigade back to camp. He invited me to accompany him, and without delay we started at a gallop.

Never shall I forget that ride. The evening was deliciously cool. My horse was strong and fresh, for I had changed him at midday. The ground was rough with many stones, but we cared little for that. Beyond the next ridge, or the rise beyond that, or around the corner of the hill, was Ladysmith—the goal of all our hopes and ambitions during weeks of almost ceaseless fighting. Ladysmith— the centre of the world's attention, the scene of famous deeds, the cause of mighty efforts—Ladysmith was within our reach at last. We were going to be inside the town within an hour. The excitement of the moment was increased by the exhilaration of the gallop. Onward wildly, recklessly, up and down hill, over the boulders, through the scrub, Hubert Gough with his two squadrons, Mackenzie's Natal Carabineers and the Imperial Light Horse, were clear of the ridges already. We turned the shoulder of a hill, and there before us lay the tin houses and dark trees we had come so far to see and save.

The British guns on Caesar's Camp were firing steadily in spite of the twilight. What was happening? Never mind, we were nearly through the dangerous ground. Now we were all on the flat. Brigadier, staff, and troops let their horses go. We raced through the thorn bushes by Intombi Spruit.

Suddenly there was a challenge. "Halt, who goes there?" "The Ladysmith Relief Column," and thereat from out of trenches and rifle pits artfully concealed in the scrub a score of tattered men came running, cheering feebly, and some were crying. In the half light they looked ghastly pale and thin. A poor, white-faced officer waved his helmet to and fro, and laughed foolishly, and the tall strong colonial horsemen, standing up in their stirrups, raised a loud resounding cheer, for then we knew we had reached the Ladysmith picket line.

Presently we arranged ourselves in military order, Natal Carabineers and Imperial Light Horse riding two and two abreast so that there might be no question about precedence, and with Gough, the youngest regimental commander in the army, and one of the best, at the head of the column, we forded the Klip River and rode into the town.

That night I dined with Sir George White, who had held the town for four months against all comers, and was placed next to Hamilton, who won the fight at Elandslaagte and beat the Boers off Wagon Hill, and next but one to Hunter, whom everyone said was the finest man in the world. Never before had I sat in such brave company nor stood so close to a great event.

★    ★    ★

On 3 March the relieving army made its triumphal entry into Ladysmith, and passing through the town camped on the plain beyond. The scene was solemn and stirring, and only the most phlegmatic were able to conceal their emotions. The streets were lined with the brave defenders, looking very smart and clean in their best clothes, but pale, thin, and wasp-waisted—their belts several holes tighter than was satisfactory.

Before the little town hall, the tower of which, sorely battered, yet unyielding, seemed to symbolize the spirit of the garrison, Sir George White and his staff sat on their skeleton horses. Opposite to them were drawn up the pipers of the Gordon Highlanders. The townsfolk, hollow-eyed but jubilant, crowded the pavement and the windows of the houses. Everyone who could find a flag had hung it out, but we needed no bright colours to raise our spirits.

At eleven o'clock precisely the relieving army began to march into the town. First of all rode Sir Redvers Buller with his head-quarters staff and an escort of the Royal Dragoons. The infantry and artillery followed by brigades, but in front of all, as a special recog-nition of their devoted valour, marched the Dublin Fusiliers, few, but proud.

Many of the soldiers, remembering their emerald island, had fastened sprigs of green to their helmets, and all marched with a swing that was wonderful to watch. Their Colonel and their four officers looked as happy as kings are thought to be. As the regiments passed Sir George White, the men recognized their former general, and, disdaining the rules of the service, waved their helmets and rifles, and cheered him with intense enthusiasm. Some even broke from the ranks. Seeing this the Gordon Highlanders began to cheer the Dublins, and after that the noise of cheering was continual, every regiment as it passed giving and receiving fresh ovations.

All through the morning and on into the afternoon the long stream of men and guns flowed through the streets of Ladysmith, and all marvelled to see what manner of men these were—dirty, war-worn, travel-stained, tanned, their uniforms in tatters, their boots falling to pieces, their helmets dinted and broken, but never-theless magnificent soldiers, striding along, deep-chested and broad-shouldered, with the light of triumph in their eyes and the blood of fighting ancestors in their veins. It was a procession of lions. And presently, when the two battalions of Devons met—both full of honours—and old friends breaking from the ranks gripped each other's hand and shouted, everyone was carried away, and I waved my feathered hat, and cheered and cheered until I could cheer no longer for joy that I had lived to see the day.

At length all was over. The last dust-brown battalion had passed away and the roadway was again clear. Yet the ceremony was incomplete. Before the staff could ride away the Mayor of Ladysmith advanced and requested Sir George White to receive an address which the townspeople had prepared and were anxious to present to him. The General dismounted from his horse, and standing on the steps of the town hall, in the midst of the inhabitants whom he had ruled so rigorously during the hard months of the siege, listened while their Town Clerk read their earnest grateful thanks to him for saving their town from the hands of the enemy. The General replied briefly, complimented them on their behaviour during the siege, thanked them for the way in which they had borne their many hardships and submitted to the severe restrictions which the circumstances of war had brought on them, and rejoiced with them that they had been enabled by their devotion and by the bravery of the soldiers to keep the Queen's flag flying over Ladysmith. And then everybody cheered everybody else, and so, very tired and very happy, we all went home to our belated luncheons.

*    *    *

But there was one who found, to use his own words, "a strange sideway out of Ladysmith", whose memory many English-speaking people will preserve. I do not write of Steevens as a journalist, nor as the master of a popular and pleasing style, but as a man. I knew him, though I had met him rarely. A dinner up the Nile, a chance meeting at an Indian junction, five days on a Mediterranean steamer, two in a Continental express, and a long Sunday at his house near Merton—it was a scanty acquaintance, but sufficient to be quite certain that in all the varied circumstances and conditions to which men are subjected Steevens rang true. Modest yet proud, wise as well as witty, cynical but above all things sincere, he combined the characters of a charming companion and a good comrade.

His conversation and his private letters sparkled like his books and articles. Original expressions, just similitudes, striking phrases, quaint or droll ideas welled in his mind without the slightest effort. He was always at his best. I have never met a man who talked so well, so easily. His wit was the genuine article—absolutely natural and spontaneous.

I once heard him describe an incident in the Nile campaign, and the description amused me so much that I was impatient to hear it again, and when a suitable occasion offered I asked him to tell his tale to the others. But he told it quite differently, and left me wondering which version was the better. He could not repeat himself if he tried, whereas most of the renowned talkers I have met will go over the old impression with the certainty of a phonograph.

But enough of his words. He was not a soldier, but he walked into the Atbara *zeriba* with the leading company of the Seaforth Highlanders. He wrote a vivid account of the attack, but there was nothing in it about himself.

When the investment of Ladysmith shut the door on soldiers, townspeople, and war correspondents alike, Steevens set to work to do his share of keeping up the good spirits of the garrison and of relieving the monotony of the long days. Through the first three months of the siege no local event was awaited with more interest than the publication of a *Ladysmith Lyre*, and the weary defenders had many a good laugh at its witticisms.

Sun, stink, and sickness harassed the beleaguered. The bombardment was perpetual, the relief always delayed; hope again and again deferred. But nothing daunted Steevens, depressed his courage, or curbed his wit. What such a man is worth in gloomy days those may appreciate who have seen the effect of public misfortunes on a modern community.

At last he was himself stricken down by enteric fever. When it seemed that the worst was over there came a fatal relapse, and the brightest intellect yet sacrificed by this war perished; nor among all the stubborn garrison of Ladysmith was there a stouter heart or a more enduring spirit.

Dismal scenes were to be found at the hospital camp by Intombi Spruit. Here, in a town of white tents, under the shadow of Bulwana, were collected upwards of two thousand sick and wounded —a fifth of the entire garrison. They were spared the shells, but exposed to all the privations of the siege.

Officers and men, doctors and patients, presented alike a most melancholy and even ghastly appearance. Men had been wounded, had been cured of their wounds, and had died simply because there was no nourishing food to restore their strength. Others had become convalescent from fever, but had succumbed from depression and lack of medical comforts. Hundreds required milk and brandy, but there was only water to give them. The weak died: at one time the death rate averaged fifteen a day. Nearly a tenth of the whole garrison died of disease. A forest of crosses, marking the graves of six hundred men, sprang up behind the camp.

It was a painful thing to watch the hungry patients, so haggard and worn that their friends could scarcely recognize them; and after a visit to Intombi I sat and gloated for an hour at the long train of wagons filled with all kinds of necessary comforts which crawled along the roads, and the relief of Ladysmith seemed more than ever worth the heavy price we had paid.

# IAN HAMILTON'S MARCH

*A continuation of the author's letters to the "Morning Post"
published in "London to Ladysmith via Pretoria". Lieutenant-General Sir Ian Hamilton's march on the flank of Lord
Roberts's main army from Bloemfontein to Pretoria was one
of the outstanding operations of the war. This force, as the
author states, "encountered and overcame the brunt of the
Boer resistance, marched more than 400 miles, fought ten
general actions and fourteen smaller affairs and captured five
towns." The book was first published in 1900.*

AFTER THE relief of Ladysmith four courses offered themselves to
Sir Redvers Buller. To stand strictly on the defensive in Natal and
to send Lord Roberts every man and gun who could be spared; to
break into the Free State by forcing Van Reenen's Pass or the
Tintwa; to attack the twelve thousand Boers in the Biggarsberg,
clear Natal, and invade the Transvaal through the Vryheid district;
and, lastly, to unite and reorganize and co-operate with Lord
Roberts's main advance either by striking west or north.

Which course would be adopted? I made inquiries. Staff officers,
bland and inscrutable—it is wonderful how well men can keep
secrets they have not been told—continued to smile and smile.
Brigadiers frankly confessed their ignorance. The general-in-chief
observed pleasantly that he would "go for" the enemy as soon as
he was ready, but was scarcely precise about when and where.

It was necessary to go to more humble sources for truth, and
after diligent search I learned from a railway porter, or somebody
like that, that all attempts to repair the bridge across the Sunday's
River had been postponed indefinitely. This, on further inquiry,
proved to be true.

Now, what does this mean? It means, I take it, that no direct
advance against the Biggarsberg is intended for some time; and as
the idea of reducing the Natal Army to reinforce the Cape Colony

215

forces has been definitely abandoned the western line of advance suggests itself.

It would be absurd to force Van Reenen's Pass with heavy loss of life, when by waiting until the main Army has reached, let us say, Kroonstad, we could walk through without opposition; so that it looks very likely that the Natal troops will do nothing until Lord Roberts's advance is more developed, and that then they will enter the Free State and operate in conjunction with him, all of which is strategy and common sense besides. At any rate there will be a long delay.

★    ★    ★

I left the camp of Dundonald's Brigade early in the morning of 29 March, and riding through Ladysmith, round the hill on which stands the battered convent, now serving as headquarters, and down the main street, along which the relieving Army had entered the city, reached the railway station and caught the 10 a.m. down train.

We were delayed for a few minutes by the departure for Elandslaagte of a trainload of Volunteers, the first to reach the Natal Army, and the officers hastened to look at these citizen soldiers. There were five companies in all, making nearly a thousand men, fine-looking fellows, with bright intelligent eyes, which they turned inquiringly on every object in turn, pointing and laughing at the numerous shell holes in the corrugated iron engine sheds and other buildings of the station.

A few regulars—sunburnt men, who had fought their way in with Buller—sauntered up to the trucks, and began a conversation with the reinforcement. I caught a fragment: "Cattle trucks, are they? Well, they didn't give us no blooming cattle trucks. No, no. We came into Ladysmith in a first-class doubly extry Pullman car. 'Oo sent 'em? Why, President —— Kruger, of course," whereat there was much laughter.

I must explain that the epithet which the average soldier uses so often as to make it perfectly meaningless, and which we conveniently express by a ——, is always placed immediately before the noun it is intended to qualify. For instance, no soldier would under any circumstances say "—— Mr. Kruger has pursued a —— reactionary policy," but "Mr. —— Kruger has pursued a reactionary —— policy." Having once voyaged for five days down the Nile in a sailing boat with a company of Grenadiers, I have had the best opportunities for being acquainted with these idiomatic constructions, and I insert this little note in case it may be useful to some of our national poets and minstrels.

★       ★       ★

"Are there many troops here?" [At Bethany.] They replied, "The whole of the Third Division." "Who commands?" "Gatacre." That decided me.

I knew the General slightly, having made his acquaintance up the Nile in pleasant circumstances, for no one was allowed to pass his mess hungry or thirsty. I was very anxious to see him and hear all about Stormberg and the rest of the heavy struggle along the eastern line of rail. I found him in a tin house close to the station. He received me kindly, and we had a long talk. The General explained to me many things which I had not understood before, and after we had done with past events he turned with a hopeful eye to the future. At last, and for the first time, he was going to have the division of which he had originally been given the command.

"You know I only had two and a half battalions at Sterkstroom and a few colonial horse; but now I have got both my brigades complete."

I thought him greatly altered from the dashing, energetic man I had known up the river, or had heard about on the frontier or in plague-stricken Bombay. Four months of anxiety and abuse had left their mark on him. The weary task of keeping things going with utterly insufficient resources, and in the face of an adroit and powerful enemy in a country of innumerable kopjes, where every advantage lay with the Boer, had bowed that iron frame and tired the strange energy which had made him so remarkable among soldiers. But when he thought of the future his face brightened. The dark days were over. The broken rocky wilderness lay behind, and around rolled the grassy plains of the Free State. He had his whole division at last. Moreover, there was prospect of immediate action. So I left him, for it was growing late, and went my way. Early next morning he was dismissed from his command and ordered to England, broken, ruined, and disgraced.

217

Because General Gatacre has been cruelly persecuted in England by people quite ignorant of the difficulties of war or of the conditions under which it is carried on in this country, it is perhaps not out of place to write a few words of different tenor.

Gatacre was a man who made his way in the army, not through any influence or favour which he enjoyed, but by sheer hard work and good service. Wherever he had served he had left a high record behind him. His courage has never been questioned, because the savage critics did not wish to damage their cause by obvious absurdities. If I were to discuss his tactics in the Boer War here I should soon get on to ground which I have forbidden myself. It is sufficient to observe that Gatacre retained the confidence and affection of his soldiers in the most adverse circumstances. When the weary privates struggled back to camp after the disastrous day at Stormberg they were quite clear on one point: "No one could have got us out but him." Two days before he was dismissed the Cameron Highlanders passed through Bethany, and the men recognized the impetuous leader of the Atbara charge; and, knowing he had fallen among evil days, cheered him in the chivalry of the common man. The poor general was much moved at this spontaneous greeting, which is a very rare occurrence in our phlegmatic, well-ordered British Army. Let us hope the sound will long ring in his ears, and, as it were, light a bright lamp of memory in the chill and dreary evening of life.

Exit General Gatacre. "Now," as my Parsee merchant remarked, "he is gone"; and I suppose there are, here and there, notes of triumph. But among them I will strike a note of warning. If the War Office breaks generals not so much for incapacity as for want of success with any frequency, it will not find men to fight for it in brigade and divisional commands. Every man who knows the chances of war feels himself insecure. The initiative which an unsympathetic discipline has already killed, or nearly killed, in younger officers, will wither and die in their superiors. You will have generals as before, but they will not willingly risk the fruits of long years of service in damnable countries and of perils of all kinds. They will look at the enemy's position. They will endeavour to divide responsibility. They will ask for orders or instructions. But they will not fight—if they can possibly help

it, and then only on the limited liability principle, which means
the shedding of much blood without any result. Besides, as an
irreverent subaltern remarked to me: "If you begin with Gatacre,
where are you going to end? What about poor old ——?"

I dare not pursue the subject further.

*    *    *

Bloemfontein—a town of brick and tin—stands at the apparent
edge of a vast plain of withered grass, from whose inhospitable
aspect it turns and nestles, as if for protection, round the scrub-
covered hills to northward. From among the crowd of one-storied
dwelling-houses, more imposing structures, the seats of government
and commerce, rise prominently to catch the eye and impress the
mind with the pleasing prospect of wealthier civilization. Here and
there are towers and pinnacles, and, especially remarkable, a handsome building surrounded in the classic style by tall white pillars,
and, surmounted by a lofty dome, looks like a Parliament House,
but for the Red Cross flag which flies from the summit and proclaims that, whatever may have been its former purposes, the
spacious hall within is at last devoted to the benefit of mankind.
The dark hills—their uncertain outline marked at one point by the
symmetrical silhouette of a fort—form the background of the
picture: Bloemfontein, April, 1900.

It is five o'clock in the afternoon. The market-square is crowded
with officers and soldiers listening to the band of the Buffs. Every
regiment in the service, every colony in the Empire is represented;
all clad in uniform khaki, but distinguished by an extraordinary
variety of badges.

Each group is a miniature system of Imperial Federation. The City
Volunteer talks to a Queensland Mounted Infantryman, who hands
his matchbox to a private of the Line. A Bushman from New
Zealand, a Cambridge undergraduate, and a tea-planter from
Ceylon stroll up and make the conversation general. On every side
all kinds of men are intermingled, united by the sympathy of a
common purpose and soldered together in the fire of war. And this
will be of great consequence later on.

The inhabitants—bearded Burghers who have made their peace,
townsfolk who never desired to make a quarrel—stand round and

watch complacently. After all, there are worse things than to be defeated. Demand is keen, the Army is wealthy, and prices are high. Trade has followed hard on the flag which waves from every building; and, whether it be for merchandise or farm produce, the market is buoyant.

The officers congregate about the pretentious building of the club, and here I find acquaintances gathered together from all the sentry beats of the Empire, for the Regular Army usually works like a kaleidoscope, and, new combinations continually forming, scatter old friends in every direction. But here all are collected once more, and the man we met on the frontier, the man we met "up the river", the man we met at manoeuvres with the comrade of Sandhurst, the friend or enemy of Harrow days, and the rival of a Meerut tournament, stand in a row together. Merry military music, laughing faces, bright, dainty little caps, a moving throng, and the consciousness that this means a victorious British Army in the capital of the Free State, drive away all shadows from the mind.

One cannot see any gaps in the crowd; it is so full of animation that the spaces where Death has put his hand are not to be seen. The strong surges of life have swept across them as a sunny sea closes over the foundered ship. Yet they are not quite forgotten.

"Hallo, my dear old boy, I am glad to see you. When did you get up here? Have you brought —— with you? Oh, I am sorry. It must have been a fever-stricken hole, that Ladysmith. Poor chap! Do you remember how he. . . . Charlie has gone home. He can never play polo again—expanding bullet smashed his arm all to bits. Bad luck, wasn't it? Now we've got to find a new back . . . and —— was killed at Paardeberg . . . spoiled the whole team." The band struck into a lively tune. "How long is it going to last?"

"With luck it ought to be over by October, just a year from start to finish."

"I thought you said something about Pretoria the third week in March."

"Ah, I must have meant May, or, perhaps, June."

"Or August."

"Who can tell? But I think this is the half-way house.'

The conversation stops abruptly. Everyone looks round. Strolling across the middle of the square, quite alone, was a very small grey-haired gentleman, with extremely broad shoulders and a most unbending back. He wore a staff cap with a broad red band and a heavy gold-laced peak, brown riding boots, a tightly-fastened belt, and no medals, orders or insignia of any kind. But no one doubted his identity for an instant, and I knew that I was looking at the Queen's greatest subject[1], the commander who had in the brief space of a month revolutionized the fortunes of the war, had turned disaster into victory, and something like despair into almost inordinate triumph.

★     ★     ★

Our rapid advance, almost into the heart of the Boer position, had disturbed and alarmed them. They were doubtful whether this was reconnaissance or actual attack. They determined to make certain by making an attempt to outflank the outflanking cavalry; and no sooner had our long-range rifle fire compelled them to take cover behind the hill than a new force, as it seemed, of two hundred rode into the open and, passing across our front at a distance of, perhaps, two thousand yards, made for a white stone kopje on our right.

Angus McNeill ran up to the General: "Sir, may we cut them off? I think we can just do it." The scouts pricked up their ears. The General reflected. "All right," he said, "you may try."

"Mount, mount, mount, the scouts!" cried their impetuous officer, scrambling into his saddle. Then, to me, "Come with us, we'll give you a show now—first-class."

A few days before, in an unguarded moment, I had promised to follow the fortunes of the scouts for a day. I looked at the Boers: they were nearer to the white stone kopje than we, but, on the other hand, they had the hill to climb, and were probably worse mounted. It might be done, and if it were done how dearly they would have to pay in that open plain. So, in the interests of the *Morning Post*, I got on my horse and we all started—forty or fifty scouts, McNeill and I, as fast as we could, by hard spurring, make the horses go.

It was from the very beginning a race, and recognized as such by both sides. As we converged I saw the five leading Boers, better mounted than their comrades, outpacing the others in a desperate

[1] Lord Roberts.

resolve to secure the coign of vantage. I said, "We cannot do it"; but no one would admit defeat or leave the matter undecided. The rest is exceedingly simple.

We arrived at a wire fence 100 yards—to be accurate, 120 yards—from the crest of the kopje, dismounted, and, cutting the wire, were about to seize the precious rocks when—as I had seen them in the railway cutting at Frere, grim, hairy, and terrible—the heads and shoulders of a dozen Boers appeared; and how many more must be close behind them?

There was a queer, almost inexplicable, pause, or perhaps there was no pause at all; but I seem to remember much happening. First the Boers—one fellow with a long, drooping, black beard, and a chocolate-coloured coat, another with a red scarf round his neck. Two scouts cutting the wire fence stupidly. One man taking aim across his horse, and McNeill's voice, quite steady: "Too late; back to the other kopje. Gallop!"

Then the musketry crashed out, and the "swish" and "whirr" of the bullets filled the air. I put my foot in the stirrup. The horse, terrified at the firing, plunged wildly. I tried to spring into the saddle; it turned under the animal's belly. He broke away, and galloped madly off. Most of the scouts were already 200 yards off. I was alone, dismounted, within the closest range, and a mile at least from cover of any kind.

One consolation I had—my pistol. I could not be hunted down unarmed in the open as I had been before. But a disabling wound was the brightest prospect. I turned, and, for the second time in this war, ran for my life on foot from the Boer marksmen, and thought to myself, "Here at last I take it." Suddenly, as I ran, I saw a scout. He came from the left, across my front; a tall man, with skull and crossbones badge, and on a pale horse. Death in Revelation, but life to me.

I shouted to him as he passed: "Give me a stirrup." To my surprise he stopped at once. "Yes," he said shortly. I ran up to him, did not bungle in the business of mounting, and in a moment found myself behind him on the saddle.

Then we rode. I put my arms round him to catch a grip of the mane. My hand became soaked with blood. The horse was hard hit; but, gallant beast, he extended himself nobly. The pursuing bullets piped and whistled—for the range was growing longer—overhead.

"Don't be frightened," said my rescuer; "they won't hit you." Then, as I did not reply, "My poor horse, oh, my poor —— horse; shot with an explosive bullet. The devils! But their hour will come. Oh, my poor horse!"

I said, "Never mind, you've saved my life." "Ah," he rejoined, "but it's the horse I'm thinking about." That was the whole of our conversation.

Judging from the number of bullets I heard I did not expect to be hit after the first 500 yards were covered, for a galloping horse is a difficult target, and the Boers were breathless and excited. But it was with a feeling of relief that I turned the corner of the further kopje and found I had thrown double sixes again.

The result of the race had been watched with strained attention by the rest of the troops, and from their position they knew that we were beaten before we ever reached the wire fence. They had heard the sudden fierce crackle of musketry and had seen what had passed. All the officers were agreed that the man who pulled up in such a situation to help another was worthy of some honourable distinction. Indeed, I have heard that Trooper Roberts—note the name, which seems familiar in this connexion—is to have his claims considered for the Victoria Cross. As to this I will not pronounce, for I feel some diffidence in writing impartially of a man who certainly saved me from a great danger.

\* \* \*

When Ian Hamilton was born his father was serving with a detachment of the 92nd Highlanders at Corfu. His mother died in 1856, and for the next ten years, the father being constantly on duty with the regiment, he and his younger brother, Vereker Hamilton, who was born in 1856, lived with their grandparents at Hafton, in the Holy Loch in Argyllshire. Such a childhood on moor and loch in a fine wild country was likely to develop and brace nerve and muscle, and stir the keen blood inherited from many generations of warlike ancestors. He was educated first at Cheam, and as he grew sufficiently old at Wellington College. Here he was very happy, and although he was not especially noted for industry, his success in the examinations at the end of each term excused any neglect in its course. In 1872 he passed the tests for the Army, and, according to the system at that time in force, was offered the choice of going to Sandhurst or living for a year abroad to learn a foreign language thoroughly. The cadet chose the latter, and was sent to Germany. Here he had the good luck to make the close friendship of a most distinguished old man. General Dammers was a Hanoverian who had fought against the Prussians at Langesalze, and who, refusing a very high command under the Prussians, lived at Dresden. Although he himself remained the aide-de-camp to the ex-King of Hanover, he became the centre of a group of Hanoverian officers who had entered the Saxon service. He was thus in touch with the latest school of military thought, stimulated to its utmost activity by the lessons of the great war which had lately been concluded. From General Dammers, Ian Hamilton learned the German language, military surveying, something of military history, and something doubtless of strategy and the art of war. The year thus passed very profitably. On his return to England, however, the War Office announced that they had changed their minds and that for the future everybody must go through Sandhurst. Such protests as his father, himself an officer, was entitled to make were overruled by the authorities, and Ian Hamilton embarked upon his military career having lost, through no fault of his own, one year of seniority—a year which Fortune had perhaps even then determined to restore to him manifold.

In 1873 he entered the 12th Foot, and after some months joined his father's old regiment, the 92nd. At first with the 92nd, and after 1881 with the 2nd battalion of the regiment, the Gordon Highlanders, Ian Hamilton followed the drum from garrison to garrison, going through the military routine, and plodding slowly up the first few steps of the long ladder of promotion. From the very first he interested himself in musketry. He became himself a keen and good rifle shot, and not with the military rifle alone. He spent a long leave in Kashmir on the fringe of the snows, and made a remarkable bag. Indeed, some of his heads attained nearly to the record dimensions, and one big single-horned markhor enjoyed the actual supremacy for several months.

Then came the Afghan war. Ian Hamilton, although only an infantry soldier, became aide-de-camp, with Brabazon as Brigade

Major, to the unfortunate commander of the British Cavalry Brigade. Early in the campaign he was stricken down with fever, and so avoided being drawn into the controversy which raged for several years in military circles around the actions in the Chardeh valley. It would indeed have been unfortunate if at this early stage in his career he had been led into any antagonism to the great General with whom his fortunes were afterwards so closely associated.

*     *     *

The Boer war of 1881 found Hamilton still a subaltern. He was ordered to South Africa with his regiment, and went full of eager anticipation. The regiment, composed almost entirely of soldiers inured to the hardships and disdainful of the dangers of war, was in the most perfect condition to encounter the enemy, and, as is usual in British expeditions on the outward voyage, they despised him most thoroughly. It was not to be dreamed of that a parcel of ragged Boers should stand against the famous soldiers of Kabul and Kandahar. They discussed beforehand the clasps which would be given upon the medal for the campaign. They were to be Laing's Nek, Relief of Potchefstroom, and Pretoria 1881. No one had then ever heard the name of Majuba Mountain. Yet there was to be the first encounter between Highlanders and Dutchmen.

The dismal story of Majuba is better known than its importance deserves. Had that action been fought in this war it would perhaps have gone down to history as the affair of 27 February. Instead, it was accepted as a stricken field, and might, such was the significance that was attached to it, have changed the history of nations. It needs no repetition here save in so far as it is concerned with Ian Hamilton. Majuba Mountain may in general terms be described as a saucer-topped hill. Sir George Colley and his six hundred soldiers, picked from various units (that all might share the glory), sat themselves down to rest and sleep, and dig a well in the bottom of the saucer. One weak picket of Gordon Highlanders was thrust forward over the rim on to the outer slope of the hill to keep an eye on those silent grey patches which marked the Boer laagers far below. Hamilton was the subaltern in command. As the day gradually broke and the light grew stronger, he saw from the very lifting of the curtain the course of the tragedy. Boers awoke, bustled about

225

their encampments; looked up just as Symons' Brigade looked up on the morning of Talana Hill, and saw the sky-line fringed with men. More bustle, long delay, much argument and hesitation below, a little boasting rifle fire from some of the British soldiers: "Ha, ha! got you this time I think!"—and then. straggle of horsemen riding in tens and twenties towards the foot of the mountain. Hamilton reported accordingly. The action of Majuba Hill had begun. Pause.

There was—so it has been described to me—a long donga that led up the steep slope. Into the lower end of this the Boer horsemen disappeared. Hamilton moved his score of men a little to their right, where they might command this zig-zag approach as much as the broken ground would allow, and reported again to the General or whoever was directing affairs—for Colley, wearied with the tremendous exertion of the night climb, was sleeping—"Enemy advancing to attack". He also made a few stone shelters. Pause again. Suddenly, quite close, darting forward here and there among the rocks and bushes of the donga—Boers! Fire on them, then. The Gordons' rifles spluttered accordingly, and back came the answer hot and sharp—a close and accurate musketry fire pinning the little party of Regulars to the earth behind their flimsy shelters. No one could show his head to fire. Soldiers would hold a helmet up above the sheltering stone and bring it down with two and three bullets through it. Could half a company fight a battle by itself? What were others doing? Hamilton felt bound to send another report. He left the half company in charge of the sergeant, got up, ran up the slope, and dropped into safety the other side of the saucer-shaped rim. The distance was scarcely forty yards, yet two bullets passed through his kilt in crossing it. Where was the General? A staff officer, ignorant and therefore undisturbed, said that the General was sleeping. "He knew," said the staff officer, "what was going on. No need for a subaltern of Highlanders to concern himself." Hamilton returned, running the gauntlet again, to his men. The fire grew hotter. The Boers began to creep gradually nearer. Their front of attack widened and drew around the contours of the hill. Were all the force asleep? One more warning at any rate they should have. Again he darted across the open space with the swish of bullets around him. Again he found the staff. But this time they were annoyed. It is such a bore when young officers are jumpy and alarmist. "It's all right," they said: and so it was within the saucer. The bullets piped overhead as the wind howls outside the well warmed house. But a sudden change impended.

Hamilton rejoined his men just as the Boers attacked at all points. The little picket of Highlanders, utterly unable to withstand the weight of the enemy's advance, ran back to the rim of the saucer intermingled with the Boers, who fired their rifles furiously at them, even putting the muzzles to the men's heads and so destroying them. Of the seventeen men under Ian Hamilton in this advanced position twelve were shot dead.

Without orders or order, exposed to a terrible fire, ignorant of what was required of them, the soldiers wavered. One last chance presented itself. Hamilton rushed up to the General in the impetuosity of youth: "I hope you'll forgive my presumption, sir, but will you let the Gordon Highlanders charge with the bayonet?"

"No presumption, young gentleman," replied Colley, with freezing calmness. "We'll let them charge us, and then we'll give them a volley and a charge."

On the word the whole scene broke into splinters. The British troops abandoned their positions and fled from the ground. The Boers, standing up along the rim, shot them down mercilessly—sporting rifles, crack shots, eighty yards' range. Hamilton saw a figure scarcely ten yards away aiming at him, raised the rifle he found himself somehow possessed of to reply. Both fired simultaneously. The British officer went down with his wrist smashed to pieces. He rose again: the rear crest was near. The last of the fugitives were streaming over it. One dash for liberty! The fire was murderous. Before the distance was covered his tunic was cut by one bullet, his knee by another, and finally a splinter of rock striking him behind the head brought him down half stunned to the ground.

The firing stopped. The Boers began to occupy the position. Two discovered the wounded man. The younger, being much excited, would have shot him. The elder restrained him. "Are you officer, you damned Englishman?" said they.

"Yes."

"Give your sword."

Now Hamilton's sword had belonged to his father before him. He replied by offering them money instead.

"Money!" they cried; "give it up at once," and were about to snatch it away when a person of authority—it is said Joubert himself —arrived. "*Voorwärts*," he said to the burghers, and in spite of their desire to plunder he drove them on. Hamilton thanked him. "This is a bad day for us."

"What can you expect," was the answer characteristic of the Boer—the privileged of God—"from fighting on a Sunday?"

Then they collected the prisoners and helped Hamilton to walk back to the British position. Colley lay dead on the ground. The Boers would not believe it was the General. "Englishmen are such liars." Hector Macdonald—grim and sad—hero of the Afghan War now a prisoner in the enemy's hand, watched the proceedings sullenly. The Boers picked out the surrendered prisoners. They looked at Hamilton. He was covered with blood from head to foot. They said: "You will probably die. You may go." So he went; staggered, and crawled back to camp, arrived there delirious the next morning. The wrist joint is composed of eight separate bones. The bullet, breaking through, had disarranged them sadly, had even carried one or two away. If he had consented to amputation he would soon have been convalescent. But a soldier must preserve all he can. What with fever and shock he nearly died. For six months he was an invalid. But the hand was saved, so that now the General can hold an envelope between its paralysed and withered fingers, and sometimes hold a cigarette. For all other purposes it is useless, and when he rides it flaps about helplessly—a glorious deformity.

After some months of doubt as to whether he should leave the army and throw himself entirely into the literary pursuits which had always possessed for him a keen attraction, Hamilton decided to remain a soldier.

★   ★   ★

Ian Hamilton's part in the Boer War is so well known that it will be unnecessary to do more than refer to it here. He displayed a curious facility for handling troops in close contact with the enemy, and practically from the beginning of the fighting he held the command of a brigade. It was Hamilton whose influence went so far to counteract the astounding optimism of the gallant Penn Symons.

It was Hamilton who was to have led the bayonet attack by night on the Boer laagers two days before Talana Hill was fought. It was Hamilton to whom French entrusted the entire disposition of the Infantry and Artillery at Elandslaagte, who arranged the attack, rallied the struggling line, and who led the final charge upon the Boer entrenchment. Again after Lombard's Kop, when the army reeled back in disorder into Ladysmith, it was Hamilton's brigade which, judiciously posted, checked the onset of the victorious enemy. During the defence of Ladysmith Hamilton's section of the defence included Caesar's Camp and Wagon Hill. He has been censured in the press for not having fortified these positions on their outer crests, and it was said in the Army after 6 January that this neglect caused unnecessary loss of life. How far this criticism may be just I do not now propose to examine. The arguments against entrenching the outer crest were that heavy works there would draw the enemy's artillery fire, and that the Imperial Light Horse, who were to have defended this section, said they preferred to avail themselves of the natural cover of rocks and stones.

Whatever the rights of this question may be, it is certain that on 6 January Ian Hamilton, by his personal gallantry and military conduct, restored the situation on Wagon Hill. Indeed, the Homeric contest, when the British General and Commandant Prinsloo of the Free State fired at each other at five yards' range, the fierce and bloody struggle around the embrasure of the naval gun, and the victorious charge of the Devons, may afterwards be found to be the most striking scene in the whole war.

*　　*　　*

Hamilton found that no force of the enemy stood between him and Winburg.

He therefore sent, shortly after noon, a staff officer, Captain Balfour to wit, under flag of truce, with a letter to the mayor of the town summoning him forthwith to surrender the town and all stores therein, and promising that if this were done he would use every effort to protect private property, and that whatever food-stuffs were required by the troops should be paid for. This message, which was duly heralded by the sound of a trumpet, concluded by saying that unless an acceptance was received within two hours

229

the General would understand that his offer had been declined.

Thus accredited, Captain Balfour made his way into the town and was soon the centre of an anxious and excited crowd of burghers and others who filled the market square. The mayor, the landdrost, and other prominent persons—indeed, all the inhabitants—were eager to avail themselves of the good terms, and a satisfactory settlement was almost arranged when, arriving swiftly from the north-east, Philip Botha and a commando of five hundred men, mostly Germans and Hollanders, all very truculent since they were as yet unbeaten, entered the town.

A violent and passionate scene ensued. Botha declared he would never surrender Winburg without a fight. Dissatisfied with the attentions paid him by Captain Balfour, he turned furiously on him and rated him soundly. Several of the Free Staters had asked what would be done to them if they laid down their arms. Balfour had replied that they would be permitted to return to their farms, unless actually captured on the field. This Botha held to be a breach of the laws of war, and he thereupon charged the officer with attempting to suborn his burghers. What had he to say that he should not be made a prisoner? "I ask favours of no Dutchman," replied Balfour, sternly.

"Arrest that man!" shouted Botha, in a fury; "I shall begin shooting soon." At these shameful words a great commotion arose. The women screamed, the mayor and landdrost rushed forward in the hopes of averting bloodshed. The Boers raised their rifles in menace, and the unarmed British envoy flourished his white flag indignantly.

For several minutes it seemed that an actual scuffle, possibly a tragedy, would occur. But the influence of the townsfolk, who knew that their liberty and property lay in the hands of the Imperial General, and that the great siege guns were even then being dragged into effective range, prevailed, and Philip Botha, followed by his men, galloped furiously from the square towards the north.

That afternoon General Ian Hamilton entered Winburg at the head of his troops. Under a shady tree outside the town the mayor and landdrost tendered their submission and two large silver keys. The Union Jack was hoisted in the market-place amid the cheers of the British section of the inhabitants, and, as each battalion marching through the streets saw the famous emblem of pride and power, bright in the rays of the setting sun, these feeble or interested plaudits were drowned in the loud acclamations of the victorious invaders.

\*　　\*　　\*

In the afternoon I rode into Lindley to buy various stores in which my wagon was deficient. It is a typical South African town, with a large central market square and four or five broad unpaved streets radiating therefrom. There is a small clean-looking hotel, a substantial jail, a church and a school-house. But the two largest buildings are the general stores. These places are the depots whence the farmers for many miles around draw all their necessaries and comforts. Owned and kept by Englishmen or Scotsmen, they are built on the most approved style. Each is divided into five or six large well-stocked departments. The variety of their goods is remarkable. You may buy a piano, a kitchen range, a slouch hat, a bottle of hair wash, or a box of sardines over the same counter. The two stores are the rival Whiteley's of the countryside; and the diverse tastes to which they cater prove at once the number of their customers, and the wealth which even the indolent Boer may win easily from his fertile soil.

Personally I sought potatoes, and after patient inquiry I was directed to a man who had by general repute twelve sacks. He was an Englishman, and delighted to see the British bayonets at last. "You can't think," he said, "how we have looked forward to this day."

I asked him whether the Dutch had ill-used him during the war.

"No, not really ill-used us; but when we refused to go out and fight they began commandeering our property, horses and carts at first and latterly food and clothing. Besides, it has been dreadful to have to listen to all their lies and, of course, we had to keep our tongues between our teeth."

It was evident that he hated the Boers among whom his lot had been cast with great earnestness. This instinctive dislike which the British settler so often displays for his Dutch neighbour is a perplexing and not a very hopeful feature of the South African problem. Presently we reached his house (where the potatoes were stored). Above the doorway hung a Union Jack. I said:

"I advise you to take that down."

"Why?" he asked, full of astonishment. "The British are going to keep the country, aren't they?"

"This column is not going to stay here for ever."

"But," with an anxious look, "surely they will leave some soldiers behind to protect us, to hold the town."

I told him I thought it unlikely. Ours was a fighting column. Other troops would come up presently for garrison duty. But there would probably be an interval of at least a week. Little did I foresee the rough fighting which would rage round Lindley for the next three months. He looked very much disconcerted; not altogether without reason.

"It's very hard on us," he said after a pause. "What will happen when the Boers come back? They're just over the hill now."

"That's why I should take the flag down if I were you. If you don't fight, keep your politics till the war is over!" He looked very disappointed, and I think was asking himself how much his enthusiasm had compromised him. After we had settled the potato question to his satisfaction and I had sent the sack away upon my pack pony, he perked up. "Come and see my garden," he said, and nothing loth I went. It was not above a hundred yards square, but its contents proclaimed his energy and the possibilities of the soil. He explained how he had dammed a marshy sluit in the side of the hills to the eastward. "Plenty of water at all seasons: this pipe you see, only a question of piping: as much water as ever I want: twenty gardens: grow anything you like, potatoes mostly, cabbages (they were beauties), tomatoes and onions, a vine of sweet white grapes, a bed of strawberries over there—anything: it only wants water, and there's plenty of that if you take the trouble to get it."

The signs of industry impressed me. "How long," I asked, "have you been here?"

"Eight years last February," he replied; "see those trees?"

He pointed to a long row of leafy trees about twenty feet high, which gave a cool shade and whose green colour pleased the eye.

"I planted those myself when I came: they grow quickly, don't they? Only a question of water, and that is only a question of work."

Then I left him and returned to the camp with my potatoes and some information thrown in.

The next morning before breakfast-time there was firing in the picket line south of Lindley. The patter of shots sounded across the valley, and upon the opposite slopes the British patrols could be seen galloping about like agitated ants. I was at the moment with General Hamilton. He watched the distant skirmish from his tent door for a little while in silence. Then he said:

"The scouts and the Kaffirs report laagers of the enemy over there, and over there, and over there" (he pointed to the different quarters). "Now either I must attack them today or they will attack me tomorrow. If I attack them today, I weary my troops; and if I don't we shall have to fight an awkward rearguard action to get out of this place tomorrow."

★   ★   ★

Heilbron lies in a deep valley. About it on every side rolls the grassy upland country of the Free State, one smooth grey-green surge beyond another, like the after-swell of a great gale at sea; and here in the trough of the waves, hidden almost entirely from view, is the town itself, white stone houses amid dark trees, all clustering at the foot of a tall church spire. It is a quiet, sleepy little place, with a few good buildings and pretty rose gardens, half a dozen large stores, a hotel, and a branch line of its own.

For a few days it had been capital of the Free State. The President, his secretaries, and his councillors arrived one morning from Lindley, bringing the "seat of government" with them in a Cape cart. For nearly a week Heilbron remained the chief town. Then, as suddenly as it had come, the will-o'-the-wisp dignity departed, and Steyn, secretaries, councillors, and Cape cart, hurried away to the eastward, leaving behind them rumours of advancing hosts— and (to this I can testify) three bottles of excellent champagne. That was on Sunday night. The inhabitants watched and wondered all the next day.

On the Tuesday morning, shortly after the sun had risen, Christian De Wet appeared with sixty wagons, five guns, and a thousand burghers, very weary, having trekked all night from the direction of Kroonstadt, and glad to find a place of rest and refreshment. "What of the English?" inquired the newcomers, and the Heilbron folk replied that the English were coming, and so was Christmas,

233

and that the country to the southward was all clear for ten miles. Thereat the war-worn commando outspanned their oxen and settled themselves to coffee. Forty minutes later the leading patrols of Broadwood's Brigade began to appear on the hills to the south of the town.

Looked at from any point of view, the British force was a formidable array: Household Cavalry, 12th Lancers and 10th Hussars, with P and Q Batteries Royal Horse Artillery (you must mind your P's and Q's with them), two "pom-poms", and two galloping Maxims; and, hurrying up behind them, Light Horse, Mounted Infantry, 19th and 21st Brigades, thirty field-guns, more "pom-poms", two great 5-in. ox-drawn siege pieces ("cow guns" as the army calls them), and Ian Hamilton. It was an army formidable to any foe; but to those who now stared upwards from the little town and saw the dark, swift-moving masses on the hills—an avalanche of armed men and destructive engines about to fall on them—terrible beyond words.

"And then," as the poet observes, "there was mounting in hot haste," saddling up of weary ponies, frantic inspanning of hungry oxen cheated of their well-earned rest and feed, cracking of long whips, kicking of frightened Kaffirs; and so pell-mell out of the town and away to the northward hurried the commando of Christian De Wet.

The cavalry halted on the hills for a while, the General being desirous of obtaining the formal surrender of Heilbron, and so preventing street-fighting or bombardment. An officer—Lieutenant M. Spender-Clay, of the 2nd Life Guards—was despatched with a flag of truce and a trumpeter; message most urgent, answer to be given within twenty minutes, or Heaven knows what would happen; but all these things take time. Flags of truce (prescribe the customs of war) must approach the enemy's picket line at a walk; a mile and a half at a walk—twenty minutes; add twenty for the answer, ten for the return journey, and nearly an hour is gone. So we wait impatiently watching the two solitary figures with a white speck above them draw nearer and nearer to the Boer lines; "and," says the brigadier, "bring two guns up and have the ranges taken."

There was just a chance that while all were thus intent on the

234

town, the convoy and commando might have escaped unharmed, for it happened that the northern road runs for some distance eastward along the bottom of the valley, concealed from view. But the clouds of dust betrayed them.

"Hallo! what the deuce is that?" cried an officer.

"What?" said everyone else.

"Why, that! Look at the dust. There they go. It's a Boer convoy. Gone away."

And with this holloa the chase began. Never have I seen anything in war so like a fox hunt. At first the scent was uncertain, and the pace was slow with many checks.

Before us rose a long smooth slope of grass, and along the crest the figures of horsemen could be plainly seen. The tail of the wagon train was just disappearing. But who should say how many rifles lined that ridge? Besides, there were several barbed-wire fences, which, as anyone knows, will spoil the best country.

Broadwood began giving all kinds of orders—Household Cavalry to advance slowly in the centre; 12th Lancers to slip forward on the right, skirting the town, and try to look behind the ridge, and with them a battery of horse guns; 10th Hussars, to make a cast to the left, and the rest of the guns to walk forward steadily.

Slowly at first, and silently besides; but soon the hounds gave tongue. Pop, pop, pop—the advanced squadron—Blues—had found something to fire at, and something that fired back, too; pip-pop, pip-pop came the double reports of the Boer rifles. Bang—the artillery opened on the crest-line with shrapnel, and at the first few shells it was evident that the enemy would not abide the attack. The horsemen vanished over the sky-line.

The leading squadron pushed cautiously forward—every movement at a walk, so far. Infantry brigadiers and others, inclined to impatience, ground their teeth, and, thinking there would be no sport that day, went home criticizing the master. The leading squadron reached the crest, and we could see them dismount and begin to fire.

We were over the first big fence, and now the scent improved. Beyond the first ridge was another, and behind this, much nearer now, dust clouds high and thick. The General galloped forward himself to the newly-captured position and took a comprehensive view. "Tell the brigade to come here at once—sharp."

A galloper shot away to the rear. Behind arose the rattle of trotting batteries. The excitement grew. Already the patrols were skirting the second ridge. The Boer musketry, fitful for a few minutes, died away. They were abandoning their second position. "Forward, then." And forward we went accordingly at a healthy trot.

In front of the jingling squadrons two little galloping Maxims darted out, and almost before the ridge was ours they were spluttering angrily at the retreating enemy, so that four burghers, as I saw myself, departed amid a perfect hail of bullets, which peppered the ground on all sides.

But now the whole hunt swung northward towards a line of rather ugly-looking heights. Broadwood looked at them sourly. "Four guns to watch those hills, in case they bring artillery against us from them." Scarcely were the words spoken, when there was a flash and a brown blurr on the side of one of the hills, and with a rasping snarl a shell passed overhead and burst among the advancing cavalry. The four guns were on the target without a moment's delay.

The Boer artillerists managed to fire five shots, and then the place grew too hot for them—indeed, after Natal, I may write, even for them. They had to expose themselves a great deal to remove their gun, and the limber and its six horses showed very plainly on the hillside, so that we all hoped to smash a wheel or kill a horse, and thus capture a real prize. But at the critical moment our "pompoms" disgraced themselves. They knew the range, they saw the target. They fired four shots; the aim was not bad. But four shots— four miserable shots! Just pom-pom, pom-pom. That was all. Whereas, if the Boers had had such a chance, they would have rattled through the whole belt, and sent eighteen or twenty shells in a regular shower. So we all saw with pain how a weapon, which is so terrible in the hands of the enemy, may become feeble and ineffective when used on our side by our own gunners.

After the menace of the Boer artillery was removed from our right flank, the advance became still more rapid. Batteries and squadrons were urged into a gallop. Broadwood himself hurried forward. We topped a final rise.

Then at last we viewed the vermin. There, crawling up the opposite slope, clear cut on a white roadway, was a long line of wagons—ox wagons and mule wagons—and behind everything a small cart drawn by two horses. All were struggling with frantic energy to escape from their pursuers. But in vain.

The batteries spun round and unlimbered. Eager gunners ran forward with ammunition, and some with belts for the "pom-poms". There was a momentary pause while ranges were taken and sights aligned, and then ——! Shell after shell crashed among the convoys. Some exploded on the ground; others, bursting in the air, whipped up the dust all round mules and men. The "pom-poms", roused at last from their apathy by this delicious target and some pointed observations of the General, thudded out strings of little bombs. For a few minutes the wagons persevered manfully. Then one by one they came to a standstill. The drivers fled to the nearest shelter, and the animals strayed off the road or stood quiet in stolid ignorance of their danger.

And now at this culminating moment I must, with all apologies to "Brooksby", change the metaphor, because the end of the chase was scarcely like a fox hunt. The guns had killed the quarry, and the cavalry dashed forward to secure it. It was a fine bag—to wit, fifteen laden wagons and seventeen prisoners. Such was the affair of Heilbron, and it was none the less joyous and exciting because, so far as we could learn, no man on either side was killed, and only one trooper and five horses wounded. Then we turned homewards.

*   *   *

The orders from headquarters for the 29th [May] were such as to involve certain fighting should the enemy stand. French, with the Cavalry Division, was to march around Johannesburg to Driefontein; Ian Hamilton was directed on Florida; the main army, under the Field-Marshal, would occupy Germiston and seize the junctions of the Natal, Cape Colony and Potchefstroom lines. These movements, which the chief had indicated by flags on the map, were now to be executed—so far as possible—by soldiers on the actual field.

At three o'clock precisely the infantry advanced to the attack. Major-General Bruce-Hamilton directed the left attack with the

237

21st Brigade, and Colonel Spens the right with the 19th Brigade. The whole division was commanded by General Smith-Dorrien. The lateness of the hour gave scarcely any time for the artillery preparation, and the artillery came into action only a few minutes before the infantry were exposed to fire.

The leading battalion of the 19th Brigade chanced—for there was no selection—to be the Gordon Highlanders; nor was it without a thrill that I watched this famous regiment move against the enemy. Their extension and advance were conducted with machine-like regularity. The officers explained what was required to the men. They were to advance rapidly until under rifle fire, and then to push on or not as they might be instructed.

With impassive unconcern the veterans of Chitral, Dargai, the Bara Valley, Magersfontein, Paardeberg, and Houtnek walked leisurely forward, and the only comment recorded was the observation of a private: "Bill, this looks like being a kopje day." Gradually the whole battalion drew out clear of the covering ridge, and long dotted lines of brown figures filled the plain. At this moment two batteries and the two 5-in. guns opened from the right of the line, and what with the artillery of French and Bruce-Hamilton there was soon a loud cannonade.

The Dutch replied at once with three or four guns, one of which seemed a very heavy piece of ordnance on the main Rand ridge, and another fired from the kopje against which the Gordons were marching. But the Boer riflemen, crouching among the rocks, reserved their fire for a near target. While the troops were thus approaching the enemy's position, the two brigades began unconsciously to draw apart. Colonel Spens's battalions had extended further to the right than either Ian Hamilton or Smith-Dorrien had intended. Bruce-Hamilton, pressing forward on the left, found himself more and more tempted to face the harassing attack on his left rear. Both these tendencies had to be corrected. The Gordons were deflected to their left by an officer, Captain Higginson, who galloped most pluckily into the firing line in spite of a hail of bullets. Bruce-Hamilton was ordered to bear in to his right and disregard the growing pressure behind his left shoulder. Nevertheless a wide gap remained. But by this mischance Ian Hamilton contrived to profit.

Smith-Dorrien had already directed the only remaining battalion—the Sussex—to fill up the interval, and the General-in-Chief now thrust a battery forward through the gap, almost flush with the skirmish line of the infantry on its left and right.

The fire of these guns, combined with the increasing pressure from the turning movements both of Bruce-Hamilton and French, who was now working very far forward in the west, weakened the enemy's position on the kopje which the Gordons were attacking. Yet, when every allowance has been made for skilful direction and bold leading, the honours, equally with the cost of the victory, belong more to the Gordon Highlanders than to all the other troops put together.

The rocks against which they advanced proved in the event to be the very heart of the enemy's position. The grass in front of them was burnt and burning, and against this dark background the khaki figures showed distinctly. The Dutch held their fire until the attack was within eight hundred yards, and then, louder than the cannonade, the ominous rattle of concentrated rifle fire burst forth. The black slope was spotted as thickly with grey puffs of dust where the bullets struck as with advancing soldiers, and tiny figures falling by the way told of heavy loss. But the advance neither checked nor quickened.

With remorseless stride, undisturbed by peril or enthusiasm, the Gordons swept steadily onward, changed direction half left to avoid, as far as possible, an enfilade fire, changed again to the right to effect a lodgement on the end of the ridge most suitable to attack, and at last rose up together to charge. The black slope twinkled like jet with the unexpected glitter of bayonets. The rugged sky-line bristled with kilted figures, as, in perfect discipline and disdainful silence, those splendid soldiers closed on their foe.

The Boers shrank from the contact. Discharging their magazines furiously, and firing their guns twice at point-blank range, they fled in confusion to the main ridge, and the issue of the action was no longer undecided.

Still the fight continued. Along the whole infantry front a tremendous rifle fire blazed. Far away to the left French's artillery pursued the retreating Boers with shells. The advanced batteries of Hamilton's force fired incessantly. The action did not cease with the daylight. The long lines of burning grass cast a strange, baleful glare on the field, and by this light the stubborn adversaries maintained their debate for nearly an hour.

At length, however, the cannonade slackened and ceased, and the rifles soon imitated the merciful example of the guns. The chill and silence of the night succeeded the hot tumult of the day. Regiments assembled and re-formed their ranks, ambulances and baggage wagons crowded forward from the rear, the burning veldt was beaten out, and hundreds of cooking fires gleamed with more kindly meaning through the darkness.

The General rode forward, to find the Gordons massed among the rocks they had won. The gallant Burney, who commanded the firing line, was severely wounded. St. John Meyrick was killed. Nine officers and eighty-eight soldiers had fallen in the attack; but those that remained were proud and happy in the knowledge that they had added to the many feats of arms which adorn the annals of the regiment—one that was at least the equal of Elandslaagte or Dargai; and, besides all this, they may have reflected that by their devotion they had carried forward the British cause a long stride to victory, and, better than victory, to honourable peace. Ian Hamilton spoke a few brief words of thanks and praise to them—"the regiment my father commanded and I was born in"—and told them that in a few hours all Scotland would ring with the tale of their deeds. And well Scotland may, for no men of any race could have shown more soldier-like behaviour.

A melancholy spectacle broke upon my view. Near a clump of rocks eighteen Gordon Highlanders lay dead in a row. Their faces were covered with blankets, but their grey stockinged feet—for the boots had been removed—looked very pitiful. There they lay stiff and cold on the surface of the great Banket Reef. I knew how much more precious their lives had been to their countrymen than all the gold mines the lying foreigners say this war was fought to win. And yet, in view of the dead and the ground they lay on, neither I nor the officer who rode with me could control an emotion of illogical anger, and we scowled at the tall chimneys of the Rand.

General Ian Hamilton, General Smith-Dorrien, all their staffs, and everyone who wished to pay a last tribute of respect to brave men, attended the funerals. The veteran regiment stood around the grave, forming three sides of a hollow square—Generals and staff filled the other. The mourning party rested on their arms, reversed; the Chaplain read the Burial Service, the bodies were lowered into the trench, and the pipes began the lament. The wild, barbaric music filled the air, stirring the soldiers, hitherto quite unmoved, with a strange and very apparent force. Sad and mournful was the dirge wailing of battles ended, of friendships broken, and ambitions lost; and yet there were mingled with its sadness many notes of triumph, and through all its mourning rang the cry of hope.

★ ★ ★

After lunch I became very anxious to go into, and, if possible, through, Johannesburg. An important action had been fought, witnessed by only two or three correspondents; and since the enemy lay between the force and the telegraph wire no news could have been sent home. Hamilton, indeed, had sent off two of Rimington's Guides early in the morning with despatches; but they were to make a wide sweep to the south, and it was not likely, if they got through at all, that they would reach Lord Roberts until late. The shortest, perhaps the safest, road lay through Johannesburg itself. But was the venture worth the risk? While I was revolving the matter in my mind on the veranda of the temporary head-quarters, there arrived two cyclists from the direction of the town. I got into conversation with one of them, a Frenchman, Monsieur Lautré by name. He had come from the Langlaagte mine, with which undertaking he was connected. There were no Boers there, according to him. There might or might not be Boers in the town. Could a stranger get through? Certainly, he thought, unless he were stopped and questioned. He undertook there and then to be my guide if I wished to go; and it being of considerable importance to get the telegrams through to London, I decided, after a good many misgivings, to accept his offer. The General, who wanted to send a more detailed account of his action, and to report his arrival at Florida, was glad to avail himself even of this precarious channel. So the matter was immediately settled. Lautré's friend, a most accommodating person, got off his bicycle without demur and placed it at my disposal. I doffed my khaki and put on a suit of plain clothes which I had in my valise, and exchanged my slouch hat for a soft cap. Lautré put the despatches in his pocket, and we started without more ado.

The tracks were bad, winding up and down hill, and frequently deep in sand; but the machine was a good one, and we made fair progress. Lautré, who knew every inch of the ground, avoided all highways, and led me by devious paths from one mine to another, around huge heaps of tailings, across little private tram lines, through thick copses of fir trees, or between vast sheds of machinery, now silent and idle. In three-quarters of an hour we reached Langlaagte, and here we found one of Rimington's scouts pushing cautiously forward towards the town. We held a brief parley with him, behind a house, for he was armed and in uniform. He was very doubtful of the situation ahead; only knew for certain that the troops had not yet entered Johannesburg. "But," said he, "the correspondent of *The Times* passed me more than two hours ago."

"Riding?" I asked.

"Yes," he said, "a horse."

"Ah," said my Frenchman, "that is no good. He will not get through on a horse. They will arrest him." And then, being quite fired with the adventure: "Besides, we will beat him, even if, unhappily, he escape the Boers."

So we hurried on. The road now ran for the most part downhill, and the houses became more numerous. The day was nearly done, and the sun drew close to the horizon, throwing our long shadows on the white track before us. At length we turned into a regular street.

"If they stop us," said my guide, "speak French. *Les Français sont en bonne odeur ici.* You speak French, eh?"

I thought my accent might be good enough to deceive a Dutchman, so I said yes; and thereafter our conversation was conducted in French.

Suddenly, as we crossed a side lane, I saw in the street parallel to that we followed three mounted men with slouch hats, bandoliers, and that peculiar irregular appearance which I have learned to associate with Boers. But to stop or turn back was now fatal. After all, with the enemy at their gates, they had probably concerns of their own to occupy them. We skimmed along unhindered into the central square, and my companion, whose coolness was admirable, pointed me out the post office and other public buildings, speaking all the time in French. The slope now rose against us so steeply that we dismounted to push our machines. While thus circumstanced I was alarmed to hear the noise of an approaching horse behind me. With an effort I controlled my impulse to look back.

"*Encore un Boer*," said Lautré lightly. I was speechless. The man drew nearer, overtook and pulled his horse into a walk beside us. I could not help—perhaps it was the natural, and, if so, the wise, thing to do—having a look at him. He was a Boer sure enough, and I think he must have been a foreigner. He was armed *cap-à-pie*. The horse he rode carried a full campaigning kit on an English military saddle. Wallets, saddle-bags, drinking-cup, holsters—all were there. His rifle was slung across his back, he wore two full bandoliers over his shoulders and a third round his waist—evidently a dangerous customer. I looked at his face and our eyes met. The light was dim, or he might have seen me change colour. He had a pale, almost ghastly visage, peering ill-favoured and cruel from beneath a slouch hat with a large white feather. Then he turned away carelessly. After all, I suppose he thought it natural a poor devil of a townsman should wish to look at so fine a cavalier of fortune. Presently he set spurs to his horse and cantered on. I breathed again freely. Lautré laughed.

"There are plenty of cyclists in Johannesburg," he said. "We do not look extraordinary. No one will stop us."

Then we met a shabby-looking man, and now, no one else being in sight, the night dark, and the man old and feeble, we decided to ask him.

"The English," he said with a grin, "why, their sentinels are just at the top of the hill."

"How far?"

"Five minutes—even less."

Two hundred yards further on three British soldiers came in sight. They were quite unarmed, and walking casually forward into the town. I stopped them and asked what brigade they belonged to. They replied Maxwell's.

"Where is the picket line?"

"We haven't seen no pickets," said one of them.

"What are you doing?"

"Looking for something to eat. We've had enough of 'arf rations."

I said, "You'll get taken prisoners or shot if you go on into the town."

"Wot's that, guvnor?" said one of them, deeply interested in this extraordinary possibility.

I repeated, and added that the Boers were still riding about the streets.

"Well, then, I ain't for it," he said with decision. "Let's go back and try some of them 'ouses near the camp."

So we all proceeded together.

I soon found some officers of my acquaintance, and from them we learned that Lord Roberts's headquarters were not at Elandsfontein (South), but back at Germiston, nearly seven miles away. It was now pitch dark, and all signs of a road had vanished; but Lautré declared he knew his way, and, in any case, the messages—press and official —had to go through.

We left the camp of Maxwell's Brigade and struck across country in order to cut into the main southern road. A bicycle now became a great encumbrance, as the paths wound through dense fir woods, obstructed by frequent wire fences, ditches, holes, and high grass. Lautré, however, persisted that all was well, and, as it turned out, he was right. After about an hour of this slow progress we reached the railway, and, seeing more camp fires away to the left, turned along it.

Another half-hour of walking brought us, as Lautré had promised, to a good firm road, and the bicycles quickly made amends for their previous uselessness. The air was cold, and we were glad to spin along at a fair ten miles an hour. At this rate twenty minutes brought us into Germiston. Not knowing where I should be likely to find dinner, or a bed, I dismounted opposite the hotel, and, seeing lights and signs of occupation, went inside.

We dined hastily and not too well, secured the reversion of half the billiard table, should all other couches fail, and set out again, this time tired and footsore. After two miles of dusty track the camp was reached. I found more officers who knew where Army

Headquarters were, and at last, at about half-past ten, we reached the solitary house. We sent the despatches in by an orderly, and after a few minutes Lord Kerry came out and said that the Chief wanted to see the messengers.

Now, for the first time in this war, I found myself face to face with our illustrious leader, Lord Roberts. The room was small and meanly furnished, and he and his staff, who had just finished dinner, sat round a large table which occupied the greater part of the floor. With him were Sir William Nicholson (who arranges all the transport of the army, a work the credit of which is usually given to Lord Kitchener) and Colonel Neville Chamberlayne, his private secretary, both of them soldiers of the practical Indian school, where you have real fighting, both of them serving once more under their commander of Afghan days. There, too, was Sir Henry Rawlinson, whom I had last seen round Sir George White's table, the night Dundonald broke into Ladysmith; and Sir James Hills-Johnes, who won the Victoria Cross in the Indian Mutiny, and aides-de-camp and others whom I cannot remember.

The Field-Marshal rose from his place, shook hands, and bade us, in most ceremonious fashion, to be seated. He had read half of Hamilton's despatch.

"The first part of this," he said, "we knew already. Two guides—Rimington's, I think—got in here about an hour ago. They had a dangerous ride, and were chased a long way, but escaped safely. I am glad to hear Hamilton is at Florida. How did you get through?"

I told him briefly. His eyes twinkled. I have never seen a man before with such extraordinary eyes. I remember to have been struck with them on several occasions. The face remains perfectly motionless, but the eyes convey the strongest emotions. Sometimes they blaze with anger, and you see hot yellow fire behind them. Then it is best to speak up straight and clear, and make an end quickly. At others there is a steel grey glitter—quite cold and uncompromising—which has a most sobering effect on anyone who sees it. But now the eyes twinkled brightly with pleasure or amusement or approbation, or, at any rate, something friendly.

"Tell me about the action," he said.

So I told him all I knew, and I don't think the tale lost in the telling. From time to time he asked questions about the artillery concentration, or the length of front of the infantry attack, and other technical matters, on which I was luckily well-informed. The fact that the troops had no rations seemed to disturb him very much. He was particularly interested to hear of Hamilton's novel attack "at thirty paces extension"; of the manner in which the batteries had been rammed almost into the firing line; but most of all he wanted to hear about the Gordons' charge. When I had done he said: "The Gordons always do well."

\*　　\*　　\*

The Guards, fixing bayonets, began to enter Pretoria, marching through the main street, which was crowded with people, towards the central square, and posting sentries and pickets as they went. We were naturally very anxious to know what had befallen our comrades held prisoners all these long months. Rumour said they had been removed during the night to Waterfall Boven, two hundred miles down the Delagoa Bay line. But nothing definite was known.

The Duke of Marlborough, however, found a mounted Dutchman who said he knew where all the officers were confined, and who undertook to guide us, and without waiting for the troops, who were advancing with all due precautions, we set off at a gallop.

The distance was scarcely three-quarters of a mile, and in a few minutes, turning a corner and crossing a little brook, we saw before us a long tin building surrounded by a dense wire entanglement. Seeing this, and knowing its meaning too well, I raised my hat and cheered. The cry was instantly answered from within. What followed resembled the end of an Adelphi melodrama.

The Duke of Marlborough called on the commandant to surrender forthwith. The prisoners rushed out of the house into the yard, some in uniform, some in flannels, hatless or coatless, but all violently excited. The sentries threw down their rifles. The gates were flung open, and while the rest of the guards—they numbered fifty-two in all—stood uncertain what to do, the long-penned-up officers surrounded them and seized their weapons. Someone—Grimshaw of the Dublin Fusiliers—produced a Union Jack (made during imprisonment out of a Vierkleur). The Transvaal emblem was torn down, and, amid wild cheers, the first British flag was hoisted over Pretoria. Time 8.47, 5 June.

The commandant then made formal surrender to the Duke of Marlborough of 129 officers and 39 soldiers whom he had in his custody as prisoners of war, and surrendered, besides himself, 4 corporals and 48 Dutchmen. These latter were at once confined within the wire cage, and guarded by their late prisoners; but, since they had treated the captives well, they have now been permitted to take the oath of neutrality and return to their homes. The anxieties which the prisoners had suffered during the last few hours of their confinement were terrible, nor did I wonder, when I heard the account, why their faces were so white and their manner so excited.

At two o'clock Lord Roberts, the staff, and the foreign attachés entered the town, and proceeded to the central square, wherein the Town Hall, the Parliament House, and other public buildings are situated. The British flag was hoisted over the Parliament House amid some cheers. The victorious army then began to parade past it, Pole-Carew's Division, with the Guards leading, coming from the south, and Ian Hamilton's force from the west. For three hours the broad river of steel and khaki flowed unceasingly, and the townsfolk gazed in awe and wonder at those majestic soldiers, whose discipline neither perils nor hardships had disturbed, whose relentless march no obstacles could prevent.

With such pomp and the rolling of drums the new order of things was ushered in. The former government had ended without dignity. One thought to find the President—stolid old Dutchman —seated on his stoep reading his Bible and smoking a sullen pipe. But he chose a different course. On the Friday preceding the British occupation he left the capital and withdrew along the Delagoa Bay Railway, taking with him a million pounds in gold, and leaving behind him a crowd of officials clamouring for pay, and far from satisfied with the worthless cheques they had received, and Mrs. Kruger, concerning whose health the British people need not further concern themselves.

# THE FIRST WORLD WAR

# THE WORLD CRISIS

## 1911–1918

*The author's history of the First World War and of the Second, taken in conjunction, are unique among all personal books on politics and war. In the First World War he was First Lord of the Admiralty and Minister of Munitions, and in the Second was regarded by many as the greatest of all Prime Ministers. He was in the happy position as an historian of being able to record and explain stupendous events in which he himself not only participated, but which he helped to direct, mould and control.*

*"The World Crisis", like "The Second World War", was, as the author says, strung throughout on the strong thread of personal reminiscence. The selections from "The World Crisis" are taken from the abridged and revised edition which presents a continuous narrative in one volume, and which contains all the main facts, foundations and conclusions drawn by the author in the full work.*

*"In presenting the complete story," he writes in his Preface to the abridged edition, "I have a sure conviction that it will not in essentials be overturned by the historians of the future."*

*The four volumes of the original edition were published between 1923 and 1927. The abridged and revised edition was first published in 1931.*

THE GREAT WAR [1914–1918] differed from all ancient wars in the immense power of the combatants and their fearful agencies of destruction, and from all modern wars in the utter ruthlessness with which it was fought. All the horrors of all the ages were brought together, and not only armies but whole populations were thrust into the midst of them. The mighty educated States involved conceived with reason that their very existence was at stake. Germany having let Hell loose kept well in the van of terror; but she was followed step by step by the desperate and ultimately avenging nations she had assailed. Every outrage against humanity or international law was repaid by reprisals often on a greater scale and of longer duration. No truce or parley mitigated the strife of the armies. The wounded died between the lines: the dead mouldered into the soil. Merchant ships and neutral ships and hospital ships were sunk on the seas and all on board left to their fate, or killed as they swam. Every effort was made to starve whole nations into submission without regard to age or sex. Cities and monuments were smashed by artillery. Bombs from the air were cast down indiscriminately. Poison gas in many forms stifled or seared the soldiers. Liquid fire was projected upon their bodies. Men fell from the air in flames, or were smothered, often slowly, in the dark recesses of the sea. The fighting strength of armies was limited only by the manhood of their countries. Europe and large parts of Asia and Africa became one vast battlefield on which after years of struggle not armies but nations broke and ran. When all was over, Torture and Cannibalism were the only two expedients that the civilized, scientific, Christian States had been able to deny themselves: and these were of doubtful utility.

But nothing daunted the valiant heart of man. Son of the Stone Age, vanquisher of nature with all her trials and monsters, he met the awful and self-inflicted agony with new reserves of fortitude. Freed in the main by his intelligence from medieval fears, he marched to death with inherent dignity. His nervous system was found in the twentieth century capable of enduring physical and moral stresses before which the simpler natures of primeval times would have collapsed. Again and again to the hideous bombardment, again and again from the hospital to the front, again and again to the hungry submarines, he strode unflinching. And withal, as an individual, preserved through these torments the glories of a reasonable and compassionate mind.

The Victorian Age was the age of accumulation; not of a mere piling up of material wealth, but of the growth and gathering in every land of all those elements and factors which go to make up the power of States. Education spread itself over the broad surface of the millions. Science had opened the limitless treasure-house of nature. Door after door had been unlocked. One dim mysterious gallery after another had been lighted up, explored, made free for all: and every gallery entered gave access to at least two more. Every morning when the world woke up, some new machinery had started running. Every night while the world had supper, it was running still. It ran on while all men slept.

And the advance of the collective mind was at a similar pace. Disraeli said of the early years of the nineteenth century: "In those days England was for the few—and for the very few." Every year of Queen Victoria's reign saw those limits broken and extended. Every year brought in new thousands of people in private stations who thought about their own country and its story and its duties towards other countries, to the world and to the future, and understood the greatness of the responsibilities of which they were the heirs. Every year diffused a wider measure of material comfort among the higher ranks of labour. Substantial progress was made in mitigating the hard lot of the mass. Their health improved, their lives and the lives of their children were brightened, their stature grew, their securities against some of their gravest misfortunes were multiplied, their numbers greatly increased.

Thus when all the trumpets sounded, every class and rank had something to give to the need of the State. Some gave their science and some their wealth, some gave their business energy and drive, and some their wonderful personal prowess, and some their patient strength or patient weakness. But none gave more, or gave more readily, than the common man or woman who had nothing but a precarious week's wages between them and poverty, and owned little more than the slender equipment of a cottage, and the garments in which they stood upright. Their love and pride of country, their loyalty to the symbols with which they were familiar, their keen sense of right and wrong as they saw it, led them to outface and endure perils and ordeals the like of which men had not known on earth.

In the year 1895 I had the privilege, as a young officer, of being invited to lunch with Sir William Harcourt. In the course of a conversation in which I took, I fear, none too modest a share, I asked the question, "What will happen then?" "My dear Winston," replied the old Victorian statesman, "the experiences of a long life have convinced me that nothing ever happens." Since that moment, as it seems to me, nothing has ever ceased happening. The growth of the great antagonisms abroad was accompanied by the progressive aggravation of party strife at home. The scale on which events have shaped themselves has dwarfed the episodes of the Victorian Era. Its small wars between great nations, its earnest disputes about superficial issues, the high, keen intellectualism of its personages, the sober, frugal, narrow limitations of their action, belong to a vanished period. The smooth river with its eddies and ripples along which we then sailed, seems inconceivably remote from the cataract down which we have been hurled and the rapids in whose turbulence we are now struggling.

I date the beginning of these violent times in our country from the Jameson Raid, in 1896. This was the herald, if not indeed the progenitor, of the South African War. From the South African War was born the Khaki Election, the Protectionist Movement, the Chinese Labour cry and the consequent furious reaction and Liberal triumph of 1906. From this sprang the violent inroads of the House of Lords upon popular government, which by the end of 1908 had reduced the immense Liberal majority to virtual impotence, from which condition they were rescued by the Lloyd George Budget in 1909. This measure became, in its turn, on both sides, the cause of still greater provocations, and its rejection by the Lords was a constitutional outrage and political blunder almost beyond compare. It led directly to the two General Elections of 1910, to the Parliament Act, and to the Irish struggle, in which our country was brought to the very threshold of civil war. Thus we see a succession of partisan actions continuing without intermission for nearly twenty years, each injury repeated with interest, each oscillation more violent, each risk more grave, until at last it seemed that the sabre itself must be invoked to cool the blood and the passions that were rife.

\*     \*     \*

As soon as I knew for certain that I was to go to the Admiralty I sent for Lord Fisher: he was abroad in sunshine. We had not seen each other since the dispute about the Naval Estimates of 1909. He conceived himself bound in loyalty to Mr. McKenna [Mr. Churchill succeeded Mr. McKenna at the Admiralty], but as soon as he learned that I had had nothing to do with the decision which had led to our changing offices, he hastened home. We passed three days together in the comfort of Reigate Priory.

I found Fisher a veritable volcano of knowledge and of inspiration; and as soon as he learnt what my main purpose was, he passed into a state of vehement eruption. It must indeed have been an agony to him to wait and idly watch from the calm Lake of Lucerne through the anxious weeks of the long-drawn Agadir crisis, with his life's work, his beloved Navy, liable at any moment to be put to the supreme test. Once he began, he could hardly stop. I plied him with questions, and he poured out ideas. It was always a joy to me to talk to him on these great matters, but most of all was he stimulating in all that related to the design of ships. He also talked brilliantly about Admirals, but here one had to make a heavy discount on account of the feuds. My intention was to hold the balance even, and while adopting in the main the Fisher policy, to insist upon an absolute cessation of the vendetta.

I began our conversations with no thought of Fisher's recall. But the power of the man was deeply borne in upon me, and I had almost made up my mind to do what I did three years later, and place him again at the head of the Naval Service. It was not the outcry that I feared; that I felt strong enough at this time to face. But it was the revival and continuance of the feuds; and it was clear from his temper that this would be inevitable. Then, too, I was apprehensive of his age. I could not feel complete confidence in the poise of the mind at seventy-one. All the way up to London the next morning I was on the brink of saying "Come and help me," and had he by a word seemed to wish to return, I would surely have spoken. But he maintained a proper dignity, and in an hour we were in London. Other reflections supervened, adverse counsels were not lacking, and in a few days I had definitely made up my mind to look elsewhere for a First Sea Lord.

I wonder whether I was right or wrong.

For a man who for so many years filled great official positions and was charged with so much secret and deadly business, Lord Fisher appeared amazingly voluminous and reckless in correspondence. When for the purpose of this work and for the satisfaction of his biographers I collected all the letters I had received from the Admiral in his own hand, they amounted when copied to upwards of three hundred closely typewritten pages. In the main they repeat again and again the principal naval conceptions and doctrines with which his life had been associated. Although it would be easy to show many inconsistencies and apparent contradictions, the general message is unchanging. The letters are also presented in an entertaining guise, interspersed with felicitous and sometimes recondite quotations, with flashing phrases and images, with mordant jokes and corrosive personalities. All were dashed off red-hot as they left his mind, his strong pen galloping along in the wake of the imperious thought. He would often audaciously fling out on paper thoughts which other people would hardly admit to their own minds. It is small wonder that his turbulent passage left so many foes foaming in his wake. The wonder is that he did not shipwreck himself a score of times. The buoyancy of his genius alone supported the burden. Indeed, in the process of years the profuse and imprudent violence of his letters became, in a sense, its own protection. People came to believe that this was the breezy style appropriate to our guardians of the deep, and the old Admiral swept forward on his stormy course.

To me, in this period of preparation, the arrival of his letters was always a source of lively interest and pleasure. I was regaled with eight or ten closely-written double pages, fastened together with a little pearl pin or a scrap of silken ribbon, and containing every kind of news and counsel, varying from blistering reproach to the highest forms of inspiration and encouragement. From the very beginning his letters were couched in an affectionate and paternal style. "My beloved Winston," they began, ending usually with a variation of "Yours to a cinder", "Yours till Hell freezes", or "Till charcoal sprouts", followed by a P.S. and two or three more pages of pregnant and brilliant matter. I have found it impossible to re-read these letters without sentiments of strong regard for him, his fiery soul, his volcanic energy, his deep creative mind, his fierce outspoken hatreds, his love of England. Alas, there was a day when Hell froze and charcoal sprouted and friendship was reduced to cinders; when "My beloved Winston" had given place to "First Lord: I can no longer be your colleague". I am glad to be able to chronicle that this was not the end of our long and intimate relationship.

Winston Churchill in 1904

Lord Balfour with Winston Churchill, 1915

A few weeks after my arrival at the Admiralty I was told that among several officers of Flag rank who wished to see me was Rear-Admiral Beatty. I had never met him before, but I had the following impressions about him. First, that he was the youngest Flag Officer in the Fleet. Second, that he had commanded the white gunboat which had come up the Nile as close as possible to support the 21st Lancers when we made the charge at Omdurman. Third, that he had seen a lot of fighting on land with the Army, and that consequently he had military as well as naval experience. Fourth, that he came of a hard-riding stock; his father had been in my own regiment, the 4th Hussars, and I had often heard him talked of when I first joined. The Admiral, I knew, was a very fine horseman, with what is called "an eye for country". Fifth, that there was much talk in naval circles of his having been pushed on too fast. Such were the impressions aroused in my mind by the name of this officer, and I record them with minuteness because the decisions which I had the honour of taking in regard to him were most serviceable to the Royal Navy and to the British arms.

I was, however, advised about him at the Admiralty in a decisively adverse sense. He had got on too fast, he had many interests ashore. His heart it was said was not wholly in the Service. He had been offered an appointment in the Atlantic Fleet suited to his rank as Rear-Admiral. He had declined this appointment—a very serious step for a naval officer to take when appointments were few in proportion to candidates—and he should in consequence not be offered any further employment. It would be contrary to precedent to make a further offer. He had already been unemployed for eighteen months, and would probably be retired in the ordinary course at the expiration of the full three years' unemployment.

My first meeting with the Admiral induced me immediately to disregard this unfortunate advice. He became at once my Naval Secretary (or Private Secretary, as the appointment was then styled). Working thus side by side in rooms which communicated, we perpetually discussed during the next fifteen months the problems of a naval war with Germany. It became increasingly clear to me that he viewed questions of naval strategy and tactics in a different light from the average naval officer: he approached them, as it seemed to me, much more as a soldier would. His war experiences on land had illuminated the facts he had acquired in his naval training. He was no mere instrumentalist. He did not think of *matériel* as an end in itself but only as a means. He thought of war problems in their unity by land, sea and air. His mind had been rendered quick and supple by the situations of polo and the hunting-field, and enriched by varied experiences against the enemy on Nile gunboats, and ashore. It was with equal pleasure and profit that I discussed with him our naval problem, now from this angle, now from that; and I was increasingly struck with the shrewd and profound sagacity of his comments expressed in language singularly free from technical jargon.

I had no doubts whatever when the command of the Battle-Cruiser Squadron fell vacant in the spring of 1913, in appointing him over the heads of all to this incomparable command, the nucleus as it proved to be of the famous Battle-Cruiser Fleet—the strategic cavalry of the Royal Navy, that supreme combination of speed and power to which the thoughts of the Admiralty were continuously directed. And when two years later (3 February, 1915) I visited him on board the *Lion*, with the scars of victorious battle fresh upon her from the action of the Dogger Bank, I heard from his Captains and his Admirals the expression of their respectful but intense enthusiasm for their leader. Well do I remember how, as I was leaving the ship, the usually imperturbable Admiral Pakenham caught me by the sleeve, "First Lord, I wish to speak to you in private," and the intense conviction in his voice as he said, "Nelson has come again." Those words often recurred to my mind.

We made a great assembly of the Navy in the spring of 1912 at Portland. The flags of a dozen admirals, the broad pennants of as many commodores and the pennants of a hundred and fifty ships were flying together. The King came in the Royal Yacht, the Admiralty flag at the fore, the Standard at the main, and the Jack at the mizzen, and bided among his sailors for four days. One day there is a long cruise out into the mist, dense, utterly baffling—the whole Fleet steaming together all invisible, keeping station by weird siren screamings and hootings. It seemed incredible that no harm would befall. And then suddenly the fog lifted and the distant targets could be distinguished and the whole long line of battleships, coming one after another into view, burst into tremendous flares of flame and hurled their shells with deafening detonations while the water rose in tall fountains. The Fleet returns—three battle squadrons abreast, cruisers and flotillas disposed ahead and astern. The speed is raised to twenty knots. Streaks of white foam appear at the bows of every vessel. The land draws near. The broad bay already embraces this swiftly moving gigantic armada. The ships in their formation already fill the bay. The foreign officers I have with me on the *Enchantress* bridge stare anxiously. We still steam fast. Five minutes more and the van of the Fleet will be aground. Four minutes, three minutes. There! At last. The signal! A string of bright flags is hauled down from the *Neptune's* halyards. Every anchor falls together; their cables roar through the hawser holes; every propeller whirls astern. In a hundred and fifty yards, it seems, every ship is stationary. Look along the lines, miles this way and miles that, they might have been drawn with a ruler. The foreign observers gasped.

These were great days. From dawn to midnight, day after day, one's whole mind was absorbed by the fascination and novelty of the problems which came crowding forward. And all the time there was a sense of power to act, to form, to organize: all the ablest officers in the Navy standing ready, loyal and eager, with argument, guidance, information; everyone feeling a sense that a great danger had passed very near us; that there was a breathing space before it would return; that we must be better prepared next time. Saturdays, Sundays and any other spare day I spent always with the Fleets at Portsmouth or at Portland or Devonport, or with the Flotillas at Harwich. Officers of every rank came on board to lunch or dine and discussion proceeded without ceasing on every aspect of naval war and administration.

The Admiralty yacht *Enchantress* was now to become largely my office, almost my home; and my work my sole occupation and amusement. In all, I spent eight months afloat in the three years before the war. I visited every dockyard, shipyard and naval establishment in the British Isles and in the Mediterranean and every important ship. I examined for myself every point of strategic consequence and every piece of Admiralty property. I got to know what everything looked like and where everything was, and how one thing fitted into another. In the end I could put my hand on anything that was wanted and knew thoroughly the current state of our naval affairs.

I recall vividly my first voyage from Portsmouth to Portland, where the Fleet lay. A grey afternoon was drawing to a close. As I saw the Fleet for the first time drawing out of the haze a friend reminded me of "that far-off line of storm-beaten ships on which the eyes of the grand Army had never looked", but which had in their day "stood between Napoleon and the dominion of the world". In Portland Harbour the yacht lay surrounded by the great ships; the whole harbour was alive with the goings and comings of launches and small craft of every kind, and as night fell ten thousand lights from sea and shore sprang into being and every masthead twinkled as the ships and squadrons conversed with one another. Who could fail to work for such a service? Who could fail when the very darkness seemed loaded with the menace of approaching war?

For consider these ships, so vast in themselves, yet so small, so easily lost to sight on the surface of the waters. Sufficient at the moment, we trusted, for their task, but yet only a score or so. They were all we had. On them, as we conceived, floated the might, majesty, dominion and power of the British Empire. All our long history built up century after century, all our great affairs in every part of the globe, all the means of livelihood and safety of our faithful, industrious, active population depended upon them. Open the sea-cocks and let them sink beneath the surface, as another Fleet was one day to do in another British harbour far to the North, and in a few minutes—half an hour at the most—the whole outlook of the world would be changed. The British Empire would dissolve like a dream; each isolated community struggling forward by itself; the central power of union broken; mighty provinces, whole Empires in themselves, drifting hopelessly out of control, and falling a prey to strangers; and Europe after one sudden convulsion passing into the iron grip and rule of the Teuton and of all that the Teutonic system meant. There would only be left far off across the Atlantic unarmed, unready, and as yet uninstructed America, to maintain, single-handed, law and freedom among men.

Guard them well, admirals and captains, hardy tars and tall marines; guard them well and guide them true.

At the end of June [1914] the simultaneous British naval visits to Kronstadt and Kiel took place. For the first time for several years some of the finest ships of the British and German Navies lay at their moorings at Kiel side by side surrounded by liners, yachts and pleasure craft of every kind. Undue curiosity in technical matters was banned by mutual agreement. There were races, there were banquets, there were speeches. There was sunshine, there was the Emperor. Officers and men fraternized and entertained each other afloat and ashore. Together they strolled arm in arm through the hospitable town, or dined with all goodwill in mess and wardroom. Together they stood bareheaded at the funeral of a German officer killed in flying an English seaplane.

In the midst of these festivities, on 28 June, arrived the news of the murder of the Archduke Charles at Sarajevo. The Emperor was out sailing when he received it. He came on shore in noticeable agitation, and that same evening, cancelling his other arrangements, quitted Kiel.

Like many others, I often summon up in my memory the impression of those July days. The world on the verge of its catastrophe was very brilliant. Nations and Empires crowned with princes and potentates rose majestically on every side, lapped in the accumulated treasures of the long peace. All were fitted and fastened—it seemed securely—into an immense cantilever. The two mighty European systems faced each other glittering and clanking in their panoply, but with a tranquil gaze. A polite, discreet, pacific, and on the whole sincere diplomacy spread its web of connections over both. A sentence in a despatch, an observation by an ambassador, a cryptic phrase in a Parliament seemed sufficient to adjust from day to day the balance of the prodigious structure. Words counted, and even whispers. A nod could be made to tell. Were we after all to achieve world security and universal peace by a marvellous system of combinations in equipoise and of armaments in equation, of checks and counter-checks on violent action ever more complex and more delicate? Would Europe thus marshalled, thus grouped, thus related, unite into one universal and glorious organism capable of receiving and enjoying in undreamed-of abundance the bounty which nature and science stood hand in hand to give? The old world in its sunset was fair to see.

But there was a strange temper in the air. Unsatisfied by material prosperity the nations turned restlessly towards strife internal or external. National passions, unduly exalted in the decline of religion, burned beneath the surface of nearly every land with fierce, if shrouded, fires. Almost one might think the world wished to suffer. Certainly men were everywhere eager to dare. On all sides the military preparations, precautions and counter-precautions had reached their height. France had her Three Years' military service; Russia her growing strategic railways. The Ancient Empire of the Hapsburgs, newly smitten by the bombs of Sarajevo, was a prey to intolerable racial stresses and profound processes of decay. Italy faced Turkey; Turkey confronted Greece; Greece, Serbia and Roumania stood against Bulgaria. Britain was rent by faction and seemed almost negligible. America was three thousand miles away. Germany, her fifty million capital tax expended on munitions, her army increases completed, the Kiel Canal open for Dreadnought battleships that very month, looked fixedly upon the scene and her gaze became suddenly a glare.

Our *Entente* with France and the military and naval conversations that had taken place since 1906 had led us into a position where we had the obligations of an alliance without its advantages. An open alliance, if it could have been peacefully brought about at an earlier date, would have exercised a deterring effect upon the German mind, or at the least would have altered their military calculations. Whereas now we were morally bound to come to the aid of France and it was our interest to do so, and yet the fact that we should come in appeared so uncertain that it did not weigh as it should have done with the Germans. Moreover, as things were, if France had been in an aggressive mood, we should not have had the unquestioned right of an ally to influence her action in a pacific sense: and if as the result of her aggressive mood war had broken out and we had stood aside, we should have been accused of deserting her, and in any case would have been ourselves grievously endangered by her defeat.

However, in the event there was no need to moderate the French attitude. Justice to France requires the explicit statement that the conduct of her government at this awful juncture was faultless. She assented instantly to every proposal that could make for peace. She abstained from every form of provocative action. She even compromised her own safety, holding back her covering troops at a considerable distance behind her frontier, and delaying her mobilization in the face of continually gathering German forces till the latest moment. Not until she was confronted with the direct demand of Germany to break her Treaty and abandon Russia, did France take up the challenge; and even had she acceded to the German demand, she would only, as we now know, have been faced with a further ultimatum to surrender to German military occupation as a guarantee for her neutrality the fortresses of Toul and Verdun. Thus there never was any chance of France being allowed to escape the ordeal. Even cowardice and dishonour would not have saved her. The Germans had resolved that if war came from any cause, they would take and break France forthwith as its first operation. The German military chiefs burned to give the signal, and were sure of the result. She would have begged for mercy in vain. She did not beg.

The more I reflect upon this situation, the more convinced I am that we took the only practical course that was open to us or to any British Cabinet; and that the objections which may be urged against it were less than those which would have attended any other sequence of action.

★   ★   ★

On Saturday evening [31 July] I dined alone at the Admiralty. The foreign telegrams came in at short intervals in red boxes which already bore the special label "Sub-Committee", denoting the precautionary period. The flow was quite continuous, and the impression produced on my mind after reading for nearly an hour was that there was still a chance of peace. Austria had accepted the conference, and intimate personal appeals were passing between the Tsar and the Kaiser. It seemed to me, from the order in which I read the series of telegrams, that at the very last moment Sir Edward Grey might succeed in saving the situation. So far no shot had been fired between the Great Powers. I wondered whether armies and fleets could remain mobilized for a space without fighting and then demobilize.

I had hardly achieved this thought when another Foreign Office box came in. I opened it and read "Germany has declared war on Russia". There was no more to be said. I walked across the Horse Guards Parade and entered 10 Downing Street, by the garden gate. I found the Prime Minister upstairs in his drawing-room: with him were Sir Edward Grey, Lord Haldane and Lord Crewe; there may have been other Ministers. I said that I intended instantly to mobilize the Fleet notwithstanding the Cabinet decision, and that I would take full personal responsibility to the Cabinet the next morning. The Prime Minister, who felt himself bound to the Cabinet, said not a single word, but I was clear from his look that he was quite content. As I walked down the steps of Downing Street with Sir Edward Grey, he said to me, "You should know I have just done a very important thing. I have told Cambon that we shall not allow the German fleet to come into the Channel." I went back to the Admiralty and gave forthwith the order to mobilize. We had no legal authority for calling up the Naval Reserves, as no proclamation had been submitted to His Majesty in view of the Cabinet decision, but we were quite sure that the Fleet men would unquestioningly obey the summons. This action was ratified by the Cabinet on Sunday morning, and the Royal Proclamation was issued some hours later.

All through the tense discussions of the Cabinet one had in mind another greater debate which must begin when these were concluded. Parliament, the nation, the Dominions, would have to be convinced. That the cause was good, that the argument was overwhelming, that the response would be worthy, I did not for a moment doubt. But it seemed that an enormous political task awaited us, and I saw in the mind's eye not only the crowded House of Commons, but formidable assemblies of the people throughout the land requiring full and swift justification of the flaming action taken in their name. But such cares were soon dispersed. When the Council doors had opened and ministers had come into the outer air, the British nation was already surging forward in its ancient valour, and the Empire had sprung to arms.

\*　　\*　　\*

Now, after all the stress and convulsion, there came to us at the

Admiralty a strange interlude of calm. All the decisions had been taken. The ultimatum to Germany had gone: it must certainly be rejected. War would be declared at midnight. As far as we had been able to foresee the event, all our preparations were made. Mobilization was complete. Every ship was in its station: every man at his post. All over the world, every British captain and admiral was on guard. It only remained to give the signal. What would happen then? It seemed that the next move lay with the enemy. What would he do? Had he some deadly surprise in store? Some awful design, long planned and perfected, ready to explode upon us at any moment NOW? Would our ships in foreign waters have been able to mark down their German antagonists? If so, morning would witness half a dozen cruiser actions in the outer seas. Telegrams flowed in from the different naval stations round our coasts reporting the movements of vessels and rumours of sighting of enemies. Telegrams still flowed in from the Chancelleries of Europe as the last futile appeals of reason were overtaken by the cannonade. In the War Room of the Admiralty, where I sat waiting, one could hear the clock tick. From Parliament Street came the murmurs of the crowd; but they sounded distant and the world seemed very still. The tumult of the struggle for life was over: it was succeeded by the silence of ruin and death. We were to awake in Pandemonium.

I had the odd sense that it was like waiting for an election result. The turmoil of the contest seemed finished: the votes were being counted, and in a few hours the announcement would be made. One could only wait; but for what a result! Although the special duties of my office made it imperative that I, of all others, should be vigilant and forward in all that related to preparation for war, I claim that in my subordinate station I had in these years before the war done nothing wittingly or willingly to impair the chances of a peaceable solution, and had tried my best as opportunity offered to make good relations possible between England and Germany. I thank God I could feel also in that hour that our country was guiltless of all intended purpose of war. Even if we had made some mistakes in the handling of this awful crisis, though I do not know them, from the bottom of our hearts we could say that we had not willed it. Germany it seemed had rushed with head down and

THE FIRST WORLD WAR

settled resolve to her own undoing. And if this were what she had meant all along, if this was the danger which had really menaced us hour by hour during the last ten years, and would have hung over us hour by hour until the crash eventually came, was it not better that it should happen now: now that she had put herself so hopelessly in the wrong, now that we were ready beyond the reach of surprise, now that France and Russia and Great Britain were all in the line together?

The First Sea Lord and the Chief of the Staff came in with French Admirals who had hurried over to concert in detail arrangements for the co-operation of the two Fleets in the Channel and in the Mediterranean. They were fine figures in uniform, and very grave. One felt in actual contact with these French officers how truly the crisis was life or death for France. They spoke of basing the French Fleet on Malta—that same Malta for which we had fought Napoleon for so many years, which was indeed the very pretext of the renewal of the war in 1803. Little did the Napoleon of St. Helena dream that in her most desperate need France would have at her disposal the great Mediterranean base which his strategic instinct had deemed vital. I said to the Admirals, "Use Malta as if it were Toulon."

The minutes passed slowly.

Once more now in the march of centuries Old England was to stand forth in battle against the mightiest thrones and dominations. Once more in defence of the liberties of Europe and the common right must she enter upon a voyage of great toil and hazard across waters uncharted, towards coasts unknown, guided only by the stars. Once more the "far-off line of storm-beaten ships" was to stand between the Continental Tyrant and the dominion of the world.

It was 11 o'clock at night—12 by German time—when the ultimatum expired. The windows of the Admiralty were thrown wide open in the warm night air. Under the roof from which Nelson had received his orders were gathered a small group of Admirals and Captains and a cluster of clerks, pencil in hand, waiting. Along the Mall from the direction of the Palace the sound of an immense concourse singing "God Save the King" floated in. On this deep wave there broke the chimes of Big Ben; and, as the first stroke of the hour boomed out, a rustle of movement swept across the room.

The war telegram, which meant "Commence hostilities against Germany", was flashed to the ships and establishments under the White Ensign all over the world.

I walked across the Horse Guards Parade to the Cabinet room and reported to the Prime Minister and the Ministers who were assembled there that the deed was done.

★     ★     ★

Since 1 August the armies of Europe had been mobilizing. Millions of men pouring along the roads and railroads, flowing across the Rhine bridges, entraining from the farthest provinces of the Russian Empire, streaming northwards from Southern France and Northern Africa, were forming in immense masses of manoeuvre or in the line of battle. Yet the silence at sea was accompanied by suspense on land. There was a long stifling pause before the breaking of the storm. The combatants were taking up their stations with every precaution and strictest secrecy; and apart from the splutters of cannon fire at Liége and Belgrade—in the little countries first to be attacked—and unrecorded frontier bickering, there reigned over Europe for the first fortnight of Armageddon a strange, dull hush.

The opening was not only the first, but incomparably the greatest, crisis of the war. From 18 August to the middle of September all the best-trained troops of the seven warring states were continuously hurled against one another in open warfare with ample ammunition and in all the ardour of warlike inexperience arising from what, for most, had been a generation of peace. In this awful month more divisions fought on more days, and more men were killed and wounded than in any whole year of the struggle. There were in fact two crises—one in the West and one in the East—each surpassing in scale and intensity anything subsequently endured, and each reacting reciprocally upon the other.

There had arisen for Germany the long foreseen and profoundly studied case of the War on Two Fronts. For this she had prepared the Schlieffen plan. The main German effort was directed against France. More than seven-eighths of the German armies was employed in the West. Out of forty German Army Corps less than five were left to defend the eastern provinces of Germany against the onslaught of the Russian Empire. The Schlieffen plan staked everything upon the invasion of France and the destruction of the French armies by means of an enormous turning march through Belgium. In order to strengthen this movement by every means, General von Schlieffen was resolved to run all risks and make all sacrifices in every other quarter. He was prepared to let the Austrians bear the brunt of the Russian attack from the east, and to let all East Prussia be overrun by the Russian armies, even if need be to the Vistula. He was ready to have Alsace and Lorraine successfully invaded by the French. The violation and trampling down of Belgium, even if it forced England to declare war, was to him only a corollary of his main theme. In his conception nothing could resist the advance of Germany from the north into the heart of France, and the consequent destruction of the French armies, together with the incidental capture of Paris and the final total defeat of France within six weeks. Nothing, as he saw it, would happen anywhere else in those six weeks to prevent this supreme event from dominating the problem and ending the war in victory.

No one can say that the Schlieffen plan was wrong. However, Schlieffen was dead. His successors on the German General Staff applied his plan faithfully, resolutely, solidly—but with certain reservations enjoined by prudence. These reservations were fatal. Moltke, the nephew of the great Commander, assigned 20 per cent more troops to the defence of the German western frontier and 20 per cent less troops to the invasion of northern France than Schlieffen had prescribed. Confronted with the Russian invasion of East Prussia he still further weakened the Great Right Wheel into France. Thus as will be seen the Schlieffen plan applied at four-fifths of its intensity just failed, and we survive.

At 7 o'clock on the morning of 24 August I was sitting up in bed in Admiralty House working at my boxes, when the door of my bedroom opened and Lord Kitchener appeared. These were the days before he took to uniform, and my recollection is that he had a bowler hat on his head, which he took off with a hand which also held a slip of paper. He paused in the doorway and I knew in a flash and before ever he spoke that the event had gone wrong. Though his manner was quite calm, his face was different. I had the subconscious feeling that it was distorted and discoloured as if it had been punched with a fist. His eyes rolled more than ever. His voice, too, was hoarse. He looked gigantic. "Bad news," he said heavily and laid the slip of paper on my bed. I read the telegram. It was from Sir John French.

["My troops have been engaged all day with the enemy on a line roughly east and west through Mons. The attack was renewed after dark, but we held our ground tenaciously. I have just received a message from G.O.C. Fifth French Army that his troops have been driven back, that Namur has fallen, and that he is taking up a line from Maubeuge to Rocroi. I have therefore ordered a retirement to the line Valenciennes-Longueville-Maubeuge, which is being carried out now. It will prove a difficult operation, if the enemy remains in contact. I remember your precise instructions as to method and direction of retirement if necessity arises.

"I think that immediate attention should be directed to the defence of Havre."]

I did not mind it much till I got to Namur. Namur fallen! Namur taken in a single day—although a French brigade had joined the Belgians in its defence. We were evidently in the presence of new facts and of a new standard of values. If strong fortresses were to melt like wisps of vapour in a morning sun, many judgments would have to be revised. The foundations of thought were quaking. As for the strategic position, it was clear that the encircling arm was not going to be hacked off at the shoulder, but would close in a crushing grip. Where would it stop? What of the naked Channel ports? Dunkirk, Calais, Boulogne! "Fortify Havre," said Sir John French. One day's general battle and the sanguine advance and hoped-for counterstroke had been converted into "Fortify Havre". "It will be difficult to withdraw the troops if the enemy remains in contact"—a disquieting observation. I forget much of what passed between us. But the apparition of Kitchener *Agonistes* in my doorway will dwell with me as long as I live. It was like seeing old John Bull on the rack!

★     ★     ★

One must suppose upon the whole that the Marne was the greatest battle ever fought in the world. The elemental forces which there met in grapple and collision of course far exceeded anything that has ever happened. It is also true that the Marne decided the World War. Half a dozen other cardinal crises have left their gaunt monuments along the road of tribulation which the nations trod; and it may well be argued that any of these might in part at least have reversed the decision of the Marne. The Allies might have been beaten on other occasions, and Germany might have emerged from the World War upon a victorious peace. If in 1917 the French Army had succumbed, if the British Navy had not strangled the submarine, if the United States had not entered the war, students of today and tomorrow would bend over different history books and different maps. But never after the Marne had Germany a chance of absolute triumph. Never again was there the possibility of all the claims of their proud militarism receiving complete vindication. Never again could the domination of scientific force have achieved its lasting establishment. Deep changes took place in the world and among warring powers in the terrible years that followed. The nations fought desperately, but they fought in a different atmosphere and on a lower plane. The carnage and the cannonade increased; but never were the moral or the military issues at the same pitch of intensity. By the end of 1915 England was a great warlike power, and the whole British Empire was roused and marshalling its strength. By the end of 1916 Germany was deeply conscious of her weakness. In 1917 the United States had been drawn into the conflict. It is obvious that the British Empire and the United States could in the long run have crushed Germany, even if France had been completely subjugated. But the battle of the Marne might have ended the war in six weeks; and the Kaiser and his twenty kinglets and their feudal aristocracy might have founded for many generations the legend of invincible military force.

We must remember that on 3 September the Emperor William II and the German General Staff knew that they were victorious in the East and had every reason to believe that within a week they would capture or destroy all the armies that withstood them in the West. On the 10th, according to wide report, Moltke informed his master with rugged truth that "Germany had lost the war". Evidently an immense transformation took place. Something of enormous and mysterious potency had worked its will, and the question which will puzzle posterity as much as it astonished those who lived through the deluge, is—what?

At the time nobody worried about the causes. Everyone facing the new perils of the hour or the week, was concerned only with the result. The German invasion of France was stopped. The obsession of German invincibility was dispersed. There would be time for all the world to go to war—time even for the most peaceful and unprepared countries to turn themselves into arsenals and barracks. Surely that was enough. All bent their backs or their heads to the toil of war; and in the instructed circles of the allies none, and in those of the Germans few, doubted which way the final issue would go. Never again need we contemplate the entire surrender of the French Army before any other armies were afoot to take its place. At the very worst there would be parley, negotiation, barter, compromise, and a haggled peace.

I do not remember any period when the weight of the war seemed to press more heavily on me than these months of October and November, 1914. In August one was expecting the great sea battle and the first great battles on land; but our course was obvious, and, when taken, we had only to wait for decisions. All September was dominated by the victory of the Marne. But in October and November the beast was at us again. The sense of grappling with and being overpowered by a monster of appalling and apparently inexhaustible strength on land, and a whole array of constant, gnawing anxieties about the safety of the Fleet from submarine attack at sea and in its harbours, oppressed my mind. Not an hour passed without the possibility of some disaster or other in some part of the world. Not a day without the necessity of running risks.

My own position was already to some extent impaired. The loss of three cruisers had been freely attributed to my personal interference. I was accused of having overridden the advice of the Sea Lords and of having wantonly sent the squadron to its doom. Antwerp became a cause of fierce reproach. One might almost have thought I had brought about the fall of the city [Antwerp] by my meddling. The employment of such untrained men as the Naval Brigades was generally censured. The internment in Holland of three of their battalions was spoken of as a great disaster entirely due to my inexcusable folly. One unhappy phrase—true enough in thought, and indeed in the event—about "Digging rats out of holes", which had slipped from my tongue in a weary speech at Liverpool, was fastened upon and pilloried. These were the only subjects with which my name was connected in the newspapers. My work at the Admiralty—such as it was—was hidden from the public. No Parliamentary attack gave me an opportunity of defending myself. In spite of being accustomed to years of abuse, I could not but feel the adverse and hostile currents that flowed about me. One began to perceive that they might easily lead to a practical result. Luckily there was not much time for such reflections.

The Admiralty had entered upon the war with commanding claims on public confidence. The coincidence of the test mobilization with the European crisis was generally attributed to profound design. The falsification one after another of the gloomy predictions that we should be taken unawares, that the German commerce destroyers would scour the seas, and that our own shipping, trade and food would be endangered, was recognized with widespread relief. The safe transportation of the Army to France and the successful action in the Heligoland Bight were acclaimed as fine achievements. But with the first few incidents of misfortune a different note prevailed in circles which were vocal. The loss of the three cruisers marked a turning point in the attitude of those who in the evil times of war are able to monopolize the expression of public opinion. As the expectation of an imminent great sea battle faded, the complaint began to be heard, "What is the Navy doing?" It was perhaps inevitable that there should be a sense of disappointment as week succeeded week and the tremendous engine of British naval power seemed to be neither seen nor heard. There was a general opinion that we should have begun by attacking and destroying the German Fleet. Vain to point to the ceaseless stream of troops and supplies to France, or to the world-wide trade of Britain proceeding almost without hindrance. Impossible, in the hearing of the enemy, to explain the intricate movement of reinforcements or expeditions escorted across every ocean from every part of the Empire, or to unfold the reasons which rendered it impossible to bring the German Fleet to battle. There was our little Army fighting for its life, and playing to British eyes almost as large a part as all the armies of France; and meanwhile our great Navy—the strongest in the world—lay apparently in an inertia diversified only by occasional mishap.

Eaten bread is soon forgotten. Dangers which are warded off by effective precautions and foresight are never even remembered. Thus it happened that the Admiralty was inconsiderately judged in this opening phase. To me, who saw the perils against which we had prepared and over which we had triumphed, and who felt a sense of profound thankfulness for the past and absolute confidence for the future, these manifestations of discontent seemed due only to lack of understanding and to impatience pardonable in the general stress of the times. But they were none the less disquieting. Nor was it easy to deal with them. The questions could not be argued out in public or in Parliament. No formal indictment was ever preferred; nor could one have been fully answered without injury to national interests. We had to endure all this carping in silence. A certain proportion of losses at sea was inevitable month by month; and in each case it was easy to assert that someone had blundered. In most cases indeed this was true. With a thousand ships upon the sea and a thousand hazards, real or potential, every day to menace them, accidents and mistakes were bound to happen. How many were made for which no forfeit was claimed by Fortune! There was never an hour when risks against which no provision could be made were not being run by scores of vessels, or when problems of novelty and difficulty were not being set to sea captains, scarcely any of whom had ever been tried in war. Was it wonderful that we fell occasionally into error, or even into loss? "Another naval disaster. Five hundred men drowned. What are the Admiralty doing?" While all the time the armies reeled about in the confusion of the mighty battles, and scores of thousands were sent, often needlessly or mistakenly, to their deaths: while all the time every British operation of war and trade on the seas proceeded without appreciable hindrance.

*　　*　　*

Lord Fisher used to come occasionally to the Admiralty, and I watched him narrowly to judge his physical strength and mental alertness. There seemed no doubt about either. On one occasion, when inveighing against someone whom he thought obstructive, he became so convulsed with fury that it seemed that every nerve and blood-vessel in his body would be ruptured. However, they stood the strain magnificently, and he left me with the impression of a terrific engine of mental and physical power burning and throbbing in that aged frame. I was never in the least afraid of working with him, and I thought I knew him so well, and had held an equal relationship and superior constitutional authority so long, that we could come through any difficulty together. I therefore sounded him in conversation without committing myself, and soon saw that he was fiercely eager to lay his grasp on power, and was strongly inspired with the sense of a message to deliver and a mission to perform. I therefore determined to act without delay. I sought the Prime Minister and submitted to him the arguments which led me to the conclusion that Fisher should return, and that I could work with no one else. I also spoke of Sir Arthur Wilson as his principal coadjutor. I was well aware that there would be strong, natural and legitimate, opposition in many quarters to Fisher's appointment, but having formed my own conviction I was determined not to remain at the Admiralty unless I could do justice to it. So in the end, for good or for ill, I had my way.

The decision to recall Lord Fisher to the Admiralty was very important. He was, as has been here contended, the most distinguished British naval officer since Nelson. The originality of his mind and the spontaneity of his nature freed him from conventionalities of all kinds. His genius was deep and true. Above all, he was in harmony with the vast size of events. Like them, he was built upon a titanic scale.

Lord Fisher's age and the great strain to which he was now to be subjected made it necessary for him to lead a very careful life. He usually retired to rest shortly after 8 o'clock, awaking refreshed between four and five, or even earlier. In these morning hours he gave his greatest effort, transacting an immense quantity of business, writing innumerable letters and forming his resolutions for the day. Indeed, his methods corresponded closely to the maxims of the poet Blake: "Think in the morning; act in the noon; eat in the evening; sleep in the night." But I never heard him use this quotation.

As the afternoon approached the formidable energy of the morning gradually declined, and with the shades of night the old Admiral's giant strength was often visibly exhausted. Still, judged from the point of view of physical and mental vigour alone, it was a wonderful effort, and one which filled me, who watched him so closely, with admiration and, I will add, reassurance.

I altered my routine somewhat to fit in with that of the First Sea Lord. I slept usually an hour later in the morning, being called at eight instead of seven, and I slept again, if possible, for an hour after luncheon. This enabled me to work continuously till one or two in the morning without feeling in any way fatigued. We thus constituted an almost unsleeping watch throughout the day and night. In fact, as Fisher put it, "very nearly a perpetual clock". Telegrams came in at the Admiralty at all hours of the day and night, and there was scarcely an hour when an immediate decision could not be given, if necessary, by one or the other of us always awake.

This arrangement was also convenient from the point of view of business. The First Lord completed everything with which he was concerned before going to bed, and three hours later the First Sea Lord addressed himself to the whole budget, and I, awaking at eight, received his dawn output. I had not previously seen the pulse of the Admiralty beat so strong and regular.

We made the agreement between ourselves that neither of us should take any important action without consulting the other, unless previous accord had been reached. To this agreement we both scrupulously adhered. We had thus formed, for the first time, an overwhelmingly strong control and central authority over the whole course of the naval war, and were in a position to make our will prevail throughout the fleets and all branches of the naval administration, as well as to hold our own against all outside interference. I had for a long time been accustomed to write my minutes in red ink. Fisher habitually used a green pencil. To quote his words, "it was the port and starboard lights". As long as the port and starboard lights shone together, all went well. We had established a combination which, while it remained unbroken, could not have been overthrown by intrigue at home or the foe on the sea.

German naval chroniclers are accustomed to dwell in biting terms upon the failure of the British Fleet to attack them at the beginning of the war. They describe the martial ardour which inspired the German Navy, and their constant and instant expectation of battle. Admiral Scheer relates how as early as 2 August, 1914, his colleague commanding the 1st German Squadron urged him to come through the Kiel Canal that very night to join the rest of the Fleet at Wilhelmshaven lest if he waited till daylight he should be too late. He describes the feverish energy with which every scrap of woodwork and paint was stripped from the interiors of German ships the better to prepare them for action. He professes astonishment, not unmingled with derision, that the British disappointed his hope. Considering that the German Fleet remained for the first four months of the war absolutely motionless in its strongly fortified river mouths and harbours protected by its minefields and its submarines, this attitude of mind on the part of a skilful sailor appears to be somewhat forced.

If the Germans really believed that the Grand Fleet would be sent through their minefields to give them battle in their war harbours, they must have rated our intelligence very low. Such a course could only have cast away the British Fleet and achieved our ruin in a few hours. Nor would empty demonstrations off Heligoland, Sylt or Borkum have achieved any useful object. Both Scheer and Tirpitz write as if we had only to appear off these islands to compel the German High Sea Fleet to put to sea for the decisive battle. Yet at the same time we are told that the orders to the German Navy were not to fight a general battle until the British Fleet had been worn down by minor losses to a condition of equality. Why then should the Germans come out and fight a battle at heavy odds because British warships were exchanging shells with the batteries on the German islands? A much more sensible course for the Germans would be to send submarines by day and destroyers by night to torpedo the demonstrators and to sow the area with mines in case they should return. In this way the German equalization policy would have had a very good chance; and one can believe that such action by the British Fleet would have been very agreeable to German wishes. What more, indeed, could they want than that the British Fleet should be swiftly worn down in patrolling boastfully and idiotically outside the German harbours?

We also were anxious for a battle; but not a fool's battle, or even an equal battle. It was our duty to take the fullest advantage of our superiority, and to fight only under conditions which gave solid assurances of victory. Moreover, while the Germans lay in harbour we had secured and were enjoying the full command of the sea. On the outbreak of war the British Fleet, from its war station at Scapa Flow, cut Germany off from the rest of the world. This was in itself an offensive act of prime intensity. It was for the Germans to prevent it if they dared and if they could. We had to convoy our Army to France and collect our forces from all parts of the British Empire. These armies were being sent to the decisive battle front on land. To hinder this transportation was surely a highly important strategic object for Germany and her Navy. If the British Army could have been prevented from reaching its station on the French left, who shall say whether the war might not have ended at the Battle of the Marne? Yet the German Navy, with the formal and explicit assent of the German General Staff, remained inert, impassive behind its minefields and fortifications, while the whole business of the world and of the war proceeded under British authority on the high seas.

★   ★   ★

The German grip was strengthening every day on Turkey. The distresses of her peoples and the improvement of her military organization were advancing together. Under the guns of the *Goeben* and *Breslau*, doubt, division and scarcity dwelt in Constantinople. Outside the Straits the British Squadron maintained its silent watch. Greece, perplexed at the attitude of Britain, distracted by the quarrels of Venizelos and King Constantine, had fallen far from the high resolve of August. Serbia stoutly contended with the Austrian armies. Roumania and Bulgaria brooded on the past and watched each other with intense regard. In Egypt the training of the Australian and New Zealand Army Corps perfected itself week by week.

Thus, as this act in the stupendous world drama comes to its close, we see already the scene being set and the actors assembling for the next. From the uttermost ends of the earth ships and soldiers are approaching or gathering in the Eastern Mediterranean in fulfilment of a destiny as yet not understood by mortal man. The clearance of the Germans from the oceans liberated the Fleets, the arrival of the Anzacs in Egypt created the nucleus of the Army needed to attack the heart of the Turkish Empire. The deadlock on the Western Front, where all was now frozen into winter trenches, afforded at once a breathing space and large possibility of further troops. While Australian battalions trampled the crisp sand of the Egyptian desert in tireless evolutions, and Commander Holbrook in his valiant submarine dived under the minefields of Chanak and sank a Turkish transport in the throat of the Dardanelles, far away in the basins of Portsmouth the dockyard men were toiling night and day to mount the fifteen-inch guns and turrets of the *Queen Elizabeth*. As yet all was unconscious, inchoate, purposeless, uncombined. Any one of a score of chances might have given, might still give, an entirely different direction to the event. No plan has been made, no resolve taken. But new ideas are astir, new possibilities are coming into view, new forces are at hand, and with them there marches towards us a new peril of the first magnitude. Russia, mighty steam-roller, hope of suffering France and prostrate Belgium—Russia is failing. Her armies are grappling with Hindenburg and Ludendorff, and behind their brave battle fronts already the awful signs of weakness, of deficiency, of disorganization, are apparent to anxious Cabinets and Councils. Winter has come and locked all Russia in its grip. No contact with her Allies, no help from them, is possible. The ice blocks the White Sea. The Germans hold the Baltic. The Turks have barred the Dardanelles. It needs but a cry from Russia for help, to make vital what is now void, and to make purposeful what is now meaningless. But as yet no cry has come.

\*      \*      \*

It may be claimed that during these months we met every single call that was made upon us, guarded every sea, carried every expedition, brought every convoy safely in, discharged all our obligations both to the Army in France and to the Belgians, and all the time maintained such a disposition of our main forces that we should never have declined battle had the enemy ventured to offer it.

Then suddenly all over the world the tension was relaxed. One after another the German cruisers and commerce destroyers were blocked in or hunted down. The great convoys arrived. The Expeditions were safely landed. Ocean after ocean became clear. The boom defences of our harbours were completed. A score of measures for coping with the submarine were set on foot. Large reinforcements of new ships of the highest quality and of every class began to join the Fleet. The attack on the Suez Canal was stemmed. The rebellion in South Africa was quelled. The dangers of invasion, if such there were, diminished every day with the increasing efficiency of the Territorials and the New Armies. The great battle for the Channel ports ended in decisive and ever glorious victory. And finally with the Battle of the Falkland Islands the clearance of the oceans was complete, and soon, except in the land-locked Baltic and Black Seas and in the defended area of the Heligoland Bight, the German flag had ceased to fly on any vessel in any quarter of the world. [The *Dresden* and two armed merchant cruisers were alive for a few weeks more, but in complete inactivity.]

As December passed, a sense of indescribable relief stole over the Admiralty. We had made the great transition from peace to war without disaster, almost without mishap. All the perils which had haunted us before the war, and against which we had prepared, had been warded off or surmounted or had never come to pass. There had been no surprise. The Fleet was ready. The Army had reached the decisive battlefield in time and was satisfactorily maintained. The mine danger had been overcome. We thought we had the measure of the submarine, and so indeed we had for nearly two years to come. All the enemy's plans for commerce destruction and all our alarms about them had come to nought. British and allied commerce proceeded without hesitation throughout the world; the trade and food of Britain were secured; the war insurance dropped to one per cent. A feeling of profound thankfulness filled our hearts as this first Christmas of the war approached; and of absolute confidence in final victory.

The mighty enemy, with all the advantages of preparation and design, had delivered his onslaught and had everywhere been brought to a standstill. It was our turn now. The initiative had passed to Britain—the Great Amphibian. The time and the means were at our command. It was for us to say where we would strike and when. The strength of the Grand Fleet was, as we believed, ample; and in addition the whole of those numerous squadrons which hitherto had been spread over the outer seas now formed a surplus fleet capable of intervening in the supreme struggle without in any way compromising the foundation of our naval power.

But these realizations were only permissible as the prelude to fresh and still more intense exertions. It would indeed be shameful, so it seemed at least to me, for the Admiralty to rest contented with the accomplishment of the first and most hazardous stage of its task and to relax into a supine contemplation of regained securities and dangers overcome. Now was the time to make our weight tell, perhaps decisively, but certainly most heavily, in the struggle of the armies. Now was the time to fasten an offensive upon the Germans, unexpected and unforeseeable, to present them with a succession of surprising situations leading on from crisis to crisis and from blow to blow till their downfall was achieved.

Moreover, these same Germans were, of all the enemies in the world, the most to be dreaded when pursuing their own plans; the most easily disconcerted when forced to conform to the plans of their antagonist. To leave a German leisure to evolve his vast, patient, accurate designs, to make his slow, thorough, infinitely far-seeing preparations, was to court a terrible danger. To throw him out of his stride, to baffle his studious mind, to break his self-confidence, to cow his spirit, to rupture his schemes by unexpected action, was surely the path not only of glory but of prudence.

Here then ends the first phase of the naval war. The first part of the British task is done both by land and sea. Paris and the Channel ports are saved, and the oceans are cleared. It is certain that the whole strength of the British Empire can be turned into war power and brought to bear upon the enemy. There is no chance of France being struck down, before the British Empire is ready; there is no chance of the British Empire itself being paralysed, before its full force can be applied to the struggle. The supreme initiative passes from the Teutonic Powers to the Allies. Resources, almost measureless and of indescribable variety in ships, in men, in munitions and devices of war, will now flow month by month steadily into our hands. What shall we do with them? Strategic alternatives on the greatest scale and of the highest order present themselves to our choice. Which shall we choose? Shall we use our reinforced fleets and great new armies of 1915, either to turn the Teutonic right in the Baltic or their left in the Black Sea and the Balkans? Or shall we hurl our manhood against sandbags, wire and concrete in frontal attack upon the German fortified lines in France? Shall we by a supreme effort make direct contact with our Russian ally or leave her in a dangerous isolation? Shall we by decisive action, in hopes of shortening the conflict, marshal and draw in the small nations in the North and in the South who now stand outside it? Or shall we plod steadily forward at what lies immediately in our front? Shall our armies toil only in the mud of Flanders, or shall we break new ground? Shall our fleets remain contented with the grand and solid results they have won, or shall they ward off future perils by a new inexhaustible audacity?

★ ★ ★

The year 1915 was fated to be disastrous to the cause of the Allies and to the whole world. By the mistakes of this year the opportunity was lost of confining the conflagration within limits which though enormous were not uncontrolled. Thereafter the fire roared on till it burnt itself out. Thereafter events passed very largely outside the scope of conscious choice. Governments and individuals conformed to the rhythm of the tragedy, and swayed and staggered forward in helpless violence, slaughtering and squandering on ever-increasing scales, till injuries were wrought to the structure of human society which a century will not efface, and which may conceivably prove fatal to the present civilization. But in January, 1915, the terrific affair was still not unmanageable. It could have been grasped in human hands and brought to rest in righteous and fruitful victory before the world was exhausted, before the nations were broken, before the empires were shattered to pieces, before Europe was ruined.

It was not to be. Mankind was not to escape so easily from the catastrophe in which it had involved itself. Pride was everywhere to be humbled, and nowhere to receive its satisfaction. No splendid harmony was to crown the wonderful achievements. No prize was to reward the sacrifices of the combatants. Victory was to be bought so dear as to be almost indistinguishable from defeat. It was not to give even security to the victors. To the convulsions of the struggle must succeed the impotent turmoil of the aftermath. Noble hopes, high comradeship and glorious daring were in every nation to lead only to disappointment, disillusion and prostration. The sufferings and impoverishment of peoples might arrest their warfare, the collapse of the defeated might still the cannonade, but their hatreds continue unappeased and their quarrels are still unsettled. The most complete victory ever gained in arms has failed to solve the European problem or remove the dangers which produced the war.

No war is so sanguinary as the war of exhaustion. No plan could be more unpromising than the plan of frontal attack. Yet on these two brutal expedients the military authorities of France and Britain consumed, during three successive years, the flower of their national manhood. Moreover, the dull carnage of the policy of exhaustion did not even apply equally to the combatants. The Anglo-French offensives of 1915, 1916 and 1917 were in nearly every instance, and certainly in the aggregate, far more costly to the attack than to the German defence. It was not even a case of exchanging a life for a life. Two, and even three, British or French lives were repeatedly paid for the killing of one enemy, and grim calculations were made to prove that in the end the Allies would still have a balance of a few millions to spare. It will appear not only horrible but incredible to future generations that such doctrines should have been imposed by the military profession upon the ardent and heroic populations who yielded themselves to their orders.

It is a tale of the torture, mutilation or extinction of millions of men, and of the sacrifice of all that was best and noblest in an entire generation. The crippled, broken world in which we dwell today is the inheritor of these awful events. Yet all the time there were ways open by which this slaughter could have been avoided and the period of torment curtailed. There were regions where flanks could have been turned; there were devices by which fronts could have been pierced. And these could have been discovered and made mercifully effective, not by any departure from the principles of military art, but simply by the true comprehension of those principles and their application to the actual facts.

Battles are won by slaughter and manoeuvre. The greater the general, the more he contributes in manoeuvre, the less he demands in slaughter. The theory which has exalted the "bataille d'usure" or "battle of wearing down" into a foremost position, is contradicted by history and would be repulsed by the greatest captains of the past. Nearly all the battles which are regarded as masterpieces of the military art, from which have been derived the foundation of states and the fame of commanders, have been battles of manoeuvre in which very often the enemy has found himself defeated by some novel expedient or device, some queer, swift, unexpected thrust or stratagem. In many such battles the losses of the victors have been small. There is required for the composition of a great commander not only massive common sense and reasoning power, not only imagination, but also an element of legerdemain, an original and sinister touch, which leaves the enemy puzzled as well as beaten. It is because military leaders are credited with gifts of this order which enable them to ensure victory and save slaughter that their profession is held in such high honour. For if their art were nothing more than a dreary process of exchanging lives, and counting heads at the end, they would rank much lower in the scale of human esteem.

There are many kinds of manoeuvres in war, some only of which take place upon the battlefield. There are manoeuvres far to the flank or rear. There are manoeuvres in time, in diplomacy, in mechanics, in psychology; all of which are removed from the battlefield, but react often decisively upon it, and the object of all is to find easier ways, other than sheer slaughter, of achieving the main purpose. The distinction between politics and strategy diminishes as the point of view is raised. At the summit true politics and strategy are one. The manoeuvre which brings an ally into the field is as serviceable as that which wins a great battle. The manoeuvre which gains an important strategic point may be less valuable than that which placates or overawes a dangerous neutral. We suffered grievously at the beginning of the war from the want of a common clearing house where these different relative values could be established and exchanged. A single prolonged conference, between the allied chiefs, civil and martial, in January, 1915, might have saved us from inestimable misfortune. Nothing could ever be thrashed out by correspondence. Principals must be brought together, and plans concerted in common. Instead each allied state pursued in the main its own course, keeping the others more or less informed. The armies and navies dwelt in every country in separate compartments. The war problem, which was all one, was tugged at from many different and disconnected standpoints. War, which knows no rigid divisions between French, Russian and British Allies, between Land, Sea and Air, between gaining victories and alliances, between supplies and fighting men, between propaganda and machinery, which is, in fact, simply the sum of all forces and pressures operative at a given period, was dealt with piecemeal. And years of cruel teaching were necessary before even imperfect unifications of study, thought, command, and action were achieved. The men of the Beginning must not be judged wholly by the light of the End. All had to learn and all had to suffer. But it was not those who learned the slowest who were made to suffer most.

There can be few purely mental experiences more charged with cold excitement than to follow, almost from minute to minute, the phases of a great naval action from the silent rooms of the Admiralty. Out on blue water in the fighting ships amid the stunning detonations of the cannonade, fractions of the event unfold themselves to the corporeal eye. There is the sense of action at its highest; there is the wrath of battle; there is the intense, self-effacing, physical or mental toil. But in Whitehall only the clock ticks, and quiet men enter with quick steps laying slips of pencilled paper before other men equally silent who draw lines and scribble calculations, and point with the finger or make brief subdued comments. Telegram succeeds telegram at a few minutes' interval as they are picked up and decoded, often in the wrong sequence, frequently of dubious import; and out of these a picture always flickering and changing rises in the mind, and imagination strikes out around it at every stage flashes of hope or fear.

The tests to which the Admirals in high command are subjected during a naval engagement are far more searching than those of Generals in a battle on land. The Admiral actually leads the Fleet in person and is probably under as severe fire and in as great danger as any man in it; a General, whatever his wishes, has no choice but to remain in his headquarters in complete tranquillity, ten, fifteen or even twenty miles away. The General is forced to rely on the reports of others which flow upwards to him from Brigades, Divisions and Corps, and transmits his orders through the same channel after consultation with his staff; the Admiral sees with his own eyes, and with his own lips pronounces the orders which move the whole mighty event. The phases of a naval action succeed one another at intervals of two or three minutes; whereas in modern battles two or three hours, and sometimes even days, elapse before fresh decisions are required from an Army Commander. Once the sea battle is joined the whole event is in the hand of the Admiral or his successor as long as he can signal; whereas on land, after zero hour has struck, it escapes for the time being almost entirely from the control of the General. There are a hundred ways of explaining a defeat on land and of obscuring the consequences of any mistake. Of these the simplest is to continue the attack next day in a different direction or under different conditions. But on the sea no chance returns. The enemy disappears for months and the battle is over. The Admiral's orders uttered from minute to minute are recorded for ever in the log-book of every vessel engaged. The great ships, unless their mechanism ceases to function, obey punctually and inexorably the directions they receive from the human will. The course and speed of every vessel at every moment are recorded. The value of every vessel sunk is known. Their names are published. The charts and compasses are produced, and with almost exact accuracy the position and movement of every ship can be fixed in relation to every other. The battlefield is flat and almost unvarying. Exact explanations can be required at every point, and the whole intense scene can be reconstructed and analysed in the glare of history. This should always be borne in mind in forming judgments.[1]

---

[1] These are the author's comments and reflections on the action of the Dogger Bank on the 24 January, 1915, written several years afterwards.

I have asked myself, what would have happened if I had taken Lord Fisher's advice and refused point-blank to take any action at the Dardanelles unless or until the War Office produced on their responsibility an adequate army to storm the Gallipoli Peninsula? Should we by holding out in this way have secured a sufficient army and a good plan? Should we have had all the advantages of the Dardanelles policy without the mistakes and misfortunes for which we had to pay so dearly? The Dardanelles Commissioners, studying the story from an entirely different angle, obviously felt that if there had been no naval plan in the field, there would later on have been a really well-conceived and well-concerted amphibious attack. No one can probe this imaginary situation very far, and it is impossible to pronounce. But I think myself that nothing less than the ocular demonstration and practical proof of the strategic meaning of the Dardanelles, and the effects of attacking it on every Balkan and Mediterranean Power, would have lighted up men's minds sufficiently to make a large abstraction of troops from the main theatre a possibility. I do not believe that anything less than those tremendous hopes, reinforced as they were by dire necessity, would have enabled Lord Kitchener to wrest an army from France and Flanders. In cold blood, it could never have been done. General Headquarters, and the French General Staff would have succeeded in shattering any plan put forward so long as it was a mere theoretical proposal for a large diversion of force to the Southern theatre. At one moment they would have told us that, owing to the Russian failure, great masses of Germans were returning to the West to deliver an overwhelming offensive: at another that they could not spare a round of ammunition and were in desperate straits for the want of it: at a third, that they had a wonderful plan for a great offensive which would shatter the German line and drive them out of a large portion of France. All these arguments were in fact used, and their effect was, as will be seen, to cripple the Dardanelles operations even after they had actually begun. How much more would they have overwhelmed any paper plan for an Eastern campaign. There would have been no Dardanelles with its hopes, its glories, its losses and its ultimate heart-breaking failure.

But who shall say what would have happened instead? A few weeks' more delay in the entry of Italy into the war, and the continuance of the great Russian defeats in Galicia, would have rendered that entry improbable in the extreme. A few more months' acceleration of the Bulgarian declaration of war against us, and the whole of the Balkans, except Serbia, might have been rallied to the Teutonic standards. The flower of the Turkish Army, which was largely destroyed on the Gallipoli Peninsula, would certainly have fought us or our Allies somewhere else. The destruction of the Russian Army of the Caucasus could not have been long averted. I do not believe that by adopting the negative attitude we should ever have got our good and well-conceived amphibious operation. We should have got no operation at all. We should have done nothing, and have been confronted with diplomatic and military reactions wholly unfavourable throughout the Southern and Eastern theatre. Searching my heart, I cannot regret the effort. It was good to go as far as we did.

Not to persevere—that was the crime.[1]

*      *      *

The workings of Lord Kitchener's mind constituted at this period [early in 1915] a feature almost as puzzling as the great war problem itself. His prestige and authority were immense. He was the sole mouthpiece of War Office opinion in the War Council. Everyone had the greatest admiration for his character, and everyone felt fortified, amid the terrible and incalculable events of the opening months of the war, by his commanding presence. When he gave a decision it was invariably accepted as final. He was never, to my belief, overruled by the War Council or the Cabinet in any military matter, great or small. No single unit was ever sent or withheld contrary, not merely to his agreement, but to his advice. Scarcely anyone ever ventured to argue with him in Council. Respect for the man, sympathy for him in his immense labours, confidence in his professional judgment, and the belief that he had plans deeper and wider than any we could see, silenced misgivings and disputes,

[1] The failure of the Dardanelles campaign, one of the author's most ambitious naval and military conceptions, provoked violent attacks upon him and resulted in his replacement as First Lord of the Admiralty by Mr. Balfour. (Mr. Asquith had decided to form a national government but the author was not included in it. For some time he was in political eclipse, and endured one of the most bitter experiences in the whole of his career. When Mr. Asquith was succeeded as Prime Minister by Mr. Lloyd George, the author was appointed Minister of Munitions.)

whether in the Council or at the War Office. All-powerful, imperturbable, reserved, he dominated absolutely our counsels at this time in all that concerned the organization and employment of the armies.

Yet behind this imposing and splendid front lay many weaknesses, evidences of which became increasingly disquieting. The Secretary of State for War had burdens laid upon him which no man, no three men even of his great capacity, could properly discharge. He had absorbed the whole War Office into his spacious personality. The General Staff was completely in abeyance, save as a machine for supplying him with information. Even as such a machine it was woefully weak. All the ablest officers and leading and strongest minds in the General Staff and Army Council, with the exception of Sir John Cowans, the Quartermaster-General, had hurried eagerly out of the country with the Expeditionary Force and were now in France, feeling that they ought to control the whole conduct of the war from the highly localized point of view of the British General Headquarters at St. Omer. In their place, filling vitally important situations, were officers on the retired list or men whose opinions had never counted weightily in British military thought. These officers were petrified by Lord Kitchener's personality and position. They none of them showed the natural force and ability to argue questions out with him vigorously as man to man. He towered up in his uniform as a Field-Marshal and Cabinet Minister besides, and they saluted as subordinates on a drill-ground. They never presented him with well-considered general reasonings about the whole course of the war. They stood ready to execute his decisions to the best of their ability. It was left to the Members of the War Council to write papers upon the broad strategic view of the war. It was left to the Chancellor of the Exchequer, Mr. Lloyd George, to discern and proclaim to the Cabinet in unmistakable terms the impending military collapse of Russia. It was left to me to offer at any rate one method of influencing the political situation in the Near East in default of comprehensive military schemes. And Lord Kitchener himself was left to face the rushing, swirling torrent of events with no rock of clear, well-thought-out doctrine and calculation at his back.

Churchill welcomed on
a visit to the north of
England in 1918

Austen Chamberlain,
Stanley Baldwin and
Churchill

Winston Churchill the artist at work

Beside these trials and burdens, to which he was certainly not able to rise superior, stood the whole vast business of recruiting, organizing and equipping the New Armies; and behind this again there now marched steadily into view a series of problems connected with the manufacture and purchase of munitions upon a scale never dreamed of by any human being up till this period. These problems comprised the entire social and industrial life of the country and touched the whole economic and financial system of the world. Add to this the daily exposition of all military business in Cabinet and in Council—a process most trying and burdensome to Lord Kitchener, and one in which he felt himself at a disadvantage: add, further, the continuous series of decisions upon executive matters covering the vast field of the war, including important operations and expeditions which were campaigns in themselves, and it will be realized that the strain that descended upon the King's greatest subject was far more than mortal man could bear.

It must, however, be stated that Lord Kitchener in no way sought to lighten these terrific burdens. On the contrary, he resented promptly any attempt to interfere in and even scrutinize his vast domains of responsibility. He resisted tenaciously the efforts which were made from January onwards to remove the production of munitions of all kinds from his control as Secretary of State. He devolved on to subordinates as little as he could. He sought to manage the Great War by the same sort of personal control that he had used with so much success in the command of the tiny Nile Expedition. He kept the General Staff, or what was left of it, in a condition of complete subservience and practical abeyance. He even reached out, as his Cabinet Office justified, into political spheres in questions of Ireland, of Temperance, and of Industrial Organization.

It is idle to affect to disregard or conceal these facts. Indeed, the greatness of Lord Kitchener and his lasting claims upon the respect and gratitude of succeeding generations of his fellow-countrymen, for whose cause and safety he fought with single-hearted purpose and a giant's strength, will only be fortified by the fullest comprehension of his character and of his difficulties. If this story [*The World Crisis*] and the facts and documents on which it rests constitute any reflection upon his military policy, I must also testify to the overwhelming weight of the burdens laid upon him, to his extraordinary patience and courage in all the difficulties and perplexities through which we were passing, and to his unvarying kindness and courtesy to me.

\*       \*       \*

When Lord Kitchener undertook to storm the Gallipoli Peninsula with the Army, he was under the impression that a week would suffice to prepare and begin the operation. But when he had reversed the decision of 16 February to send the 29th Division, when he had countermanded and consequently dispersed its transports, when he had deliberately left the issue in suspense until 10 March, when he had allowed the division to be embarked otherwise than in order for battle, he had tied his own hands inextricably. He had no choice now but to wait for weeks in the face of ever-accumulating dangers and difficulties, or to abandon the enterprise. This latter solution, however, he at no time entertained. On the contrary he braced himself resolutely for the effort, and events continued to drift steadily forward.

I still hoped that the continuance of the naval pressure, even within the limits now prescribed, would yield results which would encourage the Admiral [de Robeck] to renew his attack, and thus perhaps spare the Army the dreaded ordeal.

However, he did not in the event pursue even limited operations. His energies and those of his staff soon became absorbed in the preparation of the comprehensive and complicated plans necessary for the landing of the Army. The *Queen Elizabeth* never fired a gun, and all ships remained inactive against the enemy for another month. From this slough I was not able to lift the operations. All the negative forces began to band themselves together.

Henceforward the defences of the Dardanelles were to be reinforced by an insurmountable mental barrier. A wall of crystal, utterly immovable, began to tower up in the Narrows, and against this wall of inhibition no weapon could be employed. The "No" principle had become established in men's minds, and nothing could ever eradicate it. Never again could I marshal the Admiralty War Group and the War Council in favour of resolute action. Never again could I move the First Sea Lord. "No" had settled down for ever on our councils, crushing with its deadening weight what I shall ever believe was the hope of the world. Vain was it for Admiral de Robeck a month later, inspired by the ardent Keyes, to offer to renew the naval attack. His hour had passed. I could never lift the "No" that had descended, and soon I was myself to succumb. Still vainer was it for Admiral Wemyss, when he succeeded de Robeck, to submit the Keyes plans and his own resolute convictions to the new Board of Admiralty. Vain was it for Keyes in October to resign his appointment as Chief of the Staff and hasten personally to London to plead with Lord Kitchener and my successor for permission to attack. "No" had won, with general assent and measureless ruin. Never again did the British Fleet renew the attack upon the Narrows which in pursuance of their orders they had begun on 18 March, and which they then confidently expected to continue after a brief interval. Instead, they waited for nine months the spectators of the sufferings, the immense losses and imperishable glories of the Army, always hoping that their hour of intervention would come, always hoping for their turn to run every risk and make every sacrifice, until in the end they had the sorrow and mortification of taking the remains of the Army off and steaming away under the cloak of darkness from the scene of irretrievable failure.

And yet if the Navy had tried again they would have found that the door was open. Their improved sweeping forces could have concentrated upon clearing the few remaining mines out of the Eren Keui Bay. All their losses were made good. The battle of 18 March could have been resumed a month later in overwhelming favourable conditions; and had it been resumed it would, in a few hours, have become apparent that it could have only one ending. We knew at the time from secret sources, the credit of which was unquestionable, that the Turkish Army was short of ammunition. We had only to resume a gradual naval advance and bombardment to discover the wonderful truth that they had, in fact, scarcely any more ammunition. We now know what we could have so easily found out then, that for the heavy guns which alone could injure the armoured ships, they had not twenty rounds apiece.

★   ★   ★

The operations [in Gallipoli, April, 1915] presented the most incalculable and uncertain problems of War. To land a large army in the face of a long-warned and carefully prepared defence by brave troops and modern weapons was to attempt what had never yet been dared and what might well prove impossible.

The first incalculable hazard was the landing under fire. This might well fail altogether. It was not inconceivable that most of the troops might be shot in the boats before they even reached the shore. No one could tell. But if the landing were successful, the next peril fell upon the Turks: they had for at least three days to try to hold out against superior forces. How superior no Turk could tell. It had rested entirely with Lord Kitchener how many men he would employ. If, however, the British and French forces were too few and the Turkish defence was maintained for three days, then the balance of advantage would turn against the Allies. After the third or fourth day the attackers would have expended their priceless treasure of surprise. Their choice would be disclosed and they would be committed almost irrevocably to it. Large reinforcements would reach the Turks; strong entrenchments would be completed; and ultimately the invaders would have to meet the main forces of Turkey which could gradually be brought against them from all parts of the Ottoman Empire. Rapidity and intensity of execution at the outset were therefore the essential of any sound plan.

Of the five landings in the neighbourhood of Cape Helles that of the 88th Brigade on "V" Beach close to the ruined fort of Sedd-el-Bahr was intended to be the most important. Over two thousand men of the Dublin and Munster Fusiliers and of the Hampshire Regiment packed in the hold of the *River Clyde*, a steamer specially prepared for landing troops, were carried to within a few yards of the shore. It had been planned to bridge the intervening water space by two lighters or barges. Along this causeway the troops were to rush company by company on to the Beach. At the same time the rest of the Dublin Fusiliers approached the shore in boats. There were scarcely more than four or five hundred Turks to oppose this assault, but these were skilfully concealed in the cliffs and ruined buildings reinforced by a good many machine guns and protected by mines and wire both in the water and ashore. As the Irish troops rushed from the hold of the *River Clyde*, or as the boats reached the submerged barbed wire, an annihilating fire burst upon them from all parts of the small amphitheatre. The boats were checked by the wire or by the destruction of their rowers. The lighters, swayed by the current, were with difficulty placed and kept in position. In a few minutes more than half of those who had exposed themselves were shot down. The boats, the lighters, the gangways, the water, and the edge of the beach were heaped or crowded with dead and dying. Nevertheless the survivors struggled forward through the wire and through the sea, some few reaching the Beach, while successive platoons of Dublin and Munster Fusiliers continued to leap from the hold of the *River Clyde* into the shambles without the slightest hesitation until restrained by superior authority. Commander Unwin and the small naval staff responsible for fixing the lighters, and indeed for the plan of using the *River Clyde*, persevered in their endeavours to secure their lighters and lay down gangways unremittingly in the deadly storm, while others struggled with unsurpassed heroism to save the drowning and dying or to make their way armed to the shore. The scenes were enacted once again which Napier has immortalized in the breaches of Badajoz. Nothing availed. The whole landing encountered a bloody arrest. The survivors lay prone under the lip of the Beach, and but for the fire of the machine guns of Commander Wedgwood's armoured car squadron which had been mounted in the bows of the *River Clyde*, would probably have been exterminated. The Brigadier, General Napier, being killed, the whole attempt to land at this point was suspended until dark.

Fighting scarcely less terrible had taken place at "W" Beach. Here the Lancashire Fusiliers, after a heavy bombardment from the Fleet, were towed and rowed to the shore in thirty or forty cutters. Again the Turks reserved their fire till the moment when the leading boats touched the Beach. Again its effects were devastating. Undeterred by the most severe losses from rifle and machine-gun fire, from sea mines and land mines, this magnificent battalion waded through the water, struggled through the wire, and with marvellous discipline actually re-formed their attenuated line along the Beach. From this position they were quite unable to advance, and

293

this attack also would have been arrested, but for a fortunate accident. The boats containing the company on the left had veered away towards some rocks beneath the promontory of Cape Tekke. Here the soldiers landed with little loss, and climbing the cliffs fell upon the Turkish machine guns which were sweeping the Beach and bayoneted their gunners. Profiting by this relief, the remainder of the battalion already on the Beach managed to make their way to the shelter of the cliffs, and climbing them established themselves firmly on their summit. Here at about nine o'clock they were reinforced by the Worcesters, and gradually from this direction the foothold won was steadily extended during the day.

$$\star \quad \star \quad \star$$

In spite of warnings[1] and instructions, for which the Admiralty Trade Division deserve credit, the *Lusitania* was proceeding along the usual trade route without zigzagging at little more than three-quarter speed when, at 2.10 p.m. on 7 May [1915], she was torpedoed eight miles off the Old Head of Kinsale by Commander Schweiger in the German submarine *U.20*. Two torpedoes were fired, the first striking her amidships with a tremendous explosion, and the second a few minutes later striking her aft. In twenty minutes she foundered by the head, carrying with her 1,195 persons, of whom 291 were women and ninety-four infants or small children. This crowning outrage of the U-boat war resounded through the world. The United States whose citizens had perished in large numbers, was convulsed with indignation, and in all parts of the great Republic the signal for armed intervention was awaited by the strongest elements of the American people. It was not given, and the war continued in its destructive equipoise. But henceforward the friends of the Allies in the United States were armed with a weapon against which German influence was powerless, and before which after a lamentable interval cold-hearted policy was destined to succumb.

Even in the first moments of realizing the tragedy and its horror, I understood the significance of the event. As the history of the Great War is pondered over, its stern lessons stand forth from the

---

[1] Warnings that the *Lusitania* would be sunk were given in New York before she sailed. The Admiralty sent a wireless message to the ship on 7 May: "Submarine five miles south of Cape Clear proceeding west when sighted at 10 a.m."

tumult and confusion of the times. On two supreme occasions the German Imperial Government, quenching compunction, outfacing conscience, deliberately, with calculation, with sinister resolve, severed the underlying bonds which sustained the civilization of the world and united even in their quarrels the human family. The invasion of Belgium and the unlimited U-boat war were both resorted to on expert dictation as the only means of victory. They proved the direct cause of ruin. They drew into the struggle against Germany mighty and intangible powers by which her strength was remorselessly borne down. Nothing could have deprived Germany of victory in the first year of war except the invasion of Belgium; nothing could have denied it to her in its last year except her unlimited submarine campaign. Not to the number of her enemies, nor to their resources or wisdom; not to the mistakes of her Admirals and Generals in open battle; not to the weakness of her Allies; not assuredly to any fault in the valour or loyalty of her population or her armies; but only to these two grand crimes and blunders of history, were her undoing and our salvation due.

\*     \*     \*

For thirty-four months of preparation and ten months of war I had borne the prime responsibility [at the Admiralty] and had wielded the main executive power. Dubious years, many misfortunes, enormous toils, bitter disappointments, still lay before the Royal Navy. But I am entitled to place on record the situation and condition in which the mighty instrument of our sea power and of our salvation passed into the hands of my successors. At no moment during all the wars of Britain had our command of the seas been more complete, and in no previous war had that command been asserted more rapidly or with so little loss. Not only had the surface ships of the enemy been extirpated from the oceans of the world; not only in the North Sea had his fleets and squadrons been beaten, cowed and driven into port; but even the new and barbarous submarine warfare had been curbed and checked. For more than a year to come the German High Seas Fleet scarcely quitted its harbours, and even when they did so, it was with no intention of fighting a battle and in the unfounded hope that they could return unperceived or unmolested. For eighteen months their submarine campaign was virtually suspended. In spite of modern complications, the economic blockade of Germany was established and maintained, so far as it rested with the Navy, with the utmost strictness: scarcely any ship that the Navy had authority to touch ever passed our far-spread cordons. The maintenance of the armies in France and in the East proceeded every month on a vaster scale, without the slightest substantial hindrance upon their communications becoming apparent to our commanders at the Front. The mercantile fleets of Britain and of her allies moved with freedom in all directions about the seas and oceans: and an insurance rate of 1 per cent left a substantial profit to the Government Fund. These conditions lasted during all the year 1915 and up to the last quarter of the year 1916. There never was in all the history of war such an unchallenged reign of sea power.

Meanwhile the British Navy was growing continually and rapidly in strength. The fruits of the exertions which had been made before and since the outbreak of the war were being reaped with each successive month. Battleships, battle-cruisers, light cruisers in dozens, submarines in scores, destroyers in hundreds, small craft in thousands, were being armed and built, and were coming into commission in an unceasing and broadening tide. The manning arrangements to meet this enormous new construction were perfected for a year in advance. Every requirement known to the naval science of the day in guns, in torpedoes, in shells, in explosives, in propellant, in coal, in oil, and in auxiliary services had been foreseen and provided for in harmonious relation to the expansion of our naval power. At the Admiralty we were in hot pursuit of most of the great key inventions and ideas of the war; and this long in advance of every other nation, friend or foe. Tanks, smoke, torpedo-seaplanes, directional wireless, cryptography, mine fenders, monitors, torpedo-proof ships, paravanes— all were being actively driven forward or developed. Poison gas alone we had put aside—but not from want of comprehension. Even for the new submarine campaign, not to burst upon us for nearly eighteen months, the principal safeguarding measures had already been devised: the multitudes of vessels were building; the decoy ships were at work.

Moreover the true war leaders of the Navy had already emerged from the ranks of peace-time merit; and in Beatty, Keyes, Tyrwhitt,

Pakenham, and I must add, Lewis Bayly—though under a temporary cloud—we had masters of the storm capable of rivalling upon the seas and against the enemy's coasts the exploits of the famous sailor figures of the past. There remained only to devise and perfect those schemes of naval offensive which in spite, and indeed by means of, modern science and invention would have liberated the pent-up skill and daring of our officers and men. There was also at hand that prolonged interlude of ease and tranquillity upon salt water in which every plan could be worked out with sure and deliberate study.

★   ★   ★

The Christian States of the Balkans were the children of oppression and revolt. For four hundred years they had dwelt under the yoke of the Turkish conqueror. They had recovered their freedom after cruel struggles only during the last hundred years. Their national characteristics were marked by these hard experiences. Their constitutions and dynasties resulted from them. Their populations were poor, fierce and proud. Their governments were divided from one another by irreconcilable ambitions and jealousies. Every one of them at some ancient period in its history had been the head of a considerable Empire in these regions, and though Serbian and Bulgarian splendours had been of brief duration compared to the glories of Greece, each looked back to this period of greatness as marking the measure of its historic rights. All therefore simultaneously considered themselves entitled to the ownership of territories which they had in bygone centuries possessed only in succession. All therefore were plunged in convulsive quarrels and intrigues.

It is to this cause that their indescribable sufferings have been mainly and primarily due. It was not easy for all or any of these small States to lift themselves out of this dismal and dangerous quagmire or find a firm foothold on which to stand. Behind the national communities, themselves acting and reacting upon each other in confusion, there were in each country party and political divisions and feuds sufficient to shake a powerful Empire. Every Balkan statesman had to thread his way to power in his own country through complications, dangers and surprising transformations, more violent, more intense than those which the domestic affairs of great

297

nations revealed. He arrived hampered by his past and pursued by foes and jealousies, and, thus harassed and weakened, had to cope with the ever-shifting combinations of Balkan politics, as these in turn were influenced by the immense convulsions of the Great War.

In addition to all this came the policy of the three great allied Powers. France and Russia had each its own interests and outlook, its favourite Balkan State and its favourite party in each State. Great Britain had a vague desire to see them all united, and a lofty impartiality and detachment scarcely less baffling. To this were super-added the distracting influences of the various Sovereigns and their Teutonic origins or relations. In consequence, the situation was so chaotic and unstable, there were so many vehement points of view rising and falling, that British, French and Russian statesmen never succeeded in devising any firm, comprehensive policy. On the contrary, by their isolated, half-hearted and often contradictory interventions, they contributed that culminating element of disorder which led every one of these small States successively to the most hideous forms of ruin.

Yet all the time the main interests of the three great Allies and of the four Balkan kingdoms were identical, and all could have been protected and advanced by a single and simple policy. The ambitions of every one of the Balkan States could have been satisfied at the expense of the Turkish and Austrian Empires. There was enough for all, and more than enough. The interest of the three great Allies was to range the Balkan States against these Empires. United among themselves, the Balkan States were safe: joined to the three Allies, they could not fail to gain the territories they coveted.

It is astonishing that when all interests were the same, when so many powerful means of leverage and stimulus were at hand, everything should without exception have gone amiss. If in February, 1915, or possibly after the Turkish declaration of war in November, 1914, the British, French and Russian Governments could have agreed upon a common policy in the Balkans—and had sent plenipotentiaries of the highest order to the Balkan Peninsula to negotiate on a clear, firm basis with each and all of these States—a uniform, coherent action could have been devised and enforced with measureless benefits to all concerned. Instead, the situation was dealt with by partial expedients suggested by the rapid and baffling procession of events. Everything was vainly offered or done by the Allies successively and tardily, which done all at once and in good time would have achieved the result.

The Balkan States offered by far the greatest possibility open to allied diplomacy at the beginning of 1915. This was never envisaged and planned as if it were the great battle which indeed it was. Fitful, sporadic, half-hearted, changeable, unrelated expedients were all that the statesmen of Russia, France and Britain were able to employ. Nor is it right for public opinion in these countries to condemn the Balkan States and Balkan politicians or sovereigns too sweepingly. The hesitations of the King of Roumania, the craft of King Ferdinand, the shifts and evasions of King Constantine, all arose from the baffling nature of the Balkan problem and the lack of policy of the Allies. Serbia, indeed, fought on desperately and blindly without consideration for any other interests but her own and with frightful consequences to herself, ultimately repaired only by the final victory. Roumania was throughout in peril of her life and perplexed to the foundations of her being. When at last, after infinite hesitations, bargainings and precautions, she entered the war, she was too late to decide or abridge the struggle but in good time to be torn in pieces. Bulgaria turned traitor alike to her past and to her future, and after many exertions was plunged in the woe of the vanquished. Greece, rescued in the nick of time by courage and genius, and emerging with little cost upon the side of the victors, survived incorrigible to squander all that she had gained. Yet in Roumania there was Také Jonesco always pointing clear and true; in Bulgaria, Stambulisky, braving the wrath of King Ferdinand and marching proudly to his long prison with the names of England and Russia on his lips; and in Greece, Venizelos, threading his way through indescribable embarrassments and triumphing over unimaginable difficulties, preserved his country for a time in spite of herself and might well have limited the miseries of Europe.

★    ★    ★

A new tremendous event was now to strike across this darkening situation. At a Conference held at Calais early in July, 1915, the representatives of the Cabinet, viz., the Prime Minister, Lord

Kitchener and Mr. Balfour, had, in accordance with the convictions of the overwhelming majority of their colleagues, argued against a further Anglo-French offensive in the West in 1915. They had proposed that the allied operations in France and Flanders should be confined to what was described as an "offensive defensive" or, to speak more accurately, an active defensive. The French had agreed; General Joffre had agreed. The agreement was open and formal. And it was on this basis that we had looked forward and prepared for the new battle on the Gallipoli Peninsula. No sooner, however, had General Joffre left the Conference than, notwithstanding these agreements, he had calmly resumed the development of his plans for his great attack in Champagne, in which he confidently expected to break the German lines and roll them back. It was not until after the Battle of Suvla Bay had been finally lost, and we were more deeply committed in the Peninsula than ever before, that we became aware of this.

To avoid unnecessary circulation of secret documents it had been arranged that members of the War Committee wishing to read the daily War Office telegrams could do so each morning at the War Office in Lord Kitchener's ante-room. It was my practice to read every word every day. On the morning of 21 August I was thus engaged when the private secretary informed me that Lord Kitchener, who had just returned from the French Headquarters, wished to see me. I entered his room and found him standing with his back to the light. He looked at me sideways with a very odd expression on his face. I saw he had some disclosure of importance to make, and waited. After appreciable hesitation he told me that he had agreed with the French to a great offensive in France. I said at once that there was no chance of success. He said the scale would be greater than anything ever before conceived; if it succeeded, it would restore everything, including of course the Dardanelles. He had an air of suppressed excitement, like a man who has taken a great decision of terrible uncertainty and is about to put it into execution. He was of course bracing himself for the announcement he had to make that morning to the War Committee and to the Cabinet. I continued unconvinced. It was then 11 o'clock, and he drove me across in his car to Downing Street.

The Committee assembled. Lord Kitchener had no doubt apprised the Prime Minister beforehand, and he was immediately invited to make his statement. He told us that owing to the situation in Russia he could not longer maintain the attitude which was agreed upon in conjunction with the French at Calais, i.e., that a real serious offensive on a large scale in the West should be postponed until the Allies were ready. As he put it to us, he had himself urged upon General Joffre the adoption of the offensive. In view of the fact that, as we now know, the French plans and preparations had long been in progress, had indeed never been interrupted, this must have been a work of supererogation. I immediately protested against departure from the decisions of the Cabinet maturely made and endorsed by the Calais Conference, and against an operation that could only lead to useless slaughter on a gigantic scale. I pointed out that we had neither the ammunition nor the superiority in men necessary to warrant such an assault on the enemy's fortified line; that it could not take place in time effectively to relieve Russia; that it would not prevent the Germans from pursuing their initiative in theatres other than the West; and that it would rupture fatally our plans for opening the Dardanelles.

$$\ast \qquad \ast \qquad \ast$$

At dawn on 26 September, 1915, the great battle in the West began. It comprised a subsidiary attack by about thirty British and French divisions at Loos, and a main attack by forty French divisions in Champagne. Sir John French had been compelled, in order to combine with the French, to accept a sphere of attack against his better judgment; but, having agreed to conform to General Joffre's plans, he threw himself into their execution with his customary determination. The French attack in Champagne has since been described as "the unlimited method"—i.e., the armies were hurled on to advance as far as they could "into the blue", in the confident expectation that they would carry, not merely the front systems, which had been subjected to bombardment, but all intact positions and defences likely to be met with in rear. In the absurd misconceptions of the Staff, large masses of cavalry were brought up to press the victory to a decisive conclusion. At the fatal signal the brave armies marched into the firestorm. The ardour of the French infantry was not unmatched by their British comrades. The issue,

301

however, was never in doubt. The German calculations of the strength of their front and of the numbers of troops needed to defend it were accurate and sound. Their drive against Russia, their project against the Balkans proceeded unchecked. In the first week the Anglo-French attack had secured slight advances of no strategic significance at various points, a few score of guns, and a few thousand prisoners, at the expense of more than 300,000 casualties.

*    *    *

The failure of the Dardanelles Expedition was fatal to Lord Kitchener. During the whole of 1915 he had been in sole and plenary charge of the British military operations, and until November on every important point his will had been obeyed. The new Cabinet, like the leading members of the old, had now in their turn lost confidence in his war direction. The conduct of the Gallipoli campaign showed only too plainly the limitations of this great figure at this period of his life and in this tremendous situation both as an organizer and a man of action. His advocacy of the offensive in France which had failed so conspicuously at Loos and in Champagne was upon record. Under the agony of the Gallipoli evacuation his will power had plainly crumpled, and the long series of contradictory resolves which had marked his treatment of this terrible question was obvious to all who knew the facts.

Already, in November, had come direct rebuff. His plan for a fresh landing in the Gulf of Alexandretta, though devised by him in the actual theatre of operations, had been decisively vetoed by the new War Committee of the Cabinet and by the Allies in conference. In a series of telegrams the inclination of which could scarcely be obscure, he was encouraged to transform his definite mission at the Dardanelles into a general and extensive tour of inspection in the East. His prompt return to London showed that he was not himself unaware of the change in his position. The disposition of the British forces in the East which he made after the evacuation of Suvla and Anzac was certainly not such as to retrieve a waning prestige. It was natural that Egypt should loom disproportionately large in his mind. Almost his whole life had been spent and his fame won there. He now saw this beloved country menaced, as he believed, by an imminent Turkish invasion on a large scale. In an endeavour to ward off the imaginary peril he crowded division after division into Egypt, and evidently contemplated desperate struggles for the defence of the Suez Canal at no distant date. In the early days, at the end of 1914 and beginning of 1915, it had been worth while for a score of thousand Turks to threaten the Canal and create as much disturbance as possible in order to delay the movement of troops from India, Australia and New Zealand to the European battlefield. But both the usefulness and feasibility of such an operation were destroyed by the great increase in the scale of the war in the eastern Mediterranean theatre which had been in progress during the whole year.

On 3 December [1915], the War Committee determined to re-create the Imperial General Staff at the War Office in an effective form. The decision was drastic. The experiment of making a Field-Marshal Secretary of State for War had run its full course. Lord Kitchener might still hold the Seals of Office, but his power, hitherto so overwhelming that it had absorbed and embodied the authority alike of the ministerial and the professional Chief, was now to be confined within limits which few politicians would accept in a Secretaryship of State. Sir William Robertson, Chief of the General Staff in France, was brought to Whitehall, and an Order in Council was issued establishing his rights and responsibility in terms both strict and wide. Lord Kitchener acquiesced in the abrogation, not only of the exceptional personal powers which he had enjoyed, but of those which have always been inherent in the office which he retained.

The end of his great story is approaching: the long life full of action, lighted by hard-won achievement, crowned by power such as a British subject had rarely wielded and all the regard and honour that Britain and her Empire can bestow, was now declining through the shadows. The sudden onrush of the night, the deep waters of the North, were destined to preserve him and his renown from the shallows. The solemn days when he stood forth as Constable of Britain, beneath whose arm her untrained people braced themselves for war, were ended. His life of duty could only reach its consummation in a warrior's death. His record in the Great War as strategist, administrator and leader, will be judged by the eyes of other generations than our own. Let us hope they will also remember the comfort his character and personality gave to his countrymen in their hours of hardest trial.

★     ★     ★

The end of the Dardanelles campaign closed the second great period of the struggle. There was nothing left on land now but the war of exhaustion—not only of armies but of nations. No more strategy, very little tactics; only the dull wearing down of the weaker combination by exchanging lives; only the multiplying of machinery on both sides to exchange them quicker. The continuous front now stretched not only from the Alps to the Seas, but across the Balkan Peninsula, across Palestine, across Mesopotamia. The Central Empires had successfully defended their southern flank in the Balkans and in Turkey. Their victory quelled simultaneously all likelihood of any attempt against their northern flank upon the Baltic. All such ideas had received their quietus. Good, plain, straightforward frontal attacks by valiant flesh and blood against wire and machine guns, "killing Germans" while Germans killed Allies twice as often, calling out the men of forty, of fifty, and even of fifty-five, and the youths of eighteen, sending the wounded soldiers back three or four times over into the shambles—such were the sole manifestations now reserved for the military art. And when at the end, three years later, the throng of uniformed function-aries, who in the seclusion of their offices had complacently presided over this awful process, presented Victory to their exhausted nations, it proved only less ruinous to the victor than to the vanquished.

★     ★     ★

What is a battle? War between equals in power should be a succession of climaxes on which everything is staked, towards which everything tends and from which permanent decisions are obtained. These climaxes have usually been called battles. A battle means that the whole of the resources on either side that can be brought to bear are, during the course of a single episode, concentrated upon the enemy. The scale of a battle must bear due proportion to the whole fighting strength of the armies. Five divisions engaged out of an army of seven may fight a battle. But the same operation in an army of seventy divisions, although the suffering and slaughter are equal, sinks to the rank of a petty combat. A succession of such combats augments the losses without raising the scale of events.

Moreover a battle cannot, properly speaking, be considered apart from the time factor. By overwhelming the enemy's right we place ourselves in a position to attack the exposed flank or rear of his centre; or by piercing his centre we gain the possibility of rolling up his flanks; or by capturing a certain hill we command his lines of communication. But none of these consequential advantages will be gained, if the time taken in the preliminary operations is so long that the enemy can make new dispositions—if, for instance, he can bend back his lines on each side of the rupture and fortify them, or if he can withdraw his army before the hill is taken which would command his communications. If he has time to take such measures effectively, the first battle is over; and the second stage involves a second battle. Now the amount of time required by the enemy is not indefinite. One night is enough to enable a new position to be entrenched and organized. In forty-eight hours the railways can bring large reinforcements of men and guns to any threatened point. The attacker is confronted with a new situation, a different problem, a separate battle. It is a misnomer to describe the resumption of an attack in these different circumstances as a part of the original battle, or to describe a series of such disconnected efforts as one pro-longed battle. Operations consisting of detached episodes extending over months and divided by intervals during which a series of entirely new situations are created, however great their scale, cannot be compared—to take some modern instances—with Blenheim, Rossbach, Austerlitz, Waterloo, Gettysburg, Sedan, the Marne, or Tannenberg.

The Truths of War are absolute, but the principles governing their application have to be deduced on each occasion from the circumstances, which are always different; and in consequence no rules are any guide to action. Study of the past is invaluable as a means of training and storing the mind, but it is no help without selective discernment of the particular facts and of their emphasis, relation and proportion.

German, like British military policy, oscillated throughout the

Great War between two opposed conceptions of strategy. Reduced to the simplest terms the contrasted theories may be expressed as follows: To attack the strong, or to attack the weak. Once all attempts against the Dardanelles were finally excluded from consideration, little was left to Britain but to attack the strong. The Balkans were lost, and the scale of the armies required to produce decisive results in the Balkan Peninsula or in Turkey had by this time outrun the limits of available sea power. The prizes had disappeared or dwindled; the efforts required to gain them had been multiplied beyond all reason. But to Germany, with her central position and excellent railway system, both alternative policies were constantly open, and her leaders, in their torment of perplexity were drawn now in one direction and now in the other.

To contend that either of these theories was wholly and invariably right and the other wrong would be to press argument beyond the bounds of common sense. Obviously if you can beat your strongest opponent in the hostile combination you should do so. But if you cannot beat your strongest opponent in the main theatre, nor he beat you; or if it is very unlikely that you can do so, and if the cost of failure will be very great, then surely it is time to consider whether the downfall of your strongest foe cannot be accomplished through the ruin of his weakest ally, or one of his weaker allies; and in this connexion a host of political, economic and geographical advantages may arise and play their part in the argument. Every case must be judged upon its merits and in relation to the whole of the circumstances of the occasion. The issue is not one for rigid or absolute decision in general terms; but a strong inclination in theory, based upon profound reflection, is a good guide amid the conflict and confusion of facts.

\*     \*     \*

In a military sense, Verdun had no exceptional importance either to the French or to the Germans. Its forts were disarmed; it contained no substantial magazines; it guarded no significant strategic point. It was two hundred and twenty kilometres from Paris, and its capture would not have made any material difference to the safety either of the capital or of the general line. Falkenhayn and Ludendorff both speak of it as a dangerous sally-port against their main railway communications, scarcely twelve miles away. But seeing that only two inferior lines of railway served Verdun, while the German occupied area in its front was fed by no less than fifteen, it should have been easy for the Germans to provide against such a sally. At its highest, the capture of Verdun would have been a military convenience to the Germans, and in a lesser degree an inconvenience to the French.

It was not to be an attempt at a "break through". The assailants were not to be drawn into pockets from which they would be fired at from all sides. They were to fire at the French and assault them continually in positions which French pride would make it impossible to yield. The nineteen German divisions and the massed artillery assigned to the task were to wear out and "bleed white" the French Army. Verdun was to become an anvil upon which French military manhood was to be hammered to death by German cannon. The French were to be fastened to fixed positions by sentiment, and battered to pieces there by artillery. Of course this ingenious plan would be frustrated if the French did not lend themselves to it, and if they did not consider themselves bound to make disproportionate sacrifices to retain the particular hills on which stood the empty forts of Verdun.

It is certainly arguable that the French would have been wise to play with the Germans around Verdun, economizing their forces as much as possible, selling ground at a high price in German blood wherever necessary, and endeavouring to lead their enemies into a pocket or other unfavourable position. In this way they might have inflicted upon the Germans very heavy losses without risking much themselves, and as we now know they would certainly have baffled Falkenhayn's plan of wearing out the French Army and beating it to pieces upon the anvil. By the end of June the Germans might thus have exhausted the greater part of their offensive effort, advancing perhaps a dozen miles over ground of no decisive strategic significance, while all the time the French would have been accumulating gigantic forces for an overwhelming blow upon the Somme.

However, other counsels—or shall we call them passions?— prevailed, and the whole French nation and army hurled itself into the struggle around Verdun. This decision not only wore out the French reserves and consumed the offensive strength of their army, but it greatly diminished the potential weight of the British attack which was in preparation. Already before the German attack opened, Sir Douglas Haig had taken over an additional sector of the French front, liberating, as we have seen, the Second French Army which was thus enabled to restore the situation at Verdun. As soon as the Battle of Verdun had began, Joffre requested Haig to take over a fresh sector, and this was accordingly effected in the early days of March, thus liberating the whole of the Tenth French Army. Thus the number of British divisions resting and training for the great battle was at the outset sensibly diminished. As the Verdun conflict prolonged itself and deepened all through March, April and May, the inroads upon the fighting strength and disposable surplus of the French Army became increasingly grave. And as July approached the thirty-nine French divisions of the original scheme had shrunk to an available eighteen. This greatly diminished the front of the battle and the weight behind the blow. The numbers available were reduced by at least one-third, and the front to be attacked must be contracted from seventy to about forty-five kilometres. Whereas in the original conception the main onslaught would have been made by the French with the British co-operating in great strength as a smaller army, these roles had now been reversed by the force of events. The main effort must be made by the British, and it was the French who would co-operate to the best of their ability in a secondary role.

While the eyes of the world were riveted on the soul-stirring frenzy of Verdun, and while the ponderous preparations for the Allied counter-stroke on the Somme were being completed, great events were at explosion-point in the East. To those who knew that Russia was recovering her strength with every day, with every hour that passed, who knew of the marshalling of her inexhaustible manhood, and the ever-multiplying and broadening streams of munitions of war which were flowing towards her, the German attack on Verdun had come with a sense of indescribable relief. Russia had been brought very low in the preceding autumn, before the rearguards of the winter closed down on her torn and depleted line. But mortal injury had been warded off. Her armies had been extricated, her front was maintained, and now behind it, "the whole of Russia" was labouring to re-equip and reconstitute her power.

Few episodes of the Great War are more impressive than the resuscitation, re-equipment and renewed giant effort of Russia in 1916. It was the last glorious exertion of the Czar and the Russian people for victory before both were to sink into the abyss of ruin and horror.

It was, however, true that the new Russian armies, though more numerous and better supplied with munitions than ever before, suffered from one fatal deficiency which no Allied assistance could repair. The lack of educated men, men who at least could read and write, and of trained officers and sergeants, woefully diminished the effectiveness of her enormous masses. Numbers, brawn, cannon and shells, the skill of great commanders, the bravery of patriotic troops were to lose two-thirds of their power for want, not of the higher military science, but of Board School education; for want of a hundred thousand human beings capable of thinking for themselves and acting with reasonable efficiency in all the minor and subordinate functions on which every vast organization—most of all the organization of modern war—depends. The mighty limbs of the giant were armed, the conceptions of his brain were clear, his heart was still true, but the nerves which could transform resolve and design into action were but partially developed or non-existent. This defect, irremediable at the time, fatal in its results, in no way detracts from the merit or the marvel of the Russian achievement, which will for ever stand as the supreme monument and memorial of the Empire founded by Peter the Great.

\*     \*     \*

If the German Fleet had been decisively defeated on 31 May, 1916, in battle off Jutland, very great reliefs and advantages would have been gained by the Allies. The psychological effect upon the German nation cannot be estimated, but might conceivably have been profound. The elimination of the German Battle Fleet would have been an important easement to Great Britain, enabling men and material required by the Admiralty for the Grand Fleet to be diverted for the support of the Army. It would have brought the entry of the Baltic into immediate practical possibility. Whether the presence of the British squadrons in the Baltic during the winter of

1916 and the spring of 1917 would have prevented the Russian Revolution is a speculative question, but one which cannot be overlooked. The reactions of a great defeat at sea upon the U-boat attack of 1917, which the Germans were actively preparing, are diverse. On the one hand the disappearance of most of the German battleships might have led to a greater concentration of skilled men and resources upon the development of the U-boat campaign. On the other hand the liberation of the Grand Fleet flotillas and the increased sense of mastery at sea might well have led the Admiralty to more aggressive action against the German river mouths and to an earlier frustration of the U-boat attack. These important advantages must, however, be compared with the consequences to Britain and her Allies which would immediately have followed from a decisive British defeat. The trade and food-supply of the British islands would have been paralysed. Our armies on the Continent would have been cut from their base by superior naval force. All the transportation of the Allies would have been jeopardized and hampered. The United States could not have intervened in the war. Starvation and invasion would have descended upon the British people. Ruin utter and final would have overwhelmed the Allied cause.

The great disparity of the results at stake in a battle between the British and German navies can never be excluded from our thoughts. In a pitched battle fought to a conclusion on British terms between the British and German navies our preponderance was always sufficient to make victory reasonably probable, and in the spring of 1916 so great as to have made it certain. No such assurance could be felt, in the earlier days at any rate, about the results of a piecemeal pursuing engagement against a retreating enemy. If that enemy succeeded in drawing part of our Fleet into a trap of mines or submarines, and eight or nine of the most powerful ships were blown up, the rest might have been defeated by the gunfire of the German Fleet before the whole strength of the British line of battle could have reached the scene. This as we know was always the German dream: but there would certainly be no excuse for a Commander to take risks of this character with the British Fleet at a time when the situation on sea was entirely favourable to us. Neither would there be any defence for a British Admiralty which endeavoured to put pressure upon their Admiral to try to achieve some spectacular result against his better judgment, and by overstraining risks when the prizes on either side were so unequal. To be able to carry on all business on salt water in every part of the world without appreciable let or hindrance, to move armies, to feed nations, to nourish commerce in the teeth of war, implies the possession of the command of the sea. If these are the tests, that priceless sovereignty was ours already. We had the upper hand; we had the advantage; time—so it then seemed, so in the end it proved—was on our side. We were under no compulsion to fight a naval battle except under conditions which made victory morally certain and serious defeat, as far as human vision goes, impossible. A British Admiralissimo cannot be blamed for making these grave and solid reasons the basis of his thought and the foundation from which all his decisions should spring.

★     ★     ★

Sir John Jellicoe was in experience and administrative capacity unquestionably superior to any British Admiral. He knew every aspect and detail of his profession. Afloat or at the Admiralty his intellect, energy, and efficiency won equal confidence from those he served and those he led. Moreover he was a fine sea officer, capable of handling in the most difficult circumstances of weather and navigation the immense Fleet with which he was entrusted. He had served on active service in more than one campaign with courage and distinction. Before the war he was marked out above all others for the supreme command. When at its outbreak he assumed this great duty, his appointment was acclaimed alike by the nation and the Navy. Nearly two years of the full strain of war had only enhanced the confidence and affection with which he was regarded by his officers and men. In judging his discharge of his task we must consider first his knowledge and point of view; secondly the special conditions of the war; and thirdly the spirit which should impel the Royal Navy.

The standpoint of the Commander-in-Chief of the British Grand Fleet was unique. His responsibilities were on a different scale from all others. It might fall to him as to no other man—Sovereign,

Statesman, Admiral or General—to issue orders which in the space of *two or three hours* might nakedly decide who won the war. The destruction of the British Battle Fleet was final. Jellicoe was the only man on either side who could lose the war in an afternoon. First and foremost, last and dominating, in the mind of the Commander-in-Chief stood the determination not to hazard the Battle Fleet.

The safety and overwhelming strength of the Grand Fleet was Jellicoe's all-embracing aim. Its strength must be continually augmented. Every service ancillary to the Battle Fleet must be continually developed on the largest scale and to the highest efficiency. Every vessel that the northern harbours could contain must be placed at his disposal. With this object the Commander-in-Chief in his official letters to the Admiralty and by every other channel open to him continually dwelt upon the weakness and deficiencies of the force at his disposal, and at the same time magnified the power of the enemy. This habit of mind had been acquired during many years of struggle for money with peace-time Governments. It had now become ingrained in his nature.

The combat of the battle-cruisers which preceded the encounter of the main Fleets off Jutland is a self-contained episode. Both Admirals, tactics apart, wished for a trial of strength and quality. Human beings have never wielded so resolutely such tremendous engines or such intense organizations of destruction. The most powerful guns ever used, the highest explosives ever devised, the fastest and the largest ships of war ever launched, the cream of the officers and men of the British and German nations, all that the martial science of either Navy could achieve—clashed against each other in this rigorous though intermittent duel. Each in turn faced an adverse superiority of numbers; each had behind him supporting forces which, could they be made available, would have involved the destruction of the other. Hipper counted on the High Sea Fleet, and Beatty could always fall back on his four *Queen Elizabeths*. Each in turn retired before superior forces and endeavoured to draw his opponent into overwhelming disadvantage. The officers and the men on both sides showed themselves completely unaffected in their decisions and conduct by the frightful apparatus which they used upon each other; and their conflict represents in its intensity the concentration and the consummation of the war effort of men. The battle-cruiser action would of course have been eclipsed by a general battle between the main Fleets. But since this never occurred to any serious extent, the two hours' fight between Beatty and Hipper constitutes the prodigy of modern war on sea.

✱   ✱   ✱

The detailed story of the action has been told so often and told so well that it needs only brief repetition. The salient features can be recognized by anyone.

Both sides deliberately converged to effective striking distance. Fire was opened by the *Lützow* and answered by the *Lion* a little after a quarter to four. Each ship engaged its respective antagonist. As there were six British to five German battle-cruisers, the *Lion* and the *Princess Royal* were able to concentrate on the enemy's flagship *Lützow*. The chances of the battle on either side led to discrepancies in the selection of targets, and sometimes two British ships were firing at one German, while another was ignored, or *vice versa*. Two minutes after the great guns had opened fire at about 14,000 yd., the *Lion* was hit twice; and the third salvo of the *Princess Royal* struck the *Lützow*. On both sides four guns at a time were fired, and at every discharge four shells each weighing about half a ton smote target or water in a volley. In the first thirty-seven minutes of an action which lasted above two hours, one-third of the British force was destroyed. At four o'clock the *Indefatigable*, after twelve minutes at battery with the *Von der Tann*, hit by three simultaneous shells from a salvo of four, blew up and sank almost without survivors. Twenty-six minutes later the *Queen Mary*, smitten amidships by a plunging salvo from the *Derfflinger*, burst into flame, capsized, and after thirty seconds exploded into a pillar of smoke which rose 800 ft. in the air, bearing with it for 200 ft. such items as a 50-ft. steamboat. The *Tiger* and the *New Zealand*, following her at the speed of an ordinary train, and with only 500 yd. between them had barely time to sheer off port and starboard to avoid her wreck. The *Tiger* passed through the smoke cloud black as night, and her gunnery officer, unable to fire, took advantage of the pitch-darkness to reset to zero the director controls of his four turrets. Meanwhile the *Lion*, after being eight minutes in action, was hit on her midship turret (Q) by a shell which, but for a sublime act of personal devotion

313

and comprehension, would have been fatal.

All the crew of the turret except its commanding officer, Major Hervey (Royal Marine Artillery), and his sergeant were instantly killed; and Major Hervey had both his legs shattered or torn off. Each turret in a capital ship is a self-contained organism. It is seated in the hull of the vessel like a fort; it reaches from the armoured gunhouse visible to all, 50 ft. downwards to the very keel. Its intricate hydraulic machinery, its ammunition trunk communicating with the shell-rooms and magazines—all turn together in whatever direction its twin guns may point. The shell of the *Lützow* wrecked the turret and set the wreckage on fire. The shock flung and jammed one of the guns upwards, and twenty minutes later the cartridge which was in its breech slid out. It caught fire and ignited the other charges in the gun-cages. The flash from these passed down the trunk to the charges at the bottom. None but dead and dying remained in the turret. All had been finished by the original shell burst. The men in the switch-board department and the handling parties of the shell-room were instantly killed by the flash of the cordite fire. The blast passed through and through the turret in all its passages and foundations, and rose 200 ft. above its gaping roof. But the doors of the magazines were closed. Major Hervey, shattered, weltering, stifled, seared, had found it possible to give the order down the voice tube: "Close magazines doors and flood magazines." So the *Lion* drove on her course unconscious of her peril, or by what expiring breath it had been effectually averted. In the long, rough, glorious history of the Royal Marines there is no name and no deed which in its character and its consequences ranks above this.

Meanwhile the Vice-Admiral, pacing the bridge among the shell fragments rebounding from the water, and like Nelson of old in the brunt of the enemy's fire, has learned that the *Indefatigable* and the *Queen Mary* have been destroyed, and that his own magazines are menaced by fire. It is difficult to compare sea with land war. But each battle-cruiser was a unit comparable at least to a complete infantry division. Two divisions out of his six have been annihilated in the twinkling of an eye. The enemy, whom he could not defeat with six ships to five, are now five ships to four. Far away all five German battle-cruisers—grey smudges changing momentarily into "rippling sheets of flame"—are still intact and seemingly invulnerable. "Nevertheless," proceeds the official narrative, "the squadron continued its course undismayed." But the movement of these blind, inanimate castles of steel was governed at this moment entirely by the spirit of a single man. Had he faltered, had he taken less than a conqueror's view of the British fighting chances, all these great engines of sea power and war power would have wobbled off in meaningless disarray. This is a moment on which British naval historians will be glad to dwell; and the actual facts deserve to be recorded. The *Indefatigable* had disappeared beneath the waves. The *Queen Mary* had towered up to heaven in a pillar of fire. The *Lion* was in flames. A tremendous salvo struck upon or about her following ship, the *Princess Royal*, which vanished in a cloud of spray and smoke. A signalman sprang on to the *Lion*'s bridge with the words: "*Princess Royal* blown up, sir." On this the Vice-Admiral said to his Flag Captain, "Chatfield, there seems to be something wrong with our —— ships today. Turn two points to port," i.e., two points nearer the enemy.

Thus the crisis of the battle was surmounted. All the German damage was done in the first half-hour.

The supreme moment on which all the thought and efforts of the British and German Admiralties had been for many years concentrated was now at hand. On both sides nearly the whole naval effort of the nation had been devoted to the battle fleets. In the British Navy, at any rate, the picture of the great sea-battle had dominated every other thought, and its needs had received precedence over every other requirement. Everything had been lavished upon the drawing out of a line of batteries of such a preponderance and in such an order that the German Battle Fleet would be blasted and shattered for *certain* in a very short space of time. Numbers, gun power, quality, training—all had been provided for the Commander-in-Chief to the utmost extent possible to British manhood and science. Unless some entirely unforeseen factor intervened or some incalculable accident occurred, there was no reason to doubt that thirty minutes' firing within ten thousand yards between two parallel lines of battle would achieve a complete victory.

Nothing like this particular event had ever happened before, and nothing like it was ever to happen again. The "Nelson touch" arose from years of fighting between the strongest ships of the time. Nelson's genius enabled him to measure truly the consequences of any decision. But that genius worked upon precise practical data. He had seen the same sort of thing happen on a less great scale many times over before the Battle of Trafalgar. Nelson did not have to worry about underwater damage. He felt he knew what would happen in a Fleet action. Jellicoe did not know. Nobody knew. All he knew was that a complete victory would not improve decisively an already favourable naval situation, and that a total defeat would lose the war. He was prepared to accept battle on his own terms; he was not prepared to force one at a serious hazard. The battle was to be fought as he wished it or left unfought.

But while we may justify on broad grounds of national policy the general attitude of the Commander-in-Chief towards the conditions upon which alone a decisive battle should be fought, neither admiration nor agreement can adhere to the system of command and training which he had developed in the Fleet. Everything was centralized in the Flagship, and all initiative except in avoiding torpedo attack was denied to the leaders of squadrons and divisions. A ceaseless stream of signals from the Flagship was therefore required to regulate the movement of the Fleet and the distribution of the fire. These signals prescribed the course and speed of every ship, as well as every manoeuvring turn. In exercises such a centralization may have produced a better drill. But in the smoke, confusion and uncertainty of battle the process was far too elaborate. The Fleet was too large to fight as a single organization or to be minutely directed by the finger of a single man. The Germans, following the Army system of command, had foreseen before the war that the intelligent co-operation of subordinates, who knew thoroughly the general views and spirit of their Chief, must be substituted in a Fleet action for a rigid and centralized control. At this moment the line in which they were approaching was in fact three self-contained independently manoeuvring squadrons following one another. But Jellicoe's system denied initiative not only to his battle squadrons, but even to the flotillas. Throughout the battle he endeavoured personally to direct the whole Fleet. He could, as his own account describes, only see or know a small part of what was taking place; and as no human mind can receive more than a limited number of impressions in any given period of time, his control disappeared as a guiding power, and only remained as a check on the enterprise of others.

★　　★　　★

In the sphere of tactics it is evident that the danger of underwater damage by mine or torpedo, the danger of "losing half the fleet before a shot is fired", dominated the mind of the British Commander-in-Chief. This danger, though less great than was supposed at the time, was nevertheless real and terrible. Coupled with a true measure of the disproportionate consequences of battle to the rival navies, it enforced a policy of extreme caution upon Sir John Jellicoe. This policy was deliberately adopted by him after prolonged thought, and inflexibly adhered to, not only before and during the encounter at Jutland but afterwards. The policy cannot be condemned on account of the unsatisfying episodes to which it led, without due and constant recognition of the fatal consequences which might have followed from the opposite course or from recklessness. Admitting this however to the full, it does not cover several of the crucial Jutland situations, nor that which arose in the German sortie of 19 August. Tactical movements lay open on these occasions to the Grand Fleet for gripping the enemy without in any way increasing the risk of being led into an underwater trap. A more flexible system of fleet training and manoeuvring would have enabled these movements to be made. The attempt to centralize in a single hand the whole conduct in action of so vast a fleet failed. The Commander-in-Chief, with the best will in the world, could not see or even know what was going on. No attempt was made to use the fast division of battleships (*Queen Elizabeths*) to engage the enemy on the opposite side and hold him up to the battle. The British light cruiser squadrons and flotillas were not used as they ought to have been to parry and rupture hostile torpedo attacks, but these were dealt with merely by the passive turn away of the whole Fleet. The sound and prudent reasoning of the Commander-in-Chief against being led into traps did not apply to situations where the enemy was obviously himself surprised, separated from his harbours, and dealing with utterly unforeseen and unforeseeable emergencies. Praiseworthy caution had induced a defensive habit of mind and scheme of tactics which hampered the Grand Fleet even when the special conditions enjoining the caution did not exist.

The ponderous, poignant responsibilities borne successfully, if not triumphantly, by Sir John Jellicoe during two years of faithful command constitute unanswerable claims to the lasting respect of the nation. But the Royal Navy must find in other personalities and other episodes the golden links which carried forward through the Great War the audacious and conquering traditions of the past; and it is to Beatty and the battle-cruisers, to Keyes at Zeebrugge, to Tyrwhitt and his Harwich striking force, to the destroyer and sub-marine flotillas out in all weathers and against all foes, to the wild adventures of the Q-ships, to the steadfast resolution of the British Merchant Service, that the eyes of rising generations will turn.

\* \* \*

A sense of the inevitable broods over the battlefields of the Somme [1916]. The British armies were so ardent, their leaders so confident, the need and appeals of our Allies so clamant, and decisive results seemingly so near, that no human power could have prevented the attempt. All the spring the French had been battling and dying at Verdun, immolating their manhood upon that anvil-altar; and every chivalrous instinct in the new British armies called them to the succour of France, and inspired them with sacrifice and daring. Brusiloff's surprising successes redoubled, if that were possible, the confidence of the British Generals. They were quite sure they were going to break their enemy and rupture his invading lines in France. They trusted to the devotion of their troops, which they knew was boundless; they trusted to masses of artillery and shells never before accumulated in war; and they launched their attack in the highest sense of duty and the strongest conviction of success.

At seven o'clock in the morning of 1 July [1916] the British and French armies rose from their trenches steel-helmeted, gas-masked, equipped with all the latest apparatus of war, bombs, mortars, machine guns light and heavy, and, supported by all their artillery, marched against the enemy on a front of 45 kilometres. Fourteen British divisions and five French divisions were almost immediately engaged. South of the Somme on the French front the Germans were taken completely by surprise. They had not believed the French capable after their punishment at Verdun of any serious offensive effort. They expected at the most only demonstrations. They were not ready for the French, and the French attack, though unfortunately on a needlessly small scale, captured and overwhelmed the German troops throughout the whole of their first system of trenches.

Very different were the fortunes of the British. Everywhere they found the enemy fully prepared. The seven-days' bombardment had by no means accomplished what had been expected. Safely hidden in the deep dugouts, the defenders and their machine guns were practically intact. From these, they emerged with deadly effect at the moment of assault or even after the waves of attack had actually passed over and beyond them. Though the German front line was crossed at every point, the great advance into his position failed except on the right. The three British divisions on that flank captured Montauban and Mametz and an area $4\frac{1}{2}$ miles wide by $1\frac{1}{2}$ miles deep, thus isolating Fricourt on the south. The 21st Division north of this village also made progress and gained nearly a mile. But though the defenders of Fricourt were thus almost cut off, the attempt to storm the village failed. Northwards again the two divisions of the Third Army, though they advanced a thousand yards, failed in spite of repeated efforts to capture La Boiselle or Ovillers on the long spurs of the Pozières plateau. By nightfall the gain in this part of the field comprised only two pockets or bulges in the enemy's position. The attack of the X Corps with three divisions broke down before the immense defences of the Thiepval spur and plateau. Although two of its great supporting points, the Leipzig and Schwaben redoubts, were captured, all attacks on Thiepval failed, and the failure to take Thiepval entailed the evacuation of the Schwaben. Opposite Beaumont-Hamel, on the extreme left, the VIII Corps, after reaching the German front line, was driven back to its own trenches. The subsidiary attack made by the Third Army against Gommecourt completely failed, practically no damage to the German defences having been done in the long bombardment.

319

Night closed over the still-thundering battlefield. Nearly 60,000 British soldiers had fallen, killed or wounded, or were prisoners in the hands of the enemy. This was the greatest loss and slaughter sustained in a single day in the whole history of the British Army. Of the infantry who advanced to the attack, nearly half had been overtaken by death, wounds or capture. Against this, apart from territory, we had gained 4,000 prisoners and a score of cannon.

The extent of the catastrophe was concealed by the Censorship, and its significance masked by a continuance of the fighting on a far smaller scale, four divisions alone being employed. The shattered divisions on the left were placed under General Gough, whose command, originally designated the "Reserve Corps" and intended to receive resting divisions, was renamed the "Reserve Army" and given orders to maintain "a slow and methodical pressure" on the enemy's front. Henceforward the battle degenerated into minor operations which proceeded continuously on a comparatively small front. The losses were however in this phase more evenly balanced, as the Germans delivered many vigorous counter-attacks.

The anatomy of the battles of Verdun and the Somme was the same. A battlefield had been selected. Around this battlefield walls were built—double, triple, quadruple—of enormous cannon. Behind these railways were constructed to feed them, and mountains of shells were built up. All this was the work of months. Thus the battlefield was completely encircled by thousands of guns of all sizes, and a wide oval space prepared in their midst. Through this awful arena all the divisions of each army, battered ceaselessly by the enveloping artillery, were made to pass in succession, as if they were the teeth of interlocking cog-wheels grinding each other.

For month after month the ceaseless cannonade continued at its utmost intensity, and month after month the gallant divisions of heroic human beings were torn to pieces in this terrible rotation. Then came the winter, pouring down rain from the sky to clog the feet of men, and drawing veils of mist before the hawk-eyes of their artillery. The arena, as used to happen in the Coliseum in those miniature Roman days, was flooded with water. A vast sea of ensanguined mud, churned by thousands of vehicles, by hundreds of thousands of men and millions of shells, replaced the blasted dust.

Still the struggle continued. Still the remorseless wheels revolved. Still the auditorium of artillery roared. At last the legs of men could no longer move; they wallowed and floundered helplessly in the slime. Their food, their ammunition lagged behind them along the smashed and choked roadways.

\*     \*     \*

The campaign of 1916 on the Western Front was from beginning to end a welter of slaughter, which after the issue was determined left the British and French armies weaker in relation to the Germans when it opened, while the actual battle fronts were not appreciably altered, and except for the relief of Verdun, which relieved the Germans no less than the French, no strategic advantage of any kind had been gained. The German unwisdom in attacking Verdun was more than cancelled in French casualties, and almost cancelled in the general strategic sphere by the heroic prodigality of the French defence. The loss in prestige which the Germans sustained through their failure to take Verdun was to be more than counterbalanced by their success in another theatre while all the time they kept their battle front unbroken on the Somme.

But this sombre verdict, which it seems probable posterity will endorse in still more searching terms, in no way diminishes the true glory of the British Army. A young army, but the finest we have ever marshalled; improvised at the sound of the cannonade, every man a volunteer, inspired not only by love of country but by a widespread conviction that human freedom was challenged by military and imperial tyranny, they grudged no sacrifice however unfruitful and shrank from no ordeal however destructive. Struggling forward through the mire and filth of the trenches, across the corpse-strewn crater fields, amid the flaring, crashing, blasting barrages and murderous machine-gun fire, conscious of their race, proud of their cause, they seized the most formidable soldiery in Europe by the throat, slew them and hurled them unceasingly backward. If two lives or ten lives were required by their commanders to kill one German, no word of complaint ever rose from the fighting troops. No attack however forlorn, however fatal, found them without ardour. No slaughter however desolating prevented them from returning to the charge. No physical conditions however severe

321

deprived their commanders of their obedience and loyalty. Martyrs not less than soldiers, they fulfilled the high purpose of duty with which they were imbued. The battlefields of the Somme were the graveyards of Kitchener's Army. The flower of that generous manhood which quitted peaceful civilian life in every kind of workaday occupation, which came at the call of Britain, and as we may still hope, at the call of humanity, and came from the most remote parts of her Empire, was shorn away for ever in 1916. Unconquerable except by death, which they had conquered, they have set up a monument of native virtue which will command the wonder, the reverence and the gratitude of our island people as long as we endure as a nation among men.

\*     \*     \*

The conscription crisis in April, 1916, was averted by further concessions on the part of Mr. Asquith. A new National Service Bill was passed, and Mr. Lloyd George remained in the government. During the summer and autumn the Coalition Government hung uneasily together racked by many stresses and strains. The reproaches which sprang from the ruin of Roumania and the downfall of all the hopes of 1916 renewed the struggle between the two sections of the Cabinet. The resignation of Mr. Lloyd George led immediately to the fall of the government. The kaleidoscopic groupings and re-groupings of the Ministerial personages which accompanied this event will some day form a profoundly instructive chapter in British constitutional history.

On 5 December Mr. Asquith tendered to the King his resignation and that of his Ministry. Mr. Bonar Law, summoned by the Sovereign, advised that Mr. Lloyd George was the only possible successor. Every effort to induce Mr. Asquith to associate himself with the new Administration was made without success. Followed by all his Liberal colleagues, with the exception of Mr. Lloyd George, he retired into patriotic opposition, and the new Triumvirate of Mr. Lloyd George, Mr. Bonar Law and Sir Edward Carson assumed, with what were in practice dictatorial powers, the direction of affairs. These decisions were not challenged by Parliament, were accepted by the nation, and were acclaimed by the press.

The new Prime Minister wished to include me in his government;

but this idea was received with extreme disfavour by important personages whose influence during this crisis was decisive. Lord Northcliffe was animated at this time by a violent hostility to me. He made haste to announce in *The Times* and the *Daily Mail* that it had been firmly resolved to exclude from office those who had been responsible for the failures of the war, and that the public would "learn with relief and satisfaction that Mr. Churchill would not be offered any post in the new Administration". He also endeavoured—though happily without success—to veto the appointment of Mr. Balfour as Foreign Secretary. Four prominent Conservatives, judged indispensable to the new combination, signed or made a statement stipulating as a condition of taking office that neither I nor Lord Northcliffe should be Ministers. To this extent therefore—though perhaps in a manner scarcely complimentary to himself—Lord Northcliffe received a powerful reinforcement in his view. It could certainly be adduced with validity that my conduct while First Lord was *sub judice* until the Dardanelles Commission had presented its report. Mr. Lloyd George was in no position in these circumstances to resist this oddly combined but formidable cabal. He therefore sent me a message a few days later, through a common friend, Lord Riddell, that he was determined to achieve his purpose, but that the adverse forces were too strong for the moment. I replied through the same channel with a verbal declaration of political independence.

*　　*　　*

Mr. Lloyd George possessed two characteristics which were in harmony with this period of convulsion. First, a power of living in the present, without taking short views. Every day for him was filled with the hope and the impulse of a fresh beginning. He surveyed the problems of each morning with an eye unobstructed by preconceived opinions, past utterances, or previous disappointments and defeats. In times of peace such a mood is not always admirable, nor often successful for long. But in the intense crisis when the world was a kaleidoscope, when every month all the values and relations were changed by some prodigious event and its measureless reactions, this inexhaustible mental agility, guided by the main purpose of Victory, was a rare advantage. His intuition fitted the crisis better than the logical reasoning of more rigid minds.

The quality of living in the present and starting afresh each day led directly to a second and invaluable aptitude. Mr. Lloyd George in this period seemed to have a peculiar power of drawing from misfortune itself the means of future success. From the U-boat depredations he obtained the convoy system: out of the disaster of Caporetto he extracted the Supreme War Council: from the catastrophe of 21 March [1918] he drew the Unified Command and the immense American reinforcement.

His ascendancy in the high circles of British Government and in the councils of the Allies grew in the teeth of calamities. He did not sit waiting upon events to give a wiseacre judgment. He grappled with the giant events and strove to compel them, undismayed by mistakes and their consequences. Tradition and convention troubled him little. He never sought to erect some military or naval figure into a fetish behind whose reputation he could take refuge. The military and naval hierarchies were roughly handled and forced to adjust themselves to the imperious need. Men of vigour and capacity from outside the Parliamentary sphere became the ministerial heads of great departments. He neglected nothing that he perceived. All parts of the task of government claimed his attention and interest. He lived solely for his work and was never oppressed by it. He gave every decision when it was required. He scarcely ever seemed to bend under the burden. To his native adroitness in managing men and committees he now added a high sense of proportion in war policy and a power of delving to the root of unfamiliar things. Under his Administration both the Island and the Empire were effectually organized for war. He formed the Imperial War Cabinet which centred in a single executive the world-spread resources of the British Monarchy. The convoy system, which broke the U-boat attack at sea; the forward impulsion in Palestine, which overwhelmed the Turks, and the unified command which inaugurated the victories in France, belonged in their main stress and resolve as acts of policy to no one so much as to the First Minister of the Crown.

*　　*　　*

The beginning of 1917 was marked by three stupendous events:

the German declaration of unlimited U-boat war, the intervention of the United States, and the Russian revolution. Taken together these events constitute the second great climax of the war. The order in which they were placed was decisive. If the Russian revolution had occurred in January instead of in March, or if, alternatively, the Germans had waited to declare unlimited U-boat war until the summer, there would have been no unlimited U-boat war and consequently no intervention of the United States. If the Allies had been left to face the collapse of Russia without being sustained by the intervention of the United States, it seems certain that France could not have survived the year, and the war would have ended in a Peace by negotiation, or, in other words, a German victory. Had Russia lasted two months less, had Germany refrained for two months more, the whole course of events would have been revolutionized. In this sequence we discern the footprints of Destiny. Either Russian endurance or German impatience was required to secure the entry of the United States, and both were forthcoming.

The total defeat of Germany was due to three cardinal mistakes: the decision to march through Belgium regardless of bringing Britain into the war; the decision to begin the unrestricted U-boat war regardless of bringing the United States into the war; and thirdly, the decision to use the German forces liberated from Russia in 1918 for a final onslaught in France. But for the first mistake they would have beaten France and Russia easily in a year; but for the second mistake they would have been able to make a satisfactory peace in 1917; but for the third mistake they would have been able to confront the Allies with an unbreakable front on the Meuse or on the Rhine, and to have made self-respecting terms as a price for abridging the slaughter. All these three errors were committed by the same forces, and by the very forces that made the military strength of the German Empire. The German General Staff, which sustained the German cause with such wonderful power, was responsible for all these three fatal decisions. Thus nations as well as individuals come to ruin through the over-exercise of those very qualities and faculties on which their dominion has been founded.

However long the controversy may last, there will never be any agreement between the belligerent nations on the rights or wrongs of U-boat warfare. The Germans never understood, and never will understand, the horror and indignation with which their opponents and the neutral world regarded their attack. They believed sincerely that the outcry was only hypocrisy and propaganda. The law and custom of the sea were very old. They had grown up in the course of centuries and, although frequently broken in the instance, had in the main stood the stress of many bitter conflicts between nations. To seize even an enemy merchant ship at sea was an act which imposed strict obligations on the captor. To make a neutral ship a prize of war stirred whole histories of international law. But between taking a ship and sinking a ship was a gulf. The captor of a neutral ship at sea had by long tradition been bound to bring his prize into harbour and judge her before the Prize Courts. To sink her incontinently was odious; to sink her without providing for the safety of the crew, to leave that crew to perish in open boats or drown amid the waves was in the eyes of all seafaring peoples a grisly act, which hitherto had never been practised deliberately except by pirates. Thus old seagoing nations, particularly Britain, France, Holland, Norway and the United States, saw in the U-boat war against merchant ships, and particularly neutral merchant ships, depth beyond depth of enormity. And indeed the spectacle of helpless merchant seamen, their barque shattered and foundering, left with hard intention by fellow-mariners to perish in the cruel sea, was hideous.

But the Germans were newcomers on salt water. They cared little for all these ancient traditions of seafaring folk. Death for them was the same in whatever form it came to men. It ended in a more or less painful manner their mortal span. Why was it more horrible to be choked with salt water than with poison gas, or to starve in an open boat than to rot wounded but alive in No Man's Land? The British blockade treated the whole of Germany as if it were a beleaguered fortress, and avowedly sought to starve the whole population—men, women and children, old and young, wounded and sound—into submission. Suppose the issues had arisen on land instead of at sea; suppose large numbers of Americans and neutrals had carried food or shell into the zone of the armies under the fire of the German artillery; suppose their convoys were known to be traversing certain roads towards the front: who would have hesitated for a moment to overwhelm them with drum-fire and blast them from the face of the earth? Who ever hesitated to fire on towns and villages because helpless and inoffensive non-combatants were gathered there? If they came within reach of the guns, they had to take their chance, and why should not this apply to the torpedoes too? Why should it be legitimate to slay a neutral or a non-combatant on land by cannon if he got in the way, and a hideous atrocity to slay the same neutral or non-combatant by torpedo on the seas? Where was the sense in drawing distinctions between the two processes? Policy might spread its web of calculation, but in logic the path was clear. Yes, we will if necessary kill everyone of every condition who comes within our power and hinders us from winning the war, and we draw no distinction between land and sea. Thus the German Naval Staff. But the neutrals took a different view.

Coming to the end of 1916, and in the breathing space which winter still affords to warring nations, the German Chiefs haggardly surveyed the deadly scene. In spite of the disasters which had followed Falkenhayn's decision to attack Verdun and to neglect the Eastern Fronts, Germany had survived. She had bled the French at Verdun; she had withstood the British upon the Somme; she had repaired the breach made by Brusiloff; she had even found strength to strike down Roumania, and had emerged from the year's welter with this trophy of victory. But the sense of frightful peril, of increasing pressure, of dwindling resources, of hard pressed fronts, of blockade-pinched populations, of red sand running out in the time-glass, lay heavily upon the leaders of Germany. In the West the Allies were preparing still more formidable blows for the spring; Russian resistance was unweakened; it was even reviving on a scale almost incredible. But for the first time two hundred U-boats were at hand. Would it be possible with these to starve Britain and so, even if war with the United States resulted, "break the backbone" of the Allies?

During November and December the German Chancellor and the Military and Naval leaders racked the Emperor with their contentions: whether two hundred U-boats in the hand were worth 120 million Americans across the Atlantic: whether Britannia rules not only the waves but the waters underneath them too. Dire issue, exceeding in intensity the turning points in the struggles of Rome and Carthage!

There is no doubt that the responsibility for the decision rests upon Hindenburg and Ludendorff. Tirpitz was gone. He even argues that the moment for ruthless U-boat war had already passed, and records a somewhat hesitating comment of "Too late". But Main Headquarters had long been converted to the need of using the U-boat weapon at all costs to the full. In Ludendorff they had found a Chief who shrank from nothing, and upon whose mind supreme hazards exercised an evident fascination. The old Field-Marshal shared or adopted his resolve. He threw his whole weight against the Chancellor. The Admirals chimed in with promises of swift decisive success. The Civil Powers felt the balance turning against them. Their peace overtures had been unceremoniously rejected by the Allies. The stern interchange of telegrams between Hindenburg and Bethmann-Hollweg in the last week of the year marked the end of the Chancellor's resistance. His capitulation followed on 9 January [1917]. It would have been better before history to have gone down with flag flying. No one can doubt what his convictions were, and we now know that they were right. Events forthwith began their new course.

\*   \*   \*

Surely to no nation has Fate been more malignant than to Russia. Her ship went down in sight of port. She had actually weathered the storm when all was cast away. Every sacrifice had been made; the toil was achieved. Despair and Treachery usurped command at the very moment when the task was done.

The long retreats were ended; the munition famine was broken; arms were pouring in; stronger, larger, better equipped armies guarded the immense front; the depots overflowed with sturdy men. Alexeieff directed the Army and Koltchak the Fleet. Moreover, no difficult action was now required: to remain in presence: to lean with heavy weight upon the far-stretched Teutonic line: to hold without exceptional activity the weakened hostile forces on her front: in a word to endure—that was all that stood between Russia and the fruits of general victory.

It is the shallow fashion to dismiss the Czarist regime as a purblind, corrupt, incompetent tyranny. But a survey of its thirty months' war with Germany and Austria should correct these loose impressions and expose the dominant facts. We may measure the strength of the Russian Empire by the battering it had endured, by the disasters it had survived, by the inexhaustible forces it had developed, and by the recovery it had made. In the Governments of States, when great events are afoot, the leader of the nation, whoever he be, is held accountable for failure and vindicated by success. No matter who wrought the toil, who planned the struggle, to the supreme responsible authority belongs the blame or credit for the result.

Why should this stern test be denied to Nicholas II? He had made many mistakes, what ruler had not? He was neither a great captain nor a great prince. He was only a true, simple man of average ability, of merciful disposition, upheld in all his daily life by his faith in God. But the brunt of supreme decisions centred upon him. At the summit where all problems are reduced to Yea or Nay, where events transcend the faculties of men and where all is inscrutable, he had to give the answers. His was the function of the compass-needle. War or no war? Advance or retreat? Right or left? Democratize or hold firm? Quit or persevere? These were the battlefields of Nicholas II. Why should he reap no honour from them? The devoted onset of the Russian armies which saved Paris in 1914; the mastered agony of the munitionless retreat; the slowly regathered forces; the victories of Brusiloff; the Russian entry upon the campaign of 1917, unconquered, stronger than ever; has he no share in these? In spite of errors vast and terrible, the regime he personified, over which he presided, to which his personal character gave the vital spark, had at this moment won the war for Russia.

He is about to be struck down. A dark hand, gloved at first in folly, now intervenes. Exit Czar. Deliver him and all he loved to wounds and death. Belittle his efforts, asperse his conduct, insult his memory; but pause then to tell us who else was found capable. Who or what could guide the Russian State? Men gifted and daring; men ambitious and fierce; spirits audacious and commanding—of these there was no lack. But none could answer the few plain questions on which the life and fame of Russia turned. With victory in her grasp she fell upon the earth, devoured alive, like Herod of old, by worms. But not in vain her valiant deeds. The giant mortally stricken had just time, with dying strength, to pass the torch eastward across the ocean to a new Titan long sunk in doubt who now arose and began ponderously to arm. The Russian Empire fell on 16 March [1917]; on 6 April the United States entered the war.

\*　　\*　　\*

Of all the grand miscalculations of the German High Command none is more remarkable than their inability to comprehend the meaning of war with the American Union.

The war had lasted nearly three years; all the original combatants were at extreme tension; on both sides the dangers of the front were matched by other dangers far behind the throbbing lines of contact. Russia has succumbed to these new dangers; Austria is breaking up; Turkey and Bulgaria are wearing thin; Germany herself is forced even in full battle to concede far-reaching Constitutional rights and franchise to her people; France is desperate; Italy is about to pass within an ace of destruction; and even in stolid Britain there is a different light in the eyes of men. Suddenly a nation of one hundred and twenty millions unfurls her standard on what is already the stronger side; suddenly the most numerous democracy in the world, long posing as a judge, is hurled, nay, hurls itself into the conflict. The loss of Russia was forgotten in this new reinforcement. Defeatist movements were strangled on the one side and on the other inflamed. Far and wide through every warring nation spread these two opposite impressions—"The whole world is against us"—"The whole world is on our side".

American historians will perhaps be somewhat lengthy in explaining to posterity exactly why the United States entered the Great War on 6 April, 1917, and why they did not enter at any earlier moment. American ships had been sunk before by German submarines; as many American lives were lost in the Lusitania as in all the five American ships whose sinking immediately preceded the declaration of war. As for the general cause of the Allies, if it was good in 1917 was it not equally good in 1914? There were plenty of reasons of high policy for staying out in 1917 after waiting so long.

It was natural that the Allies, burning with indignation against Germany, breathless and bleeding in the struggle, face to face with mortal dangers, should stand amazed at the cool, critical, detached attitude of the great Power across the Atlantic. In England particularly, where laws and language seemed to make a bridge of mutual comprehension between the two nations, the American abstention was .hard to understand. But this was to do less than justice to important factors in the case. The United States did not feel in any immediate danger. Time and distance interposed their minimizing perspectives. The mass of the people engaged in peaceful industry, grappling with the undeveloped resources of the continent which was their inheritance, absorbed in domestic life and politics, taught by long constitutional tradition to shun foreign entanglements, had an entirely different field of mental interest from that of Europe. World Justice makes its appeal to all men. But what share, it was asked, had Americans taken in bringing about the situation which had raised the issue of World Justice? Was even this issue so simple as it appeared to the Allies? Was it not a frightful responsibility to launch a vast, unarmed, remote community into the raging centre of such a quarrel? That all this was overcome is the real wonder. All honour to those who never doubted, and who from the first discerned the inevitable path.

At the Ministry of Munitions [the author was appointed Minister of Munitions on 17 July, 1917] I worked with incomparably the largest and most powerful staff in my experience. Here were gathered the finest business brains of the country working with might and main and with disinterested loyalty for the common cause. Many if not most of the leading men stood at the head of those industries which were most expanded by war needs. They therefore resigned altogether the immense fortunes which must inevitably have come to them, had they continued as private contractors. They served the State for honour alone. They were content to see men of lesser standing in their own industries amass great wealth and extend the scale of their business. In the service of the Crown there was a keen rivalry among them; and the position of Member of Council with its general outlook was deeply prized. According to the Statute constituting the office, the whole authority rested with the Minister; but in practice the Council had a true collective responsibility.

If I dwell with pride upon the extraordinary achievements of the Munitions Council in the field of supply, it is not to appropriate the credit. That belongs in the first instance to Mr. Lloyd George, who gathered together the great majority of these able men, and whose foresight in creating the national factories laid the foundations for subsequent production. It belongs also to the men who did the work, who quarried and shaped the stones, and to whose faithful, resourceful, untiring contrivance and exertion the Army and the nation owe a lasting debt.

*　　*　　*

The British offensive against Passchendaele [in the autumn of 1917] unrolled its sombre fate. The terrific artillery pulverized the ground, smashing simultaneously the German trenches and the ordinary drainage. By sublime devotion and frightful losses small indentations were made upon the German front. In six weeks at the farthest point we had advanced four miles. Soon the rain descended, and the vast crater fields became a sea of choking fetid mud in which men, animals and tanks floundered and perished hopelessly. The few tracks which alone could be preserved across this morass were swept with ceaseless shell fire, through which endless columns of transport marched with fortitude all night long. The impossibility of supplying the British field and medium batteries with ammunition, at any distance from the only road maintained in being, led to their being massed in line by its side. Thus there could be no concealment, and the German counterfire caused very heavy losses in gunners and guns and killed nearly all the artillery horses.

The disappointing captures of ground were relieved by tales of prodigious German slaughter. The losses and anxieties inflicted upon the enemy must not be underrated. Ludendorff's admissions are upon record. These violent sustained thrusts shook the enemy to their foundations. But the German losses were always on a far smaller scale. They always had far fewer troops in the cauldron. They always took nearly two lives for one and sold every inch of ground with extortion.

In Flanders the struggle went on. New divisions continued to replace those that were shattered. The rain descended and the mud sea spread. Still the will-power of the Commander and the discipline of the Army remained invincible. By measureless sacrifices Passchendaele was won. But beyond, far beyond, still rose intact and unapproachable the fortifications of Klercken. August had passed away; September was gone; October was far spent. The full severity of a Flanders winter gripped the ghastly battlefield. Ceaselessly the Menin gate of Ypres disgorged its streams of manhood. Fast as the cannons fired, the ammunition behind them flowed in faster. Even in October the British Staff were planning and launching offensives and were confident of reaching the goal of decisive results. It was not until the end of November that final failure was accepted.

The Passchendaele offensive had ended in mire and carnage, when suddenly there emerged from the British sector opposite Cambrai a battle totally different in character from any yet fought in the war. For the first time the mechanical method of securing Surprise was effectively used. Here was a superb example of scientific novelty and audacious tactics combined into a conception of military genius. But this conception, not only its underlying idea but its methods and even its instruments, had been pressed upon the British High Command for almost exactly two years. The plan of attack at Cambrai was inherent in the original conception of the tank. It was for this, and for this precisely, that tanks had been devised.

Tanks in considerable and growing numbers had been in action on the British front since their conception had been improvidently exposed to the enemy on the Somme in 1916. At the headquarters of the Tank Corps the original tactical ideas inspiring their conception had been earnestly and thoroughly developed. The Tank Corps had never yet been allowed to put them into practice. These engines had been used in small numbers as mere ancillaries to infantry and artillery battles. They had been condemned to wallow in the crater fields under the full blast of massed German artillery, or to founder in the mud of Passchendaele. Never had they been allowed to have their own chance in a battle made for them, adapted to their special capacities, and in which they could render the inestimable service for which they had been specially designed.

If British and French war leaders had possessed—not more genius, for the possibilities had by this time been obvious to all who were studying the tank problem—but the vision and comprehension which is expected from the honoured chiefs of great armies, there was no reason why a battle like Cambrai could not have been fought a year before, or better still, why three or four concerted battles like Cambrai could not have been fought simultaneously in the spring of 1917. Then indeed the enemy's front line pierced at once in three or four places might have been completely overwhelmed on a front of fifty miles. Then indeed the roll forward of the whole army might have been achieved and the hideous deadlocks broken.

But, it will be said, such assertions take insufficient account of the practical difficulties, of the slowly gathered experience, of the immense refinements of study, discipline and organization required. Could, for instance, three thousand tanks have been manufactured by the spring of 1917? Could the men to handle them have been spared from the front? Could their tactical training have been perfected behind the line and out of contact with the enemy? Could the secret have been kept? Would not preparation on so large a scale, even behind the line, have become apparent to the enemy? To all these questions we will answer that one-tenth of the mental effort expended by the Headquarters Staff on preparing the old-fashioned offensives of which the war had consisted, one-twentieth of the influence they used to compel reluctant Governments to sanction these offensives, one-hundredth of the men lost in them, would have solved all the problems easily and overwhelmingly before the spring of 1917. As for the Germans getting to hear of it, learning, for instance, that the British were practising with Caterpillar armoured cars at dummy trenches behind their lines on a large scale—what use would they have made of their knowledge? What use did Ludendorff make of the awful disclosure, not as a mere rumour or questionable Intelligence report, but of the actual apparition of the tanks in September, 1916? There is a melancholy comfort in reflecting that if the British and French commands were short-sighted, the ablest soldier in Germany was blind. In truth, these high military experts all belong to the same school. Haig at least moved faster and farther along the new path, and in consequence, doubtingly and tardily, he reaped in the end a generous reward.

Accusing as I do without exception all the great ally offensives of 1915, 1916, and 1917, as needless and wrongly conceived operations of infinite cost, I am bound to reply to the question, What else could be done? And I answer it, pointing to the Battle of Cambrai, "*This* could have been done." This in many variants, this in larger and better forms ought to have been done, and would have been done if only the generals had not been content to fight machine-gun bullets with the breasts of gallant men, and think that that was waging war.

It remains only to be said of the Battle of Cambrai that the initial success so far exceeded the expectations of the Third Army Staff that no suitable preparations had been made to exploit it. The Cavalry who scampered forward were naturally soon held up by snipers and machine guns, and no important advance beyond the first day's gains was achieved. The railways at this part of the German front favoured a rapid hostile concentration, and ten days after the victory the Germans delivered a most powerful counter-stroke in which they recaptured a large portion of the conquered ground and took in their turn ten thousand prisoners and two hundred guns. In this counter-attack the enemy used for the first time those tactics of "infiltration" by small highly competent parties of machine-gunners or trench-mortar men, which they were soon to employ on a larger scale. The bells which had been rung for Cambrai were therefore judged premature, and the year 1917 closed on the allied fronts, British, French, Italian, Russian and Balkan, in a gloom relieved only by Allenby's sword-flash at Jerusalem.

\*    \*    \*

It is commonly said that the German drive on Paris in 1914 and the unlimited U-boat warfare both "nearly succeeded". But this expression requires analysis, and also differentiation between the issues on land and sea. A partisan watching an evenly contested football match, an engineer watching a vehicle whose weight he does not know exactly, crossing a bridge whose strength he has never been able to measure, experience no doubt similar sensations of anxiety or excitement. The processes, however, are different. A football match like a great battle on land is in a continual state of flux and chance. But whether the vehicle will break down the bridge does not depend on chance. It depends on the weight of the vehicle and the strength of the bridge. When both these are unknown beforehand, anxiety is natural. But once it is known that the bridge will bear at least ten tons and the vehicle at the most weighs no more than eight, all misgivings are proved to have been unfounded. To say that the vehicle "nearly" broke down the bridge is untrue. There was never any chance of it. Whereas any one of a score of alternative accidents would have given the German Army Paris in 1914, the seafaring resources of Great Britain were in fact and in the circumstances always superior to the U-boat attack. Moreover, that attack was inherently of a character so gradual that these superior resources could certainly obtain their full development.

The shortcomings in the higher command of the British Navy, afloat and at home, which had led to Admiral de Robeck's failure to force the Dardanelles, to the abortive conclusion of Jutland, and to the neglect to carry the fighting into the German Bight, had given to the enemy during 1915 and 1916 the means of developing an entirely novel form of sea attack upon a scale the potential intensity of which no one could measure beforehand, and which if successful would be fatal. At first sight all seemed to favour the challengers. Two hundred U-boats each possessing between three and four weeks' radius of action, each capable of sinking with torpedo, gun fire or bomb four or five vessels in a single day, beset the approaches to an island along which there passed in and out every week several thousand merchant vessels. The submarine, with only a periscope showing momentarily like a broomstick above the waves, could discharge its torpedo unseen. It could rise to the surface and fire its gun to sink, burn or induce the surrender of a defenceless vessel, and disappear into the invisible depths of the vast waste of water without leaving a trace behind. Of all the tasks ever set to a Navy none could have appeared more baffling than that of sheltering this enormous traffic and groping deep below the surface of the sea for the deadly elusive foe. It was, in fact, a game of blind man's buff in an unlimited space of three dimensions.

Had the problem been surveyed in cold blood beforehand it might well have seemed insoluble. But in the event as the danger grew, so grew also the will-power of the threatened State and the courage, endurance and ingenuity of its servants. At the summit through the authority of the Prime Minister all misgivings were suppressed, all croakers silenced, and all doubters banished from executive responsibility. But strict inquiry was made into facts, and no official grimace passed long for argument. The qualities of audacity, initiative and seamanship inbred in the sailors and young officers of the Navy found in this new warfare their highest opportunity. But without the unquenchable spirit of the Merchant Service nothing would have availed. The foundation of all defence lay in the fact that Merchant-seamen three or four times "submarined" returned unfalteringly to the perilous seas, and even in the awful month when one ship out of every four that left the United Kingdom never came home, no voyage was delayed for lack of resolute civilian volunteers.

As the U-boats were forced by the progressive arming of the British Mercantile Marine to rely increasingly on under-water attacks, they encountered a new set of dangers. The submerged U-boat with its defective vision ran the greatest risk of mistaking neutral for British vessels and of drowning neutral crews, and thus of embroiling Germany with other great Powers. We also resorted to the well-known *ruse de guerre* of hoisting false colours in order further to baffle and confuse the enemy. Thus from a very early stage the U-boats were forced to choose between all the practical inconveniences and far-reaching diplomatic consequences of under-water attack with the torpedo, or on the other hand facing the disproportionate hazards of the gun duel on the surface. It was at this stage that we developed the stratagem of the Q-ship. A number of merchant vessels were specially equipped with torpedo tubes and with concealed guns firing from behind trap-door bulwarks, and sent along the trade routes to offer themselves to the hostile submarines. When the U-boat, wishing to economize torpedoes, attacked the Q-ship by gun fire on the surface, a portion of the British crew took to the boats and by every device endeavoured to entice the Germans to close quarters. Once the enemy was within decisive range, the White Ensign was hoisted, the trap-doors fell and a deadly fire by trained gunners was opened upon them. By these means in 1915 and 1916 eleven U-boats were destroyed and the rest, rendered far more nervous of attacking by gun fire, were thrown back more and more upon their torpedoes. By the end of 1917 this process was complete. The German submarine commanders would not face the unequal gun-fire combat. The stratagem of the Q-ship was thus exhausted, and its last victim, U.88, perished in September, 1917.

*    *    *

There was no surprise about the time or general direction of the German attack [21 March, 1918]. The surprise consisted in its weight, scale and power.

After a bombardment of incredible fury for not more than two to four hours, accompanied at certain points by heavy discharges of poison gas, the German infantry began to advance. The whole of this region had been in their possession during 1915 and the greater part of 1916, and there was no lack in any unit of officers and men who knew every inch of the ground. The form of attack which they adopted was an extension of the method of "infiltration" first tried by them in their counter-stroke after the Battle of Cambrai. A low-lying fog, which was in some places dense, favoured their plan at any rate in the initial stages. The system of detached posts on which the British relied, and which their comparatively small numbers had made necessarily rather open in character, depended to a very large extent upon clear vision, both for the machine gunners themselves and to a lesser extent for their protecting artillery. Aided by the mist, the German infantry freely entered the Forward Zone in small parties of shock troops, carrying with them machine guns and trench mortars. They were followed by large bodies, and even by noon had at many points penetrated the Battle Zone. The British posts, blasted, stunned or stifled by the bombardment or the gas, mystified and baffled by the fog, isolated and often taken in the rear, defended themselves stubbornly and with varying fortunes. Over the whole of the battlefield, which comprised approximately 160 square miles, a vast number of bloody struggles ensued. But the Germans, guided by their excellent organization and their local knowledge, and backed by their immense superiority in numbers, continued during the day to make inroads upon the Battle Zone, and even to pierce it at several points. When darkness fell, nearly all the British divisions had been forced from their original fighting line, and were intermingled at many points with the enemy in the Battle Zone.

The devoted resistance of the isolated British posts levied a heavy toll upon the enemy and played a recognizable part in the final result. From the outset the Germans learned that they had to deal with troops who would fight as long as they had ammunition, irrespective of what happened in any other quarter of the field or whether any hope of success or escape remained.

The conflict was continuous. Fresh German troops poured ceaselessly into action. By the evening of the 22nd the British Fifth Army had been driven completely beyond its battle zone and half the Army was beyond its last prescribed defensive line. The British Third Army still fought in and around the Battle Zone. The German penetration south of the Oise had made serious progress. The British losses by death, wounds or capture exceeded one hundred thousand men; and nearly five hundred guns were already lost. An immense slaughter was also wrought upon the German side. At every step they paid the price of the offensive, but their great numbers rendered their losses inappreciable during the crisis. Overwhelming reserves were close at hand. The British on the other hand had only eight divisions in general reserve of which five were readily available; and the French were too slowly moved or too far away to give effective assistance for several days. Therefore on the night of the 22nd, Sir Hubert Gough ordered a general retreat of the Fifth Army behind the Somme. His orders had been "to protect at all costs the important centre of Péronne and the River Somme to the South" of it. He was fully justified in retiring in a general rear-guard action up to this line. But once the retreat of so thin a line on such a wide front had begun, it was very difficult to stop as long as the enemy pressure continued. The circumstances of each corps or division were so various that those who made a stand found their flanks exposed by others falling back. A great many of the bridges across the Somme were blown up; but enough were left—and among them the most important bridges, confided to the railway authorities and not to the troops—to enable the Germans to pass artillery rapidly across. Moreover, the river was easily fordable at this time.

Backward then across the hideous desolation of the old craterfields rolled the British front for five days in succession. The Cavalry Corps filled the gaps in the line, and the Air Force, concentrating all its strength upon the battle, flying low, inflicted heavy losses on the endless marching columns. Meanwhile reserves drawn from other parts of the line, and improvised forces from the schools and technical establishments, continually reached the scene. At the same time, with every day's advance, the strength and momentum of the German thrust abated. The actual fighting gave place to the painful toiling westward of two weary armies; and when the retreating British were sufficiently reinforced to come to a general halt, their pursuers found themselves not less exhausted, and far in front of their own artillery and supplies. By the evening of the 27th the first crisis of the great battle was over.

*     *     *

Let us focus what had actually happened. With whom lay the victory? Contrary to the generally accepted verdict, I hold that the Germans, judged by the hard test of gains and losses, were decisively defeated. Ludendorff failed to achieve a single strategic object. By the morning of the 23rd he had been forced to resign his dream of overwhelming and crumpling back upon the sea the main strength of the British armies, and to content himself with the hope of capturing Amiens and perhaps dividing the British from the French. After 4 April he abandoned both these most important but to him secondary aims. What then had been gained? The Germans had reoccupied their old battlefields and the regions they had so cruelly devastated and ruined a year before. Once again they entered into possession of those grisly trophies. No fertile province, no wealthy cities, no river or mountain barrier, no new untapped resources were their reward. Only the crater-fields extending abominably wherever the eye could turn. The old trenches, the vast graveyards, the skeletons, the blasted trees and the pulverized villages—these, from Arras to Montdidier and from St. Quentin to Villers-Bretonneux, were the Dead Sea fruits of the mightiest military conception and the most terrific onslaught which the annals of war record. The price they paid was heavy. They lost for the first time in the war, or at any rate since Ypres in 1914, two soldiers killed for every one British, and three officers killed for every two British. They made sixty thousand prisoners and captured over a thousand guns, together with great stores of ammunition and material. But their advantage in prisoners was more than offset by their greater loss in wounded. Their consumption of material exceeded their captures. If the German loss of men was serious, the loss of time was fatal. The great effort had been made and had not succeeded. The German Army was no longer crouched, but sprawled. A great part of its reserves had been exposed and involved. The stress of peril on the other hand wrung from the Allies exertions and sacrifices which, as will be seen, far more than made good their losses.

Hard measure was meted out to General Gough. The Fifth Army from the 28th onwards ceased to exist. Its shattered divisions were painfully reorganized behind the line. The gap was filled by the now rapidly arriving French, by the cavalry, by the improvised forces collected from the schools, and by General Rawlinson who began, from scanty and diverse materials, to constitute a "Fourth Army" and to maintain the tottering and fluctuating line of battle.

Gough never received another fighting command. The Cabinet insisted on his removal on the ground, probably valid, that he had lost the confidence of his troops. This officer had fought his way upwards through the whole war from a Cavalry Brigade to the command of an Army. He was held to have greatly distinguished himself on the Ancre at the close of 1916. With Plumer he bore the brunt of Passchendaele while it continued, and its blame when it ended rested upon him. He was a typical cavalry officer, with a strong personality and a gay and boyish charm of manner. A man who never spared himself or his troops, the instrument of costly and forlorn attacks, he emerged from the Passchendaele tragedy pursued by many fierce resentments among his high subordinates, rumours of which had even reached the rank and file. For over a year his reputation had been such that troops and leaders alike disliked inclusion in the Fifth Army. There was a conviction that in that Army supplies were awkward and attacks not sufficiently studied. In these circumstances Gough was not in a position to surmount the impression of a great disaster. The sternest critic has, however, been unable to find ground for censuring his general conduct of the battle of 21 March. It appears that he took every measure, both before and during the battle, which experience and energy could devise and of which his utterly inadequate resources admitted; that his composure never faltered, that his activity was inexhaustible, that his main decisions were prudent and resolute, and that no episode in his career was more honourable than the disaster which entailed his fall.

From the general not less than from the British point of view, 12 April [1918] is probably, after the Marne, the climax of the war. It looked as if the Germans had resolved to stake their fate and their regathered superiority on battering the life out of the British Army. During twenty days they had hurled nearly ninety divisions in three great battles upon an Army which counted no more than fifty-eight, and of these nearly half were fastened to fronts not under attack. With a superiority of numbers in the areas of assault of three and often four to one, with their brilliantly trained shock troops, with their extraordinary skill and enterprise in manoeuvring with machine guns and trench mortars, with their new infiltration scheme, with their corroding mustard gas, with their terrific artillery and great science of war, they might well succeed. The French seemed to the British Headquarters sunk in stupor and passivity. Since the Nivelle disaster they had been grappling with mutiny and nursing their remaining resources. With the exception of the "set piece" battle of Malmaison in the winter, and the stinted and tardy divisions which had been involved south of the Somme in the later stages of 21 March, they had only fought in ordinary trench warfare for nearly nine months. During that time the much smaller British Army had fought almost unceasingly, and wisely or unwisely had sacrificed in the common cause, apart from the prolonged Arras-Messines offensive of 1917, more than four hundred thousand men in the Passchendaele tragedy, and had now lost nearly three hundred thousand more under Ludendorff's terrible hammer. It was upon an Army bled white by frightful losses, its regimental officers shorn away by scores of thousands, its batteries and battalions filled and refilled with young soldiers plunged into battle before they knew their officers or each other, that the massed might of the desperate German Empire now fell.

Moreover, the shock could not be deadened nor breathing space gained by ceding ground. No large retirement was open to Sir Douglas Haig A few kilometres might be yielded here and there. The dearly bought ground of Passchendaele could be given up and some relief obtained thereby. Ypres could in the last resource be let go. But in front of Amiens, in front of Arras, in front of Béthune, in front of Hazebrouck he must stand or fall. All units and all ranks of the British Expeditionary Force therefore prepared themselves to conquer or die.

The convulsion continued. The reinforcements closed the gaps that were hourly torn in the struggling line. Companies, battalions, even whole brigades were obliterated where they stood. Ludendorff, resolute, ruthless, hazard-loving, raised his stakes. More and more of the German reserves were committed to the onset. The roar of the cannonade resounded through Flanders and reverberated across the Channel. But nothing could move the 55th Division on the right nor the 9th on the left. The Australians were coming, and the 4th Guards Brigade all through the 12th and 13th may be discerned, where all was valour, barring the path to Hazebrouck. So intermingled were the units and formations in the fighting line, that across the Bailleul-Armentières road, Freyberg, V.C., four years before a Sub-Lieutenant, found himself holding a front of four thousand yards with elements of four different divisions, and covered by the remnants of two divisional artilleries that had drifted back with the line. Neuve Eglise was lost, and Bailleul and Méteren; and under the intense pressure the front bent backwards. But it did not break. When on the 17th eight German divisions—seven of them fresh—were violently repulsed in their attack on the famous hill of Kemmel, the crisis of the Battle of the Lys was over. The orders of the Commander had been strictly and faithfully fulfilled.

\* \* \*

A drear panorama confronted the rulers of Germany in the month that followed the Battle of Noyon [opened on 9 June, 1918], and a growing sense of the inevitable began to chill all hearts. No rift, no crack, no crevice appeared in the mighty concourse of States, almost the world in arms, which glared stonily across the lines of battle at Germany and her Allies. France under Clemenceau was flint. The British Army was known to be rapidly recovering, and under Lloyd George's leadership the whole Empire resounded with the clang of redoubled exertion. The Americans were pouring in across the open seas. Italy, so nearly extinguished in the preceding winter, renewed her strength. Meanwhile from every quarter dark tidings flowed in upon Great Headquarters. Turkey was desperate. A sinister silence brooded in Bulgaria. The Austro-Hungarian Empire was upon the verge of dissolution. A mutinous outbreak had occurred in the German Navy. And now the valiant German Army itself, the foundation and life of the whole Teutonic Powers, showed disquieting symptoms. The German nation had begun to despair, and the soldiers became conscious of their mood. Ugly incidents occurred. Desertion increased, and the leave men were reluctant to return. The German prisoners liberated from Russia by the Treaty of Brest-Litovsk returned infected with the Lenin virus. In large numbers they refused to go again to the front. A campaign of unmerited reproach was set on foot against the German officer class. Their painstaking and thorough routine, which had enabled them on all the fronts to exact two Ally lives for every German, was no protection from the charge that they did not share the privations of the troops. The British fire had bitten deep in March and April, and for the first time since the earliest days of the war Germany felt the swift blood-drain she was accustomed to exact from others. Still the majestic war machine obeyed the levers of authority, and the teeth of its thousand wheels, in spite of occasional jars and tremors, kept grinding on remorselessly.

Haig directed Rawlinson to prepare an offensive by the Fourth Army against the German salient before Amiens. Rawlinson's plans were in consequence well advanced. He had accepted with logic and conviction the whole model of a tank battle. There were available in all nearly six hundred tanks, of which, apart from spare machines, ninety-six were supply tanks, twenty-two gun carriers and four hundred and twenty fighting tanks. Of the fighting tanks three hundred and twenty-four were of the new Mark 5 pattern of superior speed and manoeuvring power, and weighed over thirty tons apiece. Everything was subordinated to the surprise of the tank attack. One hundred and twenty brigades of British artillery of all natures were assembled, but all preliminary bombardment was prohibited. Not a shot was to be fired even for registration. The tanks were to advance, unfettered and unprejudiced, simultaneously

344

with the infantry and about two hundred yards behind the creeping barrage. Their approach was assisted by special noise barrages, by the morning mist, and by artificial fog. The British heavy and medium artillery was mainly to be directed upon the enemy's similar guns. The infantry, closely accompanied by numerous field batteries and with large bodies of cavalry at hand, were to exploit the success of the tanks. The essence of the whole plan was surprise. Rawlinson's army had a restricted position of assembly, and German counter-preparation, if it caught our troops in the act of assembling, would have serious results. For these reasons, Rawlinson did not wish to fight hand in hand with the French on his right. He feared lest secrecy should be endangered by a joint operation. Moreover, Debeney's French army had few tanks and could not attack without artillery preparation. To ensure complete co-operation Foch placed all the troops, British and French, under Sir Douglas Haig. The danger lest the French preliminary bombardment should spoil the surprise was overcome by timing the French infantry attack three-quarters of an hour later than the British. Thus not a shot would be fired before zero. On the second and third days of the battle the rest of Debeney's army and Humbert's army were in succession to intervene.

At 4.20 a.m. on 8 August, in the half light of a misty dawn, the British tanks rolled forward into No Man's Land, and simultaneously the Allied artillery opened fire. Four Canadian, four Australian and two British divisions, followed by three more in reserve and the Cavalry Corps, advanced on the British front. Eight French divisions co-operated later in echelon on their right. All along the line, but especially in the centre where the Canadians and Australians fought, victory declared itself forthwith. In less than two hours sixteen thousand prisoners and more than two hundred guns were taken by the British, and by noon tanks and armoured motor cars, followed by cavalry, were scouring the country fourteen kilometres behind the German front. The French, who attacked without tanks, advanced about half as far. But the British advance enabled Chaulnes junction to be brought under close fire and consequently destroyed the German communications on which their whole front from Montdidier to Lassigny depended. This was decisive. Two days later, when Humbert's army joined the battle, the high ground near

Lassigny was found abandoned; and the advance of the Allies was general along a front of 120 kilometres.

*　　*　　*

I spent the 9th and 10th [August] on the battlefield. I had been at the War Cabinet the day before when Sir Henry Wilson had announced the opening of the attack, and when in the afternoon the first reports of a great tank victory began to come through, I decided to get into my aeroplane and take a couple of days' holiday. Rawlinson's Headquarters were at Flixicourt, near Amiens. I was much delayed in reaching them by enormous columns of German prisoners which endlessly streamed along the dusty roads. No one who has been a prisoner of war himself can be indifferent to the lot of the soldier whom the fortunes of war condemn to this plight. The woe-begone expression of the officers contrasted sharply with the almost cheerful countenances of the rank and file. All had passed through a severe experience, the crashing bombardment, the irresistible on-rush of the tanks spurting machine-gun bullets from every unexpected quarter, the catastrophe of surrender, the long march from the battlefield with many claims to consideration in front of theirs, night in the advanced cages—now another long march since dawn.

The General received me with his customary good humour, and at luncheon, while the tramp of new columns of prisoners proclaimed his victory, explained how it had been achieved. It was, truly, *his* victory, and that of the Fourth Army which he directed. He had put aside old-fashioned ideas, he had used new weapons as they should be used, he had reaped swift and rich reward. I had known him since Omdurman, where he was one of Kitchener's leading Staff Officers. In the Great War we had met in every variety of fortune. First on the Aisne in September, 1914, before he had any command at all, when we lay on an unfinished haystack watching the shells play on the Soissons road: next at Antwerp, where he arrived to take over the command at the moment when further defence had become extremely questionable: next in my room at the Admiralty, after the Seventh Division under his command had been virtually destroyed in the first battle of Ypres and when many were ready to lay blame on his tactics. In April, 1918, I had been with him at Dury in the last extremes of 21 March, when with a few cavalry and machine-guns and details from the training establishments he was covering and enduring the dissolution of the Fifth Army. Now we met at the zenith of his career, when he had largely by his personal contribution gained a battle which ranks among the decisive episodes of war.

During these vicissitudes he was always the same. In the best of fortunes or the worst, in the most dangerous and hopeless position or on the crest of the wave, he was always the same tough, cheery gentleman and sportsman. He had always the same welcome for a friend, be he highly or lowly placed, and the same keen, practical, resolute outlook on facts however they might be marshalled.

★   ★   ★

Before the war it had seemed incredible that such terrors and slaughters, even if they began, could last more than a few months. After the first two years it was difficult to believe that they would ever end. We seemed separated from the old life by a measureless gulf. The adaptive genius of man had almost habituated him to the horrors of his new environment. Far away shone a pale star of home and peace; but all around the storm roared with unabated and indeed increasing fury. Year after year every optimist had been discredited, every sober hope cast down, and the British nation had doggedly resigned itself to pursue its task without inquiry when the end would come. In the circles of Government, where so many plans had to be made for more than a year ahead, this mood formed the subconscious foundation of our thoughts. Ultimate victory seemed certain. But how it would come, and whether it would come in 1919 or in 1920, or later, were inquiries too speculative to pursue amid the imperious needs of each day. Still less would anyone dare to hope for peace in 1918. Nevertheless, when from time to time the mental eye fell upon these puzzles, this question immediately presented itself: Would Germany collapse all of a sudden as she had done after Jena, or would she fight it out to the bitter end like the French under Napoleon or the Confederates under Lee? The Great War came when both sides were confident of victory. Would it continue after one side was sure it had no hope? Was it in the

German nature, so valiant yet at the same time so logical, to fight on in revengeful despair? Should we have a year of battle on the Rhine, the march to Berlin, the breaking up of the armies in the open field, the subjugation of the inhabitants; or would there be some intense nervous spasm, some overwhelming and almost universal acceptance of defeat and all that defeat involved? We had always fancied it would be Jena. But all our plans were for a long-drawn alternative.

It was galling to the British Headquarters, justly conscious of the predominant part which our armies were beginning to play in these great successes, to find the credit ascribed by their own Cabinet and public opinion to Marshal Foch. The part the Prime Minister had played in establishing unity of command led him unconsciously to dwell upon the brilliant conceptions of the Generalissimo, and to view only in a half light the potent forward heave of the British Army without which the results would have been mediocre. The Press and public at home followed the lead thus given, and the prevailing impression was that after many disasters and much mismanagement, an extraordinary genius had obtained the supreme command and had almost instantaneously converted defeat into victory. Care has been taken [in *The World Crisis*] to describe some of the splendid decisions on which the fame of Marshal Foch is founded; but this in no way diminishes the services in this campaign of the British Commander-in-Chief. His armies bore the lion's share in the victorious advance, as they had already borne the brunt of the German assault. Foch took a wider survey because he had a higher sphere. It was Haig's duty to take a more restricted view.

But nevertheless, on more than one cardinal occasion, Haig by strenuous insistence deflected the plans of the Supreme Commander with results which were glorious. And ever his shot-pierced divisions, five times decimated within the year, strode forward with discipline, with devotion and with gathering momentum.

Reaction from the mode in fashion at home led the British Headquarters into some disparagement of the French contribution to the final advance. In this they were as far from the truth in one direction as their own Government in the other. In the victorious period from July to 11 November, the French suffered no less than 531,000 casualties themselves, and inflicted 414,000 upon the enemy. That an army and a nation engaged at their full strength from the beginning of the war, which had sustained 700,000 casualties in the first few weeks and nearly 3 million in the first three years, should have been capable of so noble an effort at the end will ever command the admiration and gratitude of their Ally.

\*    \*    \*

The British armies had now [4 November] passed the Selle River, taking in the process 21,000 prisoners and 450 guns, and were marching swiftly forward on Valenciennes, Mons and Maubeuge, driving the enemy before them. The ardour of the troops knew no bounds. The conviction that the terrible enemy they had fought so long was breaking up under their hammer blows, and the rapture and joy of the liberated populations, made them more ready to sacrifice their lives in these last days than even in the darkest periods of the war. Every soldier felt himself at once a Conqueror and a Deliverer. The same impulses inflamed the Americans. As for the French, who shall describe the emotions with which haggard and torn, but regardless of a loss which in these last months (July to November) exceeded half a million men, they day by day battered down their ancient foe, and redeemed the sacred soil of France?

The armistice for which Hindenburg and Ludendorff had argued wore by now the aspect of an unconditional surrender. Ludendorff thereupon wished to fight on, declaring with truth that nothing could worsen the terms which Germany would receive. On the 27th the German Government, being resolved on total submission, moved the Emperor to dismiss him from his post. Hindenburg remained "greatly falling with a falling State". To him and to the German machine gunners belong the honours of the final agony.

When the great organizations of this world are strained beyond breaking point, their structure often collapses at all points simultaneously. There is nothing on which policy, however wise, can build; no foothold can be found for virtue or valour, no authority or impetus for a rescuing genius. The mighty framework of German Imperial Power, which a few days before had overshadowed the nations, shivered suddenly into a thousand individually disintegrating fragments. All her Allies whom she had so long sustained, fell down broken and ruined, begging separately for peace. The faithful armies were beaten at the front and demoralized from the rear. The proud, efficient Navy mutinied. Revolution exploded in the most disciplined and docile of States. The Supreme War Lord fled.

Such a spectacle appals mankind; and a knell rang in the ear of the victors, even in their hour of triumph.

\*　　\*　　\*

It was a few minutes before the eleventh hour of the eleventh day of the eleventh month. I stood at the window of my room looking up Northumberland Avenue towards Trafalgar Square, waiting for Big Ben to tell that the war was over. My mind strayed back across the scarring years to the scene and emotions of the night at the Admiralty when I listened for these same chimes in order to give the signal of war against Germany to our Fleets and squadrons across the world. And now all was over! The unarmed and untrained island nation, who with no defence but its Navy had faced unquestioningly the strongest manifestation of military power in human record, had completed its task. Our country had emerged from the ordeal alive and safe, its vast possessions intact, its war effort still waxing, its institutions unshaken, its people and Empire united as never before. Victory had come after all the hazards and heartbreaks in an absolute and unlimited form. All the Kings and Emperors with whom we had warred were in flight or exile. All their Armies and Fleets were destroyed or subdued. In this Britain had borne a notable part, and done her best from first to last.

The minutes passed. I was conscious of reaction rather than elation. The material purposes on which one's work had been centred, every process of thought on which one had lived, crumbled into nothing. The whole vast business of supply, the growing outputs, the careful hoards, the secret future plans—but yesterday the whole duty of life—all at a stroke vanished like a nightmare dream leaving a void behind. My mind mechanically persisted in exploring the problems of demobilization. What was to happen to our three million munition workers? What would they make now? How would the roaring factories be converted? How in fact are swords beaten into ploughshares? How long would it take to bring the Armies home? What would they do when they got home? We had, of course, a demobilization plan for the Ministry of Munitions.

It had been carefully worked out, but it had played no part in our thoughts. Now it must be put into operation. The levers must be pulled—*Full Steam Astern*. The Munitions Council must meet without delay.

And then suddenly the first stroke of the chime. I looked again at the broad street beneath me. It was deserted. From the portals of one of the large hotels absorbed by Government Departments darted the slight figure of a girl clerk, distractedly gesticulating while another stroke resounded. Then from all sides men and women came scurrying into the street. Streams of people poured out of all the buildings. The bells of London began to clash. Northumberland Avenue was now crowded with people in hundreds, nay, thousands, rushing hither and thither in a frantic manner, shouting and screaming with joy. I could see that Trafalgar Square was already swarming. Around me in our very headquarters, in the Hotel Metropole, disorder had broken out. Doors banged. Feet clattered down corridors. Everyone rose from the desk and cast aside pen and paper. All bounds were broken. The tumult grew. It grew like a gale, but from all sides simultaneously. The street was now a seething mass of humanity. Flags appeared as if by magic. Streams of men and women flowed from the Embankment. They mingled with torrents pouring down the Strand on their way to acclaim the King. Almost before the last stroke of the clock had died away, the strict, war-straitened, regulated streets of London had become a triumphant pandemonium. At any rate it was clear that no more work would be done that day. Yes, the chains which had held the world were broken. Links of imperative need, links of discipline, links of brute-force, links of self-sacrifice, links of terror, links of honour which had held our nation, nay, the greater part of mankind, to grinding toil, to a compulsive cause—every one had snapped upon a few strokes of the clock. Safety, freedom, peace, home, the dear one back at the fireside—all after fifty-two months of gaunt distortion. After fifty-two months of making burdens grievous to be borne and binding them on men's backs, at last, all at once, suddenly and everywhere the burdens were cast down. At least so for the moment it seemed.

My wife arrived, and we decided to go and offer our congratulations to the Prime Minister, on whom the central impact of the home struggle had fallen, in his hour of recompense. But no sooner had we entered our car than twenty people mounted upon it, and in the midst of a wildly cheering multitude we were impelled slowly forward through Whitehall. We had driven together the opposite way along the same road on the afternoon of the ultimatum. There had been the same crowd and almost the same enthusiasm. It was with feelings which do not lend themselves to words that I heard the cheers of the brave people who had borne so much and given all, who had never wavered, who had never lost faith in their country or its destiny, and who could be indulgent to the faults of their servants when the hour of deliverance had come.

$$\star \qquad \star \qquad \star$$

The curtain falls upon the long front in France and Flanders. The soothing hands of Time and Nature, the swift repair of peaceful industry, have already almost effaced the crater-fields and the battle lines which in a broad belt from the Vosges to the sea lately blackened the smiling fields of France. The ruins are rebuilt, the riven trees are replaced by new plantations. Only the cemeteries, the monuments and stunted steeples, with here and there a mouldering trench or huge mine-crater lake, assail the traveller with the fact that twenty-five millions of soldiers fought here and twelve millions shed their blood or perished in the greatest of all human contentions less than twenty years ago. Merciful oblivion draws its veils; the crippled limp away; the mourners fall back into the sad twilight of memory. New youth is here to claim its rights, and the perennial stream flows forward even in the battle zone, as if the tale were all a dream.

Is this the end? Is it to be merely a chapter in a cruel and senseless story? Will a new generation in their turn be immolated to square the black accounts of Teuton and Gaul? Will our children bleed and gasp again in devastated lands? Or will there spring from the very fires of conflict that reconciliation of the three giant combatants, which would unite their genius and secure to each in safety and freedom a share in rebuilding the glory of Europe?

# THE WORLD CRISIS
## THE EASTERN FRONT

*First published in 1931, "The Eastern Front" is an additional volume to "The World Crisis 1911-1918" and describes the great conflict between Russia and the two Teutonic Empires —Germany and Austria. In "The World Crisis 1911-1918" the author was unable to give full accounts of the war in the east and its effects upon the campaign and the fortunes of the Allies on their particular fronts. This book was written to fill the gaps, and records the events leading up to the war, the battles in the eastern theatre and the collapse of Russia in 1917.*

IF FOR a space we obliterate from our minds the fighting in France and Flanders, the struggle upon the Eastern Front is incomparably the greatest war in history. In its scale, in its slaughter, in the exertions of the combatants, in its military kaleidoscope, it far surpasses by magnitude and intensity all similar human episodes.

It is also the most mournful conflict of which there is record. All three empires, both sides, victors and vanquished, were ruined. All the Emperors or their successors were slain or deposed. The Houses of Romanov, Hapsburg and Hohenzollern woven over centuries of renown into the texture of Europe were shattered and extirpated. The structure of three mighty organisms built up by generations of patience and valour and representing the traditional groupings of noble branches of the European family, was changed beyond all semblance. Ten million homes awaited the return of the warriors. A hundred cities prepared to acclaim their triumphs. But all were defeated; all were stricken; everything that they had given was given in vain. The hideous injuries they inflicted and bore, the privations they endured, the grand loyalties they exemplified, all were in vain. Nothing was gained by any. They floundered in the mud, they perished in the snowdrifts, they starved in the frost. Those that survived, the veterans of countless battle-days, returned, whether with the laurels of victory or tidings of disaster, to homes engulfed already in catastrophe.

We may make our pictures of this front from Napoleon's campaigns. Hard and sombre war; war of winter; bleak and barren regions; long marches forward and back again under heavy burdens; horses dying in the traces; wounded frozen in their own blood; the dead uncounted, unburied; the living pressed again into the mill. Eylau; Aspern; Wagram; Borodino; The Beresina—all the sinister impressions of these names revive, divested of their vivid flash of pomp, and enlarged to a hideous size. Here all Central Europe tore itself to pieces and expired in agony, to rise again, unrecognizable.

Whole libraries have been written about the coming of the war. Every government involved has laboured to prove its guiltlessness. Every people casts the odium upon some other. Every statesman has been at pains to show how he toiled for peace, but was nevertheless a man of action whom no fears could turn from the path of duty. Every soldier has found it necessary to explain how much he loved peace, but of course neglected no preparations for war. Whereas the causes of old wars are often obscure from lack of records, a vast fog of information envelops the fatal steps to Armageddon. A hundred reasons are offered to show why all the governments and potentates acted as they did, and how good their motives were. But in this cloud of testimony the few gleaming points of truth are often successfully obscured. In the mood of men, in the antagonisms between the Powers, amid the clash of interests and deep promptings of self-preservation or self-assertion in the hearts of races, there lay mighty causes. Then came a few short sharp individual acts, and swiftly the final explosion. It is these acts and their doers that we must seek to discern.

There was the man who fired the shots that killed the Archduke and his wife in Sarajevo. There was the man who, deliberately, accepting the risk of a world war, told the Austrian Emperor that Germany would give him a free hand against Serbia and urged him to use it. There was the man who framed and launched the ultimatum to Serbia. These men took the fatal decisive steps. Behind them hundreds of high functionaries laboured faithfully and energetically in that state of life unto which God had been displeased to call them; and each has his tale to tell. But no one except the doers of these particular deeds bears the direct concrete responsibility for the loosing upon mankind of incomparably its most frightful misfortune since the collapse of the Roman Empire before the Barbarians.

★    ★    ★

The plans and compacts which underlay the civilization of Europe had been worked out to the minutest detail. They involved the marshalling for immediate battle of nearly twelve million men. For each of these there was a place reserved. For each there was a summons by name. The depots from which he would draw his uniform and weapons, the time-tables of the railways by which he would travel, the roads by which he would march, the proclamations which would inflame or inspire him, the food and munitions he would require, the hospitals which would receive his torn or shattered body—all were ready. Only his grave was lacking; but graves do not take long to dig. We know no spectacle in human history more instinct with pathos than that of these twelve million men, busy with the cares, hopes and joys of daily life, working in their fields or mills, or seated these summer evenings by their cottage doors with their wives and children about them, making their simple plans for thrift or festival, unconscious of the fate which now drew near, and which would exact from them their all. Only a signal is needed to transform these multitudes of peaceful peasants and workmen into the mighty hosts which will tear each other to pieces year after year with all the machinery of science, with all the passions of races, and all the loyalties of man.

Yet it should not be supposed by future generations that much direct compulsion was required. Of all the millions who marched to war in August, 1914, only a small proportion went unwillingly away. The thrill of excitement ran through the world, and the hearts of even the simplest masses lifted to the trumpet-call. A prodigious event had happened. The monotony of toil and of the daily round was suddenly broken. Everything was strange and new. War aroused the primordial instincts of races born of strife. Adventure beckoned to her children. A larger, nobler life seemed to be about to open upon the world. But it was, in fact, only Death.

To read many modern writers one would suppose that the war came by itself, and that no person in authority ever thought of such a wicked thing. Berchtold did this and Conrad that, and Jagow was on his honeymoon, and Tschirschky was snubbed by the Kaiser, and Bethmann-Hollweg did not understand the situation, and the Russians got excited and Moltke alarmed, and then all of a sudden all the greatest nations in the world fell upon each other with fire and sword. It was a case of spontaneous combustion. The theory that it all happened by itself, that Germany carelessly gave Austria a blank cheque to correct Serbia, that Russia was indignant at the spectacle, that Germany was alarmed because Russia mobilized, that France and England did not tell Russia she must give in, that England did not tell Germany in time that she would fight, that all Berchtold wanted was his little private war with Serbia, that all Germany wanted was not to be forced to desert her ally, that all the Kaiser wanted was a diplomatic triumph—all these cases find ample documentary support. Still certain stark facts which no elaboration can veil stand forth for all time.

Berchtold and his circle meant to use armed violence upon Serbia. The Kaiser encouraged and urged them to do so. Both parties knew that such an event must arouse not only the Czar and his government, but the Russian nation. Both decided to accept this risk and whatever else it might entail. The Kaiser, having given Berchtold and Vienna a free hand, deliberately absented himself until the ultimatum to Serbia had been dispatched. The German Chancellor and Foreign Secretary instructed their Ambassadors to declare that Germany considered the ultimatum right and proper, before they had even seen its terms. When the Serbians returned a soft answer, Jagow and others delayed the presentation of this document to the Kaiser until it was too late for him to prevent Austria declaring war upon Serbia. Berchtold issued his declaration of war with precipitate haste and obtained its signature from the Emperor Francis Joseph, partly under false pretences. Every request for delay was refused by Vienna. Every proposal, whether for conference of the Powers or direct negotiations between Austria and Russia, was refused or resisted until too late. At St. Petersburg the Russian Government, Court and military men extracted first a partial and then a complete mobilization decree from the reluctant

Czar. Germany fastened upon Russia a deadly quarrel about her mobilization. Germany sent an ultimatum to Russia requiring her to cancel it within twelve hours. At this moment the German mobilization, although not officially proclaimed, was already in progress. Germany declared war upon Russia. Germany summoned France to repudiate the terms of the Franco-Russian Alliance and hand over to German keeping her key fortresses as gages of faithful neutrality. Germany declared war upon France. Germany violated the treaty protecting the Duchy of Luxembourg. Germany violated the neutrality of Belgium. When Belgium resisted, Germany declared war upon Belgium, and marched across Belgium to the invasion of France. It was not till then that Great Britain declared war upon Germany, and we are still disinclined to say that she was wrong.

*     *     *

The end of the year [1914] and the severities of winter closed what has been called "The Second Round" of the struggle. In the West after the battle of Ypres, in the East after the battle of Lodz, the fronts became stationary in close contact behind ever-growing entrenchments. Sovereigns, statesmen and commanders on both sides surveyed the ghastly scene, weighed the results of all the battles, and set themselves to plan the future. An immense feeling of relief inspired the leaders of the Allies. The terrific onslaught of Germany upon France had failed. Time would now be given for the whole armed strength of the British Empire to be brought to bear. The naval victory of the Falkland Islands had exterminated the German cruiser warfare. The British command alike of the oceans and the narrow seas was absolute. Very large surplus naval forces released from the cruiser warfare came back into the hands of the Admiralty. The blockade of the enemy Empires was complete and its pressures began to grow.

Different indeed were the feelings with which the German Chiefs measured the past and faced the future. They had no illusions upon the results which had so far declared themselves. Although their armies stood almost everywhere on conquered soil and they disposed of enormous and still-growing resources, they cast about earnestly for some means of escape from the deadly toils into which they had incontinently plunged. The causes of British and French satisfaction were perfectly appreciated by them, and struck a knell in their hearts. To the problems of their Generals the German Chancellor and Foreign Office now made an unwelcome contribution. All hopes of inducing Italy or Roumania to join them had long vanished. On Christmas Day Count Czernin, Austrian Ambassador at Bucharest, had declared to Conrad that Italy and Roumania "would enter the war upon the side of the Entente, unless the Central Empires could achieve a far-reaching victory by the spring". Italy was pressing with increasing plainness and slowly unveiling menace her demands for grievous cessions of Austrian territory. Roumania seemed to be keeping step with Italy, and a hostile declaration by both Powers might well be simultaneous.

It became obvious that the attitude of the Balkan States was of decisive importance. Turkey—the one new adherent—had been defeated in the Caucasus, and was already in internal stress. No military communication existed between her and the Central Powers. Serbia had not been defeated, on the contrary, she was triumphant; Bulgaria had not been won over; Greece was adverse; and Roumania refused to allow the transport of munitions to Turkey. Already on 14 December General von der Goltz had written from Constantinople to Falkenhayn that the decision of the whole war rested with the small Balkan powers. Their by no means negligible forces and influence might turn the scale either way. It was evident to the German Foreign Office that the whole of the Balkan States and Italy might come into the war against the Teutonic and Turkish Empires. This would involve the speedy collapse of Austria-Hungary, the destruction of Turkey, and the final fatal isolation of Germany. All this pointed to the strongest action against Russia, to the imperative upholding of Austria, and to opening direct access to Turkey. To the East must the Germans go.

In the East great victories had been won, with hundreds of thousands of captives, and whole hostile armies destroyed, as the result of what were undoubtedly finely-conceived manoeuvres modelled upon the classics of war. All Germany shone with the glory of Tannenberg. The Supreme Command, which had been thankful to see the failure of the Marne thus masked, now found with some disquietude that they cut a less impressive figure in the national eye than the triumphant warriors of the East. Hindenburg and Ludendorff, while comporting themselves with decorum, met in conferences men who, though in a superior station, bore the taint of failure. But the Supreme Command with its galaxy of Generals and Staff Officers, albeit discomfited, held nearly all the machinery of the German Army and five-sixths of its strength. Patriotism, public service, military discipline, personal courtesy, spread their emollients upon the sore places. Still the underlying facts remained; and the East said in unspoken words, "Why don't you let us go on winning the war for you?" and the West replied by thunderous looks, "Win the war! Why, you have only been collecting Russians!"

Even now the German Supreme Command had not divined the root fact that they were in the presence of an enormous inherent superiority of the defensive. At this time in the West, that is to say between armies of equal quality and in a theatre with closed flanks, the offensive could make no headway. Once the war subsided into the trench lines and barbed wire, the advantage of the defenders was overwhelming. The attacking troops had not got at this time the weight of artillery necessary to pulverize the trenches. Still less had they the volume of artillery capable of lining the whole front, so that an attack on a great scale could be launched on any one of three or four different sectors. The offensive therefore could not acquire the virtue of surprise. They had no tanks to crush down the barbed wire. They had not yet developed poison-gas. Even the creeping barrage was unknown. In short, the offensive possessed none of the processes or apparatus capable of making headway against a continuous line of bravely-defended trenches supported by the ordinary artillery of a field army, reinforced by many fortress guns. Falkenhayn did not understand this, nor did Joffre, nor did French, nor Foch, nor apparently any of the high military officers on either side. But it remained for several years the dominant fact in the Western theatre. With the armies matched as they were, no means of advance was open.

*     *     *

The year [1915] that opened so darkly for Germany was to be for her the most prosperous of the war. In Artois and Champagne the French, at Neuve Chapelle and Loos the British, were doomed to wear themselves out upon the barbed wire and machine-guns of the German defence. With the loss of all her fortresses Russia was to be driven out of Poland and Galicia. Bulgaria was gained as an ally by the Central Powers; Serbia was invaded and for a space annihilated; Greece was distracted and paralysed. While Roumania was awed into a continuing neutrality and Italy was left to break her teeth on the Isonzo, the German road to Constantinople was opened and Turkey, saved from destruction, fought on reinvigorated. To observe the other side of these surprising transformations and mighty achievements we must now repair to London.

We had been absorbed in securing the command of the seas, in sending the British Army to France and keeping it alive under the terrible hammer-blows which it endured; in gathering together the forces of the Empire, and in mobilizing for the struggle all the wealth, influence and manhood—not inconsiderable in any quarter of the globe—on which His Britannic Majesty could make a claim. The French told us little except their wishes, and the Russians less. We had sustained generally the impression that Russia had defeated Austria in a great battle called Lemberg, and that Germany had successfully defended East Prussia. We had the feeling that the Russian "steam-roller" which the Western Powers had expected would smooth the path to victory, was moving backwards as well as forwards, as is indeed the habit of steam-rollers. But the full significance of Tannenberg was only gradually understood. Like the French, we were in contact with immeasurable events and occupied from hour to hour with vital details. Masses of information were provided in the Intelligence reports. Every day there lay upon my table twenty or thirty flimsies recording the ceaseless movement of troops to and fro across Europe and every kind of rumour true or false. From the Admiralty we asked the War Office repeatedly for general appreciations. But all the British General Staff had gone to the war, and had been entirely preoccupied ever since in keeping together the body and soul of the Expeditionary Army. No adequate machine existed for sifting, clarifying and focusing the multitudinous reports. Lord Kitchener, calm, Olympian, secretive and imperfectly informed, endeavoured in these months to discharge in his own person the functions of Secretary of State for War, Commander-in-Chief and of the collective intelligence of a General Staff.

Yet somehow things had not gone wrong. The seas were clear; the island was safe; the army had reached its battle station; the front was held; the Empire was forming in the fighting line. Therefore there was not at this juncture any very decided questioning of our impressions acquired from day to day, nor of our primitive methods of war-control. Indeed, up to the end of 1914, we were, I feel, entitled to be proud of our conduct of the war. All our ships and men were being used to the full and in the right way.

No more elaborate organization would up to this point have produced better results. But a change had now come over the war. Its scale and complications grew ceaselessly; and we now had broadening surpluses of men and ships to employ. Here was the question which demanded scientific study.

During the whole of the summer and autumn of 1915 the Russians had to face the almost ceaseless attack of nearly forty German divisions and of nearly the whole of the Austrian armies. Already weakened in quality and structure by the injuries they had received, and in the worst phase of their munition supply, the armies of the Czar presented an 800-mile front to the successive German thrusts which now here, now there, broke the line or forced deep and rapid retirements. The consequences of such defeats, wherever they had occurred, endangered the life of Russian armies far beyond the reverberations of the cannonade. We have the spectacle of the German warrior setting himself with prodigious energy to beat the life out of the Russian giant.

The tale is one of hideous tragedy and measureless and largely unrecorded suffering. Considering the state of their armies and organization, the Russian resistance and constancy are worthy of the highest respect. The strategy and conduct of the Grand Duke, bearing up amid ceaseless misfortune, with crumbling fronts, with congested and threatened communications, with other anxieties still further in rear, which most military commanders are spared, fills a chapter in military history from which a future generation of

Russians will not withhold their gratitude. He yielded provinces; he yielded cities; one after another he yielded river lines. He was driven from Galicia; he was driven from Poland; in the north he was driven far back upon Russian soil. He gave up his conquests; he gave up Warsaw; he gave up all his fortresses. The whole defended front broke under the hammer. All its railways passed to the service of the invader. The entire population fled in terror and agony before the advancing storm. When at last the autumn rains choked the roads with mud, and winter raised its shield before a tortured nation, the Russian armies, extricated from their perils, stood along a still continuous line from Riga on the Baltic to the Roumanian frontier, with a future before them from which the hopes of general victory were not banished.

★   ★   ★

The time was now come for the Emperor Francis Joseph to die. He had witnessed with frigid satisfaction the vast recoil of Russia in 1915. The dismissal of the Grand Duke Nicholas from the command of the Russian armies had seemed to him a signal of Teutonic victory more indubitable even than the fall of Warsaw. He had followed with measured approval the over-ripe, but at last condign chastisement of Serbia. He had welcomed the Kaiser on his way to the celebrations of that joyous event. All was then a feast of mutual congratulation. Yet intimate observers had noticed that the high spirits of both potentates had seemed rather forced, and Baron Margutti, to whose records we are indebted, felt at the time that both really wanted peace. They looked upon victory as the means of gaining peace, not, like their generals, as the means of further victories. They had preoccupations not shared by their servants. Nations may fall and rise again; but dynasties in modern times can only stand or fall. Still, at the beginning of 1916 the sun shone so brightly on the bristling bayonets of the Central Empires that the general staffs were everywhere in the ascendant. Falkenhayn, it was said, had new wonders to produce, and Conrad too, as we have seen, had his plans.

The Emperor lived long enough to endure the news of Brusiloff's offensive, to receive the Roumanian declaration of war which he had so long dreaded, to see Falkenhayn, the glittering deliverer of the spring, dismissed by the Kaiser in the autumn. The old man's inveterate pessimism and deeply ingrained expectation of misfortune returned with doubled force. How often had he not seen these false dawns before? True, the Prussian military flame seemed unquenchable, and Roumania was already suffering the penalty of her faithlessness. But the clouds had gathered again. The summer of success had been bright, but also brief. Evidently, as he had always been convinced, and so often declared, the road was to be uphill to the very end. The end had now come for him.

Since the War began, he had scarcely been seen in public. He refused all holidays and ploughed methodically through his daily routine at Schönbrunn. The care of the Court Chamberlain had forbidden the Park before the Imperial windows to the public. It was widely rumoured that the Emperor was already dead, and was being preserved as a fetish and a symbol. Unpleasant details about the social and economic life of his peoples were sedulously kept from him: but his immense experience enabled him to understand better than his courtiers or his generals how grave the food-shortage and popular discontents had become; and when his Prime Minister, Count Stürgkh, was pistolled to death by the son of the leader of the Democratic Party, Francis Joseph formed a perfectly clear resolve to make peace as soon as possible. He determined to make peace by any means at latest in the spring of 1917. As a first step he replaced his murdered minister by a politician of the Left, Koerber, a man who was honoured by the hungry millions, and distrusted by the well-fed tens of thousands. This was his last contribution to the affairs of the Austro-Hungarian Monarchy.

Bronchitis at eighty-five is always serious. The Emperor coughed much and passed bad nights. Nevertheless, the dawn of 20 November saw him already seated in his old blue uniform at his writing-desk. It was the practice to send him three portfolios a day. The first was punctually discharged. Before the second was completed his condition of weakness and fever was such that his granddaughter brought him a special blessing from the Pope and persuaded him to receive the sacraments. Four chickens were made into a broth for him at noon. He could not eat it. But the midday files were duly dispatched to the Departments. In the afternoon the doctors succeeded in inducing him to go to bed. He rose from his table, but had to be supported to the neighbouring room. The immense fatigue of years of care overwhelmed him. Sleep and death drew quickly near. With an effort he said to his valet, "Call me at seven. I am behindhand with my work," and sank almost immediately into coma. The Departments inquired about the evening portfolio. The aide-de-camp on duty replied that it would not be delivered that night. A few hours later, the sixty-six years' reign of Francis Joseph was completed. He died in harness.

Although the War weighed oppressively upon Vienna, the funeral of the departed ruler was magnificent. The populace, sorely tried, silent, helpless, hungry, understood that a long chapter in the history of Central Europe had closed. New pages must be turned; nay, a new volume must open. The aged Count Paar would not see this volume. "I died yesterday," he said to Margutti on the morrow of his master's death. In fact, he expired during the memorial service two days later. The ties of a lifetime which had been snapped were also the heartstrings of this faithful servitor.

But the War rolled on.

\*     \*     \*

During the afternoon of 13 March, 1917, the Russian Embassy in London informed us that they were no longer in contact with Petrograd. For some days the capital had been a prey to disorders which it was believed were being effectively suppressed. Now suddenly for a space there was a silence. Volumes have been written upon the causes and consequences of this silence. For us it draws the curtain upon the tale.

The Allies, startled and disappointed by the German recovery at the end of 1916, had planned in closer concert than ever before what they hoped would be the decisive operations of the coming year. Each and all of the Allies were to attack at the selected moments upon all their fronts—French, British, Russian, Italian, Roumanian, Salonican. The prospects were good. The Allies now disposed of a superiority of nearly five to two, and the factories of the whole world outside enemy territory were pouring munitions and implements of war to them across the seas and oceans. Russia, from whose fathomless man-power so much was still hoped, was for the first time since the opening battles to be properly equipped. The doubled broad-gauge railway to the never-ice-bound port of Murmansk on the White Sea was now at last completed. The labours, the sufferings and dying gasps of thousands of prisoners-of-war inter-mingled with criminals and Chinese, toiling for months in perpetual night, had built these sixteen hundred miles of line across the frozen plains and marshes; and Russia was now for the first time in per-manent contact with her Allies. Nearly two hundred new battalions had been added to her forces; and behind the armies large deposits of all kinds of shell had been amassed. There seemed to be no military reason why the year 1917 should not witness the final triumph of the Allies, and bring to Russia the reward which she had sought through infinite agonies.

Now suddenly there was this silence. The great Power with whom we had been in such intimate comradeship, without whom all plans were meaningless, was stricken dumb. With Russian effective aid, all the Allied fronts could attack together. Without that aid it might well be that the war was lost. It was therefore with strained attention that we watched for the reopening of the telegraph lines to Petrograd.

★    ★    ★

Many streams had flowed together to bring the deluge. The Russian revolution was begun by social, military and political forces which within a week were left aghast behind it. In its opening paroxysm all conscious Russia participated. It was primarily a patriotic revolt against the misfortunes and mismanagement of the War. Defeats and disasters, want of food and prohibition of alcohol, the slaughter of millions of men, joined with inefficiency and corruption to produce a state of exasperation among all classes which had no outlet but revolt, could find no scapegoat but the Sovereign. For a year past the Czar and his wife had been the objects of growing universal resentment. The fond, obstinate husband and father, the absolute monarch obviously devoid of all the qualities of a national ruler in times of crisis, bore the burden of all the sufferings which the German Armies had inflicted on the Russian State. Behind him the Empress, a still more hated figure, dwelt in her tiny circle listening only to her cronies—her lady companion Madame Virubova, her spiritual adviser the sensual mystic Rasputin—and presumed

365

thence and on such promptings to sway the whole policy and fortunes of the tormented Empire.

In vain the Imperial family, deeply concerned for their own existence—apart from all other issues—approached their Head. In vain the leaders of the Duma and every independent figure in Russia made their protests. In vain the Ambassadors of the Allied Powers dropped their elaborate hints, or even uttered solemn and formal warnings under the direction of their governments. Nicholas II, distressed, remained immovable. He saw as clearly as they did the increasing peril. He knew of no means by which it could be averted. In his view nothing but autocracy established through centuries had enabled the Russians to proceed thus far in the teeth of calamity. No people had suffered and sacrificed like the Russians. No State, no nation, had ever gone through trials on such a scale and retained its coherent structure. The vast machine creaked and groaned. But it still worked. One more effort and victory would come. To change the system, to òpen the gate to intruders, to part with any portion of the despotic power, was in the eyes of the Czar to bring about a total collapse. Therefore, though plunged daily deeper in anxiety and perplexity, he was held alike by all his instincts and his reasoning faculties in a fixed position. He stood like a baited animal tied to a stake and feebly at bay.

It is easy for critics never subjected to such ordeals to recount lost opportunities. They speak lightly of changing the fundamental principles of the Russian State in the stress of the War from absolute monarchy to some British or French parliamentary system. It would be a thankless task to assail convictions so confidently asserted. Nevertheless, the martial and national achievements of Russia in the three terrible campaigns constitute a prodigy no less astounding than the magnitude of her collapse thereafter. The very rigidity of the system gave it its strength and, once broken, forbade all recovery. The absolute Czar in spite of all his lamentable deficiencies commanded Russia. It can never be proved that a three-quarters-Czar or half-Czar, and the rest a Parliament, could in such a period have commanded anything at all. In fact, once the Czar was gone, no Russian ever commanded again. It was not until a fearsome set of internationalists and logicians built a sub-human structure upon the ruins of Christian civilization that any form or order or design again emerged. Thus it is by no means certain that the generally accepted view upon the practical steps is right, or that the Czar for all his errors and shortcomings was wrong. After all, he was within an ace of safety and success. Another month and the accession of the United States to the cause of the Allies would have brought a flood of new energy, encouragement, and moral stimulus to Russian society. The certainty of victory, never again lost, was to dawn like a new sun beyond the wastes of Asia and the Pacific Ocean. Only another month till daybreak! Only another month and the world might have been spared the tribulations of the two most grievous years of the war. That month was lacking. A brief but hideous hiatus marred the scene. Meanwhile Nicholas II, casting his eyes now towards the Providence he sought to serve, now towards the family group he loved so well, clung chained to his post.

*     *     *

All sorts of Russians made the revolution. No sort of Russian reaped its profit. Among the crowds who thronged the turbulent streets and ante-rooms of Petrograd in these March days, with resolve for "Change at all costs" in their hearts, were found Grand Dukes, fine ladies, the bitterest die-hards and absolutists like Purishkevitch and Yusupov; resolute, patriotic politicians like Rodzianko and Guchkov; experienced Generals; diplomatists and financiers of the old regime; Liberals and Democrats; Socialists like Kerensky; sturdy citizens and tradesfolk; faithful soldiers seeking to free their Prince from bad advisers; ardent nationalists resolved to purge Russia from secret German influence; multitudes of loyal peasants and workmen; and behind all, cold, calculating, ruthless, patient, stirring all, demanding all, awaiting all, the world-wide organization of International Communism.

Actually the deposition of the Czar was effected by the Chiefs of his Army. Nicholas was at his Headquarters at Mohilev when on the afternoon of 11 March the first telegrams about the disorders in Petrograd began to flow in. It was reported at first that they were of no great consequence. Had he been in his capital accessible to all the moderate forces now inflamed, there might still have been time, not indeed as we hold to avert disaster, but to lessen its shock. But he was at Mohilev, and the Grand Duke Nicholas who should have ruled the armies was far off in the half-banishment of Tiflis. On the 12th Rodzianko, President of the Duma, confronted with a swiftly mounting crisis, sent the following telegram to his master: "The situation is growing worse. Immediate steps must be taken, for tomorrow will be too late. The final hour has come when the fate of the country and the dynasty must be decided."

To such grave tidings was added scarcely less disturbing news from Tsarskoe Selo. The Royal children had sickened of the measles. The Czar replied to his counsellors with hard defiance, and to his wife with overflowing sympathy. He called for the Imperial train. His duties as a Sovereign and as a father equally demanded his return to the seat of government. The train was ready at midnight; but it took six hours more to clear the line. The Dowager-Empress had arrived. Mother and son travelled together. The next afternoon the train stopped at Dno. Impossible to proceed! A bridge had been, it was said, blown up or damaged. The Czar indicated an alternative route, and for the first time came in contact with naked resistance. Such authority as now reigned in Petrograd refused to permit his further approach. Where to turn? Some hours passed. Back to Mohilev? We do not know how far he tested this possibility. Perhaps he had been conscious of the unspoken reproach with which the atmosphere of the Stavka was loaded. To the Northern Front then—to General Ruzski. Here at least he would find a trusty commander, whose armies lay nearest to the rebellious capital.

The train reached Pskov. Ruzski was there with grave salutes. But with him also very soon were Guchkov and Shulguin as a deputation from the Duma. Here were able, determined public men with plain advice: immediate abdication in favour of his son, and the Regency of his brother, the Grand Duke Michael Alexandrovich. The Czar appealed to Ruzski. Ruzski, anticipating his responsibilities, had felt that the matter was too serious for him. Already before the Czar's arrival he had consulted the Stavka and the other commanders. Accordingly fateful telegrams had been dispatched through the Stavka along the whole length of the Russian front. All the Army Group Commanders, Brusilov, Ewarth, the Grand Duke, and finally, with many reservations, Sakharov from distant

Roumania, declared in favour of abdication. The document was drawn. Guchkov presented the pen. Nicholas was about to sign. Suddenly he asked whether he and his family could reside in the Crimea, in that palace of Livadia whose sunlit gardens seemed green and calm and tranquil. Bluntly he was told he must leave Russia forthwith, and that the new sovereign must remain among his people. On this his fatherly love triumphed over his public duty and indeed over his coronation oath. Rather than be separated from his son, he disinherited that son. The paper was redrafted and Nicholas II abdicated in favour of his brother. Thus all claim of legitimacy was shivered; and everything in a second stage was thrown into redoubled confusion.

However, it is over now. The Czar has ceased to reign. The brother, around whom everything is melting, fears to seize the abandoned reins of power without the vote of a National Assembly, impossible to obtain. Nothing could ever bring stabilizing ideas together again. We cannot here follow the long, swift, splintering, crashing descent which ended, as it could only end, in the abyss. The dynasty was gone. Vainly did leaders of the Duma and the Zemstvos strive to clutch at handholds. In their turn they broke. Vainly did Kerensky with his nationalist democracy try to stop the fall a long leap lower down. Vainly did the great men of action, Kornilov the warrior, Savinkov the terrorist-patriot, strive to marshal the social revolutionary forces in defence of Russia. All fell headlong into the depths where Lenin, Trotsky, Zinoviev and other unnatural spirits awaited their prey.

# THE PROBLEMS OF PEACE

# THE AFTERMATH

*First published in March, 1929, "The Aftermath" is a sequel
to "The World Crisis", the author's history of the First
World War. This whole history is regarded by many as
the best of its kind ever written.*

*"The Aftermath" is a personal and authoritative account of
what happened during the four years which followed the
Armistice. Unhappily, as the author states, the book is for the
most part "a chronicle of misfortune and tragedy".*

THE CONCLUSION of the Great War raised England to the highest
position she has yet attained. For the fourth time in four successive
centuries she had headed and sustained the resistance of Europe to
a military tyranny; and for the fourth time the war had ended
leaving the group of small states of the Low Countries, for whose
protection England had declared war, in full independence. Spain,
the French Monarchy, the French Empire and the German Empire
had all overrun and sought to possess or dominate these regions.
During four hundred years England had withstood them all by war
and policy, and all had been defeated and driven out. To that list
of mighty Sovereigns and supreme military Lords which already
included Philip II, Louis XIV and Napoleon, there could now be
added the name of William II of Germany. These four great series
of events, directed unswervingly to the same end through so many
generations and all crowned with success, constitute a record of
persistency and achievement, without parallel in the history of
ancient or modern times.

But other substantial advantages had been obtained. The menace
of the German navy was destroyed and the overweening power of
Germany had been for many years definitely set back. The Russian
Empire which had been our Ally had been succeeded by a revolutionary government which had renounced all claims to Constantinople, and which by its inherent vices and inefficiency could not
soon be a serious military danger to India. On the other hand,

England was united with her nearest neighbour and oldest enemy —France—by ties of comradeship in suffering and in victory which promised to be both strong and durable. British and United States troops had fought for the first time side by side, and the two great branches of the English-speaking world had begun again to write their history in common. Lastly, the British Empire had stood every shock and strain during the long and frightful world convulsion. The parliamentary institutions by which the life of the Mother Country and the self-governing Dominions found expression had proved themselves as serviceable for waging war as for maintaining freedom and progress in times of peace. The invisible ties of interest, sentiment and tradition which across all the waters of the world united the Empire had proved more effective than the most binding formal guarantees, and armies of half a million Canadians, Australians and New Zealanders had been drawn by these indefinable and often imperceptible attractions across greater distances than any armies had travelled before, to die and conquer for a cause and quarrel which only remotely affected their immediate material safety. All the peoples and all the creeds of India during the years of crisis had made in their own way a spontaneous demonstration of loyalty, and sustained the war by arms and money on a scale till then unknown. The rebellion in South Africa in 1914 had been repressed by the very Boer generals who had been our most dangerous antagonists in the South African War, and who had signed with us the liberating treaty of Vereeniging. Only in parts of Ireland had there been a failure and a repudiation, and about that there was a lengthy tale to tell.

The pageant of victory unrolled itself before the eyes of the British nation. All the Emperors and Kings with whom we had warred had been dethroned, and all their valiant armies were shattered to pieces. The terrible enemy whose might and craft had so long threatened our existence, whose force had destroyed the flower of the British nation, annihilated the Russian Empire and left all our Allies except the United States at the last gasp, lay prostrate at the mercy of the conquerors. The ordeal was over. The peril had been warded off. The slaughter and sacrifices had not been in vain and were at an end; and the overstrained people in the hour of deliverance gave themselves up for a space to the sensations of triumph. Church and State united in solemn thanksgiving. The whole land made holiday. Triple avenues of captured cannon lined the Mall. Every street was thronged with jubilant men and women. All classes were mingled in universal rejoicing. Feasting, music and illuminations turned the shrouded nights of war into a blazing day. The vast crowds were convulsed with emotions beyond expression; and in Trafalgar Square the joy of the London revellers left enduring marks upon the granite plinth of Nelson's column.

Who shall grudge or mock these overpowering entrancements? Every Allied nation shared them. Every victorious capital or city in the five continents reproduced in its own fashion the scenes and sounds of London. These hours were brief, their memory fleeting; they passed as suddenly as they had begun. Too much blood had been spilt. Too much life-essence had been consumed. The gaps in every home were too wide and empty. The shock of an awakening and the sense of disillusion followed swiftly upon the poor rejoicings with which hundreds of millions saluted the achievement of their hearts' desire. There still remained the satisfactions of safety assured, of peace restored, of honour preserved, of the comforts of fruitful industry, of the home-coming of the soldiers; but these were in the background; and with them all there mingled the ache for those who would never come home.

★　　★　　★

Along the British lines in France and Belgium eleven o'clock had produced a reaction revealing the mysterious nature of man. The cannonade was stilled; the armies halted where they stood. Motionless in the silence the soldiers looked at each other with vacant eyes. A sense of awe, of perplexity, and even of melancholy stole coldly upon men who a few moments before had been striding forward in the ardour of hot pursuit. It was as though an abyss had opened before the conquerors' feet.

The fighting troops seemed for a time incapable of adjusting themselves to the abrupt relaxation of strain. So quiet were the forward camps on the night of victory that one would have thought they belonged to brave men after doing their best at last defeated. This wave of psychological depression passed as quickly as the opposite mood in Britain; and in a few days Home had become the foundation of all desires. But here again were disillusion and hope deferred.

On the night of the Armistice I dined with the Prime Minister at Downing Street. We were alone in the large room from whose walls the portraits of Pitt and Fox, of Nelson and Wellington, and —perhaps somewhat incongruously—of Washington then looked down. One of the most admirable traits in Mr. Lloyd George's character was his complete freedom at the height of his power, responsibility and good fortune from anything in the nature of pomposity or superior airs. He was always natural and simple. He was always exactly the same to those who knew him well: ready to argue any point, to listen to disagreeable facts even when controversially presented. One could say anything to him, on the terms that he could say anything back. The magnitude and absolute character of the victory induced a subdued and detached state of mind. There was no feeling that the work was done. On the contrary, the realization was strong upon him that a new and perhaps more difficult phase of effort was before him. My own mood was divided between anxiety for the future and desire to help the fallen foe. The conversation ran on the great qualities of the German people, on the tremendous fight they had made against three-quarters of the world, on the impossibility of rebuilding Europe except with their aid. At that time we thought they were actually starving, and that under the twin pressures of defeat and famine the Teutonic peoples—already in revolution—might slide into the grisly gulf that had already devoured Russia.

*     *     *

Great allowances must be made for the behaviour of all the peoples and of all their governments—victors and vanquished alike —as they emerged from the furnace of fifty-two months' world war. The conditions were outside all previous experience. At the outbreak with all its unknown and measureless possibilities the flood of crisis flowed along channels which for some distance had already been prepared. The naval and military leaders and the staffs behind them assumed the immediate direction; and they had plans which, whether good or bad, were certainly worked out in the utmost detail. These plans of scientific havoc were put into execution; and the second series of events arose out of their clashings. Every War Office and every Admiralty emitted laconic orders, and for a while the consequences followed almost automatically. The immense forces of destruction, long gathered and stored, were released. When a battleship is launched the operation is short and simple. A few speeches are made; a few prayers are said; a bottle of champagne is broken; a few wedges are knocked away; and thousands of tons of steel swiftly gathering momentum glide irrevocably into the water. Very different are the problems of bringing that same ship, shattered in action, ripped by torpedoes, crowded with wounded, half full of water, safely back to harbour through storm and mist and adverse tides.

The men at the head of the victorious states were subjected to tests of the most trying kind. They seemed all-powerful: but their power was departing. Although it was departing, the appearance of it remained for a space: and it might perhaps be recalled by great action. But time was paramount. With every day's delay it became more difficult to gather the fruits of victory. With every day the power not only of statesmen, but of the Allied nations themselves, and their unity, must decline. Their armies must come home; their electorates must regain their sway. Jealousies, factions, revenges long pent up now advanced on every side. Yet every day was so full of important and urgent business, and so disturbed by jostling personalities and events, that human nature could not cope with the task. Was it strange that these men should yield themselves to the illusion of power, to the relief of victory and to the press of business? Was it strange that they should wish to draw breath before beginning new tasks? They remained for some time under the impression that the same strenuous controls would continue in other forms and that equal powers and sanctions would be available for overcoming the new difficulties. In fact, however, just as the ship was coming into port more than half the rudder had dropped off without the men at the helm perceiving it.

The former peace-time structure of society had for more than four years been superseded and life had been raised to a strange intensity by the war spell. Under that mysterious influence, men and women had been appreciably exalted above death and pain and toil. Nothing had been too hard to bear or too precious to cast away. Unities and comradeships had become possible between men and classes and nations and grown stronger while the hostile pressure and the common cause endured. But now the spell was broken: too late for some purposes, too soon for others, and too suddenly for all! Every victorious country subsided to its old levels and its previous arrangements; but these latter were found to have fallen into much disrepair, their fabric was weakened and disjointed, they seemed narrow and out of date. The boundless hopes that had cheered the soldiers and the peoples in their tribulations died swiftly away. The vision of a sunlit world redeemed by valour, where work would be less and its recompense more, where Justice and Freedom reigned together through centuries of unbroken peace—that vision which had flickered over the battlefields and beckoned from behind the German or Turkish trenches, comforting the soldier's heart and fortifying his strength, was soon replaced by cold, grey reality. How could it have been otherwise? By what process could the slaughter of ten million men and the destruction of one-third of the entire savings of the greatest nations of the world have ushered in a Golden Age? A cruel disillusionment was at hand for all. All men, all women, all soldiers, all citizens were looking forward to some great expansion, and there lay before them nothing but a sharp contraction; a contraction in material conditions for the masses; a contraction in scope and command for those who had raised themselves by their qualities—and they too were numbered by the hundred thousand—to stations of responsibility.

With the passing of the spell there passed also, just as the new difficulties were at their height, much of the exceptional powers of guidance and control. The triumphant statesmen, the idols of the masses, acclaimed as saviours of their countries, were still robed with the glamour of war achievement and shod with the sanctions of Democracy. But their hour was passing; their work was almost done, and Wilson, Clemenceau and Lloyd George were soon to follow into retirement or adversity the Kings and Emperors they had dethroned.

To the faithful, toil-burdened masses the victory was so complete that no further effort seemed required. Germany had fallen, and with her the world combination that had crushed her. Authority was dispersed; the world unshackled; the weak became the strong; the sheltered became the aggressive; the contrast between victors and vanquished tended continually to diminish. A vast fatigue dominated collective action. Though every subversive element endeavoured to assert itself, revolutionary rage like every other form of psychic energy burnt low. Through all its five acts the drama has run its course; the light of history is switched off, the world stage dims, the actors shrivel, the chorus sinks. The war of the giants has ended; the quarrels of the pigmies have begun.

★     ★     ★

For the moment, however, all eyes were turned upon the approaching Peace Conference and historical pictures of the Congress of Vienna rose in the political mind. Paris became the centre of the world, and thither as soon as the urgent domestic business could be dispatched all the leading statesmen of all the victorious countries were intending or eager to repair. The choice before Mr. Lloyd George was not free from embarrassment. His right-hand colleague must obviously be the Conservative leader, Mr. Bonar Law. Mr. Barnes must represent Labour. The limit provisionally imposed upon national delegations for the sake of convenience was three, and it was already complete. But two personages, very different in character and methods, and each with much to give or to withhold, had also to be considered. The first was Lord Northcliffe who, armed with *The Times* in one hand and the ubiquitous *Daily Mail* in the other, judged himself at least the equal of any political leader and appeared prepared to assert his claims or resent their disregard with a directness scarcely open to a statesman. A general election was imminent, and the wise and helpful behaviour of these great newspapers, obedient as they were to the orders of their proprietor, seemed to the Prime Minister a serious factor. The appointment of Lord Northcliffe as a principal peace delegate over the heads of Mr. Balfour, the Foreign Secretary, and all the Prime Ministers of the British Empire was not, however, to be conceded.

The remaining figure was the leader of the Liberal Party. Mr. Asquith both at the moment and after his fall from power had steadily refused to contemplate serving under or even with Mr.

379

Lloyd George; and he and his friends had been accustomed to treat any suggestion of that kind as highly offensive. Nevertheless, in the weeks which immediately followed the victory, it was indicated that he would not be unwilling to join as the head of his party in the national making of a peace. Such a development would in many ways have strengthened the Prime Minister's position. The peace negotiations must last for many months and the close co-operation between the Prime Minister and the Liberal leader could scarcely have failed to heal the breach between them. Mr. Asquith's own qualities would also have been of inestimable service at the Conference. On the other hand, his inclusion would still further have angered Lord Northcliffe. Weighing all these somewhat ill-assorted considerations, Mr. Lloyd George decided not to increase the size of the delegation beyond the limits already agreed upon with the other Powers.

I have no doubt that from his own point of view his decision was a mistake. He had no real knowledge of the Conservative Party; he must soon expect to lose the Labour Ministers; and here at hand was the opportunity of at once making amends to the chief to whom he had owed so much, and of reuniting the Liberal forces with which alone he could work contentedly in times of peace. But far above all personal and political considerations the association of all parties in the peace treaty was an object of national importance, and no one was more fitted than Mr. Asquith to enrich the councils of the Allies. We should have had a more august delegation, a better treaty and a more friendly atmosphere at home.

While these delicate issues remained unsettled, except in his own mind, the Prime Minister resolved upon an immediate appeal to the country. He was armed with victory, complete, absolute, tremendous; victory beyond the dreams of the most ardent, the most resolute, the most exacting. The whole nation was eager to acclaim "the pilot who weathered the storm". Was it wonderful that that pilot should turn from aggrieved and resentful associates of former days who sourly awaited the hour of peace to call him to account, and from Conservatives with whom he had no real sympathy, to the vast electorate who sought only to testify their gratitude by their votes?

To this Election I was a consulted and consenting party. I thought we had need of all the strength we could get to face the problems of bringing home and disbanding our armies which then numbered at home and abroad nearly four million men, of reconstructing our industry, and making the treaty of peace. Moreover, I had in the stress of war resumed intimate contact with the Conservative Party and with the friends of my youth. Having seen so many implacable party quarrels swept away by the flood, I was in no mind to go back and look for them. The idea of methodically fishing up and revitalizing all the old pre-war party controversies, and of fabricating disagreements even where none existed, was absurd and abhorrent. I therefore swam with the stream. If I had taken the opposite course it would not have made the slightest difference to the event. But candour compels acknowledgment of this measure of responsibility.

But when the Election came it woefully cheapened Britain. The Prime Minister and his principal colleagues were astonished and to some extent overborne by the passions they encountered in the constituencies. The brave people whom nothing had daunted had suffered too much. Their unpent feelings were lashed by the popular Press into fury. The crippled and mutilated soldiers darkened the streets. The returned prisoners told the hard tale of bonds and privation. Every cottage had its empty chair. Hatred of the beaten foe, thirst for his just punishment, rushed up from the heart of deeply injured millions. Those that had done the least in the conflict were as might be expected the foremost in detailing the penalties of the vanquished. A police report thrust under my eye at this time said: "The feelings of all classes are the same. Even those who a few weeks ago were agitating for peace now say, 'The Germans should pay every penny of the damage even if it takes them a thousand years.'" In my own constituency of Dundee, respectable, orthodox, life-long Liberals demanded the sternest punishment for the broken enemy. All over the country the most bitter were the women, of whom seven millions were for the first time to vote. In this uprush and turmoil state policy and national dignity were speedily engulfed.

Three demands rose immediate and clangorous from the masses of the people, viz. to hang the Kaiser; to abolish conscription; and to make the Germans pay the uttermost farthing.

In the summer of 1917 a draft scheme of demobilization had been prepared partly in the War Office but mainly in accordance with civilian opinion.

According to the logic of this scheme the first men to be released were what were called "key men", i.e. men who were asked for by employers at home to restart the industries. These "key men" were therefore being picked out by scores of thousands from all the units of the Army and hurried back across the Channel. But these "key men" who were to be the first to come home had been in many cases the last to go out. The important parts they played in war industry had retained them at home until the needs of the Army became desperate after 21 March, 1918. In practice also the system lent itself to inevitable abuse. Those who were so fortunate as to be able to present letters and telegrams from employers at home offering them employment and claiming their services were immediately released. Influence was not slow to procure such credentials. Several thousands while on leave at home were actually excused from returning to the Army. The ordinary soldier without these advantages saw his lately joined comrade hurrying home to take his job, or somebody's job, in England, while he, after years of perils and privations on a soldier's pay, wounded and sent back to the carnage three or sometimes four times, was to be left until all the plums at home had been picked up and every vacancy filled. The fighting man has a grim sense of justice, which it is dangerous to affront. As the result the discipline of every single separate unit throughout the whole of our Army in all the theatres of war was swiftly and simultaneously rotted and undermined. For nearly two months this process had continued, and it had become intolerable to the fighting troops.

The study I gave to the matter in the five days which intervened between the acceptance and the assumption of my new office left me in no doubt upon the course to pursue. Mutinies and disorders had already taken place on both sides of the Channel. In particular a mutiny had occurred at Folkestone on 3 January. Sir Eric Geddes had newly succeeded General Smuts in dealing with the restarting of Industry. A few days before I entered the War Office the approaches to the building were blocked by lorry-loads of insubordinate Army Service Corps men who had seized these vehicles and driven them up to London. On each lorry was painted the legend borrowed from a *Daily Express* cartoon, "Get on or Get out Geddes". A wave of intense impatience and resentment accompanied by serious breaches of discipline spread across the splendid armies which had never faltered in the direst stress of war.

If the cause was plain, so was the remedy. My only difficulty was to procure the assent of others; my only apprehension, whether we were not already too late. I had before taking up my new duties insisted that the Secretary of State for War should have the final word against all civilian departments in matters affecting the discipline of the troops. In the situation which had now developed this could hardly be denied, and was readily conceded.

I propounded forthwith the following policy—

First: Soldiers should as a general rule only be released from the front in accordance with their length of service and age. Those who had served the longest at the front were to be the first to be demobilized, and any man with three wound stripes or more was to be discharged forthwith. Everyone must take his turn in accordance with this order.

Secondly: The pay of the Army must be immediately increased to more than double the war rate, in order to lessen the gap between the rewards of military and civilian employment.

Thirdly: In order, whilst still maintaining the necessary forces in the field, to release the men who had fought in as large numbers and as quickly as possible, the 80,000 young lads, who had been trained but had not quitted our shores, must be retained compulsorily for a period of two years and sent abroad.

\*      \*      \*

Certainly there were factors which nobody could measure and which no one had ever before seen at work. Armies of nearly four million men had been suddenly and consciously released from the iron discipline of war, from the inexorable compulsions of what they believed to be a righteous cause. All these vast numbers had been taught for years how to kill; how to punch a bayonet into the vital organs; how to smash the brains out with a mace; how to make and throw bombs as if they were no more than snowballs. All of them had been through a mill of prolonged inconceivable pressures and innumerable tearing teeth. To all, sudden and violent death, the woeful spectacle of shattered men and dwellings was, either to see in others or expect and face for oneself, the commonest incident of daily life. If these armies formed a united resolve, if they were seduced from the standards of duty and patriotism, there was no power which could even have attempted to withstand them.

This was the testing time, if there ever was one, for the renowned sagacity and political education of the British Democracy.

In a single week more than thirty cases of insubordination among the troops were reported from different centres. Nearly all were repressed or appeased by the remonstrances of their officers. But in several cases considerable bodies of men were for some days entirely out of control. The chief offenders were the Army Service Corps in the Grove Park and Kempton Park Mechanical Transport Depots. Some units informed their officers that they had constituted themselves a Soldiers' Council and intended to march to the nearest township and fraternize with the workmen. Usually they were dissuaded by reasonable arguments. Sometimes the officers cycling by a circuitous route intercepted their men before the town was reached and induced them to return to their duty. The influence of the regimental officers was nearly always successful. Although the situation was very threatening in many places, almost the only spot where there was actual and serious rioting was at Luton, where owing to the weakness of the civic authorities, the town hall was burnt by the mob.

A regular mutiny broke out at Calais. Between 27 and 31 January the Army Ordnance detachments and the Mechanical Transport, which were the least-disciplined part of the army, had seen least of the fighting and were most closely associated with political Trade Unionism, refused to obey orders. They met the leave-boats and induced a large number of the returning soldiers to join them. In twenty-four hours the ringleaders were at the head of about three or four thousand armed men and in complete possession of the town. All the fighting divisions had moved on towards or into Germany, and there was no force immediately at hand to cope with the mutineers. The Commander-in-Chief accordingly recalled two divisions from their forward march, and placing them under the personal control of a most trusted and respected Army Commander, General Byng, directed them upon the scene of the disorders. The soldiers of these divisions were roused to indignation at the news that demobilization was being obstructed by comrades of theirs who had in no wise borne the brunt of the fighting. By nightfall of the second day the disaffected soldiery were encircled by a ring of bayonets and machine guns. At daylight a converging advance was made upon them. In front, officers, unarmed, called upon them to return to duty; behind them deadly overwhelming force was arrayed. Thus confronted, most of the men drifted to the rear, but several hundreds stood their ground with obstinacy. A shocking explosion would have been precipitated by a single shot; but self-restraint and good feeling triumphed. The ringleaders were arrested, and the rest returned to their obedience without the shedding of a drop of blood.

Simultaneously with this came the news of serious riots in Glasgow and Belfast. Both these riots were fomented by the Communists. The Army was called upon to aid the civil power. Two Brigades were moved into Glasgow. These were only second-line troops consisting of the least efficient soldiers or young recruits. They had not, like those at the front, been tempered in war nor had they tasted victory. However, officers and men discharged their duty faultlessly. Order was restored. Very few lives were lost, and when blood flowed, it was mostly from the nose.

$$* \quad * \quad *$$

The last incident that I shall record came under my personal notice. At half-past eight on the morning of 8 February I was summoned urgently to the War Office. As I drove thither I observed a battalion of Guards drawn up along the Mall. I passed through the Admiralty Arch and reached my office without remarking anything else unusual. Arrived there I received a disagreeable report: About three thousand soldiers of many units and all arms of the service had gathered at Victoria Station to catch the early train for those returning from leave. The Director of Movements had failed to make adequate arrangements for the transport, feeding and housing of leave men coming in this case principally from the North. The poor soldiers, many of whom had waited all night on the platform, none of whom could obtain food or tea, felt it very hard to be going back to France now that the fighting was over and the war was won, while so many of their comrades were, as they had been told, snapping up the best billets in England. They had suddenly upon some instigation resorted in a body to Whitehall, and were now filling the Horse Guards' Parade armed and in a state of complete disorder. Their leader, I was informed, was at that very moment prescribing conditions to the Staff of the London Command in the Horse Guards building.

Sir William Robertson and General Feilding, commanding the London District, presented themselves to me with this account, and added that a reserve Battalion of Grenadiers and two troops of the Household Cavalry were available on the spot. What course were they authorized to adopt? I asked whether the Battalion would obey orders, and was answered "The officers believe so." On this I requested the Generals to surround and make prisoners of the disorderly mass. They departed immediately on this duty.

I remained in my room a prey to anxiety. A very grave issue had arisen at the physical heart of the State. Ten minutes passed slowly. From my windows I could see the Life Guards on duty in Whitehall closing the gates and doors of the archway. Then suddenly there appeared on the roof of the Horse Guards a number of civilians, perhaps twenty or thirty in all, who spread themselves out in a long black silhouette and were evidently watching something which was taking place, or about to take place, on the Parade Ground below them. What this might be I had no means of knowing, although I was but a hundred yards away. Another ten minutes of tension passed and back came the Generals in a much more cheerful mood. Everything had gone off happily. The Grenadiers with fixed bayonets had closed in upon the armed crowd; the Household Cavalry had executed an enveloping movement on the other flank; and the whole three thousand men had been shepherded and escorted under arrest to Wellington Barracks, where they were all going to have breakfast before resuming their journey to France. No one was hurt, very few were called to account, and only one or two were punished and that not seriously. A large portion of the blame lay upon the administration which had made no change in its routine at the railway stations since the fighting had stopped. For years men had gone back punctually and faithfully to danger and death with hardly any officers or organization just as if they were ordinary passengers on an excursion train, and those responsible had not realized that much more careful arrangements were required in the mild reign of Peace.

The history books boast of the way in which twenty or thirty thousand of Cromwell's Ironsides laid down the panoply of war and resorted to peaceful occupations. But what was this compared with the noble behaviour of nearly four million British soldiers who without confusion or commotion of any kind—once they were treated as they deserved—merged themselves unostentatiously in the mass of the nation and gathered together again the severed threads of their former lives? One had expected, after all the methodically inculcated butchery and barbarism of five years of war, that acts of murder and pillage, brutality and rapine, would for some years at any rate be rife in the land. On the contrary, such are the powers of civilization and education, and such are the qualities of our people, that crimes of violence actually diminished and prisons had to be closed and sold, when four million trained and successful killers, or nearly one-third of the whole manhood of the nation, resumed their civic status.

\*     \*     \*

From the circle of panoplied and triumphant States soon to gather from all over the world to the Peace Conference in Paris there was one absentee.

At the beginning of the war France and Britain had counted heavily upon Russia. Certainly the Russian effort had been enormous. Nothing had been stinted; everything had been risked. The forward mobilization of the Imperial Armies and their headlong onslaught upon Germany and Austria may be held to have played an indispensable part in saving France from destruction in the first two months of the war. Thereafter in spite of disasters and slaughters on an unimaginable scale Russia had remained a faithful and mighty ally. For nearly three years she had held on her fronts considerably more than half of the total number of enemy divisions, and she had lost in this struggle nearly as many men killed as all the other allies put together. The victory of Brusiloff in 1916 had been of important service to France and still more to Italy; and even as late as the summer of 1917, *after the fall of the Czar*, the Kerensky Government was still attempting offensives in aid of the common cause. The endurance of Russia as a prime factor, until the United States had entered the war, ranked second only to the defeat of the German submarines as a final turning-point of the struggle.

But Russia had fallen by the way; and in falling she had changed her identity. An apparition with countenance different from any yet seen on earth stood in the place of the old Ally. We saw a State without a nation, an army without a country, a religion without a God. The government which claimed to be the new Russia sprang from Revolution and was fed by Terror. It had denounced the faith of treaties; it had made a separate peace; it had released a million Germans for the final onslaught in the West. It had declared that between itself and non-Communist society no good faith, public or private, could exist and no engagements need be respected. It had repudiated alike all that Russia owed and all that was owing to her. Just when the worst was over, when victory was in sight, when the fruits of measureless sacrifice were at hand, the old Russia had been dragged down, and in her place there ruled "the nameless beast" so long foretold in Russian legend. Thus the Russian people were deprived of Victory, Honour, Freedom, Peace and Bread.

★     ★     ★

In the middle of April [1917] the Germans took a sombre decision. Ludendorff refers to it with bated breath. Full allowance must be made for the desperate stakes to which the German war leaders were already committed. They were in the mood which had opened unlimited submarine warfare with the certainty of bringing the United States into the war against them. Upon the Western front they had from the beginning used the most terrible means of offence at their disposal. They had employed poison gas on the largest scale and had invented the "Flammenwerfer". Nevertheless it was with a sense of awe that they turned upon Russia the most grisly of all weapons. They transported Lenin in a sealed truck like a plague bacillus from Switzerland into Russia. Lenin arrived at Petrograd on 16 April. Who was this being in whom there resided these dire potentialities? Lenin was to Karl Marx what Omar was to Mahomet. He translated faith into acts. He devised the practical

388

methods by which the Marxian theories could be applied in his own time. He invented the Communist plan of campaign. He issued the orders, he prescribed the watchwords, he gave the signal and he led the attack.

Lenin was also Vengeance. Child of the bureaucracy, by birth a petty noble, reared by a locally much respected Government School Inspector, his early ideas turned by not unusual contradictions through pity to revolt extinguishing pity. Lenin had an unimpeachable father and a rebellious elder brother. This dearly loved companion meddled in assassination. He was hanged in 1894. Lenin was then sixteen. He was at the age to feel. His mind was a remarkable instrument. When its light shone it revealed the whole world, its history, its sorrows, its stupidities, its shams, and above all its wrongs. It revealed all facts in its focus—the most unwelcome, the most inspiring—with an equal ray. The intellect was capacious and in some phases superb. It was capable of universal comprehension in a degree rarely reached among men. The execution of the elder brother deflected this broad white light through a prism: and the prism was red.

But the mind of Lenin was used and driven by a will not less exceptional. The body tough, square and vigorous in spite of disease was well fitted to harbour till middle age these incandescent agencies. Before they burnt it out his work was done, and a thousand years will not forget it. Men's thoughts and systems in these ages are moving forward. The solutions which Lenin adopted for their troubles are already falling behind the requirements and information of our day. Science irresistible leaps off at irrelevant and henceforth dominating tangents. Social life flows through broadening and multiplying channels. The tomb of the most audacious experimentalist might already bear the placard "Out of date". An easier generation lightly turns the pages which record the Russian Terror. Youth momentarily interested asks whether it was before or after the Great War; and turns ardent to a thousand new possibilities. The educated nations are absorbed in practical affairs. Socialists and Populists are fast trooping back from the blind alleys of thought and scrambling out of the pits of action into which the Russians have blundered. But Lenin has left his mark. He has won his place.

And in the cutting off of the lives of men and women no Asiatic conqueror, not Tamerlane, not Jenghiz Khan can match his fame.

Implacable vengeance, rising from a frozen pity in a tranquil, sensible, matter-of-fact, good-humoured integument! His weapon logic; his mood opportunist. His sympathies cold and wide as the Arctic Ocean; his hatreds tight as the hangman's noose. His purpose to save the world: his method to blow it up. Absolute principles, but readiness to change them. Apt at once to kill or learn: dooms and afterthoughts: ruffianism and philanthropy. But a good husband; a gentle guest; happy, his biographers assure us, to wash up the dishes or dandle the baby; as mildly amused to stalk a capercailzie as to butcher an Emperor. The quality of Lenin's revenge was impersonal. Confronted with the need of killing any particular person he showed reluctance—even distress. But to blot out a million, to proscribe entire classes, to light the flames of intestine war in every land with the inevitable destruction of the well-being of whole nations—these were sublime abstractions.

Lenin was the Grand Repudiator. He repudiated everything. He repudiated God, King, Country, morals, treaties, debts, rents, interest, the laws and customs of centuries, all contracts written or implied, the whole structure—such as it is—of human society. In the end he repudiated himself. He repudiated the Communist system. He confessed its failure in an all-important sphere. He proclaimed the New Economic Policy and recognized private trade. He repudiated what he had slaughtered so many for not believing. They were right it seemed after all. They were unlucky that he did not find it out before. But these things happen sometimes: and how great is the man who acknowledges his mistake! Back again to wash the dishes and give the child a sweetmeat. Thence once more to the rescue of mankind. This time perhaps the shot will be better aimed. It may kill those who are wrong: not those who are right. But after all what are men? If Imperialism had its cannon food, should the Communist laboratory be denied the raw material for sociological experiment?

When the subtle acids he had secreted ate through the physical texture of his brain Lenin mowed the ground. The walls of the Kremlin were not the only witnesses of a strange decay. It was reported that for several months before his death he mumbled old prayers to the deposed gods with ceaseless iteration. If it be true, it shows that Irony is not unknown on Mount Olympus. But this gibbering creature was no longer Lenin. He had already gone. His body lingered for a space to mock the vanished soul. It is still preserved in pickle for the curiosity of the Moscow public and for the consolation of the faithful.

Lenin's intellect failed at the moment when its destructive force was exhausted, and when sovereign remedial functions were its quest. He alone could have led Russia into the enchanted quagmire; he alone could have found the way back to the causeway. He saw; he turned; he perished. The strong illuminant that guided him was cut off at the moment when he had turned resolutely for home. The Russian people were left floundering in the bog. Their worst misfortune was his birth: their next worst—his death.

\*    \*    \*

President Wilson reached at the Armistice the zenith of his power and fame. Since the United States had entered the war in its thirty-second month he had proclaimed more vehemently, and upon occasion more powerfully, than anyone else the righteousness of the Allied cause. Coming into the struggle fresh and cool, he had seemed to pronounce the conclusions of an impartial judge upon the terrible and frantic disputation. High above the swaying conflict, speaking in tones of majesty and simplicity, deeply instructed in all the arts of popular appeal, clad with power unmeasured and certainly unexhausted, he had appeared to the tortured and toiling combatants like a messenger from another planet sent to the rescue of freedom and justice here below. His words had carried comfort to every Allied people, and had been most helpful in silencing subversive peace propaganda in all its forms.

From time to time during the war the various Allies had declared their war aims. In the bleak January of 1918 both Great Britain and the United States had sought to restate their case in the most reasonable terms. In particular on 8 January President Wilson had delivered a speech to Congress in which he had mentioned fourteen points which should in his opinion guide American aspiration. These "Fourteen Points", admirably, if vaguely, phrased, consisted in the main of broad principles which could be applied in varying degrees according to the fortunes of war. They included however two perfectly definite conditions, the reconstitution of an independent Poland, and the retrocession to France of Alsace-Lorraine. The adhesion by the United States to these profoundly important war-objectives, involving as it did a fight to a finish with Germany, was very satisfactory to the Allies. None of them was concerned to examine the whole speech meticulously or felt committed except in general sympathy. In the meanwhile the President's declaration played an important part in holding the Western Democracies firmly and unitedly to the prosecution of the war, and also encouraged defeatist and subversive movements among the enemy populations.

When on 1 October Ludendorff made his panic demand that the German Government should immediately ask for an armistice, it was on the basis of these Fourteen Points that Prince Max of Baden addressed himself to President Wilson. Wilson seized the opportunity of keeping the negotiations in his own hands in their first and all-important phase. He exploited the advantages of his position energetically both against the enemy and against the Allies, so as to engross to himself the whole task and its responsibility. He refused to transmit the appeals of the despairing enemy to the Allies until he was himself satisfied of their sincerity. He dealt with the suppliant Germans in the sternest manner. He used the weapon of delay with masterly skill. No armistice was possible, he declared, without "absolutely satisfactory safeguards and guarantees of the maintenance of the present military supremacy of the armies of the United States and of its Allies". The terms of the armistice must be settled by the Allied Commanders. There could be no question of discussing peace until Germany had deprived herself of all power of resuming the war. The Germans were to deliver themselves naked and defenceless to the discretion and judgment of their conquerors. The month occupied by these parleyings had been one incessant gigantic battle on the whole front. The armies of the United States had lost over 100,000 men killed and wounded, and the French, British and Italians about 380,000. Their advance had been continuous. German resistance had crumpled under the double pressure of the terrors of war and the hopes of peace. At the end they had fallen prostrate at the Presidential footstool.

Wilson's conduct of these negotiations had been so strong and skilful that France and Britain, though at first startled by his self-assertion, were content to leave them in his hands. Even the most rigorous against the enemy could find no fault with his sword-play. He had thus been in the closing stages of the war the spokesman, for all purposes, not only of the United States but of the Allies. He had enunciated the highest principles; he had driven the hardest of bargains.

The European statesmen whom President Wilson was about to meet in Paris to discuss the Peace Treaty represented only too well, in the assertion of national claims and in severity to the beaten enemy, the views and wishes of their own peoples. They ceased and failed to represent them only in so far as they diverged from these hard standards, and guided by experience, tolerance and detachment sought to mitigate the misfortunes of the vanquished, or to disappoint their own national expectations. Orlando, in making the most extreme claims, fell short of Italian aspirations. The iron Clemenceau, the prop of France, was throughout condemned by the French for weakness in championing his country. As for Lloyd George, he was not only fortified by an overwhelming majority but actually embarrassed by the demands of the multitude for the unsparing punishment of the guilty. So far from these national leaders thrusting forward upon their own impulse a ruthless claim against the defeated, they were every one of them in danger of censure for lukewarmness. The Parliaments and Press of every country stood vigilant to detect the slightest symptoms of tenderheartedness or philosophic indifference. Even the prestige which sprang from absolute victory did not protect them from constant scrutiny and suspicion. In every victorious State there rose the cry: "Our soldiers have won the war; let us make sure our politicians do not throw away the peace." These European leaders represented their democracies best in all in which they differed from President Wilson most.

And where was he? He had pledged and was about to recommit the United States to the service of mankind.

The American populace fell as far short of their Chief in disinterested generosity to the world, as the peoples of the Allied countries exceeded their own leaders in severity to the enemy. The President himself was without a majority both in the Senate and in the newly elected Congress. Already ex-President Roosevelt had brutally proclaimed: "Our Allies and our enemies and Mr. Wilson himself should all understand that Mr. Wilson has no authority whatever to speak for the American people at this time." Much lower and cruder views than his were to prevail on both sides of the Atlantic. The Allies were destined to settle their affairs among themselves. The agreements to which President Wilson sought to commit the United States, for which the Allies would be asked to concede many grave things, were to be swiftly repudiated by the American Senate and electors. After immense delays and false hopes that only aggravated her difficulties, Europe was to be left to scramble out of the world disaster as best she could; and the United States, which had lost but 125,000 lives in the whole struggle, was to settle down upon the basis of receiving through one channel or another four-fifths of the reparations paid by Germany to the countries she had devastated or whose manhood she had slain.

To write thus is not to blame peoples or their leading men. It is only to recognize the comparatively low level upon which the intercourse of vast communities can proceed at the present stage in human development. How could the peoples know? Through what channel could they receive their instruction? What choate and integral conviction could they form? How could they express it? Vague, general ideas, some harsh, some noble, attracted them from day to day. But in the main they were so glad the war had stopped that each individual family was thinking of nothing so much as reunion, and building up again the home, the business, the old life. Wilson created world democracy in his own image. In fact, however, the "plain people" of whom he spoke so much, though very resolute and persevering in war, knew nothing whatever about how to make a just and durable peace. "Punish the Germans", "No more War", and "Something for our own country", above all "Come Home", were the only mass ideas then rife.

If Wilson had been either simply an idealist or a caucus politician, he might have succeeded. His attempt to run the two in double harness was the cause of his undoing. The spacious philanthropy which he exhaled upon Europe stopped quite sharply at the coasts of his own country. There he was in every main decision a party politician, calculating and brazen. A tithe of the fine principles and generous sentiments he lavished upon Europe, applied during 1918 to his Republican opponents in the United States, would have made him in truth the leader of a nation. His sense of proportion operated in separate water-tight compartments. The differences in Europe between France and Germany seemed trivial, petty, easy to be adjusted by a little good sense and charity. But the differences between Democrat and Republican in the United States! Here were really grave quarrels. He could not understand why the French should not be more forgiving to their beaten enemy; nor why the American Republicans should not expect cold comfort from a Democratic Administration. His gaze was fixed with equal earnestness upon the destiny of mankind and the fortunes of his party candidates. Peace and goodwill among all nations abroad, but no truck with the Republican Party at home. That was his ticket and that was his ruin, and the ruin of much else as well. It is difficult for a man to do great things if he tries to combine a lambent charity embracing the whole world with the sharper forms of populist party strife.

★     ★     ★

However keen may be the feelings excited by the distribution of tropical colonies, of compensation in money or in kind and of retributive justice; high as are the hopes centred in the League of Nations, it is by the territorial settlements in Europe that the Treaties of 1919 and 1920 will finally be judged. Here we are in contact with those deep and lasting facts which cast races of men into moulds and fix their place and status in the world. Here we stir the embers of the past and light the beacons of the future. Old flags are raised anew; the passions of vanished generations awake; beneath the shell-torn soil of the twentieth century the bones of long dead warriors and victims are exposed, and the wail of lost causes sounds in the wind.

The treaties with which we now have to deal take their place in the great series which includes the Treaty of Westphalia, the Treaty of Utrecht and the Treaties of Vienna. They are at once the latest and the largest link in the chain of European history. They will be memorable for three events of the first magnitude: the dissolution of the Austro-Hungarian Empire; the rebirth of Poland; and the preservation of united Germany. Even the short distance we have travelled since the Conference in Paris reveals the scale of these monarch-peaks, and how they tower above the range and dominate the wide regions of mountainous and hilly country. Already through the clearer air we can discern the proportions of the vast landscape and its massive simplicity. The Empire of Charles V, and with it the Hapsburg Monarchy, the survivor of so many upheavals, the main structure of central and southern Europe, is represented only by a chasm. The three sundered parts of Poland are reunited into a sovereign independent republic of thirty million souls; and Germany, beaten and disarmed upon the field of battle, defenceless before her outraged conquerors, rises the largest and incomparably the strongest racial mass in Europe.

These dominant facts in the life of Europe did not spring solely, or even mainly, from the volcanic violence of the war. They were the result of the methodical application of a principle. If the treaty makers of Vienna in 1814 were ruled by the principle of Legitimacy, those of Paris in 1919 were guided by the principle of Self-determination. Although the expression "Self-determination" will rightly be forever connected with the name of President Wilson, the ideal was neither original nor new. The phrase itself is Fichte's "*Selbst bestimmung*". The conception has never been more forcefully presented than by Mazzini. Throughout the British Empire it had long been known and widely practised under the somewhat less explosive precepts of "Self-government" and "Government by Consent". During the nineteenth century the rise of Nationalism made it increasingly plain that all great Empires must reckon with this principle and increasingly conform to it, if they were to survive united and vital in the modern world. The almost complete exclusion of religion in all its forms from the political sphere had left Nationalism the most powerful moulding instrument of mankind in temporal affairs.

*       *       *

During the year 1919 there was fought over the whole of Russia a strange war; a war in areas so vast that considerable armies, armies indeed of hundreds of thousands of men, were lost—dispersed, melted, evaporated; a war in which there were no real battles, only raids and affrays and massacres, as the result of which countries as large as England or France changed hands to and fro; a war of flags on the map, of picket lines, of cavalry screens advancing or receding by hundreds of miles without solid cause or durable consequence; a war with little valour and no mercy. Whoever could advance found it easy to continue; whoever was forced to retire found it difficult to stop. On paper it looked like the Great War on the Western and Eastern fronts. In fact it was only its ghost: a thin, cold, insubstantial conflict in the Realms of Dis. Koltchak first and then Denikin advanced in what were called offensives over enormous territories. As they advanced they spread their lines ever wider and ever thinner. It seemed that they would go on till they had scarcely one man to the mile. When the moment came the Bolsheviks lying in the centre, equally feeble but at any rate tending willy-nilly constantly towards compression, gave a prick or a punch at this point or that. Thereupon the balloon burst and all the flags moved back and the cities changed hands and found it convenient to change opinions, and horrible vengeances were wrought on helpless people, vengeances perseveringly paid over months of fine-spun inquisition. Mighty natural or strategic barriers, like the line of the Volga River or the line of the Ural Mountains, were found to be no resting places; no strategic consequences followed from their loss or gain. A war of few casualties and unnumbered executions! The tragedy of each Russian city, of loyal families, of countless humble households might fill libraries of dreary volumes.

The population of Russia is a village population. The peasant millions dwell in scores of thousands of villages. There was always the land, and Nature brought forth her fruits. What was the life of these villages in this period? Savinkov gave a convincing account of it when we lunched together one day with Lloyd George. It was in some ways the story of the Indian villages over whose heads the waves of conquest swept and recoiled in bygone ages. They had the land. They had murdered or chased away its former owners. The village society had flowed over into new and well cultivated fields. They now had these long coveted domains for themselves. No more landlords: no more rent. The earth and its fullness—no more—no less. They did not yet understand that under Communism they would have a new landlord, the Soviet State—a landlord who would demand a higher rent to feed his hungry cities. A collective landlord who could not be killed but who could and would without compunction kill them.

Meanwhile they were self-supporting. Their rude existence could be maintained apart altogether from the outer world or modern apparatus. From the skins of beasts they made garments and footwear. The bees gave them honey in place of sugar. They gave them also wax for such lights as might be needed after sundown. There was bread; there was meat; there were roots. They ate and drank and squatted on the land. Not for them the causes of men. Communism, Czarism; the World Revolution, Holy Russia; Empire or Proletariat, civilization or barbarism, tyranny or freedom—these were all the same to them in theory; but also—whoever won—much the same in fact. There they were and there they stayed; and with hard toil, there they gained their daily bread. One morning arrives a Cossack patrol. "Christ is risen; the Allies are advancing; Russia is saved; you are free." "The Soviet is no more." And the peasants grunted, and duly elected their Council of Elders, and the Cossack patrol rode off, taking with it what it might require up to the limit of what it could carry. On an afternoon a few weeks later, or it may be a few days later, arrived a Bolshevik in a battered motor-car with half a dozen gunmen, also saying: "You are free; your chains are broken; Christ is a fraud; religion is the opiate of democracy; Brothers, Comrades, rejoice for the great days that have dawned." And the peasants grunted. And the Bolshevik said: "Away with this Council of Elders, exploiters of the poor, the base tools of reaction. Elect in their place your village Soviet, henceforward the sickle and hammer of your Proletarian rights." So the peasants swept away the Council of Elders and re-elected with rude ceremony the village Soviet. But they chose exactly the same people who had hitherto formed the Council of Elders and the land also remained in their possession. And presently the Bolshevik and his gunmen got their motor-car to start and throbbed off into the distance, or perhaps into the Cossack patrol.

Moscow held the controls of Russia; and when the cause of the Allies burnt itself out in victory, there were no other controls: just chatter and slaughter on a background of Robinson Crusoe toil. The ancient capital lay at the centre of a web of railroads radiating to every point of the compass. And in the midst a spider! Vain hope to crush the spider by the advance of lines of encircling flies! Still I suppose that twenty or thirty thousand resolute, comprehending, well-armed Europeans could, without any serious difficulty or loss, have made their way very swiftly along any of the great railroads which converged on Moscow; and have brought to the hard ordeal of battle any force that stood against them. But twenty or thirty thousand resolute men did not exist or could not be brought together. Denikin's forces foraged over enormous areas. They boasted a superficial political sway. They lived on the country and by so doing soon alienated the rural population which at first had welcomed them. Had he collected the necessary supplies at one spot in the south for a direct dash to Moscow, and had he seized the psychological moment just before the Siberian armies began to fade away, he would have had a good chance of success. Master of Moscow and its unequalled railway centre with a corps of trustworthy troops, his power and prestige might have been unshakable. But there never was a thrust; no Napoleon eagle-swoop at the mysterious capital; only the long thin lines wending on ever thinner, weaker and more weary. And then finally when the Bolsheviks in the centre of the circle were sufficiently concentrated by the mere fact of retirement, they in their turn advanced and found in front of them—nothing!—nothing but helpless populations and scores of thousands of compromised families and individuals.

*       *       *

The story of the human race is War. Except for brief and precarious interludes there has never been peace in the world; and before history began murderous strife was universal and unending. But the modern developments surely require severe and active attention.

Up to the present time the means of destruction at the disposal of man have not kept pace with his ferocity. Reciprocal extermination was impossible in the Stone Age. One cannot do much with a clumsy club. Besides, men were so scarce and hid so well that they were hard to find. They fled so fast that they were hard to catch. Human legs could only cover a certain distance each day. With the best will in the world to destroy his species, each man was restricted to a very limited area of activity. It was impossible to make any effective progress on these lines. Meanwhile one had to live and hunt and sleep. So on the balance the life-forces kept a steady lead over the forces of death, and gradually tribes, villages, and governments were evolved.

The effort at destruction then entered upon a new phase. War became a collective enterprise. Roads were made which facilitated the movement of large numbers of men. Armies were organized. Many improvements in the apparatus of slaughter were devised. In particular the use of metal, and above all, steel, for piercing and cutting human flesh, opened out a promising field. Bows and arrows, slings, chariots, horses, and elephants lent a valuable assistance. But here again another set of checks began to operate. The governments were not sufficiently secure. The armies were liable to violent internal disagreements. It was extremely difficult to feed large numbers of men once they were concentrated, and consequently the efficiency of the efforts at destruction became fitful and was tremendously hampered by defective organization. Thus again there was a balance on the credit side of life. The world rolled forward, and human society entered upon a vaster and more complex age.

But all that happened in the four years of the Great War was only a prelude to what was preparing for the fifth year. The campaign of the year 1919 would have witnessed an immense accession to the power of destruction. Had the Germans retained the morale to make good their retreat to the Rhine, they would have been assaulted in the summer of 1919 with forces and by methods incomparably more prodigious than any yet employed. Thousands of aeroplanes would have shattered their cities. Scores of thousands of cannon would have blasted their front. Arrangements were being made to carry simultaneously a quarter of a million men, together with all their requirements, continuously forward across country in mechanical vehicles moving ten or fifteen miles each day. Poison gases of incredible malignity, against which only a secret mask (which the Germans could not obtain in time) was proof, would have stifled all resistance and paralysed all life on the hostile front subjected to attack. No doubt the Germans too had their plans. But the hour of wrath had passed. The signal of relief was given, and the horrors of 1919 remained buried in the archives of the great antagonists.

The War stopped as suddenly and as universally as it had begun. The world lifted its head, surveyed the scene of ruin, and victors and vanquished alike drew breath. In a hundred laboratories, in a thousand arsenals, factories, and bureaux, men pulled themselves up with a jerk, turned from the task in which they had been absorbed. Their projects were put aside unfinished, unexecuted; but their knowledge was preserved; their data, calculations, and discoveries were hastily bundled together and docketed "for future reference" by the War Offices in every country. The campaign of 1919 was never fought; but its ideas go marching along. In every army they are being explored, elaborated, refined under the surface of peace, and should war come again to the world it is not with the weapons and agencies prepared for 1919 that it will be fought, but with developments and extensions of these which will be incomparably more formidable and fatal.

# STEP BY STEP

## 1936–1939

*In May, 1935, Hitler instituted compulsory military service; later in that year Mussolini invaded Abyssinia and the foundation of the Berlin-Rome Axis was laid. German rearmament was unchecked by collective action. In March, 1936, Hitler reoccupied the Rhineland and denounced the Treaties of Versailles and Locarno. These defiant actions were warnings of grave dangers of war to the author, and in writings and speeches he constantly repeated them up to the outbreak of war. This book, published in June, 1939, collects together some of his comments and forecasts which were in the end seen to be completely justified.*

It is a mistake to suppose that the problem of averting another European or probably a world war depends to any important extent either upon the reply which Herr Hitler has made to the Locarno Powers, or to staff conversations now decided upon between Great Britain and France or Belgium. Herr Hitler is continuing his efforts to separate Great Britain from France, and also to separate British public opinion from the British Government and House of Commons. The British Government, on the other hand, is anxious to comfort France in view of the great restraint which France, largely in deference to British wishes, has observed in presence of the German breach of treaties and military reoccupation of the Rhine zone. The realities are far larger and more profound than either of these moves upon the diplomatic chessboard.

First stands the rapid and tremendous rearmament of Germany, which is proceeding night and day and is steadily converting nearly seventy millions of the most efficient race in Europe into one gigantic, hungry war-machine. The second is that the recent actions of Germany have destroyed all confidence in her respect for treaties, whether imposed as the result of defeat in war or freely entered into by post-War Germany and confirmed by the Nazi regime. The third is that practically the whole of the German nation has been taught to regard the incorporation in the Reich of the Germanic population of neighbouring states as a natural, rightful and inevitable aim of German policy. The fourth is that the financial and economic pressures in Germany are rising to such a pitch that Herr Hitler's government will in a comparatively short time have only to choose between an internal and an external explosion.

The dear desire of all the peoples, not perhaps even excluding a substantial portion of the German people themselves, is to avoid another horrible war in which their lives and homes will be destroyed or ruined and such civilization as we have been able to achieve reduced to primordial pulp and squalor. Never till now were great communities afforded such ample means of measuring their approaching agony. Never have they seemed less capable of taking effective measures to prevent it. Chattering, busy, sporting, toiling, amused from day to day by headlines and from night to night by cinemas, they yet can feel themselves slipping, sinking, rolling backward to the age when "the earth was void and darkness moved upon the face of the waters". Surely it is worth a supreme effort— the laying aside of every impediment, the clear-eyed facing of fundamental facts, the noble acceptance of risks inseparable from heroic endeavour—to control the hideous drift of events and arrest calamity upon the threshold. Stop it! Stop it!! Stop it now!!! NOW is the appointed time.

When, on that Friday night three weeks ago, Herr Hitler, against the advice of his generals, ordered his redoubtable troops to march through the "scraps of paper" to occupy and entrench the Rhineland, he set in motion a trend of events which offered nothing less than blessing or cursing to mankind. Which fate shall befall us rests no longer with him, but with the world. The world, nay, Europe alone, is overwhelmingly strong compared to any single member of its family. But there must be Concert and Design guided by far-sighted unselfishness and sustained by inexorable resolve. This is no task for France; no task for Britain; no task for the Locarno Powers or any group of Powers; no task for small Powers nor for great; it is a task for all. The means are at hand; the occasion has come. There may still be time.

Let the States and peoples who lie in fear of Germany carry their alarms to the League of Nations at Geneva. Let the greatest among them lead the way and marshal the assembly. Let none be a laggard or a doubter. Let the League, if satisfied that their fears are well-founded, authorize, nay, adjure them, to take forthwith all necessary measures for mutual protection, and require them to stand in readiness alike to submit themselves to, or, if need be, enforce the reign of international law. Let us have, in the words of a writer in *The Times*: "A block of peaceable but resolute nations determined to make a stand against aggression in any form". Let the League then address Germany *collectively*, not only upon her treaty breaches but also upon her own grievances and anxieties, and, above all, upon her armaments. Let Germany receive from united nations a guarantee of the inviolability of her own soil unless she invades the soil of others. Let unchallengeable power and fair play march hand in hand. Let us move forward by measured steps to a faithful and a lasting settlement in accordance with the general need.       [3 April, 1936]

\*       \*       \*

Ever since the fall of the Lloyd George Coalition we have dwelt under what may be known as the "Baldwin-MacDonald Regime". At first in alternation, but since 1931 in political brotherhood, these two statesmen have governed the country. Nominally the representatives of opposing parties, of contrary doctrines, of antagonistic interests, they proved in fact to be more nearly akin in outlook, temperament and method than any other two statesmen who have been Prime Ministers since that office was known to the Constitution. Curiously enough the sympathies of each extended far into the territory of the other. Ramsay MacDonald nursed many of the sentiments of the old Tory. Stanley Baldwin, apart from a manufacturer's ingrained approval of Protection, was by disposition a truer representative of mild Socialism than any to be found in the Labour ranks. Especially upon Imperial questions like India, Egypt, the mandated territories, and above all National Defence, his temper and feelings corresponded to what used to be called "Lib.-Lab." standards.

404

Both men excelled in the art of minimizing political issues, of frustrating large schemes of change, of depressing the national temperature, and reducing Parliament to a humdrum level. Their ideal of government appears to be well expressed by the noble lord in the Gilbert and Sullivan opera who "did nothing in particular, but did it very well". No wonder they agreed so happily when, instead of throwing the ball to one another across the Parliamentary table, they settled down as colleagues side by side.

When it began to be apparent that the Teutonic giant was stealthily regathering the weapons with which he had almost conquered the world, a dire change affected the whole situation. This unwelcome —nay, hateful—intrusion of the external upon our two poor eminent friends was received by them at first with inveterate incredulity. So unwilling were they to accept the plainest evidence of danger that they covered themselves contentedly with a cloud of well-meaning platitudes. They closed their eyes to what they did not wish to see. Thus the seasons passed swiftly away, and all the time the sombre processes which were to undermine the peace of Europe hurried forward amain.

By the spring of 1934 incredulity was worn threadbare. It was succeeded by half-measures and dismay. No attempt was made to grapple courageously with the European situation while it could have been controlled. Nor were even those simple precautions taken which would have enabled Great Britain to be placed swiftly in a state of security. A year ago Mr. MacDonald transferred the growing burden with exhausted strength to his co-partner. Mr. Baldwin became for the third time Prime Minister. He appealed to the country most urgently to rearm; but at the same time he stipulated that there should be no large rearmament. It may well be that he sustained the impression at the General Election that he won it himself. In fact it was won by the clear resolve of the British people not, amid multiplying dangers, to entrust their affairs to the weak and discredited Socialist Party.

The new Parliament met at Westminster under the impact of realities. Almost every month it has been smitten by fresh hammer-blows. The country is slowly but undoubtedly awakening to the fact that world peace is menaced, and that our island safety is no longer unquestioned. Gradually it is being understood that whereas four years ago all was sure and easy, all has now become dark, doubtful and hazardous in the extreme. It is this growing comprehension that the times have changed, that woeful miscalculations have been made, that a violent period is drawing near, and that we ourselves are neither ready for it nor even making the exertions which are now possible, that has weakened so profoundly the position of the Prime Minister.                    [13 July, 1936]

*     *     *

If we look back only across the year that has nearly passed since the General Election, the most thoughtless person will be shocked at the ceaseless degeneration abroad, and also of our own interests on the Continent. Abyssinia has been conquered. The League of Nations and all that it stands for has been grievously stricken. The old friendship between Great Britain and Italy is sundered. In its place there has arisen a dangerous association between the martial dictators. France is passing through a phase of apparent weakness and acute anxiety. Upon all this there has supervened the hideous Spanish Civil War, now raging towards its climax.

Meanwhile, Germany, whose annual quota of manhood reaching the military age is already double that of France, has increased her period of service from one year to two. She has taken armed possession of the demilitarized zone in the Rhineland. Her fortification of it is far advanced and growing every week. Her armoured divisions, each comprising thousands of vehicles, present themselves as a vast new definite source of aggressive strength. Her terrific expenditure upon war preparations goes forward to the full limit of national capacity and regardless of financial embarrassment and food stringency.

All the while Great Britain has drifted along her fatuous feckless course, the sport of every wind that blows. Chatter to uphold the League of Nations and defend the rights of Abyssinia; chatter for the Hoare-Laval pact; chatter for its reversal; cheers for Mr. Eden and the policy of more vigorous sanctions; cheers and chatter for their total abandonment; chatter about reforming the League of Nations without decision whether to strengthen it or weaken it;

chatter for a new Locarno in the West—all in a year; only a year! Thus did the people of Madrid sit in their cafés, visit their cinemas, shout in their demonstrations, while day after day some strong point of their defences was torn away and the iron ring of consequences contracted remorselessly upon them. But why worry? The Ministers have had good holidays. Except for the derelict areas, the country is fat, prosperous and contented, and every eye is fixed upon the joyous festivities of the approaching Coronation.

What has happened to our defences in the meanwhile? Three years ago there was time. Two years ago there was danger. One year ago great new programmes of rearmament, and especially of expansion in the Air, were announced. What has happened to them? Are they being fulfilled? Are we making up for lost time? Are we overtaking foreign countries? Will the goods be delivered at the dates promised? How long must we wait in a condition, apart from the Navy, of lamentable weakness and confusion?

Surely Parliament should take some effective interest in a matter which so vitally affects the safety of the State. Surely Members of the House of Commons have a responsibility towards their constituents to find out where we stand, and to make sure that everything possible is being done to remedy our admitted weakness. The Parliaments of the past would never have been content with smooth generalities or partial illustrations. They would have been ashamed to dwell in supine ignorance of the true state of our affairs. They would have insisted upon searching inquiry, conducted in secret where necessary, and on receiving a report upon the facts from persons independent of Ministerial control. A new session is about to open. Is it to be marked only by a series of fitful, disjointed and inconclusive debates where nothing is brought to a head and a few new Ministerial announcements are sufficient to tide over the afternoon, or are the Houses of Parliament going to satisfy themselves definitely that everything that is possible is being done, and done in the best way; that the organization for the production of munitions of all kinds is really harmonious, symmetrical and comprehensive? Are the members going to discharge their responsibilities to the Empire and to the nation, and earnestly associate themselves with the business of national defence? Or will they simply shrug their shoulders, admit their impotency, and await in docile resignation the impending teachings of events? [30 October, 1936]

* * *

The Coronation is over. A new King and Queen are seated upon their thrones amid the acclamations of the British people. The Abdication has been digested. The Duke of Windsor is married according to his resolve and with the good wishes of all that is decent in Britain. After a period of pageantry and of domestic stress the British public may be invited to turn again to Europe.

How has it all gone in Europe while we have been thinking about our own affairs? I, personally, have never been able to forget Europe. It hangs over my mind like a vulture. How are we going to prevent our happy, peaceful, free, progressive life from being destroyed by what may happen in Europe? All the time the German armament hammers have been descending. All the time the great flow of destructive weapons has been passing from the factories to fighting units of brave, virile, competent men improving in their training month by month. All the time the German Army has been increasing its numbers above those of the French Army. All the time the efficiency and ripeness of the German Officer-Corps has been improving. All the time the German Air Force in quantity and in quality has been gaining on our British effort.

What is the precise character of the arrangements between Germany and Italy? Here are these two dictators seated on their thrones high above the common mass of peaceful, well-disposed, heavily burdened mankind. Both have plenty of obedient men. Both are hard pressed for money. Both have to ask their obedient men to tighten their belts. Both are confronted with the awkward sense that though Germany is all for Hitler, it wishes to be known as Germany; and though Italy is all for Mussolini, it would like to be known as Italy. Both are disquieted by the fact that large sections of their population would like to stand in with the general efflorescence of the world, and that quite large numbers of Fascists and Nazis would be very much inclined to vote "that a good time should be had by all". Grim dictators glowering over gaunt populations! What are their personal relations to be?

Who shall presume to lift the veils of the future, and who would be believed if he reported what he saw? Evidently we are approaching the point in European history where the League of Nations, if properly supported, will have an immense and perhaps decisive part to play in the prevention of a brutal trial of strength. How else are we going to marshal adequate and if possible overwhelming forces against brazen, unprovoked aggression, except by a grand alliance of peace-seeking peoples under the authority of an august international body? One is astonished to hear the vain talk and chatter that proceeds in certain social and political circles in London against the League of Nations. Only by a European union spreading gradually to a world union against war can the dreaded catastrophe, which nevertheless approaches inch by inch and day by day, be warded off. I hold that at the present time an alliance of an offensive or even of a defensive character between Italy and Germany is far from being achieved. There is still time to build Europe into a better framework. There is still time to conciliate existing grievances. There is still time, if all friendly efforts for peace are futile, to forge and weld a grand alliance for international law and justice, which will arrest armaments, avert war and confound the wicked of every land.                                    [11 June, 1937]

\*       \*       \*

Although the Spanish Civil War and its surrounding complications have lately held the first place in the public mind, Czechoslovakia remains beyond all question the immediate danger-point of Europe.

The Czechoslovakian Government have decided to keep strong forces on guard along their frontiers. Their object is no doubt to make the invasion of their country an operation which will require very large troop movements in Germany. The larger the scale of the movements the harder it is to conceal them. Thus there should be time to mobilize the whole national defence. This constitutes a very substantial deterrent upon a sudden onslaught.

Thus, whatever else may happen, an easy walkover transforms itself into a grave and costly operation of war. Before embarking on such a plan, an aggressive government would have to contemplate general mobilization, the employment of a large portion of its whole army, and at least three or four hundred thousand casualties. Even taken by itself, such an enterprise would be heart-shaking to any modern Power, especially to one just recovering from a defeat in which nearly the whole world gradually came against her. But would the issue stand by itself? Would Czechoslovakia be left to struggle week after week against an avalanche of fire and steel? There is the explicit French declaration to the contrary. There is the Russian engagement, which should not be lightly discounted. There is the statement which the Prime Minister made in the House of Commons about Czechoslovakia. No poorer service can be done to peace than to belittle these massive deterrents. We have only to recall the swift rise of temperature which occurred in British public opinion during the annexation of Austria, bloodless as it was, to imagine the effects of a fearful conflict raging day by day between the invading armies of a great Power and the heroic defenders of a small civilized State. [23 June, 1938]

★     ★     ★

How heavily do the destinies of this generation hang upon the government and people of the United States! From many lands in Europe and in Asia eyes are turned towards this large, strong English-speaking community, which lies doubly shielded by its oceans, and yet is responsive to the surge of world causes. Will the United States throw their weight into the scales of peace and law and freedom while time remains, or will they remain spectators until the disaster has occurred; and then, with infinite cost and labour, build up what need not have been cast down? This is the riddle of a Sphinx who under the mask of loquacity, affability, sentimentality, hard business, machine-made politics, wrong-feeling, right-feeling, vigour and weakness, efficiency and muddle, still preserves the power to pronounce a solemn and formidable word.

When things are going well in America, the more solid pedestrian forces in the free countries of Europe are conscious of a new draught of strength. When things go ill, they are weakened through a hundred channels in those very elements of strength which ought to reward law-respecting, peace-interested, civilized States.

Economic and financial disorder in the United States not only depresses all sister countries, but weakens them in those very forces which might either mitigate the hatreds of races or provide the means to resist tyranny. The first service which the United States can render to world causes is to be prosperous and well-armed.

The arming part is being achieved on a very large scale. Enormous supplies have been voted by Congress for the expansion of the armed forces, particularly the Navy, to levels far above what any immediate direct danger would seem to require. No American party resists the President's desire to make the United States one of the most heavily armed, scientifically prepared countries in the world. Pacifism and the cult of defencelessness have been discarded by all parties. There never was in peace a time when the American armaments by land, air and sea, reached so imposing a height, or were sustained by so much national conviction.

In the meanwhile, the movement of American opinion upon world affairs is remarkable. Side by side with the loudest reiterations of "Never again will we be drawn in", there is a ceaselessly growing interest in the great issues which are at stake both in Europe and the Far East. There never was a peace-time when the newspapers of the United States carried more foreign news to their readers, or when those readers showed themselves more anxious to be informed about affairs taking place thousands of miles away, or more inclined to develop strong intellectual and moral convictions about them. There are literally scores of millions of men and women in the United States who feel as much opposed to the tyrannies of totalitarian governments, Communist or Nazi, as their grandfathers were to the continuance of slavery.

The feeling, not against Germany, but against the Nazi regime, is more pronounced and outspoken throughout the United States than in Great Britain. It is far more active and widespread than it was before 1914. This mood is not at all discouraged by the Administration. The speeches of important Ministers express, in ardent terms, all the feelings of British, French and Scandinavian liberal democracies. The American ex-Servicemen confront the Nazi movement with a stern, unrelenting hostility. German espionage in America rivets public attention. The New Yorkers have to be restrained from mobbing German ships. Hardly a week passes without some incident arising in politics or sport which affords the five-hundred-headed newspaper Press an opportunity of writing against Nazism the kind of things their readers want to read.

All these facts should be noted by those whom they concern. It would be foolish of the European democracies, in their military arrangements, to count on any direct aid from the United States. It would be still more foolish for war-making forces in the Dictator Governments of Europe to ignore or treat with contempt this slow but ceaseless marshalling of United States opinion around the standards of freedom and tolerance. The more weightily the personality of the United States is accounted in Europe in these years, perhaps even in these months, the better are our chances of escaping another lurch into the pit.                                    [4 August, 1938]

*       *       *

Fear, not unmanly fear, but none the less wearing, broods over Europe in these fateful days.

Germany is very largely mobilized. The fleet is mobilized; the Air Force is ready, and two-thirds of the army are on a war footing. The economic and industrial organization of the country and its general life approximate to conditions of war. The chiefs of the Nazi regime have made these enormous demands upon their country, and nothing like it has happened before in time of peace. It seems impossible that these extreme conditions could remain in their present tension for very long. The armies must act, or they must disperse. Winter is approaching, and after the middle of October the weather may become severe. Therefore, it seems that the limit of time when these great forces are either launched in war, or sent to their homes, is very short. If they are dispersed without some clear triumph, the Nazi regime, already the object of much criticism in Germany, will have sustained a rebuff which may affect its future life.

Many credible witnesses declare that a programme is being executed step by step. Certainly the troop movements which carried great forces from Central Germany to the Rhine frontier, and have produced very heavy concentrations all around Czechoslovakia, and

412

particularly in the newly conquered Austrian Province, seem to be all part of a plan which will reach its climax before the end of the present month. The time that is passing has been well spent by the mobilized troops in welding the reservists into the formations, and shaking them together into fighting efficiency. We must suppose that everything is ready, or will be ready in the next ten days, for a converging attack upon Czechoslovakia with troops and weapons which the Nazi Party believe to be overwhelming. All that remains is for some bloody incident, or actual revolt, to be created at the moment prescribed by Hitler, and for the signal to advance to be given. It is not probable there would be any ultimatum. "When I strike," said Hitler a year ago in a little-remembered speech, "I shall not waste time like Mussolini in discussion. I shall strike like lightning in the night."

Some people still profess to believe that Herr Hitler and his confederates would never dream of using violence against the Czechs; that these vast preparations are only after all small local manoeuvres entirely normal in their character, though perhaps a little extensive in their scale; and that soon the armies will disperse. If that be true, then we may all rejoice. But on the assumption that it is not true, and that the crime is planned and imminent, the question before us is whether we can stop it, and how? The British Government sustained by a united nation have made it clear that should a major war explode, they would be almost inevitably involved. But it is not enough to say that we shall probably be in the war if it happens. What above all is important is to prevent it happening. The ordinary smooth and balanced phrases of diplomacy, with all their refinements and reserves, are of little use in dealing with the fierce chiefs of German Nazidom. Only the most blunt, plain, even brutal language will make its effect. Moreover, whatever words are used must carry with them the conviction that they are spoken in deadly earnest. This is no time to bluff.

Everyone will sympathize with the high-minded statesmen who have laboured so patiently for peace. But one must ask whether they would add appreciably to our danger by declaring themselves unmistakably, while time remains. If, for instance, Great Britain, France and Russia were even now to present a joint or simultaneous note to Herr Hitler personally, setting forth that an attack on Czechoslovakia would immediately be followed by common action; and if at the same time President Roosevelt would proclaim that this note carried with it the moral sympathy of the United States, with all that would follow therefrom—there would be good hopes, if not intended almost a certainty, of warding off the catastrophe which may so easily engulf our civilization.

[15 September, 1938]

\* \* \*

British sympathy goes out in generous measure to France as she stands by this fateful milestone in her long history. It is a duty binding upon all public men, on both sides of the Channel, who write or speak about the tremendous events of the last fortnight, to make sure that no words of theirs weaken the ties which unite our two countries. That would be the last and crowning service that could be rendered to the triumphant Nazi power. If the French Republic and the British Empire were necessary to each other in days of war and in days of success, they are still more necessary in these times when conditions are so different. Above all, there must be no recrimination between the two countries whose future security and independence is more than ever bound up with their unity.

It would be affectation to deny that the whole basis of French foreign policy in Central and Eastern Europe has disappeared. On the other hand, no charge can be made against France of having broken her military engagement with Czechoslovakia. That promise did not become operative until the act of aggression was in fact perpetrated. It was the outbreak of an armed conflict which alone would have brought the French obligation into absolute being. "Unbearable pressure" was brought by France and Great Britain upon the Czechoslovak Government, and beneath that pressure they bent and yielded.

An injury has, however, been sustained by the prestige and authority of both the Western democracies which must woefully reduce their influence with small countries of all kinds. It will not be easy to regain the lost confidence. All those statesmen in the minor countries of Europe who have consistently endeavoured to incline their policy towards the Nazi channels, who have pointed out the weakness of the democracies and the impediments to action

414

provided by their parliamentary systems, are now, of course, vindicated.

Much will depend upon the attitude of the British and French Parliaments, and upon the new measures which they may consider necessary for meeting the grave deterioration in their positions. It is, no doubt, heartbreaking to look back over the last few years and see the enormous resources of military and political strength which have been squandered through lack of leadership and clarity of purpose. There has never been a moment up to the present when a firm stand by France and Britain together with the many countries who recently looked to them would not have called a halt to the Nazi menace. At each stage, as each new breach of treaties was effected, timidity, lack of knowledge and foresight have prevented the two peaceful Powers from marching in step. Thus we have the spectacle of a handful of men, who have a great nation in their grip, outfacing the enormously superior forces lately at the disposal of the Western democracies.

It is a crime to despair. We must learn to draw from misfortune the means of future strength. There must not be lacking in our leadership something of the spirit of that Austrian corporal who, when all had fallen into ruins about him, and when Germany seemed to have sunk for ever into chaos, did not hesitate to march forth against the vast array of victorious nations, and has already turned the tables so decisively upon them. It is the hour, not for despair, but for courage and rebuilding; and that is the spirit which should rule our minds. [4 October, 1938]

\* \* \*

Everyone must recognize that the Prime Minister is pursuing a policy of a most decided character and of capital importance. He has his own strong view about what to do, and about what is going to happen. He has his own standard of values; he has his own angle of vision. He believes that he can make a good settlement for Europe and for the British Empire by coming to terms with Herr Hitler and Signor Mussolini. No one impugns his motives. No one doubts his conviction or his courage. Besides all this, he has the power to do what he thinks best.

The Prime Minister is persuaded that Herr Hitler seeks no further territorial expansion upon the continent of Europe; that the mastering and absorption of the Republic of Czechoslovakia has satiated the appetite of the German Nazi regime. It may be that he wishes to induce the Conservative Party to return to Germany the mandated territories in British possession, or what are judged to be their full equivalent. He believes that this act of restoration will bring about prolonged, good and secure relations between Great Britain and Germany. He believes further that these good relations can be achieved without weakening in any way the fundamental ties of self-preservation which bind us to the French Republic, which ties, it is common ground between us all, must be preserved. Mr. Chamberlain is convinced that all this will lead to general agreement; to the appeasement of the discontented Powers, and to a lasting peace.

By this time next year we shall know whether the Prime Minister's view of Herr Hitler and the German Nazi Party is right or wrong. By this time next year we shall know whether the policy of appeasement has appeased, or whether it has only stimulated a more ferocious appetite. All we can do in the meanwhile is to gather together forces of resistance and defence, so that if the Prime Minister should unhappily be wrong, or misled, or deceived, we can at the worst keep body and soul together.

But these issues, although painful and important, are dwarfed by the dangers of what is called disarmament. What does that mean? Everyone would like to see it. Everyone would rejoice if the resources of all the great nations of the world could be turned into channels more fruitful to the mass of the peoples. But surely we have to take care that what is called disarmament does not in fact mean leaving Britain where she can be blackmailed out of her skin. I fear that seductive proposals will be thrust upon us, perhaps at very short notice.

But above all, I fear a proposal that we should abandon the right to have an Air Force, in Mr. Baldwin's words, at least "equal to that of any Power within striking distance of these shores". I fear the kind of argument which will say, if Germany consents to be only a third as strong as Britain on the seas, is it not reasonable that

416

Britain should consent to be only a half, or a third, or some fraction, of the strength of Germany in the air? To agree to that would be to betray the life and independence of the British nation. All these matters must weigh heavily with us while we are awaiting the results of the Prime Minister's impending negotiations with Herr Hitler. And the government would do well to speak with more plainness upon these issues and give reassurance to the country, in so far as they are in a position to do so.     [17 November, 1938]

*     *     *

There is, alas, insufficient justification for the ripples of optimism which have spread across the surface of British and European opinion since Herr Hitler's last speech. From every quarter comes the tale of heavy movements of German munitions and supplies through Prague, Vienna and Munich. The ordinary railway services are restricted while these great convoys pass. What is their destination? What is their purpose? The German Army is maintaining with the Colours a far larger number of troops than even its own immense establishment requires. Many straws of technical information show the way the wind is blowing. There is no doubt that Signor Mussolini will soon focus upon France demands of a serious character, and although the German Nazi Government have by no means spurred him to this, Herr Hitler has declared that he will support him. Indeed, it is clear that the German Dictator could not afford to witness the downfall of his Italian colleague.

The momentous declaration made by Mr. Chamberlain in the House of Commons that an act of aggression against France from any quarter would be equally resisted by Great Britain shows that the two Western democracies are resolved to act as one and stand together. Few can escape the feeling that the next few months will witness another confrontation and trial of strength and will-power between the rival forces in Europe. When Herr Hitler expressed his belief that a long period of peace lay ahead, it was no doubt in the expectation that matters would, after a time of tension, be adjusted to the satisfaction of the two Dictatorial Powers. Whether this will be so or not no man can predict.

It would not, however, be right only to look upon the darker side. The remarkable action of President Roosevelt, undoubtedly sustained by the government and people of the United States, in letting it be widely known that not only American moral support but also practical aid in munitions and supplies will be accorded to the Western democracies should they become the victims of unprovoked aggression, is a potent stabilizing force. It may well be that the preservation of European peace will be secured through his far-sighted and courageous policy. The spirit of resistance to Nazi encroachment has not been extinguished in Eastern and South-eastern Europe. Countries which before Munich were under the impression that they were being asked to confer favours on France and Great Britain, have now realized forcibly that it is their own lives which are endangered.

Here at home in England there has been a reconsolidation of national union. The attitude of the government has stiffened, and some past differences are fading into history. Above all, there is a sense of gathering strength. The power and condition of the Royal Navy relatively to its possible tasks is unprecedented. The long-delayed flow of aircraft and munitions is now arriving. If redoubled exertions are made, a far greater measure of security may be procured for the civil population against air raids. While only astrologers and other merchants of superstition can declare the future, the day may yet come when the peaceful, law-respecting British nation may once again be able to pursue its journey without having to wait and listen on the wireless from week to week to the dictatorial orations of countries they defeated or succoured in the past.

[9 February, 1939]

\*     \*     \*

A month ago I used the phrase "the European crunch" because it seemed certain that some great trial of strength impended between Nazidom and its opponents.

The blow has been struck. Hitler, following exactly the doctrines of *Mein Kampf*, has broken every tie of good faith with the British and French statesmen who tried so hard to believe in him. The Munich Agreement which represented such great advantages for Germany has been brutally violated. Mr. Chamberlain has been ill-used and affronted. The entire apparatus of confidence and goodwill which was being sedulously constructed in Great Britain has been shattered into innumerable fragments. It can never again be mended while the present domination rules in Germany. This melancholy fact must be faced. A veritable revolution in feeling and opinion has occurred in Britain, and reverberates through all the self-governing Dominions. Indeed, a similar process has taken place spontaneously throughout the whole British Empire.

One can understand very readily how Hitler's mind has worked. He regarded Munich as an act of submission on the part of Britain and France under the threat of war. No one knew better than he the inherent weakness of his own position at that time. His generals and financial experts had warned him of the risks he ran. He felt that he knew the limits of the will-power of those against whom he was matched. He was sure that the sincere love of peace which inspired the British and French governments would lead them to give way under pressure. He ascribed their action when they did so only to the basest motives. All their conscientious scruples about self-determination for the Sudeten-Germans were to him only the evidences of their lack of fighting quality. When what he had predicted to his circle was confirmed by the event, his confidence in his instinct and in his star bounded high.

If the Nazi Dictator had the time to study English history he would see that on more than one famous occasion this island had lost great military advantages in Europe by its intense reluctance to be involved in Continental struggles, and has yet in the end led the way to victory. He had only to read the last two years of the reign of King William III and the opening years of Queen Anne to learn that an improvident unwillingness to enter a quarrel may be succeeded by unwearying and triumphant leadership in that same quarrel at a later date and more difficult stage. How could Louis XIV believe that the England which had tamely watched his occupation of all the Belgian fortresses in 1701 would reach a long arm to strangle his armies on the Danube in 1704?

The situation which confronts Hitler is therefore stern; and the question which now lies in suspense is how he and his circle will respond to it. It is certain that no tolerable relations will be possible for Germany with the outer world until Czechoslovakia has been liberated. There can be no question of Trade Pacts or cordiality while that crime still calls for justice and reparation. On the other hand, for a dictator to recede and disgorge is a step fraught with mortal danger. It is for this reason that the whole world position must be regarded as tense and grievous in the last degree.

One thing only is certain: the forces opposed to Nazidom are, in spite of what has happened, still by far the stronger. A period of suffering resulting from the air-slaughter of non-combatants may lie before us; but this, if borne with fortitude, will only seal the comradeship of many nations to save themselves and the future of mankind from a tyrant's grip.                    [24 March, 1939]

# ON FAMOUS MEN

# LORD RANDOLPH CHURCHILL

*The author's biography of his father, Lord Randolph Churchill, was begun in the summer of 1902 and was first published in 1906. The last edition, with a new Introduction by the author, appeared in 1952.*

*The book is now generally accepted as one of the best political biographies in the English language. It deals more particularly with Lord Randolph Churchill's public career than with his private life. It is a biography inspired by the deepest feelings of love and loyalty between father and son.*

*Lord Randolph is revealed in exact detail as a remarkable but incalculable man who left his mark upon our political history. The author describes the long and complicated story of his father's unsuccessful efforts to found the Party of Tory Democracy, and the courageous ways in which he dealt with the activities of all the difficult and opposing political forces— within and without the Conservative Party—without regard to his own political future.*

IN AUGUST of 1873 Lord Randolph went to Cowes upon what proved to him a memorable visit. In honour of the arrival of the Czarewich and the Czarevna the officers of the cruiser *Ariadne*, then lying as guard-ship in the Roads, gave a ball, to which all the pleasure-seekers who frequent the Solent at this season of the year made haste to go in boats and launches from the shore and from the pleasure fleet. Here for the first time he met Miss Jerome, an American girl whose singular beauty and gifted vivacity had excited general attention. He was presented to her by a common friend. Waltzing made him giddy, and he detested dancing of all kinds; so that after a formal quadrille they sat and talked. She was living with her mother and eldest sister at Rosetta Cottage, a small house which they had taken for the summer, with a tiny garden facing the sea. Thither the next night, duly bidden, he repaired to dine. The dinner was good, the company gay and attractive, and with the two young ladies chatting and playing duets at the piano the evening passed very pleasantly. She was nineteen, and he scarcely twenty-four; and, if Montaigne is to be believed, this period of extreme youth is Love's golden moment. That very night Miss Jerome told her laughing and incredulous sister of a presentiment that their new friend was the man she would marry; and Lord Randolph confided to Colonel Edgecumbe, who was of the party, that he admired the two sisters and meant, if he could, to make "the dark one" his wife.

Next day they met again "by accident"—so runs the account I have received—and went for a walk. That evening he was once more a guest at Rosetta Cottage. That night—the third of their acquaintance—was a beautiful night, warm and still, with the lights of the yachts shining on the water and the sky bright with stars. After dinner they found themselves alone in the garden, and—brief courtship notwithstanding—he proposed and was accepted.

So far as the principals were concerned, everything was thus easily and swiftly settled, and the matter having become so earnest all further meetings were suspended until the Duke of Marlborough and Mr. Jerome, who was in America, had been consulted. Lord Randolph returned to Blenheim shaken by alternating emotions of joy and despondency. He had never been in love before and the force and volume of the tide swept him altogether off his feet. At one moment he could scarcely believe that one so unworthy as he could have been preferred; the next he trembled lest all his hopes should be shattered by circumstances unforeseen. Nor indeed was his anxiety without reason; for many and serious obstacles had yet to be encountered and smoothed away.

The Duke was very seriously disturbed at the news of his son's intention and declined to commit himself to any expression of approval until he had made searching inquiry into the standing and circumstances of the Jerome family. He deplored the precipitancy with which the decision had been taken. "It is not likely," he wrote upon 31 August, "that at present you can look at anything except from your own point of view; but persons from the outside cannot but be struck with the unwisdom of your proceedings, and the uncontrolled state of your feelings, which completely paralyses your judgment." His rebuke was supported by his wife, who urged affectionate counsels of caution, patience and self-restraint, and was pointed by a set of witty and satirical verses from his brother, Lord Blandford, setting forth the unhappy fate of those who marry in haste and repent at leisure.

It will easily be understood how this attitude—most Americans being proud as the devil—raised corresponding objections on the other side. Mr. Jerome was himself in many ways a remarkable personality. He had made and lost and made again considerable fortunes in the enterprise and struggle of American life. He had founded the first two great American racecourses, Jerome Park and Coney Island Jockey Club, and divides with Mr. August Belmont the claim to be the father of the American Turf. He owned and edited the *New York Times*. A vehement Federalist in the Civil War, he was said to have subscribed nearly half his fortune to the Federal war funds. When in 1862 the war party in New York was discredited by the disasters of the campaign, and riotous mobs attacked the *Times* office, Mr. Jerome—having purchased a battery of cannon and armed his staff with rifles—beat them off, not without bloodshed. Altogether he was a man of force and versatility. He had at first, indeed, written a conditional assent to his daughter's engagement, but he withdrew it with promptness as soon as he heard a murmur of opposition. Mrs. Jerome and her daughters retreated to France; and all interviews, and even communications, were forbidden by all the parents. Randolph Churchill, however, knew his own mind in many things, and most especially in this. Such was his vehemence that the Duke was soon persuaded, for the sake of his son's peace of mind and of his own authority, to acquiesce —at any rate, provisionally—in a formal engagement. But he insisted upon delay. Nothing, he declared, but time could prove an affection so rapidly excited; and with this decision, supported and emphasized by the Jeromes, the lovers had perforce to be content.

The parents on both sides only wished to be assured that the attachment of their children was no passing caprice, but a sincere and profound affection; and as the weeks grew into months this conviction was irresistibly borne in upon them. In October the Duke was willing to admit that the period of probation might be considerably curtailed. But he still had strong reasons for not wishing the marriage to take place immediately. The dissolution was certainly in the air. By-election after by-election had gone against Mr. Gladstone's Government. Greenwich, Stroud, Dover, Hull, Exeter, East Staffordshire and Renfrewshire had renounced their allegiance; Bath had been barely retained, and the Solicitor-General, whose victory at Taunton had been a much-paraded compensation, was threatened with a petition for bribery. It was most important that Woodstock should be held for the Conservatives. No one could possibly have so good a chance as the young cadet born and bred on the soil, who knew half the farmers and local magnates personally, whose excursions with the harriers had made him familiar with all parts of the constituency and whose gay and stormy attractiveness had won him a host of sworn allies.

He had often in words and in letters expressed a disinclination for public life. It is curious to notice how even in the days of buoyant unconquered youth, moods of depression cast their shadows across his path. Although possessed of unusual nervous energy, his whole life was a struggle against ill health. Excitement fretted him cruelly. He smoked cigarettes "till his tongue was sore" to soothe himself. Capable upon emergency of prolonged and vehement exertion, of manifold activities and pugnacities, of leaps and heaves beyond the common strength of men, he suffered by reaction fits of utter exhaustion and despondency. Most people grow tired before they are over-tired. But Lord Randolph Churchill was of the temper that gallops till it falls. An instinct warned him of the perils which threatened him in a life of effort. He shrank from it in apprehension. Peace and quiet, sport and friends, agricultural interests—above all a home—offered a woodland path far more alluring than the dusty road to London. The Duke felt, and with reason, that unless Lord Randolph were member for Woodstock before his marriage, not only would the borough be seduced to Radicalism, but that the son in whom all the hopes and ambitions of his later life were centred might never enter Parliament at all.

Lord Randolph was very grateful for the friendly attitude his family had now assumed and was quite prepared to repay concession by patience in one direction and by energy in another.

The Woodstock election being out of the way, the road was cleared for more important matters. The Duke, his political anxieties laid to rest, journeyed to Paris, saw the young lady for himself, and, returning completely converted, withdrew all remaining stipulations for delay. But further difficulties presented themselves. The question of settlements proved delicate and thorny. Mr. Jerome had strong and, it would seem, not unreasonable views, suggested by American usage, about married women's property and made some propositions which Lord Randolph considered derogatory to him. Although he was to benefit considerably under the arrangement proposed, he refused utterly to agree to any settlement which contained even technical provisions to which he objected; and after an embarrassing discussion went off to prepare determined plans to earn a living "in England or out of it", as fortune should dictate, for himself and his future wife—"a course in which," so he wrote to his father, "I am bound to say she thoroughly agrees with me."

Face to face with this ultimatum—the first of any importance and not the least successful in Lord Randolph's forceful career—Mr. Jerome, who after all only wished to make a proper and prudent arrangement, capitulated after twenty-four hours' consideration. A satisfactory treaty was ratified, and it only remained to fulfil the conditions. The negotiations had already extended over seven months and the ceremony was appointed without further delay. The Duke, though unable to be present himself, sent his blessing in a most cordial letter. "Although, my dear Randolph, you have acted in this business with less than usual deliberation, you have adhered to your choice with unwavering constancy and I cannot doubt the truth and force of your affection." On 15 April, 1874, the marriage was celebrated at the British Embassy in Paris, and after a tour—not too prolonged—upon the Continent, Lord Randolph Churchill returned in triumph with his bride to receive the dutiful laudations of the borough of Woodstock and enjoy the leafy glories of Blenheim in the spring.

In the spring of 1875 Lord and Lady Randolph installed themselves in a larger house in Charles Street, where they continued their gay life on a somewhat more generous scale than their income warranted. Fortified by an excellent French cook, they entertained with discrimination. The Prince of Wales, who had from the beginning shown them much kindness, dined sometimes with them. Lord Randolph's college friend, Lord Rosebery, was a frequent visitor. One night Mr. Disraeli was among their guests, and an anecdote of his visit may be preserved. "I think," said Lord Randolph, discussing with his wife their party after it had broken up, "that Dizzy enjoyed himself. But how flowery and exaggerated is his language! When I asked him if he would have any more wine, he replied: 'My dear Randolph, I have sipped your excellent champagne; I have drunk your good claret; I have tasted your delicious port—I will have no more'!" "Well," said Lady Randolph, laughing, "he sat next to me, and I particularly remarked that he drank nothing but a little weak brandy-and-water." In August, 1875, Lord Randolph went with his wife to America to spend ten bustling days at the Philadelphia Exhibition; and in the United States, as in Paris, he made the acquaintance of many politicians and persons of public note.

Thus for two years his days were filled with social amusements and domestic happiness.

He was embarrassed chiefly by the necessity, which time imposed, of having to select from a superfluity of pleasures. The House of Commons was but one among various diversions. His occasional attendances contributed an element of seriousness to his life, good in itself, attractive by contrast, that provided, moreover, a justification (very soothing to the conscience) for not engaging in more laborious work. But for the recurring ailments to which his delicate constitution was subject and the want of money which so often teases a young married couple, his horizon had been without a cloud, his career without a care. But in the year 1876 an event happened which altered, darkened, and strengthened his whole life and character. Engaging in his brother's quarrels with fierce and reckless partisanship, Lord Randolph incurred the deep displeasure of a great personage. The fashionable world no longer smiled. Powerful enemies were anxious to humiliate him. His own sensitiveness and pride magnified every coldness into an affront. London became odious to him. The breach was not repaired for more than eight years, and in the interval a nature originally genial and gay contracted a stern and bitter quality, a harsh contempt for what is called "Society", and an abiding antagonism to rank and authority. If this misfortune produced in Lord Randolph characteristics which afterwards hindered or injured his public work, it was also his spur. Without it he might have wasted a dozen years in the frivolous and expensive pursuits of the silly world of fashion; without it he would probably never have developed popular sympathies or the courage to champion democratic causes.

The position of the Conservative Party [in 1880] was weak and miserable in the extreme. The sympathies and the intellect of the nation were estranged. Lord Beaconsfield, the only man who could touch the imagination of the people, was withdrawn from the popular assembly. Many of the Tory strongholds—family boroughs and the like—were threatened by approaching Redistribution. The Front Opposition Bench, cumbered with the ancient and dreary wreckage of the late Administration, was utterly unequal to the government in eloquence or authority. The attendance of Conservative members, as in all dispirited Oppositions, was slack and fitful.

Outmatched in debate, outnumbered in division, the party was pervaded by a profound feeling of gloom. They had nothing to give to their followers, nothing to promise to the people: no Garters for Dukes, no peerages for wealth, no baronetcies or knighthoods or trinkets for stalwarts. Although the new spirit created by Disraeli— Imperium abroad, Libertas at home—still lived in the Tory Party, it had been profoundly discouraged by the results of the election; and many of those who swayed Conservative counsels could think of no plan of action except an obstinate but apathetic resistance to change. Jeered at as "the stupid party", haunted by profound distrust of an ever-growing democracy, conscious that the march of ideas was leaving them behind, these desponding counsellors could discern in the future no sign of returning fortune and seemed to find the sole function of the Conservative minority in delaying and restricting the movements of the age by means of electoral inequalities, by Parliamentary procedure, and through the prejudices of interest and of class.

What political prophet or philosopher, surveying the triumphant Liberal array, would have predicted that this Parliament, from

429

which so much was hoped, would be indeed the most disastrous and even fatal period in their party history? Or who could have foreseen that these dejected Conservatives in scarcely five years, with the growing assent of an immense electorate, would advance to the enjoyment of twenty years of power? It needed a penetrating eye to discover the method, and a bold heart first to stem and finally to turn the tide. Who would have thought of breaking up the solid phalanx of Liberalism by driving in a wedge between the Radicals and the Whigs; or dreamt of using the Irish to overthrow the great apostle of reconciliation between peoples; and who without the audacity of genius would have dared to force the Conservative Party to base the foundations of their authority with confidence upon the very masses they dreaded and to teach those masses to venerate and guard the institutions they had formerly despised?

\* \* \*

Lord Beaconsfield's death early in the year 1881 had been a heavy blow to the Fourth Party. Great men at the height of their power often, to their cost, refuse to recognize the ability of newcomers. Peel had scorned Disraeli. Gladstone never understood Mr. Chamberlain's capacity till he faced him as a foe. Smaller persons, called from time to time to the conduct of public affairs, exhibit the same failing in an aggravated degree with greater regularity and more disastrous results to themselves. The jealousy and dislike with which the leaders of the Conservative Party in the House of Commons regarded the activities of Lord Randolph and his friends, had been apparent even before the session of 1880 had come to an end. From all such feelings Lord Beaconsfield was free. His character and the hard experiences of his earlier years made him seek eagerly for the first signs of oncoming power. He was an old man lifted high above his contemporaries and he liked to look past them to the new generation and to feel that he could gain the sympathy and confidence of younger men. If he liked youth, he liked Tory Democracy even more. He had, moreover, good reason to know how a Parliamentary Opposition should be conducted. He saw with perfect clearness the incapacity above the gangway and the enterprise and pluck below it. Had his life been prolonged for a few more years the

Fourth Party might have marched, as his Young Guard, by a smoother road, and this story might have reached a less melancholy conclusion. He stood above personal rivalries. He was removed from the petty vexations of the House of Commons. Surely he would not have allowed these clever ardent men to drift into antagonism against the mass of the Conservative Party and into fierce feud with its leaders. He alone could have kept their loyalty, as he alone commanded their respect; and never would he have countenanced the solemn excommunication by dullness and prejudice of all that preserved the sparkling life of Toryism in times of depression and defeat. But Lord Beaconsfield was gone; and those whom he had left behind had other views of how his inheritance—such as it was—should be divided.

The conditions of British politics during the Parliament of 1880, whether in the House of Commons or abroad in the country, were peculiar—perhaps unprecedented. Mr. Gladstone's Administration, outwardly so powerful alike in the capacity of its members and the number and fidelity of its supporters, was divided by zigzag, oblique, inconsistent yet fundamental dissensions. Nor were these disturbances the temporary or accidental effect of particular men or measures. There were important measures. There were earnest, ambitious men. But something more lay behind the unrest and uncertainties of the day. Not merely the decay of a government or the natural overripeness of a party produced the agitations of 1885 and 1886. It was the end of an epoch. The long dominion of the middle classes which had begun in 1832 had come to its close and with it the almost equal reign of Liberalism. The great victories had been won. All sorts of lumbering tyrannies had been toppled over. Authority was everywhere broken. Slaves were free. Conscience was free. Trade was free. But hunger and squalor and cold were also free; and the people demanded something more than liberty. The old watchwords still rang true; but they were not enough. And how to fill the void was the riddle that split the Liberal Party. It happened, moreover, that at this very time, already so critical, a Liberal Government had been forced to deal with all kinds of affairs for the efficient conduct of which their formulas furnished no clue. They were compelled to intervene by force of arms in Egypt, to repress popular movements, to banish popular leaders, to hang revolutionaries, to devise ingenious instruments of coercion, to mutilate Parliamentary procedure and to curtail the freedom of debate. And thus, while half the Cabinet were ransacking the past for weapons of Executive authority, others were groping dimly towards a vague Utopia.

All·this confusion was still worse confounded by the imminence of a further extension of the franchise. The "ten-pounder" and the "householder" had been stages of growth. The evolution was now to be completed, or practically completed. The government of a world-wide empire was, for the first time in human experience, to be thrown unreservedly to the millions. And no man could predict the results of that experiment. There seemed to be no reason to assume that any large body of working-class electors would ever vote Tory. Who could possibly have foreseen that, whether from conscious choice between men and parties or from the unsuspected operation of irresistible forces till then latent, the millions would peacefully hand back their powers to political organizations and so to established authority; that enfranchised multitudes would constitute themselves the buttresses of privilege and property; that a free press would by its freedom sap the influence of debate and through its prosperity become the implement of wealth; that members and constituencies would become less independent, not more independent; that Ministers would become more powerful, not less powerful; that the march would be ordered backward along the beaten track, not forward in some new direction; and that, after a period of convulsion and flux, twenty years of Tory Government would set in? Who would have listened to such paradox with patience?

By the end of 1882 Lord Randolph Churchill was already unquestionably the most popular speaker in the Conservative Party. In 1884 and 1885 he equalled, if he did not surpass, Mr. Gladstone himself in the interest and enthusiasm which his personality aroused. Wherever he went he was received by tremendous throngs and with extraordinary demonstrations of goodwill. In times when good Conservatives despaired of the fortunes of their party under a democratic franchise and even, making a virtue of necessity, regarded it as almost immoral to court a working-class vote, and when the chiefs of Toryism looked upon the resisting powers of small shop and lodging-house keepers, of suburban villadom, and of the genial and seductive publican as almost the only remaining bulwarks of the Constitution, Lord Randolph Churchill boldly enlisted the British nation in defence of Church and State. At a time when Liberal orators and statesmen, "careering about the country," as Lord Randolph described them, "calling themselves 'the people of England', " were looking forward to an election which should relegate the Conservative Party to the limbo of obsolete ideas, they were disconcerted by the spectacle, repeatedly presented, of multitudes of working men hanging upon the words of a young aristocrat; and Radicals, bidding higher and higher to catch the popular fancy, heard with disgust the loudest acclamations of the crowd accorded to Lord Randolph Churchill as he denounced "the Moloch of Midlothian" (Mr. Gladstone) or "the pinchbeck Robespierre" (Mr. Chamberlain) for war and tyranny beyond the sea, profusion and misgovernment at home.

Abuse was retorted on his head in vain. "Yahoo Churchill", "Little Randy", "Cheeky Randy", "the music-hall cad", "the Champagne Charley of politics", were designations which measured at once his popularity and the rising fury of his foes. His fierce moustache and "note of interrogation" had lent themselves to caricature. He was drawn as a pigmy, a pug dog, a gnat, a wasp, a ribald and vicious monkey, so habitually, that nearly everyone who had not seen him in the flesh believed that his physical proportions were far below the common standards of humanity; but the contrast between his reputed stature and the majestic outlines of Mr. Gladstone and Sir William Harcourt only enhanced his fighting qualities in the public eye. "Give it 'em hot, Randy," cried the crowds in the streets and at the meetings, till he himself was forced to complain that he was expected to salute his opponents with every species of vituperation. But, to tell the truth, he responded to the public demand with inexhaustible generosity. He spared no one. Neither persons nor principles escaped an all-embracing ridicule. The most venerated leaders of the Liberal Party, famous in the great days of its rise, fared no better at his hands than the crudest and most violent of the New Radicals. One by one Mr. Bright, Mr. Gladstone, Lord Hartington, Lord Granville, Sir Charles Dilke, Mr. Chamberlain,

Mr. Bradlaugh and Mr. Schnadhorst were summoned before that irreverent tribunal and exhibited to popular censure and derision.

★    ★    ★

"The work of inspiring a beaten and depressed party with hope and courage," wrote Mr. Jennings in 1888,[1] "was substantially left to one man." What had become meanwhile of the acknowledged leaders of Toryism? Where were the names which in after years were to fill the newspapers and the government offices? It is curious to reflect that all this time, while Lord Randolph Churchill was straining every nerve in the service of his party, he was the object of almost passionate jealousy and dislike in its high places. The world of rank and fashion had long been hostile to him. The prominent people and party officials who formed and guided opinion at the Carlton Club, on the Front Opposition Bench, and in the central Conservative offices, regarded him with aversion and alarm. They could not understand him. Still less could they explain his growing influence. He was as unwelcome and insoluble a riddle to them as ever Disraeli had been. To them he seemed an intruder, an upstart, a mutineer who flouted venerable leaders and mocked at constituted authority with a mixture of aristocratic insolence and democratic brutality. By what warrant did he pronounce in accents of command on all the controverted questions of the day, when men grey in the service of the State, long installed in the headship of the party, held their peace or dealt in platitude and ambiguity? By what strange madness of the hour had this youth, who derided Radicals for abandoning their principles and preached Liberalism from Tory platforms, gained acceptance throughout the land? The Conservative benches were rich in staid, substantial merchants and worthy squires. They had their blameless young men of good family and exemplary deportment who never gave the party Whips an anxious moment and used their talents only to discover what "older and therefore wiser" people would wish to have them say. Why was no honour shown to them? Did not they address meetings in the provinces? Did they not utter sentiments to which every sensible and patriotic man might listen with unruffled contentment? And no one marked them! Was there not enough in these evil days to bear

[1] Preface to *Lord Randolph Churchill's Speeches*, by L. J. Jennings, p. xxiv.

from Mr. Gladstone and his legions, without this turbulent uprising in their own ranks?

In truth, at this crisis in their fortunes the Conservative Party were rescued in spite of themselves. A very little and they would never have won the new democracy. But for a narrow chance they might have slipped down into the gulf of departed systems. The forces of wealth and rank, of land and Church, must always have exerted vast influence in whatever confederacy they had been locked. Alliances or fusions with Whigs and moderate Liberals must from time to time have secured them spells of office. But the Tory Party might easily have failed to gain any support among the masses. They might have lost their hold upon the new foundation of power; and the cleavage in British politics must have become a social, not a political, division—upon a line horizontal, not oblique.

There are, without doubt, some who will be inclined to think that no element of the heroic enters into these conflicts, and that political triumphs are necessarily tarnished by vulgar methods. The noise and confusion of election crowds; the cant of phrase and formula, the burrowings of rival caucuses, fill with weariness, and even terror, persons of exquisite sensibility. It is easy for those who take no part in the public duties of citizenship under a democratic dispensation to sniff disdainfully at the methods of modern politics and to console themselves for a lack of influence upon the course of events by the indulgence of a fastidious refinement and a meticulous consistency. But it is a poor part to play. Amid the dust and brawling, with rude weapons and often unworthy champions, a real battle for real and precious objects is swaying to and fro. Better far the clamour of popular disputation, with all its most blatant accessories, hammering out from month to month and year to year the laboured progress of the common people in a work-a-day world, than the poetic tragedies and violence of chivalric ages. The splintering of lances and clashing of swords are not the only tests by which the natural captains and princes among men can be known. The spirit and emotions of war do not depend upon the weapons or conditions of the conflict. A bold heart, a true eye—clear, plain, decided leading—count none the less, although no blood is spilled. "To rally the people round the Throne," cried Lord Randolph Churchill, "to unite the Throne with the people, a loyal Throne and a patriotic people—that is our policy and that is our faith." Much of the work that he did was turned to purposes very different from his own. His political doctrines were not free from error and contradiction. But he accomplished no mean or temporary achievement in so far as he restored the healthy balance of parties, and caused the ancient institutions of the British realm once again to be esteemed among the masses of the British people.

But whether, in these vexed and protracted debates, Lord Randolph Churchill attacked the Prime Minister or harassed his own leaders; whether he was supported by loud applause of Conservative members or heard by them in chilly silence; whether he seemed to be the accepted spokesman of the Opposition or a solitary politician—his hand against every man and every man's hand against him—his almost unerring eye for a Parliamentary situation, his mastery over the House and his formidable power for good or evil upon the fortunes of his party became continually more evident. Alone, or almost alone, he waged his double warfare against Government and Opposition. Assailed on all sides—from the Ministerial box, from the Front Opposition Bench, from those who sat before him and behind him and even beside him; confronted with his own contradictory statements; now by one side, now by the other; rebuked by the Prime Minister, repeatedly repudiated by his colleagues and leaders, he nevertheless preserved throughout an air of haughty composure and met or repelled all attacks with resourceful and undaunted pluck.

*     *     *

The reconciliation of Lord Randolph Churchill with Lord Salisbury which followed on the Sheffield Conference was comprehensive and loyally observed. The tactics of the Opposition became more effective in the House of Commons and their councils more harmonious. But strife in the constituencies was to succeed this session of storm and effort. To mark and proclaim the newly compacted alliance within the Conservative Party, Sir Stafford Northcote came during the autumn recess to speak in Lord Randolph's support at Birmingham. Of all the demonstrations organized against the House of Lords for its rejection of the Franchise Bill scarcely any had exceeded that held at Soho Pool, near Birmingham, on Bank Holiday. Aston Park, in the same neighbourhood, had been secured on 13 October by the Conservatives for a counter-demonstration, which was to open a week of campaigning throughout the district. Besides Sir Stafford and Lord Randolph Churchill, Colonel Burnaby and many other members of Parliament and candidates were to address the concourse at five simultaneous political meetings, and the well-known attractions of the Park and of the orators were to be strengthened by bands of music and a firework display. According to the Conservatives, the Aston demonstration was to represent the Midlands in general and Birmingham in particular, and special trains were run from all the surrounding constituencies with detachments of enthusiastic Tories and holiday-makers.

These well-conceived arrangements caused much offence to the Radicals of Birmingham. They declared that an attempt was to be made to misrepresent the feeling of their city by importing outsiders and excursionists to swell the numbers of the demonstrators; and as the meetings had been called from the citizens of Birmingham and were in local parlance "town meetings", rather than ordinary "party meetings", they resolved to attend them, too. Admission to Aston Park was by ticket. It was stated that 120,000 tickets would be issued to those who applied for them. Everyone applied. Trade Union secretaries, great Liberal manufacturers like the Tangyes, officials of the Radical organizations, applied for, in some cases, as many as eight hundred at a time. The promoters of the demonstration became alarmed; and as it was now clear—and even avowed—that the Radicals would attend in force and spoil the effect, the issue of tickets was stopped and the applications were refused. Elaborate, formidable, and, as it proved, thoroughly effective measures were thereupon adopted to enable the voice of Birmingham to be heard. It became known that large numbers of tickets were being forged. Of course, no one in authority in the Liberal Party lent any countenance to such proceedings. Mr. Schnadhorst went away for the day upon important business. A few working men—a mere handful of trampled toilers—spontaneously, with no help from their party, inspired by no other emotion than zeal for freedom and Reform, organized a counter-demonstration. The place of meeting was selected, by an unlucky coincidence, just outside the walls of Aston Park; and there also it happened that, on the appointed day, a cart containing ladders and other useful appliances drew up. The bills announcing this innocent counter-demonstration summoned the "Men of Birmingham and the Midlands" to assemble for deliberation in Witton Road (just outside the Park), after which "let all who can get admittance attend the Tory meetings, wear the Gladstone badge, and show you are not ashamed of your colours". In order that nothing should interfere with the discharge of these civic duties, Tangye's and other large works in the city closed for the afternoon.

The day arrived. The weather was suitable to outdoor political debate. The holders of tickets—forged or genuine—assembled by road and rail from all parts of the Midlands. The Aston grounds were soon crowded with demonstrators. Outside, the counter-demonstration, made up of three large processions, estimated at fifteen thousand strong, converged upon a waste plot of land hard by the Park wall. Individuals began to climb over but were stopped by broken glass. Earnest hands seized the ladders which stood there by chance and the broken glass was demolished. A waggon which had served as the platform was dragged towards the wall; and by this, by the ladders, and also, it appears, by a convenient tree, many persons swarmed over. Inside they found a single police-man, who could do nothing to gainsay them, and a tool-house containing a number of planks. By using the planks as battering-rams a breach was made in the wall and thousands of excited people poured through it into the Park to join by force their friends who had entered by fraud.

The open-air meetings were broken up by riot. Stones, potatoes and even chairs were flung at the members of Parliament who attempted to address the crowd. The platform of the great hall was stormed. Sir Stafford Northcote, who showed much pluck through-out these turbulent experiences which his physical condition ill fitted him to endure, and Lord Randolph Churchill were over-whelmed by furious clamour and finally driven from the hall in the midst of a battle royal of sticks and chair-legs. Lord Randolph, not following promptly enough, was picked up and carried away bodily by a burly admirer from Wolverhampton. The crowd at

438

first followed at a walk and afterwards at a run and so menacing and dangerous was their temper that Sir Stafford Northcote was dragged along by his guards at full speed and, even so, narrowly avoided capture. Other members of Parliament had rougher experiences and Mr. Darling [later Sir Charles Darling] was lucky to make an escape from a window before the door of the room in which he had taken refuge was battered down. The platform of the Skating Rink collapsed while a free-fight was raging upon it. The fireworks perished ignominiously in broad daylight; the set-piece of Sir Stafford Northcote being received with storms of groans and fired off, by a refinement of cruelty, *upside down*. Such were the Aston riots. No persons were actually killed in them, but not a few were seriously injured, and hundreds carried away scars and bruises from the fray.

★    ★    ★

The first trials of a Prime Minister are often the most severe. The most formidable obstacles lie at the beginning. Once these have been surmounted, the path is comparatively smooth. Nearly all the rest of Lord Salisbury's life was spent at the head of the government. In a period of seventeen years he filled for more than twelve the greatest office in the State. Four separate Administrations were formed under his hand. Responsibilities not less grave than those of 1885, far more important legislation, wide acquisitions of territory, vast decisions of peace and war attended their course. But, as with Mr. Pitt, the first two years of his service perhaps exceeded in personal stress all the years that were to follow. And it is probable that no part of those two years was more clouded with anxious perplexity than the autumn of 1885. His own position was not assured. Public confidence in his character and judgment had yet to be won; his authority within his party had yet to be consolidated. That party itself had struggled back to power, weak in numbers, nervously excited by its efforts, upon curious and compromising terms. It was torn by the very inspiration that revived its strength. It awaited in acute apprehension an imminent and momentous election, the result of which no man could foretell. Very different were those after-years, when the old statesman, towering above his colleagues in the Cabinet and commanding the implicit obedience of his followers, had gathered patiently together round the standards of Conservatism almost all the strongest forces in the country.

Yet while resources were still slender the difficulties and dangers of the situation were tremendous. The dispute with Russia about the Afghan boundary was in its most critical stage. For at least two months the Cabinet faced the chance of war with a formidable military empire. The triumphant Mahdi was ravaging the Sudan, and Egypt, withdrawn behind her narrowest frontiers, was threatened without and utterly disorganized within. The British finances were oppressed by a deficit. Ireland smouldered. All the elements of Irish national life were banded together under the supreme authority of Parnell and that efficient Protestant rebel was methodically preparing his campaign for an Irish Parliament. In the English provinces Mr. Chamberlain, released from such partial restraint as official obligations had hitherto imposed, unfolded the "Unauthorized Programme" to an exulting Radical democracy. And behind all "two million intelligent citizens", newly enfranchised, impatiently awaited the opportunity of casting their votes. Such were the perils and embarrassments amid which the "Ministry of Caretakers" came into being. Nor was it strange that eminent politicians were willing to prophesy that after a brief and inglorious career they would be "swept off the face of the earth".

Among the millions who at the General Election of 1885 exercised, many of them for the first time, the proud privilege of the franchise, no human being could have explained with any approach to accuracy what a vote for either of the great parties in the State actually involved, whether in principle or action. Leaders on both sides, swept to and fro by turbulent cross-currents, took refuge in ambiguous obscurity, even where the most fiercely contested questions were concerned. Official Liberalism had no decided opinion about Disestablishment, nor Toryism about Fair Trade. Every politician had his own ideas about a social programme; and Ireland was a riddle at which neither party cared to guess in the absence of the electoral returns. What a mockery of statesmen's leadership and foresight the future was to unveil! The Parnellite manifesto and the Irish vote weakened, perhaps fatally, the Liberals who a few months later were to stake their fortunes upon Home Rule. Sir William Harcourt, who derided the Conservative Party for "stewing in Parnellite juice", was himself to stew in that juice for the rest of his life. Lord Salisbury, whose philosophic defence of boycotting had excited general consternation, stood on the threshold of a Coercion Bill and "twenty years of resolute government". Mr. Gladstone, appealing for a majority independent of Irish members, became ever more dependent upon them. Mr. Chamberlain was soon to fight for political existence side by side with that same Lord Hartington whom he now described as Rip Van Winkle, to sit for years in the same Cabinet as the Mr. Goschen he now ran up and down the land to denounce, and to be driven from the Liberal Party, locked in fast alliance with the very Whigs he was now striving in the name of Radicalism to expel. Whether Lord Randolph Churchill surpassed these standards of consistency the reader will be able to judge.

These were perhaps the busiest days of his life, and the amount of work of the most exhausting character which he contrived to discharge astonished all who knew him. Besides the anxious and incessant attention which the India Office required, and the ordinary labours of a Cabinet Minister, he had to watch the Irish situation and to prosecute his Birmingham candidature from week to week. In addition to all this he darted to and fro about the country—to Dorsetshire, Sheffield, Worcester, Lynn, Manchester—commending the Conservative cause to the electors in speeches in which serious argument was garnished with a vigour of metaphor and a raciness of language that delighted the Tory Democracy and attracted universal attention. Lord Salisbury, who knew what the management of the India Office at this time involved, seems to have been genuinely concerned lest his lieutenant should break himself down by attempting a platform campaign as well as his departmental work.

★　　★　　★

At the Treasury the appointment of [Lord Randolph Churchill as] the new Chancellor of the Exchequer had been received with no little apprehension. Every great department has an atmosphere and identity of its own. No politician, however popular in the country or influential in Parliament, can afford to be indifferent to the opinion formed of him by the civil servants through whom and by whom he works. Concealed from the public eye among the deeper recesses of Whitehall, seeking no fame, clad with the special knowledge of lifelong study, armed with the secrets of a dozen Cabinets, the slaves of the Lamp or of the Ring render faithful and obedient service to whomsoever holds the talisman. Whatever task be set, wise or foolish, virtuous or evil, as they are commanded, so they do. Yet their silent judgments of their masters and their projects do not pass unheeded. Although the spell still works, it loses half its potency if these spirits are offended or alarmed; and padded walls of innumerable objections, backed by the masonry of unanswerable argument, restrain the irreverent or unworthy from the fullest exercise of the powers they may have won by force or favour.

Over all public departments the department of finance is supreme. Erected upon the vital springs of national prosperity, wielding the mysterious power of the purse, the final arbiter in the disputes of every other office, a good fairy or a perverse devil, as "My Lords" may choose, to every imaginative Secretary of State, the Treasury occupies in the polity of the United Kingdom a central and superior position. No school of thought is so strong or so enduring as that founded on the great traditions of Gladstonian and Peelite finance. Reckless Ministers are protected against themselves, violent Ministers are tamed, timid Ministers are supported and nursed. Few, if any, are insensible to the influences by which they are surrounded. Streams of detailed knowledge, logic and experience wash away fiscal and financial heresies; and a baptism of economic truth inspires the convert not merely with the principles of a saint but—too often —with the courage of a martyr.

To many who had spent their lives at the Treasury, Lord Randolph's arrival was a shock. They had instinctively resented the assaults he had delivered against Mr. Gladstone, "the best friend the Civil Service ever had". They remembered that, not long before, Lord Randolph had made himself the mouthpiece of a harsh attack upon one of their number. He was known to have expressed privately a candid opinion that they were "a knot of damned Gladstonians". Lastly, they had read his Fair Trade speeches; and, notwithstanding the reputation he had made at the India Office as a departmental chief, he still appeared in the eyes of Treasury officials as a Minister who would ride roughshod over their habits and violate all their most cherished financial canons.

This mood was short-lived. The disquieted officials found a Minister assiduous and thorough in work and scrupulously patient and quiet in discussion. He possessed the very rare gift of keeping his mind exclusively devoted to the subject in hand, and impressed on all those with whom he worked the idea that the business on which they were employed was the only one of interest to him. No time spent with the Chancellor of the Exchequer was ever wasted. No interruption of any sort was suffered. No one ever left his room after an interview without having at any rate gained a clear knowledge of his views and intentions. Around all played an old-fashioned ceremony of manner, oddly mingled with a sparkle of pure fun, which charmed everybody. In a month the conquest was complete. Every official worked with enthusiasm in his service and all their mines of information were laid open to his hand. It has often been said that Lord Randolph won his popularity among permanent officials by his subservience to their views. This is by no means true. If he cast away altogether as vicious and unpractical the Fair Trade opinions which he had urged, and which commanded so much support among the Tory democracy, it will also be seen that he was able to enlist the interest and positive support of his subordinates in schemes far outside the orthodoxy of the official mind. His stay at the Treasury was short; but his memory was long respected. He left behind him golden opinions and dearly treasured reminiscences. He took away with him friendships which lasted him his life.

Many tales of Lord Randolph in these days have been preserved. We have a glimpse of his first meeting with a rather dismayed subordinate in the historical Board Room at the Treasury—the stiff and formal cut of his frock-coat, the long amber cigarette-holder, so soon produced, the eternal cigarette, and "an old-world courtesy of manner" which surprised and disarmed a preconceived dislike. We see him going down to the City with Sir Edward Hamilton to lunch formally with the Governor and Directors of the Bank of England and hovering for half an hour outside in a panic of nervousness which robbed him for the time of his self-confidence. We see him once, and once only, when the Court of Exchequer, presided over by its Chancellor, settles the list from which Sheriffs are selected, in his robes of office—those imposing and expensive robes which seem to assert the opulence which should result from thrift, rather than thrift itself. His cynicism was disarming. We are told how, when the dreadful subject of bimetallism cropped up, he turned to Sir Arthur Godley and said: "I forget. Was I a bimetallist when I was at the India Office?" When he received an influential deputation of sugar-refiners and sugar-planters in protest against the foreign Sugar Bounties, he created general consternation by inquiring, with immense gravity, "Are the consumers represented upon this deputation?" We are even told how he complained to a clerk who put some figures before him that they were not clear and he could not understand them. The clerk said that he had done his best, and, pointing them out, explained that he had reduced them to decimals. "Oh," said Lord Randolph, "I never could make out what those damned dots meant." But this was surely only to tease.

★    ★    ★

On the morning of 23 December, 1886, all who took an interest in politics—and in those days these were a very great number—were startled to read in *The Times* newspaper that Lord Randolph Churchill had resigned the offices of Chancellor of the Exchequer and Leader of the House of Commons and had retired altogether from the government. As the news was telegraphed abroad, it became everywhere the chief subject of rumour and discussion, and Cabinet Ministers—dispersed on their holidays—hurried back to London to find out the truth of the matter and to prepare for the changes that must follow. To the political world the event came as a complete surprise. No important issue had arisen in foreign or domestic affairs; no great question likely to lead to such a breach was before the country; there had been hardly a whisper of Cabinet dissension.

After writing his letter of resignation to Lord Salisbury on 22 December, 1886, Lord Randolph Churchill went down to *The Times* office, imparted his priceless information to Mr. Buckle, authorized him to make it public, and so to bed. Lord Salisbury received this second letter at half-past one in the morning of the

LORD RANDOLPH CHURCHILL

23rd, and realized that the breach was definite. He posted the news at once to the Queen; but he was already too late. With the first light of the morning the announcement appeared in *The Times*.

This action of Lord Randolph Churchill in resigning the office he held in such a manner and on such an occasion has two aspects— a smaller and a larger. Both are partly true: neither by itself is comprehensive. The smaller aspect is that of a proud, sincere, over-strained man conceiving himself bound to fight certain issues, at whatever cost to himself, believing at each movement that victory would be won, and drawn by every movement further into a position from which he could not or would not retreat. The larger aspect deserves somewhat longer consideration. The differences between the Chancellor of the Exchequer and his colleagues were matters of detail and might easily have been compacted. The difference between the Leader of the House of Commons and the Prime Minister was fundamental. It was a difference of belief, of character, of aspiration—and by nothing could it ever have been adjusted. There were many considerations and influences which worked powerfully for their agreement. In the Union they found a common cause; in Mr. Gladstone they faced a common antagonist. Lord Randolph's fiercest invective did not jar upon the "master of flouts and jeers". Neither could be insensible to the personal fascination of the other. Both rejoiced in a wide and illuminating survey of public affairs; both dwelt much upon the future; both preserved a cynical disdain of small men seeking paltry ends. But the gulf which separated the fiery leader of Tory Democracy—with his bold plans of reform and dreams of change, with his record of storm and triumph and slender expectations of a long life—from the old-fashioned Conservative statesman, the head of a High Church and High Tory family, versed in diplomacy, representative of authority, wary, austere, content to govern—was a gulf no mutual needs, no common interests, no personal likings could permanently bridge. They stood for ideas mutually incompatible. Sooner or later the breach must have come; and no doubt the strong realization of this underlay the action of the one and the acquiescence of the other.

It seems, however, very surprising that Lord Randolph Churchill

445

should at this period have overlooked the anger and jealousy that his sudden rise to power had excited. In little more than a year two Administrations had been formed from the Conservative Party. In the making of both of these his influence had been almost supreme; and it had been an influence which, from the point of view of ordinary Parliamentary promotion, had been disturbing and even revolutionary. Men who in quieter times would have received office had been disappointed. Others who had enjoyed what they considered almost prescriptive right had been forced out. The former leader of the Conservative Party had been driven from the House of Commons. Mr. Matthews had been raised from private life to one of the highest posts in the Cabinet. This one, hitherto unknown, had been jumped up: that one, so long respected, had been thrust down. Malice proved a stronger motive power than gratitude; and, although unquestioned success had crowned the struggle, bitterness and resentment gathered behind the conqueror.

Nor, indeed, do we think he should have counted much upon the goodwill of the plain member. He was often—and seemed to be, more often still—in things political a hard man, reaping where he had not sown, severe to exact service and obedience, hasty in judgment, fierce in combat; and many a black look or impatient word had been remembered against him by those of whose existence he was perhaps scarcely conscious. Friends he had in plenty—some of them true ones; but, for all the personal charm he could exert at will, his manner had added to his enemies. Venerable Ministers saw a formidable intruder who had entered the Cabinet by adventurous and unusual paths. Austere Conservatives shrank from this alarming representative of the New Democracy. Worthy men thoughtlessly slighted, tiresome people ruthlessly snubbed, office-seekers whose pretensions had been ignored, Parliamentary martinets concerned for party discipline, all were held in check only so long as he was powerful. His position had been won by the sword, and he must be armed to keep it.

Yet at this moment, when he proposed to try conclusions with all the strongest forces in the Conservative Party, he seems to have taken no single precaution to safeguard himself. He gave the Cabinet long and ample notice of his intention. He reiterated his determination at intervals through the autumn. He knew that Smith and

Hamilton took counsel together: he knew that they had prevailed upon Lord Salisbury; and that if in the end they should resist stubbornly, their resistance would not be ill-considered or unprepared. Upon the other hand, he made no effort to rally his own friends. A third at least of the government were men of his own choice. Beach would have made great exertions on his behalf. But no one was consulted. He was in constant and intimate intercourse with Chamberlain. Their views at this time were almost identical; their relations most cordial. Yet he gave him no knowledge of the situation, nor dreamed of inviting his support: so strictly—quixotically even—did he interpret the idea of Cabinet loyalty.

Few men then alive were more skilled in political tactics, or knew better how to deal with a crisis. If he had made up his mind to break with the government, there were many ways in which the severance might have been made effective. First, as to time. I have said a more patient man would have waited; a more unscrupulous man would most certainly have waited. The power of a Leader of the House of Commons whose chief is in the House of Lords, always immense, is far greater when Parliament is sitting. He is the general in the field at the head of the army. The other waits at home, trying to make what he can of the dispatches. Moreover, the House of Commons, for all its staid and sober qualities, is sometimes, and was particularly in times like these, an organism of impulse. A sudden announcement; a brilliant and persuasive speech; powerful support coming from an unexpected quarter; panic, emotion, or excitement, and fine majorities may crumble into dust.

He could with perfect ease and candour have postponed the issue; and had he done so the danger to the government must have been enormously increased. He resigned, however, at Christmastime, when politicians were scattered far and wide on their holidays, when the temperature was low, and when three clear weeks intervened before the reconstructed government would have to meet Parliament, and before he would have an opportunity of explanation. It was scarcely possible to have chosen a season better suited to the interests of his colleagues or more unpromising to his own.

★     ★     ★

There is scarcely any more abundant source of error in history than the natural desire of writers—regardless of the overlapping and interplay of memories, principles, prejudices and hopes, and the reaction of physical conditions—to discover or provide simple explanations for the actions of their characters. It would be a barren task to set forth the motives of this affair in a schedule. Yet the main causes emerge—shadowy perhaps, but unmistakable. Lord Randolph Churchill did not think of himself as a man, but rather as the responsible trustee and agent of the Tory Democracy; and this temper, overpowering even the most attractive personal associations, impelled him by deliberate steps—yet not without deep despondency—towards a fateful issue: and all the while a feeling, partly of sombre pride, partly of loyalty, forbade him to take the necessary and obvious steps to protect himself. Ambushes, intrigues, cabals, might suit the freelance of Fourth Party days; but an official leader of a great party could only state the terms on which his assistance could be obtained, and, if it were not worth while to grant them, could only go.

It may no doubt be observed that this was the highest imprudence; that it agreed very little with much that he had done before, and not at all with the impression formed in the public mind. If he had put away for a season his pledges and his pride, both might have been recovered with interest later on. As it was, he delivered himself, unarmed, unattended, fettered even, to his enemies; and therefrom ensued not only his own political ruin, but grave injury to the causes he sustained. Yet it is noteworthy that he never repented of the course he had taken. Bitterly as he regretted the consequences, and felt the abuse and misrepresentation of which he was the object, and the exclusion from the fascinating and exciting life into which he had been drawn, he was not wont by word or letter to admit that he was wrong to resign, or assert that, having again the opportunity, he would do otherwise. He looked upon the action as the most exalted in his life, and as an event of which, whatever the results to himself, he might be justly proud. "I had to do it—I could be no longer useful to them."

It should, indeed, not escape notice that there was among the principal characters in English politics during this momentous time a high and disinterested air, very refreshing in contrast with the humiliating antics of the place-hunters and trinket-seekers who surrounded them, and more admirable than the selfish ambitions of the statesmen of a sterner age. Sir Michael Hicks-Beach refuses the Leadership of the House of Commons, and insists upon serving under a younger man who in his opinion can better fill the place. Sir Stafford Northcote in the interests of party union voluntarily effaces himself in a peerage. Lord Salisbury twice offers to be a member of a Hartington Administration, and Lord Hartington twice refuses to be the First Minister of the Crown. Sir Henry James on a matter of principle severs himself from Mr. Gladstone and refuses the Woolsack. Lastly, Mr. Chamberlain leaves the party of which he must one day have been the leader, relinquishes the great office and power he had already obtained, and, confronted at every step by distrust and pursued at every step by obloquy, sets forth upon his long, eventful pilgrimage. Among all these indications of the healthy and generous conditions of English public life, so full of honour for our race and of vindication for its institutions, the resignation of Lord Randolph Churchill need not suffer by any impartial comparison.

Why, then, was Lord Randolph Churchill so hardly used by the party which owed so much to his efforts up till the year 1887, and might have often been grateful for support, and more often still for silences afterwards? Why was such unusual and uncompromising advantage taken of the false step he had made? No doubt much must be set down to the animosities he had excited; much to the alarm of a Cabinet at so impulsive and imperious a colleague; something to Lord Salisbury's desire that the leadership of the House of Commons, and all that might follow therefrom, should be secured to Mr. Balfour. Perhaps they thought that ten years later, or twenty years even, he might serve with his own con-temporaries or lead a younger generation. Time would cool the blood of the Reformer, and the experience of adversity might temper an impatience born of extraordinary success. Little did they know how short was the span, or at what a cost in life and strength the immense exertions of the struggle had been made. That frail body, driven forward by its nervous energies, had all these last five years been at the utmost strain. Good fortune had sustained it; but disaster, obloquy and inaction now suddenly descended with crushing force, and the hurt was mortal.

Looking back on the circumstances and events of those years in the light of after-knowledge, there may be some who will find it easy to say what Lord Randolph should have done after his resignation. He should have stated the whole grounds of his difference with the Tory Cabinet, minimizing nothing, keeping nothing back. In two or three speeches in Parliament and in the country he should broadly have outlined his general political conception of the course the Conservative Party should follow, and then, unless he was prepared to wage relentless war upon the government for the purpose of compelling them to adopt that course, he should forthwith have withdrawn himself entirely from public life. Leaving his party in the place of power to which he had raised them, with all the glamour of three years of cumulative and unexampled success still untarnished, he might well have been content to stand for a season apart from the floundering progress of the Administration, leaving others to muddle away the majority he had made. And he could have counted, not without reason, upon the continued affection of the Conservative working classes. The party press would have been silent or even conciliatory. The relentless irritation of the machine would have been prevented. As the years passed by and the discredit of the government increased, the Tory Democracy would have turned again to the lost leader by whom the victories of the past had been won.

In three speeches which he delivered during the month of April to public audiences at Paddington (where he defended particularly his resignation), at Birmingham, and at Nottingham, he made clear what his attitude towards Lord Salisbury's Government would be. He was entirely independent of that government. He had resigned from it on important grounds of difference. He desired a liberal and progressive policy in domestic affairs, and he was determined to wage war on extravagance and expenditure. But in the main lines of their policy he was a supporter of the government; and to the cause of the Union, as to the large and permanent interests of the Conservative Party, he remained perfectly loyal. From these

450

intentions he never in any degree varied or departed in the years that followed. "You are quite right," he wrote to FitzGibbon (5 November, 1887), "in supposing that mere returning to office has never been in my mind. I fight for a policy and not for place; and when I go back to office (if ever) I shall have secured my policy." A Tory Democratic policy could only be furthered from within the Conservative Party, and to that party he faithfully adhered. Besides Mr. Jennings, Lord Randolph had two good friends among the younger men in the House of Commons—his brother-in-law, Lord Curzon, and Mr. Ernest Beckett, the member for Whitby. These gentlemen stood by him, worked with him, and rendered him many political services in the years that followed his resignation, for which they were not extravagantly beloved in the high places of their party.

With these three exceptions the late Leader of the House of Commons was entirely alone. To do him justice he made no effort to increase his following and discouraged several who would have willingly worked with him. Profoundly as he disagreed with much that the government did, and disliked the temper that inspired it, fiercely as he resented the Lobby slanders and the steady detraction of the party press, never in the five years that followed—the last five years, as they were fated to be, of his physical strength—did he contemplate alliance of any sort with the Liberal Party or seek to cause cave, clique or faction in the Conservative ranks.

★ ★ ★

Meanwhile, outside the House of Commons and the forbidding circles of politics Lord Randolph was developing during these years new interests and amusements. Excitement in one form or another always attracted him, and after his resignation he sought it on the Turf. In partnership with Lord Dunraven he soon acquired a number of horses, to whose training and running he paid the closest attention. He became a shrewd judge of "form". In handicaps especially his forecasts were so often fulfilled that he acquired quite a reputation among his sporting friends. On the morning of a race meeting he would sit for hours pencilling upon the card, by the aid of *Ruff's Guide*, calculations which led very often to conclusions that were right and still more often to conclusions that were nearly right.

Under his eye Sherwood's stable became successful and for two years at least stood high in the winning lists. His footsteps fell upon some odd streaks of luck. While he was away fishing in Norway, in the summer of 1889, his mare the Abbesse de Jouarre won the Oaks at odds of twenty to one. At Doncaster, the year before, he dreamed he saw a number hoisted. On consulting his card the next day he found that only one horse running had so high a number. Inquiries led to the belief that this horse had a much better chance than the odds at which it stood suggested. Lord Randolph backed it heavily and won a considerable sum. Against the advice of his trainer he insisted on running the Abbesse de Jouarre for the Manchester Cup in 1889, and her victory constituted perhaps his most fortunate speculation. Of other horses which he owned or leased it is not necessary to speak, but during the years 1887 to 1891 Lord Randolph's colours—"chocolate, pink sleeves and cap"—were often to the fore.

His own society was eagerly sought by his friends; for he had much treasure to give as a companion, if only he were in the giving vein. The gay and reckless brilliancy of his conversation fascinated all who came within its range. He would talk and argue with entire freedom on every subject. He loved to defend daring paradoxes; and when forced to exert himself he would produce arguments so original and ingenious that the listeners were delighted, even if they were unconvinced. He sometimes amused himself by saying things on purpose to shock ponderous people, and in painting himself extravagantly in the darkest hues, so that they departed grieved to think there was so much wickedness left in the world. He excelled in all kinds of chaff and conversational sword-play—from sombre irony to schoolboy fun. When he wanted to persuade people to do any particular thing, he took enormous pains, seeming to touch by instinct all the feelings and reasons which moved or disturbed them, and very often he coaxed or compelled them to his wishes. On the other hand, he did not care how rude he was to those who wearied or irritated him, and he would toss and gore fools with true Johnsonian vigour and zest. In this abrupt and impulsive way he hurt the feelings of some harmless people and disquieted a good many more; but if he were sorry afterwards, as he very often was, he could nearly always make amends by a word or a smile or some little courtesy, and the sun shone out all the brighter for the storm. Although in his later years the nervous irritability of his nature became extreme, he steadily enlarged the circle of his private friends, and those who had known him long were increasingly attached to him.

It is instructive to notice that Lord Randolph's conduct during the years that followed his resignation will bear a far more exacting scrutiny than the years of his good fortune. Differing as he did on many questions from the government, separated from them by the personal dislike or distrust with which he was regarded, he had nevertheless given them, so far as he conscientiously could, a loyal and regular support. He had never spoken against them except when compelled by opinions plainly declared in former years, or moved by deep feeling; and then he had always practised a moderation in tone and language foreign to his disposition. He had done nothing to embarrass them or hamper them. He had never made a personal attack on any of his late colleagues, nor can I discover any unkind or acrimonious word used about them. From time to time he had tried to influence their policy in directions which he believed the public interest and their own equally required; but these occasions had been rare and he had usually been right. Although the object of much abuse and even hatred from his old friends, he nourished no thoughts of permanent separation.

These were the best years of his intellectual power—a short summer when his mind was most fertile and his judgment ripe and prescient. Almost alone and unsupported he had by sheer personal force and persuasive speech commanded respect and procured important decisions. Grave or gay, in attack, defence, or exposition, on all sorts of subjects and in all sorts of humours, the House of Commons had delighted to hear him; and what he said in Parliament or out of doors, whether about politics or other matters, was received and examined with national attention. But let it be observed that Lord Randolph Churchill was beaten, whatever he did, when he played the national game; and was victorious, whatever he did, while he played the party game. No question of "taste" or "patriotism" was raised when what he said, however outrageous, suited his party. No claim of truth counted when what he said, however incontrovertible, was awkward for his party. Yet almost fiercely he asserted his loyalty to the Unionist cause.

★     ★     ★

It had been proved to utter conviction in those barren years that "ten men armed can subdue one man in his shirt". One friend after another had fallen away from Lord Randolph. The hostility of the Prime Minister and the tireless machine-like detraction of the party press had not been without effect. His Parliamentary position was one of complete isolation and his popularity in the country had declined. Others—scarcely heard of in the days of battle—were now bearing the burden of the Unionist cause, and the public eye was fixed upon a stout-hearted bookseller whose perseverance as Leader was making of his repeated failures a curious but undoubted success, and upon an Irish Secretary whose reputation was every day enhanced by the taunts and revilings he provoked from his opponents. The Minister who seemed so powerful in 1886, the people's favourite, the necessary Parliamentarian, the central link of the Unionist alliance, certainly its most redoubtable champion, stood outside all political combinations, actual or potential. The government of such a sickly infancy was grown up into a strong, if not a healthy, manhood. The sunrise of wealth and extending comfort which in every nation lighted up the last quarter of the nineteenth century was strengthening by an unseen yet irresistible process the forces upon which Conservatism depends; and the millstone of Home Rule bowed and strangled the Liberals. There was neither need nor place for a leader of Tory Democracy.

All this was perfectly appreciated by Lord Randolph Churchill, and his detached contented mood and habit of thought were carefully and laboriously assumed and fortified by every trick of mental discipline he knew. A studied disdain of the course of public events, the influence of movement and of changing scenes, the delights of summer lands, books, friends and mild Egyptian cigarettes—all were to him the incidents of an elaborate art. But the characters of valetudinarian, pleasure-seeker, traveller, sportsman, failed to satisfy, and served scarcely to distract. Always at hand, though forbidden his mind, lurked the hopes and the schemes, once so real, now turned to shadows: and the thought—never quite to be chased away—of that multitude of working people he knew so well, who had trusted him as their champion; who were still ready, if they knew how, to do him honour; but for whom—though their problems were still unsolved, uncared for, or cared for only as counters in the game of politics—it was beyond his power to do the smallest service. And although the great river, gliding impassively along by the sands of the desert and the temples of forsaken faiths, might seem to smile at fretful aspirations, the reproach and disappointment silently consumed him.

Farther and farther afield! After the session of 1890 Lord Randolph Churchill abandoned the House of Commons. He attended seldom; he never spoke. In the summer of 1891 he sailed for South Africa in quest of sport and gold—and peace. A journey to Mashonaland was in those days an enterprise of some difficulty; nor, indeed, before the overthrow of the Matabele power, devoid of risk. Elaborate arrangements were required to conduct even a small party in comfort through these untrodden fields. The command of the miniature expedition was entrusted to Major Giles, a traveller well acquainted with the country. As killing game was a necessity as well as an amusement, one of the best hunters in South Africa, Hans Lee, was included in the party; and Mr. Perkins, a mining engineer of the highest eminence, was engaged to search for gold.

The interest with which Lord Randolph was regarded by the public had survived his popularity and all these preparations excited general curiosity and afforded fertile themes· for comment and satire. He was persuaded to write a long series of letters for the *Daily Graphic* by the extraordinary offer of a hundred pounds for each letter. Every incident of his journey, even the most trivial, especially the most personal that could be discovered, was telegraphed to England by assiduous reporters and discussed with genial malice by the Conservative newspapers. He was burlesqued on the Gaiety stage with a wit so pointed that the song was stopped by the intervention of the Lord Chamberlain. While paragraphs, lampoons and caricatures exhibited him daily to the ridicule of his countrymen; while the delegates of the National Union hooted his name at their annual conference; and while the chiefs of the Tories complacently admired the fullness of their triumph, the ex-Minister plunged into vast solitudes. Across the veldt by bush and kloof and kopje, through the drifts of flooded rivers, by mining camps and frontier posts into magnificent wildernesses toiled the tiny caravan. A gust of bracing air and rough exertion breaks in upon the artificial ventilation of the House of Commons. The crowded benches, with the yellow light streaming down upon them from the ceiling, recede into the distance. Waggons creak and jolt along stony tracks, camp-fires twinkle in the waste, antelope gallop over spacious pastures, lions roar beneath the stars——

\* \* \*

With the opening of the Session in January, 1893, and the beginning of the fight came full and complete reconciliation. Lord Randolph was urged to take his place again upon the Front Bench. He declared his willingness to serve, to the best of his ability, in the House of Commons under his friend and political chief, Mr. Balfour.

But now, when a new prospect was opening to his view, when he had been welcomed by the mass of the party, when he had returned to its inmost councils and ranged himself once again with his old friends and colleagues in wholehearted support of a cause which he had long defended, a dark hand intervened. The great strain to which he had subjected himself during the struggle against Mr. Gladstone, the vexations and disappointments of later years and finally the severe physical exertions and exposure of South Africa had produced in a neurotic temperament and delicate constitution a very rare and ghastly disease. During the winter of '92 symptoms of vertigo, palpitation, and numbness of the hands made themselves felt, and his condition was already a cause of the deepest anxiety to his friends. But it was not till he rose on the occasion of the introduction of the Home Rule Bill that the political world realized how great was the change. It happened that the debate was unexpectedly delayed by a question of privilege. The suspense proved a strain greater than he could bear with composure and when he rose his nervousness was extreme, and more to be looked for in some novice presuming for the first time than in a Parliamentarian of near twenty years' standing. He no longer dared to trust his memory: while the notes of his speech on the first Home Rule

Bill had been written on a single sheet of paper, he now required eighteen. The House, crowded in every part to hear him, was shocked by his strangely altered appearance. It seemed incredible that this bald and bearded man with shaking hands and a white face drawn with pain and deeply marked with the lines of care and illness, and with a voice whose tremulous tones already betrayed the fatal difficulty of articulation, could be that same brilliant audacious leader who in the flush of exultant youth had marched irresistibly to power through the stormy days of 1886.

Yet the quality of his speech showed no signs of intellectual failing. Avoiding the network of details in which so many speakers had stumbled, he presented a broad intelligible picture. Lucid and original expression, close and careful reasoning, wealth of knowledge, quaint Randolphian witticisms—all were there. Although much of the charm and force of his manner was gone, his statement was considered by good and impartial judges to have been, with the exception of Mr. Chamberlain's, the best speech delivered against the Bill.

And he was destined to have one last flicker of success. Once again was he to encounter, not unequally, his majestic antagonist; once again those he had been so proud to lead were to sustain him with triumphant acclamation. Exactly a week after his reappearance he was entrusted with the conclusion of the debate on the Welsh Church Suspensory Bill. The trying circumstances of his first effort were no longer present and the feeling that he had broken the ice comforted him. His whole condition varied sensibly from day to day. This was his good day. The House seemed friendly to him; his spirits responded to its mood, and for the moment he seemed to recover all, or nearly all, of his former power. Anyone who will take the trouble to read in Hansard the intricate and sustained argument and the ready rejoinders of the speech will see that the vigour of his mind was unimpaired. Triumph came at the end. Putting aside his notes, he began a fierce and sparkling attack on Mr. Gladstone.

Lord Randolph's speech on the Welsh Church was his last Parliamentary success. Throughout the passage of the Home Rule Bill he held his place in the front rank of the Opposition and took a regular and not undistinguished part in the debates. In the Easter recess his speeches to large audiences at Liverpool and Perth commanded the attention of the country, and now, as in former years, he provided his party with an inexhaustible supply of catchwords and homely arguments. But the fire and force of his oratory were gone, never to return; and as the Session drew on, his difficulties of utterance and of memory increased, and the severe and unrelenting labour exhausted the remnants of his strength. Several times in the hot summer months he failed to hold the attention of the House and even sometimes to make himself understood. Once, indeed, the members grew impatient and the House was filled with restless murmurs. But his friends—some of them his most distinguished opponents—rallied to him, checked the interruptions, and tried perseveringly to make all look smooth and successful. And in these days it was observed that Mr. Gladstone would always be in his place to pay the greatest attention to his speeches and to reply elaborately to such arguments as he had advanced.

Lord Randolph Churchill was acutely conscious of his failing powers and the realization roused him to immense exertions. A year before he had hardly cared for political affairs. Now he plunged desperately into the struggle. Others around him encountered the measures of a Liberal Administration. He faced a different foe. With the whole strength of his will he fought against the oncoming decay. He refused to accept defeat. He redoubled his labours. If five hours no longer sufficed for the preparation of a speech—he would take five days. If his memory played him false, it must be exercised the more.

He spent Christmas [1893] at Howth. The old circle of friends were gathered once more, and they saw with sadness that their hopes of his return to power, cherished for so many years, would never be fulfilled. When he came back to England for the beginning of the Session, the hounds were hard upon his track. But it was not till June that he consented to yield. The doctors ordered complete rest.

And now followed only a few dinners of farewell to good friends— who knew they would never see him again—and busy preparations for a long journey. He sailed, with his wife, for America on 27 June

[1894] under a sentence of death, operative within twelve months; and he realized perfectly that his time was very short. But now nature began mercifully to apply increasing doses of her own anaesthetics, and for the space there was yet to travel he suffered less than those who watched him. Indeed, in an odd way he was positively happy in these last few months; for the changing scenes kept him from sombre reflections, and the increasing attention which he paid to details of all kinds occupied his mind. Nothing was too small to command his interest, and neither in America nor in Japan was ever seen so methodical a tourist. The light faded steadily. At intervals small blood-vessels would break in the brain, producing temporary coma, and leaving always a little less memory or faculty behind. His physical strength held out till he reached Burma, "which I annexed", and which he had earnestly desired to see. But when it failed, the change was sudden and complete. The journey was curtailed, and in the last days of 1894 he reached England as weak and helpless in mind and body as a little child. For a month, at his mother's house, he lingered pitifully, until very early in the morning of 24 January the numbing fingers of paralysis laid that weary brain to rest.

*　　*　　*

The story of Lord Randolph Churchill's life is complete in itself and needs no comment from the teller. It is idle to speculate upon what his work and fortunes might have been, had he continued to lead the House of Commons and influence against its inclinations the Conservative Party. It is certain only that the course of domestic policy in Finance, in Temperance and other social questions would have been widely deflected from that which has been in fact pursued. Most of all, perhaps, was Ireland a loser by his downfall; for more than any other Unionist of authority he understood the Irish people —their pride, their wants, their failings, their true inspiration. What would have happened to him, aye, and to others, had he lived the ordinary span of men—after all, he was but forty-six—are questionings even more shadowy and unreal. How would he have regarded a naval and military expenditure of seventy millions in time of peace? What would he have thought of the later developments of those Imperialistic ideas, the rise of which he had powerfully, yet almost unconsciously, aided? What action would have been wrung from him by the stresses of the South African war? Would he, under the many riddles the future had reserved for such as he, have snapped the tie of sentiment that bound him to his party, resolved at last to "shake the yoke of inauspicious stars"; or would he by combining its Protectionist appetites with the gathering forces of labour have endeavoured to repeat as a Tory-Socialist in the new century the triumphs of the Tory-Democrat in the old?

For all its sense of incompleteness, of tragic interruption, his life presents a harmony and unity of purpose and view. Verbal consistency is of small value. Yet even his verbal consistency was not especially open to challenge. But the "climate of opinion" in which he lived, the mood and intention with which he faced the swiftly changing problems of a stormy period, were never sensibly or erratically altered. The principles and convictions which he developed in the Parliament of 1874, and professed during the Parliament of 1880, were those which guided him to the end. That the period was brief in which he swayed and almost dominated the Conservative Party is not wonderful. The marvel is that he should ever have won to power in it at all.

He contained in his nature and in his policy all the elements necessary to ruin and success. If the principles he championed from 1880 to 1885 were the cause of his rise, they were also the cause of his fall. All his pledges he faithfully fulfilled. The government changed. The vast preponderance of power in the State passed from one great party to the other. Lord Randolph Churchill remained exactly the same. He thought and said the same sort of things about foreign and domestic policy, about armaments and expenditure, about Ireland, about Egypt, while he was a Minister as he had done before. He continued to repeat them after he had left office for ever. The hopes he had raised among the people, the promises he had made, the great support and honour he had received from them, seemed to require of him strenuous exertions. And when all exertions had failed, he paid cheerfully the fullest and the only forfeit in his power.

Lord Randolph Churchill's name will not be recalled upon the bead-roll of either party. The Conservatives, whose forces he so greatly strengthened, the Liberals, some of whose finest principles he notably sustained, must equally regard his life and work with mingled feelings. A politician's character and position are measured in his day by party standards. When he is dead, all that he achieved in the name of party is at an end. The eulogies and censures of partisans are powerless to affect his ultimate reputation. The scales wherein he was weighed are broken. The years to come bring weights and measures of their own.

There is an England which stretches far beyond the well-drilled masses who are assembled by party machinery to salute with appropriate acclamation the utterances of their recognized fuglemen; an England of wise men who gaze without self-deception at the failings and follies of both political parties; of brave and earnest men who find in neither faction fair scope for the effort that is in them; of "poor men" who increasingly doubt the sincerity of party philanthropy. It was to that England that Lord Randolph Churchill appealed; it was that England he so nearly won; it is by that England he will be justly judged.

461

# MARLBOROUGH
## HIS LIFE AND TIMES

*"Every taunt, however bitter; every tale, however petty;*
*every charge, however shameful, has been levelled against him*
*(John Churchill, Duke of Marlborough). Swift, Pope,*
*Thackeray and Macaulay have vied with one another in*
*presenting an odious portrait to posterity."*

*These pungent phrases are quoted from the author's Preface*
*to "Marlborough, His Life and Times", the biography of*
*his illustrious ancestor, in which he defends Marlborough*
*and rebuts the charges made against him. In his judgment*
*Marlborough was one of the greatest commanders in military*
*annals and, until Napoleon, no other wielded such widespread*
*power on the continent of Europe. The work was originally*
*published in four volumes between 1933 and 1938.*

AT THE beginning of 1671 John Churchill, grown a man, bronzed by African sunshine, close-knit by active service and tempered by discipline and danger, arrived home from the Mediterranean. He seems to have been welcomed with widespread pleasure by the Court, and by none more than by Barbara, now become Duchess of Cleveland. She was twenty-nine and he twenty. They were already affectionate friends. The distant degree of cousinly kinship which had hitherto united them had sanctioned intimacy, and did not now prohibit passion. Affections, affinities, and attractions were combined. Desire walked with opportunity, and neither was denied. John almost immediately became her lover, and for more than three years this wanton and joyous couple shared pleasures and hazards. The cynical, promiscuous, sagacious-indulgent sovereign was outwitted or outfaced. Churchill was almost certainly the father of Barbara's last child, a daughter, born on 16 July, 1672, and the ties between them were not severed until the dawn of his love for Sarah Jennings in 1675.

If anyone in 1672 computed the relative forces of France and England, he could only feel that no contest was possible; and the apparent weakness and humiliation of the pensioner island was aggravated by the feeble, divided condition of Europe. No dreamer, however romantic, however remote his dreams from reason, could have foreseen a surely approaching day when, by the formation of mighty coalitions and across the struggles of a generation, the noble colossus of France would lie prostrate in the dust, while the small island, beginning to gather to itself the empires of India and America, stripping France and Holland of their colonial possessions, would emerge victorious, mistress of the Mediterranean, the Narrow Seas, and the oceans. Aye, and carry forward with her, intact and enshrined, all that peculiar structure of law and liberty, all her own inheritance of learning and letters, which are today the treasure of the most powerful family in the human race.

This prodigy was achieved by conflicting yet contributory forces, and by a succession of great islanders and their noble foreign comrades or guides. We owe our salvation to the sturdy independence of the House of Commons and to its creators, the aristocracy and country gentlemen. We owe it to our hardy tars and bold sea-captains, and to the quality of a British Army as yet unborn. We owe it to the inherent sanity and vigour of the political conceptions sprung from the genius of the English race. But those forces would have failed without the men to use them. For the quarter of a century from 1688 to 1712 England was to be led by two of the greatest warriors and statesmen in all history: William of Orange and John, Duke of Marlborough. They broke the military power of France, and fatally weakened her economic and financial foundations. They championed the Protestant faith, crowned Parliamentary institutions with triumph, and opened the door to an age of reason and freedom. They reversed the proportions and balances of Europe. They turned into new courses the destinies of Asia and America. They united Great Britain, and raised her to the rank she holds today.

There are two main phases in the military career of John, Duke of Marlborough. In the first, which lasted four years, he rose swiftly from ensign to colonel by his conduct and personal qualities and by the impression he made on all who met him in the field. In the second, during ten campaigns he commanded the main army of the Grand Alliance with infallibility. An interval of more than a quarter of a century separates these two heroic periods. From 1671 to 1675 he exhibited all those qualities which were regarded as the fore-runners in a regimental officer of the highest military distinction. He won his way up from grade to grade by undoubted merit and daring. But thereafter was a desert through which he toiled and wandered. A whole generation of small years intervened. He was like young men in the Great War [1914–18] who rose from nothing to the head of battalions and brigades, and then found life suddenly contract itself to its old limits after the Armistice. His sword never rusted in its sheath. It was found bright and sharp whenever it was needed, at Sedgemoor, at Walcourt, or in Ireland. There it lay, the sword of certain victory, ready for service whenever opportunity should come.

In the early seventies a new star began to shine in the constellations of the English Court. Frances Jennings—"la belle Jenyns" of Gram-mont—beautiful as "Aurora or the promise of Spring", haughty, correct, mistress of herself, became a waiting-woman of the Duchess of York. She soon had no lack of suitors.

In 1673 Frances brought her younger sister Sarah, a child of twelve, into the Court circle. She too was attached to the household of the Duke of York. There she grew up, and at the mature age of fifteen was already a precocious, charming figure. She was not so dazzling as her sister, but she had a brilliancy all her own; fair, flaxen hair, blue eyes sparkling with vivacity, a clear, rosy com-plexion, firm, engaging lips, and a nose well chiselled, but with a slightly audacious upward tilt. She also, from her tenderest years, was entirely self-possessed and self-confident, and by inheritance she owned, when roused, the temper of the devil.

Towards the end of 1675 she began to dance with John Churchill at balls and parties. He, of course, must have been acquainted with her ever since she arrived at St. James's, but after one night of dancing at the end of that year they fell in love with each other. It was a case of love, not at first sight indeed, but at first recognition. It lasted for ever; neither of them thenceforward loved anyone else in their whole lives, though Sarah hated many. The courtship was obstructed and prolonged. Meanwhile Sarah grew to her beauty and power, and her personality, full of force, woman's wiles, and masculine sagacity, became manifest.

This [the surrender to Sarah] was the only surrender to which the Duke of Marlborough was ever forced. It was to the fan of a chit of seventeen. Moreover, so far as we have been able to ascertain, his courtship of Sarah affords the only occasions in his life of hazards and heart-shaking ordeals when he was ever frightened. Neither the heat of battle nor the long-drawn anxieties of conspiracy, neither the unsanctioned responsibilities of the march to the Danube nor the tortuous secret negotiations with the Jacobite Court, ever disturbed the poise of that calm, reasonable, resolute mind. But in this love-story we see him plainly panic-stricken. The terror that he and Sarah might miss one another, might drift apart, might pass and sail away like ships in the night, overpowered him. A man who cared less could have played this game of love with the sprightly Sarah much better than he. A little calculation, a little adroitness, some studied withdrawals, some counter-flirtation, all these were the arts which in every other field he used with innate skill. He has none of them now. He begs and prays with bald, homely, pitiful reiteration. We see the power of the light which sometimes shines upon the soul. These two belonged to one another, and, with all their faults, placarded as we know them, their union was true as few things of which we have experience here are true. And at this moment in the depth of his spirit, with the urge of uncounted generations pressing forward, he feared lest it might be cast away.

*　　*　　*

The lines of battle were now slowly yet remorselessly drawing up in our island. Everything pointed, as in 1642, to the outbreak of civil war; but now the grouping of the forces was far different from the days when Charles I had unfurled his standard at Nottingham. The King had a large, well-equipped regular army, with a powerful artillery. He believed himself master of the best, if not at the moment the largest, navy afloat. He could call for powerful armed aid from Ireland and from France. He held the principal seaports and arsenals under trusty Catholic governors. He enjoyed substantial revenues. He had on his side his Catholic co-religionists, all the personal following which the government and the Court could command, and, strangely assorted with these, a very considerable concourse of Dissenters and traditional Roundheads. He assumed that the Church of England was paralysed by its doctrine of non-resistance, and he had been careful not to allow any Parliament to assemble for collective action.

Ranged against him were not only the Whigs, but almost all the old friends of the Crown. The men who had made the Restoration, the sons of the men who had fought and died for his father at Marston Moor and Naseby, the Church whose bishops and ministers had so long faced persecution for the principle of Divine Right, the universities who had melted their plate for King Charles's coffers and sent their young scholars to his armies, the nobility and landed gentry whose interests had seemed so bound up with the monarchy: all, with bent heads and burning hearts, must now prepare themselves to outface their King in arms.

It would indeed have been a strange war in which the sons of Puritans, Roundheads, and regicides would have marched for a Catholic and catholicizing King against Churchmen and Cavaliers, while the mass of the people remained helpless, passionate, terrified spectators. It would have been a war of the extremes against the means; a war of heterogeneous coalition against the central body of English wealth, rank, and grit. Few there were who could truly measure the value of all these various elements and the force of their harmonious combination, should it occur. And above and beyond all lay the incalculable hazards and accidents of the battlefield.

Very fearsome and dubious must the prospect have seemed to the nobility, gentry, and clergy who embodied the life and meaning of the England that we still know. They had no army; they had no lawful means of resistance, expression, or debate. They could not appeal to the unenfranchised millions of peasants and townsmen. They saw in mental eye the King in martial panoply advancing upon them with all that royal power in whose sanctity they themselves were the chief believers, with French troops ready to descend at any moment upon their shores to quell rebellion, with the children of the Ironsides hand in hand with Jesuit priests. Never did the aristocracy or the Established Church face a sterner test or serve the nation better than in 1688. They never flinched; they never doubted. They faced this hideous, fraudulent, damnable hotch-potch of anti-national designs without a tremor, and they conquered without a blow. Why they conquered and, above all, why they conquered bloodlessly, turned upon the action of no more than as many men and women as can be counted upon one's fingers.

Marlborough's childhood had been lived in penury. In Ashe House [near Axminster, the home of the widow of Sir John Drake, sister of the third Duchess of Marlborough] food and clothing for Sir Winston Churchill's lusty brood were inferior in quantity and quality, and above all in variety, to the standard of a well-to-do modern English artisan or strong, industrious navvy. While old silver appeared upon the tables, while the living-rooms contained pieces of furniture which persons of taste would now value and admire, while the family escutcheon boasted the achievements of many generations, the physical conditions were primitive and narrow. But to Marlborough's early years there was an added sting. He learned almost as soon as he could walk and speak that he and his father and mother were dependants upon the charity and good will of his grandmother. As he grew older he saw the straits to which the impoverishments of a Cavalier had reduced his father. He heard the talk of the exactions of the Roundheads and of the frequent litigation for quite small sums in which all the grown-ups of the household were engaged with the government or with the other members of their family. When, for his father's services and his own good looks, he was taken as a page at Court, he was penniless. He might be finely dressed and well fed, but he was penniless among those who monopolized a large proportion of the entire wealth of the kingdom. On every side his seeming equals were youths of noble fortune, heirs to vast estates and splendid titles. He was the earthenware pot among the iron ones. This was his second strong impression of life.

Before he was eighteen he realized that, unless he could make and save money, he could neither have a career, nor a bride, nor a home, nor even a modest independence. It is therefore not at all surprising, however unromantic, that his first preoccupation was the gathering of money. In his twenties and thirties his temper was very similar to that which we have attributed to the French nation —always more generous of life than treasure, ready to encounter every personal hazard, prodigal of blood, but deeply concerned about money. His thrift was not without a certain grandeur, a habit of self-denial differing altogether from a miser's sordidness. We have seen how when, after heartbreaking postponements, he married a girl almost as poor as himself he could offer her no home. We have seen him at twenty-eight marrying for love, and at the same time helping his father out of debt by resigning his own reversionary interest in the small family estate. In all supreme matters his actions were those of a generous spirit. His need and desire to possess a competence and not to be crippled in his career did not outweigh—nay, were cast aside by—true love and family duty.

But these great decisions only made thrift and circumspection more imperative. He could not afford to gamble and carouse with his equals. He could not indulge in the slightest personal extravagance. He ate sparingly, drank little, always more readily at the expense of others than his own, and eschewed all kind of display in dress. He was always strict and punctilious in money matters. He paid his bills with the utmost promptitude. He condescended to keep careful accounts in his own handwriting about quite small household affairs, and generally behaved more like a tradesman whose livelihood depends upon his honesty and solvency than like a gay and gallant courtier and fine gentleman. Even now, fifteen years later, after having held several lucrative posts, he was by far the poorest man in the high circle in which he had taken his natural place. He was an Earl, but the most impecunious in England. He was the first Lieutenant-General, but unemployed. He had braved the displeasure of the Crown. It might well be that his career was closed for many years. The slightest financial imprudence would be fatal to his future. Thus he continued those habits of strict and austere personal economy which had been ingrained in childhood and youth, and without which he would certainly have been submerged.

It is probably a just conclusion that Marlborough's conduct was above and not below the standards of his time; that though he took all the emoluments, perquisites, and commissions which belonged to his offices and appointments, he never took bribes or any money that was not his by usage or law. Although he always recognized the claims of natural love and affection, as in choosing his wife, in helping his father, or providing for his children, and set these far above riches, his own deep-rooted habits of personal thrift and self-denial were carried to a point which drew upon him the mockery of his envious contemporaries and of malicious historians. Yet these same habits, unpleasing though they may seem, were an essential part of his character as a gatherer, as a builder and a founder. They were mitigated or often baffled by the pervasive kindness of his nature. They arose from the same methodical, patient, matter-of-fact spade-work which characterizes all his conduct of war, and formed the only basis upon which the great actions for which he is renowned could have sprung. His handling of his private affairs was as grave, as strongly marked by common sense, and as free from indulgence or unwisdom as his conduct of politics and war. His private fortune was amassed upon the same principles as marked the staff-work of his campaigns, and was a part of the same design. It was only in love or on the battlefield that he took all risks. In these supreme exaltations he was swept from his system and rule of living, and blazed resplendent with the heroic virtues. In his marriage and in his victories the worldly prudence, the calculation, the reinsurance, which regulated his ordinary life and sustained his strategy, fell from him like a too heavily embroidered cloak, and the genius within sprang forth in sure and triumphant command.

*　　*　　*

It is difficult for a modern officer, with his ideas of individual foot soldiers working and scrambling separately or in small groups across or through any kind of country, and feeling the safer the more it is accidented, to realize what tiny obstacles were serious to the infantry of this period. Most of these historic features would hardly be noticed by a tourist in his walk. But the infantry of Marlborough and Louis XIV depended for their existence in battle upon keeping close and perfect order. Although their fire-power was growing, they must still depend largely upon their strict array and their bayonets, while all around, close at hand, often within hailing distance, moved the flashing squadrons which upon the slightest disorder could crumple them almost instantaneously into bloody and fatal confusion. Thus passing even a small hedge or ditch, which unarmed men could easily jump or perhaps step over, was in the presence of the enemy a most anxious business, and every movement, even of a hundred yards, had to be judiciously foreseen as to the ground and timed as to the enemy.

It would, however, be a mistake to infer that battles under these conditions were slow conflicts of feeble forces. On the contrary, they were far more sudden and intense than those of the Great War. Instead of struggles lasting for several weeks along fronts of seventy or eighty miles, all was brought into a small compass and a single day. Sometimes two hundred thousand men fought for an afternoon in a space no larger than the London parks put together, and left the ground literally carpeted with a quarter of their number, and in places heaped with maimed or slaughtered men. The spectacle of one of the battlefields of Marlborough, Frederick, or Napoleon was for these reasons incomparably more gruesome than any equal sector of the recent fronts in France or Flanders.

We do not think that the warriors of our own time, unsurpassed in contempt of death or endurance of strain, would have regarded these old battles as a light ordeal. Instead of creeping forward from one crater to another or crouching low in their trenches under the blind hail of death and amid its shocking explosions, Marlborough's men and their brave, well-trained opponents marched up to each other shoulder to shoulder, three, four, or six ranks deep, and then slowly and mechanically fired volley after volley into each other at duelling distance until the weaker wavered and broke. This was the moment when the falcon cavalry darted in and hacked and slashed the flying men without mercy. Keeping an exact, rigid formation under the utmost trial, filling promptly all the gaps which at every discharge opened in the ranks, repeating at command, platoon by platoon, or rank by rank, the numerous unhurried motions of loading and firing—these were the tests to which our forebears were not unequal. In prolonged severe fighting the survivors of a regiment often stood for hours knee-deep amid the bodies of comrades writhing or for ever still. In their ears rang the hideous chorus of the screams and groans of a pain which no anaesthetic would ever soothe.

The task of the commander in Marlborough's wars was direct. There were no higher formations like divisions and corps. Even the brigade was an improvisation adopted for the campaign. The armies were often divided into wings. There were for each wing generals of cavalry and infantry. Each, like the Chief, was assisted by lieutenant-generals. These high executive officers were available either to carry out particular tasks assigned to them often in the heat of action, or to see that the main plan, with which they were made acquainted, was carried out. The control of the battle was maintained on each side by eight or ten superior officers who had no permanent commands of their own, and were virtually the general staff officers of modern times, working in a faithful subordination. It was with and through these that the commander-in-chief acted, and it is astonishing how smoothly and effectually the troops were often handled and great changes of plan and formation effected even in the stress of action.

All this was quite different from the trials of our latter-day generals. We will not belittle them, but they were the trials of mind and spirit working in calm surroundings, often beyond even the sound of the cannonade. There are no physical disturbances: there is no danger: there is no hurry. The generalissimo of an army of two million men, already for ten days in desperate battle, has little or nothing to do except to keep himself fit and cool. His life is not different, except in its glory, from that of a painstaking, punctual public official, and far less agitating than that of a Cabinet Minister who must face an angry Chamber on the one hand or an offended party upon the other. There is no need for the modern commander to wear boots and breeches: he will never ride a horse except for the purposes of health. In the height of his largest battles, when twenty thousand men are falling every day, time will hang heavy on his hands. The heads of a dozen departments will from hour to hour discreetly lay significant sheets of paper on his desk. At intervals his staff will move the flags upon his map, or perhaps one evening the Chief of Staff himself will draw a blue line or a brown line or make a strong arrow upon it. His hardest trials are reduced to great simplicity. "Advance", "Hold", or "Retreat". His personal encounters are limited to an unpleasant conversation with an army commander who must be dismissed, an awkward explanation to a harassed Cabinet, or an interview with a representative of the neutral press. Time is measured at least by days and often by weeks. There is nearly always leisure for a conference even in the gravest crises. It is not true that the old battle has merely been raised to a gigantic scale. In the process of enlargement the sublime function of military genius—perhaps happily—has been destroyed for ever.

But in the times of which we tell the great commander proved in the day of battle that he possessed a combination of mental, moral, and physical qualities adapted to action which were so lifted above the common run as to seem almost godlike. His appearance, his serenity, his piercing eye, his gestures, the tones of his voice—nay, the beat of his heart—diffused a harmony upon all around him. Every word he spoke was decisive. Victory often depended upon whether he rode half a mile this way or that. At any moment a cannon-shot or a cavalry inrush might lay him with thousands of his soldiers a mangled bundle on the sod. That age has vanished for ever. Other trials are reserved for the human spirit. New and vaguer problems overtop such minds as are available. But let us not pretend that modern achievements can be compared, except by million-tongued propaganda, with the personal feats which the very few great captains of the world performed.

★    ★    ★

In the midst of activities [mainly political] almost the greatest sorrow that can come to man fell upon Marlborough. His only surviving son was now sixteen. We remember him as a playmate of the poor little Duke of Gloucester. He had been at Eton and had already gone to Cambridge. Life began early in those days, and this handsome, eager youth wanted, of course, to go with his father to the wars. Bred in a martial atmosphere, he was thrilled by camps and soldiers, and especially by reviews and processions. His father would have liked to have him with him at the front; but his mother thought he was too young. In those days an officer on the staff of the Commander-in-Chief must be frequently under fire, and might be required at any moment to ride with a message into the hottest of the fighting. Sarah could not bring herself to let him go so young—while still a child. Let him stay one more year at Cambridge and finish his studies. Thus was it settled. But Death

472

knows where to keep his appointments.

During the autumn of 1702 Lord Blandford often came over from Cambridge to stay with Lord Godolphin close by at Newmarket, and apparently made the best impression upon the Treasurer. There was smallpox in the town.

It was at the end of his long visit to Godolphin that the infection fell upon him. He had scarcely returned to Cambridge in February when he was struck down by virulent smallpox. Sarah was there as fast as horses could bear her, nursing him herself and invoking all that the medical knowledge of those days could do. The Queen hurried her own physicians into the royal coach and sent them posting to Cambridge. It was less than three years since the same scourge had carried off her own child.

Till all hope was abandoned John was kept away. He received his summons and, hurrying to Cambridge, arrived as his son expired. On the morning of Saturday, 20 February, John and Sarah crept off to Holywell to endure their pangs.

This blow not only cut at the natural feelings of John and Sarah, but seemed to ruin their future. Both were dynasts. To gather wealth and fame and found a family to run on down the ages was their dear—indeed, their over-dear—ambition. Now it was ended.

Even the most hostile Continental historians are struck by Marlborough's resiliency. Every action that he thought vital to the success of the war was denied him. His opinion as Captain-General and deputy Captain-General of the two armies was brushed aside, as though he were a suitor with a doubtful case before some small tribunal. He preserved an imperturbable demeanour.

But his stress of soul and inward vexation were so great as to make him physically ill. To be thus continually thwarted and forbidden to carry out what his genius told him was right, and what his knowledge of the whole war declared vital to the Common Cause, roused passions in his breast, the more tormenting because borne with apparent composure. He burned with suppressed anger; he was racked with headaches; a profound loathing for the conditions of his task possessed him. He spoke no word of complaint or menace before subordinates, but he resolved to be quit of such stifling responsibilities. This should be his last campaign. He would serve no more under intolerable conditions. He bore all the responsibility before Europe and before his professional opponents, and yet was constantly prevented from doing justice to his task.

*          *          *

The annals of the British Army contain no more heroic episode than the march from the North Sea to the Danube [May, 1704]. The strategy which conceived, the secrecy and skill which performed, and the superb victory which crowned the enterprise have always ranked among the finest examples of the art of war. But a brighter and truer glory shines upon the Man than can be won by military genius alone. Never did lifeboat captain launch forth to the rescue of a ship in distress with more selfless devotion to duty. Not Wolfe before Quebec, not Nelson before Trafalgar, nursed a purer love of his country's cause than Marlborough in this supreme passage in his career. The profound calculations which he made, both political and military, could only present a sum of dangers against which forethought could make no provision. All that gallant army that marched with him risked life and honour: but he alone bore the burden. It was for them to obey the lawful authorities. For him the task was to persuade, deceive, and defy them for their own salvation.

Marlborough was the champion of the entire confederacy, accountable for all time for the common cause and the general deliverance. He could not retire. He could not escape. To withdraw to peace and quiet, ease and affluence; to mingle in the vivid politics of the day; to live the interesting and varied life of an English duke, in days when dukes were dukes: nay, to be happy with Sarah, surrounded in the home he had built and was building at Holywell by children and grandchildren—all were temptations to be put aside. But for what? Ambition? Not certainly in any base sense. He had already all its material rewards. He was only a subject and a servant under a monarchy and patriciate and the House of Commons. He might be the greatest of servants. He could never be more. Monarchies and empires were dissolving or being framed upon the Continent. Perhaps they would be made or marred by his sword. But not for him the prizes of Napoleon, or in later times of cheaper types. His toils could only be for England, for that kind of law the

474

English called freedom, for the Protestant religion, and always in the background for that figure, half mystic symbol and the best cherished friend, the Queen. But these incentives were respectable He had to respond to them no matter at what cost in peril or care They were also impersonal. A page in history, a niche in Valhalla, and a good conscience to have used well the gifts which God had given: these must be the sole reward of a moral and mental exertion which, for its comprehension and power, has not often been surpassed in history.

But Marlborough felt the greatest compulsion that can come to anyone—the responsibility of proprietorship. It had become his war. He was the hub of the wheel. He was bound to function. He had made the treaties. He had accepted William's bequest. He must discharge it faithfully. He must bring it all to success and safety. The task was his. These foolish-frantic Parliaments, jealous princes, hungry generals, and bitter politicians were all, as he conceived it, in his care. He alone knew the path which would lead them out of their tangles and tribulations, and he was bound to force or trick them to salvation if he could.

★     ★     ★

[Before the Battle of Blenheim] Marlborough had spent some of the night in prayer. He received the sacrament from Dr. Hare. "The religion he had learned as a boy" fortified his resolution and sealed his calm. While the advance guards were moving into the night he visited Prince Eugene, whom he found writing letters. They mounted their horses. It is said by several authorities that on being in the saddle he declared, "This day I conquer or die." Nothing was more unlike him. Months before in England he had used such words to Wratislaw, and assuredly they did not go beyond the truth. But, arrived at the point of action, it is more probable that he made some considerate inquiry about his horse's forage or his man's rations.

The army filed off at three o'clock in eight columns, preceded by 40 squadrons, along tracks which had been carefully marked and prepared, through darkness intensified by the gathering mists of dawn. As day broke they crossed the watercourse by Tapfheim, and here the advance guards were merged in their respective columns.

Here also a ninth column was formed close to the river. It comprised all the troops of the outpost line, and included the two English brigades of Rowe and Ferguson, in all 20 battalions and 15 squadrons. Of this powerful body Lord Cutts took command. The artillery and the pontoons marched by the main road with the Duke's six-horse coach at their tail. The whole force numbered 66 battalions, 160 squadrons, and 66 guns, or about fifty-six thousand men. Daylight came, but at first the sun only drew more vapours from the marshes and shrouded densely the crawling masses. Thus the heads of the columns arrived in line with Schwenningen village, scarcely two miles from the enemy's camp, about six.

Here Marlborough and Eugene remained together for some time in company with the Prussian Major-General Natzmer, who had fought at Höchstädt in the previous year. The plan of the two commanders was that Eugene should attack and hold the enemy's left wing while Marlborough overwhelmed his right. If Marlborough succeeded he carried forward Eugene's battle with him. The more decisively Eugene could attack, the greater the chances of Marlborough's success. If both allied wings were defeated, retreat would be difficult, especially for Eugene, most of whose troops could only have fallen back into trackless wooded heights. On the other hand, the advance of Marlborough along the Danube and towards Höchstädt would not only conquer the enemy in his own front, but would threaten the retreat of the whole of the French opposite Eugene.

The mists began to thin as the sun rose higher, and the enemy outposts became aware of large numbers of men gathering along their front. They sent back speedy warnings, and at the same time the mists dispersing revealed from the French camp large forces covering the whole space from the Danube to the hills. Even now the Marshal and the Elector held to their prepossession that the confederate army was retiring under a bold display through the shallow valley which led back to Nördlingen.

Marlborough, resplendent in scarlet, wearing his Garter ribbon and riding his white horse, paced slowly in front of his harassed lines. A roundshot, striking at his horse's feet, enveloped him in a cloud of earth, and wrung an anxious gasp from the watching troops he had led so far from home. But he continued his progress uninjured. He had found the time to choose the sites for the field hospitals, such as they were, and had posted every battery himself. He spent the dragging hours in watching their shooting or conversing with the commanding officers. After a while he dismounted and lunched with his attendants, probably on the rising ground behind Unterglau village. In these conditions, where every man's bearing could be so closely scrutinized, he seemed entirely free from care; yet a grave anxiety was growing in his heart. What had happened to [Prince] Eugene? He should have been in position by eleven. It was now nearly noon. Messengers had gone and returned with vague reports. The columns were struggling on as fast as they could. At length he sent Cadogan to find the Prince, and to see for himself. Cadogan returned shortly after twelve with the news that Eugene was nearly ready. All the bridges were now finished, and so far the enemy opposite Marlborough showed no mind to dispute the passage. But the day was wasting. Each minute now acquired a value. At last an aide-de-camp arrived at a gallop. "His Highness will give the signal for attack at half-past twelve." Marlborough rose, called for his horse, and mounted saying to the group of officers, "Gentlemen, to your posts." All the troops stood up and dressed their ranks. The infantry fixed their bayonets, and Cutts launched his attack upon Blenheim. At the same time the first line of General Churchill's infantry began slowly to move towards the Nebel.

High and proud was the bearing of these regular soldiers as they strode into battle. Among those who now advanced was Captain Blackadder, and as he gazed upon the mass and pomp of the enemy covering the whole plain before him his heart was so filled with a sense of the infinite mercy and power of God that he could not help exclaiming aloud to his company, "How easy it would be for the Lord to slay or take captive all those thousands before nightfall!" whereat his men, seeing their commander thus transported, were mightily heartened. "And moreover," adds the Captain, in proof of the efficacy of faith and prayer, "before night it was even so."

The British brigade of five battalions which had been sheltering as much as possible in the stream-bed from the artillery now rose up and marched upon the palisades and enclosures of Blenheim.

Their brigadier, General Rowe, had ordered that there should be no firing till he struck his sword upon the pales. The distance was perhaps a hundred and fifty yards, and almost immediately, owing to the ground, the troops passed out of the fire of the hostile battery. They marched in silence and perfect order to within thirty yards of the defences. Then the French fired a deadly volley, and General Rowe, who was still unscathed, struck the palisade with his sword; whereupon the survivors of the leading companies fired in their turn, and came to grips with the French through the palisades and across the obstacles which they tried by main force to tear to pieces. Their efforts were vain. Although here and there small parties penetrated, the French, who so greatly outnumbered their assailants, repulsed the attack, inflicting a loss of one man in three. Here fell General Rowe mortally wounded, and both his staff officers were killed in trying to carry him away. As the assault recoiled in disorder three squadrons of the celebrated French Gendarmerie, also clothed in red, charged round the outskirts of the village and fell upon their flank. Rowe's own regiment [the 21st Foot, the Royal Scots Fusiliers] lost its colours. The Gendarmes, pressing on, encountered the Hessian brigade at the edge of the marsh, but these good troops by a well-directed fire routed them in their turn and rescued and restored the colours of the 21st.

There were crowded into Blenheim no fewer than twenty-seven battalions, together with the four regiments of horseless dragoons who held the ground between the village and the river. As these excessive reinforcements arrived when the French in the village were already being forced to contract their front line a disastrous congestion resulted. Nearly twelve thousand men were crammed into Blenheim, so closely packed that the bulk could neither move nor use their arms. All the ground before the village was heaped with nearly two thousand dead and wounded, including many hundreds of the British. Lord Cutts had still an intact Hanoverian brigade, and was preparing himself to lead the third attack when, about half-past two, Marlborough, who was watching the struggle at some distance, sent him orders to desist, and to hold the enemy pinned down. Cutts therefore withdrew his infantry just beyond musket-shot, and made his colonels advance their platoons from each company in succession to deliver their fire and retire out of range. Thus the repulse was accepted. At this moment, however, though it was not fully realized, twenty-seven French battalions were occupied by sixteen of the allies. It is probable that Cutts' unused Hanoverian brigade, moving to its right, rejoined the main body of Churchill's infantry.

The whole front from the Danube to the hills was roaring with fire and conflict. Marlborough, who had lately been watching the battle from the rising ground behind Unterglau, attended by his retinue, now came quickly forward, passed the burning villages, crossed the Nebel by a causeway, and took personal control at the danger-point. He led forward three Hanoverian battalions from Holstein-Beck's reserve. He made Colonel Blood bring a battery of cannon across the streamlet. With these he threw the Irish back some distance towards Oberglau. In this breathing-space the rest of Holstein-Beck's command began to form a line on the firm ground. This was the moment for Marsin's cavalry beyond Oberglau to renew their charges, and strenuous efforts were made to gather a strong force and set it in motion.

★ ★ ★

A lull now descended upon the battlefield. The firing had lasted more than six hours and physical contact for nearly two, and everywhere it seemed that the armies reeled. These perils had been surmounted. But, indeed, many an experienced officer in Europe, impartially surveying the scene, would have pronounced the allies defeated. They had failed with ghastly slaughter to take Blenheim. Nothing but deadlock existed there. They had equally failed to take Oberglau, and only narrowly escaped a severance of their wings. The whole of Prince Eugene's attack had come to a standstill. For nearly three-quarters of an hour the two lines of cavalry in this quarter stood facing each other at sixty yards' distance, neither of them able to move forward or strike another blow. In vain did Eugene on one side and the Elector on the other ride along the ranks animating, commanding, entreating, and taunting their exhausted and shaken soldiers to a renewed effort. At no point, it seemed, could the allies move forward. Yet it was certain they could not

479

stay where they were. If they could not advance they must soon retreat. If they retreated they were lost.

Nevertheless at this moment Marlborough was sure of victory. Shortly after three o'clock he sent one of his aides, Lord Tunbridge, to Eugene, announcing that all was well in the centre. From the tumult of battle his design was now emerging. Although his total army had at the beginning been several thousands fewer than the French, and although it had suffered up to this point perhaps double their losses, he was now in a position of overwhelming strength. By four o'clock the whole of the cavalry and the whole of Churchill's infantry were formed in good order on the farther side of the Nebel opposite the French centre. The cavalry now formed the first two lines and the infantry the second pair. The English field batteries were moving forward to join them. Upon the two-mile stretch from Blenheim to Oberglau he had now nearly 80 squadrons, only a few of which had yet charged, against 50 or 60 French, many of whom had been several times engaged. Upon the same front he had 23 battalions against only 9. Leaving the bloody local fight around Oberglau, he now rode to conduct the advance of this formidable array.

The pause in the battle continued for a while. The reason for it is plain. Marlborough wished to concert the attack upon the whole front, and Eugene after his second repulse required time to reorganize. At half-past four, when the Danish infantry had worked their way round the Bavarians on the extreme left of Lutzingen, the battle was renewed at all points. The Prince of Anhalt-Dessau, carrying a regimental colour in his hand, led forward for the third time the redoubtable Prussian Foot. Eugene advanced again at the head of the Imperial cavalry. And now between Blenheim and Oberglau Marlborough's long lines, horse and foot together, were set in motion. The impact of so great a body of troops, comparatively fresh, upon the weakest part of a wasted front everywhere closely engaged, after so many hours, might reasonably be expected to be decisive. It was not in character different from the march of the French centre against the plateau of Pratzen by which Napoleon so suddenly yet so surely gained the battle of Austerlitz. There is a grand simplicity in two or three to one at the decisive point. To procure it—there lies the secret.

When Marshal Marsin saw Tallard's line broken and the wide plain between Oberglau and Blenheim occupied by Marlborough's troops advancing in solid formations, he resolved to retreat. The Elector and the other generals were all in agreement. The disengagement and withdrawal were effected with skill and discipline, and the army of the French left wing marched in the direction of Lauingen in admirable order. This was indeed necessary, for they must expect to have to fight hard to gain the exit between the hills and the marsh of Höchstädt. Marsin's army was by no means exhausted. They had no reason to boast about their battle. With more squadrons, with nearly double the battalions and more than double the cannon of Prince Eugene, they had been hard put to it to defend themselves. They had even ceded important ground to the attack of far less numerous forces. They had fought a self-centred battle, and had been able to give no help to their friends on the right, with whose defeat their own was now involved. These facts attest the glory of Prince Eugene, whose fire and spirit had extorted the wonderful exertions of his troops; who after contending all day against very heavy odds held the initiative and the offensive to the end; and who, moreover, in the midst of local disaster had not hesitated to answer Marlborough's call for the Cuirassier brigade. By seven o'clock the whole of Marsin's army, escorting their prisoners and rescuing on their way two of Tallard's battalions who had already surrendered, were making for the gap above Morselingen, followed by all the troops that Prince Eugene could muster.

General Churchill, with the bulk of his 23 battalions, besides supporting the front, had the duty of protecting both flanks of Marlborough's advance against sorties from Blenheim or a counter-attack from the direction of Oberglau. As soon as Marlborough's cavalry rode on ahead in pursuit of the French his brother wisely turned his main force to the left against Blenheim in order to encircle and capture the mass of French infantry known to be in the village. The process of hemming in Blenheim was thus in full progress. To deter the enemy from breaking out, Churchill at a little after six asked Lord Cutts to make another attack or at least hold the enemy tight. Cutts and his troops responded generously. The remains of Rowe's British brigade headed a new assault, the third, upon the deadly defences. This time they broke in, and fierce hand-to-hand fighting was resumed all along the Nebel side of the village, as well as round the corner between the Nebel and the Maulweyer brook. Marshal Tallard, being conducted down the main road to Marlborough's coach, which we suppose was still some distance behind the Nebel, saw this furious combat flare up on his right hand. He induced one of the officers escorting him to bear a message from him to the Duke offering, if he would "let these poor fellows retire", to prevent all further firing by the French. Marlborough had now joined Hompesch between Oberglau and Morselingen, and was organizing a cavalry charge upon the flank of Marsin's columns, which could be seen approaching half a mile away. He was surprised at Tallard's presumption. He replied severely, "Inform Monsieur de Tallard that in the position in which he now is, he has no command."

Meanwhile Marsin's army in three columns, the outer ones of cavalry, was drawing near, and Hompesch was about to charge, when another large body of troops in good formation came in sight from behind Oberglau village. These were thought to be Marsin's rearguard. They were so disposed as to take in flank such a charge as Hompesch was about to make. They were in fact the leading brigades of Prince Eugene following the French, and themselves seeking a chance of attack. Marlborough, in no mood to compromise his victory, sent out patrols to make sure of the truth, and meanwhile waited. Eugene in his turn mistook Hompesch for a part of Tallard's cavalry, and likewise paused to assure himself. By the time these mistakes were discovered Marsin and the Elector had made such progress across Marlborough's front that a new attack meant a new battle. The Duke surveyed the scene against the setting sun. He observed the firm attitude of the enemy and their superior numbers. He knew that he had the bulk of Tallard's infantry—how many he could not tell—behind him in Blenheim, still to be mastered. He decided to break off the pursuit of Marsin, and in all the circumstances his judgment should be accepted.

The last scene in the drama of Blenheim lay around the village which finally gave its name to the battle. The garrison comprised the best infantry of France and its proudest regiments. They had repulsed every attack with heavy slaughter and so far with no great loss to themselves. But many had seen—and it needed no military knowledge to understand—what had happened on the plain and what its consequences to them would be. Their army was routed, and they were cut off. The Marquis de Clérambault, whose nervousness or folly had crowded Tallard's reserves into the village, saw himself the cause of the disaster which had befallen the army and was now to overtake himself and all those for whom he was responsible. His brain reeled. He sought in flight a still more fearful safety. Without a word to his subordinates or giving anyone a chance to assume the command, he rode to the river, attended only by his groom. The man tried the passage and escaped: his master followed. But the swirl of the Danube mercifully extinguished a life for which there was no room on earth. More charitable tales have been told of his conduct. He had gone to examine the river-bank—a cannon-ball had startled his horse, and he had fallen into the river; or again that he sought in its wave the death he found.

From seven o'clock, when he disappeared, till nearly eight the twenty-seven battalions in Blenheim had no leader, and received no orders. Meanwhile they were attacked on every side. Three or four battalions of British infantry under Lord Orkney, with the Greys and the 5th Dragoons and four guns, had cut off all retreat shortly after seven o'clock. Cutts, Churchill, and Orkney assaulted continually. Orkney from the back of the village reached the church-yard, the Buffs in the van, while at the same time every cannon and howitzer within reach fired into the crowded streets from the north and the east. All the assailants were driven out. M. de Blansac now assumed command, and strenuous efforts were made to sally forth at several points. The fire of the surrounding troops, which were constantly reinforced, shattered the heads of every formation. The three British Generals, working in spontaneous combination, all realized the tremendous prize they had in their grip. A French brigade which had actually debouched was brought to parley, and its commander allowed himself to be sent in to bring the rest to reason. Agitated argument began about capitulation. Orkney, whose line across the rear of the village was none too strong, used bold language. Resistance was impossible. The Duke, he said, was coming with the whole army. All must surrender at once as prisoners of war. The one concession granted by Churchill, to whom the issue was referred, was that the officers should not be searched.

The grief and fury of these unbeaten troops have often been described. The regiment of Navarre burned its standards, and many officers refused to sign the convention; but this could hardly avail them much. Before nine o'clock the surrender was complete. It was not till then that Marlborough's orders arrived. The Duke, concerned at the very great numbers he now knew to be in the place, would run no risks. All the troops were to lie on their arms, and by morning he would bring the entire army. But the work had already been completed by his competent lieutenants.

*　　*　　*

Colonel Parke rode fast across Europe, spreading the good tidings [the victory of Blenheim] through the German and Dutch cities as he passed. On the morning of the 10th/21st [August, 1704] he delivered his note to Sarah at St. James's, who sent him on with it at a gallop to Windsor. Queen Anne sat in the big bay-window of the long gallery overlooking the Terrace, and serious must have been her thoughts. Here, at the summit of England's war effort, many grievous pressures met in a sovereign's breast. It was but five days before that she had been forced to assent to the Security Act of the Scots Parliament with all the injury which it threatened to her island. She knew that far away in Germany Mr. Freeman meant to strike some blow that should kill or cure. Rulers in constitutional states hear tales from many quarters, and the Queen understood only too well that the entire political system of her reign was under grave and pent-up challenge. She could read the stress of the times in Mr. Montgomery's anxious eyes. With all her patient courage and, let us add, Stuart obstinacy—she had sustained the men she trusted against the gathering antagonism of Parliament and society, and amid the growing degeneration of her affairs both at home and abroad.

A scarlet horseman has crossed the river: news of battle is in the air. They bring the weary messenger to her presence. He falls on his knee, but before he speaks she knows that all is well. He hands her Marlborough's note to Sarah, and tells her that with his own eyes he has seen the first army of France broken into flight and ruin, and the celebrated Marshal Tallard led off prisoner by the Duke's officers.

This was no regular dispatch. That would follow in a day or so. It was but a message to the Cockpit circle; but as the Queen read its pencilled lines she knew that something very great had happened to her country and to the world. It was the custom to give the messenger of victory five hundred guineas, but Colonel Parke, invited to name his reward, asked instead a miniature of the Queen. His request was granted, and in addition Anne gave him a thousand guineas in her relief and joy.

Meanwhile from Whitehall Godolphin spread the news throughout the town. The cannon of the Tower were fired; the bells were rung; copies of Marlborough's note, struck off upon the presses, passed from hand to hand. A wave of enthusiasm swept all classes. The streets were filled with cheering crowds. Bonfires and illuminations disputed the night. Nor were these rejoicings unwarranted. Indeed, they arose from the smallest part of what had happened. Every one could understand that the Grand Monarch had had a drubbing, and that Marlborough had caught his famous general, old Tallard, the Ambassador, well known at St. James's, and packed him in his coach. But few could measure the consequences, and none could foresee how the fortunes of Britain would now broaden through the centuries.

Blenheim is immortal as a battle not only because of the extraordinary severity of the fighting of all the troops on the field all day long, and the overwhelming character of the victory, but because it changed the political axis of the world. This only gradually became apparent. Even a month after all the facts were known, measured, and discounted, scarcely anyone understood what transformations had been wrought. Until that August day the statesmen of every country must contemplate the prospect of the Elector of Bavaria supplanting the House of Hapsburg in the Imperial crown, with Munich instead of Vienna as the capital of Central Europe. Yet this Prince, should he become so bright a luminary, would be himself a planet only in the system of the Sun King. Spain and Italy would have their appointed orbits around the parent of light. The vast new regions opening beyond the oceans to the consciousness of man, those distant constellations, would shine with brightening gleams upon a French Monarchy of Europe and a dominant Gallican Church. The sullen and awkward Dutch and boorish English would perforce conform to the august design. Their recalcitrancy would be but the measure of their sufferings.

All this glittering fabric fell with a crash. From the moment when Louis XIV realized, as he was the first to realize, the new values and proportions which had been established on 13 August [1704], he decided to have done with war. Although long years of bloodshed lay before him, his object henceforward was only to find a convenient and dignified exit from the arena in which he had so long stalked triumphant. His ambition was no longer to gain a glorious dominion, but only to preserve the usurpations which he regarded as his lawful rights, and in the end this again was to shrink to no more than a desperate resolve to preserve the bedrock of France.

★     ★     ★

The terror of the French armies was broken. Forty years of successful war, the invasion of so many countries, few and minor reverses, and these repaired by victory upon a hundred fields, had brought a renown before which, even while they still resisted, the most stubborn opponents bowed their heads. French generals and French troops believed themselves to be, and were largely accepted throughout the Continent as, a superior military order. All this was changed by the Danube battle. Here was defeat, naked, brutal, murderous; defeat in spite of numbers; defeat by manoeuvre and defeat by force. The prolonged severity of the fighting and the extraordinary losses of the victors proved the reality of the test. But to all this was added the sting of disgrace and ridicule. A surrender in mass of the finest infantry of France, the most famous regiments disarmed wholesale on the battlefield, the shameful confusion and collapse of command in Blenheim village, the overthrow of the French cavalry front to front by sword against pistol, their flight while their comrades perished—all these hideous disillusionings had now to be faced. And with them also arose the red star of the island troops. Their discipline, their fighting energy, their readiness to endure extraordinary losses, the competence and team-play of their officers, the handiness of their cavalry and field artillery, their costly equipment and lavish feeding, their self-assured, unaffected disdain of foreigners, became the talk of Europe.

In the first days of the new year (3 January [1705]) all London crowded to a pageant the like of which England had never seen. [A celebration of the victories of Marlborough's troops.] A long procession of the household troops and footguards bore the captured standards and colours from the Tower to Westminster Hall amid the salutes of the "great guns" and the cheers of the people. The thirty-four French standards were borne by the gentlemen of the Blues, and the 128 French colours by the pikemen of the Guards. Through the city, down the Strand, along "the Pall-Mall", before St. James's Palace, through St. James's Mews, they marched into the Park, where two salvos of forty cannon were fired. Queen Anne had let it be known that she would see them pass, and did so from Lord Fitzharding's lodgings in the Palace. These banners of mighty France, that nation of twenty millions, whom men in middle age could remember as England's disdainful paymaster, were received and set up in Westminster Hall for all to see. But more significant than this well-organized ceremonial was the temper of the masses who lined the route or thronged behind the procession. The foreign Ambassadors, bred in countries where Court, nobles, and magnates counted for all, were struck by a manifestation of a national self-consciousness unique among the nations. Here was a society which did not end with the powerful and the rich, which descended through every class of citizen down to the very poorest and most humble, all of whose hearts responded to the feeling that it was *their* victory, that *their* cause had triumphed, and that *their* England was growing great. Even while foreign observers cavilled with some reason that the London populace claimed for themselves a victory in which their troops had formed but a quarter of the army, they admired the integral force and comprehension of the vigorous islanders, who could quarrel so fiercely with one another and yet rejoice together in national glory.

\*     \*     \*

Ramillies, with its prelude and its sequel, was the most glorious episode in Marlborough's life. Whether as the victorious commander, the sagacious Minister, or the disinterested servant of the allied cause, his personal conduct was noble. Before the battle he had sacrificed as he believed his prospects of a fine campaign in the Low Countries for the sake of the armies in other theatres, and especially for Prince Eugene. He had gained a great battle by consummate art. He had used the military pursuit and the political consequences to such deadly profit as to drive the French out of the Netherlands. After the victory he had handsomely renounced his own interests in order to preserve the harmony of the Alliance. To procure from Max Emmanuel the four French key-fortresses he had not hesitated to throw his own principality of Mindelheim into the scale. How vain are those writers in so many lands who suppose that the great minds of the world in their supreme activities are twisted or swayed by sordid or even personal aims. These, indeed, may clog their footsteps along the miry road of life; but soaring on the wings of victory all fall away. It is Marlborough's true glory that the higher his fortune, the higher rose his virtue. In 1706 he shines as genius and hero, wise, valiant, and stainless, striving only for the best for England and the best for all.

*   *   *

England had now [the winter of 1708] been raised by Marlborough's victories to the summit of the world. Many living men could remember the island as a paid dependant of France. The Constitution and the religion of the nation had repeatedly lain under mortal challenge. Only twenty years before, with Ireland in rebellion and Scotland separate and estranged, the English people, led by the aristocracy, had been reduced to the desperate remedy of bringing in a foreign ruler and foreign troops to protect them against betrayal by their own sovereign and invasion by Louis XIV. Even after the wars of William III, as it seemed but yesterday, the nation, disarmed by an insensate economy, had quaked to see the Grand Monarch occupying without the firing of a shot all the fortresses of the Spanish Netherlands, and adding, apparently without opposition, the mighty empire of Spain and the Indies to the already paramount and overweening power of France. Protestantism and Parliamentary institutions crouched behind the dykes of

Holland or stood ill-guarded and downcast beyond the Strait of Dover. The discordant petty states of Germany could make no headway against the gleaming arms and all-embracing diplomacy of France. Not only European hegemony, but even the dominion of the whole world seemed about to fall to a glorified, triumphant, Catholic ruler, as intolerant as he was cultured, as cruel and ambitious as he was strong, and sole autocrat of twenty million Frenchmen.

One man and three battles had transformed all. The Grand Monarch was beaten to his knees. His armies would no longer face in the open field the men who had conquered at Blenheim, Ramillies, and Oudenarde, or the Commander who led them. The whole of the Netherlands, all their fortresses, had been regained and now stood as the barrier of salvation for world causes dear to Dutch and English hearts. The three parts of the British Isles were united under one Queen and one Parliament. The French fleets had been driven from the seas. The Mediterranean had become an English lake. The treasures of the ocean, the wonders of the New World, seemed to be the appointed inheritance of the islanders.

An intense desire to take part in these splendid events inspired the nobility, the country gentlemen, and even the city merchants. There was a galaxy of talent at the disposal of the Crown. Not merely profit, though profit there was in plenty, but even more fame and the chance to attempt great deeds, allured with their magnetic spell ability and rank. Eloquence in Parliament, valour in the field or afloat, wealth, broad acres, ancient lineage, bore the eager competitors to the arena. Political intrigue, party faction, royal favour, prescribed the conditions of their strife for power. The Continent laboured to understand the English political system. The eyes of Europe were fixed upon the Court of Queen Anne. Every word, every whisper, every gesture, every combination or counter-combination of the leading figures of British public life, were eagerly reported. Above all, the minutest indications of the Queen's mood and leanings were reported far and wide. The persons she saw, the bishops she made, the honours she bestowed, the jewels she chose to wear, the bedchamber women who presented them to her—all these were scrutinized by rulers of a score of states with as much attention as was paid to the march of a substantial corps from one theatre to another.

We have now [the end of 1708] reached the culmination of the eighteenth-century world war. The foundations of Marlborough's authority in England had been destroyed, and the national and European cause which he served was triumphant. His power had gone, but his work was done. We have witnessed the spectacle of a league of twenty-six signatory states successfully resisting and finally overcoming a mighty coherent military despotism. It was a war of the circumference against the centre. When we reflect upon the selfish aims, the jealousies and shortcomings of the Allies, upon their many natural divergent interests, upon the difficulties of procuring common and timely agreement upon any single necessary measure, upon the weariness moral and physical which drags down all prolonged human effort; when we remember that movement was limited to the speed of a marching soldier or a canal barge, and communication or correspondence to that of a coach, or at the best of a horseman, we cannot regard it as strange that Louis XIV should so long have sustained his motto, "*Nec pluribus impar*". Lying in his central station with complete control of the greatest nation of the world in one of its most remarkable ebullitions, with the power to plan far in advance, to strike now in this quarter, now in that, and above all with the certainty of implicit obedience, it is little wonder how well and how long he fought. The marvel is that any force could have been found in that unequipped civilization of Europe to withstand, still less to subdue him. In Marlborough the ramshackle coalition had found, if not its soul, its means of effective expression, its organic unity, and its supreme sword. Thus the circle of quaking states and peoples, who had almost resigned themselves to an inevitable overlordship, became a ring of fire and steel, which in its contraction wore down and strangled their terrible foe.

This result had in fact been achieved. Behind the lines of the French armies, beneath the glitter of Versailles, all was exhausted, all lay in ruin. The Grand Monarch still stood magnificent at bay; but his heart was broken. When he looked out upon his wasted realm, upon the depleted manhood of France, upon his pillaged treasury and half-tilled fields, upon his cowed armies and sunken fleet, despair and remorse swelled upon him in a dark flood, and peace at any price became his dearest, all-compelling wish.

Marlborough, Heinsius, Eugene, the Triumvirate of executive action, could not as yet see the dust and ashes which lay behind the fortresses, the rivers, and the mountain-chains of the French front. They saw that front was still unbroken; they were sure it was crumbling. One more campaign, one effort stronger than any yet made, and the prize of their long toils would be won. This was their conviction at the fall of Ghent and Bruges. They could not foresee the crowning calamity of the great frost which was to fall on France in the winter of 1708. Neither, on the other hand, were they or any of their generation conscious of the new strength which the French people could supply if a war of monarchical aggrandizement should be transformed into a war of national survival. They all three under-rated both the present prostration and the latent final resources of France. None of these facts presented themselves to the breathless actors in this struggle in the clear light, shape, and proportion in which we now see them. They could not tell how soon or with what exertions they were going to win. But that they were winning, and had only to hold together and drive on, was their absolute conviction.

But when they looked behind them to their own countries they saw themselves at the last gasp. The Empire, including Austria and all Germany, could not put forty thousand men in the field, apart from the troops paid for by the Sea Powers. The Dutch were worn to the bone by the endless struggles of the Republic. Their Barrier was in their hands to take and hold. They longed for peace. All future war-effort depended upon Marlborough and England, and from this moment Marlborough and England were no longer one.

The Captain-General and the Lord Treasurer, Marlborough and Godolphin, had spent upon the seven campaigns all their political capital. The Queen was estranged. Instead of being their strength, she was henceforth their bane. Sarah and Godolphin were her aversion, Marlborough a splendid but oppressive fact. The Tories banished from power, united by misfortune, nursed revenge. The Whigs had arrived. They had forced their way into what the Queen regarded as her own apartments. They had gained control of all the great offices and assets of State, including the services of Marlborough. They had the majorities of the Lords and Commons at their backs. They cared nothing for Sarah and Godolphin; for these were blunted tools which could be thrown aside. They knew they owed nothing to Marlborough. He constantly vowed that he would align himself with no party. In so far as he had used his influence in their behalf upon the Queen it had been in vain. He had not only had no part in their success, but had even been grievously offended by the actual methods by which they had succeeded in gaining their ends. They recognized him as their greatest possession. They were sure he was in their hands, or at least that without them his power was at an end. He knew this too. He was inflexibly resolved not to play the game of any party. From the bottom of his heart, and with forty years' experience in court, camp, and council, he despised both Whigs and Tories with a cordiality which history has readily understood. Henceforward he regarded himself not as a leader, but as a functionary. He would serve the government as a soldier or as a diplomatist. He would not be answerable for their relations with the Queen or with Parliament. He would lead such armies as they provided, and negotiate such treaties as they prescribed. In this humbler guise he might still procure the means to fight the final campaign and march to Paris.

\*      \*      \*

Europe was appalled at the slaughter of Malplaquet. The battle of Landen, to which its features have sometimes been compared, had not been nearly so bloody. The losses of the Allies were returned at twenty-four thousand officers and men; those of the French were not fewer than twelve thousand, and probably nearer fifteen thousand. Not until Borodino in 1812 was the carnage of this day surpassed. Our modern mass minds, brutalized by the tenfold figures of the [first] Great War, spread over wider fronts and often weeks of fighting, measure only with some difficulty the shock which the intricate polite society of the old world sustained. Upon no one was the impression of the slaughter more deeply marked than upon Marlborough. It disturbed his mind; it affected his health; it changed his sense of values. As he rode through the ghastly woods of Taisnières, or up the trough across which the Dutch had attacked, the heaps of stripped corpses affected him profoundly.

All his long years of war—almost from childhood—had not been able to impart to Marlborough that detachment from human suffering which has often frozen the hearts of great captains. Considering all the rough work he had had to do, he was astonishingly sensitive. He had none of the fanatical ruthlessness of Cromwell at Wexford and Drogheda. He could not, like Napoleon on the field of Eylau, remark unconcernedly upon the physique of the dead. He was unmanned by the plight of the wounded, of whom at least fifteen thousand of all nations and both armies were left upon his hands. "I have hardly had time to sleep, being tormented by the several nations for care to be taken of their wounded." His resources and the science of those days were hopelessly inadequate. For days the woods were crawling with shattered beings. From all sides it is testified that he did his utmost to succour them. He invited Boufflers to send waggons without formality or delay to take back all French wounded, officers or men, upon the simple promise not to serve again. He sent back the wounded Irish himself. He took all the money in his military chest and spent it on relief. His behaviour at this time was greatly respected in all countries. It was known how hard and well he had fought in the battle, and also that his compassion for the wounded was sincere.

Marlborough, like his army, was morally and physically exhausted by the battle. He had fought it with all the skill and vehemence he had shown at Blenheim. His plans had proved successful. He had won at every point. The enemy had been beaten out of all their defences and driven from the field as a result of the heart-shaking struggle. But they had not been routed: they had not been destroyed. They had got off as an army, and, indeed, as a proud army. They retreated, but they cheered. They were beaten, but they boasted.

Villars has been blamed by many French writers for fighting a defensive battle; but what he did was in fact to make the best use of his forces. In particular Feuquières, the most pretentious, censorious, and misleading of military critics, has outlined fancy schemes either for a French attack beyond the woods or for a broader line of defence behind them. Modern thought may, on the contrary, regard Villars's decision as both simple and sensible, as all great things in war should be. Unable to face the Allies in the open, he contrived to bring about the main trial of strength under conditions which were most costly to them. Resting his wings upon the woods and covering his centre with intermittent entrenchments, he presented a front which no army but that commanded by Marlborough and Eugene, with superior numbers and eight years of unbroken success behind them, would have dared to attack. He exacted from the Allies a murderous toll of life by his entrenchments and abattis; but all the time he fought a manoeuvre battle around and among these created or well-selected obstacles. By a prodigy of valour, tactical skill, and bloodshed they drove him from the field. The victory was theirs; but not one of the allied generals, if he could have gone back upon the past, would have fought the battle, and none of them ever fought such a battle again.

All England awaited the arrival of King George I. An epoch glorious in its prime, shameful in its close, had passed away. The famous Age of Anne, the supreme manifestation of British genius, its virtues and vices, in peace and war, by land and sea, in politics, letters, and architecture, was over. A new scene opens with different patterns, lights, and values. All the old actors quit the stage—some in ignominy, some in splendour. Younger men of high gifts and proved capacity present the drama of national life after the triumphs and intense passions of the war. Milder, easier, more comfortable, less romantic themes rule in British society for many years. England had gained heights in the world that she had never reached before. She sat exhausted after prodigious exertions upon these commanding uplands, and regathered her strength and poise.

The contrary wind which had detained Marlborough for a momentous fortnight was at last changed to "fair". He landed at Dover on 2 August, and there learned the news of the Queen's death. On this homecoming he did not attempt concealment.

He was everywhere received with demonstrations of welcome and regard. Notables and populace thronged the streets of every town and village through which he and Sarah passed, and when they entered the City they were escorted by hundreds of gentlemen on horseback, a body of grenadiers, the civic authorities, a long train of attendant coaches, and an immense concourse of all classes, who accompanied him with loud, unceasing cheers, drowned amid which, we are assured, there were also boos.

\* \* \*

The span of mortals is short, the end universal; and the tinge of melancholy which accompanies decline and retirement is in itself an anodyne. It is foolish to waste lamentations upon the closing phase of human life. Noble spirits yield themselves willingly to the successively falling shades which carry them to a better world or to oblivion. Of course, it is more becoming for a warrior to die in battle on the field, in command, with great causes in dispute and strong action surging round; like Charles XII at Frederikshald, like Berwick at Philippsburg, or Wolfe on the Heights of Abraham, or Nelson at Trafalgar. But these swift exits are not in human choice. Great captains must take their chance with the rest. Caesar was assassinated by his dearest friend. Hannibal was cut off by poison. Frederick the Great lingered out years of loneliness in body and soul. Napoleon rotted at St. Helena. Compared with these, Marlborough had a good and fair end to his life.

Early in June, 1722, at Windsor Lodge, he was attacked with further paroxysms, and though his reason was unclouded, his strength began to fail rapidly. He was aware that his end was near.

He lay quietly or in a coma for some hours, and died with the dawn of 16 June in the seventy-third year of his age.

His funeral was a scene of solemn splendour and martial pomp. Sarah would not accept the offers of the State, wishing to bear the expense herself; but the nobility, the Army, and the College of Heralds surrounded and followed the funeral car as it made its way through immense crowds to Westminster Abbey. Eight Dukes, Knights of the Garter, followed the Duke of Montagu, chief mourner, and in the procession walked Cadogan, now Commander-in-Chief, and a group of generals who had shared equally in Marlborough's glories and misfortunes. The coffin was lowered into the vault at the east end of Henry VII's Chapel, and rested there for some years.

Marlborough's death stirred his old soldiers wherever they might be.

Sarah survived John by twenty-two years. She lived entirely for her husband's memory. At sixty-two she was still remarkably handsome, and her high, keen intelligence also exercised a powerful attraction. Although hitherto she had never cared for Blenheim, she made it her duty to fulfil in letter and in spirit Marlborough's wishes for its completion. She threw herself into this task with characteristic efficiency, and the fifty thousand pounds he had left to finish it went double as far as equal sums spent by the government in previous years. Besides this she herself built a triumphal arch at the entrance to the park from Woodstock. On the rise opposite the palace she set up a pillar of a hundred and thirty feet, surmounted by a leaden statue of the Duke, which looks from the ground no larger than human, but is actually twenty-five feet high. On three sides of the plinth of this fine monument she had inscribed the Acts of Parliament setting forth the gift of Blenheim by the nation and Queen Anne, and on the fourth an inscription recounting the ten campaigns. This inscription is said to be by the hand of Bolingbroke, and is a masterpiece of compact and majestic statement. In fact, it would serve as a history in itself, were all other records lost.

She was no doubt the richest woman alive in any country, having at least £40,000 a year in the commanding currency of those days. She used her fortune to sustain her ideas and assert her power. She lived in some state in her various homes, and even built, and rebuilt to her liking, a fifth house for herself at Wimbledon. She also gave largely to charity. She built almshouses in Woodstock and in St. Albans, and helped a surprising number of people whose misfortunes or qualities appealed to her, some of whose cases have become known. She administered her estates with broad-minded capacity, and distributed her favours among her descendants according to her likes and dislikes, both of which continued to be vehement. Her most remarkable gift was the ten thousand pounds and landed property with which she presented William Pitt, then comparatively a small figure in national affairs, in order to make him independent of Court or Cabinet favour. Although her relish for his attacks upon Walpole affords one explanation of her motive, it is nevertheless an extraordinary fact that in the bloom of youth and in extreme old age her instinct discerned undiscovered genius in the two greatest builders of British imperial power.

After her death, in accordance with her wish, Marlborough's body was removed from King Henry VII's Chapel in Westminster Abbey to the tomb she had built at Blenheim. There they lie side by side in victorious peace.

# GREAT CONTEMPORARIES

*Most of these studies of famous men were written in the period
1928-31, others a few years later. The first edition of the
book was published in 1937 and the enlarged edition in 1939.
The studies reveal the author's shrewd judgment of the
characters, personalities, careers and achievements of many
strangely different men ranging from the first, on the Earl
of Rosebery, to the last, on President Roosevelt.*

★

## THE EARL OF ROSEBERY

IT MIGHT be said that Lord Rosebery outlived his future by ten
years and his past by more than twenty. The brilliant prospects
which had shone before him until he became Prime Minister in 1894
were dispersed by the break-up of his government and the decisive
defeat of the Liberal Party in 1895. The part he took as an Imperialist
and a patriot in supporting, four years later, the South African War
destroyed his hold upon the regard and confidence of a large section
of the Radical masses. His resignation of the Leadership of the
Liberal Party had already released them from their allegiance. By
his definite declaration against Home Rule when Mr. Balfour's fall
in 1905 was approaching, he cut himself off deliberately and resolutely
from all share in the impending Liberal triumph and long reign of
power. He severed himself by purposeful action from his friends
and followers. "Content to let occasion die", he withdrew from all
competition for leadership in the political arena; he erected barriers
against his return which he meant to be insurmountable; he isolated
himself in cool and unaffectedly disdainful detachment. It was known
only too well that overtures would be useless. By 1905 his political
career was closed for ever. It was only in 1929 that his long life
ended.

Dwelling in his wide and beautiful estates, moving frequently
from one delightful house and one capacious library to another, he

lived to sustain the burden of an eightieth birthday, lighted by the refinements of profound and astonishingly wide-ranging literary knowledge, amused by the Turf, and cheered and companioned by his children and his grandchildren. The afflictions of old age fell successively with gathering weight upon him in his ever-deepening retirement; and when he died his name and actions had faded entirely from the public mind, and were only revived and presented to the eyes of a new generation by the obituary notices. But those actions, and still more the character and personality which lay behind them, are worthy of most careful study, not only for the sake of their high merit, but at least as much for their limitations.

Lord Rosebery was probably my father's greatest friend. They were contemporaries at Eton and at Oxford. Although apparently divided by party, they moved in the same society, had many friends in common, and pursued the same pleasures and sports—of which racing was ever the sovereign. Their correspondence was sparkling and continuous, and their intimate personal relations were never affected by the fierce political struggles of the eighties, or by any vicissitudes of fortune.

I inherited this friendship, or rather the possibility of renewing it in another generation. I was anxious to cultivate it for many reasons, of which the first was to learn more about my father from his contemporary, his equal and his companion. With some at least of those feelings of awe and attraction which led Boswell to Dr. Johnson, I sought occasions to develop the acquaintance of childhood into a grown-up friendship. At first he did not seem to approve of me: but after the South African War, when I had at least become well known and was a young M.P., he began to show me marked kindness. The biography of my father by which I was soon absorbed opened a wide and fertile field of common interest. He assisted actively in the enterprise, drew richly upon his fund of choice reminiscence, collected letters and documents, read proofs, criticized sympathetically but penetratingly both the subject and the work. This formed a theme of common interest between us and built a bridge across the gulf of a different generation.

During the years of my literary task, from 1900 to 1905, I was often his guest in all his houses, at Mentmore, in Berkeley Square, at the Durdans hard by Epsom Downs, on the Firth of Forth at

Dalmeny, at his shooting lodge, Rosebery; and we also met year after year on long visits to common friends in the delicious autumn of the Scottish Highlands. Politics provided additional links and ties; for we were both adrift from our parties. He was out of sympathy with the Liberals: I was soon quarrelling with the Tories. We could both toy with the dream of some new system and grouping of men and ideas, in which one could be an Imperialist without swallowing Protection, and a social reformer without Little Englandism or class bitterness. We had certainly that solid basis of agreement and harmony of outlook upon middle courses, which is shared by many sensible people and was in those days abhorrent to party machines. Need one add that the party machines always prove the stronger?

He made many things not only arresting, but merry. He seemed as much a master of trifles and gossip as of weighty matters. He was keenly curious about every aspect of life. Sportsman, epicure, bookworm, literary critic, magpie collector of historical relics, appreciative owner of veritable museums of art treasures, he never needed to tear a theme to tatters. In lighter vein he flitted jauntily from flower to flower like a glittering insect, by no means unprovided with a sting. And then in contrast, out would come his wise, matured judgments upon the great men and events of the past. But these treats were not always given. He was at his best with two or three and on his day; and sometimes in larger company he seemed shy and ill at ease. When he was out of humour, he could cast a chill over all, and did not hesitate to freeze and snub. On these occasions his face became expressionless, almost a slab, and his eyes lost their light and fire. One saw an altogether different person. But after a bit one knew the real man was there all the time, hiding perversely behind a curtain. And all the more agreeable was it when he came out.

Hardest of all is it to revive the impression which he produced upon his hearers when dealing with the greatest affairs. His life was set in an atmosphere of tradition. The Past stood ever at his elbow and was the counsellor upon whom he most relied. He seemed to be attended by Learning and History, and to carry into current events an air of ancient majesty. His voice was melodious and deep, and often, when listening, one felt in living contact with the centuries which are gone, and perceived the long continuity of our island tale.

Rosebery's Eton tutor in something of a spirit of prophecy said of him that he "sought the palm without the dust". This was not true in the sense in which the phrase is often used—that of avoiding hard work. Rosebery was capable of very hard work and of long hours of daily concentration both on politics and literature. He sought indeed the palm, but the dust had never come his way; and when in high station the compromises, the accommodations, the inevitable acquiescence in inferior solutions, were forced upon him, he was not toughened against these petty vexations, or trained to see them in their true light. Although equipped with capacious knowledge of the part of a modern statesman, he was essentially a survival from a vanished age, when great Lords ruled with general acceptance and strove, however fiercely, only with others like themselves. While he stood under the aegis of Mr. Gladstone, the Radical masses presented themselves as devoted, loyal, enthusiastic adherents. It was not until the Gladstonian spell had passed away that he realized how very imperfect was his contact with them. He did not think as they thought, or feel as they felt, or understand the means of winning their unselfish and unbounded allegiance. He understood the hard conditions of their lives, and was intellectually indignant at their wrongs and sufferings. His mind ranged back across centuries of their history, and selected with shrewd and wise judgment the steps required to sustain their progress and welfare. But actually to handle them, to wrestle with them, to express their passion and win their confidence, this he could not do.

The milestones of Rosebery's public life stand forth abruptly along the track. He was one of the first Whig nobles who as a young man embraced the Liberal and democratic conceptions of the later nineteenth century. The stir and enthusiasm of Mr. Gladstone's Midlothian campaign carried him into politics. There he was, on the spot, a gifted, bright figure in Edinburgh and Scotland, thirty-one or thirty-two, with all that rank and fortune could bestow. And here was the Grand Old Man, to listen to whose words rich and poor travelled for days and stood in rain and mist for hours, fighting in Rosebery's own Scottish domain for what seemed to be a world cause. Rosebery plunged into politics as "a chivalrous adventure". "When I found myself in this evil-smelling bog, I was always trying to extricate myself. That is the secret of what people used to call my lost opportunities and so forth."

These rather bitter words written in the years of eclipse did not in any way represent the effort, the industry, the resolution or the robust citizenship which Rosebery contributed for a quarter of a century to British and Imperial affairs.

The disharmonies and the eventual rupture of his political career sprang from his proud and at times supercilious inability to subject himself to the mechanism of modern democracy and to the exigencies of the party caucus. Had he possessed Mr. Baldwin's phlegmatic capacity of putting up with a score of unpleasant and even humbling situations, in order to be master of something very big at the end of a blue moon, he would indeed have been not only a Prophet but a Judge in Israel. He was far too sensitive, too highly strung, for these compromises and submissions. He was a child and brilliant survivor of the old vanishing, and now vanished, oligarchic world which across the centuries had built the might and the freedom of Britain. He was often palpably out of touch with his environment; perhaps that is no censure upon him. It must however be emphasized that physically he did not stand the stresses well. In times of crisis and responsibility his active, fertile mind and imagination preyed upon him. He was bereft of sleep. He magnified trifles. He failed to separate the awkward incidents of the hour from the long swing of events, which he so clearly understood. Toughness when nothing particular was happening was not the form of fortitude in which he excelled. He was unduly attracted by the dramatic, and by the pleasure of making a fine gesture. He would not join Mr. Gladstone's Government in 1880, for that might seem to be the direct reward of his share in the Midlothian campaign. He volunteered to join after the death of General Gordon at Khartoum, because then it was a case of "all hands to the pumps". In a wearing ordeal his thoughts strayed to the fine speech he could make on resignation. And then he was of course never given the chance of wielding real power. He never held office with a large, loyal, solid majority behind him. He never had a united party at his back, and could never plan ahead for two or three years at a time.

How these Victorians busied themselves and contended about minor things! What long, brilliant, impassioned letters they wrote each other about refined personal and political issues of which the modern Juggernaut progression takes no account! They never had to face, as we have done, and still do, the possibility of national ruin. Their main foundations were never shaken. They dwelt in an age of British splendour and unchallenged leadership. The art of government was exercised within a limited sphere. World-revolution, mortal defeat, national subjugation, chaotic degeneration, or even national bankruptcy, had not laid steel claws upon their sedate, serene, complacent life. Rosebery flourished in an age of great men and small events.

It was in the sphere of Foreign Affairs that Rosebery found his home. Here he was Master. He combined the knowledge of the historian or of a Foreign Office official with the practical understanding and the habit of command of a Statesman. He did not have to form his views from the files of papers set before him. He knew the whole long history about how all these nations had lived their lives for two or three hundred years, and what they had fought about, and which ones had been subjugated and were boiling with ancient wrongs under the smooth surface of modernism. He knew with pregnant conviction much that other leading men in England —and may we add the United States—only found out during and after the Peace Conference. He knew not only the British share in bygone events, but the whole European tale. He felt in his bones, with his finger-tips, all that subterranean, subconscious movement whereby the vast antagonisms of the Great War were slowly, remorselessly, inexorably assembling. He had laboriously inspected the foundations of European Peace; he saw where the cracks were, and where a subsidence would produce a crash. His heart responded instinctively to any readjustment or disturbance of the balance of power. In Rosebery's time Foreign Affairs and war dangers were invested with a false glamour and shrouded in opaque ignorance. But when some schoolteacher was dismissed in Upper Silesia Rosebery said to me, "All Prussia has been shaken." When Delcassé was forced to resign, he said that the German Army corps were afoot. And when Lord Lansdowne signed the Anglo-French Agreement of August, 1904, with all the prestige of the Conservative Party behind him, and amid the tributes of Liberals and Pacifists all over the world, Rosebery said in public that "it was far more likely to lead to War than to Peace."

There was another sphere in which Rosebery moved with confidence and distinction. He was one of those men of affairs who add to the unsure prestige of a minister and the fleeting successes of an orator the more enduring achievements of literature. Some of his most polished work is found in his Rectorial Addresses and in his appreciations of great poets and writers like Burns and Stevenson. His private letters, of which he wrote so many, are alive with Byronic wit and colour. His style, lucid, pointed, musical and restrained, was an admirable vehicle for conveying his treasure of historical research to the world. He has enriched our language with a series of biographical studies, terse, pregnant and authoritative, which will long be read with pleasure and instruction on both sides of the Atlantic. *Pitt, Peel, Randolph Churchill,* are literary gems, and on the larger scale *Chatham* and *Napoleon* make definite contributions to the judgment of history. Yet even in this field there are some characteristic, self-imposed limitations. He never planned or executed a work of the first magnitude—a work to hold the field against all comers for a century. His taste, discernment, and learning were directed to partial tasks, and in these he attracts and stimulates the reader, only to leave his main curiosities unsatisfied. Rosebery's *Chatham* ends before the great period has begun: his *Napoleon* begins only when it has ended. We are excited; we demand more; we seek the climax. But the author has retired again to his solitudes. The curtain is pulled down and the gleaming lights extinguished— and now, alas, extinguished for ever.

The war he had dreaded came to pass by the paths he had foreseen, but his heart beat high for Britain. His younger son, the charming, gifted Neil, was killed in Palestine. The old man sank, bowed and broken under the blow. Years of infirmity followed, and what to an Imperial spirit must ever be a pang—powerlessness. A month before the Armistice he had a stroke. He lay unconscious or delirious in a small house in Edinburgh when the bells of victory rang through its streets. The Scots do not easily forget those who have been their leaders. Spontaneously in the joy of the hour a great crowd gathered with torches and beset his door in thousands to share their triumph with him. But he lay stricken, prostrate, paralysed.

He lived for ten years more, and all the qualities of his mind resumed their play. He reached the age of eighty. If he enjoyed life in a mild way from week to week, he also thought of Death as a deliverance. He made one statement which should be helpful to all of us. For some time he had received a special insulin treatment. One day by mistake the dose was doubled. He fell down in a total stupor, and his attendants were sure the end had come. He remained in this condition for many hours. His daughter, Lady Crewe, summoned from Paris, reached his bedside the next morning and to her relief and surprise found him alive with his mental faculties restored. "If this is Death," he said with the air of one who has been on a voyage and made a discovery, "it is absolutely nothing."

He was happy and at peace: but his steps became more weary. Although a religious man, a regular church-goer, and a frequent Communicant, he made one odd, characteristic preparation for his departure. He bade his servant buy a gramophone, and told him that when Death came upon him, he was to make it play the "Eton Boating Song". This was actually done, though perhaps he did not hear it. Thus he wished the gay memories of boyhood to be around him at his end, and thus he set Death in its proper place as a necessary and unalarming process.

## GEORGE BERNARD SHAW

Mr. Bernard Shaw was one of my earliest antipathies. Indeed, almost my first literary effusion, written when I was serving as a subaltern in India in 1897 (it never saw the light of day), was a ferocious onslaught upon him, and upon an article which he had written disparaging and deriding the British Army in some minor war. Four or five years passed before I made his acquaintance. My mother, always in agreeable contact with artistic and dramatic circles, took me to luncheon with him. I was instantly attracted by the sparkle and gaiety of his conversation, and impressed by his eating only fruit and vegetables, and drinking only water. I rallied him on the latter habit, asking: "Do you really never drink any wine at all?" "I am hard enough to keep in order as it is," he replied. Perhaps he had heard of my youthful prejudice against him.

Few people practise what they preach, and no one less so than Mr. Bernard Shaw. Few are more capable of having the best of everything both ways. His spiritual home is no doubt in Russia; his native land is the Irish Free State; but he lives in comfortable England. His dissolvent theories of life and society have been sturdily banished from his personal conduct and his home. No one has ever led a more respectable life or been a stronger seceder from his own subversive imagination. He derides the marriage vow and even at times the sentiment of love itself; yet no one is more happily or wisely married. He indulges in all the liberties of an irresponsible Chatterbox, babbling gloriously from dawn to dusk, and at the same time advocates the abolition of Parliamentary institutions and the setting up of an Iron Dictatorship, of which he would probably be the first victim. It is another case for John Morley's comment upon Carlyle, "the Gospel of silence in thirty volumes by Mr. Wordy". He prattles agreeably with the tame English Socialists, and preens himself with evident satisfaction in the smiles alike of Stalin or Mussolini. He promulgates in stern decree that all incomes should be equalized and that anyone who has more than another is guilty—unconsciously perhaps—of personal meanness, if not fraud; he has always preached the ownership of all forms of wealth by the State; yet when the Lloyd George Budget imposed for the first time the slender beginnings of the super-tax, no one made a louder squawk than this already wealthy Fabian. He is at once an acquisitive capitalist and a sincere Communist. He makes his characters talk blithely about killing men for the sake of an idea; but would take great trouble not to hurt a fly.

He seems to derive equal pleasure from all these contrary habits, poses and attitudes. He has laughed his sparkling way through life, exploding by his own acts or words every argument he has ever used on either side of any question, teasing and bewildering every public he has addressed, and involving in his own mockery every cause he has ever championed. The world has long watched with tolerance and amusement the nimble antics and gyrations of this unique and double-headed chameleon, while all the time the creature was eager to be taken seriously.

If the truth must be told, our British island has not had much help in its troubles from Mr. Bernard Shaw. When nations are fighting for life, when the Palace in which the Jester dwells not uncomfortably is itself assailed, and everyone from prince to groom is fighting on the battlements, the Jester's jokes echo only through deserted halls, and his witticisms and commendations, distributed evenly between friend and foe, jar the ears of hurrying messengers, of mourning women and wounded men. The titter ill accords with the tocsin, or the motley with the bandages. But these trials are over; the island is safe, the world is quiet, and begins again to be free. Time for self-questioning returns; and wit and humour in their embroidered mantles take again their seats at a replenished board. The ruins are rebuilt; a few more harvests are gathered in. Fancy is liberated from her dungeon, and we can afford, thank God, to laugh again. Nay more, we can be proud of our famous Jester, and in regathered security rejoice that we laugh in common with many men in many lands, and thereby renew the genial and innocent comradeship and kinship of mankind. For when all is said and done, it was not the Jester's fault there was a war. Had we all stayed beguiled by his musings and his sallies, how much better off we should be! How many faces we should not have to miss! It is a source of pride to any nation to have nursed one of those recording sprites who can illuminate to the eye of remote posterity many aspects of the age in which we live. Saint, sage, and clown; venerable, profound, and irrepressible, Bernard Shaw receives, if not the salutes, at least the hand-clappings of a generation which honours him as another link in the humanities of peoples, and as the greatest living master of letters in the English-speaking world.

# JOSEPH CHAMBERLAIN

The career of Joseph Chamberlain, that strong actuator of world movements, is divided between the period when he was making his way towards the world scene and the period when he acted upon it. In the first he was a ruthless Radical and, if you challenged him, a Republican; in the second he was a Jingo Tory and Empire Builder. All followed naturally and sincerely from the particular pressures and environment affecting an exceptional being at one stage or the other of his life.

Thus we have Chamberlain the Radical Mayor—far worse than any naughty Socialist of today—who questioned whether he could condescend to drive as Mayor in the carriage which received the Prince of Wales (afterwards King Edward VII) on his visit to Birmingham, and Chamberlain who popularized or promulgated the conception of a vast Empire centring mainly upon the golden circle of the Crown. Thus we have Chamberlain the most competent, the most searching, the most entirely convinced protagonist of Free Trade; and Chamberlain who lighted the torch of Tariff Reform and Food Taxation. An immense force was exerted with complete sincerity in different phases in opposite directions. We have a splendid piebald; first black then white; or in political terms, first Fiery Red, then True Blue.

First there is the tale of "Radical Joe". We see this robust, virile, aggressive champion of change and overturn marching forward into battle against almost all the venerable, accepted institutions of the Victorian epoch. We see him fighting now with a rapier, now with a bludgeon, to establish quite new levels for the political and social status of the mass of the people. In his stride he shrinks from nothing and turns away from no antagonist. The monarchy, the church, the aristocracy, the House of Lords, the "country party", London Society, the limited franchise, the great vested interests and professions—all in their turn became his targets.

But this was no campaign of mere demagogy, of ranting and denouncing, of pushing and brawling. It was the hard, cold, deeply informed effort of a man who, though removed by superior education and an adequate income from the masses, nevertheless under-

508

stood their lives, the pressures under which they bent, the injustices and inequalities which rankled in their bosoms, the appetites and aspirations to which they would respond; and who, with heart-whole resolve, offered himself to them as a leader whom nothing should daunt.

At forty-nine Chamberlain stood on the threshold of a complete change. His outlook upon our national life, which although always intense, had up to this point been narrow and short, broadened and lengthened; and he perceived that the remorseless unfolding of events had proved contrary to expectations both of his youth and of his prime. The rest of his life was to be spent fighting against the forces he had himself so largely set in motion. In 1870 he had made a tremendous onslaught upon Forster's Education Bill. Repulsed by the Church and Mr. Gladstone at the time, he lived to support —reluctantly, no doubt—Balfour's Education Act of 1902, which finally established sectarian education as a vital element in English life. He believed in his early phase that the British monarchy was doomed; he lived to see it the lynch-pin of the entire Imperial structure to the building of which his later years were devoted. As President of the Board of Trade he delivered the most masterly condemnations of Protection and food taxes which are upon record; his memory will be ever associated with their adoption.

In wider spheres his policy led to results he had not foreseen. He was prime mover in the events which produced the South African War, and there are some who say that that war inaugurated an era of armaments and violence which ultimately led to the supreme catastrophe. He was foremost in the denial to Ireland of Home Rule, with the result that a generation later a settlement was reached on terms from which Mr. Gladstone himself would have recoiled and after episodes among the most odious in living memory.

It will be difficult for the present generation to understand the overpowering part which the Home Rule struggle played in the lives of their fathers and grandfathers. The insurgent Ireland that we now see merely as a group of ill-mannered agricultural counties, outside the march of British affairs, in the eighties bestrode the Imperial Parliament. Irish passions, Irish ideals, Irish leaders, Irish crimes, swayed the whole structure of English public life. The Irish parliamentary party, with their wit, their eloquence and their malice, destroyed the ancient and characteristically English procedure of the House of Commons. They riveted world attention upon their actions. They made and unmade governments and statesmen. Like the Praetorians of old, they put the Empire up to auction and knocked it down to the highest bidder. Thus the Irish problem was for more than twenty years the supreme issue. It was the pivot around which the whole political life of England revolved, and men rose or fell in power or fame according as they were able to comprehend how it might be solved or burked.

Between the winters of 1885 and 1886 Chamberlain sustained a succession of staggering blows such as have rarely fallen in our country to the lot of a public man. All the political work of his life was swept away. All his hold upon Radical democracy was destroyed. His most intimate friends and comrades became henceforward his life-long opponents. The political rupture with John Morley, the tragedy of Charles Dilke, broke the circle not only of his public but of his private life and thought. His friendship with Morley had to be preserved across the gulf of party antagonism. His friendship with Dilke was valiantly but vainly extended above the abyss of personal disaster. He had to make friends and work for long bleak years in a narrow grouping with that same Hartington and those same Whigs he had been about to drive from the parliamentary scene. He had to learn the language of those very Tories against whom he had sought to rouse the new electorate.

All these trials show Chamberlain at his best. His warm heart, his constancy, his perfect self-control, his "genius for friendship", as Morley years afterwards called it, all shine amid these stresses. He was a faithful friend. No one differed from him more, or resisted him more consistently, than his comrade and colleague, John Morley. Home Rule, Free Trade, the South African War, furnished ever fresh causes of public strife between them. Yet they preserved their private relation. There never was a year in which they could not find opportunities of meeting, and when they met, they talked with all the freedom and zest of old confederates. Morley had an affection for him which the tumults of politics and the pangs of blows and injuries given and taken in the arena were powerless to affect.

I have many vivid memories of the famous "Joe". He was always very good to me. He had been the friend, foe, and friend again of my father. He was sometimes a foe in my father's days of triumph and sometimes a friend in his days of adversity; but always there had subsisted between them a quarrelsome comradeship and a personal liking. At the time when I looked out of my regimental cradle and was thrilled by politics, Mr. Chamberlain was incomparably the most live, sparkling, insurgent, compulsive figure in British affairs. Above him in the House of Lords reigned venerable, august Lord Salisbury, Prime Minister since God knew when. Beside him on the Government Bench, wise, cautious, polished, comprehending, airily fearless, Arthur Balfour led the House of Commons. But "Joe" was the one who made the weather. He was the man the masses knew. He it was who had solutions for social problems; who was ready to advance, sword in hand if need be, upon the foes of Britain; and whose accents rang in the ears of all the young peoples of the Empire and of lots of young people at its heart.

After he had split the Conservative Party and convulsed the country by raising the Protectionist issue, I had my last important conversation with him. I was writing my father's life, and wrote to him asking for copies of letters in his possession. We were at that time in full political battle, and although I was of small consequence I had attacked him with all the ferocity of youth, face to face in Parliament and throughout the country. I was one of those younger Conservatives most prominent in resisting the policy on which he had set his heart and the last efforts of his life. To my surprise he replied to my letter by suggesting that I should come and stay with him for a night at Highbury to see the documents. So I went, not without some trepidation. We dined alone. With the dessert a bottle of '34 port was opened. Only the briefest reference was made to current controversies. "I think you are quite right," he said, "feeling as you do, to join the Liberals. You must expect to have the same sort of abuse flung at you as I have endured. But if a man is sure of himself, it only sharpens him and makes him more effective." Apart from this our talk lay in the controversies and personalities of twenty years before.

We sat up until two. "Joe" produced diaries, letters and memoranda of the eighties, and as each fragment revived memories of those bygone days, he spoke with an animation, sympathy and charm which delighted me. I think it is a pleasing picture of this old statesman, at the summit of his career and in the hardest of his fights treating with such generous detachment a youthful, active, truculent and, as he well knew, irreconcilable political opponent. I doubt whether the English tradition of not bringing politics into private life has often been carried much farther.

## JOHN MORLEY

John Morley was a Victorian. He grew and flourished in the long era of peace, prosperity and progress which filled Queen Victoria's famous reign. This was the British Antonine Age. Those who were its children could not understand why it had not begun earlier or why it should ever stop. The French Revolution had subsided into tranquillity; the Napoleonic Wars had ended at Waterloo; the British Navy basked in the steady light of Trafalgar, and all the navies of the world together could not rival its sedate strength. The City of London and its Gold Standard dominated the finance of the world. Steam multiplied the power of man; Cottonopolis was fixed in Lancashire; railroads, inventions, unequalled supplies of superior coal, abounded in the island; the population increased; wealth increased; the cost of living diminished; the conditions of the working classes improved with their expanding numbers.

Morley was the intellectual child of John Stuart Mill. He sat at his feet and fed upon his wisdom. "In such ideas as I have about political principles," he said in his Indian Budget Speech of 1907, "the leader of my Federation was Mr. Mill. There he was, a great and benignant lamp of wisdom and humanity, and I and others kindled our modest rushlights at that lamp." To me, when I first saw it, John Morley's "modest rushlight" had become a very bright ray. I admired it without seeking to borrow its flame. I approached near enough to read by its light, and to feel its agreeable, genial, companionable warmth. From 1896 onwards I began to meet him and to delight in his company. Rosebery was often more impressive in conversation; Arthur Balfour always more easy and encouraging; Chamberlain more commanding and forceful; but there was a rich and positive quality about Morley's contributions, and a sparkle of phrase and drama which placed him second to none among the four most pleasing and brilliant men to whom I have ever listened. His manner and aspect were captivating. His art in private was to understand the opposite point of view, and to treat it with so much sympathy and good humour, while adhering to his own, that the hearers were often led to believe themselves in agreement with him, or at any rate that the remaining differences were small and not final. This sometimes led to disappointment; for Morley, though in conversation he paraded and manoeuvred nimbly and elegantly around his own convictions, offering his salutations and the gay compliments of old-time war to the other side, always returned to his fortified camp to sleep.

As a speaker, both in Parliament and on the platform, Morley stood in the front rank of his time. There was a quality about his rhetoric which arrested attention. He loved the pageantry as well as the distinction of words, and many passages in his speeches dwell in my memory. As may be guessed, he was better on a set occasion than in the movement of debate. He pleaded unpopular causes with a courage and sincerity which commanded the respect of the House.

At the India Office he was an autocrat and almost a martinet. After several years, he shaped the first modest proposals for Indian representative government, now known as the "Morley-Minto Reforms". He, the ardent apostle of Irish self-government, felt no sense of contradiction in declaring his hostility to anything like "Home Rule for India". He went out of his way to challenge Radical opinion on this issue and, in an impressive speech, he warned his own supporters of the perils of applying to the vast

Indian scene the principles which he applauded in Ireland and in South Africa. "There is I know a school of thought who say that we might wisely walk out of India, and that the Indians can manage their own affairs better than we can. Anyone, who pictures to himself the anarchy, the bloody chaos that would follow, might shrink from that sinister decision." And again: "When across the dark distances, you hear the sullen roar and scream of carnage an d confusion, your hearts will reproach you with what you have done." All his thought and outlook made a strong impression u pon me. But times have changed, and I have lived to see the chiefs of the Conservative Party rush in where Radical Morley feared to tread.

His literary output was very large. He earned his living by his pen. His celebrated essay on "Compromise" was for many years a guide to Liberal youth, and its insistence on the duty of independent individual judgment in every sphere of life and in respect of every creed and institution is a healthy tonic in these days of totalitarian heresy. He was a formidable critic and reviewer. He edited the series of "Twelve English Statesmen", of which Rosebery's "Pitt" was one. Amid the general chorus of p raise which acclaimed this work, Morley's comment strikes a different note: "Nothing can be more agreeable to read, or more brightly written, in spite of a certain heaviness, due partly to excess of substantives, and partly to too great a desire to impress not only the author's meaning, but his opinion." Tart!

Another and larger series was "English Men of Letters", to which he himself contributed "Burke". His friendship for my father, in whose company he had delighted, induced him to turn a kindly eye upon the proof-sheets of my *Life of Lord Randolph Churchill.* Like Lord Rosebery, he took a keen interest in this record, and I have a file of long and deeply instructive letters of comment and suggestion from him upon it, all written in his magnificent handwriting.

From 1908 onwards my seat in the Cabinet was next to his. Six years of constant, friendly, and to me stimulating propinquity! Week after week, often several times a week, we had faced side by side the national, party, and personal troubles and business of a period of hard political strife. Cabinet neighbours, if they are friends, have a natural tendency to share confidences, especially about their colleagues and their colleagues' performances. Whispered and scribbled comments pass to and fro. Physically they survey the council scene from the same point of view. Personally they become much engaged to one another. And to me John Morley was always a fascinating companion, a man linked with the past, the friend and contemporary of my father, the representative of great doctrines, an actor in historic controversies, a master of English prose, a practical scholar, a statesman-author, a repository of vast knowledge on almost every subject of practical interest. It was an honour and privilege to consult and concert with him on equal terms, across the gulf of thirty-five years of seniority, in the swift succession of formidable and perplexing events.

Such men are not found today. Certainly they are not found in British politics. The tidal wave of democracy and the volcanic explosion of the war have swept the shores bare. I cannot see any figure which resembles or recalls the Liberal statesmen of the Victorian epoch. To make head against the aristocratic predominance of those times, a Lancashire lad, the son of a Blackburn doctor without favour or fortune, had need of every intellectual weapon, of the highest personal address, and of all that learning, courtesy, dignity and consistency could bestow. Nowadays when "one man is as good as another—or better", as Morley once ironically observed, anything will do. The leadership of the privileged has passed away; but it has not been succeeded by that of the eminent. We have entered the region of mass effects. The pedestals which had for some years been vacant have now been demolished. Nevertheless, the world is moving on; and moving so fast that few have time to ask—whither. And to these few only a babel responds.

But in John Morley's prime the course was clear and conscious, and the issues not so large as to escape from human control.

It was from my close and intimate proximity and friendship that I witnessed the horrible impact of the Great War upon the statesman who above all others then alive represented the Victorian Age and the Gladstonian tradition. I found that my neighbour was dwelling in a world which was far removed from the awful reality. At such a juncture his historic sense was no guide; it was indeed an impediment. It was vain to look back to the Crimean War, to the wars of

1866 and 1870, and to suppose.that any of the political reactions which had attended their declaration or course would repeat themselves now. We were in the presence of events without their equal or forerunner in the whole experience of mankind. This frightful, monstrous thing, that had been so long whispered, was now actually upon us. All the greatest armies were mobilizing. Twelve or fourteen millions of men were getting into harness, raising deadly weapons, and rolling forward by every road and railway towards long-appointed destinations.

Morley, resolute for neutrality, not indeed at all costs, but—as it seemed to me—at fatal cost in days, was absorbed by ideas of parley, of the fate of Liberalism, of the party situation. He had spent his life building up barriers against war in Parliament, in the constituencies, and in the national mind. Surely all these ramparts of public opinion would not collapse together. He was old; he was frail; but outside this Cabinet room, were there not forces of Radical democracy strong and fierce enough to make head against the madness that was sweeping across Europe, and even, alas! infecting the Liberal Administration, originally formed by Sir Henry Campbell-Bannerman himself. My responsibility on the other hand was to make sure that whatever else happened or did not happen, the British Fleet was ready and in its proper station in good time. This involved the demanding of certain measures from the Cabinet one after another as they fell due. So there we sat side by side, hour after hour, through this flaming week.

The majority of the Cabinet was for leaving France and Germany and the other Powers great and small to fight it out as they pleased, and Morley found himself looked to as leader by a gathering band. But the issues were clouded and tangled. There was Belgium and the faith of treaties. There were the undefended coasts of France, and the possibility of the German fleet "on our very doorstep" cannonading Calais, while the French battleships as the result of tacit agreement with us were stationed in the Mediterranean. Morley was no doctrinaire or fanatic. The "doorstep" argument weighed with him. It persuaded the Cabinet. John Burns alone resisting and resigning, they agreed unitedly that the Germans should be told we could not allow them in the Channel. This was a far-reaching decision. From that moment Morley, too, was on the slippery slope. The week wore on. The Fleet went silently to its Northern base. The "Precautionary Period" measures were authorized by the Cabinet.

"One of these days," writes Morley, "I tapped Winston on the shoulder, as he took his seat next me. 'Winston, we have beaten you after all.' He smiled cheerfully. Well he might. *O pectora caeca!*"

But it was not me he had to beat. It was the avalanche, the whirlwind, the earthquake, roaring forth in triple alliance. So when later on he told me he must resign, I said in effect that if he would wait for two or three days more, everything would be clear, and we should be in full agreement. The Germans would make everyone easy in his conscience. They would accept all responsibilities and sweep away all doubts. Already their vanguards pouring through Luxembourg approached the Belgian frontier. Nothing could recall or deflect them. They were launched; and the catastrophe now imminent and certain would convince and unite the British Empire as it had never been convinced and united before. "They cannot stop now. If they tried, they would be thrown into utter confusion. They must go on in spite of frontiers, treaties, threats, appeals, through cruelties and horrors, trampling on until they meet the main French Armies and the largest battles of history are fought. Remember all the others are marching too."

I offered to illustrate the position on the map. But he took another line. "You may be right—perhaps you are—but I should be no use in a War Cabinet. I should only hamper you. If we have to fight, we must fight with single-hearted conviction. There is no place for me in such affairs." To this I could find no answer, except to repeat that all would speedily be made plain, and that in forty-eight hours what was going to happen in Belgium, and perhaps in the North Sea, would make him feel quite differently about things. But he persisted. Gently, gaily almost, he withdrew from among us, never by word or sign to hinder old friends or add to the nation's burden.

I can only surmise his action had he taken my counsel. What would have been the effect upon his strong, courageous and authoritarian spirit of the German invasion of Belgium, of the resistance of the Belgian King and people, of the struggle at Liége, of the horrors of Louvain? Personally, I believe he would have marched heart and soul at the head of his fellow-countrymen, if he had waited only for forty-eight hours. But looking back I am glad I did not prevail upon him. It was better for him, for his repute and for the great period and conceptions he embodied, that he should "testify" however impotently, and raise unavailing hands of protest and censure against the advancing deluge. The old world of culture and quality, of hierarchies and traditions, of values and decorum deserved its champions. It was doomed: but it did not lack its standard-bearer.

Morley had risen to eminence and to old age in a brilliant, hopeful world. He lived to see that fair world shattered, its hopes broken, its wealth squandered. He lived to see the fearful Armageddon, "the angry vision of this hideous war", the nations hurled against each other in the largest, the most devastating, and nearly the most ferocious of all human quarrels. He lived to see almost everything he toiled for and believed in dashed to pieces. He endured the cataclysm of fire and sword; but he also survived to see the island he loved so well emerge once again victorious in the supreme ordeal. He lived even to recognize the immense, fascinating, yet mysterious and unmeasured new growths which everywhere are bursting forth amid the ruins of the structures he had known.

# HINDENBURG

Hindenburg! The name itself is massive. It harmonizes with the tall thick-set personage with beetling brows, strong features, and heavy jowl, familiar to the modern world. It is a face that you could magnify tenfold, a hundredfold, a thousandfold, and it would gain in dignity, nay, even in majesty; a face most impressive when gigantic. In 1916 the Germans made a wooden image of him, colossal, towering above mankind; and faithful admirers, by scores of thousands, paid their coins to the War Loan for the privilege of hammering a nail into the giant who stood for Germany against the world. In the agony of defeat the image was broken up for firewood. But the effect remained—a giant: slow-thinking, slow-moving but sure, steady, faithful, war-like yet benignant, larger than the ordinary run of men.

He loved the old world of Prussia. He lived in the famous tradition of Frederick the Great. *"Toujours en vedette"*, as the German military saying goes—"Always on the look-out." He revelled in the "good old Prussian spirit of Potsdam"; the officer class, poor, frugal, but pursuing honour with feudal fidelity, their whole existence devoted to King and country; a class most respectful to the aristocracy and the lawfully constituted authorities; a class, the enemy of change. Hindenburg had nothing to learn from modern science and civilization except its weapons; no rule of life but duty; no ambition but the greatness of the Fatherland.

The years rolled by. The subaltern rose in the military hierarchy. He held a succession of important commands. He was one of the leading generals of the German Army. Always he waited for the day when he would be leading into battle not a mere company but whole army corps against the accursed Frenchmen. Still the years rolled on. A younger generation came knocking at the door. Deep peace lapped the nations. At the top of the ladder of promotion Hindenburg found only the shelf of retirement. So, then, the great day would be for others. He retired in modest circumstances to his home. From 1911 he dwelt like Cincinnatus on his farm.

The call came. The Russian masses wended on victoriously in the East. The advance in the West approached its climax. Suddenly there is a telegram—3 p.m., 22 August, 1914. It is from Main Headquarters: "Are you prepared for immediate employment?" Answer: "I am ready." Within a few hours he was speeding eastwards to command the German armies against Russia, against odds of between three or four to one. In the train he met his chief of staff, who was already managing everything and issuing all the orders with the underlying, over-riding authority of the German General Staff. Nothing is more becoming than the relations which Hindenburg preserved with Ludendorff. Certainly it was a marvellous partnership. His lieutenant was a prodigy of mental energy, cast in a military form. Hindenburg was not jealous; he was not petty; he was not fussy. He took the responsibility for all that his brilliant, much younger, subordinate conceived and did. There were moments when the nerve of Ludendorff flickered, and in these moments the solid, simple strength of Hindenburg sustained him.

The awful battle of Tannenberg destroyed the Russian armies in the north; the invaders were swept from German soil by little more than one-third of their number. Their losses exceeded twice over the total numbers of their conquerors.

Thenceforward Hindenburg with his astounding Chief Staff Officer, Ludendorff, became the main pillar of German hope. The English military historians have used the cabalistic symbol HL to represent this famous combination which during the war and to the outer world at least presented itself as a pendant to the comradeship of Lee and Jackson and farther back to the brotherhood of Marlborough and Eugene. HL swiftly became the rival of Main Headquarters. Moltke had disappeared with the failure at the Marne, and a new chief, perhaps the ablest of German commanders, Falkenhayn, directed the German armies. He still looked to the West as the scene upon which the decision would be obtained. Here were the greatest forces, here were the hated French, here above all in his own words was "our most dangerous enemy . . . England, with whom the conspiracy against Germany stands and falls".

Henceforward the entire direction of the German war machine fell into the hands of the redoubtable pair. Not only this, but they increasingly absorbed to themselves the main political authority in Germany. They stabilized the Austrian front against Russia. They destroyed Roumania. They preserved their lines unbroken against the British until the longed-for winter days came. With the new year they made a prudent withdrawal in the West which completely disconcerted the Allied plans. Suddenly, swiftly and silently the Germans withdrew to the new immense fortifications of the Hindenburg Line, and gained a four months' breathing space. The stakes were raised on both sides and the fury of the War intensified. Russia disintegrated into revolution and ruin. The peace of Brest-Litovsk was signed. HL could now look forward to a last supreme opportunity in 1918. Their plans were not interrupted by the murderous struggles with the British at Passchendaele. They knew themselves in a position to bring a reinforcement of a million men and five thousand guns from the Russian front, and to have in 1918 for the first time since the very beginning of the war a large and substantial superiority in the West.

But these great measures of generalship were accompanied by a fatal error. HL were led to believe that a submarine campaign on a gigantic scale would starve England and force the British Empire to make peace. Against the wish of the Kaiser, against the appeals of the German Chancellor and the Foreign Office, they insisted on unlimited submarine warfare, and on 6 April, 1917, the United States declared war upon Germany. Here Hindenburg was acting outside the military sphere in which he and his colleagues were expert. They staked too much upon a purely mechanical device. They looked too little to the tremendous psychological reactions upon the Allies, upon the whole world, above all upon their own people, which must follow the apparition of a fresh, mighty antagonist among the forces against Germany. They utterly underrated the power of the United States. Moreover they had miscalculated the mechanical aspect. The British Navy was not unequal to the extraordinary strain of the submarine attack. By no great margin, but quite decisively, they reached beneath the surface of the seas, groped for, found and strangled the German submarines. By the summer of 1917 it was certain that the seas would remain open, that Britain would be fed, and that American troops in millions could be carried to France.

The American weight grew unceasingly. In the end, under the pressure of superior cannon and superior numbers, the armies of the Kaiser bent and bowed, and behind them the civil population, long pinched by the British blockade, broke into turbulent confusion. It was indeed now the world that was coming against them in an irresistible tide. Millions of men, scores of thousands of cannon, thousands of tanks; the heroic constancy of France and the unrelenting willpower, which they always recognized, of England. And behind, the measureless, now rapidly gathering forces of the United States. Too much!

The German front was broken, and the homeland behind the front crumpled beneath the strain. The proud armies recoiled; Ludendorff was dismissed. Hindenburg bided with his sovereign to the end. We must suppose that he approved, and perhaps enjoined, the Kaiser's departure to Holland. For himself he went home with the troops. What was Revolution compared to Defeat?

Events rolled forward with gathering momentum. The transition from Papen to Schleicher (now murdered) and from Schleicher to Hitler were but an affair of months. In the last phase we see the aged President, having betrayed all the Germans who had re-elected him to power, joining reluctant and indeed contemptuous hands with the Nazi leader. There is a defence for all this, and it must be made on behalf of President von Hindenburg. He had become senile. He did not understand what he was doing. He could not be held physically, mentally or morally responsible for opening the flood-gates of evil upon German, and perhaps upon European civilization. We may be sure that the renowned veteran had no motive but love of his country, and that he did his best with declining mental strength to cope with problems never before presented to a ruler.

Dusk deepens into dark. It is time to sleep. Nightmares, hideous choices, unanswerable riddles, pistol-shots disturb an old man's torpor. Where is the path? Always uphill! Worse to come? *Vorwärts* —always *vorwärts*—then silence.

## HERBERT HENRY ASQUITH

Asquith was a man who knew where he stood on every question of life and affairs in altogether unusual degree. Scholarship, politics, philosophy, law, religion, were all spheres in which at the time when I knew him best he seemed to have arrived at definite opinions. On all, when the need required it, his mind opened and shut smoothly and exactly, like the breech of a gun. He always gave me the impression—perhaps natural for a younger man in a subordinate station—of measuring all the changing, baffling situations of public and Parliamentary life according to settled standards and sure con-victions: and there was also the sense of a scorn, lightly and not always completely veiled, for arguments, for personalities and even for events which did not conform to the pattern he had with so much profound knowledge and reflection decidedly adopted.

In some respects this was a limitation. The world, nature, human beings, do not move like machines. The edges are never clear-cut, but always frayed. Nature never draws a line without smudging it. Conditions are so variable, episodes so unexpected, experiences so conflicting, that flexibility of judgment and a willingness to assume a somewhat humbler attitude towards external phenomena may well play their part in the equipment of a modern Prime Minister. But Asquith's opinions in the prime of his life were cut in bronze. Vast knowledge, faithful industry, deep thought were imbedded in his nature; and if, as was inevitable in the rough and tumble of life, he was forced to submit and bow to the opinions of others, to the force of events, to the passions of the hour, it was often with barely concealed repugnance and disdain.

At the time when I knew him best he was at the height of his power. Great majorities supported him in Parliament and the country. Against him were ranged all the stolid Conservative forces of England. Conflict unceasing grew year by year to a more dangerous intensity at home, while abroad there gathered sullenly the hurricane that was to wreck our generation. Our days were spent in the furious party battles which arose upon Home Rule and the Veto of the House of Lords, whilst always upon the horizon deadly shapes grew or faded, and even while the sun shone there was a curious whisper in the air.

He was always very kind to me and thought well of my mental processes; was obviously moved to agreement by many of the State papers which I wrote. A carefully marshalled argument, cleanly printed, read by him at leisure, often won his approval and thereafter commanded his decisive support. His orderly, disciplined mind delighted in reason and design. It was always worth while spending many hours to state a case in the most concise and effective manner for the eye of the Prime Minister. In fact I believe I owed the repeated advancement to great offices which he accorded me more to my secret writings on government business than to any impressions produced by conversation or by speeches on the platform or in Parliament. One felt that the case was submitted to a high tribunal, and that repetition, verbiage, rhetoric, false argument, would be impassively but inexorably put aside.

In Cabinet he was markedly silent. Indeed he never spoke a word in Council if he could get his way without it. He sat, like the great judge he was, hearing with trained patience the case deployed on every side, now and then interjecting a question or brief comment, searching or pregnant, which gave matters a turn towards the goal he wished to reach; and when at the end, amid all the perplexities and cross-currents of ably and vehemently expressed opinion, he summed up, it was very rarely that the silence he had observed till then did not fall on all.

He disliked talking "shop" out of business hours, and would never encourage or join in desultory conversation on public matters. Most of the great Parliamentarians I have known were always ready to talk politics and let their fancy play over the swiftly-moving scene—Balfour, Chamberlain, Morley, Lloyd George, threw themselves with zest into the discussion of current events. With Asquith, either the Court was open or it was shut. If it was open, his whole attention was focused on the case; if it was shut, there was no use knocking at the door. This also may have been in some respects a limitation. Many things are learnt by those who live their whole lives with their main work; and although it is a great gift at once to have an absorbing interest and to be able to throw it off in lighter hours, it seemed at times that Asquith threw it off too easily, too completely. He drew so strict a line between work and play that one might almost think work had ceased to attract him. The habit, formed in the life of a busy lawyer, persisted. The case was settled and put aside; judgment was formed, was delivered, and did not require review. The next case would be called in its turn and at the proper hour. Of course he must have communed deeply with himself, but less I believe than most men at the summit of a nation's affairs. His mind was so alert, so lucid, so well stored, so thoroughly trained that once he had heard the whole matter thrashed out, the conclusion came with a snap; and each conclusion, so far as lay with him, was final.

In affairs he had that ruthless side without which great matters cannot be handled. When offering me Cabinet office in his government in 1908, he repeated to me Mr. Gladstone's saying: "The first essential for a Prime Minister is to be a good butcher," and he added "there are several who must be pole-axed now." They were. Loyal as he was to his colleagues, he never shrank, when the time came and public need required it, from putting them aside—once and for all. Personal friendship might survive if it would. Political association was finished. But how else can States be governed?

His letters to colleagues were like his conduct of government business. They were the counterpart of his speeches. Innately conservative and old-fashioned, he disliked and disdained telephones and typewriters. He who spoke so easily in public had never learnt to dictate. All must be penned by him. A handwriting at once beautiful and serviceable, rapid, correct and clear, the fewest possible words and no possibility of misunderstanding; and if argument or epigram or humour found their place, it was because they slipped from the pen before they could be bridled. He wrote other letters in which no such compression was practised. They were addressed to brighter eyes than peer through politicians' spectacles.

When work was done, he played. He enjoyed life ardently; he delighted in feminine society; he was always interested to meet a new and charming personality. Women of every age were eager to be taken in to dinner by him. They were fascinated by his gaiety and wit, and by his evident interest in all their doings. He would play bridge for modest stakes for hours every evening, no matter what lightnings were flashing around the house or what ordeals the morrow would swiftly be thrusting upon him.

I saw him most intimately in the most agreeable circumstances. He and his wife and elder daughter were our guests on the Admiralty yacht for a month at a time in the three summers before the War. Blue skies and shining seas, the Mediterranean, the Adriatic, the Aegean; Venice, Syracuse, Malta, Athens, the Dalmatian coast; great fleets and dockyards; the superb setting of the King's Navy; serious work and a pleasure cruise filled these very happy breathing-spaces. In one whole month, with continuous agitation at home and growing apprehension abroad, he maintained towards me, who stood so near him in responsibility, a reserve on all serious matters which was unbreakable. Once and once only did he invite discussion. Important changes impended in the government. He asked my opinion about men and offices, expressed agreement or difference in the most confiding manner. He weighed the persons concerned in nicely balanced scales, then closed and locked the subject, put the invisible key in his pocket, and resumed a careful study of a treatise on the monuments and inscriptions of Spalato before which the yacht had just dropped anchor. But some weeks later the appointments were made in the exact sense of the discussion.

For the rest, you would not have supposed he had a care in the world. He was the most painstaking tourist. He mastered Baedeker, examined the ladies upon it, explained and illuminated much, and evidently enjoyed every hour. He frequently set the whole party competing who could write down in five minutes the most Generals beginning with L, or Poets beginning with T, or Historians with some other initial. He had innumerable varieties of these games and always excelled in them. He talked a great deal to the captain and the navigators about the ship and the course and the weather. His retort in Parliament, "The Right Honourable Gentleman must wait and see", was then current. There was a cartoon in *Punch* in which he was depicted asking the young officer on the bridge, "Why is she pitching so much this morning?" To which the response was alleged to have been, "Well, you see, sir, it is all a question of Weight and Sea." Although only an apocryphal pun, this deserves to survive.

For the rest he basked in the sunshine and read Greek. He fashioned with deep thought impeccable verses in complicated metre, and recast in terser form classical inscriptions which displeased him. I could not help much in this. But I followed with attention the cipher telegrams which we received each day, and of course we were always on the new wireless of the Fleet.

One afternoon we drove along a lovely road near Cattaro—a harbour in those days of peculiar interest, not merely for its scenery. We suddenly met endless strings of mules and farm horses. We asked where they were going and what for? We were told "They are dispersing. The manoeuvres are cancelled." The Balkan and European crisis of 1913 was over!

Mr. Asquith was probably one of the greatest peace-time Prime Ministers we have ever had. His intellect, his sagacity, his broad outlook and civic courage maintained him at the highest eminence in public life. But in war he had not those qualities of resource and energy, of prevision and assiduous management, which ought to reside in the executive. Mr. Lloyd George had all the qualities which he lacked. The nation, by some instinctive, almost occult process, had found this out. Mr. Bonar Law was the instrument which put

Mr. Asquith aside and set another in his stead. Asquith fell when the enormous task was but half completed. He fell with dignity. He bore adversity with composure. In or out of power, disinterested patriotism and inflexible integrity were his only guides. Let it never be forgotten that he was always on his country's side in all her perils, and that he never hesitated to sacrifice his personal or political interests to the national cause. In the Boer War, in the Great War, whether as Prime Minister or Leader of the Opposition, in the constitutional outrage of the General Strike—in every one of these great crises he stood firm and unflinching for King and Country. The glittering honours, his Earldom and his Garter, which the Sovereign conferred upon him in his closing years, were but the fitting recognition of his life's work, and the lustre and respect with which the whole nation lighted his evening path were a measure of the services he had rendered, and still more of the character he had borne.

## "F.E."
## FIRST EARL OF BIRKENHEAD

A hundred years ago, Thomas Smith was the best runner and the most redoubtable knuckle-fighter in the West Riding of Yorkshire. He earned his living as a miner. In those days the miners were a class apart. They were "bound" to their employers by engagements whose terms recalled the serfdom of the Middle Ages; they lived, for the most part, in self-contained communities, lives of hard privation, and were regarded by more fortunate workers as little better than savages. It was a fierce world. According to routine the pit, its darkness, its thousand lurking dangers, and its warlike comradeships, swallowed up the son of a mining family.

But Thomas Smith resolved that his boy, for one, should have a different life. With great pains he had him educated, and the youth, seizing his opportunities, obtained a post as schoolmaster, first at Wakefield, and afterwards at Birkenhead. A devout and uncompromising Nonconformist of the harshest and narrowest school, this Thomas Smith had brought home as bride a strange, wild creature of swift, fierce moods and a will that matched his own. It is said she was of gipsy stock; she certainly possessed the dark but vivid beauty that sometimes goes with Romany blood. A curious match, but a happy one; nay, with remarkable consequences; for students of heredity may note that the grandchild of Thomas and Bathsheba Smith became Lord Chancellor of England. He was Frederick Edwin Smith, first Earl of Birkenhead.

An uncle was prepared to help him through Oxford, but only on condition that he won an open scholarship. He won it. After much pleasant idleness and whole-hearted enjoyment of university life, he found himself in debt and with no prospect of extricating himself from his difficulties unless he took a First Class in Schools. He shut himself up in his lodgings, and for six months worked fourteen hours a day. He got his First Class, and next year became Vinerian Law Scholar and a Fellow of Merton College. He was called to the Bar in 1899. By 1904 he was earning £6,000 a year, and in 1908 he took silk. His Parliamentary reputation was by then already firmly established. He had become a national figure with his maiden speech.

That speech was a daring gamble. He knew it to be so. As he drove to Westminster with his wife on the evening that he expected to catch the Speaker's eye, he told her of his resolve to stake all upon this single throw, and that he had counted the cost of failure.

"If I fail," he said, "there will be nothing for me but to remain silent for three years until my disgrace is forgotten."

"Must you risk so much?" she asked.

The speech was a triumph. I only heard the latter part. But I could feel from the moment I came in that the crowded House was listening to a new figure of the first rank. Tim Healy, the Irish Nationalist, a master of invective and one of the most brilliant debaters in the House, scribbled a note as the young member sat down amid a storm of cheering. It was passed along the benches. "I am old, and you are young," it said, "but you have beaten me at my own game."

I did not come to know him until he was thirty-four. An ardent Conservative, he was angry with me for leaving that party on the Protection issue. His own father had been in the eighties a keen admirer of Lord Randolph Churchill, and had taught him to embrace not only the conceptions of Tory Democracy, but to think kindly of one who had done much to make it a living force in modern politics. "F. E.", to use his famous soubriquet, felt a strong antagonism to me for breaking a continuity. He did not wish to meet me. It was only after the Parliament of 1906 had run some months of its course that we were introduced to one another by a common friend as we stood at the bar of the House of Commons before an important division. But from that hour our friendship was perfect. It was one of my most precious possessions. It was never disturbed by the fiercest party fighting. It was never marred by the slightest personal difference or misunderstanding. It grew stronger as nearly a quarter of a century slipped by, and it lasted till his untimely death. The pleasure and instruction of his companionship were of the highest order. The world of affairs and the general public saw in F. E. Smith a robust, pugnacious personality, trampling his way across the battlefields of life, seizing its prizes as they fell, and exulting in his prowess. They saw his rollicking air. Acquaintances and opponents alike felt the sting of his taunts or retorts in the House of Commons and at the Bar. Many were prone to regard him as a mere demagogue whose wits had been sharpened upon the legal grindstone. It is a judgment which those who practise the popular arts before working-class audiences in times of faction are likely to incur. The qualities which lay behind were not understood by his fellow-countrymen till the last ten years of his life.

But his close friends, and certainly I, acclaimed him for what he was—a sincere patriot; a wise, grave, sober-minded statesman; a truly great jurist; a scholar of high attainments; and a gay, brilliant, loyal, lovable being. We made several considerable journeys together. We both served for many years in the Oxfordshire Hussars. We were repeatedly together at Blenheim. We met and talked on innumerable occasions: never did I separate from him without having learnt something, and enjoyed myself besides. He was always great fun; but more than that he had a massive common sense and a sagacious comprehension which made his counsel invaluable, whether in public broil or private embarrassment. He had all the canine virtues in a remarkable degree—courage, fidelity, vigilance, love of the chase. He had reached settled and somewhat sombre conclusions upon a large number of questions, about which many people are content to remain in placid suspense. Man of the world; man of affairs; master of the law; adept at the written or spoken word; athlete; sportsman; book-lover—there were few topics in which he was not interested, and whatever attracted him he could expound and embellish.

I cannot speak at first hand of his forensic success, for I only once heard him address a Court of Law. I did not think him so good in the House of Commons as upon the platform or at a public dinner. He was only a comparatively short time—ten or twelve years—in the House, and his character and style were formed upon other moulds. Still, no one can contest his many remarkable Parliamentary feats. He seemed to me more at home in the House of Lords, and more dominating upon that assembly than ever in the Lower Chamber. To hear him wind up a debate from the Woolsack, speaking for an hour at a time without a note, without a gesture, with hardly an alteration of tone, dealing with point after point, weaving them all into an ordered texture of argument, darting aside, now here, now there, upon some retaliatory foray, but returning always surely and easily to his main theme, and reaching his conclusion without the slightest appearance of effort; all this constituted an impressive and enviable gift. For this gift he was grateful. He rejoiced in using it. "I always feel best," he said to me, "when I am on the unpinioned wing."

He was good upon the platform because he understood thoroughly the outlook, feelings and prejudices of the ordinary patriotic Tory man-in-the-street. This same quality helped him with a jury. He could strike with faultless accuracy the simple major keynotes to which the full-blooded English father or husband or eager youngster would respond; and he spoke with the greatest sureness and freedom upon all the most delicate questions of life and morals, sportsmanship and fair play.

But most of all I liked to hear him in the Cabinet. He was a singularly silent member. He had acquired in the legal profession the habit of listening mute and motionless hour after hour, and he rarely spoke until his counsel was sought. Then his manner was so quiet, so reasonable, so matter-of-fact and sensible, that you could feel opinion being changed; and promptly, as he warmed to his subject, there grew that glow of conviction and appeal, instinctive and priceless, which constitutes true eloquence. Often I have thought of Mr. Pitt's famous translation of some Latin epigram, which if he were here F. E. would tell me—"Eloquence is like the flame. It requires fuel to feed it, motion to excite it, and it brightens as it burns." In my experience he and Mr. Lloyd George were both at their best in gatherings of ten or a dozen men, every one of whom was well informed upon the question at issue, and upon whom the effect of claptrap in any of its innumerable varieties would only be disastrous.

I have said he was remarkably consistent in opinion. He was more; he was persistent. In every affair, public or personal, if he was with you on the Monday, you would find him the same on the Wednesday, and on the Friday when things looked blue, he would still be marching forward with strong reinforcements. The opposite type of comrade or ally is so very common that I single this out as a magnificent characteristic. He loved pleasure; he was grateful for the gift of existence; he loved every day of his life. But no one could work harder. From his youth he worked and played with might and main. He had a singular power of concentration, and five or six hours sustained thought upon a particular matter was always within his compass. He possessed what Napoleon praised, the mental power *"de fixer les objets longtemps sans être fatigué"*. No doubt he presumed often in his legal work upon his great quickness in mastering a difficult field and getting to the roots. He was never entangled in the briars of detail. I remember after he had taken silk and was in the front rank at the Bar, how it was the fashion in the Liberal Government circles of those days to say that he had no real grasp of the fundamentals of the law. I lived to see him take his place among the great Lord Chancellors who have interpreted that marvellous structure of English good sense and right feeling.

Looking back, I think that the post-war years of the Coalition must be regarded as the great period of F. E.'s life. And there was nothing in it that became him more than the part he played in the final settlement of the difficult and dangerous Irish controversy that had distorted English politics for over thirty years. The general public, and particularly that section of it which supported Conservative principles, still remember him as "Galloper Smith", and one of the most bitter and able opponents of Home Rule in pre-war years. The efforts he had made to secure a solution of the Irish question on the basis of the exclusion of Ulster were either not known or had been forgotten. Since then, the Easter Rebellion had revealed the Irish Sinn Feiners as striking at the British Empire in extremity; and after came assassination and terrorism.

F. E. felt that it was his duty to aid a final effort to end the long, deadly, and obsolete quarrel. He took a leading part in the negotiations with the Sinn Fein delegates. He was one of the signatories of the Irish Treaty.

"I may have signed my political death-warrant tonight," he remarked, as he laid down his pen.

"I may have signed my actual death-warrant," said Michael Collins.

F. E. was the only one of my contemporaries from conversation with whom I have derived the same pleasure and profit as I got from Balfour, Morley, Asquith, Rosebery and Lloyd George. One did feel after a talk with these men that things were simpler and easier, and that Britain would be strong enough to come through all her troubles. His record remains. It is not in every aspect a model for all to copy. Whose is? He seemed to have a double dose of human nature. He burned all his candles at both ends. His physique and constitution seemed to be capable of supporting indefinitely every form of mental and physical exertion. When they broke the end was swift. Between the setting of the sun and night there was only the briefest twilight. It was better so. Prolonged ill health and deprivation of all the activities upon which his life was built would have pressed very hard upon him.

## MARSHAL FOCH

A singular degree of integrity and harmony pervades the life of Marshal Foch. The drama of the conflict between France and Germany has fascinated the attention of the whole world, and ruined the prosperity of a large part of it. The life of Marshal Foch lay in the centre of this drama. He felt its passions and its pangs perhaps more intensely than any other human being; and he wielded the supreme executive power in its climax and decision. He was just old enough to serve as a volunteer lieutenant in the Franco-German War of 1870; but he was employed with troops so young and raw that they were never exposed to the fire of the enemy. He saw, he suffered, he comprehended. He could do nothing. The ardent youth in whose veins flowed Gascon and warrior blood, whose keen intelligence revealed the high issues, whose well-nerved sensitiveness responded to every touch, was forced to be the helpless witness of his country's downfall. He was fitted in an extraordinary degree to feel alike her agony and his own impotence.

But he was also fitted to nourish within himself those deep and in some respects mystic forces which were the resultants of his pain. Fortified by a simple, practical but intense religious conviction, animated by natural love of his country and focused by the highest forms of professional military intellectualism, Foch from the year 1870 onward embodied within the brain and frame of a mortal the spirit which the French call *La Revanche* and which is ill-translated by the word Revenge. Ill-translated, because in this revenge there was no zest of spite or cruelty, no greed of material gains or personal splendours, no desire however deeply concealed to humiliate or maltreat the German enemy—only a life-long wish and aim and toil to see the France which had been levelled in the dust of 1870 some day restored to her honourable seat. He began his career a little cub brushed aside by the triumphant march of the German armies to Paris and victory; he lived to see all the might of valiant Germany prostrate and suppliant at his pencil tip. In the weakest position he endured the worst with his country; at the summit of power he directed its absolute triumph.

Let us first dwell upon the most lovable traits of this remarkable and, it may well be argued, predestined being. His personal charm and deft address made its persistent appeal to all with whom he came in contact. His fidelity to his country, whatever its government or form of government and to his religion, no matter what obstacle it imposed upon his military career, constituted for him an abiding element of strength. His undaunted and ever-flowing combative energy, as a man in contact with other personalities and harrying remorseless detail, as a Commander with a front crumbling under the German flail, was proved inexhaustible even by the Great War. His power of cold endurance was the equal of his energy. He preserved a strict respect for the Constitution of his country, and for the position of the Ministerial Chiefs of a system which was certainly not his. He nourished an understanding, impartial and detached we must admit, of the feelings of the allied armies and countries gathered under his command, and lastly a chivalry—all a soldier's—to the ancient and terrible foe beneath whose heel he had writhed and over whose head he was in turn to triumph. When, after the hard terms of the Armistice had been accepted by the Germans, prudent and vigilant civilian counsel urged the immediate disarmament of the German fighting troops, Foch exclaimed: "They have fought well, let them keep their weapons."

I had made the acquaintance of Foch at manoeuvres before the war; and during the struggle I came in contact with him on three occasions which illustrated not inaptly his chequered fortunes. The first was in 1917 when, though myself out of office, I made a considerable tour of the French front upon the courteous invitation of M. Painlevé. This was for Foch a period of eclipse. The reaction and recrimination which followed the awful slaughters of the Somme and its disappointment had been finally fatal to Joffre, and Foch as his fighting lieutenant had followed him into disfavour. The brilliant part he had played in the battles on the Marne and the Yser in 1914 had been overlaid by the ghastly losses sustained by the French Army in his obstinate and ill-starred offensive in Artois in the spring of 1915. France shuddered at her dwindling manhood, and turned to other leaders and new methods. Foch was assigned a high advisory post in Paris, and it was here in a modest office near the Invalides that he received me. Certainly no one ever appeared less downcast or conscious of being at a discount. He discussed with utmost frankness and vigour the whole scene of the war, and particularly those Eastern spheres in which I had been so much interested. His postures, his captivating manner, his vigorous and often pantomimic gestures—comical, if they had not been fully expressive—the energy of his ideas when his interest was aroused, made a vivid impression upon me. He was fighting all the time, whether he had armies to launch or only thoughts.

The disaster of 21 March, 1918, and the bitter wisdom of the Doullens Conference had forced Haig to propose and Pétain, the French Commander-in-Chief, to accept, his over-lordship. He had succeeded to a fearsome inheritance. A wide gap had been torn in the Allied front; the British Fifth Army was broken and largely destroyed; the French relief had not yet arrived; only a thin and ragged line of dismounted cavalry, of improvised detachments from the schools of instruction and of exhausted survivors from the disaster, stood between the German advance and Amiens with its almost vital railway lines. Farther to the south in the French zone Montdidier had just fallen. Foch, with a handful of Staff Officers, his "military family", and with an authority none too clearly defined, had to demand further sacrifices from the British and draw from Pétain northwards the reserves which that General always thought should be kept to cover the capital. Certainly a terrible hour. I can see him now as, for the benefit of Clemenceau and me, he described the situation and explained with map and pencil, like a schoolmaster teaching a class with a blackboard, the reasons for his confidence. He showed how each succeeding day the wave of invasion was smaller and how the tremendous initial impulse was dying away. Calm he certainly was not. He was vehement, passionate, persuasive, but clairvoyant and, above all, indomitable.

I did not see him again until the early autumn when the German offensive had been decisively mastered, when the tide had finally turned, when all was well and would undoubtedly be better. Now he was at the summit of power. His word was law. French, British, American and Belgian armies conformed with dutiful precision to the directions of a victorious leader, and the German line rolled ever backward before them.

The six-weeks period from the first of June to the middle of July, 1918, must be recorded as the climax of Foch's ordeal. So far he had nothing to show but a first-class French disaster and a deep British sensation of ill-usage. His claim to enduring military greatness must be founded largely upon his conduct in this test. He could never have survived if behind him there had not been a being of a different order, of equal courage and of even greater personal force. Clemenceau, the faithful and dreaded Tiger, prowled the French capital and guarded from all subversion the authority of the commanding Chief. It was in this situation, depressed, precarious, disputed, half undermined, that Marshal Foch, faced by the new German offensive of 12 July, did not hesitate to overrule Pétain, to withdraw the reserves which stood between Paris and the enemy, and hurl them under Mangin at the German flank. This decision judged in its circumstances and in its results, must ever be regarded as one of the greatest deeds of war and examples of fortitude of soul which history has recorded.

But all this was over now. The Allies were united, the enemy were beaten. Foch was supreme and victory certain. I find myself at his chateau on a lovely autumn afternoon trying to win his enthusiasm for a vast tank programme for the campaign of 1919 with a grave, quiet and courteous gentleman who knew he had nothing before him but measureless success and immortal fame.

The magnitude of the events which Marshal Foch directed is of course beyond compare in the annals of war. But it will be found, I believe, as time passes, that the valour of his spirit and the shrewd sagacity of his judgment were of the highest order. Fortune lighted his crest. His peculiar gift of obstinate combativeness which had gained his laurels at the Marne and the Yser, when the only hope was not to despair, led him to serious disasters in the offensive battles of Artois and the Somme. In 1914 he had saved the day by refusing to recognize defeat. In 1915 and in 1916 he broke his teeth upon the Impossible. But 1918 was created for him. In the first phase of the Ludendorff offensive no one knew so well as he how to use every ounce of strength to defend every inch of ground, and so to hoard reserves. In the second phase, when the initiative passed to the Allies, they had for the first time in the war not only the superior numbers, but the cannon, the shells, the tanks and the aeroplanes—in short the apparatus indispensable for a successful advance. Then it was that the characteristic genius of Foch attained its full and decisive expression, and with cries of "*Allez à la bataille*", "*Tout le monde à la bataille*", he heaved the mighty wave of allied armies, French, British, American and Belgian, forward in vast, united, irresistible attack.

Arthur Balfour did not mingle in the hurly-burly. He glided upon its surface. He was born to substantial wealth. After more than fifty years of service he died with a reduced, but still adequate estate, derived from ancient title. He was never seriously worried about money; he never had to face the problem of earning his livelihood, or of paying the bills for the common necessities of life. He had a beautiful home in Scotland and a comfortable mansion in Carlton House Terrace, maintained automatically by a solid capital. This was his lot in life. He shared the gradual, steady impoverishment of the class of landed gentlefolk to which he belonged. Although he lost a good deal of his fortune by an unlucky speculation in later life, he never bothered much about it. His wants were small; his habit of life austere; he always had enough, and security for having enough.

Biographers of eminent persons are prone to ignore or slur over these harshly practical considerations. They have their value however in the career of any public man. Throughout his life the late Lord Balfour, fortunately for himself, still more fortunately for his country, was removed from vulgar necessities. He never had to make any of those compromises, increasing under modern conditions, between an entirely dispassionate outlook upon affairs and his daily bread. This was for him a great advantage and source of strength.

He was a bachelor. All that tremendous process of keeping a home together and rearing a family, which is the main preoccupation of the human race, was by a romantic tragedy far removed from his ken. Henceforward he was self-contained; he was entirely independent. His thought was national, his interests were world-wide. That Britain should be powerful and prosperous, that the Empire should gather more closely around her, that she should be the champion of right and peace; that her own ambitions and aspirations should fit harmoniously into the requirements of an ever-widening and strengthening Cosmopolis, and that he should play a worthy part in all this, was his life's aim.

He was in fact a lay-priest seeking a secular goal. He acquired and possessed from earlier life profound and definite conceptions; and by a marvellous gift of comprehension and receptivity he was able to adjust all the new phenomena and the ever-changing currents of events to his solidly wrought convictions. His interest in life, thought and affairs, as Mr. MacDonald observed, was as keen at eighty as it was at twenty: but his purpose, his foundation, and his main theme were obstinate, obdurate and virtually unchanged throughout the memorable times in which he lived, played his part, and even ruled. He was a man to whom without commonplace extravagance one might apply the word "Statesman". His aversion from the Roman Catholic faith was dour and inveterate. Otherwise he seemed to have the personal qualifications of a great Pope. He had that composed, detached, uplifted mental and moral vision combined with the art of dexterous and practical management requisite for those who guide the course of permanent societies. To the defence of his principles and prejudices he summoned every resource of conduct, oratory and dialectic. But he knew when to change, and not only when to change, but how to change, in accordance with the pressures of events. Holding to his own convictions, steering always by the same stars, diverging only so far as was inevitable under the thrust of adverse winds, he moved with the times, and lived in the forefront of nearly three generations. He was never stranded; he was never out-of-date. He loved youth and accepted, nay, encouraged its demands. In mind he was always young, and yet he inspired the feeling that he possessed the wisdom of the ages.

The Wykehamists have the motto, "Manners makyth Man". If this be so, Arthur Balfour was the most perfect of men. He was the best-mannered man I ever met—easy, courteous, patient, considerate, in every society and with great and small alike. But this urbane and graceful air, which was entirely natural to him and effortless, was the least part of his manners, which were equal to every situation, pleasant or awkward. Not only was he never embarrassed or at a loss himself, but he seemed to impart this gift in large measure to any company while he was among them. He put everyone at their ease and sailed with them smoothly through the most disconcerting and painful situations. Whatever had to be said, he knew how to say it; and when others blundered into foolish or offensive remarks, he knew how to defend himself or retaliate with point, justice or severity. At the right time and in the right place he could and did say with dignity and suavity any hard things which were necessary. Such occasions were rare. He was always the most agreeable, affable and amusing of guests or companions; his presence was a pleasure and his conversation a treat.

He possessed and practised the art of always appearing interested in any subject that was raised, or in any person with whom he was talking. He had not perhaps in conversation the vivid, vibrant qualities of John Morley, nor the brilliance, often disconcerting, of Rosebery; but he excelled both in the pleasure he gave. His contribution was less positive. He allowed the talk to flow as his companion wished, appreciating in the most complimentary manner anything that was said in good will, taking up every point, and lifting the discussion step by step—yet often himself speaking very little. All who met him came away feeling that *they* had been at their very best, and that they had found someone who, whether he agreed or differed, understood their point of view. Very often they remembered the things they had said to him, which he had welcomed or seemed to agree with, better than what he had said to them. He loved general conversation, and knew exactly how to rule it, so that no one was left out, and it never degenerated into "damned monologue".

All his life he dwelt in circles of admiring friends. He was for many years the mainspring of a society of brilliant men and women known as "The Souls", who dined together, travelled together and stayed constantly in each other's delightful houses. He accepted, besides, invitations from all sorts of people, never broke an engagement for something more tempting, and left behind him a trail of satisfaction and even happiness.

I must present a few blades from my sheaf of Balfouriana. A comment upon a speech: "Asquith's lucidity of style is a positive disadvantage when he has nothing to say." A retort on another occasion. "In that oration there were some things that were true, and some things that were trite: but what was true was trite, and what was not trite was not true." And again: "There were some things in it meant seriously which were humorous, and there were others meant humorously which were serious." Here is a remark which when pessimists are prating I have often found helpful: "This is a singularly ill-contrived world; but not so ill-contrived as that." Of a supporter somewhat over-ripe, "He pursues us with malignant fidelity." At a luncheon Mr. Frank Harris, wishing to shine, blurted out, "All the evil in the world is due to Christianity and Journalism." Arthur Balfour, contemplating this proposition for a moment, replied, "Christianity of course, but why Journalism?" Once when I was very young I asked him whether he ever prepared his perorations. "No," he said, "I say what occurs to me, and sit down at the end of the first grammatical sentence."

He had many habits which conserved his vigour. He never answered an invitation except by telegram. People were glad to have an answer quickly, and regarded a telegram as a mark of consideration. Thirty years ago the arrival of the pale orange envelope made our fathers and mothers sit up; if it did not contain bad news, they took it as a compliment; so all was well at that end. On the other hand, you could dictate a telegram instead of having to write *with your own hand* a ceremonious letter.

He very rarely rose before luncheon. He rested in bed, unapproachable, transacting business, reading, writing, ruminating, and at weekends appeared, whatever the crisis, composed and fresh shortly after 1 p.m. His work for the day was done; he seemed carefree, even at the head of a tottering government, even in the darkest hours of the war. He would sit and talk gaily for a half-hour after luncheon; he hoped to be able to play a round of golf or in later years lawn tennis. Uninstructed persons who saw him thus in private life, while the newspapers growled in double-headed columns about the political situation, were surprised and even scandalized. They thought he did not care or did not reck. But he had often been at his affairs since dawn. He was never excited, and in the House of Commons was very hard indeed to provoke. I tried often and often, and only on a few occasions, which I prefer to forget, succeeded in seriously annoying him in public debate.

Curiously enough this most easy, sure and fluent of speakers was the most timid, laborious of writers. He would go to a meeting of ten thousand people when every kind of consequence hung upon

540

his words and their reception, with a preparation often completed by a conversation upon important points in the cab that drove him there. Once he saw in his mind's eye a reasoned proposition, he was certain he could unfold it intelligently and with distinction; but when he took up the pen "he came all over of a tremble", and crossed out and transposed and re-wrote to an amazing extent. He would spend hours upon a paragraph and days upon an article. This was a strange inversion. The spoken word, uttered from the summit of power, gone beyond recall, had no terrors for him; but he entered the tabernacles of literature under a double dose of the humility and awe which are proper. He was sure of the movement of his thought; he was shy in the movement of his pen. The history of every country abounds with brilliant and ready writers who have quailed and faltered when called upon to compose in public, or who have shrunk altogether from the ordeal. Balfour was the reverse example, and in this lies a considerable revelation of his character. His was a mind to weigh and balance, to see both sides, especially all the flaws and all the faults in his own case. The emergency and compulsion of public speech forced upon him at a high rate of speed the exposition of his thought. His mind was in action and every second he had to take mental decisions; but in his bedroom with his writing-pad on his lap and fountain-pen poised judicially over the blank sheet of paper, a score of arguments against every case and against every phrase and almost every word paraded themselves and marched and counter-marched before his speculative gaze. Everything he wrote was upon a high level; but its excellence was purchased by inconceivable labour.

Amid universal goodwill and widespread affection he celebrated triumphantly his eightieth birthday. But thereafter hungry Time began to revenge itself upon one who had so long disdained its menace. He became an invalid. His body was stricken; but his mind retained, almost to the very end, its clear, tranquil outlook upon the human scene, and its inexhaustible pleasure in the processes of thought.

I had the privilege of visiting him several times during the last months of his life. I saw with grief the approaching departure, and —for all human purposes—extinction, of a being high-uplifted above the common run. As I observed him regarding with calm, firm and cheerful gaze the approach of Death, I felt how foolish the Stoics were to make such a fuss about an event so natural and so indispensable to mankind. But I felt also the tragedy which robs the world of all the wisdom and treasure gathered in a great man's life and experience, and hands the lamp to some impetuous and untutored stripling, or lets it fall shivered into fragments upon the ground.

# GEORGE NATHANIEL CURZON

George Curzon was born with all the advantages of moderate affluence and noble descent. A stately home, beautiful surroundings, ancestral trees, every material ministration nurtured his youth. But at the same time a strict Miss Paraman and a stern Mr. Campbell, his governess and private schoolmaster respectively, applied disciplinary spurs and corrections in a most bracing and even severe degree. A rigorous and pious upbringing proceeded in an atmosphere of old-world dignity and on the basis of adequate funds. Shot like a long-range projectile from this domestic gun, the youth arrived in the early seventies at Eton. No less than ten years were lavished upon his education. He writes of the six he spent at Eton as the most enjoyable of his life. Certainly they were years of constant and almost unbroken triumph. He stood out at once beyond his contemporaries as one endowed with superabundant powers. He rose rapidly in the school. He rose eventually to be virtually head of the school. He captured a record number of prizes of every kind. Latin, French, Italian, history and, above all, English prose and English verse came to him with precocious facility. At Eton he was the best and most industrious scholar of his day. But to all these achievements he added a strong, rebellious and scornful temper which made him at once admired and feared by his teachers. Armed with his terrific powers of work and easy swiftness of assimilation, he repulsed all favour and loved to excel in despite. He quitted the classes of the French, Italian and historical professors in order by private exertions to win the prizes from their most cherished pupils.

But with all this, his charm, his good looks, his fun and his natural ascendancy won him without question the acceptance of the boys and extorted the respect of the scored-off masters. He was certainly not the model pupil, but far and away the most proficient. He matured at an uncanny speed.

His four years at Oxford were not less conspicuous. He focused his main attention directly upon politics. His academic studies took a second place in his interest and gained him only a Second Class in the examination. But he swiftly rose to be the leader of youthful Tory opinion. He sustained the Chatham and Canning Clubs. He became President of the Union. He wrote voluminously and spoke continually. He infused energy into everything he touched. His infant reputation spread beyond the University and throughout the aristocratic circles which in those days dominated the political scene. He was at twenty-one notorious as "The Coming Man".

The word "notorious" is used advisedly, for with all this early glitter there mingled an innocent but none the less serious tarnish. His facility carried him with a bound into prolixity; his ceremonious diction wore the aspect of pomposity; his wide knowledge was accused of superficiality; his natural pre-eminence was accompanied by airs of superiority. Nevertheless, all these were but the under-currents to a tide that flowed strongly and hopefully forward.

It was easy in those days—indeed it is fortunately still easy—for a young man of such parts and influence to enter the House of Commons as the freely chosen representative of a large constituency. But here for the first time he came in contact with a set of tests to which his gifts were not wholly suited. The House of Commons of the late eighties was very different in its social levels from the assemblies of our day. But it was then, as now, the most competent and comprehending judge of a man. It found something lacking in Mr. Curzon.

I first cast an admiring, measuring eye upon him at the time of his second appointment as Under-Secretary, and was instantly attracted by the geniality, candour and fullness of his conversation. I saluted him at the Devonshire House reception which celebrated in the summer of 1895 the return of the Conservatives to power. A year later I was several times his guest as a subaltern officer when he was Viceroy of India. He had, or at any rate practised, that admirable habit, in which politicians excel, of treating quite young men on absolutely equal terms in conversation. At his table in Calcutta I hugely enjoyed his sprightly and none too merciful chaff of his close friend, my late Harrow Headmaster, Bishop Welldon, then Bishop Metropolitan of India. "I presume," he said to me, "it will not be long before we hear you declaim in the House of Commons." Though greatly hampered by inability to compose at the rate necessary for public speaking, I was strongly of the same opinion myself.

The contradictory qualities which dwell in the characters of so many individuals can rarely have formed more vivid contrasts than in George Curzon. The world thought him pompous in manner and in mind. But this widespread and deep impression, arising from the experience and report of so many good judges, was immediately destroyed by the Curzon one met in a small circle of intimate friends and equals or those whom he treated as equals. Here one saw the charming, gay companion adorning every subject that he touched with his agile wit, ever ready to laugh at himself, ever capable of conveying sympathy and understanding. It seemed incredible that this warm heart and jolly, boyish nature should be so effectually concealed from the vast majority of those he met and with whom he worked. Most difficult in all small matters of business, disputing pettifogging details of private life to the point of quarrel with well-proved friends, he none the less was never happier or seen to better advantage than when he dispensed the splendid hospitalities of his various palatial homes. Helpful with comfort and sympathy on every occasion of sickness or sorrow in his wide circle, unpopular with most of those who served him, the master of scathing rebuke for subordinates, he seemed to sow gratitude and resentment along his path with evenly lavish hands. Bespangled with every quality that could dazzle and attract, he never found himself with a following. Majestic in speech, appearance and demeanour, he never led. He often domineered; but at the centre he never dominated.

Curzon's Viceroyalty of India was his greatest period. For nearly seven years he reigned imperially over the vast Indian scene. He brought to that task intellectual powers never yet surpassed by his successors. Everything interested him, and he adorned nearly all he touched.

Yet it closed in sorrow and anger. A first-class quarrel developed between the Viceroy and the Commander-in-Chief, Lord Kitchener. On the merits there is, I believe, at this distance of time no question that Curzon was right. But in craft, in slow intrigue, in strength of personality, in doubtful dangerous manoeuvres, the soldier beat the politician every time. Lord Kitchener established his own secret contacts with the Home Government and with the Secretary of State. He had his own agents and channels of communication. He selected the fighting positions with Lloyd Georgian skill. In the climax the government of Curzon's own friends and the Secretary of State, Mr. Brodrick, almost his best friend, pronounced against him, and pronounced against him in error.

He resigned in just indignation. He returned to England with his sword drawn against his former colleagues, and chiefly against his two most intimate friends, Mr. Balfour and Mr. Brodrick. But the redoubtable conflict never took place.

We now come forward into Armageddon. In this phase Curzon came into contact with a personality almost exactly the opposite of his own. You could hardly imagine two men so diverse as Curzon and Lloyd George. Temperament, prejudices, environment, up-bringing, mental processes were utterly different and markedly antagonistic. There never of course was any comparison in weight and force between the two. The offspring of the Welsh village whose whole youth had been rebellion against the aristocracy, who had skipped indignant out of the path of the local Tory magnate driving his four-in-hand, and revenged himself at night upon that magnate's rabbits, had a priceless gift. It was the very gift which the product of Eton and Balliol had always lacked—the one blessing denied him by his fairy godmothers, the one without which all other gifts are so frightfully cheapened. He had the "seeing eye". He had that deep original instinct which peers through the surfaces of words and things—the vision which sees dimly but surely the other side of the brick wall or which follows the hunt two fields before the throng. Against this, industry, learning, scholarship, eloquence, social influence, wealth, reputation, an ordered mind, plenty of pluck, counted for less than nothing. Put the two men together in any circumstances of equality and the one would eat the other. Lloyd George used Curzon for his purposes, rewarded him handsomely when it suited him to do so, flattered him frequently, but never admitted him to the inner chambers of his decisions.

I remember in 1903 during his Viceroyalty in India going to see the first Lady Curzon, formerly Miss Leiter—("the Leiter of Asia", as the wags said)—one of the most beautiful, delightful women of her day, when she was recovering in England from the first attack of her ultimately fatal illness. She showed me a letter from her husband in India. It was a hundred pages long! She showed me the numbers on the pages. All was written in his graceful legible flowing hand. But a hundred pages!

When I left the Cabinet, because I saw what was coming, and went out to France at the end of 1915, Curzon and I had been in close collaboration to prevent the evacuation of the Dardanelles. He wrote me a letter of certainly twenty pages, describing in vivid style the whole of the struggle within the Cabinet on that grievous issue and deploring my absence—"You who have always led us"—from the discussion. I was in the line when this rather deadly document reached me. A little later he was much concerned to retrieve it. But although I have hardly ever lost an important letter in my life, I have never been able to find it or find out what happened to it. However if it turns up now, it no longer matters.

One of Curzon's characteristic weaknesses was that he thought too much about stating his case, and too little about getting things done. When he had written his cogent dispatch, or brought a question before the Cabinet in full and careful form with all his force and knowledge, he was inclined to feel that his function was fulfilled. He had done his best. Events must take their course. He was too much concerned with what might be said about things, and too little with the things themselves.

It is customary, of course, for the outgoing Prime Minister, who is, presumably, the head of the stronger party, and of the majority in the House of Commons, to advise the King who should be his successor. Thus, the risks of the Crown making an unacceptable choice are greatly diminished, and in any case, whatever happens, the Sovereign is protected by the fact that he has acted upon responsible advice. If trouble arises, the outgoing Prime Minister is there to bear the brunt. In the majority of cases, the advice is obvious. But there are occasions when the matter is doubtful. This was one of them. Moreover, Mr. Bonar Law had only a few weeks earlier come to the conclusion that Curzon would not do. The incident which determined him must be mentioned.

A promoter, wishing to start an enterprise in Turkey before the conclusion of a formal peace with Mustapha Kemal, had applied to Mr. Bonar Law. The Prime Minister, about to depart upon his melancholy, almost despairing, voyage in search of health, referred the matter to the Foreign Office in a brief letter. Lord Curzon found in this an occasion to write back with acerbity. He criticized in scathing terms the character of the promoter, and in his most lecturing manner dwelt upon the inconveniences which arise when persons are led to suppose they can apply to No. 10 Downing Street, upon questions within the province of the Foreign Office. Such a practice, he remarked, would only revive one of the worst traditions of the late regime. The Prime Minister who had done nothing to deserve this rebuke, was too ill to be angry: but undoubtedly he became acutely conscious of the difficulties which would arise in a government, and in a party, if they fell into the hands of one who could write on such a small pretext so hectoring an effusion.

Mr. Bonar Law's malady was gaining daily upon him, and he did not feel himself justified in pronouncing. All he was sure of was that he would not recommend Curzon. He therefore wrote to Lord Curzon on 20 May [1923]: "I understand that it is not customary for the King to ask the Prime Minister to recommend his successor in circumstances like the present, and I presume he will not do so; but if, as I hope, he accepts my resignation at once, he will have to take immediate steps about my successor." This, of course, recognized the priority of Curzon's claim, but was noncommittal.

On Monday, 21 May, 1923, Lord Curzon was at Montacute House in Somersetshire, where he was spending the Whitsun recess. The morning post brought Mr. Bonar Law's letter. The moment then at which his life had aimed, had come. Curzon surveyed the political scene, and could discern no serious rival. Of the great figures of Conservatism there was none likely to dispute his claims. Lord Balfour was in his seventy-fifth year. Mr. Austen Chamberlain and Lord Birkenhead had not yet been forgiven for their loyalty to Mr. Lloyd George. Of Curzon's colleagues in the Bonar Law administration only one was a possible competitor, and it is doubtful whether Curzon ever considered him. Nor was this unreasonable. In official experience, in mental calibre, in Parliamentary rank and reputation, he far surpassed the only conceivable rival.

Mr. Baldwin was at that time a new and almost unknown figure. He had only been six months Chancellor of the Exchequer, and scarcely three years in the Cabinet. He had never made a noticeable speech in Parliament or elsewhere. Curzon on the other hand was Leader in the House of Lords. He had filled a prominent position in the public eye for a quarter of a century, and at the moment he occupied the Foreign Office with his customary distinction. All Monday Lord Curzon waited for the summons that was sure to come. At last it arrived. Towards evening a telegram from Lord Stamfordham was delivered, calling the Secretary of State to London. The journey to town on Tuesday was filled with the making of plans. There was no doubt in Curzon's mind—nor indeed should there have been—as to the meaning of the summons.

He was to become Prime Minister.

But as the inquiries of the King had proceeded, what may at first have seemed the obvious choice appeared in a new and doubtful light. Lord Balfour's great influence was thrown into the scales against the former Viceroy. He was summoned specially from Sheringham in Norfolk where he lay ill of phlebitis. The doctors protested that travelling would be dangerous. Balfour was undeterred. He felt he had a duty to perform. Arrived at the Palace, he expressed with conviction the view that in these days a Prime Minister must be in the House of Commons. He confined himself strictly to this point. He was careful to use no other argument. It was enough. When late that night Balfour returned to his sick-bed at Sheringham after his fatiguing journey, he was asked by some of his most cherished friends who were staying with him, "And will

548

dear George be chosen?" "No," he replied placidly, "dear George will not."

While Curzon was journeying to London, debating what he should do with No. 10 Downing Street, the King sent for Mr. Baldwin. When, that afternoon, Lord Stamfordham was announced at Carlton House Terrace, it was only to tell him that Mr. Baldwin was already at Buckingham Palace. The blow was bitter, and for the moment overwhelming.

Now that these matters can be viewed in the afterlight, opinion has declared itself, that the right choice was made. It is more doubtful whether it was made in the right way. But had Curzon been able to foresee events, his personal fortunes might yet have been retrieved. The new Prime Minister was deeply anxious to retain his services. No sooner did Mr. Baldwin receive the commission than his first visit was made to Curzon to ask him to remain at the Foreign Office. Curzon agreed at once. He had no wish to give up the Foreign Office. He did not allow his grief to distort his action. He did not give way to pique. He played his part loyally in the new team. This right and public-spirited conduct, though creditable to his character, was finally fatal to his ambitions. If he had stood aside from the government, there can be little doubt that after the electoral disaster which befell the Conservative Party six months later, he would have been in a position of greater strength than ever before. Baldwin was judged to have blundered. Curzon, uncompromised by the miscalculation, and representing the Free Trade policy now again perforce adopted by the Conservatives, might well have been the indispensable man. When therefore at the end he lost the game, it was because he played it fairly and like a man. This was one of those cases in which virtue is not its own reward.

A final disillusionment for Curzon resulted from the next turn of Fortune's wheel; and when the government of 1924 was formed, he yielded the Foreign Office to another.

These heavy reverses were supported after the initial shocks with goodwill and dignity. But undoubtedly they invested the long and strenuous career with ultimate disappointment. The morning had been golden; the noontide was bronze; and the evening lead. But all were solid, and each was polished till it shone after its fashion.

# PHILIP SNOWDEN

It would be wrong to think of Mr. Snowden as the spiteful, vindictive Death's-head of his caricatures; as a sworn tormentor who used the Rack, the Thumbscrew, and the Little Ease of taxation with gusto upon his victims. He was really a tender-hearted man, who would not have hurt a gnat unless his party and the Treasury told him to do so, and then only with compunction. Philip Snowden was a remarkable figure of our time. He was among the chief architects of the Labour-Socialist Party. He was the first Socialist Chancellor of the Exchequer. He played a decisive part in the political convulsion which hurled the Socialists from power in 1931, and inaugurated the National Government regime twice acclaimed by enormous majorities.

For nearly forty years Philip Snowden steadily and consistently built up the Socialist Party. He faced all its misfortunes, swallowed and reproduced most of its follies; and he held an indisputable right to share its years of prosperity. The first quality that the British nation approved in Philip Snowden was that they knew where he stood.

He was no more a doctrinaire Socialist than Ramsay MacDonald, but he revolted from Socialism at a different angle. MacDonald liked the Tory atmosphere and tradition; the glamour of old England appealed to him. Snowden viewed the Socialist creed with the blistering intellectual contempt of the old Gladstonian Radical. To him Toryism was a physical annoyance, and militant Socialism a disease brought on by bad conditions or contagion, like rickets or mange. His heart was filled with an equal measure of disgust and pity when he contemplated the true-blue Conservative or the green-eyed Socialist.

We must imagine with what joy Mr. Snowden was welcomed at the Treasury by the permanent officials. All British Chancellors of the Exchequer have yielded themselves, some spontaneously, some unconsciously, some reluctantly to that compulsive intellectual atmosphere. But here was the High Priest entering the sanctuary. The Treasury mind and the Snowden mind embraced each other with the fervour of two long-separated kindred lizards, and the reign of joy began. Unhappily a lot of things cropped up which were very tiresome. First of all the Chancellor of the Exchequer had to go on pretending he was a Socialist, the wordy champion of the class war and so on. This was awkward when a "statesmanlike" speech had to be made to the Bankers, or an appeal made to the public to buy Savings Certificates. Then the finances had been left in such a shocking state by that profligate Mr. Churchill, that the new Chancellor of the Exchequer in his difficulties had to adopt just the same kind of devices he had blamed so harshly in his predecessor. Economy, too, was very baffling when the Tories had kept the military services at the minimum, and all the Socialists put their trust in the Dole as the last hope of party salvation. Upon these incongruities there is no need to dwell.

After thirty years of faithful, tireless labour in building up this new party Philip Snowden found himself compelled by public duty to turn the whole of his vitriolic eloquence and propagandism against his own creation, and chose to end his political life as a Viscount in the hereditary Assembly which he had so long laboured to destroy. The apparent contradiction of spending a lifetime in creating the Socialist Party and then striking it with unconcealed relish its fatal blow does not, when all is considered, expose him to any charge of instability or inconsistency of purpose. All his life he sincerely hated Toryism, Jingoism, Vested Interests, and what are called "The Upper Classes". On the other hand, he never had the slightest intention of taking part in any revolutionary movement, nor would he in any circumstances have become responsible for a state of laxity and demoralization, financial or political, which would endanger the solid foundations of the established monarchial, parliamentary and capitalist system. On the contrary, confronted with the imminence of a breakdown in the existing order of things and national bankruptcy, he not only withstood his own friends and colleagues, but fell upon them with a whole-hearted ferocity which astounded the public and delighted the greater part of it.

A distinction must be drawn between his conduct and that of Mr. Ramsay MacDonald. In the hour of national emergency Snowden quitted and at the same time almost destroyed the party he had made. But as soon as the crisis had passed he sought occasion to break with his new allies, and become again the lively exponent of the ideas he had championed all his life. He did not dream of continuing in his office as a quasi-Conservative Minister. Whether if he had been the head of the government, he would have acted differently, cannot be known. The pleasures and pomps of ministerial life, such as they are, the amenities of elegant and opulent society, made no appeal to him. Nothing that could be offered by the ruling forces in our Commonwealth swayed his judgment or his action.

The crisis surmounted, he shook off his new friends with the same thorough-paced vigour as he had his old. The violence of his denunciations of the Socialists in 1931 was matched by the terms in which he upbraided the National Government in 1935. This apparent catholicity of animosities gave him the appearance of a kind of fierce dog who would bite anyone and everyone for biting's sake. Actually it arose from an extreme integrity of personal conviction from which only a supreme emergency justified a temporary departure. Such a man, had he been a Spaniard, might have saved Spain the horrors of civil war by upholding democratic and parliamentary government with an iron hand. Such a man was the German Socialist Noske who saved Germany from Communism in 1919. Snowden knew exactly how far he meant to go, and when pushed beyond that limit reacted with a violence at once salutary and astonishing.

I first met him many years ago when I was a young Liberal Minister and he one of the small band of Independent Labour men who nevertheless found themselves forced to conform to the main policy of the Asquith Government. We travelled for four hours together to Lancashire. Then for the first time I saw beneath this apparently bitter and even spiteful spirit and regard something of the appeal and kindliness of his nature. His face, though in a way twisted by pain, ill health and the mood of revolt, was lighted by a smile truly disarming, comprehending and delightful. Afterwards it fell to my lot for seven years to wrangle with him about finance as Chancellor of the Exchequer, or in opposition to his Chancellorship, and we hit each other as hard as we could within the wide rules of Order. But never have I had any feelings towards him which destroyed the impression that he was a generous, true-hearted man.

The Marxian aberration never obsessed his keen intelligence. One who knew him well said to me, "No one will ever know what a Labour Government will be like till they see one without Snowden at the Exchequer." Arrived at the post, he confronted his colleagues with a resistance to wild and sloppy extravagance, however popular, which staggered them. Although overborne on many points, he continued to fight for what he regarded as the essential principles of sound finance, and the friction of this conflict roused him to the fury and even hatred with which he eventually assailed his friends and colleagues.

The British democracy should be proud of Philip Snowden. He was a man capable of maintaining the structure of Society while at the same time championing the interests of the masses. His long life of effort, self-denial, and physical affliction was crowned by honourable success. His fearlessness, his rectitude, his austerity, his sobriety of judgment, his deep love of Britain and his studiously concealed, but intense, pride in British greatness, distinguish him as one of the true worthies of our age.


# CLEMENCEAU

The truth is that Clemenceau embodied and expressed France. As much as any single human being, miraculously magnified, can ever be a nation, he was France. Fancy paints nations in symbolic animals—the British Lion, the American Eagle, the Russian double-headed ditto, the Gallic Cock. But the Old Tiger, with his quaint, stylish cap, his white moustache and burning eye, would make a truer mascot for France than any barnyard fowl. He was an apparition of the French Revolution at its sublime moment, before it was overtaken by the squalid butcheries of the Terrorists. He represented the French people risen against tyrants—tyrants of the mind, tyrants of the soul, tyrants of the body; foreign tyrants, domestic tyrants, swindlers, humbugs, grafters, traitors, invaders, defeatists—all lay within the bound of the Tiger; and against them the Tiger waged inexorable war. Anti-clerical, anti-monarchist, anti-Communist, anti-German—in all this he represented the dominant spirit of France.

Clemenceau's story is familiar to most of us. A life of storm, from the beginning to the end; fighting, fighting all the way; never a pause, never a truce, never a rest. His blade was forged and tempered in the fires and chills of half a century. He was Mayor of Montmartre amid the perils of the Commune. His assault upon the crumbling Empire and his resistance to the excesses of the revolutionaries; his vain attempt to save the lives—almost at the cost of his own—of Generals Clément Thomas and Lecomte, concentrated upon him the malice both of extremists opposed in their atrocities, and of reactionaries victorious and seeking the punishment of those who had stirred the mob, and could no longer lead it. He struggled long and arduously to earn his daily bread as a doctor, as a teacher, as a journalist. All these trials were but the early morning of his long and long-threatened life. When he entered Parliament another series of conflicts began. The unswerving Radical Republican; the destroyer of Ministers and Ministries; the Parliamentary Tiger whom all politicians feared; the iconoclast, the duellist, the merciless assailant of men who were building the new French Colonial Empire, gathered against him foes on every side. He followed Gambetta and repudiated him. He was duped by Boulanger and became his greatest enemy. The existence of the Republic hung for years by a thread. In Clemenceau, at least, the thread had one unsleeping guardian.

Excluded from the Chamber, his voice could no longer be heard. Never mind! He had another weapon. He had a pen. He wrote for bread and life: for life and honour! And far and wide what he wrote was read. Thus he survived. He survived not to recover only, but to assault: not to assault, but to conquer. The worst of all the scandals had yet to come. Clemenceau became the champion of Dreyfus. Here he had to fight, to him the most sacred thing in France—the French Army. The Church, Society, High Finance, the Press—these, as before, were ranged against him. But now, in addition, was that splendid organization upon whose bayonets the liberties of Europe were soon to depend. "Destroy confidence in the Army chiefs and you will have imperilled the safety of the country!" exclaimed the generals in chorus. "Is it to a butchery you wish us to lead your sons?" cried General de Pellieu at one of the Dreyfus trials. But after all, the question at issue was whether Dreyfus was a traitor or not. And he was innocent. The whole nation took sides. Friendships were ruptured and families divided. But the genius of France was not darkened. Truth and justice marched forward: and along the path which he had helped to clear for them, Clemenceau came back into his own. He even became for a space Prime Minister.

Such was the man who, armed with the experience and loaded with the hatreds of half a century, was called to the helm of France in the worst period of the war. Many of the French generals were discredited, and all their plans had failed. Widespread mutinies had been with difficulty suppressed at the front. Profound and tortuous intrigues gripped Paris. Britain had bled herself white at Passchendaele, the Russians had collapsed, the Italians were at the last gasp, and the Americans were far away. The giant enemy towered up, brazen, and so far as we could see, invulnerable. It was at this moment, after every other conceivable combination had been tried, that the fierce old man was summoned to what was in fact the Dictatorship of France. He returned to power as Marius had returned to Rome; doubted by many, dreaded by all, but doomsent, inevitable.

It was at this time I first began to know him. My work as Minister of Munitions brought me frequently to Paris, and involved me constantly with French Ministers. My close association with Mr. Lloyd George afforded additional intimate contacts. I was with Clemenceau for half an hour on the morning when he was forming his Ministry. I listened to his opening speech in the Chamber. My friend, colleague, and opposite number, Albert Thomas, had only a day or two before losing office in the ministerial earthquake. We had been drawn so closely together in the details of business, that I ventured an appeal to the Tiger not to disturb a cross-channel combination that was working smoothly. I thought I had made an impression; but meanwhile Thomas, supported by the Socialists, had declared that Clemenceau as Premier "was a danger to national defence". This of course was mortal.

One day he said to me: "I have no political system, and I have abandoned all political principles. I am a man dealing with events as they come in the light of my experience," or it may be it was "according as I have seen things happen." I was reminded of Monsieur de Camors' letter to his son: "All principles are equally true or equally false, according to circumstances." Clemenceau was quite right. The only thing that mattered was to beat the Germans.

Presently came the supreme crisis. The Germans were again on the Marne. From the heights of Montmartre the horizon could be seen alive with the flashes of artillery. The Americans were pitchforked in at Château-Thierry. I had important munition and aeroplane factories all around Paris: we had to prepare to move them and to improvise shelters farther south: so I was much in the French capital. Before a war begins one should always say, "I am strong, but so is the enemy." When a war is being fought one should say, "I am exhausted, but the enemy is quite tired too." It is almost impossible to say either of these two things at the time they matter. Until the Germans collapsed, they seemed unconquerable; but so was Clemenceau. He uttered to me in his room at the Ministry of War words he afterwards repeated in the tribune: "I will fight in front of Paris; I will fight in Paris; I will fight behind Paris." Everyone knew this was no idle boast. Paris might have been reduced to the ruins of Ypres or Arras. It would not have affected Clemenceau's resolution. He meant to sit on the safety-valve, till he won or till all his world blew up. He had no hope beyond the grave; he mocked at death; he was in his seventy-seventh year. Happy the nation which when its fate quivers in the balance can find such a tyrant and such a champion.

Whenever I visited Paris on public business, whatever the government in power, I made a point of calling on him. "I invite no one here," he said, "but whenever you come you will be welcome." He even on one occasion went to the point of saying in "an unforgettable manner" to his eldest daughter, from whom I have it, "Mr. Winston Churchill is very far from being an enemy of France." I have my last picture of him a year before he died. The little house in the Rue François: a small library-sitting-room. It is winter, and the room seems to be unheated. There is a large fireplace; but it is piled full of books. Evidently no fires this year! I wish I had kept on my overcoat. The old man appears, in his remarkable black skull-cap, gloved and well wrapped up. None of the beauty of

Napoleon, but I expect some of his St. Helena majesty; and far back beyond Napoleon, Roman figures come into view. The fierceness, the pride, the poverty after great office, the grandeur when stripped of power, the unbreakable front offered to this world and the next —all these belong to the ancients.

## CHARLES STEWART PARNELL

In the eighties a new figure appeared upon the Irish benches whose character, manner and method seemed to contradict all the ordinary traits of Irishmen. Here was a man, stern, grave, reserved, no orator, no idealogue, no spinner of words and phrases; but a being who seemed to exercise unconsciously an indefinable sense of power in repose—of command awaiting the hour. When the House of Commons became aware of Parnell's growing influence with the Irish Party, nearly all of whom were Catholics, it was noted with surprise that the new or future leader of Ireland was a Protestant and a delegate to the Irish Church Synod. It was also said, "He is the most English Irishman ever yet seen." Indeed, during the eighties it was upon English politics that Parnell chiefly laid his hand at Westminster. He became the ally and to some extent the spear-point of English Radicalism, then rising sharp and keen into prominence. To him perhaps more than anyone else the British Army owes the abolition of the cruel and senseless flogging then considered inseparable from effective military discipline. In every movement of reform, now achieved and long surpassed, Parnell brought the Irish parliamentary party to the aid of the most advanced challenging forces in British public life. Yet he was himself a man of Conservative instincts, especially where property was concerned. Indeed, the paradoxes of his earnest and sincere life were astonishing: a Protestant leading Catholics; a landlord inspiring a "No Rent" campaign; a man of law and order exciting revolt; a humanitarian and anti-terrorist controlling and yet arousing the hopes of Invincibles and Terrorists.

An air of mystery and legend had hung about Parnell from his Cambridge days. He was the reverse of a demagogue and agitator.

He studied mathematics and metallurgy. He was the heir to a landed estate. He was a Sheriff and a keen cricketer. His permanent ambition was to find the gold veins in the Wicklow mountains, and through all his political triumphs and agonies he could turn for peace and diversion to the laboratory with its scales, retorts and test-tubes. His Irish nationalism, which persisted and grew upon this unusual background, has been traced to his mother and her admiration for the idealistic Fenians. Assassinations he abhorred. He was too practical to harbour Fenian dreams of insurrection against the might of Britain. As his authority grew, Fenians and Invincibles stayed the bloody hand for fear of a Parnell resignation.

Without Parnell Mr. Gladstone would never have attempted Home Rule. The conviction was borne in upon the Grand Old Man in his hey-day that here was a leader who could govern Ireland, and that no one else could do it. Here was a man who could inaugurate the new system in a manner which would not be insupportable to the old. Parnell with his dogged tenacity and fascination over his followers became the keystone of the Home Rule arch which Gladstone tried to erect and beneath whose ruins he and his adherents fell. Parnell was the last great leader who could hold all the Irish. As a Protestant he was probably the only one who might eventually have conciliated Ulster. Lord Cowper once said that he had neither the virtues nor the vices of an Irishman. He was a great moderate who held back the powers of revolution as an unflung weapon in his hand. If he accepted Boycotting, it was only as a half-way house between incendiarism and constitutionalism. One of his followers, Frank O'Donnell, used to say Parnell talked daggers, but used none. In the first phase in 1881 Mr. Gladstone arrested Parnell and threw him into Kilmainham jail. But the forces at work within the Liberal Party were such as to compel the Prime Minister of Great Britain to parley with his political prisoner. After much difficulty an agreement was reached. Parnell was liberated with redoubled prestige.

But the fight grew more bitter. It wrecked the old liberties of the House of Commons. Obstruction was practised as a Parliamentary art, and the ancient freedom of debate was destroyed by the closure —"Clôture", Lord Randolph Churchill always used to call it, to brand it with its foreign origin—and ever-tightening rules of order. Parnell said that he based his tactics on those of General Grant, namely, slogging away by frontal attack. He met English hatred with obstruction, and coercion with a bitterness which destroyed the old amenities of Parliamentary debate. In Ireland, neither the Church nor the Revolutionaries liked him, but both had to submit to his policy. He was a Garibaldi who compelled at once the allegiance of the Pope and of the *Carbonari* in the national cause. When taunted with stimulating outrage and even murder, he thought it sufficient to reply, "I am answerable to Irish opinion, and Irish opinion alone."

The love of Charles Stewart Parnell and Kitty O'Shea holds its place among the romances of political history. Since 1880 Parnell had loved Kitty, or as he called her, "Queenie". This lady was an attractive adventuress, bored with her husband—no wonder!—and aching for a sip in the secret brew of politics. The sister of an English Field-Marshal, she was not very deeply vowed to the cause of Ireland. She heard of Parnell as a rising portent when he was living in solitary lodgings in London. She invited him to dinner for a wager. She sent her card to him at the House of Commons. When he appeared she dropped a red rose. He picked it up; its shrivelled petals were buried with him in his coffin.

If ever there was a monogamist it was Parnell. Early in life he had been jilted. He had only taken to politics as an anodyne. Kitty became all-important and absorbing to him. She was at once mistress and nurse, queen and companion, and the lonely man fighting the might of Britain, afflicted by ill health, drew his life from her smile and presence. By a strange telepathy he could tell whenever she entered the Ladies' Gallery in the House. In her strange book she describes the life they lived together, first at Eltham and then at Brighton. It was a mixture of secrecy and reck-lessness. From a very early stage the complaisance of the husband was indispensable. Collision with Captain O'Shea passed swiftly into collusion. O'Shea accepted the position. He even profited by it, though not in the base way sometimes represented. He too was under the spell of the great man. By Parnell's support O'Shea was returned as an Irish Nationalist for Galway, although all the other leading Home Rulers thought him but a poor champion of the Irish cause. When murmurs broke out in the election at the advancement of this lukewarm, unsuitable candidate, Parnell silenced them with an imperious gesture. "I have a Parliament for Ireland in my hand. Forbear to dispute my will."

Thus we see Parnell and Kitty living as man and wife year after year in love none the less true because illicit; while the Captain following the Irish leader enjoyed the opportunities of being a go-between with Chamberlain, with Dilke, and with other prominent men in the great world of London. But always in his heart lurked the spirit of revenge. Often he writhed and cursed, and then subsided. As long as the supreme political interest held, he endured. We have the incident in O'Shea's triangular household of Parnell finding him in Kitty's bedroom, a conjuncture forbidden by their unwritten law. Instead of kicking out O'Shea, Parnell slung Kitty on to his shoulder and carried her off to another room. It was said of Parnell that he was himself a volcano under an ice-cap. He certainly lived upon the brink of a geyser which might at any moment erupt in scalding water. The public knew nothing of all this secret drama, but as early as the Kilmainham Treaty it became a matter of knowledge to the Cabinet. Parnell hastened from the jail to visit her, and received their dead child in his arms. Sir William Harcourt as Home Secretary informed the Cabinet that the Kilmainham Treaty had been engineered by the husband of Parnell's mistress. Kitty played a vital part in Parnell's action. She prevented him from abandoning politics after the Phoenix Park murders. She was always the intermediary between him and Mr. Gladstone. O'Shea has been as bitterly blamed by his countrymen as anyone in Irish history. There is no doubt that he was thrilled to see his wife adjusting enormous State issues between Parnell and the Prime Minister. His own relations with Chamberlain, of whom he was a frequent attendant, made a compulsive appeal to his sense of self-importance and even to his price. The story was neither so simple nor so contemptible as it has been painted.

Parnell was so early interwoven with the O'Sheas that there was no time in the eighties in which he could have disentangled himself. Before Gladstone cast him into Kilmainham Jail he was deep in their toils and enchantments. Mrs. O'Shea's book pretends that she continued to deceive O'Shea, but there is no doubt that from 1881 onwards he was fully apprised. The opening of letters by close friends in the party had made them aware of the intrigue, and both Healy and Biggar repeatedly warned Parnell that the O'Sheas would be his ruin. Parnell cared nothing for this. His was a love stronger than death, defiant of every social ordinance, scornfully superior not only to worldly ambitions, but even to the Cause entrusted to his hands.

In 1887, *The Times* newspaper began to publish a series of articles under the heading of "Parnellism and Crime". Then, in order to substantiate the charges made by its correspondent, it reproduced, in what Morley calls "all the fascination of facsimile", a letter in Parnell's handwriting which directly connected the Irish leader with the murder campaign. The story of this letter is without compare in the annals of the Press. In 1885 there lived in dishonourable poverty in Dublin a broken-down journalist named Richard Pigott. For years he had preyed upon a credulous public. He had raised subscriptions for the defence of the accused in Fenian trials and the relief of their wives and children, and then embezzled the moneys received. That source of income failing, he had turned to the writing of begging letters. But the wells of Christian charity yielded little to his pump. According to rumour, he was about this time supplementing their scanty flow by the sale of indecent books and photographs. And even that could not procure sufficient for his moderate needs. In this crisis of his fate there came to him a gentleman convinced that Parnell and his colleagues were parties to the crimes of the extremists. But he wanted proof, and he offered Pigott a guinea a day, hotel and travelling expenses, and a round price for documents, if he could supply the necessary evidence. Of course Pigott could supply it. And so the famous Parnell letter and a host of other incriminating documents, came into being, and ultimately found their way into the offices of *The Times*.

The manager of *The Times*, unfortunately, did not investigate the origin of these letters. He paid, in all, over £2,500 for them. But he asked no questions. He believed that the letters were genuine because he wanted them to be genuine. And the government took the same view for precisely the same reason. They believed that here they had a weapon of the first importance, not only against Parnell but against Gladstone. Against Lord Randolph Churchill's earnest advice, embodied in a secret memorandum, they set up a Special Commission of three judges to investigate the connection of Parnell and his colleagues, and the movement of which they were the leaders, with agrarian political crime assassination.

It was, in effect, a State trial—but a State trial without a jury. For over a year the Judges toiled and laboured. Many of the secrets of terrorism and of counter-espionage were laid bare. Strange figures like Le Caron, in the deep-hidden employ of the British Government, told their tale of conspiracies in England, Ireland and America. The whole political world followed the case with fascination. Nothing like it had been seen since the impeachment of Sacheverell. The brilliant Irish advocate who was afterwards Lord Russell of Killowen, Lord Chief Justice of England, was principal counsel for his compatriots. He was aided by a young Radical lawyer, by name Herbert Henry Asquith. The climax was not reached until February, 1889, when Pigott was put in the box and broke down in fatal cross-examination. His exposure by Russell was complete and remorseless. He was asked to write down the words "likelihood" and "hesitancy" which he had misspelt in the forged letter. He repeated his misspellings. He wrote "hesitency" as it had appeared in the accusing document. Letters which he had written, begging for money, were read out, and greeted with mocking laughter from all parts of the Court. There was another day of damning exposure. The fact of forgery was established. Then, on the third day, when Pigott's name was called, he did not answer. He had fled from justice. Detectives tracked him to an hotel in Madrid, and he blew out his brains to escape the punishment of his crime.

The effect of these proceedings on the British electorate was profound. A general election could not long be delayed, and the prospect of a sweeping Liberal victory seemed certain. Parnell was widely regarded throughout Britain as a deeply wronged man who had at length been vindicated. He had been cleared of a horrible charge brought against him by political malice. The prospects of a Home Rule victory were never so bright. Making allowance for the differences between countries, the charge against Parnell was invested with all the significance attached in France to the Dreyfus case. All the political forces were stirred by vehement passion. Then came the counterstroke. Someone detonated O'Shea. The husband who for ten years had been inert suddenly roused himself to strike a deadly blow. He opened proceedings for divorce against his wife, naming Parnell as co-respondent.

Parnell and Mrs. O'Shea were at first unperturbed by the proceedings. Parnell was sure he could hold Ireland, and even Irish Conservatism. To Kitty divorce promised the end of a false and odious situation and of long apprehension, and she saw a sure and quick way to becoming Mrs. Parnell. If Parnell had defended the suit, he could, in the opinion of his renowned solicitor Sir George Lewis, have certainly won by proving the long collusion. But Kitty and he could never then be united before the whole world in wedlock. It must be admitted that Parnell inclined to this course. But Mrs. O'Shea's counsel, Frank Lockwood, a man of exceptional brilliancy, persuaded him to let the case go forward without resistance. In after years Lockwood said, "Parnell was cruelly wronged all round. There is a great reaction in his favour. I am not altogether without remorse myself."

The furious political world of the early nineties learned with delight or consternation that Parnell was adjudged a guilty co-respondent. The details of the case, published verbatim in every newspaper, fed the prudish curiosity of the public. According to one story Parnell had made his exit on one occasion from her room down the fire-escape, and this tale aroused unpitying laughter. But the reaction which followed was different from what Parnell had foreseen. Mr. Gladstone did not appear at the first blush so shocked as might have been expected from so saintly a figure. It was only when he realized the violent revolt of English Nonconformity against a "convicted adulterer" that he saw how grievous was the injury to his political interests and how inevitable his severance from Parnell had become. He repudiated Parnell, and Ireland was forced to choose between the greatest of English Parliamentarians, the statesman who had made every sacrifice for the Irish cause, who alone could carry the victory in the larger island, and the proud chieftain under whom the Irish people might have marched to a free and true partnership in the British Empire. The choice was bitter, but the forces inexorable. A meeting of the Irish Party was called on a requisition signed by thirty-one members. Parnell, re-elected leader only the day before, was in the chair, looking, as one of those present put it, "as if it were we who had gone astray, and he were sitting there to judge us". An appeal was made to him to retire temporarily, leaving the management of the party in the hands of a committee to be nominated by himself: then, after the excitement had died down, he could resume the leadership. Parnell said nothing. But equally strong appeals were made by other members that he should not retire. In the end, the meeting adjourned.

Parnell now fought for time. He believed that Ireland was behind him, and that if he could only delay decision long enough, he must win. But when the party meeting resumed, his opponents were taking a stronger line. Mr. T. M. Healy was leading the rebels. "I say to Mr. Parnell his power has gone," he declared. "He derived that power from the people. We are the representatives of the people." Parnell was stung to reply: "Mr. Healy has been trained in this warfare," he said. "Who trained him? Who gave him his first opportunity and chance? Who got him his seat in Parliament? That Mr. Healy should be here today to destroy me is due to myself." Day after day the debate went on, Parnell fighting more and more desperately to avoid a vote on the real issue, still clinging to the belief that the people of Ireland would support him against the insurgent M.P.s. But he knew that the tide was turning against him. His eyes blazed ever more fiercely in his pallid face: it was only by an intense effort that he still held himself in check. On every side tempers were taut, at the breaking-point. On the fifth day Healy quoted a speech of Parnell's, six months before, in which he had referred to an alliance with the Liberals, "an alliance which I venture to believe will last". "What broke it off?" demanded Healy. "Gladstone's letter," said Parnell. "No," retorted Healy. "It perished in the stench of the Divorce Court."

The end came on the seventh day of the meeting, 6 December, 1890. There were disorderly scenes. John Redmond, who had stuck to Parnell through thick and thin, used the phrase, "the master of the Party". "Who is to be the mistress of the Party?" cried the bitterest tongue in Ireland. Parnell rose, his eyes terrible. For a moment it seemed that he was going to strike Healy, and some of the rebels even hoped that he would. But: "I appeal to my friend the chairman," said one of them. "Better appeal to your own friends," said Parnell, "better appeal to that cowardly scoundrel there, that in an assembly of Irishmen dares to insult a woman." There was more barren argument, more recriminations. Finally, Justin M'Carthy rose. "I see no further use carrying on a discussion which must be barren of all but reproach, ill-temper, controversy and indignity," he said, "and I therefore suggest that all who think with me at this grave crisis should withdraw with me from this room." Forty-five members filed out silently, twenty-seven remained behind. And Ireland, Parnell was soon to discover, was with the majority.

The Catholic Church swung decidedly against him. In vain he asserted his vanished authority. In vain he fought with frantic energy at savage Irish by-elections. Another year of grim struggle at hopeless odds sapped a constitution always frail. Then in Morley's moving words, "the veiled shadow stole upon the scene", and Charles Stewart Parnell struggled for the last time across the Irish Channel to die at Brighton on 6 October, 1891, in the arms of the woman he loved so well.

# SPLENDID VARIETY

# THOUGHTS
# AND ADVENTURES

*A collection of articles first published in newspapers and periodicals between 1924 and 1931 and in book form in 1932. They are reminiscences and reflections covering a wide variety of subjects such as the "Battle of Sidney Street"; "My Spy Story"; "A Day with Clemenceau"; "Election Memories"; "Shall We All Commit Suicide?"; "Fifty Years Hence" and "Painting as a Pastime".*

★

## A SECOND CHOICE

IF I HAD to live my life over again in the same surroundings, no doubt I should have the same perplexities and hesitations; no doubt I should have my same sense of proportion, my same guiding lights, my same onward thrust, my same limitations. And if these came in contact with the same external facts, why should I not run as the result along exactly the same grooves? Of course if the externals are varied, if accident and chance flow out through new uncharted channels, I shall vary accordingly. But then I should not be living my life over again, I should be living another life in a world whose structure and history would to a large extent diverge from this one.

If, for instance, when I went to Monte Carlo and staked my money on red, as I usually do, having a preference for the optimistic side of things, and the whirling ivory ball had fallen into a red slot in the roulette wheel instead of falling, as it nearly always did on these occasions, into a black slot, I might have made a lot of money. If I had invested this money twenty years ago in plots of land on the lake shore at Chicago and had never gone to Monte Carlo any more, I might be a multi-millionaire. On the other hand, if fired by my good luck I had continued to gamble, I might have become an habitué of the tables, and should now be one of those melancholy shadows we see creeping in the evening around the gaming and so-called pleasure resorts of Europe. Clearly two processes are at work, the first dictating where the ivory ball is to come to rest and the second what reaction it is to produce in me. If both these are to vary, their interplay becomes too intricate for us even to catch one glimpse of what might have been! Therefore let us suppose that the march of events and its freaks and accidents remain as we now know them and that all that happens is that I have another choice.

But now I must ask an important question: Do I have my new choice *with my present knowledge* of what has actually happened? Or am I to have nothing better in health, character, knowledge and faith to guide me next time than I had before? If the latter, our argument comes very quickly to a dead end. If the same choice and the same environment were at any given moment to be repeated, and I were the same person, I should infallibly take the same step. If, for instance, I were the sort of person who would spin a coin to settle whether he should take a journey, or buy a house, or open a lawsuit, or join a government, and the coin in fact came down tails up as it had before, I should certainly act as I did then.

If, then, there is to be any reality in the new choice offered to me to live my life over again, I must have foreknowledge. I must carry back with me to this new starting-point the whole picture and story of the world and of my own part in it, as I now know them. Then surely I shall know what to make for and what to avoid; then surely I shall be able to choose my path with certainty. I shall have success in all my dealings. Thus armed I shall be able to guide others and, indeed, guide the human race away from the follies in which they wallow, away from the errors to which they are slaves, away from the endless tribulations in which they plunge themselves.

But wait a minute. All that I was offered was one choice, to live my life over again. I take back with me to that moment all that I know today. But once I have exercised my choice my present picture of existing world's history and all my own life-story is out of date, or rather it will never happen. Of course if I use my foreknowledge only in some trifling matter, that will not make much appreciable difference in the currents of cause and effect. But it will nevertheless make immediately a different world around me.

I might, for instance, without altering the economy of the universe, use my foreknowledge to back the winner of the Derby at the first moment that I began to live my life over again. But my foreknowledge would give me no assurance about the next Derby. True that in the life of the world as it has worked out, I know the name of the horse which won. But now something new has happened. I have won such an enormous stake that several important bookmakers have defaulted. One of their richest clients was ruined in the crash. In despair he jumped into a pond. The client happened to be the owner of the horse that was going to win the Derby next year. His untimely death of course disqualified his horse. Under our silly rules it was struck out of the race, and I, proceeding to Epsom next year with all my foreknowledge, found myself the most ignorant man on the Downs about what was going to happen. I was so cluttered up with all my recollections of the way the other horses had run in the world as it would have been, that I made the most foolish speculations about what would now happen in the new world which my supernatural intuition had made. Thus we may say that if one had the chance to live one's life over again foreknowledge would, in important decisions, be only fully effective once. Thereafter I should be dealing with a continually diverging skein of consequence which would increasingly affect my immediate environment.

If we look back on our past life we shall see that one of its most usual experiences is that we have been helped by our mistakes and injured by our most sagacious decisions. I suppose if I had to relive my life I ought to eschew the habit of smoking. Look at all the money I have wasted on tobacco. Think of it all invested and mounting up at compound interest year after year. I remember my father in his most sparkling mood, his eye gleaming through the haze of his cigarette, saying, "Why begin? If you want to have an eye that is true, and a hand that does not quiver, if you want never to ask yourself a question as you ride at a fence, don't smoke."

But consider! How can I tell that the soothing influence of tobacco upon my nervous system may not have enabled me to comport myself with calm and with courtesy in some awkward personal encounter or negotiation, or carried me serenely through some critical hours of anxious waiting? How can I tell that my temper would have been as sweet or my companionship as agreeable if I had abjured from my youth the goddess Nicotine? Now that I think of it, if I had not turned back to get that matchbox which I left behind in my dug-out in Flanders, might I not just have walked into the shell which pitched so harmlessly a hundred yards ahead?

So far as my own personal course has been concerned, I have mostly acted in politics as I felt I wanted to act. When I have desired to do or say anything and have refrained therefrom through prudence, slothfulness or being dissuaded by others, I have always felt ashamed of myself at the time; though sometimes afterwards I saw that it was lucky for me I was checked. I do not see how it would have been possible for me in the mood I was in after the South African War to have worked enthusiastically with the Conservative Party in the mood they were in at that time. Even apart from the Free Trade quarrel, I was in full reaction against the war and they in full exploitation in the political sphere of the so-called victory. Thus when the Protection issue was raised I was already disposed to view all their actions in the most critical light. The flood tides of a new generation long pent-up flowed forward with the breaking of the dikes upon the low-lying country. Of course it is a lamentable thing to leave the party which you have been brought up in from a child, and where nearly all your friends and kinsmen are. Still, I am sure that in those days I acted in accordance with my deepest feeling and with all that recklessness in so doing which belongs to youth and is indeed the glory of youth and its most formidable quality.

When the Great War broke out and I started with the enormous prestige of having prepared the fleet in spite of so much opposition and of having it ready according to the science of those days, almost to a single ship, at the fateful hour, I made the singular mistake of being as much interested in the military as in the naval operations. Thus, without prejudice to my Admiralty work, I was led into taking minor military responsibilities upon my shoulders which exposed me to all those deadly risks on a small scale that await those in high stations who come too closely in contact with action in detail.

I ought, for instance, never to have gone to Antwerp. I ought to have remained in London and endeavoured to force the Cabinet and Lord Kitchener to take more effective action than they did, while I all the time sat in my position of great authority with all the precautions which shield great authority from rough mischance. Instead, I passed four or five vivid days amid the shells, excitement and tragedy of the defence of Antwerp. I soon became so deeply involved in the local event that I had in common decency to offer to the government my resignation of my office as First Lord of the Admiralty in order to see things through on the spot. Lucky indeed it was for me that my offer was not accepted, for I should only have been involved in the command of a situation which locally at any rate had already been rendered hopeless by the general course of the war. In all great business very large errors are excused or even unperceived, but in definite and local matters small mistakes are punished out of all proportion. I might well have lost all the esteem I gained by the mobilization and readiness of the fleet, through getting mixed up in the firing-lines at Antwerp. Those who are charged with the direction of supreme affairs must sit on the mountain-tops of control; they must never descend into the valleys of direct physical and personal action.

Sometimes our mistakes and errors turn to great good fortune. When the Conservatives suddenly plunged into Protection in 1923, a dozen Liberal constituencies pressed me to be their candidate. And clearly Manchester was for every reason the battleground on which I should have fought. A seat was offered me there, which, as it happened, I should in all probability have won. Instead, through some obscure complex I chose to go off and fight against a Socialist in Leicester, where, being also attacked by the Conservatives, I was of course defeated. On learning of these two results in such sharp contrast, I could have kicked myself. Yet as it turned out, it was the very fact that I was out of Parliament, free from all attachment and entanglement in any particular constituency, that enabled me to make an independent and unbiased judgment of the situation when the Liberals most unwisely and wrongly put the Socialist minority government for the first time into power, thus sealing their own doom.

Thus I found myself free a few months later to champion the anti-Socialist cause in the Westminster by-election, and so regained for a time at least the goodwill of all those strong Conservative elements, some of whose deepest feelings I share and can at critical moments express, although they have never liked or trusted me. But for my erroneous judgment in the General Election of 1923 I should never have regained contact with the great party into which I was born and from which I had been severed by so many years of bitter quarrel.

When I survey in the light of these reflections the scene of my past life as a whole, I have no doubt that I do not wish to live it over again. Happy, vivid and full of interest as it has been, I do not seek to tread again the toilsome and dangerous path. Not even an opportunity of making a different set of mistakes and experiencing a different series of adventures and successes would lure me. How can I tell that the good fortune which has up to the present attended me with fair constancy would not be lacking at some critical moment in another chain of causation?

Let us be contented with what has happened to us and thankful for all we have been spared. Let us accept the natural order in which we move. Let us reconcile ourselves to the mysterious rhythm of our destinies, such as they must be in this world of space and time. Let us treasure our joys but not bewail our sorrows. The glory of light cannot exist without its shadows. Life is a whole, and good and ill must be accepted together. The journey has been enjoyable and well worth making—once.

## CONSISTENCY IN POLITICS

A distinction should be drawn at the outset between two kinds of political inconsistency. First, a statesman in contact with the moving current of events and anxious to keep the ship on an even keel and steer a steady course may lean all his weight now on one side and now on the other. His arguments in each case when contrasted can be shown to be not only very different in character, but contradictory in spirit and opposite in direction: yet his object will throughout have remained the same. His resolves, his wishes, his outlook may have been unchanged; his methods may be verbally irreconcilable. We cannot call this inconsistency. In fact it may be claimed to be the truest consistency. The only way a man can remain consistent amid changing circumstances is to change with them while preserving the same dominating purpose. It is inevitable that frequent changes should take place in the region of action. A policy is pursued up to a certain point; it becomes evident at last that it can be carried no further. New facts arise which clearly render it obsolete; new difficulties, which make it impracticable. A new and possibly the opposite solution presents itself with overwhelming force. To abandon the old policy is often necessarily to adopt the new. It sometimes happens that the same men, the same government, the same party have to execute this *volte face*. It may be their duty to do so because it is the sole manner of discharging their responsibilities, or because they are the only combination strong enough to do what is needed in the new circumstances. In such a case the inconsistency is not merely verbal, but actual, and ought to be boldly avowed. In place of arguments for coercion, there must be arguments for conciliation; and these must come from the same lips as the former. But all this may be capable of reasonable and honourable explanation. Statesmen may say bluntly, "We have failed to coerce; we have now to conciliate," or alternatively, "We have failed to conciliate; we have now to coerce."

Apart from action in the march of events, there is an inconsistency arising from a change of mood or heart. *"Le cœur a ses raisons que la raison ne connaît pas."* Few men avoid such changes in their lives, and few public men have been able to conceal them. Usually youth is for freedom and reform, maturity for judicious compromise, and old age for stability and repose. The normal progression is from Left to Right, and often from extreme Left to extreme Right. Mr. Gladstone's progress was by a striking exception in the opposite direction. In the immense period covered by his life he moved steadily and irresistibly from being "the rising hope of stern unbending Tories" to become the greatest Liberal statesman of the nineteenth century. Enormous was the change of mood which this august transition represented. From the young Member of Parliament whose speech against the abolition of slavery attracted the attention of the House of Commons in 1833, from the famous Minister who supported the Confederate States against the North in the sixties, to the fiery orator who pleaded the cause of Bulgarian independence in the eighties, and the veteran Premier, the last scraps of whose matchless strength were freely offered in the nineties to the cause of Irish self-government—it was a transit almost astronomical in its scale.

A change of Party is usually considered a much more serious breach of consistency than a change of view. In fact as long as a man works with a Party he will rarely find himself accused of inconsistency, no matter how widely his opinions at one time on any subject can be shown to have altered. Yet Parties are subject to changes and inconsistencies not less glaring than those of individuals. How should it be otherwise in the fierce swirl of Parliamentary conflict and Electoral fortune? Change with a Party, however inconsistent, is at least defended by the power of numbers. To remain constant when a Party changes is to excite invidious challenge. Moreover, a separation from Party affects all manner of personal relations and sunders old comradeship. Still, a sincere conviction, in harmony with the needs of the time and upon a great issue, will be found to override all other factors; and it is right and in the public interest that it should. Politics is a generous profession. The motives and characters of public men, though constantly criticized, are in the end broadly and fairly judged.

## THE BATTLE OF SIDNEY STREET

At about ten o'clock on the morning of 3 January [1911] I was in my bath, when I was surprised by an urgent knocking at the door.

"There is a message from the Home Office on the telephone absolutely immediate."

Dripping wet and shrouded in a towel I hurried to the instrument, and received the following news:

"The Anarchists who murdered the police have been surrounded in a house in the East End—No. 100 Sidney Street—and are firing on the police with automatic pistols. They have shot one man and appear to have plenty of ammunition. Authority is requested to send for troops to arrest or kill them."

I replied at once, giving the necessary permission and directing the police to use whatever force was necessary. In about twenty minutes I was at the Home Office. There I found my principal adviser, Mr. Ernley Blackwell, who told me that no further information had been received, except that the Anarchists had been effectually surrounded, but were still firing in all directions. No one knew how many Anarchists there were or what measures were going to be taken. In these circumstances I thought it my duty to see what was going on myself, and my advisers concurred in the propriety of such a step. I must, however, admit that convictions of duty were supported by a strong sense of curiosity which perhaps it would have been well to keep in check.

We started at once in a motor-car. Down the Strand, through the City towards Houndsditch, until at length at about noon we reached the point where all traffic was stopped. We got out of the car. There was a considerable crowd of angry and alarmed people, and I noticed the unusual spectacle of Metropolitan constables armed with shotguns hastily procured from a local gunsmith. The attitude of the crowd was not particularly friendly, and there were several cries of "Oo let 'em in?" in allusion to the refusal of the Liberal Government to introduce drastic laws restricting the immigration of aliens. Just at this moment, however, a shot rang out perhaps a couple of hundred yards away, followed by another and another, until there was a regular fusillade. Accompanied by an inspector, we proceeded down the empty street, turned a corner, turned another corner, and reached a group of policemen, several of whom were armed, and a number of onlookers and journalists who had found themselves within the police cordon when it was originally closed and had been permitted to remain. Another street ran at right angles across our path. Up this street fifty or sixty yards to the left was the house (No. 100) in which the murderers had barricaded themselves. On the opposite side in front of us, police, Scots Guardsmen, and spectators were crouching behind the projecting corners of the buildings; and from both sides of the street, from the street itself, and from numerous windows, policemen and other persons were firing rifles, pistols, and shotguns with increasing frequency at the house which harboured the desperadoes. These replied every minute or two, shooting sometimes up and down the street and sometimes at their assailants in front. The bullets struck the brickwork and ricocheted hither and thither. We have since become only too familiar with scenes of this kind, and the spectacle of street fighting has long lost its novelty in Europe. But nothing of the sort had ever been seen within living memory in quiet, law-abiding, comfortable England; and from this point of view at least my journey was well repaid.

But the situation almost immediately became embarrassing. Some of the police officers were anxious to storm the building at once with their pistols. Others rightly thought it better to take more time and to avoid the almost certain loss of three or four valuable lives. It was no part of my duty to take personal control or to give executive decisions. From my chair in the Home Office I could have sent any order and it would have been immediately acted on, but it was not for me to interfere with those who were in charge on the spot. Yet, on the other hand, my position of authority, far above them all, attracted inevitably to itself direct responsibility. I saw now that I should have done much better to have remained quietly in my office. On the other hand, it was impossible to get into one's car and drive away while matters stood in such great uncertainty, and moreover were extremely interesting.

Being anxious to have a direct view of the besieged house, I now crossed the street and took shelter in the doorway of a ware-house on the opposite side. Here I found Lord Knutsford, the Chairman of the London Hospital, and together we watched the closing scenes of the drama.

Plans were now made to storm the building from several sides at once. One party, emerging from the next-door house, was to rush the front door and charge up the stairs; another party of police and soldiers would break into the second floor at the back through a window; a third, smashing-in the roof, would leap down on the assassins from above. There could be no doubt about the result of such an attack, but it certainly seemed that loss of life would be caused, not only by the fire of the Anarchists, but also from shots fired by the attackers in the confusion. My own instincts turned at once to a direct advance up the staircase behind a steel plate or shield, and search was made in the foundries of the neighbourhood for one of a suitable size. Meanwhile, however, the problem settled itself. At about half-past one a wisp of smoke curled out of the shattered upper windows of the besieged house, and in a few minutes it was plainly on fire. The conflagration gained apace, burning downwards. To the crackling of wood succeeded the roar of flames. Still the Anarchists, descending storey by storey, kept up their fire, and bullets continued to strike the brickwork of the surrounding houses and pavement.

Now occurred a curious incident, which, for the first time, made my presence on the spot useful. The ordinary functions of British life had been proceeding inflexibly to within a few feet of the danger-zone, and the postman on his rounds actually delivered his letters at the house next door. Suddenly, with a stir and a clatter, up came the fire brigade, scattering the crowds gathered on the approaches to the scene and thrusting through them until they reached the police cordon at the beginning of the danger-zone. The inspector of police forbade further progress, and the fire brigade officer declared it his duty to advance. A fire was raging, and he was bound to extinguish it. Anarchists, automatic pistols, danger-zones, nothing of this sort was mentioned in the Regulations of the London Fire Brigade. When the police officer pointed out that his men would be shot down, he replied simply that orders were orders and that he had no alternative. I now intervened to settle this dispute, at one moment quite heated. I told the fire brigade officer on my authority as Home Secretary, that the house was to be allowed to burn down and that he was to stand by in readiness to prevent the conflagration from spreading. I then returned to my coign of vantage on the opposite side of the road.

The flames were now beginning to invade the ground floor of the doomed house. Some minutes had passed without a shot being fired by the Anarchists. No human being could live longer in the building. Everyone expected to see the Anarchists—how many there were was not known for certain—sally out, pistol in hand, into the open street. A hundred rifles, revolvers, and shotguns were levelled at the smouldering doorway. The minutes passed in intense excitement, and the flames invaded the whole ground floor. At last it became certain that these human fiends had perished. Suddenly, upon a spontaneous impulse which led everyone into the open, a detective inspector walked quickly to the door and kicked it open. I followed a few yards behind, accompanied by a police sergeant with a double-barrelled shotgun. There was nothing but smoke and flame inside the building. The firemen rushed forward into the empty street with their hoses, and behind them surged a crowd of soldiers, journalists, photographers, and spectators. It was already three o'clock, and leaving the now-dying fire to be dealt with by the fire brigade and the ruins to be searched by the police, I went home.

Besides the police inspector shot in the morning, a colour sergeant of the Guards and three civilians had been wounded by bullets, and a police sergeant struck, but not seriously injured, by a ricochet. Up to this moment no lives had been lost except those of the murderers. Alas, the day was not yet done! A falling wall injured five of the firemen, two in the most grave manner. There were found in the ruins of Sidney Street two charred bodies, one shot by a British bullet and one apparently suffocated by smoke. These were established to be the corpses of Fritz Svaars and Jacob Vogel, both members of "Peter the Painter's" Anarchist gang, and both certainly concerned in the police murders. One Browning and two Mauser pistols and six gun-metal bomb-cases were found amid the ruins, together with many cartridges.

Thus ended the battle of Sidney Street. Of "Peter the Painter" not a trace was ever found. He vanished completely. Rumour has repeatedly claimed him as one of the Bolshevik liberators and saviours of Russia. Certainly his qualities and record would well have fitted him to take an honoured place in that noble band. But of this Rumour is alone the foundation.

Party controversy was then at its height in England, and I was much criticized in the newspapers and in Parliament for my share in this curious episode. Mr. Balfour in the House of Commons was especially sarcastic.

"We are concerned to observe," he said in solemn tones, "photographs in the illustrated newspapers of the Home Secretary in the danger-zone. I understand what the photographer was doing, but why the Home Secretary?"

And with this not altogether unjust reflection I may bring the story to an end.

Here is my own true spy story, and the only one with which I have ever been directly concerned.

In September, 1914, the state of our northern war harbours caused us lively anxiety. In all our Channel ports there were anchorages secured by moles and breakwaters, and the gates to these were closed with nets and booms capable of resisting not only the entrance of a destroyer or submarine but of stopping a torpedo fired through from outside. But the Fleet had now moved to the North, and since Rosyth was not yet completed, it used in general the enormous anchorage of Scapa Flow in the Orkney Islands, or alternatively Cromarty Firth a little to the southward. Up to the outbreak of the war the only danger which had been apprehended in these northern harbours had been an attack by destroyers; and against these, temporary booms and improvised batteries, rapidly called into being in the early weeks of the war, were held to be a sufficient defence. But now in September the fear of the submarine actually coming into the harbours and attacking the sleeping ships laid its pressure on every responsible mind. Once this idea had been formed it was insistently magnified in everyone's consciousness. Alarms were raised by night and day without foundation. Periscopes that never existed were seen, and more than once the whole Grand Fleet proceeded to sea in order to find on the broad waters that assurance and safety which it had lost in those places of rest where above all it ought to have been able to feel secure. At this time therefore, while measures of netting the northern harbours with anti-submarine obstructions were being pressed forward with feverish activity, the Grand Fleet was encouraged to change its anchorages at frequent and uncertain intervals. Sometimes in the North, sometimes on the East and sometimes on the West coast of Scotland the great vessels which were our safeguard and on which the issue of the whole war depended, found a series of temporary habitations. The solitary condition of their safety was that not one single enemy should know where they were and that they should not remain in any one place long enough for anyone to find out. We were therefore passing through a period of exceptional tension.

I had occasion to visit the Fleet in order to discuss personally with the Commander-in-Chief these and other urgent problems, and one evening, in the middle of that trying September, I travelled from London in a special train with several high officers and technical authorities from the Admiralty. Our train pulled up at daybreak at a wayside station somewhere in the Highlands, and from here a motor trip of fifty or sixty miles would take us to the bay on the West Coast in which the Grand Fleet was at that moment sheltering—one cannot refuse to say "hiding"—from a danger which though exaggerated by our imaginations, was also terribly real, and potentially fatal.

We started off by motor in a clear delicious autumn morning, myself, my Naval Secretary, the Director of Intelligence (now Admiral of the Fleet Sir Henry Oliver), and a Flotilla Commodore since renowned as Sir Reginald Tyrwhitt. It was a charming drive through the splendid scenery of the Scottish Highlands, and absorbed in the topics we were to discuss with the Commander-in-Chief, to which swift motion, cool air and a changing landscape were an agreeable accompaniment, we said little to one another. Suddenly the Flotilla Commodore, who was sitting in the back of the car with the Director of Intelligence, said so loud that I could hear him, "Look, there is a searchlight on the top of that house." "What's that?" I said, turning round, following with my eye the gaze of the two officers. But before I could see what had struck their attention the car swung quickly round a corner and the object, whatever it was, was invisible. "A searchlight, sir," said the Commodore, "is mounted on top of one of the houses over there" (pointing). A searchlight, I must explain, is a considerable apparatus of about the size of a big drum.

"Surely," I said, "that is unlikely in the middle of the Highlands."

"Sir," said the Commodore, "I know a searchlight when I see one."

"Well, but what could it be for, why should we have mounted one here? Do you know anything about it, Admiral?"

The Director of Intelligence knew nothing. He was sure however that it could serve no British naval purpose. On the other hand both officers were certain they had seen it.

In war time everything that is unexplained requires to be probed, and here we were confronted with a complete mystery. We racked our brains for the rest of the journey and no one could suggest any reasonable or innocent explanation.

At last the road went winding downwards round a purple hill, and before us far below there gleamed a bay of blue water in which rode at anchor, outlined in miniature as in a plan, the twenty Dreadnoughts and Super-Dreadnoughts on which the command of the seas depended. Around them and darting about between them were many scores of small craft. The vessels themselves were painted for the first time in the queer mottled fashion which marked the early beginnings of the science of *Camouflage*. The whole scene bursting thus suddenly upon the eye, and with all its immense significance filling the mind, was one which I shall never forget. Not a house, not a building of any kind disfigured the splendid hills and cliffs that ran down on either side to ocean water. Yet gathered together in this solitude and narrow compass was the floating steel city with its thirty or forty thousand inhabitants upon whose strength, loyalty, courage and devotion our lives and freedom, and as we may perhaps assert still the freedom of the world, from minute to minute depended. Last night not a vessel had been there; tomorrow morning perhaps the bay would again be empty; but today the vital and all-powerful instrument of the world war was reposing on its bosom.

"What would the German Emperor give," I said to my companions, "to see this?"

"He would have to get the news back," said the Commodore, "if he was to do any good with it." "And then," added the Admiral, who was a man of facts and figures, "it would take about forty-eight hours before anything could get at us." "But," I persisted, drawn on by the sombre current of reflection, "suppose a submarine flotilla were lurking about behind some of the islands and suppose a Zeppelin came over and saw the Fleet, couldn't she tell them and lay them on at once?" "By day," was the reply, "she would be seen and we should put to sea, by night she would probably not see the Fleet. The whole coast is full of bays."

"Suppose there was a spy on shore who signalled to the Zeppelin, and that the Zeppelin without coming near the bay signalled to the submarines," I persevered. "Suppose, for instance, sir," responded the Admiral, "someone had a *searchlight*. . . ."

Then we went on board the *Iron Duke*, and all the morning we were locked in conference on the many grave matters which had to be discussed with Sir John Jellicoe and his Admirals, nor was it until we lunched on board the Flagship that anything like ordinary conversation was possible. Then someone started the topic of the searchlight forty miles inland on the top of what looked like a shooting-lodge in the middle of a deer-forest.

"We have seen a very suspicious thing this morning," I said half seriously to the Commander-in-Chief. "What do you think of it?"

"Whereabouts was it?"

My companions explained the general position. The Commander-in-Chief paused and reflected before he answered, then he said, "There might be something in it. We have heard several bad rumours about that place." He mentioned the name of the shooting estate. "It is said that there are a number of foreigners there. We have had a report that an aeroplane had an accident there before the war, and also that one has been seen in the neighbourhood since, which we were not able to trace. Anyhow," he added, "what do they want a searchlight for?"

I said to the Director of Intelligence. "You are a properly constituted authority under the Defence of the Realm Act, are you not?" "You mean, sir," he replied, "that we might go and look them up ourselves on the way back." "If we have half an hour to spare," I answered, "we might just as well find out what the searchlight is wanted for."

It was dark when our conferences were finished, but before leaving we requisitioned four pistols from the armoury of the *Iron Duke* and put them under the seat of the car. As we swept along through the night I could not help thinking perhaps we might fall into a hornets' nest. If the sinister hypothesis was justified, if the searchlight was an enemy signal and a Scotch shooting-lodge a nest of desperate German spies, we might receive the sort of welcome the police had had at Houndsditch. However, suspicion and curiosity went hand in hand, and the excitement of adventure spurred them both.

"We are quite close here now, sir," said the Commodore, directing the driver to reduce speed, "the entrance gate is in this clump of trees. I marked it myself this morning."

"We had better get out," I said, "and walk up, and the chauffeur can report if anything goes wrong." Accordingly with our pistols in our pockets we marched up the drive, and after a couple of hundred yards arrived at the entrance of a good-sized stone house at one end of which there stood a tall square tower. We rang the front-door bell. It was duly answered by a portly respectable butler. My three companions were in naval uniform, and the butler seemed startled at such a visit.

"Whose house is this?" we asked. The name was given. "Is your master at home?" "Yes, sir," he said, "he is at dinner with the house-party." "Tell him that some officers from the Admiralty wish to see him at once."

The butler departed and we pushed into the hall.

There was a pause, and presently the dining-room door opened and a clatter of conversation suddenly stilled, and out came a ruddy grey-headed gentleman who, as we thought with some perturbation, inquired, "What can I do for you?"

"Have you got a searchlight on the top of your tower?" asked the Admiral.

I must interpolate here that I was still sceptical about the existence of the searchlight. If there were a searchlight, if that fact were established, I could not think of any alternative but treason. I was therefore startled at the admission which followed.

"Yes, we have a searchlight on the tower."

"When did you put it up?"

"Some time ago, two or three years ago, I think."

"What did you put it up for?"

"To what do I owe the honour of this visit?" countered the host, "and what right have you to put me these questions?"

"We have every right," replied Admiral Oliver. "I am the Director of Naval Intelligence, and I possess full authority under the law to inquire into any suspicious circumstances. Will you kindly explain at once what you use this searchlight for?"

"Ah," said the host, peering at me, "I recognize you, Mr. Winston Churchill."

"The question is," I replied, "what do you use your searchlight for?"

There was a strained silence, and then the old gentleman replied,

"We use it to locate the game on the hillsides. From the tower we can see several of the beats, and the searchlight gleams on the eyes of the deer, and shows us where they are lying, so we know where to send the stalkers in the morning. And," he added, warming to his subject, "we can tell deer from cattle by the searchlight, as the glint of the eyes of the cattle is white and that of the deer has a greenish tint." This farrago of improbabilities and impossibilities confirmed my deepest suspicions, and I think those of my companions. At any rate we made no comment upon them.

"We wish to see the searchlight," I said. "We wish you to show it to us yourself."

"Certainly," replied our unwilling host. "You will have to climb up the spiral staircase of the tower."

"You go ahead," we answered.

He opened a door leading out of the hall and disclosed the first steps of a stone staircase. We made a military disposition to guard against foul play. The Naval Secretary remained at the bottom of the stairs, and the Admiral, the Commodore and I followed the old gentleman up their winding course. At any rate we had a hostage, we had a stronghold and, outside the gate, we had a connecting link with unlimited reinforcements.

It was a high tower, and the stairs corkscrewed several times; at length, however, we reached the top and emerged on a fairly broad square platform with low battlements. There in the middle, sure enough, was the searchlight. It was a 24-in. medium Destroyer instrument, bolted strongly into the roof. It was, as far as we could see, quite capable of being used.

"Do you expect us to believe this story of yours," I asked the old gentleman, "that you use this searchlight to pick up game on distant hillsides and that you can tell deer from cattle by the glint in their eyes?"

"Well, it is quite true, whatever you think."

"You will have to give these explanations to the proper authorities. For the present we are going to dismantle your searchlight so that it cannot be used."

"You can do what you choose," he replied, evidently very indignant.

"We are going to," I said, and we proceeded accordingly.

Then we descended the stairs, bearing with us various parts of the mechanism, and after sullen adieux we joined our motor-car outside the entrance gate.

I have told this story exactly as it happened; but the most extraordinary part in my opinion is yet to come. There was nothing in it at all. The most searching investigations of the local and central authorities discovered no grounds for the slightest suspicion. The searchlight had been erected four years before and had apparently been used at that date for sweeping the hillsides. It had not been used, according to overwhelming testimony, since the war began. It was not in fact capable of being used at the moment when we examined it. The owner of the house was a gentleman of high reputation and undoubted patriotism. He was entertaining a party of thoroughly respectable people. There were no foreigners in the house or on the estate. No confirmation could be obtained of the rumour which we had heard on the *Iron Duke* of an aeroplane accident on the estate before the war or of an unaccountable aeroplane having been seen in the neighbourhood. There was nothing in fact, except the searchlight on the castle tower and the unreasonable explanation given for its presence there.

Although the owner of the castle may have experienced a natural anger at this sudden nocturnal call and the suspicions which it implied, he could at least solace himself by the reflection that grounds far less disquieting had consigned many other persons during the war period to far greater inconvenience; and for myself I say without hesitation that in similar circumstances I should do the same again.

# WITH THE GRENADIERS

When the British Government determined to abandon the campaign at the Dardanelles and all the hopes that had been placed upon it, and when the evacuation of Gallipoli was impending, I thought it necessary to quit their counsels and betook myself to the armies. I had asked to be allowed to join my Yeomanry Regiment, at that time serving in the French theatre and quartered in rest billets not far from Boulogne. As the crowd of officers and men returning from leave was streaming off the steamer in the French port, I heard my name called out by the Military Landing Officer and was told that the Commander-in-Chief, Sir John French, had sent a car to take me at once to his headquarters. Sir John had been hostile to me in South Africa, but for many years we had been friends. We had faced the vicissitudes of prewar years together; we had collaborated closely in all the work of preparation for the movement of the Expeditionary Force to France in the event of war; and in the early critical months I had been thrown constantly into the most intimate relations with him. The fast staff car soon carried me to the Chateau of Blondecque near St. Omer, where his headquarters lay. We dined together almost alone, and talked long on the war situation on the same footing as if I had still been First Lord of the Admiralty, responsible for carrying his armies across the Channel in the feverish hours of August, 1914.

It was not until the next morning that he said to me, "What would you like to do?"

I said that I would do whatever I was told.

He said, "My power is no longer what it was. I am, as it were, riding at single anchor. But it still counts for something. Will you take a Brigade?"

I answered that of course I should be proud to do so, but that before I could undertake any such responsibility, I must learn first-hand the special conditions of trench warfare.

I must explain to the reader that, having been trained profession-ally for about five years as a soldier, and having prior to the Great War seen as much actual fighting as almost any of the Colonels and Generals in the British Army, I had certain credentials which were accepted in military circles. I was not a Regular, but neither was I a civilian volunteer. I fell in that intermediate category described as "the Dug-outs". However presumptuous it may have been, I did not feel incapable of discharging the duties in question, provided I had a month or two in the line to measure the novel conditions of the Great War for myself.

The Commander-in-Chief said that this was quite right and that he would attach me for instruction to any Division I liked. I said that the Guards was the best school of all. He thereupon invited Lord Cavan, who commanded the Guards Division, to come and see him a few days later; and after a pleasant conversation I found myself duly posted to this famous unit.

The Guards were then holding the line in front of Merville. It was the depth of winter, and this part of the front was fairly active.

"I will send you," said Lord Cavan, "to one of the best Colonels I have. You will learn more from —— than from anyone else. His battalion goes into the line tomorrow. If you come and lunch with me at La Gorgue at one o'clock, you will be in plenty of time."

Accordingly the next day, having packed what I thought was a very modest kit, I repaired to the headquarters of the Guards Division and was most kindly welcomed by its gallant Commander. As soon as a frugal lunch was over, the General took me himself in his car to the Grenadier battalion I was to join as a major under instruction previous to higher appointment. The Companies had already begun their march to the trenches, and the Colonel, the Adjutant and the Battalion staff were on the point of setting out. There were salutes and smiles and clickings of heels. A few friendly commonplaces were exchanged between the Divisional General and the Battalion officers; and then His Lordship got into his car and drove off, leaving me very like a new boy at school in charge of the headmaster, the monitors and the senior scholars. We were to ride on and overtake the Battalion a mile or so ahead of us. My new host had considerately provided a pony; and jogging along we soon caught up the marching troops and reined our horses into a walk among them. It was a dull November afternoon, and an icy drizzle fell over the darkening plain. As we approached the line, the red flashes of the guns stabbed the sombre landscape on either side of the road, to the sound of an intermittent cannonade. We paced onwards for about half an hour without a word being spoken on either side.

Then the Colonel: "I think I ought to tell you that we were not at all consulted in the matter of your coming to join us."

I replied respectfully that I had had no idea myself which battalion I was to be sent to, but that I dared say it would be all right. Anyhow we must make the best of it.

There was another prolonged silence.

Then the Adjutant: "I am afraid we have had to cut down your kit rather, Major. There are no communication trenches here. We are doing all our reliefs over the top. The men have little more

589

than what they stand up in. We have found a servant for you, who is carrying a spare pair of socks and your shaving gear. We have had to leave the rest behind."

I said that was quite all right and that I was sure I should be very comfortable.

We continued to progress in the same sombre silence. Presently the landscape began to change. The shell-holes in the neighbouring fields became more numerous and the road broken and littered with debris. The inhabited country was left behind. The scattered houses changed to ruins. The leafless trees were scarred and split and around them grass and weeds grew tall and rank. Night descended and no sound was heard but the crunch of marching feet and the occasional bang of an adjacent gun.

At length there was a halt. Orderlies advanced to take our horses. From this point we must proceed on foot. The four Companies quitted the road and moved slowly off in various directions into the darkness across the two miles of sopping fields beyond which an occasional Very light, rising bright and blue, betokened the position of the line.

The headquarters of the Battalion were established in a pulverized ruin called Ebenezer Farm. Enough brickwork remained to afford some protection from shells and bullets, but not enough to make an enemy suppose it was a likely abode of men. Behind these crumbling walls a small sandbag structure with three or four compartments served as the Colonel's headquarters. A charcoal fire added the un-usual element of warmth. It had taken us nearly three hours to reach this place, and it was, I suppose, about half-past six by the clock. The Colonel and the Adjutant were busy getting the Battalion into the line and receiving reports as to how the relief of the Cold-streamers we were replacing was proceeding. When all this was over, we had some food and strong tea with condensed milk. There was a little general conversation during this meal. But his subordinates evidently stood in the gravest awe of their Commanding Officer, and very few remarks were made except on topics which he himself initiated. At about eight o'clock a dead Grenadier was brought in and laid out in the ruined farmhouse for burial next day. The Second-in-Command asked me where I would sleep. There was a signal office in the Battalion Headquarters, or there was a dug-out

590

two hundred yards away. The signal office was about eight feet square occupied by four busy Morse signallers, and was stifling hot. Having surveyed it, I said I should like to see the dug-out. Accordingly we walked out into the sleet and through the dripping grass. The dug-out was very difficult to find, and it was apparently considered dangerous to show the flash of an electric torch. However, after a quarter of an hour we found it. It was a sort of pit four feet deep, containing about one foot of wa  r. I thanked the Second-in-Command for the trouble he had taken in finding me this resting place, and said that on the whole I thought I should do better in the signal office. We talked a little about "trench feet", then the prevailing malady, and he explained to me the organization of the "sockatorium", a dug-out in the trenches where wet socks were continually being dried and returned to their owners. The bullets, skimming over the front line, whistled drearily as we walked back to Ebenezer Farm. Such was my welcome in the Grenadier Guards.

It will always be a source of pride to me that I succeeded in making myself perfectly at home with these men and formed friendships which I enjoy today. It took about forty-eight hours to wear through their natural prejudice against "politicians" of all kinds, but particularly of the non-Conservative brands. Knowing the professional Army as I did and having led a variegated life, I was infinitely amused at the elaborate pains they took to put me in my place and to make me realize that nothing counted at the front except military rank and behaviour.

The longer one lives, the more one realizes that everything depends upon chance, and the harder it is to believe that this omnipotent factor in human affairs arises simply from the blind interplay of events. Chance, Fortune, Luck, Destiny, Fate, Providence seem to me only different ways of expressing the same thing, to wit, that a man's own contribution to his life story is continually dominated by an external superior power. If anyone will look back over the course of even ten years' experience, he will see what tiny incidents, utterly unimportant in themselves, have in fact governed the whole of his fortunes and career. This is true of ordinary life. But in war, which is an intense form of life, Chance casts aside all veils and disguises and presents herself nakedly from moment to moment as the direct arbiter over all persons and events. Starting out in the morning you leave your matches behind you. Before you have gone a hundred yards, you return to get them and thus miss the shell which arrived for your express benefit from ten miles away, and are no doubt shocked to find how nearly you missed the appointed rendezvous. You stay behind an extra half-minute to pay some civility to a foreign officer who has unexpectedly presented himself; another man takes your place in walking up the communication trench. Crash! He is no more. You may walk to the right or to the left of a particular tree, and it makes the difference whether you rise to command an Army Corps or are sent home crippled or paralysed for life. You are walking up a duckboard track; in front of you a shell is falling at half-minute intervals; you think it foolhardy to walk straight along the track, especially as you notice that you will reach the danger-point almost on the tick of time; you deflect fifty yards to the left; but the gun is traversing at the same time, and meets you with a grim smile in the midst of your precautions.

One afternoon when I had been about a week in the line with the Company, I sat myself down in our tiny sandbagged shelter to write some letters home. On this part of the front the water was so near the surface that we were defended by breastworks rather than trenches. In consequence there were no dug-outs in the ordinary sense. Slight sandbag structures with a sheet of corrugated iron and one layer of sandbags for a roof formed our only protection. The morning shelling had stopped, and custom led to the belief that we should have a quiet interval. I got out my writing-pad and stylo and was soon absorbed in a letter. I had written for perhaps a quarter of an hour when an Orderly presented himself at the entrance to the shelter, and saluting with Guardsman-like smartness, handed me a field telegram:

"The Corps Commander wishes to see Major Churchill at four o'clock at Merville. A car will be waiting at the Rouge Croix crossroads at 3.15."

I had known General —— personally for a good many years. But it was rather unusual to bring an officer out of the line, and I wondered what this summons could mean. I did not much like the prospect of trapesing across three miles of muddy fields, the greater part under the observation of the enemy by daylight, and then toiling back all the way in the evening. However, the order brooked no question, and in a rather sulky mood I put away my unfinished letter, arrayed myself in my trappings, and prepared to set out on my trudge. The two tall Grenadiers who acted as our servants were busy tidying-up the shelter.

"You must take your man with you," said the Company Commander, "to carry your coat. It is always better not to be alone, and he knows the way back in the dark."

Accordingly in a few minutes we set out towards Rouge Croix. We had scarcely got two hundred yards from the trenches when I heard the shriek of approaching shells, and looking round I saw four or five projectiles bursting over the trenches we had left. The firing continued for about a quarter of an hour, and then ceased. I thought no more of the matter, and toiled and sweated my way through the slush towards Rouge Croix. What on earth could the General want me for? It must be something important, or he would surely not have summoned me in this way.

At last I reached the rendezvous—a shattered inn at these exceptionally unhealthy crossroads. There was no motor-car. I waited impatiently for nearly an hour. Presently there appeared a staff officer on foot.

"Are you Major Churchill?"

I said I was.

"There was a mistake," he said, "about sending the car for you. It went to the wrong place, and now it is too late for you to see the General at Merville. He has already gone back to his Headquarters at Hinges. You can rejoin your unit."

I said, "Thank you very much. Would it be troubling you too much to let me know the nature of the business on which the General required to bring me out of the line?"

"Oh," said the staff officer airily, "it was nothing in particular. He thought as he was coming up this way, he would like to have a talk with you. But perhaps there will be some other opportunity."

I was indignant; and as the staff officer was no more than a Major, I did not take any more pains to conceal my ill temper than he to conceal his indifference to it. It was now nearly dark, and I had to begin another long, sliding, slippery, splashing waddle back to the trenches. I lost my way in the dark, and it must have been nearly two hours before I got into Sign Post Lane. The cold rain descended steadily, and what with perspiration (for I was wearing my entire wardrobe) and the downpour, I was quite wet through. The bullets whistled venomously down Sign Post Lane, and I was glad when at last I came into the shelter of the breastworks of the line. I had still nearly a mile to go through a labyrinth of trenches. The sedentary life of a Cabinet Minister, which I had quitted scarcely a month before, had not left me much opportunity to keep fit. Tired out and very thirsty, I put my head into the nearest Company Mess for a drink.

"Hallo," they said, "you're in luck today."

"I haven't seen much of it," I replied. "I've been made a fool of." And I made some suitable remark about the impropriety of Corps Commanders indulging their sociable inclinations at the expense of their subordinates.

"Well, you're in luck all the same," said the Grenadier officers, "as you will see when you get back to your Company."

I did not understand their allusions at all. Having consumed a very welcome tumbler of whisky and water, I splashed out again into the rain and mud, and ten minutes later arrived at my own Company. I had got within twenty yards of my shelter when a Sergeant, saluting, said:

"We have shifted your kit to Mr. ——'s dug-out, Sir."

"Why?" I asked.

"Yours has been blown up, Sir."

"Any harm done?"

"Your kit's all right, Sir, but —— was killed. Better not go in there, Sir, it's in an awful mess."

I now began to understand the conversation in the Company Mess.

"When did it happen?" I asked.

"About five minutes after you left, Sir. A whizzbang came in through the roof and blew his head off."

Suddenly I felt my irritation against General —— pass completely from my mind. All sense of grievance departed in a flash. As I walked to my new abode, I reflected how thoughtful it had been of him to wish to see me again, and to show courtesy to a subordinate, when he had so much responsibility on his shoulders. And then upon these quaint reflections there came the strong sensation that a hand had been stretched out to move me in the nick of time from a fatal spot. But whether it was General ——'s hand or not, I cannot tell.


## "PLUGSTREET"

Everyone remembers the remark of the old man at the point of death: that his life had been full of troubles most of which had never happened. The following incident may serve as a personal example of this comforting reflection.

In February, 1916, I was commanding the 6th Royal Scots Fusiliers in Flanders. We had for some weeks been holding the well-known sector of the line near "Plugstreet" (Ploegsteert) Wood and Village. The front was comparatively calm, and the battalion moved in and out of the trenches on six-day spells with only the usual experiences of local bombardments, sniping and trench raids and counter-raids. Our so-called "rest" billets when out of the line were separated by scarcely a mile and a half of flat country from our front trenches, at this point distant about three hundred yards from those of the Germans. In this situation, living on a little more than a square mile of ground, we were destined to remain for over three months. My own headquarters when resting were only about a thousand yards away from those I occupied when we were actually holding the front. It therefore made very little difference to us whether we were in or out of the trenches, and we lost about the same number of men through shell fire.

When I had joined the army in the previous November, I had written, at the invitation of the Commander-in-Chief, a paper embodying my ideas upon new methods of attacking the enemy. This Memorandum, entitled "Variants of the Offensive", dealt with many secret projects in which I was deeply interested, including the scheme of using caterpillar vehicles (afterwards called "Tanks") in large numbers by surprise and in conjunction with smoke and other devices. The importance of this paper at the date at which it was written (3 December, 1915) can be judged from this extract:

"3. *Caterpillars.* – The cutting of the enemy's wire and the general domination of his firing-line can be effective by engines of this character. About seventy are now nearing completion in England, and should be inspected. None should be used until all can be used at once. They should be disposed secretly along the whole attacking front two or three hundred yards apart. Ten or fifteen minutes before the assault these engines should move forward over the best line of advance open, passing through or across our trenches at prepared points. They are capable of traversing any ordinary obstacle, ditch, breastwork, or trench. They carry two or three Maxims each, and can be fitted with flame-apparatus. Nothing but a direct hit from a field-gun will stop them. On reaching the enemy's wire they turn to the left or right and run down parallel to the enemy's trench, sweeping his parapet with their fire, and crushing and cutting the barbed wire in lanes and in a slightly serpentine course. While doing this the Caterpillars will be so close to the enemy's line that they will be immune from his artillery. Through the gaps thus made the shield-bearing infantry will advance.

"*If artillery is used to cut wire the direction and imminence of the attack is proclaimed days beforehand. But by this method the assault follows the wire-cutting almost immediately, i.e. before any reinforcements can be brought up by the enemy, or any special defensive measures taken.*"

At the same time as I gave a typescript copy to the Commander-in-Chief, I had sent a duplicate to the Committee of Imperial Defence, where it was printed with all precautions of secrecy, and early in February, 1916, a proof of this vital document was forwarded to me in France, reaching me through the army post office while I was actually at my headquarters in the line. The rule against taking secret documents into the front line was strict and well known, and as I gazed at the print in my sandbagged, half-demolished farm the feeling that the enemy was scarcely a thousand yards away became strangely accentuated in my mind. However, we were to go into our "rest billets" a mile farther back at daybreak. I would then make such revisions in the proof as were necessary, and send it in by an officer for transmission to London through the Army Headquarters at Bailleul.

My "rest" headquarters were in a small red-brick convent, hitherto quite intact. I had a comfortable, well-furnished room on the ground-floor, with a large bay-window looking straight out upon the front line and barely out of rifle-shot of the enemy. In this window there was a writing-table, and here, after breakfast, at about ten o'clock on the morning of which I write, I sat myself down and began to tackle my correspondence, which had accumulated during our spell in the trenches, and in particular to address myself to "Variants of the Offensive".

I must have been working on the proof for about half an hour when my attention was distracted by two or three shell-bursts about three hundred yards away in the field immediately beyond that in front of our house. Farther away, up in the line and at the corner of "Plugstreet" Wood, little white puffs of shrapnel showed an unwonted liveliness. I paused to watch the firing, as if from a box at the theatre. A few minutes passed, and two or three more shells burst with loud detonations about two hundred yards away, but this time in the field directly before my eyes. Then, after a minute or so, came another.

We had no defences of any kind, but at the back of the room in which I was writing there was a small cellar below the level of the ground and with a brick roof. In this the old lady with her daughter, who had remained in the convent after the departure of the nuns, had already taken refuge, together with two of the battalion telegraphists. It seemed foolish to go on sitting with only a sheet of glass between one and the projectiles, but, on the other hand, I did not think much of the cellar. The vaulted roof looked strong but was actually only two bricks thick. The place was so crowded that there was barely room for anyone else, so I got up from my table and, passing out of the back door, went into the adjoining building, which was used as our battalion office. Here also were large windows facing the front, but there was besides a back room where at any rate two brick walls stood between me and the fire. Against field artillery a barrier of two walls is a fair defence: the first explodes the shell, the second probably stops the pieces. Here then I sat down to wait until the shelling stopped. I left all my letters and papers, as I thought, lying on the table near the window. I do not suggest my departure was hurried, but neither was it unduly delayed. It was dignified but decided.

597

The bombardment lasted about an hour and a half. The intervals between the shells grew longer, and presently all was silent again. My second-in-command presented himself in the highest spirits. He had been making a tour of the men's billets when the enemy began to fire on the village, and had remained a serene spectator a few hundred yards away, waiting, as he put it, "until the rain stopped".

Together we returned to the "tall thin house". As we entered by the back door a scene of devastation met our eyes. The room in which I had been writing was wrecked and shattered. Daylight streamed through a large hole in the brickwork above the bay-window. The table, the furniture, papers, objects of all kinds, had been hurled into confusion. Everything was covered with thick, fine, red brick-dust. Then, from the back of the house, appeared the old woman and her daughter, completely terrified; behind them one of the signallers, grinning.

"Oh, *mon Commandant*," said the girl, "come and look at the cellar where we were; it came into the midst of us."

We followed: the brickwork which formed the roof of the cellar had been shattered, and there on the floor lay a long 30-lb. shell, unexploded. This shell had come through the architrave of the bay-window on a steep angle of descent, smashed through the brickwork of the little cellar, and fallen literally into the midst of these poor people crowded together, slightly injuring one of the signallers but otherwise doing no harm to anybody. One may imagine the spasm of terror of these two women when this monster arrived almost in their laps, and when of course they thought it would explode immediately. They had suffered far more than the pain of death.

Having told them they must pack up and quit their home at once, I returned into my wrecked writing-room. As the shell had not exploded, nothing was scorched or seriously damaged. Laboriously I collected my papers, kit and belongings. All needed only to be shaken free of thick, fine, brick-dust, and for the moment I thought nothing was missing. Still, as the letters and sheets of notepaper were gradually collected, I began to think it odd that I should not find the one paper of which I was in search and to which I attached —rightly as history has proved—extreme importance. At last everything was picked up; the soldier-servants came in and swept the room; nowhere could I find my precious document. Nothing was missing but that, and nothing mattered but that. It had gone; it had vanished completely. How and by what agency could it have been spirited away? Certainly not by the shell. If the room had been blasted by an explosion, the explanation would have been complete; but if this document alone among my papers was not found in the litter of the room, it must have been taken by someone, and by someone—observe—who comprehended its immense significance.

I now began to feel very seriously alarmed. "Plugstreet" stood on one of the last vestiges of soil left to the Belgian people. The frontier line was but a few hundred yards away. Our Intelligence reports had warned us of the probability of spies among the inhabitants who still remained. Suspicion filled every breast, and every possible precaution was always to be taken. My imagination began to construct half a dozen sinister explanations. Some sure agent of the enemy dwelling in our midst, realizing that I was a person whose correspondence would be of exceptional importance, watching day after day in the hopes of spying upon it, had entered the room in the confusion after the shell had struck it, had seized the paper, attracted no doubt by the words printed in red ink across it, "This document is the property of His Majesty's Government", and had vanished as swiftly as he came. Even now he might be making his way to some place where an enemy aeroplane could take him across the line by night. Every sort of terrifying possibility crowded in upon my mind, and no remedy of any kind suggested itself. The woman and her daughter had not seen any strangers about, but were so frightened out of their wits that they could give no assurance. The signaller had been busy with his injured comrade. We searched the house again and all in it; but not a trace! I passed the next three days in helpless anxiety. I reproached myself a thousand times with not having sent the document back by an officer the moment it had been so incontinently brought to me in the line by the military post. Why had I ever let it out of my possession for a second?

This brings me to the remark of the dying old man with which the account of this incident opens, and I may at once relieve the anxiety of the reader and clear my own character for prudence. On the third day I happened to put my hand into my right inner breast-

599

pocket, which I hardly ever used. There I found, safe and secure, the paper I had been so feverishly seeking. Instinctively, in leaving the room over which swift peril was impending, I had picked up the one thing that mattered and put it in my pocket. Seeing it once again safely in my hand, I gave a gasp of delight and relief, and the precarious, battered abodes of "Plugstreet" under rainy skies and bitter winds seemed as safe and comfortable as home.

# IN THE AIR

Except for the year 1916, I was continually in control of one or the other branch of the Air Service during the first eleven years of its existence. From 1911 to 1915 I was responsible at the Admiralty for the creation and development of the Royal Naval Air Service; from July, 1917, to the end of the war I was in charge of the design, manufacture and supply of all kinds of aircraft and air material needed for the war; and from 1919 to 1921 I was Air Minister as well as Secretary of State for War. Thus it happens to have fallen to my lot to have witnessed, and to some extent shaped in its initial phases, the whole of this tremendous new arm, undoubtedly destined to revolutionize war by land and sea, and possibly in the end to dominate or supersede armies and navies as we have known them.

From the outset I was deeply interested in the air and vividly conscious of the changes which it must bring to every form of war. On first going to the Admiralty I resolved to develop and extend the naval air service by every means in my power. I thus came into contact with a little band of adventurous young men who, under the leadership of Commander Samson, were the pioneers of naval flying. I was fascinated by the idea of flying, and yet side by side with desire was also a dread of going into the air for the first time. Indeed it must have been three or four months before I made my first flight. We had already had several accidents, and I felt a very keen sympathy with these young officers who were risking their lives in time of peace. I thought it would be a stimulus to progress generally if I, as First Lord, participated to some extent. Other ministers in charge of the Air Service have usually taken the same view.

Once I had started flying from motives in which a sense of duty, as well as excitement and curiosity, played its part, I continued for sheer joy and pleasure, going up in every kind of machine and at every air station under the Admiralty. I soon became ambitious to handle these machines myself, and took many lessons both at the Naval and Military Schools. Dual-control machines were developing fast in 1912, and I had one made where pilot and passenger could sit side by side and take control alternately.

Curiously enough my apprehensions about going into the air were apparently confirmed by a long series of dangerous or fatal accidents in which I narrowly missed being involved. The young Pilot Instructor who gave me my first lesson at Eastchurch was killed the day after we had been flying together. I was sitting in the Treasury Board Room discussing the details of the Naval Estimates of 1912 with the Chancellor of the Exchequer, when a slip of paper was put before me acquainting me with the fact that my companion of yesterday had perished in the same machine in which we had been practising for two or three hours. A few weeks later a seaplane of a new and experimental type was produced in Southampton Water, and I made a prolonged flight in it while it was being tested. It manoeuvred perfectly under every condition, and I sailed away in the Admiralty yacht *Enchantress* to Sheerness. I had no sooner arrived than I learnt that the machine had nose-dived into the sea with three officers, all of whom were killed. I was going out to fly, as I frequently did, in the sociable dual-control machine which I have mentioned, and was prevented by press of public business. The machine having flown perfectly all the morning suddenly took it into its head to plunge into a spin of a kind then quite unknown, and smashed itself to pieces on the ground, thereby gravely injuring the two officers, both personal friends of mine, who were flying it.

I had no time to fly while I was First Lord during the war, but as Minister of Munitions in 1917–18 I had to be alternately on each side of the Channel and I usually travelled by air, landing at the exact point on the front where I had to see people or where I wished to witness particular operations. My pilot in these days was a young officer who had been so shattered by wounds at Gallipoli and on the Somme that he could not endure explosions. He was insensible to any other form of danger, and as a flying officer he was as fine and skilful a pilot as one could ever wish to fly with. In this period all the best machines were of course needed for the Front, and one could not make appreciable claims upon our supply of mechanics. I remember returning from General Headquarters one afternoon to London, when we broke down twice in very awkward conditions. The first time was over the Channel. There was a sharp crack, or rather intense click, followed by a splutter from the engine. A valve had burst. We began to descend. The smooth grey Channel lay beneath us. We were five miles out from the French shore. It was a dull afternoon, and we were flying only at about two thousand feet. If the engine did not pick up again, we must reach the sea on a slant of under two miles. Usually when you look at the Channel it is crowded with traffic, but as always happens at a crucial moment, not a steamer, not a trawler, not a fishing-smack could be seen except paddling along on dim horizons. We had no means of flotation, no "bathing suits" as the inflatable air-jackets were called. My pilot made a gesture with his hand indicating that he could do nothing, and I wondered how long I could keep myself afloat in my thick clothes and heavy boots or whether it would be worth while to try to take them off. Certainly for half a minute, or it may have been a minute—it seemed quite a long time—I thought extinction certain and near. And then the old engine began to cough and splutter again with many misfires and jerks. The pilot swung the aeroplane back towards the coast of France, and after ten anxious minutes we passed over the headland of Griz Nez. We just managed to make the aerodrome of Marquise with about a hundred feet to spare, and landed safely in that gigantic war-time receiving-station for British and American outward-bound machines.

The larger resources of the Marquise aerodrome soon provided us with another indifferent aeroplane, and then we started off for the second time, with about an hour of daylight, across the Channel. The wind was against us and the engine pulling poorly, and we were nearly forty minutes before we reached the British shore. About a quarter of an hour later another snap in the engine led to a repetition on the part of my pilot of those gestures which indicated that we had no choice but to descend. He side-slipped artistically between two tall elms, just avoiding the branches on either side, and made a beautiful landing in a small field. I missed my London engagement.

It was not, and still is not, common for men over forty to become good and trustworthy pilots. Youth with its extraordinary quickness and aptitudes was almost always the first qualification for the attainment of "Flying Sense". I persevered, however, in my endeavours and continued, as I thought, to make steady progress. I was thus fated to have a much more melancholy adventure before I decided to relinquish, at any rate for the time being, the fascinating study of the art of flight. This event occurred in the summer of 1919. I had had a long day's work at the War Office, and motored down with Colonel Scott to the Croydon Aerodrome for an evening flight. I took the machine off the ground myself. The engine was pulling well, and we rose to seventy or eighty feet smoothly and swiftly. The Croydon Aerodrome was in those days bordered at several points by high elm trees, and it was necessary to make two half circles, first to the right and then to the left, in order to gain a safe height to pass over these.

The machine took its first turn perfectly, and the dial marked over sixty miles an hour, a thoroughly trustworthy flying speed. I now turned her to the left, as I had so often done before, and having put her on her bank, I began to centre the guiding-stick slowly and gently in order to resume an even keel. Anyone who has handled an aeroplane knows how delicate are its controls and how instantaneously it responds, when all is well, to the smallest movement. To my surprise the stick came home at least a foot without producing the slightest effect. The aeroplane remained inclined at about forty-five degrees and began gradually to increase its list. "She is out of control," I said through the microphone to my pilot. Instantly I felt the override of his hand and feet on stick and rudders, as by a violent effort he sought to plunge the machine head-downwards in the hope of regaining our lost flying speed. But it was too late. We were scarcely ninety feet above the ground, just the normal height for the usual side-slip fatal accident, the commonest of all. The machine rushed earthwards helplessly. Above two hundred feet there would have been no danger; in fact at a thousand or fifteen hundred feet we had over and over again deliberately stalled the machine, made it fall out of control, waited till the side-slip turned (as all side-slips do) into the ultimate nose dive, and then as the speed increased to eighty or a hundred miles an hour and the controls began again to answer, had pulled her gently out into a normal flight.

But there was no time now. I saw the sunlit aerodrome close beneath me, and the impression flashed through my mind that it was bathed in a baleful yellowish glare. Then in another flash a definite thought formed in my brain, "This is very likely Death". And swift upon that I felt again in imagination the exact sensations of my smash on the Buc Aerodrome a month before. Something like that was going to happen NOW! I record these impressions exactly as they occurred, and they probably occupied in reality about the same time as they take to read. Apart from the sinister impression of a differently lighted world, there was no time for fear. Luckily we can only take in a certain amount at a time whatever happens.

The aeroplane was just turning from its side-slip into the nose dive when it struck the ground at perhaps fifty miles an hour with terrific force. Its left wing crumpled, and its propeller and nose plunged into the earth. Again I felt myself driven forward as if in some new dimension by a frightful and overwhelming force, through a space I could not measure. There was a sense of unendurable oppression across my chest as the belt took the strain. Streams of petrol vapour rushed past in the opposite direction. I felt, as a distinct phase, the whole absorption of the shock. Suddenly the pressure ceased, the belt parted, and I fell forward quite gently on to the dial board in front of me. Safe! was the instantaneous realization. I leapt out of the shattered fuselage and ran to my companion. He was senseless and bleeding. I stood by ready to try and pull him out should the machine catch fire. Otherwise it was better to leave him till skilled help arrived.

No fire or explosion followed the crash. A year before Lord Hugh Cecil, himself an aviator, speaking to me of Jack Scott, had said, "Anyone can fly an aeroplane when things are going all right, but it is when things go wrong that the great qualities of a man like Scott are decisive." These words had indeed come true. With unfailing presence of mind he had switched off the electric current in the few seconds before the machine struck the ground, and had thus prevented the clouds of petrol vapour from exploding in flame. It was only another example of those commanding gifts which, in spite of the disabilities of his age and of the injuries he had sustained in his accident at the outset of the war, had won him the widespread fame which he enjoyed throughout the Royal Air Force.

I had two hours later to preside and speak at a House of Commons dinner to General Pershing. I managed to do this; but next day I found myself black and blue all over. Colonel Scott recovered completely from his injuries, which were severe, and actually walked better after his second accident than before.

## ELECTION MEMORIES

If you wish to know about elections I am the person to tell you. I have actually fought more parliamentary elections than any living member of the House of Commons. I have fought fifteen. [Written in 1930.] Think of that! Fifteen elections, each taking at least three weeks, with a week beforehand when you are sickening for it, and at least a week afterwards when you are convalescing and paying the bills. Since I came of age I have lived thirty-five years, and taking an election as dominating one month of your life, I have spent considerably more than a whole year of this short span under these arduous and worrying conditions. In fact I have devoted one day in thirty of my whole adult life to these strange experiences.

One has got by now pretty well to know the routine. First the negotiations and ceremonial with the local fathers and magnates, then the interviews with the Committee and the Council and the Executive: and finally confrontation with the full Association for the adoption meeting. Next the visits to the prominent people, the tour of the constituency, and study of its industries, interests, character and particular idiosyncrasies. Then decision as to the main line of the campaign. Writing the election address: alarums and excursions in the local press! Opening of the contest! Nomination day! You walk with your principal friends to the town hall or other appointed place. Here you meet your opponent or opponents for the first time. Smiles of forced geniality are interchanged. "Good morning, I am delighted to meet you. I hope we shall have a very pleasant contest." "The weather is rather cold (or hot) for this time of year, isn't it?" "Mind you let me know if there is anything I can do for your convenience," and so on. Then the fight in earnest. Every morning between nine and ten the Committee, i.e. the General Staff Meeting; all the heads of departments represented— posters, canvassers, the reports from the different committee-rooms, progress of the canvass, press-notices, advertisements, motor-cars, meetings, prevention of disorder (at your own meetings), cautioning everyone about the election laws, prominent persons who require to be attended to, and so on.

Then out and about around the constituency. When I first began, this had to be done in a two-horse landau, at about seven miles an hour. Nowadays in a whirling motor-car one sometimes goes a good deal faster. Both sides do more, so it makes no difference except that the candidates work harder. Meetings early in the mornings when the workmen have their lunch, meetings in their dinner-hour, meetings in the afternoon. Nowadays three meetings every evening, rushing from one to the other. You arrive on the platform, the other speakers sit down when the candidate is seen. (Loud cheers or boos!) Sometimes, when there are only twenty or thirty extremely stolid-looking persons in a hall which will hold six or seven hundred, this is a trial to the speaker. But think of his poor friends, of his wife and daughter who follow him round from place to place and hear the same speech let off, with variations to suit the local circumstances, again and again. Well do I know the loyal laughter of the faithful chairman or vice-chairman of the Association as he hears the same old joke trotted out for the thirty-third time. My dear friend, I sympathize with you, my heart bleeds for you. Think of all the other meetings where I shall have to make this joke, and you will have to give your enthusiastic Ha! ha! ha!—Hear, hear— Bravo! Never mind. It cannot be helped. It is the way the Constitution works. We are all galley-slaves chained to our toil. We swing forward and back, and forward again. The overseer cracks his whip and the galley goes forward through waters increasingly sullen.

Of course there are the rowdy meetings. These are a great relief. You have not got to make the same old speech. Here you have excited crowds, green-eyed opponents, their jaws twitching with fury shouting interruptions, holloing, bellowing insults of every kind, anything they can think of that will hurt your feelings, any charge that they can make against your consistency or public record, or sometimes, I am sorry to say, against your personal character; and loud jeers and scoffs arising now on all sides, and every kind of nasty question carefully thought out and sent up to the Chair by vehement-looking pasty youths or young short-haired women of bulldog appearance. An ordeal? Certainly: but still these sorts of meetings make themselves. You have not got to worry beforehand to prepare a speech. A few of the main slogans are quite enough to start with. The rest is—not silence. But how your supporters enjoy it! How much more effectually are they stimulated by the interruptions of their opponents, than convinced by the reasonings of their candidate! A long sagacious argument makes the audience yawn, a good retort at a turbulent meeting makes friends by the dozen, even sometimes of the enemy. My advice to candidates in rowdy meetings is this. First of all grin, or, as they say, "smile". There is nothing like it. Next be natural, and quite easy, as if you were talking to a single friend in some quiet place about something in which you were both much interested. Thirdly, cultivate a marked sense of detachment from the clatter and clamour proceeding around you. After all, nothing is so ludicrous as a large number of good people in a frantic state, so long as you are sure they are not going to hurt you.

Incomparably the most exciting, stirring, sensational election I have ever fought was the Westminster election of 1924. The eighteen months that had passed since the breaking up of the Coalition had produced great and lamentable changes in the political situation. Mr. Bonar Law had died, his successor Mr. Baldwin had suddenly appealed to the country upon the protectionist issue. He had been decisively defeated, and to the deep alarm of the general public the Liberal Party decided to put the Socialists in power for the first time in our history. On a vacancy occurring in the Abbey division of Westminster I decided to stand as a Liberal who wished to join with Conservatives in arresting the march of Socialism. This seemed at first a very forlorn hope. I had no organization, and no idea how to form one. All the three great parties, Conservatives, Liberals and Labour, brought forward their official candidates and backed them with their whole resources. The polling day was fixed for the earliest possible date, and less than a fortnight was available for the fight. However, I immediately felt the exhilarating sensation of being supported by a real and spontaneous movement of public opinion. From all sides men of standing and importance came to join me. With scarcely a single exception the whole London press gave its support. The Conservative Association, torn between conflicting views, split in twain. This fissure rapidly extended through the whole Conservative Party. Everyone took sides, families were divided; nearly thirty Conservative members of Parliament appeared upon my platform and worked on the committees. Energetic friends laid hold of the organization. By the end of the first week Captain Guest, my chief lieutenant, a most experienced electioneer, was able to report to me that my candidature was seriously supported.

The constituency, which includes the Houses of Parliament, the seat of government, Buckingham Palace, the principal clubs and theatres, St. James's Street, the Strand, Soho, Pimlico and Covent Garden, is one of the strangest and most remarkable in the world. The poorest and the richest are gathered there, and every trade, profession and interest finds its representative and often its headquarters in this marvellous square mile. To and fro throughout its streets flow the tides of mighty London. As the campaign progressed I began to receive all kinds of support. Dukes, jockeys, prize-fighters, courtiers, actors and business men, all developed a keen partisanship. The chorus girls of Daly's Theatre sat up all night addressing the envelopes and dispatching the election address. It was most cheering and refreshing to see so many young and beautiful women of every rank in life ardently working in a purely disinterested cause not unconnected with myself. The leaders of the Conservative Party were themselves divided. Mr. Baldwin supported the official candidate. Lord Balfour with his acquiescence wrote a letter in my support. The count at the finish was the most exciting I have ever seen. Up to the very end I was assured I had won. Someone said as the last packet was being carried up to the table: "You're in by a hundred." A loud cheer went up. The sound was caught by the crowds waiting outside and the news was telegraphed all over the world. A minute later the actual figures showed that I was beaten by forty votes out of nearly forty thousand polled. I must confess I thoroughly enjoyed the fight from start to finish.

I had now been defeated three times in succession—Dundee, West Leicester and Westminster—and it was a relief to be returned by a majority of ten thousand for West Essex at the end of the General Election of 1924. This made four elections in under two years! That is certainly enough to satisfy anyone, and makes me earnestly hope that I have now found a resting-place amid the glades of Epping which will last me as long as I am concerned with mundane affairs.

## SHALL WE ALL COMMIT SUICIDE?[1]

Except for brief and precarious interludes, there has never been peace in the world; and before history began, murderous strife was universal and unending. But up to the present time the means of destruction at the disposal of man have not kept pace with his ferocity. Reciprocal extermination was impossible in the Stone Age. One cannot do much with a clumsy club. Besides, men were so scarce and hid so well that they were hard to find. They fled so fast that they were hard to catch. Human legs could only cover a certain distance each day. With the best will in the world to destroy his species, each man was restricted to a very limited area of activity. It was impossible to make any effective progress on these lines. Meanwhile one had to live and hunt and sleep. So on the balance the life-forces kept a steady lead over the forces of death, and gradually tribes, villages, and governments were evolved.

It was not until the dawn of the twentieth century of the Christian era that War really began to enter into its kingdom as the potential destroyer of the human race. The organization of mankind into great States and Empires and the rise of nations to full collective consciousness enabled enterprises of slaughter to be planned and executed upon a scale and with a perseverance never before imagined. All the noblest virtues of individuals were gathered together to strengthen the destructive capacity of the mass. Good finances, the resources of world-wide credit and trade, the accumulation of large capital reserves, made it possible to divert for considerable periods

[1] Published in 1925.

609

the energies of whole peoples to the task of Devastation. Democratic institutions gave expression to the will-power of millions. Education not only brought the course of the conflict within the comprehension of everyone, but rendered each person serviceable in a high degree for the purpose in hand. The press afforded a means of unification and of mutual encouragement; Religion, having discreetly avoided conflict on the fundamental issues, offered its encouragements and consolations, through all its forms, impartially to all the combatants. Lastly, Science unfolded her treasures and her secrets to the desperate demands of men, and placed in their hands agencies and apparatus almost decisive in their character.

It is probable—nay, certain—that among the means which will next time be at their disposal will be agencies and processes of destruction wholesale, unlimited, and perhaps, once launched, uncontrollable.

Mankind has never been in this position before. Without having improved appreciably in virtue or enjoying wiser guidance, it has got into its hands for the first time the tools by which it can unfailingly accomplish its own extermination. That is the point in human destinies to which all the glories and toils of men have at last led them. They would do well to pause and ponder upon their new responsibilities. Death stands at attention, obedient, expectant, ready to serve, ready to shear away the peoples *en masse*; ready, if called on, to pulverize, without hope of repair, what is left of civilization. He awaits only the word of command. He awaits it from a frail, bewildered being, long his victim, now—for one occasion only—his Master.


"Wars," said a distinguished American to me some years ago, "are fought with Steel: weapons may change, but Steel remains the core of all modern warfare. France has got the Steel of Europe and Germany has lost it. Here, at any rate, is an element of permanency." "Are you sure," I asked, "that the wars of the future will be fought with Steel?" A few weeks later I talked with a German. "What about Aluminium?" he replied. "Some think," he said, "that the next war will be fought with Electricity." And on this a vista opens out of electrical rays which could paralyse the engines of a motor-car, could claw down aeroplanes from the sky, and conceivably be made destructive of human life or human vision. Then there are Explosives. Have we reached the end? Has Science turned its last page on them? May there not be methods of using explosive energy incomparably more intense than anything heretofore discovered? Might not a bomb no bigger than an orange be found to possess a secret power to destroy a whole block of buildings—nay, to concentrate the force of a thousand tons of cordite and blast a township at a stroke? Could not explosives even of the existing type be guided automatically in flying machines by wireless or other rays, without a human pilot, in ceaseless procession upon a hostile city, arsenal, camp, or dockyard?

In barbarous times superior martial virtues—physical strength, courage, skill, discipline—were required to secure such a supremacy; and in the hard evolution of mankind the best and fittest stocks came to the fore. But no such saving guarantee exists today. There is no reason why a base, degenerate, immoral race should not make an enemy far above them in quality the prostrate subject of their caprice or tyranny, simply because they happened to be possessed at a given moment of some new death-dealing or terror-working process and were ruthless in its employment. The liberties of men are no longer to be guarded by their natural qualities, but by their dodges; and superior virtue and valour may fall an easy prey to the latest diabolical trick.

Such, then, is the peril with which mankind menaces itself. Means of destruction incalculable in their effects, wholesale and frightful in their character, and unrelated to any form of human merit: the march of Science unfolding ever more appalling possibilities; and the fires of hatred burning deep in the hearts of some of the greatest peoples of the world, fanned by continual provocation and unceasing fear, and fed by the deepest sense of national wrong or national danger! Surely if a sense of self-preservation still exists among men, if the will to live resides not merely in individuals or nations but in humanity as a whole, the prevention of the supreme catastrophe ought to be the paramount object of all endeavour.

The great mass of human beings, absorbed in the toils, cares and activities of life, are only dimly conscious of the pace at which mankind has begun to travel. We look back a hundred years, and see that great changes have taken place. We look back fifty years, and see that the speed is constantly quickening. This present century has witnessed an enormous revolution in material things, in scientific appliances, in political institutions, in manners and customs. The greatest change of all is the least perceptible by individuals; it is the far greater numbers which in every civilized country participate in the fuller life of man. "In those days," said Disraeli, writing at the beginning of the nineteenth century, "England was for the few and for the very few." "The twice two thousand for whom," wrote Byron, "the world is made" have given place to many millions for whom existence has become larger, safer, more varied, more full of hope and choice. In the United States scores of millions have lifted themselves above primary necessities and comforts, and aspire to culture—at least for their children. Europe, though stunned and lacerated by Armageddon, presents a similar if less general advance. We all take the modern conveniences and facilities as they are offered to us without being grateful or consciously happier. But we simply could not live, if they were taken away. We assume that progress will be constant. "This 'ere progress," Mr. Wells makes one of his characters remark, "keeps going on. It's wonderful 'ow it keeps going on." It is also very fortunate, for if it stopped or were reversed, there would be the catastrophe of unimaginable horror. Mankind has gone too far to go back, and is moving too fast to stop. There are too many people maintained not merely in comfort but in existence by processes unknown a century ago, for us to afford even a temporary check, still less a general setback, without experiencing calamity in its most frightful form.

When we look back beyond a hundred years over the long trails of history, we see immediately why the age we live in differs from all other ages in human annals. Mankind has sometimes travelled forwards and sometimes backwards, or has stood still even for hundreds of years. It remained stationary in India and in China for thousands of years. What is it that has produced this new prodigious speed of man? Science is the cause. Her once feeble vanguards, often trampled down, often perishing in isolation, have now become a vast organized united class-conscious army marching forward upon all the fronts towards objectives none may measure or define. It is a proud, ambitious army which cares nothing for all the laws that men have made; nothing for their most time-honoured customs, or most dearly-cherished beliefs, or deepest instincts. It is this power called Science which has laid hold of us, conscripted us into its regiments and batteries, set us to work upon its highways and in its arsenals; rewarded us for our services, healed us when we were wounded, trained us when we were young, pensioned us when we were worn out. None of the generations of men before the last two or three were ever gripped for good or ill and handled like this.

Man in the earliest stages lived alone and avoided his neighbours with as much anxiety and probably as much reason as he avoided the fierce flesh-eating beasts that shared his forests. With the introduction of domestic animals the advantages of co-operation and the division of labour became manifest. In the neolithic times when cereals were produced and agriculture developed, the bleak hungry period whilst the seeds were germinating beneath the soil involved some form of capitalism, and the recognition of those special rights of landed proprietors the traces of which are still visible in our legislation. Each stage involved new problems legal, sociological and moral. But progress only crawled, and often rested for a thousand years or so.

The two ribbon States in the valley of the Nile and the Euphrates produced civilizations as full of pomp and circumstance and more stable than any the world has ever known. Their autocracies and hierarchies were founded upon the control and distribution of water and corn. The rulers held the people in an efficiency of despotism never equalled till Soviet Russia was born. They had only to cut off or stint the water in the canals to starve or subjugate rebellious provinces. This, apart from their granaries, gave them powers at once as irresistible and as capable of intimate regulation as the control of all food supplies gives to the Bolshevik commissars. Safe from internal trouble, they were vulnerable only to external attack. But in these states man had not learnt to catalyse the forces of nature. The maximum power available was the sum of the muscular efforts of all the inhabitants. Later empires, scarcely less imposing but far less stable, rose and fell. In the methods of production and communication, in the modes of getting food and exchanging goods, there was less change between the time of Sargon and the time of Louis XIV than there has been between the accession of Queen Victoria and the present day. Darius could probably send a message from Susa to Sardis faster than Philip II could transmit an order from Madrid to Brussels. Sir Robert Peel, summoned in 1841 from Rome to form a government in London, took the same time as the Emperor Vespasian when he had to hasten to his province of Britain. The bathrooms of the palaces of Minos were superior to those of Versailles. A priest from Thebes would probably have felt more at home at the Council of Trent two thousand years after Thebes had vanished, than Sir Isaac Newton at a modern undergraduate physical society, or George Stephenson in the Institute of Electrical Engineers. The changes have been so sudden and so gigantic that no period in history can be compared with the last century. The past no longer enables us even dimly to measure the future.

There are two processes which we adopt consciously or unconsciously when we try to prophesy. We can seek a period in the past whose conditions resemble as closely as possible those of our day, and presume that the sequel to that period will, save for some minor alterations, be repeated. Secondly, we can survey the general course of development in our immediate past, and endeavour to prolong it into the near future. The first is the method of the historian; the second that of the scientist. Only the second is open to us now, and this only in a partial sphere. By observing all that Science has achieved in modern times, and the knowledge and power now in her possession, we can predict with some assurance the inventions and discoveries which will govern our future. We can but guess, peering through a glass darkly, what reactions these discoveries and their applications will produce upon the habits, the outlook and the spirit of men.

Whereas formerly the utmost power that man could guide and control was a team of horses, or a galleyful of slaves; or possibly, if they could be sufficiently drilled and harnessed, a gang of labourers like the Israelites in Egypt: it is today already possible to control accurately from the bridge of a battle cruiser all the power of hundreds of thousands of men: or to set off with one finger a mine capable in an instant of destroying the work of thousands of man-years. These changes are due to the substitution of molecular energy for muscular energy, and its direction and control by an elaborate, beautifully-perfected apparatus. These immense new sources of power, and the fact that they can be wielded by a single individual, have made possible novel methods of mining and metallurgy, new modes of transport and undreamed-of machinery. These in their turn enable the molecular sources of power to be extended and used more efficiently. They facilitate also the improvement of ancient methods. They substitute the hundred-thousand-kilowatt turbo-generators at Niagara for the mill-wheel of our fore-fathers. Each invention acted and reacted on other inventions, and with ever-growing rapidity that vast structure of technical achievement was raised which separates the civilization of today from all that the past has known.

There is no doubt that this evolution will continue at an increasing rate. We know enough to be sure that the scientific achievements of the next fifty years will be far greater, more rapid and more surprising, than those we have already experienced. The slide-lathe enabled machines of precision to be made, and the power of steam rushed out upon the world. And through the steam-cloud flashed the dazzling lightning of electricity. But this is only a beginning. High authorities tell us that new sources of power, vastly more important than any we yet know, will surely be discovered. Nuclear energy is incomparably greater than the molecular energy which we use today. The coal a man can get in a day can easily do five hundred times as much work as the man himself. Nuclear energy is at least one million times more powerful still.

Up till recent times the production of food has been the prime struggle of man. That war is won. There is no doubt that the civilized races can produce or procure all the food they require. Indeed some of the problems which vex us today are due to the production of wheat by white men having exceeded their own needs, before yellow men, brown men and black men have learnt to demand and become able to purchase a diet superior to rice. But food is at present obtained almost entirely from the energy of the sunlight. The radiation from the sun produces from the carbonic acid in the air more or less complicated carbon compounds which give us our plants and vegetables. We use the latent chemical energy of these to keep our bodies warm, we convert it into muscular effort. We employ it in the complicated processes of digestion to repair and replace the wasted cells of our bodies. Many people of course prefer food in what the vegetarians call "the second-hand form", i.e. after it has been digested and converted into meat for us by domestic animals kept for this purpose. In all these processes however ninety-nine parts of the solar energy are wasted for every part used.

Even without the new sources of power great improvements are probable here. Microbes, which at present convert the nitrogen of the air into the proteins by which animals live, will be fostered and made to work under controlled conditions, just as yeast is now. New strains of microbes will be developed and made to do a great deal of our chemistry for us. With a greater knowledge of what are called hormones, i.e. the chemical messengers in our blood, it will be possible to control growth. We shall escape the absurdity of growing a whole chicken in order to eat the breast or wing, by growing these parts separately under a suitable medium. Synthetic food will, of course, also be used in the future. Nor need the pleasures of the table be banished. That gloomy Utopia of tabloid meals need never be invaded. The new foods will from the outset be practically indistinguishable from the natural products, and any changes will be so gradual as to escape observation.

If the gigantic new sources of power become available, food will be produced without recourse to sunlight. Vast cellars in which artificial radiation is generated may replace the cornfields or potato-patches of the world. Parks and gardens will cover our pastures and ploughed fields. When the time comes there will be plenty of room for the cities to spread themselves again.

But equally startling developments lie already just beyond our finger-tips in the breeding of human beings, and the shaping of human nature. It used to be said, "Though you have taught the dog more tricks, you cannot alter the breed of the dog." But that is no longer true. There seems little doubt that it will be possible to carry out in artificial surroundings the entire cycle which now leads to the birth of a child. Interference with the mental development of such beings, expert suggestion and treatment in the earlier years, would produce beings specialized to thought or toil. The production of creatures, for instance, which have admirable physical development with their mental endowment stunted in particular directions, is almost within the range of human power. A being might be produced capable of tending a machine but without other ambitions. Our minds recoil from such fearful eventualities, and the laws of a Christian civilization will prevent them. But might not lop-sided creatures of this type fit in well with the Communist doctrines of Russia? Might not the Union of Soviet Republics armed with all the power of science find it in harmony with all their aims to produce a race adapted to mechanical tasks and with no other ideas but to obey the Communist State? The present nature of man is tough and resilient. It casts up its sparks of genius in the darkest and most unexpected places. But Robots could be made to fit the grisly theories of Communism. There is nothing in the philosophy of Communists to prevent their creation.

I have touched upon this sphere only lightly, but with the purpose of pointing out that in a future which our children may live to see, powers will be in the hands of men altogether different from any by which human nature has been moulded. Explosive forces, energy, materials, machinery will be available upon a scale which can annihilate whole nations. Despotisms and tyrannies will be able to prescribe the lives and even the wishes of their subjects in a manner never known since time began. If to these tremendous and awful powers is added the pitiless sub-human wickedness which we now see embodied in one of the most powerful reigning governments, who shall say that the world itself will not be wrecked, or indeed that it ought not to be wrecked? There are nightmares of the future from which a fortunate collision with some wandering star, reducing the earth to incandescent gas, might be a merciful deliverance.

Certain it is that while men are gathering knowledge and power with ever-increasing and measureless speed, their virtues and their wisdom have not shown any notable improvement as the centuries have rolled. The brain of a modern man does not differ in essentials from that of the human beings who fought and loved here millions of years ago. The nature of man has remained hitherto practically unchanged. Under sufficient stress—starvation, terror, warlike passion, or even cold intellectual frenzy, the modern man we know so well will do the most terrible deeds, and his modern woman will back him up. At the present moment the civilizations of many different ages co-exist together in the world, and their representatives meet and converse. Englishmen, Frenchmen, or Americans with ideas abreast of the twentieth century do business with Indians or Chinese whose civilizations were crystallized several thousands of years ago. We have the spectacle of the powers and weapons of man far outstripping the march of his intelligence; we have the march of his intelligence proceeding far more rapidly than the development of his nobility. We may well find ourselves in the presence of "the strength of civilization without its mercy".

It is therefore above all things important that the moral philosophy and spiritual conceptions of men and nations should hold their own amid these formidable scientific evolutions. It would be much better to call a halt in material progress and discovery rather than to be mastered by our own apparatus and the forces which it directs. There are secrets too mysterious for man in his present state to know; secrets which once penetrated may be fatal to human happiness and glory. But the busy hands of the scientists are already fumbling with the keys of all the chambers hitherto forbidden to mankind. Without an equal growth of Mercy, Pity, Peace and Love, Science herself may destroy all that makes human life majestic and tolerable. There never was a time when the inherent virtue of human beings required more strong and confident expression in daily life; there never was a time when the hope of immortality and the disdain of earthly power and achievement were more necessary for the safety of the children of men.

After all, this material progress, in itself so splendid, does not meet any of the real needs of the human race. I read a book the other day which traced the history of mankind from the birth of the solar system to its extinction. There were fifteen or sixteen races of men which in succession rose and fell over periods measured by tens of millions of years. In the end a race of beings was evolved which had mastered nature. A state was created whose citizens lived as long as they chose, enjoyed pleasures and sympathies incomparably wider than our own, navigated the inter-planetary spaces, could recall the panorama of the past and foresee the future. But what was the good of all that to them? What did they know more than we know about the answers to the simple questions which man has asked since the earliest dawn of reason—"Why are we here? What is the purpose of life? Whither are we going?" No material progress, even though it takes shapes we cannot now conceive, or however it may expand the faculties of man, can bring comfort to his soul. It is this fact, more wonderful than any that Science can reveal, which gives the best hope that all will be well. Projects undreamed of by past generations will absorb our immediate descendants; forces terrific and devastating will be in their hands; comforts, activities, amenities, pleasures will crowd upon them, but their hearts will ache, their lives will be barren, if they have not a vision above material things. And with the hopes and powers will come dangers out of all proportion to the growth of man's intellect, to the strength of his character or to the efficacy of his institutions. Once more the choice is offered between Blessing and Cursing. Never was the answer that will be given harder to foretell.

# SAVROLA

★

## A TALE OF THE REVOLUTION
## IN LAURANIA

*The author's only novel was written in 1897 when he was
twenty-three years of age. It was first published as a serial in
"Macmillan's Magazine" and as a book in 1900. "Savrola"
is a Ruritanian story of politics and romance of a kind very
popular at the time it was written.*

THERE HAD been a heavy shower of rain, but the sun was already
shining through the breaks in the clouds and throwing swiftly
changing shadows on the streets, the houses, and the gardens of
the city of Laurania. Everything shone wetly in the sunlight: the
dust had been laid; the air was cool; the trees looked green and
grateful. It was the first rain after the summer heats, and it marked
the beginning of that delightful autumn climate which has made
the Lauranian capital the home of the artist, the invalid, and the
sybarite.

The shower had been heavy, but it had not dispersed the crowds
that were gathered in the great square in front of the Parliament
House. It was welcome, but it had not altered their anxious and
angry looks; it had drenched them without cooling their excitement.
Evidently an event of consequence was taking place. The fine
building, where the representatives of the people were wont to
meet, wore an aspect of sombre importance that the trophies and
statues, with which an ancient and an art-loving people had
decorated its façade, did not dispel. A squadron of Lancers of the
Republican Guard was drawn up at the foot of the great steps, and
a considerable body of infantry kept a broad space clear in front of
the entrance. Behind the soldiers the people filled in the rest of the
picture. They swarmed in the square and the streets leading to it;

they had scrambled on to the numerous monuments, which the taste and pride of the Republic had raised to the memory of her ancient heroes, covering them so completely that they looked like mounds of human beings; even the trees contained their occupants, while the windows, and often the roofs, of the houses and offices which overlooked the scene were crowded with spectators. It was a great multitude and it vibrated with excitement. Wild passions surged across the throng, as squalls sweep across a stormy sea. Here and there a man, mounting above his fellows, would harangue those whom his voice could reach, and a cheer or a shout was caught up by thousands who had never heard the words but were searching for something to give expression to their feelings.

It was a great day in the history of Laurania. For five long years since the Civil War the people had endured the insult of autocratic rule. The fact that the government was strong, and the memory of the disorders of the past, had operated powerfully on the minds of the more sober citizens. But from the first there had been murmurs. There were many who had borne arms on the losing side in the long struggle that had ·ended in the victory of President Antonio Molara. Some had suffered wounds or confiscation; others had undergone imprisonment; many had lost friends and relations, who with their latest breath had enjoined the uncompromising prosecution of the war. The government had started with implacable enemies, and their rule had been harsh and tyrannical. The ancient constitution to which the citizens were so strongly attached, and of which they were so proud, had been subverted. The President, alleging the prevalence of sedition, had declined to invite the people to send their representatives to that chamber which had for many centuries been regarded as the surest bulwark of popular liberties. Thus the discontents increased day by day and year by year: the National party, which had at first consisted only of a few survivors of the beaten side, had swelled into the most numerous and powerful faction in the State; and at last they had found a leader. The agitation proceeded on all sides. The large and turbulent population of the capital were thoroughly devoted to the rising cause. Demonstration had followed demonstration; riot had succeeded riot; even the army showed signs of unrest. At length the President had decided to make concessions. It was announced that on 1 September the electoral writs should be issued and the people should be accorded an opportunity of expressing their wishes and opinions.

This pledge had contented the more peaceable citizens. The extremists, finding themselves in a minority, had altered their tone. The government, taking advantage of the favourable moment, had arrested several of the more violent leaders. Others, who had fought in the war and had returned from exile to take part in the revolt, fled for their lives across the border. A rigorous search for arms had resulted in important captures. European nations, watching with interested and anxious eyes the political barometer, were convinced that the government cause was in the ascendant. But meanwhile the people waited, silent and expectant, for the fulfilment of the promise.

At length the day had come. The necessary preparations for summoning the seventy thousand male electors to record their votes had been carried out by the public officials. The President, as the custom prescribed, was in person to sign the necessary writ of summons to the faithful citizens. Warrants for election would be forwarded to the various electoral divisions in the city and the provinces, and those who were by the ancient law entitled to the franchise would give their verdict on the conduct of him whom the Populists in bitter hatred had called the Dictator.

It was for this moment that the crowd was waiting. Though cheers from time to time arose, they waited for the most part in silence. Even when the President had passed on his way to the Senate, they had forborne to hoot; in their eyes he was virtually abdicating, and that made amends for all. The time-honoured observances, the long-loved rights would be restored, and once more democratic government would be triumphant in Laurania.

\*     \*     \*

And then began a period of wild rumour. The President had refused to sign the writs; he had committed suicide; the troops had been ordered to fire; the elections would not take place, after all; Savrola had been arrested—seized in the very Senate, said one, murdered added another. The noise of the multitude changed into a dull dissonant hum of rising anger.

622

At last the answer came. There was a house, overlooking the square, which was separated from the Chamber of Representatives only by a narrow street, and this street had been kept clear for traffic by the troops. On the balcony of this house the young man, Moret, the Civic Councillor, now reappeared, and his coming.was the signal for a storm of wild, anxious cries from the vast concourse. He held up his hand for silence and after some moments his words became audible to those nearest. "You are betrayed—a cruel fraud— the hopes we had cherished are dashed to the ground—all has been done in vain. Cheated! cheated! cheated!" The broken fragments of his oratory reached far into the mass of excited humanity, and then he shouted a sentence, which was heard by thousands and repeated by thousands more. "The register of citizenship has been mutilated, and the names of more than half the electors have been erased. To your tents, oh people of Laurania!"

The President entered his carriage which, preceded by an entire troop of Lancers, immediately started at a trot. So soon as the carriage reached the edge of the open space, a rush was made by the crowd. The escort closed up; "Fall back there!" shouted an officer, but he was unheeded. "Will you move, or must we move you?" said a gruffer voice. Yet the mob gave not an inch. The danger was imminent. "Cheat! Traitor! Liar! Tyrant!" they shouted, with many other expressions too coarse to be recorded. "Give us back our rights—you, who have stolen them!"

And then someone at the back of the crowd fired a revolver into the air. The effect was electrical. The Lancers dropped their points and sprang forward. Shouts of terror and fury arose on all sides. The populace fled before the cavalry; some fell on the ground and were trampled to death; some were knocked down and injured by the horses; a few were speared by the soldiers. It was a horrible scene. Those behind threw stones, and some fired random pistol shots. The President remained unmoved. Erect and unflinching he gazed on the tumult as men gaze at a race about which they have not betted. His hat was knocked off, and a trickle of blood down his cheek showed where a stone had struck. For some moments the issue seemed doubtful. The crowd might storm the carriage and then—to be torn to pieces by a rabble! There were other and more pleasant deaths. But the discipline of the troops overcame all obstacles, the bearing of the man appeared to cow his enemies, and the crowd fell back, still hooting and shouting.

Meanwhile the officer commanding the infantry by the Parliament House had been alarmed by the rushes of the mob, which he could see were directed at the President's carriage. He determined to create a diversion. "We shall have to fire on them," he said to the Major who was beside him.

"Excellent," replied that officer; "it will enable us to conclude those experiments in penetration, which we have been trying with the soft-nosed bullet. A very valuable experiment, Sir," and then turning to the soldiers he issued several orders. "A very valuable experiment," he repeated.

"Somewhat expensive," said the Colonel dryly; "and half a company will be enough, Major."

There was a rattle of breech-blocks as the rifles were loaded. The people immediately in front of the troops struggled madly to escape the impending volley. One man, a man in a straw hat, kept his head. He rushed forward. "For God's sake don't fire!" he cried. "Have mercy! We will disperse."

There was a moment's pause, a sharp order and a loud explosion, followed by screams. The man in the straw hat bent backwards and fell on the ground; other figures also subsided and lay still in curiously twisted postures. Everyone else except the soldiers fled; fortunately there were many exits to the square, and in a few minutes it was almost deserted. The President's carriage made its way through the flying crowd to the gates of the palace, which were guarded by more soldiers, and passed through in safety.

All was now over. The spirit of the mob was broken and the wide expanse of Constitution Square was soon nearly empty. Forty bodies and some expended cartridges lay on the ground. Both had played their part in the history of human development and passed out of the considerations of living men. Nevertheless the soldiers picked up the empty cases, and presently some police came with carts and took the other things away, and all was quiet again in Laurania.

★   ★   ★

"Things are going wrong with us, my dear" [the President said to his wife]. "Savrola, the deputation, the newspapers, and, above all, the reports I receive of the people, are ominous and alarming."

"I noticed black looks this morning when I drove. Do you think there is danger?"

"I do," he answered in his precise official manner, "grave danger."

"I wish I could help you," she said, "but I am only a woman. What can I do?" He did not answer and she continued: "Señor Savrola is a kind man. I used to know him quite well before the war."

"He will ruin us."

"Surely not."

"We shall have to fly the country, if indeed they allow us to."

She turned paler. "But I know what men look like; there is a sympathy between us; he is no fanatic."

"There are powers behind and beneath him of which he knows little, which he cannot control, but which he has invoked."

"Can you do nothing?"

"I cannot arrest him; he is too popular, and besides he has broken no law. He will go on. In a fortnight are the elections; he will be returned in spite of my precautions; then the trouble will begin." He paused, and then speaking as if to himself continued: "If we could learn what he means to do, perhaps we might defeat it."

"Can I not help you?" she asked quickly. "I know him; I think he likes me. He might whisper to me what he would not tell to others." She thought of many victories in the past.

"My darling," said Molara, "why should you spoil your life by mixing in the darker side of politics? I would not ask you."

"But I want to. I will try if it would help you."

"It might do much more."

"Very well, I will find out for you; in a fortnight you shall know. He must come to the State Ball; I will meet him there."

"I am loth to let you talk to such a man, but I know your wit, and the need is great. But will he come?"

"I will write him a note with the invitation," she said, "laugh at politics and advise him to keep his private life at least free from them. I think he will come; if not, I will find some other way of seeing him."

Molara looked at her with admiration. At no time did he love her more than when he realized of what use she was to him. "I leave it to you, then. I fear you will fail, but if you can do it, you may have saved the State. If not, no harm will have been done."

"I shall succeed," she answered confidently, and rising from her seat began to walk towards the house. She saw from her husband's manner that he would like to be alone.

He remained seated there for a long time, staring into the water in which the fat, lazy, goldfish swam placidly. His face wore the expression of one who has swallowed some nasty thing.

\* \* \*

The palace of Laurania was admirably suited to the discharge of the social ceremonies of the State. The lavish expenditure on public entertainments, which the constitutional practice encouraged, allowed the hospitalities of the Republic to be extended upon the most magnificent scale. The opening State Ball of the season was in many ways the most important of these affairs. It was at this function that the great men of both parties met, for the first time after the summer heats, before the autumn session, and the brilliant society of the capital reunited after their absence in their country and mountain villas. Taste, elegance, and magnificence were equally displayed. The finest music, the best champagne, the most diverse, yet select, company were among the attractions of the evening. The spacious courtyard of the palace was completely covered by a gigantic awning. Rows of the Infantry of the Guard lined the approaches, and with their bright steel bayonets increased the splendour and the security of the occasion. The well-lit streets were crowded with the curious populace. The great hall of the palace, at all times imposing and magnificent, displayed a greater pomp when filled with a gaily dressed company.

At the head of the stairs stood the President and his wife, he resplendent in his orders and medals, she in her matchless beauty. As the guests ascended, an aide-de-camp, a gorgeous thing in crimson and gold, inquired their names and styles and announced them. Many and various was the company; every capital in Europe, every country in the world, was represented.

The guest of the evening was the King of Ethiopia, a mass of silk and jewels framing a black but vivacious face. He came early—unwisely as, had he come later, there would have been a better audience to watch his arrival; however, to his untutored mind perhaps this was a matter of little importance.

The Diplomatic Corps followed in a long succession. Coach after coach drew up at the entrance and discharged its burden of polite astuteness, clothed in every conceivable combination of gold and colour. Arrived at the top of the stairs, the Russian Ambassador, grey but gallant, paused and, bowing with a stately courtesy, kissed the hand Lucile extended.

Suddenly everyone became hushed, and above the strains of the band the distant sound of shouting was heard. Louder and louder it swelled, swiftly approaching until it was at the very gate; then it died away, and there was a silence through the hall filled only by the music. Had he been hooted or cheered? The sound had seemed strangely ambiguous; men were prepared to wager about it; his face would tell them the answer.

The swing-doors opened and Savrola entered. All eyes were turned on him, but his face showed them nothing, and the bets remained undecided. As he leisurely ascended the stairs, his eye travelled with interest round the crowded galleries and the brilliant throng who lined them. No decorations, no orders, no star relieved the plain evening dress he wore. Amid that blaze of colour, that multitude of gorgeous uniforms, he appeared a sombre figure; but, like the Iron Duke in Paris, he looked the leader of them all, calm, confident, and composed.

The President walked down a few steps to meet his distinguished guest. Both bowed with grave dignity.

"I am glad you have come, Sir," said Molara; "it is in harmony with the traditions of the State."

"Duty and inclination combined to point the way," answered Savrola with a smile marked by a suggestion of irony.

"You had no difficulty with the crowd?" suggested the President acidly.

"Oh, no difficulty, but they take politics a little seriously; they disapproved of my coming to your palace."

"You are right to come," said Molara. "Now we who are engaged in matters of State know what these things are worth; men of the world do not get excited over public affairs, nor do gentlemen fight with bludgeons."

"I prefer swords," said Savrola reflectively. He had reached the head of the stairs and Lucile stood before him. What a queen she looked, how peerless and incomparable among all women! The fine tiara she wore suggested sovereignty, and democrat as he was, he bowed to that alone. She held out her hand; he took it with reverence and courtesy, but the contact thrilled him.

Meanwhile the dances had succeeded each other and the night was passing. The King of Ethiopia, horrified at the low dresses of the unveiled women and dreading the prospect of eating with odious white people, had taken his departure. The President, approaching Savrola, invited him to take his wife down to supper; a procession was formed; he offered Lucile his arm and they descended the stairs. The supper was excellent: the champagne was dry and the quails fat. A profusion of rare and beautiful orchids covered the table; Savrola's surroundings were agreeable, and he sat next the most beautiful woman in Laurania, who, though he did not know it, was exerting herself to captivate him. At first they talked amusing frivolities. The President, whose manners were refined, showed himself a pleasant companion and an accomplished talker. Savrola, who delighted in sparkling conversation, found it difficult to keep to the part of a purely official visitor which he had determined to observe. The influence of wit, wine, and beauty were combined to break his reserve; before he knew it, he had joined in a discussion, one of those half cynical, half serious discussions which are characteristic of an age which inquires because it doubts, and doubts the more because it has inquired.

*     *     *

As Savrola walked back to the hall with Lucile, they passed an open doorway leading to the garden. A multitude of fairy lights marked out the flower-beds or hung in festoons from the trees. The paths were carpeted with red cloth; a cool breeze fanned their faces. Lucile paused.

"It is a lovely night."

The invitation was plain. She had wanted to speak to him, then, after all. How right he was to come—on constitutional grounds.

"Shall we go out?" he said.

She consented, and they stepped on to the terrace.

The night was very still. The soft breeze was not strong enough to stir even the slender palms which rose on all sides, and whose outlines, above the surrounding foliage, framed the starlit sky. The palace stood on high ground, and the garden sloped on the western side towards the sea. At the end of the terrace was a stone seat.

"Let us sit here," said Lucile.

They sat down. The dreamy music of a waltz floated down as a distant accompaniment to their thoughts. The windows of the palace blazed with light and suggested glitter, glare, and heat; in the garden all was quiet and cool.

"Why do you sneer at honour?" asked Lucile, thinking of the interrupted conversation.

"Because it has no true foundation, no ultra-human sanction. Its codes are constantly changing with times and places. At one time it is thought more honourable to kill the man you have wronged than to make amends; at another it is more important to pay a bookmaker than a butcher. Like art it changes with human caprice, and like art it comes from opulence and luxury."

"But why do you claim a higher origin for beauty and honesty?"

"Because, wherever I have looked, I see that all things are perpetually referred to an eternal standard of fitness, and that right triumphs over wrong, truth over falsehood, beauty over ugliness. *Fitness* is the general expression! Judged by this standard art and honour have little value."

"But are these things so?" she asked wonderingly. "Surely there are many exceptions?"

"Nature never considers the individual; she only looks at the average fitness of the species. Consider the statistics of mortality. How exact they are: they give to a month the expectation of life to men; and yet they tell a man nothing. We cannot say that a good man will always overcome a knave; but the evolutionist will not hesitate to affirm that the nation with the highest ideals would succeed."

"Is that the triumph of moral superiority?"

"At first it would be, for the virtues of civilization are of a higher type than those of barbarism. Kindness is better than courage, and charity more than strength. But ultimately the dominant race will degenerate, and as there will be none to take its place, the degeneration must continue. It is the old struggle between vitality and decay, between energy and indolence; a struggle that always ends in silence. After all, we could not expect human development to be constant. It is only a question of time before the planet becomes unfitted to support life on its surface."

"To what purpose then are all our efforts?"

"God knows," said Savrola cynically; "but I can imagine that the drama would not be an uninteresting one to watch."

"And yet you believe in an ultra-human foundation, an eternal ideal for such things as beauty and virtue."

"I believe that the superiority of fitness over relative unfitness is one of the great laws of matter. I include all kinds of fitness—moral, physical, mathematical."

"Mathematical!"

"Certainly; words only exist by conforming to correct mathematical principles. That is one of the great proofs we have that mathematics has been discovered, not invented. The planets observe a regular progression in their distances from the sun. Evolution suggests that those that did not observe such principles were destroyed by collisions and amalgamated with others. It is a universal survival of the fittest." She was silent. He continued: "Now let us say that in the beginning there existed two factors, matter animated by the will to live, and the eternal ideal; the great author and the great critic. It is to the interplay and counteraction of these two that all development, that all forms of life are due. The more the expression of the will to live approximates to the eternal standard of fitness, the better it succeeds."

"I would add a third," she said, "a great Being to instil into all forms of life the desire to attain to the ideal; to teach them in what ways they may succeed."

"Ah," said Lucile impetuously, "whither are you hurrying us in the future—to revolution?"

"Perhaps," said Savrola calmly. "I discharge a duty to the human species in breaking down a military despotism. I do not like to see a government supported only by bayonets.

His voice had grown strangely vehement and his manner thrilled her. "You will ruin us," she said weakly.

"No," he replied with his grand air, "you can never be ruined. Your brilliancy and beauty will always make you the luckiest of women, and your husband the luckiest of men."

His great soul was above the suspicion of presumption. She looked up at him, smiled quickly, and impulsively held out her hand. "We are on opposite sides, but we will fight under the rules of war. I hope we shall remain friends even though——"

"We are officially enemies," said Savrola, completing the sentence, and taking her hand in his he bowed and kissed it. After that they were both very silent, and walking along the terrace re-entered the palace. Most of the guests had already gone, and Savrola did not ascend the stairs, but passing through the swing-doors took his departure. Lucile walked up to the ballroom in which a few youthful and indefatigable couples were still circling. Molara met her. "My dear," he said, "where have you been all this time?"

"In the garden," she replied.

"With Savrola?"

"Yes."

The President repressed a feeling of satisfaction. "Did he tell you anything?" he asked.

"Nothing," she answered, remembering for the first time the object with which she had sought the interview; "I must see him again."

"You will continue to try and find out his political intentions?" inquired Molara anxiously.

"I shall see him again," she replied.

Her maid came in to assist her to undress.

"Is he going to make a speech tomorrow?" asked Lucile.

"So my brother says," said the maid; "he says that he is going to give them such a dressing down they will never forget it." The maid paid great attention to her brother's words. There was much sympathy between them; in fact she only called him her brother because it sounded better.

Lucile took up the evening paper which lay on the bed. There on the first page was the announcement, the great meeting would take place at the City Hall at eight the next evening. She dismissed the maid and walked to the window. The silent city lay before her; tomorrow the man she had talked with would convulse that city with excitement. She would go and hear him; women went to these meetings; why should she not go, closely veiled? After all it would enable her to learn something of his character and she could thus better assist her husband. With this reflection, which was extremely comforting, she went to bed.

★ ★ ★

The disapproval which Moret had expressed at Savrola's determination to go to the State Ball was amply justified by the result. Every paper, except those actually controlled by the party organization, commented severely or contemptuously on his action. *The Hour* alluded to the groans with which the crowd had received him, as marking the decline of his influence with the masses and the break-up of the Revolutionary party. It also reminded its readers that social distinction was always the highest ambition of the Demagogue, and declared that, by accepting the President's invitation, Savrola had revealed "his sordid personal aims". The other government organs expressed a similar opinion in an even more offensive manner. "These agitators," said *The Courtier*, "have at all times in the history of the world hankered after titles and honours, and the prospect of mixing with persons of rank and fashion has once again proved irresistible to an austere and unbending son of the people." This superior vulgarity, though more unpleasant, was less dangerous than the grave and serious warnings and protests which the Democratic journals contained. *The Rising Tide* said plainly that, if this sort of thing continued, the Popular Party would have to find another leader, "one who did not cringe to power nor seek to ingratiate himself with fashion".

Savrola read these criticisms with disdain. He had recognized the fact that such things would be said, and had deliberately exposed himself to them. He knew he had been unwise to go: he had known that from the first; and yet somehow he did not regret his mistake. After all, why should his party dictate to him how he should rule his private life? He would never resign his right to go where he

632

pleased. In this case he had followed his own inclination, and the odium which had been cast upon him was the price he was prepared to pay. When he thought of his conversation in the garden, he did not feel that he had made a bad bargain. The damage however must be repaired. He looked over the notes of his speech again, polished his sentences, considered his points, collected his arguments, and made some additions which he thought appropriate to the altered state of public feeling.

Savrola had scarcely time to smoke a cigarette before the Revolutionary leaders began to arrive. Moret was the first; he rang the bell violently, stamping about on the doorstep till it was answered, ran upstairs three steps at a time, and burst impetuously into the room, aquiver with excitement. "Ah," he cried, "the hour has come—not words but deeds now! We draw the sword in a good cause; for my part I shall fling away the scabbard; Fortune is on our side."

"Yes," said Savrola; "have some whisky and soda-water—on the sideboard there. It is a good drink to draw the sword on—the best in fact."

Moret somewhat abashed turned and walking to the table began opening a soda-water bottle. As he poured out the spirit the clinking of glass and bottle betrayed his agitation. Savrola laughed softly. Turning swiftly, his impetuous follower sought to hide his agitation by a fresh outburst. "I have told you throughout," he said, holding his glass on high, "that force was the only solution. It has come, as I predicted. I drink to it—war, civil war, battle, murder, and sudden death—by these means liberty will be regained!"

★    ★    ★

The intricate details of the plot, for plot it was, were well known to the leaders of the revolt. For several months they had looked to force as the only means of ending the government they detested. Savrola was not the man to commit himself to such an enterprise without taking every precaution. Nothing had been forgotten; the machinery of revolution only needed setting in motion. Yet in spite of the elaborate nature of the conspiracy and its great scale, the President and his police had been able to learn nothing definite. They feared that a rising was imminent; they had realized the danger for some months; but it was impossible to know where the political agitation ended, and the open sedition began. The great social position and almost European reputation of the principal leaders had rendered their arrest without certain proof a matter of extreme difficulty. The President, believing that the people would not rise unless spurred thereto by some act of power on the part of the Executive, feared to rouse them. But for this Savrola, Moret, and the others would have already filled cells in the State Prison; indeed, they would have had much to be thankful for had their lives been spared.

It had been a busy and exciting day for Savrola. He had seen his followers, had issued orders, restrained the impetuous, stimulated the weak, encouraged the timid. All day long messages and reports had reached him about the behaviour of the soldiers. The departure of the Guard, and the refusal of the supporting brigade to march, were equally pleasing events. The conspiracy had now been made known to so many persons that he doubted the possibility of keeping it much longer secret from the government agents. From every consideration he felt that the hour had come. The whole of the elaborate plan that he had devised had been put into execution. The strain had been severe, but at length all the preparations were completed, and the whole strength of the Revolutionary party was concentrated for the final struggle. Godoy, Renos, and the others were collected at the Mayoralty, whence at dawn the Provisional Government was to be proclaimed. Moret, to whom the actual duty of calling the people to arms had been assigned, instructed his agents at his own house and made arrangements for the posting of the proclamation. All was ready. The leader on whom everything depended, whose brain had conceived, whose heart had inspired, the great conspiracy, lay back in his chair. He needed and desired a few moments' rest and quiet reflection to review his schemes, to look for omissions, to brace his nerves.

A small bright fire burned in the grate, and all around were the ashes of burnt papers. For an hour he had been feeding the flames. One phase of his life was over; there might be another, but it was well to have done with this one first. Letters from friends, dead now or alienated; letters of congratulation, of praise that had inspired his younger ambitions; letters from brilliant men and some from beautiful women—all had met a common fate. Why should these records be preserved for the curious eye of unsympathetic posterity? If he perished, the world might forget him, and welcome; if he lived, his life would henceforth be within the province of the historian. A single note, preserved from the general destruction, lay on the table beside him. It was the one with which Lucile had accompanied her invitation to the State Ball, the only one he had ever received from her.

As he balanced it in his fingers, his thoughts drifted away from the busy hard realities of life to that kindred soul and lovely face. That episode too was over. A barrier stood between them. Whatever the result of the revolt, she was lost to him, unless—and that terrible unless was pregnant with suggestions of such awful wickedness that his mind recoiled from it as a man's hand starts from some filthy thing he has by inadvertence touched. There were sins, sins against the commonwealth of mankind, against the phenomenon of life itself, the stigma of which would cling through death, and for which there was pardon only in annihilation. Yet he hated Molara with a fierce hatred; nor did he care to longer hide from himself the reason. And with the recollection of the reason his mind reverted to a softer mood. Would he ever see her again? Even the sound of her name pleased him. "Lucile," he whispered sadly.

There was a quick step outside; the door opened, and she stood before him. He sprang up in mute astonishment.

Lucile looked greatly embarrassed. Her mission was a delicate one. Indeed she did not know her own mind, or did not care to know it. It was for her husband's sake, she said to herself; but the words she spoke belied her. "I have come to tell you that I did not betray your secret."

"I know—I never feared," replied Savrola.

"How do you know?"

"I have not yet been arrested."

"No, but he suspects."

"Suspects what?"

"That you are conspiring against the Republic."

"Oh!" said Savrola, greatly relieved; "he has no proofs."

"Tomorrow he may have."

"Tomorrow will be too late."

"Too late?"

"Yes," said Savrola; "the game begins tonight." He took out his watch; it was a quarter to eleven.

"At twelve o'clock you will hear the alarm-bells. Sit down, and let us talk."

Lucile sat down mechanically.

"You love me," he said in an even voice, looking at her dispassionately, and as if the whole subject of their relations was but a psychological problem, "and I love you." There was no answer; he continued: "But we must part. In this world we are divided, nor do I see how the barrier can be removed. All my life I shall think of you; no other woman can ever fill the empty space. Ambitions I still have: I always had them; but love I am not to know, or to know it only to my vexation and despair. I will put it away from me, and henceforth my affections will be as lifeless as those burnt papers. And you—will you forget? In the next few hours I may be killed; if so, do not allow yourself to mourn. I do not care to be remembered for what I was. If I have done anything that may make the world more happy, more cheerful, more comfortable, let them recall the action. If I have spoken a thought which, rising above the vicissitudes of our existence, may make life brighter or death less gloomy, then let them say, 'He said this or he did that.' Forget the man; remember, perhaps, his work. Remember too that you have known a soul, somewhere amid the puzzles of the universe, the complement of your own; and then forget. Summon your religion to your aid; anticipate the moment of forgetting; live, and leave the past alone. Can you do this?"

"Never!" she answered passionately. "I will never forget you!"

"We are but poor philosophers," he said. "Pain and love make sport of us and all our theories. We cannot conquer ourselves or rise above our state."

"Why should we try?" she whispered, looking at him with wild eyes.

He saw and trembled. Then, with the surge of impulse, he cried: "My God, how I love you!" and before she could frame a resolution or even choose her mind, they had kissed each other.

The handle of the door turned quickly. Both started back. The door swung open and the President appeared. He was in plain clothes, his right hand concealed behind his back. Miguel followed from out of the darkness of the passage.

For a moment there was silence. Then Molara in a furious voice broke out: "So, Sir, you attack me in this way also—coward and scoundrel!" He raised his hand and pointed the revolver it held full at his enemy.

Lucile, feeling that the world had broken up, fell back against the sofa, stunned with terror. Savrola rose and faced the President. Then she saw what a brave man he was, for as he did so he contrived to stand between the weapon and herself. "Put down your pistol," he said in a firm voice; "and you shall have an explanation."

"I will put it down," said Molara, "when I have killed you."

Savrola measured the distance between them with his eye. Could he spring in under the shot? Again he looked at the table where his own revolver lay. He shielded her, and he decided to stand still.

"Down on your knees and beg for mercy, you hound; down, or I will blow your face in!"

"I have always tried to despise death, and have always succeeded in despising you. I shall bow to neither."

"We shall see," said Molara, grinding his teeth. "I shall count five—one!"

There was a pause. Savrola looked at the pistol barrel, a black spot encircled by a ring of bright steel; all the rest of the picture was a blank.

"Two!" counted the President.

So he was to die—flash off this earth when that black spot burst into flame. He anticipated the blow full in his face; and beyond he saw nothing—annihilation—black, black night.

"Three!"

He could just see the rifling of the barrel; the lands showed faintly. That was a wonderful invention—to make the bullet spin as it travelled. He imagined it churning his brain with hideous energy. He tried to think, to take one grip of his philosophy or faith before the plunge; but his physical sensations were too violent. To the tips of his fingers he tingled, as the blood surged through his veins; the palms of his hands felt hot.

"Four!"

Lucile sprang up, and with a cry threw herself in front of the President. "Wait, wait!" she cried. "Have mercy!"

Molara met her look, and in those eyes read more than terror. Then at last he understood; he started as though he had caught hold of red-hot iron. "My God! it's true!" he gasped. "Strumpet!" he cried, as he pushed her from him, striking her with the back of his left hand in the mouth. She shrank into the far corner of the room. He saw it all now. Hoist with his own petard he had lost everything. Wild fury took hold of him and shook him till his throat rattled and ached. She had deserted him; power was slipping from his grasp; his rival, his enemy, the man he hated with all his soul was everywhere triumphant. He had walked into the trap only to steal the bait; but he should not escape. There was a limit to prudence and to the love of life. His plans, his hopes, the roar of an avenging crowd, all faded from his mind. Death should wipe out the long score that stood between them, death which settled all— now on the instant. But he had been a soldier, and was ever a practical man in the detail of life. He lowered the pistol and deliberately cocked it; single action would make certainty more sure; then he took good aim.

Savrola, seeing that the moment was upon him, lowered his head and sprang forward.

The President fired.

But Miguel's quick intelligence had appreciated the changed situation, and he remembered that there were consequences. He saw that the trick had become deadly earnest, and he did not forget the mob. He struck the pistol up, and the bullet, by a very little, flew high.

In the smoke and the flash Savrola closed with his adversary and bore him to the ground. Molara fell underneath and with the concussion dropped the revolver. The other seized it, wrenched himself clear, and sprang back and away from the prostrate figure. For a moment he stood there and watched, while the hungry lust of killing rose in his heart and made his trigger-finger itch. Then very slowly the President rose. The fall had dazed him; he leaned against the book-case and groaned.

Below there was a beating at the front door. Molara turned towards Lucile, who still cowered in the corner of the room, and

638

began to revile her. The common, ugly material of his character showed through the veneer and polish that varied intercourse and the conduct of great affairs had superimposed. His words were not fit to hear, nor worth remembering; but they stung her to the quick and she rejoined defiantly: "You knew I was here; you told me to come! You have laid a trap; the fault is yours!" Molara replied by a filthy taunt. "I am innocent," she cried; "though I love him, I am innocent!"

Savrola began to perceive dimly. "I do not know," he said, "what villainy you have contrived. I have wronged you too much to care to have your blood on my head; but go, and go quickly; I will not endure your foulness. Go!"

The President was now recovering his calmness. "I should have shot you myself," he said, "but I will have it done by a platoon of soldiers—five soldiers and a corporal."

"The murder will be avenged in either case."

"Why did you stop me, Miguel?"

"It is as he says, Your Excellency," replied the Secretary. "It would have been a tactical error."

The official manner, the style of address, the man's composure, restored the President to his senses. He walked towards the door and stopping at the sideboard helped himself to a glass of brandy with ostentation. "Confiscated," he said, and held it up to the light, "by order of the Government." He swallowed it. "I will see you shot tomorrow," he added, heedless that the other held the pistol.

"I shall be at the Mayoralty," said Savrola; "you may come and fetch me if you dare."

"Revolt!" said the President. "Pooh! I will stamp it out, and you too, before the sun has gone down."

"Perhaps there may be another ending to the tale."

"One or the other," said the President. "You have robbed me of my honour; you are plotting to rob me of my power. There is not room for both of us in the world. You may take your mistress with you to hell."

There was a noise of hasty footsteps on the stairs; Lieutenant Tiro flung open the door, but stopped abruptly in astonishment at the occupants of the room. "I heard a shot," he said.

"Yes," answered the President; "there has been an accident, but luckily no harm was done. Will you please accompany me to the palace? Miguel, come!"

"You had better be quick, Sir," said the subaltern. "There are many strange folk about tonight, and they are building a barricade at the end of the street."

"Indeed?" said the President. "It is time we took steps to stop them. Good night, Sir," he added, turning to Savrola; "we shall meet tomorrow and finish our discussion."

But Savrola, revolver in hand, looked at him steadily and let him go in silence, a silence that for a space Lucile's sobs alone disturbed. At length, when the retreating footsteps had died away and the street door had closed, she spoke. "I cannot stop here."

"You cannot go back to the palace."

"What am I to do, then?"

Savrola reflected. "You had better stay here for the present. The house is at your disposal, and you will be alone. I must go at once to the Mayoralty; already I am late—it is close on twelve—the moment approaches. Besides, Molara will send policemen, and I have duties to discharge which I cannot avoid. Tonight the streets are too dangerous. Perhaps I shall return in the morning."

The tragedy had stunned them both. A bitter remorse filled Savrola's heart. Her life was ruined—was he the cause? He could not say how far he was guilty or innocent; but the sadness of it all was unaltered, no matter who might be at fault.

"Good bye," he said rising. "I must go, though I leave my heart behind. Much depends on me—the lives of friends, the liberties of a nation."

And so he departed to play a great game in the face of all the world, to struggle for those ambitions which form the greater part of man's interest in life; while she, a woman, miserable and now alone, had no resource but to wait.

And then suddenly the bells began to ring all over the city with quick impatient strokes. There was the sound of a far-off bugle-call and a dull report—the boom of an alarm-gun. The tumult grew; the roll of a drum beating the *assembly* was heard at the end of the street; confused shoutings and cries rose from many quarters. At length one sound was heard which put an end to all doubts—*tap,*

*tap, tap,* like the subdued slamming of many wooden boxes—the noise of distant musketry.

The revolution had begun.

★    ★    ★

The rebels were wisely and cautiously led. They did not at once push on to the attack of the palace; sure of their prey, they could afford to wait. Meanwhile the surviving adherents of the government endeavoured to make their last foothold secure. Rough-hewn cobblestones from the pavements of the courtyard were prised up, and the windows were with these converted into loopholes through which the garrison might fire without much exposure. The gates were closed and barred, and preparations made to strut them with baulks of timber. Ammunition was distributed. The duty and responsibility of each section of the defence were apportioned to the various officers. The defenders recognized that they had entered on a quarrel which must be carried to a definite conclusion.

But Molara's mood had changed. The fury of the night had cooled into the hard, savage courage of the morning. He had led the desperate attempt to capture the Mayoralty, and had exposed himself freely and even recklessly in the tumult of the fight that followed; but now that he had come through unhurt, had regained the palace, and realized that his last chance of killing Savrola had passed, death appeared very ugly. All the excitement which had supported him had died away; he had had enough. His mind searched for some way of escape, and searched vainly. The torture of the moment was keen. A few hours might bring help: the fleet would surely come; but it would be too late. The great guns might take vengeance for his death; they could not save his life. A feeling of vexation shook him, and behind it grew the realization of the approaching darkness. Terror began to touch his heart; his nerve flickered; he had more to fear than the others. The hatred of the multitude was centred in him; after all it was his blood they wanted —his above all others. It was a dreadful distinction. He retired in deep despondency to his own room, and took no part in the defence.

"Gentlemen," cried Savrola in a loud voice, "I call upon you to surrender. Your lives shall be spared."

641

Sorrento stepped forward. "By the orders of His Excellency I surrender the palace and the government troops who have defended it. I do so on a promise that their lives shall be safe."

"Certainly," said Savrola. "Where is the President?" Sorrento pointed to the other side of the steps. Savrola turned and walked towards the spot.

Antonio Molara, sometime President of the Republic of Laurania, lay on the three lowest steps of the entrance of his palace, head downwards; a few yards away in a ring stood the people he had ruled. A man in a black suit was reloading his revolver; it was Karl Kreutze, the Number One of the Secret Society. The President had bled profusely from several bullet wounds in the body, but it was evident that the *coup de grâce* had been administered by a shot in the head. The back and left side of the skull behind the ear was blown away, and the force of the explosion, probably at close quarters, had cracked all the bones of the face so that as the skin was whole, it looked like broken china in a sponge bag.

Savrola stopped aghast. He looked at the crowd, and they shrank from his eye; gradually they shuffled back, leaving the sombre-clad man alone face to face with the great Democrat. A profound hush overspread the whole mass of men. "Who has committed this murder?" he asked in low hoarse tones, fixing his glance on the head of the Secret Society.

"It is not a murder," replied the man doggedly; "it is an execution."

"By whose authority?"

"In the name of the Society."

When Savrola had seen the body of his enemy, he was stricken with horror, but at the same time a dreadful joy convulsed his heart; the barrier was now removed. He struggled to repress the feeling, and of the struggle anger was born. Kreutze's words infuriated him. A sense of maddening irritation shook his whole system. All this must fall on his name; what would Europe think, what would the world say? Remorse, shame, pity, and the wicked joy he tried to crush, all fused into reckless ungovernable passion. "Vile scum!" he cried, and stepping down he slashed the other across the face with his cane.

The man sprang at his throat on the sudden impulse of intense pain. But Lieutenant Tiro had drawn his sword; with a strong arm and a hearty good will he met him with all the sweep of a downward cut, and rolled him on the ground.

The spring was released, and the fury of the populace broke out. A loud shout arose. Great as was Savrola's reputation among the Revolutionaries, these men had known other and inferior leaders more intimately. Karl Kreutze was a man of the people. His socialistic writings had been widely read; as the head of the Secret Society he had certain assured influences to support him, and he had conducted the latter part of the attack on the palace. Now he had been destroyed before their eyes by one of the hated officers. The crowd surged forward shouting in savage anger.

Savrola sprang backwards up the steps. "Citizens, listen to me!" he cried. "You have won a victory; do not disgrace it. Your valour and patriotism have triumphed; do not forget that it is for our ancient Constitution that you have fought." He was interrupted by shouts and jeers.

"What have I done?" he rejoined. "As much as any here. I too have risked my life in the great cause. Is there a man here that has a wound? Let him stand forth, for we are comrades." And for the first time, with a proud gesture, he lifted his left arm. Tiro perceived the reason of the start he had given when running the gauntlet in Constitution Square. The sleeve of his coat was torn and soaked with blood; the linen of his shirt protruded crimson; his fingers were stiff and smeared all over.

The impression produced was tremendous. The mob, to whom the dramatic always appeals with peculiar force, were also swayed by that sympathy which all men feel for those injured in a common danger. A revulsion took place. A cheer, faint at first, but growing louder, rose; others outside the courtyard, ignorant of the reason, took it up. Savrola continued.

"Our State, freed from tyranny, must start fair and unsullied. Those who have usurped undue authority, not derived from the people, shall be punished, whether they be presidents or citizens. These military officers must come before the judges of the Republic and answer for their actions. A free trial is the right of all Lauranians. Comrades, much has been done, but we have not finished yet. We have exalted Liberty; it remains to preserve her. These officers shall be lodged in prison; for you there is other work. The ships are coming back; it is not yet time to put away the rifles. Who is there will see the matter through—to the end?"

A man, with a bloodstained bandage round his head, stepped forward. "We are comrades," he cried; "shake hands."

Savrola gripped him. He was one of the subordinate officers in the rebel army, a simple honest man whom Savrola had known slightly for several months. "I entrust a high duty to you. Conduct these officers and soldiers to the State Prison; I will send full instructions by a mounted messenger. Where can you find an escort?" There was no lack of volunteers. "To the prison then, and remember that the faith of the Republic depends on their safety. Forward, Gentlemen," he added, turning to the surviving defenders of the palace; "your lives are safe, upon my honour."

# THE VOICE OF COURAGE

A SELECTION FROM
WINSTON CHURCHILL'S SPEECHES

# BLOOD, SWEAT AND TEARS

*

## THE CHOICE FOR EUROPE

### FROM AN ADDRESS GIVEN IN THE FREE TRADE HALL, MANCHESTER, 9 MAY, 1938

IF THE WAR breaks out in Europe, no one can say how far it will spread, or who will have it in their power to stand out of it. Is it not better then, on grounds of prudence alone, to gain the strength which comes from combined action? Is it not wise to try to invest the Covenant with reality, to unite as many nations as possible in its support, to gain a measure of protection for ourselves, in return for the risks we are to run for others. By this present policy of decrying the League and making the Covenant a matter of division between parties we are only having the disadvantage of both courses. It would indeed be disastrous if we were led into a fierce division here at home about foreign policy. An election fought on ordinary domestic issues is a process with which we are all familiar; but an election turning on the dread issues of defence and foreign policy might leave us a deeply divided nation, with an evenly balanced, incoherent Parliament, and this at the very moment when the danger on the Continent had reached its height. That is why I plead for national unity, and for a policy upon which alone it is to be achieved. We might be having a general election in this country, or preparing for one, with both sides rivalling each other as to who was most in favour of peace at any price. We might have this at the very moment when the war-lust of Dictator Powers had reached its culminating explosion point.

But we are told that we must not involve ourselves in a quarrel about ideologies. If this means that we are not to back Communism against Nazism or vice versa, we all agree. Both doctrines are equally obnoxious to the principles of freedom. Certainly we should not back one against the other. But surely we must have an opinion between Right and Wrong? Surely we must have an opinion

647

between Aggressor and Victim? This is no question of resisting Dictators because they are Dictators, but only if they attack other people. Have we not an ideology—if we must use this ugly word— of our own in freedom, in a liberal constitution, in democratic and Parliamentary government, in Magna Carta and the Petition of Right? Ought we not to be ready to make as many sacrifices and exertions for our own broad central theme and cause, as the fanatics of either of these new creeds? Ought we not to produce in defence of Right, champions as bold, missionaries as eager, and, if need be, swords as sharp as are at the disposal af the leaders of totalitarian states?

Finally, there must be a moral basis for British foreign policy. People in this country, after all we have gone through, do not mean to be drawn into another terrible war in the name of old-world alliances or diplomatic combinations. If deep causes of division are to be removed from our midst, if all our energies are to be concentrated upon the essential task of increasing our strength and security, it can only be because of lofty and unselfish ideals which command the allegiance of all classes here at home, which rouse their echoes in the breasts even of the Dictator-ridden peoples themselves, and stir the pulses of the English-speaking race in every quarter of the globe. That is why I say: "Stand by the Covenant and endeavour to revive and fortify the strength of the League."

Here is the practical plan. Britain and France are now united. Together they are an enormous force moral and physical, and one which few would dare to challenge. I should like to see these two countries go to all the smaller states that are menaced, who are going to be devoured one by one by the Nazi tyranny, and say to them bluntly, "We are not going to help you if you are not going to help yourselves. What are you going to do about it? What are you going to contribute? Are you prepared to take special service in defence of the Covenant? If you are willing to do so, and to prove it by actions, then we will join together with you, if there are enough of you, in active military association under the authority of the League in order to protect each other and the world from another act of aggression."

A large part of our dangers and the dangers of Europe is due to the fact that we did not rearm in time. It was certainly not through lack of warning, but when we at last began it was only in a half-hearted, ramshackle, confused manner, which though it has led to great outpourings of money, has not been attended by proportionate results. Is it not lamentable that our Air Force is not now fully equal to any Power within striking distance of these shores? Is it not grievous that the vast, flexible industry of Britain has not yet been able to produce a broad and copious flow of the latest weapons of all kinds? After all, it is nearly three years since Mr. Baldwin recognized the dangers which beset us. Late as we started we ought by now to be in a strong position. Parliament is to discuss this matter this week. There ought certainly to be a searching inquiry into the condition of the Air Force, and into the reasons why the solemn pledge given to the country by Mr. Baldwin of air parity has been broken.

But an equal confusion and delay covers large parts of the field of munitions supply. It is greatly to be regretted that after nearly three years since the Government became alive to the dangers, and nearly five years since the danger became apparent, the equipment of our small Regular Army should be incomplete, and that the supplying of the Territorial Army with modern weapons and appliances should be only in a rudimentary stage. As for Air Raid Precautions, artillery, balloons, organization in every form, you know for yourselves—as well as the Germans know—the unhappy and discreditable conditions which prevail. This is no case for the Opposition to make party capital against the Government. Nor for the government to try to shield incompetence and misdirection. All should set country before party. There should be a thorough and searching inquest into the mismanagement of the past and a fearless resolve to sweep away every obstacle that stands in the path of our regaining our national safety. Meanwhile everyone must do his best.

Look at the danger in which we stand. Germany has been rearming night and day for four years. For four years past they have never spent less in any year than £800,000,000 sterling on war preparation. The whole manhood of the country is harnessed to war. Even the children are organized. Every thought is turned to race assertion and the conquest of weaker, more exhausted, or less determined breeds. They are driving forward on their path. Every six weeks a new army corps is added to their active forces. Never has there been such an outpouring of munitions of war. At present we are shielded to some extent by the strength of the French army, but the German numbers are overtaking them month by month. We have still our Navy, never, happily, so supreme in European waters. But our Air Force on which so much depends, so far from overtaking Germany, is actually falling further and further behind. If we are to place ourselves in security we must throw ourselves into the business of national defence with the vigour and concentration which Germany now displays.

It is no small or local cause we plead tonight. We must march in the good company of Nations and we march under the standards of Law, of Justice and of Freedom. We must gather together round the joint strength of Britain and France and under the authority of the League all countries prepared to resist, and if possible to prevent acts of violent aggression. There is the path to safety. There are the only guarantees of Freedom. There, on the rock of the Covenant of the League of Nations alone, can we build high and enduring the temple and the towers of Peace.

## THE MUNICH AGREEMENT
### FROM A SPEECH DELIVERED IN THE HOUSE OF COMMONS
### 5 OCTOBER, 1938

All is over. Silent, mournful, abandoned, broken, Czechoslovakia recedes into the darkness. She has suffered in every respect by her association with the Western democracies and with the League of Nations, of which she has always been an obedient servant. She has suffered in particular from her association with France, under whose guidance and policy she has been actuated for so long. The very measures taken by His Majesty's Government in the Anglo-French Agreement to give her the best chance possible, namely, the 50 per cent clean cut in certain districts instead of a plebiscite, have turned to her detriment, because there is to be a plebiscite too in wide areas, and those other Powers who had claims have also come down upon the helpless victim. Those municipal elections upon whose voting the basis is taken for the 50 per cent cut were held on issues which had nothing to do with joining Germany. When I saw Herr Henlein over here he assured me that was not the desire of his people.

Positive statements were made that it was only a question of home rule, of having a position of their own in the Czechoslovakian State. No one has a right to say that the plebiscite which is to be taken in areas under Saar conditions, and the clean-cut of the 50 per cent areas—that those two operations together amount in the slightest degree to a verdict of self-determination. It is a fraud and a farce to invoke that name.

We in this country, as in other Liberal and democratic countries, have a perfect right to exalt the principle of self-determination, but it comes ill out of the mouths of those in totalitarian states who deny even the smallest element of toleration to every section and creed within their bounds. But, however you put it, this particular block of land, this mass of human beings to be handed over, has never expressed the desire to go into the Nazi rule. I do not believe that even now, if their opinion could be asked, they would exercise such an opinion.

What is the remaining position of Czechoslovakia? Not only are they politically mutilated, but, economically and financially, they are in complete confusion. Their banking, their railway arrangements, are severed and broken, their industries are curtailed, and the movement of their population is most cruel. The Sudeten miners, who are all Czechs and whose families have lived in that area for centuries, must now flee into an area where there are hardly any mines left for them to work. It is a tragedy which has occurred. There must always be the most profound regret and a sense of vexation in British hearts at the treatment and the misfortune which have overcome the Czechoslovakian Republic. They have not ended here. At any moment there may be a hitch in the programme. At any moment there may be an order for Herr Goebbels to start again his propaganda of calumny and lies; at any moment an incident may be provoked, and now that the fortress line is turned what is there to stop the will of the conqueror? Obviously, we are not in a position to give them the slightest help at the present time, except what everyone is glad to know has been done, the financial aid which the government have promptly produced.

I venture to think that in future the Czechoslovak State cannot be maintained as an independent entity. I think you will find that in a period of time which may be measured by years, but may be measured only by months, Czechoslovakia will be engulfed in the Nazi regime. Perhaps they may join it in despair or in revenge. At any rate, that story is over and told. But we cannot consider the abandonment and ruin of Czechoslovakia in the light only of what happened only last month. It is the most grievous consequence of what we have done and of what we have left undone in the last five years—five years of futile good intentions, five years of eager search for the line of least resistance, five years of uninterrupted retreat of British power, five years of neglect of our air defences. Those are the features which I stand here to expose and which marked an improvident stewardship for which Great Britain and France have dearly to pay. We have been reduced in those five years from a position of security so overwhelming and so unchallengeable that we never cared to think about it. We have been reduced from a position where the very word "war" was considered one which could be used only by persons qualifying for a lunatic asylum. We have been reduced from a position of safety and power—power to do good, power to be generous to a beaten foe, power to make terms with Germany, power to give her proper redress for her grievances, power to stop her arming if we chose, power to take any step in strength or mercy or justice which we thought right— reduced in five years from a position safe and unchallenged to where we stand now.

When I think of the fair hopes of a long peace which still lay before Europe at the beginning of 1933 when Herr Hitler first obtained power, and of all the opportunities of arresting the growth of the Nazi power which have been thrown away, when I think of the immense combinations and resources which have been neglected or squandered, I cannot believe that a parallel exists in the whole course of history. So far as this country is concerned the responsibility must rest with those who have had the undisputed control of our political affairs. They neither prevented Germany from rearming, nor did they rearm ourselves in time. They quarrelled with Italy without saving Ethiopia. They exploited and discredited the vast institution of the League of Nations and they neglected to make alliances and combinations which might have repaired previous errors, and thus they left us in the hour of trial without adequate national defence or effective international security.

What I find unendurable is the sense of our country falling into the power, into the orbit and influence of Nazi Germany, and of our existence becoming dependent upon their good will or pleasure. It is to prevent that, that I have tried my best to urge the maintenance of every bulwark of defence—first, the timely creation of an Air Force superior to anything within striking distance of our shores; secondly, the gathering together of the collective strength of many nations; and thirdly, the making of alliances and military conventions, all within the Covenant, in order to gather together forces at any rate to restrain the onward movement of this power. It has all been in vain. Every position has been successively undermined and abandoned on specious and plausible excuses.

We do not want to be led upon the high road to becoming a satellite of the German Nazi system of European domination. In a very few years, perhaps in a very few months, we shall be confronted with demands with which we shall no doubt be invited to comply. Those demands may affect the surrender of territory or the surrender of liberty. I foresee and foretell that the policy of submission will carry with it restrictions upon the freedom of speech and debate in Parliament, on public platforms, and discussions in the press, for it will be said—indeed, I hear it said sometimes now—that we cannot allow the Nazi system of dictatorship to be criticized by ordinary, common English politicians. Then, with a press under control, in part direct but more potently indirect, with every organ of public opinion doped and chloroformed into acquiescence, we shall be conducted along further stages of our journey.

I have been casting about to see how measures can be taken to protect us from this advance of the Nazi power, and to secure those forms of life which are so dear to us. What is the sole method that is open? The sole method that is open is for us to regain our old island independence by acquiring that supremacy in the air which we were promised, that security in our air defences which we were assured we had, and thus to make ourselves an island once again. That, in all this grim outlook, shines out as the overwhelming fact. An effort at rearmament the like of which has not been seen ought to be made forthwith, and all the resources of this country and all its united strength should be bent to that task. I was very glad to see that Lord Baldwin yesterday in the House of Lords said that he would mobilize industry tomorrow. But I think it would have been much better if Lord Baldwin had said that two and a half years ago, when everyone demanded a Ministry of Supply. I will venture to say to hon. Gentlemen sitting here behind the Government Bench, hon. Friends of mine, whom I thank for the patience with which they have listened to what I have to say, that they have some responsibility for all this too, because, if they had given one tithe of the cheers they have lavished upon this transaction of Czechoslovakia to the small band of Members, who were endeavouring to get timely rearmament set in motion, we should not now be in the position in which we are. Hon. Gentlemen opposite, and hon. Members on the Liberal benches, are not entitled to throw these stones. I remember for two years having to face, not only the government's deprecation, but their stern disapproval. Lord Baldwin has now given the signal, tardy though it may be; let us at least obey it.

After all, there are no secrets now about what happened in the air and in the mobilization of our anti-aircraft defences. These matters have been, as my hon. and gallant Friend the Member for the Abbey Division said, seen by thousands of people. They can form their own opinions of the character of the statements which have been persistently made to us by Ministers on this subject. Who pretends now that there is air parity with Germany? Who pretends now that our anti-aircraft defences were adequately manned or armed? We know that the German General Staff are well informed upon these subjects, but the House of Commons has hitherto not taken seriously its duty of requiring to assure itself on these matters. The Home Secretary [Sir Samuel Hoare] said the other night that he would welcome investigation. Many things have been done which reflect the greatest credit upon the administration. But the vital matters are what we want to know about. I have asked again and again during these three years for a secret Session where these matters could be thrashed out, or for an investigation by a Select Committee of the House, or for some other method. I ask now that, when we meet again in the autumn, that should be a matter on which the Government should take the House into its confidence, because we have a right to know where we stand and what measures are being taken to secure our position.

I do not grudge our loyal, brave people, who were ready to do their duty no matter what the cost, who never flinched under the strain of last week—I do not grudge them the natural, spontaneous outburst of joy and relief when they learned that the hard ordeal would no longer be required of them at the moment; but they should know the truth. They should know that there has been gross neglect and deficiency in our defences; they should know that we have sustained a defeat without a war, the consequences of which will travel far with us along our road; they should know that we have passed an awful milestone in our history, when the whole equilibrium of Europe has been deranged, and that the terrible words have for the time being been pronounced against the Western democracies: "Thou art weighed in the balance and found wanting." And do not suppose that this is the end. This is only the beginning of the reckoning. This is only the first sip, the first foretaste of a bitter cup which will be proferred to us year by year unless, by a supreme recovery of moral health and martial vigour, we arise again and take our stand for freedom as in the olden time.


## WAR

### A SPEECH DELIVERED TO THE HOUSE OF COMMONS
### 3 SEPTEMBER, 1939

In this solemn hour it is a consolation to recall and to dwell upon our repeated efforts for peace. All have been ill-starred, but all have been faithful and sincere. This is of the highest moral value—and not only moral value, but practical value—at the present time, because the wholehearted concurrence of scores of millions of men and women, whose co-operation is indispensable and whose comradeship and brotherhood are indispensable, is the only foundation upon which the trial and tribulation of modern war can be endured and surmounted. This moral conviction alone affords that ever-fresh resilience which renews the strength and energy of people in long, doubtful and dark days. Outside, the storms of war may blow and the lands may be lashed with the fury of its gales, but in our own hearts this Sunday morning there is peace. Our hands may be active, but our consciences are at rest.

We must not underrate the gravity of the task which lies before us or the temerity of the ordeal, to which we shall not be found unequal. We must expect many disappointments, and many unpleasant surprises, but we may be sure that the task which we have freely accepted is one not beyond the compass and the strength of the British Empire and the French Republic. The Prime Minister said it was a sad day, and that is indeed true, but at the present time there is another note which may be present, and that is a feeling of thankfulness that, if these great trials were to come upon our Island, there is a generation of Britons here now ready to prove itself not unworthy of the days of yore and not unworthy of those great men, the fathers of our land, who laid the foundations of our laws and shaped the greatness of our country.

This is not a question of fighting for Danzig or fighting for Poland. We are fighting to save the whole world from the pestilence of Nazi tyranny and in defence of all that is most sacred to man. This is no war of domination or imperial aggrandisement or material gain; no war to shut any country out of its sunlight and means of progress. It is a war, viewed in its inherent quality, to establish, on impregnable rocks, the rights of the individual, and it is a war to establish and revive the stature of man. Perhaps it might seem a paradox that a war undertaken in the name of liberty and right should require, as a necessary part of its processes, the surrender for the time being of so many of the dearly valued liberties and rights. In these last few days the House of Commons has been voting dozens of Bills which hand over to the executive our most dearly valued traditional liberties. We are sure that these liberties will be in hands which will not abuse them, which will use them for no class or party interests, which will cherish and guard them, and we look forward to the day, surely and confidently we look forward to the day, when our liberties and rights will be restored to us, and when we shall be able to share them with the peoples to whom such blessings are unknown.

## THE FIRST MONTH OF WAR

### AN ADDRESS BROADCAST 1 OCTOBER, 1939

The British Empire and the French Republic have been at war with Nazi Germany for a month tonight. We have not yet come

Churchill gives his famous "V" sign

Inspecting the House of Commons Home Guard, 1942, and (*below*) Mr. and Mrs. Churchill at the London Zoo in 1943

At Teheran: Stalin, Roosevelt and Churchill; (*below*) Churchill in Berlin
for the Big Three conference, July, 1945

Churchill at Croydon in 1948—Honorary Air Commodore, No. 615
County of Surrey Squadron, Royal Auxiliary Air Force

at all to the severity of fighting which is to be expected; but three important things have happened.

First, Poland has been again overrun by two of the great Powers which held her in bondage for 150 years, but were unable to quench the spirit of the Polish nation. The heroic defence of Warsaw shows that the soul of Poland is indestructible, and that she will rise again like a rock, which may for a spell be submerged by a tidal wave, but which remains a rock.

What is the second event of this first month? It is, of course, the assertion of the power of Russia. Russia has pursued a cold policy of self-interest. We could have wished that the Russian armies should be standing on their present line as the friends and allies of Poland instead of as invaders. But that the Russian armies should stand on this line, was clearly necessary for the safety of Russia against the Nazi menace. At any rate, the line is there, and an Eastern Front has been created which Nazi Germany does not dare assail. When Herr von Ribbentrop was summoned to Moscow last week, it was to learn the fact, and to accept the fact, that the Nazi designs upon the Baltic States and upon the Ukraine must come to a dead stop.

I cannot forecast to you the action of Russia. It is a riddle wrapped in a mystery inside an enigma: but perhaps there is a key. That key is Russian national interest. It cannot be in accordance with the interest or the safety of Russia that Germany should plant itself upon the shores of the Black Sea, or that it should overrun the Balkan States and subjugate the Slavonic peoples of South-Eastern Europe. That would be contrary to the historic life-interests of Russia.

But in this quarter of the world—the South-East of Europe—these interests of Russia fall into the same channel as the interests of Britain and France. None of these three Powers can afford to see Roumania, Yugoslavia, Bulgaria, and above all Turkey, put under the German heel. Through the fog of confusion and uncertainty we may discern quite plainly the community of interests which exists between England, France and Russia—a community of interests to prevent the Nazis carrying the flames of war into the Balkans and Turkey. Thus, my friends, at some risk of being proved wrong by events, I will proclaim tonight my conviction that the second great fact of the first month of the war is that Hitler, and all that Hitler stands for, have been and are being warned off the East and the South-East of Europe.

What is the third event? Here I speak as First Lord of the Admiralty, with especial caution. It would seem that the U-boat attack upon the life of the British Isles has not so far proved successful. It is true that when they sprang out upon us and we were going about our ordinary business, with two thousand ships in constant movement every day upon the seas, they managed to do some serious damage. But the Royal Navy has immediately attacked the U-boats, and is hunting them night and day—I will not say without mercy, because God forbid we should ever part company with that, but at any rate with zeal and not altogether without relish. And it looks tonight very much as if it is the U-boats who are feeling the weather, and not the Royal Navy or the world-wide commerce of Britain. A week has passed since a British ship, alone or in convoy, has been sunk or even molested by a U-boat on the high seas; and during the first month of the war we have captured by our efficient contraband control 150,000 tons more German merchandise—food, oil, minerals and other commodities—for our own benefit than we have lost by all the U-boat sinkings put together. In fact, up to date—please observe I make no promises (we must deal in performance and not in promises)—up to date we have actually got 150,000 tons of very desirable supplies into this island more than we should have got if war had not been declared, and if no U-boat had ever cast sailormen to their fate upon the stormy seas. This seems to be a very solid, tangible fact which has emerged from the first month of the war against Nazidom.

Of course, we are told that all the U-boats have gone home just to tell their master about their exploits and their experiences. But that is not true, because every day we are attacking them upon the approaches to the British Isles. Some undoubtedly have preferred to go off and sink the unprotected neutral ships of Norway and Sweden. I hope the day will come when the Admiralty will be able to invite the ships of all nations to join the British convoys, and to insure them on their voyages at a reasonable rate. We must, of course, expect that the U-boat attack upon the seaborne commerce of the world will be renewed presently on a greater scale. We hope, however, that by the end of October we shall have three times as many hunting-craft at work as we had at the beginning of the war; and we hope that by the measures we have taken, our means of putting down this pest will grow continually. I can assure you we are taking great care about all that.

Therefore, to sum up the results of the first month, let us say that Poland has been overrun, but will rise again; that Russia has warned Hitler off his Eastern dreams; and that U-boats may be safely left to the care and constant attention of the British Navy.

Now I wish to speak about what is happening in our own island. When a peaceful democracy is suddenly made to fight for its life, there must be a lot of trouble and hardship in the process of turning over from peace to war. I feel very keenly for those thousands—scores of thousands of them—who wish to throw themselves into the fight at once, but for whom we cannot find full scope at the present time. All this will clear as we get into our stride. His Majesty's Government is unitedly resolved to make the maximum effort of which the British nation is capable, and to persevere, whatever may happen, until decisive victory is gained. Meanwhile, patriotic men and women, especially those who understand the high causes in human fortunes which are now at stake, must not only rise above fear; they must also rise above inconvenience and, perhaps, most difficult of all, above boredom. Parliament will be kept in session, and all grievances or muddles or scandals, if such there be, can be freely ventilated or exposed there. In past times the House of Commons has proved itself an instrument of national will-power capable of waging stern wars. Parliament is the shield and expression of Democracy, and Ministers of the Crown base themselves upon the Parliamentary system. You have seen the power of Parliament manifested in the last week, when a Budget, gigantic in its burdens—a Budget which would have infuriated everybody a year ago—has been accepted with prompt and stolid resolve.

In other fields our work goes forward. A large army has already gone to France. British armies upon the scale of the effort of the Great War are in preparation. The British people are determined to stand in the line with the splendid army of the French Republic, and share with them, as fast and as early as we can, whatever may be coming towards us both. It may be that great ordeals are coming to us in this island from the air. We shall do our best to give a good account of ourselves; and we must always remember that the command of the seas will enable us to bring the immense resources of Canada and the New World into play as a decisive ultimate air factor, a factor beyond the reach of what we have to give and take over here.

Directions have been given by the Government to prepare for a war of at least three years. That does not mean that victory may not be gained in a shorter time. How soon it will be gained depends upon how long Herr Hitler and his group of wicked men, whose hands are stained with blood and soiled with corruption, can keep their grip upon the docile, unhappy German people. It was for Hitler to say when the war would begin; but it is not for him or for his successors to say when it will end. It began when he wanted it, and it will end only when we are convinced that he has had enough.

The Prime Minister has stated our war aims in terms which cannot be bettered, and which cannot be too often repeated. These are his words: "To redeem Europe from the perpetual and recurring fear of German aggression, and enable the peoples of Europe to preserve their independence and their liberties."

That is what the British and French nations are fighting for. How often have we been told that we are the effete Democracies whose day is done, and who must now be replaced by various forms of virile dictatorships and totalitarian despotism? No doubt at the beginning we shall have to suffer, because of having too long wished to lead a peaceful life. Our reluctance to fight was mocked at as cowardice. Our desire to see an unarmed world was proclaimed as the proof of our decay. Now we have begun. Now we are going on. Now, with the help of God, and with the conviction that we are the defenders of civilization and freedom, we are going to persevere to the end.

After all, Great Britain and France together are eighty-five millions, even in their homelands alone. They are united in their cause; they are convinced of their duty. Nazidom, with all its tyrannical power, controls no more than that. They, too, have eighty-five millions; but of these at least sixteen millions are newly conquered Czechs, Slovakians and Austrians, who are writhing under their cruel yoke and have to be held down by main force. We have other resources. We have the oceans, and with the oceans the assurance that we can bring the vast latent power of the British and French Empires to bear upon the decisive points. We have the freely given ardent support of the twenty millions of British citizens in the self-governing Dominions of Canada, Australia, New Zealand and South Africa. We have, I believe, the heart and the moral conviction of India on our side. We believe we are entitled to the respect and good will of the world, and particularly of the United States.

Here I am in the same post as I was twenty-five years ago. Rough times lie ahead; but how different is the scene from that of October, 1914! Then the French front, with its British army fighting in the line, seemed to be about to break under the terrible impact of German Imperialism. Then Russia had been laid low at Tannenberg; then the whole might of the Austro-Hungarian Empire was in battle against us; then the brave, warlike Turks were about to join our enemies. Then we had to be ready night and day to fight a decisive sea battle with a formidable German fleet almost, in many respects, the equal of our own. We faced those adverse conditions then; we have nothing worse to face tonight.

In those days of 1914 also, Italy was neutral; but we did not know the reason for her neutrality. It was only later on that we learned that by a secret clause in the original Treaty of the Triple Alliance, Italy had expressly reserved to herself the right to stand aside from any war which brought her into conflict with Great Britain. Much has happened since then. Misunderstandings and disputes have arisen, but all the more do we appreciate in England the reason why this great and friendly nation of Italy, with whom we have never been at war, has not seen fit to enter the struggle.

I do not underrate what lies before us, but I must say this: I cannot doubt we have the strength to carry a good cause forward, and to break down the barriers which stand between the wage-earning masses of every land and that free and more abundant daily life which science is ready to afford. That is my conviction, and I look back upon the history of the past to find many sources of encouragement. Of all the wars that men have fought in their hard pilgrimage, none was more noble than the great Civil War in America nearly eighty years ago. Both sides fought with high conviction, and the war was long and hard. All the heroism of the South could not redeem their cause from the stain of slavery, just as all the courage and skill which the Germans always show in war will not free them from the reproach of Nazism, with its intolerance and its brutality. We may take good heart from what happened in America in those famous days of the nineteenth century. We may be sure that the world will roll forward into broader destinies. We may remember the words of old John Bright after the American Civil War was over, when he said to an audience of English working folk: "At last after the smoke of the battlefield had cleared away, the horrid shape which had cast its shadow over the whole continent had vanished and was gone for ever."

## A TIME TO DARE AND ENDURE
### FROM AN ADDRESS GIVEN IN THE FREE TRADE HALL, MANCHESTER, 27 JANUARY, 1940

We have been five months at war against the world's greatest military power and the world's greatest air power. When the war began in September most of us expected that very soon our cities would be torn and charred by explosion and fire, and few would have dared to plan for the end of January a splendid gathering such as I see before me here this afternoon. I know of nothing more remarkable in our long history than the willingness to encounter the unknown, and to face and endure whatever might be coming to us, which was shown in September by the whole mass of the people of this island in the discharge of what they felt sure was their duty. There never was a war which seemed so likely to carry its terrors at once into every home, and there never was a war into which the whole people entered with the same united conviction that, God helping, they could do no other.

This was no war planned and entered upon by a government, or a class, or a party. On the contrary, the government laboured for peace to the very end; and during those last days the only fear in Britain was lest, weighted down by their awful responsibilities, they should fail to rise up to the height of the occasion. They did not fail, and the Prime Minister led us forward in one great body into a struggle against aggression and oppression, against wrongdoing, faithlessness and cruelty, from which there can be no turning back. We cannot tell what the course of that struggle will be, into what regions it will carry us, how long it will last, or who will fall by the way. But we are sure that in the end right will win, that freedom will not be trampled down, that a truer progress will open, and a broader justice will reign. And we are determined to play our part worthily, faithfully, and to the end.

Come then: let us to the task, to the battle, to the toil—each to our part, each to our station. Fill the armies, rule the air, pour out the munitions, strangle the U-boats, sweep the mines, plough the land, build the ships, guard the streets, succour the wounded, uplift the downcast, and honour the brave. Let us go forward together in all parts of the Empire, in all parts of the island. There is not a week, nor a day, nor an hour to lose.

# PRIME MINISTER
## A SPEECH DELIVERED IN THE HOUSE OF COMMONS
### 13 MAY, 1940

On Friday evening last I received His Majesty's Commission to form a new Administration. It was the evident wish and will of Parliament and the nation that this should be conceived on the broadest possible basis and that it should include all parties, both those who supported the late government and also the parties of the Opposition. I have completed the most important part of this task. A War Cabinet has been formed of five Members, representing, with the Opposition Liberals, the unity of the nation. The three party Leaders have agreed to serve, either in the War Cabinet or in high executive office. The three Fighting Services have been filled. It was necessary that this should be done in one single day, on account of the extreme urgency and rigour of events. A number of other key positions were filled yesterday, and I am submitting a further list to His Majesty tonight. I hope to complete the appointment of the principal Ministers during tomorrow. The appointment of the other Ministers usually takes a little longer, but I trust that, when Parliament meets again, this part of my task will be completed, and that the administration will be complete in all respects.

I considered it in the public interest to suggest that the House should be summoned to meet today. Mr. Speaker agreed, and took the necessary steps, in accordance with the powers conferred upon him by the Resolution of the House. At the end of the proceedings today, the Adjournment of the House will be proposed until Tuesday, 21 May, with, of course, provision for earlier meeting if need be. The business to be considered during that week will be notified to Members at the earliest opportunity. I now invite the House, by the Resolution which stands in my name, to record its approval of the steps taken and to declare its confidence in the new government.

To form an Administration of this scale and complexity is a serious undertaking in itself, but it must be remembered that we are in the preliminary stage of one of the greatest battles in history, that we are in action at many points in Norway and in Holland, that we have to be prepared in the Mediterranean, that the air battle is continuous and that many preparations have to be made here at home. In this crisis I hope I may be pardoned if I do not address the House at any length today. I hope that any of my friends and colleagues, or former colleagues, who are affected by the political reconstruction, will make all allowance for any lack of ceremony with which it has been necessary to act. I would say to the House, as I said to those who have joined this government: "I have nothing to offer but blood, toil, tears and sweat."

We have before us an ordeal of the most grievous kind. We have before us many, many long months of struggle and of suffering. You ask, what is our policy? I will say: it is to wage war, by sea, land and air, with all our might and with all the strength that God can give us: to wage war against a monstrous tyranny, never surpassed in the dark, lamentable catalogue of human crime. That is our policy. You ask, what is our aim? I can answer in one word: Victory—victory at all costs, victory in spite of all terror, victory, however long and hard the road may be; for without victory, there is no survival. Let that be realized; no survival for the British Empire; no survival for all that the British Empire has stood for, no survival for the urge and impulse of the ages, that mankind will move forward towards its goal. But I take up my task with buoyancy and hope. I feel sure that our cause will not be suffered to fail among men. At this time I feel entitled to claim the aid of all, and I say, "Come, then, let us go forward together with our united strength."

## "BE YE MEN OF VALOUR"

### AN ADDRESS BROADCAST 19 MAY, 1940

I speak to you for the first time as Prime Minister in a solemn hour for the life of our country, of our Empire, of our Allies, and, above all, of the cause of Freedom. A tremendous battle is raging in France and Flanders. The Germans, by a remarkable combination of air bombing and heavily armoured tanks, have broken through the French defences north of the Maginot Line, and strong columns of their armoured vehicles are ravaging the open country, which for the first day or two was without defenders. They have penetrated deeply and spread alarm and confusion in their track. Behind them there are now appearing infantry in lorries, and behind them, again, the large masses are moving forward. The re-groupment of the French armies to make head against, and also to strike at, this intruding wedge has been proceeding for several days, largely assisted by the magnificent efforts of the Royal Air Force.

We must not allow ourselves to be intimidated by the presence of these armoured vehicles in unexpected places behind our lines. If they are behind our Front, the French are also at many points fighting actively behind theirs. Both sides are therefore in an extremely dangerous position. And if the French Army, and our own Army, are well handled, as I believe they will be; if the French retain that genius for recovery and counter-attack for which they have so long been famous; and if the British Army shows the dogged endurance and solid fighting power of which there have been so many examples in the past—then a sudden transformation of the scene might spring into being.

It would be foolish, however, to disguise the gravity of the hour. It would be still more foolish to lose heart and courage or to suppose that well-trained, well-equipped armies numbering three or four millions of men can be overcome in the space of a few weeks, or even months, by a scoop, or raid of mechanized vehicles, however formidable. We may look with confidence to the stabilization of the Front in France, and to the general engagement of the masses, which will enable the qualities of the French and British soldiers to be matched squarely against those of their adversaries. For myself, I have invincible confidence in the French Army and its leaders. Only a very small part of that splendid army has yet been heavily engaged; and only a very small part of France has yet been invaded. There is good evidence to show that practically the whole of the specialized and mechanized forces of the enemy have been already thrown into the battle; and we know that very heavy losses have been inflicted upon them. No officer or man, no brigade or division, which grapples at close quarters with the enemy, wherever encountered, can fail to make a worthy contribution to the general result. The armies must cast away the idea of resisting behind concrete lines or natural obstacles, and must realize that mastery can only be regained by furious and unrelenting assault. And this spirit must not only animate the High Command, but must inspire every fighting man.

In the air—often at serious odds—often at odds hitherto thought overwhelming—we have been clawing down three or four to one of our enemies; and the relative balance of the British and German Air Forces is now considerably more favourable to us than at the beginning of the battle. In cutting down the German bombers, we are fighting our own battle as well as that of France. My confidence in our ability to fight it out to the finish with the German Air Force has been strengthened by the fierce encounters which have taken place and are taking place. At the same time, our heavy bombers are striking nightly at the tap-root of German mechanized power, and have already inflicted serious damage upon the oil refineries on which the Nazi effort to dominate the world directly depends.

We must expect that as soon as stability is reached on the Western Front, the bulk of that hideous apparatus of aggression which gashed Holland into ruin and slavery in a few days will be turned upon us. I am sure I speak for all when I say we are ready to face it; to endure it; and to retaliate against it—to any extent that the unwritten laws of war permit. There will be many men, and many women, in this island who when the ordeal comes upon them, as come it will, will feel comfort, and even a pride—that they are sharing the perils of our lads at the Front—soldiers, sailors and airmen, God bless them—and are drawing away from them a part at least of the onslaught they have to bear. Is not this the appointed time for all to make the utmost exertions in their power? If the battle is to be won, we must provide our men with ever-increasing quantities of the weapons and ammunition they need. We must have, and have quickly, more aeroplanes, more tanks, more shells, more guns. There is imperious need for these vital munitions. They increase our strength against the powerfully armed enemy. They replace the wastage of the obstinate struggle; and the knowledge that wastage will speedily be replaced enables us to draw more readily upon our reserves and throw them in now that everything counts so much.

Our task is not only to win the battle—but to win the war. After this battle in France abates its force, there will come the battle for our island—for all that Britain is, and all that Britain means. That will be the struggle. In that supreme emergency we shall not hesitate to take every step, even the most drastic, to call forth from our people the last ounce and the last inch of effort of which they are capable. The interests of property, the hours of labour, are nothing compared with the struggle for life and honour, for right and freedom, to which we have vowed ourselves.

I have received from the Chiefs of the French Republic, and in particular from its indomitable Prime Minister, M. Reynaud, the most sacred pledges that whatever happens they will fight to the end, be it bitter or be it glorious. Nay, if we fight to the end, it can only be glorious.

Having received His Majesty's commission, I have formed an administration of men and women of every party and of almost every point of view. We have differed and quarrelled in the past; but now one bond unites us all—to wage war until victory is won, and never to surrender ourselves to servitude and shame, whatever the cost and the agony may be. This is one of the most awe-striking periods in the long history of France and Britain. It is also beyond doubt the most sublime. Side by side, unaided except by their kith and kin in the great Dominions and by the wide Empires which rest beneath their shield—side by side, the British and French peoples have advanced to rescue not only Europe but mankind from the foulest and most soul-destroying tyranny which has ever darkened and stained the pages of history. Behind them—behind us —behind the armies and fleets of Britain and France—gather a group of shattered States and bludgeoned races: the Czechs, the Poles, the Norwegians, the Danes, the Dutch, the Belgians—upon all of whom the long night of barbarism will descend, unbroken even by a star of hope, unless we conquer, as conquer we must; as conquer we shall.

Today is Trinity Sunday. Centuries ago words were written to be a call and a spur to the faithful servants of Truth and Justice: "Arm yourselves, and be ye men of valour, and be in readiness for the conflict; for it is better for us to perish in battle than to look upon the outrage of our nation and our altar. As the Will of God is in Heaven, even so let it be."

## DUNKIRK
### FROM A SPEECH DELIVERED IN THE HOUSE OF COMMONS
### 4 JUNE, 1940

When a week ago today I asked the House to fix this afternoon as the occasion for a statement, I feared it would be my hard lot to announce the greatest military disaster in our long history. I thought —and some good judges agreed with me—that perhaps 20,000 or 30,000 men might be re-embarked. But it certainly seemed that the whole of the French First Army and the whole of the British Expeditionary Force north of the Amiens-Abbeville gap would be broken up in the open field or else would have to capitulate for lack of food and ammunition. These were the hard and heavy tidings for which I called upon the House and the nation to prepare themselves a week ago. The whole root and core and brain of the British Army, on which and around which we were to build, and are to build, the great British Armies in the later years of the war, seemed about to perish upon the field or to be led into an ignominious and starving captivity.

That was the prospect a week ago. But another blow which might well have proved final was yet to fall upon us. The King of the Belgians had called upon us to come to his aid. Had not this Ruler and his government severed themselves from the Allies, who rescued their country from extinction in the late war, and had they not sought refuge in what has proved to be a fatal neutrality, the French and British Armies might well at the outset have saved not only Belgium but perhaps even Poland. Yet at the last moment when Belgium was already invaded, King Leopold called upon us to come to his aid, and even at the last moment we came. He and his brave, efficient army, nearly half a million strong, guarded our left flank and thus kept open our only line of retreat to the sea. Suddenly, without prior consultation, with the least possible notice, without the advice of his Ministers and upon his own personal act, he sent a plenipotentiary to the German Command, surrendered his army and exposed our whole flank and means of retreat.

The enemy attacked on all sides with great strength and fierceness, and their main power, the power of their far more numerous air force, was thrown into the battle or else concentrated upon Dunkirk and the beaches. Pressing in upon the narrow exit, both from the east and from the west, the enemy began to fire with cannon upon the beaches by which alone the shipping could approach or depart. They sowed magnetic mines in the channels and seas; they sent repeated waves of hostile aircraft, sometimes more than a hundred strong in one formation, to cast their bombs upon the single pier that remained, and upon the sand dunes upon which the troops had their eyes for shelter. Their U-boats, one of which was sunk, and their motor launches took their toll of the vast traffic which now began. For four or five days an intense struggle reigned. All their armoured divisions—or what was left of them—together with great masses of infantry and artillery, hurled themselves in vain upon the ever-narrowing, ever-contracting appendix within which the British and French Armies fought.

Meanwhile, the Royal Navy, with the willing help of countless merchant seamen, strained every nerve to embark the British and Allied troops; 220 light warships and 650 other vessels were engaged. They had to operate upon the difficult coast, often in adverse weather, under an almost ceaseless hail of bombs and an increasing concentration of artillery fire. Nor were the seas, as I have said, themselves free from mines and torpedoes. It was in conditions such as these that our men carried on, with little or no rest, for days and nights on end, making trip after trip across the dangerous waters, bringing with them always men whom they had rescued. The numbers they have brought back are the measure of their devotion and their courage. The hospital ships, which brought off many thousands of British and French wounded, being so plainly marked were a special target for Nazi bombs; but the men and women on board them never faltered in their duty.

Meanwhile, the Royal Air Force, which had already been intervening in the battle, so far as its range would allow, from home bases, now used part of its main metropolitan fighter strength, and struck at the German bombers, and at the fighters which in large numbers protected them. This struggle was protracted and fierce. Suddenly the scene has cleared, the crash and thunder has for the moment—but only for the moment—died away. A miracle of deliverance, achieved by valour, by perseverance, by perfect discipline, by faultless service, by resource, by skill, by unconquerable fidelity, is manifest to us all. The enemy was hurled back by the retreating British and French troops. He was so roughly handled that he did not hurry their departure seriously. The Royal Air Force engaged the main strength of the German Air Force, and inflicted upon them losses of at least four to one; and the Navy, using nearly 1,000 ships of all kinds, carried over 335,000 men, French and British, out of the jaws of death and shame, to their native land and to the tasks which lie immediately ahead. We must be very careful not to assign to this deliverance the attributes of a victory. Wars are not won by evacuations. But there was a victory inside this deliverance, which should be noted. It was gained by the Air Force. Many of our soldiers coming back have not seen the Air Force at work; they saw only the bombers which escaped its protective attack. They underrate its achievements. I have heard much talk of this; that is why I go out of my way to say this. I will tell you about it.

This was a great trial of strength between the British and German Air Forces. Can you conceive a greater objective for the Germans in the air than to make evacuation from these beaches impossible, and to sink all these ships which were displayed, almost to the extent of thousands? Could there have been an objective of greater military importance and significance for the whole purpose of the war than this? They tried hard, and they were beaten back; they were frustrated in their task. We got the Army away; and they have paid fourfold for any losses which they have inflicted. Very large formations of German aeroplanes—and we know that they are a very brave race—have turned on several occasions from the attack of one-quarter of their number of the Royal Air Force, and have dispersed in different directions. Twelve aeroplanes have been hunted by two. One aeroplane was driven into the water and cast away, by the mere charge of a British aeroplane, which had no more ammunition. All of our types—the Hurricane, the Spitfire and the new Defiant—and all our pilots have been vindicated as superior to what they have at present to face.

When we consider how much greater would be our advantage in defending the air above this island against an overseas attack, I must say that I find in these facts a sure basis upon which practical and reassuring thoughts may rest. I will pay my tribute to these young airmen. The great French Army was very largely, for the time being, cast back and disturbed by the onrush of a few thousands of armoured vehicles. May it not also be that the cause of civilization itself will be defended by the skill and devotion of a few thousand airmen. There never had been, I suppose, in all the world, in all the history of war, such an opportunity for youth. The Knights of the Round Table, the Crusaders, all fall back into the past: not only distant but prosaic; these young men, going forth every morn to guard their native land and all that we stand for, holding in their hands these instruments of colossal and shattering power, of whom it may be said that

"Every morn brought forth a noble chance
And every chance brought forth a noble knight",

deserve our gratitude, as do all of the brave men who, in so many ways and on so many occasions, are ready, and continue ready, to give life and all for their native land. . . .

In the long series of very fierce battles, now on this front, now on that, fighting on three fronts at once, battles fought by two or three divisions against an equal or somewhat larger number of the enemy, and fought fiercely on some of the old grounds that so many of us knew so well, in these battles our losses in men have exceeded 30,000 killed, wounded and missing. I take occasion to express the sympathy of the House to all who have suffered bereavement or who are still anxious. The President of the Board of Trade[1] is not here today. His son has been killed, and many in the House have felt the pangs of affliction in the sharpest form. But I will say this about the missing. We have had a large number of wounded come home safely to this country, but I would say about the missing that there may be very many reported missing who will come back home, some day, in one way or another. In the confusion of this fight it is inevitable that many have been left in positions where honour required no further resistance from them.

Against this loss of over 30,000 men, we can set a far heavier loss certainly inflicted upon the enemy. But our losses in material are enormous. We have perhaps lost one-third of the men we lost in the opening days of the battle of 21 March, 1918, but we have lost nearly as many guns—nearly one thousand—and all our transport, all the armoured vehicles that were with the Army in the north. This loss will impose a further delay on the expansion of our military strength. That expansion had not been proceeding as fast as we had hoped. The best of all we had to give had gone to the British Expeditionary Force, and although they had not the numbers of tanks and some articles of equipment which were desirable, they were a very well and finely equipped Army. They had the first-fruits of all that our industry had to give, and that is gone. And now here is this further delay. How long it will be, how long it will last, depends upon the exertions which we make in this island. An effort the like of which has never been seen in our records is now being made. Work is proceeding everywhere, night and day, Sundays and weekdays. Capital and labour have cast aside their interests, rights, and customs and put them into the common stock. Already the flow of munitions has leapt forward. There is no reason why we should not in a few months overtake the sudden and serious loss that has come upon us, without retarding the development of our general programme.

Nevertheless, our thankfulness at the escape of our Army and so many men, whose loved ones have passed through an agonizing week, must not blind us to the fact that what has happened in

[1] Sir Andrew Duncan, who later became Minister of Supply.

France and Belgium is a colossal military disaster. The French Army has been weakened, the Belgian Army has been lost, a large part of those fortified lines upon which so much faith had been reposed is gone, many valuable mining districts and factories have passed into the enemy's possession, the whole of the Channel ports are in his hands, with all the tragic consequences that follow from that, and we must expect another blow to be struck almost immediately at us or at France. We are told that Herr Hitler has a plan for invading the British Isles. This has often been thought of before. When Napoleon lay at Boulogne for a year with his flat-bottomed boats and his Grand Army, he was told by someone "There are bitter weeds in England." There are certainly a great many more of them since the British Expeditionary Force returned.

We have found it necessary to take measures of increasing stringency, not only against enemy aliens and suspicious characters of other nationalities, but also against British subjects who may become a danger or a nuisance should the war be transported to the United Kingdom. I know there are a great many people affected by the orders which we have made who are the passionate enemies of Nazi Germany. I am very sorry for them but we cannot, at the present time and under the present stress, draw all the distinctions which we should like to do. If parachute landings were attempted and fierce fighting attendant upon them followed, these unfortunate people would be far better out of the way, for their own sakes as well as for ours. There is, however, another class, for which I feel not the slightest sympathy. Parliament has given us the powers to put down Fifth Column activities with a strong hand, and we shall use those powers, subject to the supervision and correction of the House, without the slightest hesitation until we are satisfied, and more than satisfied, that this malignancy in our midst has been effectively stamped out.

Turning once again, and this time more generally, to the question of invasion, I would observe that there has never been a period in all these long centuries of which we boast when an absolute guarantee against invasion, still less against serious raids, could have been given to our people. In the days of Napoleon the same wind which would have carried his transports across the Channel might have driven away the blockading fleet. There was always the chance, and it is that chance which has excited and befooled the imaginations of many Continental tyrants. Many are the tales that are told. We are assured that novel methods will be adopted, and when we see the originality of malice, the ingenuity of aggression, which our enemy displays, we may certainly prepare ourselves for every kind of novel strategem and every kind of brutal and treacherous manoeuvre. I think that no idea is so outlandish, that it should not be considered and viewed with a searching, but at the same time, I hope, with a steady eye. We must never forget the solid assurances of sea-power and those which belong to air power if it can be locally exercised.

I have, myself, full confidence that if all do their duty, if nothing is neglected, and if the best arrangements are made, as they are being made, we shall prove ourselves once again able to defend our island home, to ride out the storm of war, and to outlive the menace of tyranny, if necessary for years, if necessary alone. At any rate, that is what we are going to try to do. That is the resolve of His Majesty's Government—every man of them. That is the will of Parliament and the nation. The British Empire and the French Republic, linked together in their cause and in their need, will defend to the death their native soil, aiding each other like good comrades to the utmost of their strength. Even though large tracts of Europe and many old and famous states have fallen or may fall into the grip of the Gestapo and all the odious apparatus of Nazi rule, we shall not flag or fail. We shall go on to the end, we shall fight in France, we shall fight on the seas and oceans, we shall fight with growing confidence and growing strength in the air, we shall defend our island, whatever the cost may be, we shall fight on the beaches, we shall fight on the landing grounds, we shall fight in the fields and in the streets, we shall fight in the hills; we shall never surrender, and even if, which I do not for a moment believe, this island or a large part of it were subjugated and starving, then our Empire beyond the seas, armed and guarded by the British Fleet, would carry on the struggle, until, in God's good time, the new world, with all its power and might, steps forth to the rescue and the liberation of the old.

## A MESSAGE TO THE PEOPLE

### BROADCAST 17 JUNE, 1940

The news from France is very bad and I grieve for the gallant French people who have fallen into this terrible misfortune. Nothing will alter our feelings towards them or our faith that the genius of France will rise again. What has happened in France makes no difference to our actions and purpose. We have become the sole champions now in arms to defend the world cause. We shall do our best to be worthy of this high honour. We shall defend our island home and with the British Empire we shall fight on unconquerable until the curse of Hitler is lifted from the brows of mankind. We are sure that in the end all will come right.


## THEIR FINEST HOUR

### FROM A SPEECH DELIVERED FIRST TO THE HOUSE OF
### COMMONS AND THEN BROADCAST, 18 JUNE, 1940

During the great battle in France, we gave very powerful and continuous aid to the French Army, both by fighters and bombers; but in spite of every kind of pressure we never would allow the entire metropolitan fighter strength of the Air Force to be consumed. This decision was painful, but it was also right, because the fortunes of the battle in France could not have been decisively affected even if we had thrown in our entire fighter force. That battle was lost by the unfortunate strategical opening, by the extraordinary and unforeseen power of the armoured columns and by the great preponderance of the German Army in numbers. Our fighter Air Force might easily have been exhausted as a mere accident in that great struggle, and then we should have found ourselves at the present time in a very serious plight. But as it is, I am happy to inform the House that our fighter strength is stronger at the present time relatively to the Germans, who have suffered terrible losses, than it has ever been; and consequently we believe ourselves possessed of the capacity to continue the war in the air under better conditions than we have ever experienced before. I look forward confidently to the exploits of our fighter pilots—these splendid men, this brilliant youth—who will have the glory of saving their native land, their island home, and all they love, from the most deadly of all attacks.

There remains, of course, the danger of bombing attacks, which will certainly be made very soon upon us by the bomber forces of the enemy. It is true that the German bomber force is superior in numbers to ours; but we have a very large bomber force also, which we shall use to strike at military targets in Germany without intermission. I do not at all underrate the severity of the ordeal which lies before us; but I believe our countrymen will show themselves capable of standing up to it, like the brave men of Barcelona, and will be able to stand up to it, and carry on in spite of it, at least as well as any other people in the world. Much will depend upon this; every man and every woman will have the chance to show the finest qualities of their race, and render the highest service to their cause. For all of us, at this time, whatever our sphere, our station, our occupation or our duties, it will be a help to remember the famous lines:

"He nothing common did or mean,
Upon that memorable scene."

I have thought it right upon this occasion to give the House and the country some indication of the solid, practical grounds upon which we base our inflexible resolve to continue the war. There are a good many people who say, "Never mind. Win or lose, sink or swim, better die than submit to tyranny—and such a tyranny." And I do not dissociate myself from them. But I can assure them that our professional advisers of the three Services unitedly advise that we should carry on the war, and that there are good and reasonable hopes of final victory. We have fully informed and consulted all the self-governing Dominions, these great communities far beyond the oceans who have been built up on our laws and on our civilization, and who are absolutely free to choose their course, but are absolutely devoted to the ancient Motherland, and who feel themselves inspired by the same emotions which lead me to stake our all upon duty and honour. We have fully consulted them, and I have received from their Prime Ministers, Mr. Mackenzie King of Canada, Mr. Menzies of Australia, Mr. Fraser of New Zealand, and General Smuts of South Africa—that wonderful man, with his immense, profound mind, and his eye watching from a distance the whole panorama of European affairs —I have received from all these eminent men, who all have governments behind them elected on wide franchises, who are all there because they represent the will of their people, messages couched in the most moving terms in which they endorse our decision to fight on, and declare themselves ready to share our fortunes and to persevere to the end. That is what we are going to do.

We may now ask ourselves: In what way has our position worsened since the beginning of the war? It has worsened by the fact that the Germans have conquered a large part of the coastline of Western Europe, and many small countries have been overrun by them. This aggravates the possibilities of air attack and adds to our naval preoccupations. It in no way diminishes, but on the contrary definitely increases, the power of our long-distance blockade. Similarly, the entrance of Italy into the war increases the power of our long-distance blockade. We have stopped the worst leak by that. We do not know whether military resistance will come to an end in France or not, but should it do so, then of course, the Germans will be able to concentrate their forces, both military and industrial, upon us. But for the reasons I have given to the House these will not be found so easy to apply. If invasion has become more imminent, as no doubt it has, we, being relieved from the task of maintaining a large army in France, have far larger and more efficient forces to meet it.

If Hitler can bring under his despotic control the industries of the countries he has conquered, this will add greatly to his already vast armament output. On the other hand, this will not happen immediately, and we are now assured of immense, continuous and increasing support in supplies and munitions of all kinds from the United States; and especially of aeroplanes and pilots from the Dominions and across the oceans, coming from regions which are beyond the reach of enemy bombers.

I do not see how any of these factors can operate to our detriment on balance before the winter comes; and the winter will impose a strain upon the Nazi regime, with almost all Europe writhing and starving under its cruel heel, which, for all their ruthlessness, will run them very hard. We must not forget that from the moment when we declared war on the 3rd September it was always possible for Germany to turn all her air force upon this country, together with any other devices of invasion she might conceive, and that France could have done little or nothing to prevent her doing so. We have, therefore, lived under this danger, in principle and in a slightly modified form, during all these months. In the meanwhile, however, we have enormously improved our methods of defence, and we have learned, what we had no right to assume at the beginning, namely, that the individual aircraft and the individual British pilot have a sure and definite superiority. Therefore, in casting up this dread balance-sheet and contemplating our dangers with a disillusioned eye, I see great reason for intense vigilance and exertion, but none whatever for panic or despair.

During the first four years of the last war the Allies experienced nothing but disaster and disappointment. That was our constant fear: one blow after another, terrible losses, frightful dangers. Everything miscarried. And yet at the end of those four years the morale of the Allies was higher than that of the Germans, who had moved from one aggressive triumph to another, and who stood everywhere triumphant invaders of the lands into which they had broken. During that war we repeatedly asked ourselves the question: How are we going to win? and no one was able ever to answer it with much precision, until at the end, quite suddenly, quite unexpectedly, our terrible foe collapsed before us, and we were so glutted with victory that in our folly we threw it away.

We do not yet know what will happen in France or whether the French resistance will be prolonged, both in France and in the French Empire overseas. The French Government will be throwing away great opportunities and casting adrift their future if they do not continue the war in accordance with their Treaty obligations, from which we have not felt able to release them. The House will have read the historic declaration in which, at the desire of many Frenchmen—and of our own hearts—we have proclaimed our willingness at the darkest hour in French history to conclude a union of common citizenship in this struggle. However matters may go in France or with the French Government, or other French Governments, we in this island and in the British Empire will never lose our sense of comradeship with the French people. If we are now called upon to endure what they have been suffering, we shall emulate their courage, and if final victory rewards our toils they shall share the gains, aye, and freedom shall be restored to all. We abate nothing of our just demands; not one jot or tittle do we recede. Czechs, Poles, Norwegians, Dutch, Belgians have joined their causes to our own. All these shall be restored.

What General Weygand called the Battle of France is over. I expect that the battle of Britain is about to begin. Upon this battle depends the survival of Christian civilization. Upon it depends our own British life, and the long continuity of our institutions and our Empire. The whole fury and might of the enemy must very soon be turned on us. Hitler knows that he will have to break us in this island or lose the war. If we can stand up to him, all Europe may be free and the life of the world may move forward into broad, sunlit uplands. But if we fail, then the whole world, including the United States, including all that we have known and cared for, will sink into the abyss of a new Dark Age made more sinister, and perhaps more protracted, by the lights of perverted science. Let us therefore brace ourselves to our duties, and so bear ourselves that, if the British Empire and its Commonwealth last for a thousand years, men will still say, "This was their finest hour."

## THE WAR SITUATION
### FROM A SPEECH DELIVERED TO THE HOUSE OF COMMONS
### 20 AUGUST, 1940

The great air battle which has been in progress over this island for the last few weeks has recently attained a high intensity. It is too soon to attempt to assign limits either to its scale or to its duration. We must certainly expect that greater efforts will be made by the enemy than any he has so far put forth. Hostile airfields are still being developed in France and the Low Countries, and the movement of squadrons and material for attacking us is still proceeding. It is quite plain that Herr Hitler could not admit defeat in his air attack on Great Britain without sustaining most serious injury. If, after all his boastings and blood-curdling threats and lurid accounts trumpeted round the world of the damage he has inflicted, of the vast numbers of our Air Force he has shot down, so he says, with so little loss to himself; if after tales of the panic-stricken British crushed in their holes cursing the plutocratic Parliament which has led them to such a plight; if after all this his whole air onslaught were forced after a while tamely to peter out, the Fuhrer's reputation for veracity of statement might be seriously impugned. We may be sure, therefore, that he will continue as long as he has the strength to do so, and as long as any preoccupations he may have in respect of the Russian Air Force allow him to do so.

The enemy is, of course, far more numerous than we are. But our new production already, as I am advised, largely exceeds his, and the American production is only just beginning to flow in. It is a fact, as I see from my daily returns, that our bomber and fighter strengths now, after all this fighting, are larger than they have ever been. We believe that we shall be able to continue the air struggle indefinitely and as long as the enemy pleases, and the longer it continues the more rapid will be our approach, first towards that parity, and then into that superiority in the air, upon which in a large measure the decision of the war depends.

The gratitude of every home in our island, in our Empire, and indeed throughout the world, except in the abodes of the guilty, goes out to the British airmen who, undaunted by odds, unwearied in their constant challenge and mortal danger, are turning the tide of the world war by their prowess and by their devotion. Never in the field of human conflict was so much owed by so many to so few.

All hearts go out to the fighter pilots, whose brilliant actions we see with our own eyes day after day; but we must never forget that all the time, night after night, month after month, our bomber squadrons travel far into Germany, find their targets in the darkness by the highest navigational skill, aim their attacks, often under the heaviest fire, often with serious loss, with deliberate careful discrimination, and inflict shattering blows upon the whole of the technical and war-making structure of the Nazi power. On no part of the Royal Air Force does the weight of the war fall more heavily than on the daylight bombers who will play an invaluable part in the case of invasion and whose unflinching zeal it has been necessary in the meanwhile on numerous occasions to restrain.

# TO THE FRENCH PEOPLE

## AN ADDRESS BROADCAST TO FRANCE IN FRENCH AND ENGLISH, 21 OCTOBER, 1940

Frenchmen! For more than thirty years in peace and war I have marched with you, and I am marching still along the same road. Tonight I speak to you at your firesides wherever you may be, or whatever your fortunes are. I repeat the prayer around the *louis d'or*, *"Dieu protége la France"*. Here at home in England, under the fire of the Boche, we do not forget the ties and links that unite us to France, and we are persevering steadfastly and in good heart in the cause of European freedom and fair dealing for the common people of all countries, for which, with you, we drew the sword. When good people get into trouble because they are attacked and heavily smitten by the vile and wicked, they must be very careful not to get at loggerheads with one another. The common enemy is always trying to bring this about, and, of course, in bad luck a lot of things happen which play into the enemy's hands. We must just make the best of things as they come along.

Here in London, which Herr Hitler says he will reduce to ashes, and which his aeroplanes are now bombarding, our people are bearing up unflinchingly. Our Air Force has more than held its own. We are waiting for the long-promised invasion. So are the fishes. But, of course, this for us is only the beginning. Now in 1940, in spite of occasional losses, we have, as ever, command of the seas. In 1941 we shall have the command of the air. Remember what that means. Herr Hitler with his tanks and other mechanical weapons, and also by Fifth Column intrigue with traitors, has managed to subjugate for the time being most of the finest races in Europe, and his little Italian accomplice is trotting along hopefully and hungrily, but rather wearily and very timidly, at his side. They both wish to carve up France and her Empire as if it were a fowl: to one a leg, to another a wing or perhaps part of the breast. Not only the French Empire will be devoured by these two ugly customers, but Alsace-Lorraine will go once again under the German yoke, and Nice, Savoy and Corsica—Napoleon's Corsica—will be torn from the fair realm of France. But Herr Hitler is not thinking only of stealing other people's territories, or flinging gobbets of them to his little confederate. I tell you truly what you must believe

681

when I say this evil man, this monstrous abortion of hatred and defeat, is resolved on nothing less than the complete wiping out of the French nation, and the disintegration of its whole life and future. By all kinds of sly and savage means, he is plotting and working to quench for ever the fountain of characteristic French culture and of French inspiration to the world. All Europe, if he has his way, will be reduced to one uniform Boche-land, to be exploited, pillaged, and bullied by his Nazi gangsters. You will excuse my speaking frankly because this is not a time to mince words. It is not defeat that France will now be made to suffer at German hands, but the doom of complete obliteration. Army, Navy, Air Force, religion, law, language, culture, institutions, literature, history, tradition, all are to be effaced by the brute strength of a triumphant Army and the scientific low-cunning of a ruthless Police Force.

Frenchmen—re-arm your spirits before it is too late. Remember how Napoleon said before one of his battles: "These same Prussians who are so boastful today were three to one at Jena, and six to one at Montmirail." Never will I believe that the soul of France is dead. Never will I believe that her place amongst the greatest nations of the world has been lost for ever! All these schemes and crimes of Herr Hitler's are bringing upon him and upon all who belong to his system a retribution which many of us will live to see. The story is not yet finished, but it will not be so long. We are on his track, and so are our friends across the Atlantic Ocean, and your friends across the Atlantic Ocean. If he cannot destroy us, we will surely destroy him and all his gang, and all their works. Therefore, have hope and faith, for all will come right.

Now what is it we British ask of you in this present hard and bitter time? What we ask at this moment in our struggle to win the victory which we will share with you, is that if you cannot help us, at least you will not hinder us. Presently you will be able to weight the arm that strikes for you, and you ought to do so. But even now we believe that Frenchmen wherever they may be feel their hearts warm and a proud blood tingle in their veins when we have some success in the air or on the sea, or presently—for that will come—upon the land.

Remember we shall never stop, never weary, and never give in, and that our whole people and Empire have vowed themselves to the task of cleansing Europe from the Nazi pestilence and saving the world from the new Dark Ages. Do not imagine, as the German-controlled wireless tells you, that we English seek to take your ships and colonies. We seek to beat the life and soul out of Hitler and Hitlerism. That alone, that all the time, that to the end. We do not covet anything from any nation except their respect. Those French-men who are in the French Empire, and those who are in so-called unoccupied France, may see their way from time to time to useful action. I will not go into details. Hostile ears are listening. As for those, to whom English hearts go out in full, because they see them under the sharp discipline, oppression, and spying of the Hun—as to those Frenchmen in the occupied regions, to them I say, when they think of the future let them remember the words which Gambetta, that great Frenchman, uttered after 1870 about the future of France and what was to come: "Think of it always: speak of it never."

Good night then, sleep to gather strength for the morning. For the morning will come. Brightly will it shine on the brave and true, kindly upon all who suffer for the cause, glorious upon the tombs of heroes. Thus will shine the dawn. *Vive la France!* Long live also the forward march of the common people in all the lands towards their just and true inheritance, and towards the broader and fuller age.

# THE
# UNRELENTING STRUGGLE

*

## TRIBUTE TO NEVILLE CHAMBERLAIN
### FROM A SPEECH DELIVERED TO THE HOUSE OF COMMONS
### 12 NOVEMBER, 1940

SINCE WE last met, the House has suffered a very grievous loss in the death of one of its most distinguished Members, and of a statesman and public servant who, during the best part of three memorable years, was first Minister of the Crown.

The fierce and bitter controversies which hung around him in recent times were hushed by the news of his illness and are silenced by his death. In paying a tribute of respect and of regard to an eminent man who has been taken from us, no one is obliged to alter the opinions which he has formed or expressed upon issues which have become a part of history; but at the Lychgate we may all pass our own conduct and our own judgments under a searching review. It is not given to human beings, happily for them, for otherwise life would be intolerable, to foresee or to predict to any large extent the unfolding course of events. In one phase men seem to have been right, in another they seem to have been wrong. Then again, a few years later, when the perspective of time has lengthened, all stand in a different setting. There is a new proportion. There is another scale of values. History with its flickering lamp stumbles along the trail of the past, trying to reconstruct its scenes, to revive its echoes, and kindle with pale gleams the passion of former days. What is the worth of all this? The only guide to a man is his conscience; the only shield to his memory is the rectitude and sincerity of his actions. It is very imprudent to walk through life without this shield, because we are so often mocked by the failure of our hopes and the upsetting of our calculations; but with this shield, however the fates may play, we march always in the ranks of honour.

It fell to Neville Chamberlain in one of the supreme crises of the world to be contradicted by events, to be disappointed in his hopes, and to be deceived and cheated by a wicked man. But what were these hopes in which he was disappointed? What were these wishes in which he was frustrated? What was that faith that was abused? They were surely among the most noble and benevolent instincts of the human heart—the love of peace, the toil for peace, the strife for peace, the pursuit of peace, even at great peril, and certainly to the utter disdain of popularity or clamour. Whatever else history may or may not say about these terrible, tremendous years, we can be sure that Neville Chamberlain acted with perfect sincerity according to his lights and strove to the utmost of his capacity and authority, which were powerful, to save the world from the awful, devastating struggle in which we are now engaged. This alone will stand him in good stead as far as the verdict of history is concerned.

But it is also a help to our country and to our whole Empire, and to our decent faithful way of living that, however long the struggle may last, or however dark may be the clouds which over-hang our path, no future generation of English-speaking folks—for that is the tribunal to which we appeal—will doubt that, even at a great cost to ourselves in technical preparation, we were guiltless of the bloodshed, terror and misery which have engulfed so many lands and peoples, and yet seek new victims still. Herr Hitler protests with frantic words and gestures that he has only desired peace. What do these ravings and outpourings count before the silence of Neville Chamberlain's tomb? Long, hard, and hazardous years lie before us, but at least we entered upon them united and with clean hearts.

I do not propose to give an appreciation of Neville Chamberlain's life and character, but there were certain qualities always admired in these islands which he possessed in an altogether exceptional degree. He had a physical and moral toughness of fibre which enabled him all through his varied career to endure misfortune and disappointment without being unduly discouraged or wearied. He had a precision of mind and an aptitude for business which raised him far above the ordinary levels of our generation. He had a firmness of spirit which was not often elated by success, seldom downcast by failure, and never swayed by panic. When, contrary

685

to all his hopes, beliefs and exertions, the war came upon him, and when, as he himself said, all that he had worked for was shattered, there was no man more resolved to pursue the unsought quarrel to the death. The same qualities which made him one of the last to enter the war, made him one of the last who would quit it before the full victory of a righteous cause was won.

## THE OLD SCHOOL

### A SPEECH TO THE BOYS OF HARROW, 18 DECEMBER, 1940

It is a great pleasure and a refreshing treat to me and those of my Parliamentary Ministerial colleagues who have come to Harrow with me this afternoon to join the School in singing Harrow songs. When I was here as a boy I was thrilled by them. I had a good memory and mastered the words of many of them, and they have often come back to me in after life. I feel that they are one of the greatest treasures of the school, passing as they do from one generation to another and pointing with bright hopes towards the future.

We have sung of "the wonderful giants of old" but can anyone doubt that this generation is as good and as noble as any the nation has ever produced, and that its men and women can stand against all tests? Can any one doubt that this generation is in every way capable of carrying on the traditions of the nation and handing down its love of justice and liberty and its message undiminished and unimpaired?

I like the song "Boy", although when I was at the School I did not advance to that position of authority which entitles one to make that call. The songs and their spirit form a bond between Harrovians all over the world, and they have played a great part in the influence which has been exercised in national affairs by men who have had their education here.

Hitler, in one of his recent discourses, declared that the fight was between those who have been through the Adolf Hitler Schools and those who have been at Eton. Hitler has forgotten Harrow, and he has also overlooked the vast majority of the youth of this country who have never had the advantage of attending such schools, but who have by their skill and prowess won the admiration of the whole world.

When this war is won, as it surely will be, it must be one of our aims to work to establish a state of society where the advantages and privileges which hitherto have been enjoyed only by the few shall be far more widely shared by the many, and by the youth of the nation as a whole.

It is a great time in which you are called upon to begin your life. You have already had the honour of being under the fire of the enemy, and no doubt you acquitted yourself with befitting composure and decorum. You are here at this most important period of your lives, at a moment when our country stands forth almost alone as the champion of right and freedom all over the world. You, the young men, will be the heirs of the victory which we shall surely achieve, and perhaps some of you in this Speech Room will derive from these songs and Harrow associations the impulse to render that victory fruitful and lasting.

# A CALL TO THE ITALIAN PEOPLE

FROM A BROADCAST FROM LONDON, 23 DECEMBER, 1940

Tonight I speak to the Italian people, and I speak to you from London, the heart of the British Islands and of the British Commonwealth and Empire. I speak to you what the diplomatists call words of great truth and respect. We are at war—that is a very strange and terrible thought. Whoever imagined until the last few melancholy years that the British and Italian nations would be trying to destroy one another?

We have always been such friends. We were the champions of the Italian Risorgimento. We were the partisans of Garibaldi, the admirers of Mazzini and Cavour. All that great movement towards the unity of the Italian nation which lighted the nineteenth century was aided and was hailed by the British Parliament and public. Our fathers and our grandfathers longed to see Italy freed from the Austrian yoke, and to see all minor barriers in Italy swept away, so that the Italian people and their fair land might take an honoured place as one of the leading powers upon the Continent and as a brilliant and gifted member of the family of Europe and of Christendom.

We have never been your foes till now. In the last war against the barbarous Huns we were your comrades. For fifteen years after that war we were your friends. Although the institutions which you adopted after that war were not akin to ours, and diverged, as we think, from the sovereign impulses which had commanded the unity of Italy, we could still march forward in peace and good will. Many thousands of your people dwelt with us in England; many thousands of our people dwelt with you in Italy. We liked each other; we got on well together. There were reciprocal services; there was amity; there was esteem.

And now we are at war; now we are condemned to work each other's ruin. Your aviators have tried to cast their bombs upon London; our armies are tearing and will tear your African Empire to shreds and tatters. We are now only at the beginning of this sombre tale. Who can say where it will end? Presently we shall be forced to come to much closer grips. How has all this come about, and what is it all for?

Italians, I will tell you the truth. It is all because of one man. One man and one man alone has ranged the Italian people in deadly struggle against the British Empire, and has deprived Italy of the sympathy and intimacy of the United States of America. That he is a great man I do not deny, but that after eighteen years of unbridled power he has led your country to the horrid verge of ruin can be denied by none. It is one man who, against the Crown and Royal Family of Italy, against the Pope and all the authority of the Vatican and of the Roman Catholic Church, against the wishes of the Italian people, who had no lust for this war, has arrayed the trustees and inheritors of ancient Rome upon the side of the ferocious pagan barbarians.

There lies the tragedy of Italian history, and there stands the criminal who has wrought the deed of folly and of shame.

Why have you placed yourselves, you who were our friends and might have been our brothers, in the path of this avalanche, now only just started from its base to roll forward on its predestined track? Why, after all this, were you made to attack and invade Greece? I ask why—but you may ask why, too, because you never were consulted. The people of Italy were never consulted, the army of Italy was never consulted. No one was consulted. One man and one man alone ordered Italian soldiers to ravage their neighbour's vineyard. Surely the time has come when the Italian monarchy and people, who guard the sacred centre of Christendom, should have a word to say upon these awe-inspiring issues? Surely the Italian army, which has fought so bravely on many occasions in the past, but now evidently has no heart for the job, should take some care of the life and future of Italy?

One man and one man only was resolved to plunge Italy after all these years of strain and effort into the whirlpool of war. And what is the position of Italy today. Where is it that the Duce has led his trusting people after eighteen years of dictatorial power? What hard choice is open to them now? It is to stand up to the battery of the whole British Empire on sea, in the air, and in Africa, and the vigorous counter-attack of the Greek nation; or, on the other hand, to call in Attila over the Brenner Pass with his hordes of ravenous soldiery and his gangs of Gestapo policemen to occupy, hold down, and protect the Italian people, for whom he and his Nazi followers cherish the most bitter and outspoken contempt that is on record between races.

There is where one man and one man only has led you; and there I leave this unfolding story until the day comes—as come it will—when the Italian nation will once more take a hand in shaping its own fortunes.

## "GIVE US THE TOOLS AND WE WILL FINISH THE JOB"
### FROM A BROADCAST ADDRESS, 9 FEBRUARY, 1941

I have been so very careful, since I have been Prime Minister, not to encourage false hopes or prophesy smooth and easy things, and yet the tale that I have to tell today is one which must justly and rightly give us cause for deep thankfulness, and also, I think, for strong comfort and even rejoicing. But now I must dwell upon the more serious, darker and more dangerous aspects of the vast scene of the war. We must all of us have been asking ourselves: what has that wicked man whose crime-stained regime and system are at bay and in the toils—what has he been preparing during these winter months? What new devilry is he planning? What new small country will he overrun or strike down? What fresh form of assault will he make upon our island home and fortress; which—let there be no mistake about it—is all that stands between him and the dominion of the world?

But after all, the fate of this war is going to be settled by what happens on the oceans, in the air, and—above all—in this island. It seems now to be certain that the government and people of the United States intend to supply us with all that is necessary for victory. In the last war the United States sent two million men across the Atlantic. But this is not a war of vast armies, firing immense masses of shells at one another. We do not need the gallant armies which are forming throughout the American Union. We do not need them this year, nor next year; nor any year that I can foresee. But we do need most urgently an immense and continuous supply of war materials and technical apparatus of all kinds. We need them here and we need to bring them here. We shall need a great mass of shipping in 1942, far more than we can build ourselves, if we are to maintain and augment our war effort in the West and in the East.

These facts are, of course, all well known to the enemy, and we must therefore expect that Herr Hitler will do his utmost to prey upon our shipping and to reduce the volume of American supplies entering these islands. Having conquered France and Norway, his clutching fingers reach out on both sides of us into the ocean. I have never underrated this danger, and you know I have never concealed it from you. Therefore, I hope you will believe me when I say that I have complete confidence in the Royal Navy, aided by the Air Force of the Coastal Command, and that in one way or another I am sure they will be able to meet every changing phase of this truly mortal struggle, and that sustained by the courage of our merchant seamen, and of the dockers and workmen of all our ports, we shall outwit, outmanoeuvre, outfight and outlast the worst that the enemy's malice and ingenuity can contrive.

In order to win the war Hitler must destroy Great Britain. He may carry havoc into the Balkan States; he may tear great provinces out of Russia; he may march to the Caspian; he may march to the gates of India. All this will avail him nothing. It may spread his curse more widely throughout Europe and Asia, but it will not avert his doom. With every month that passes the many proud and once happy countries he is now holding down by brute force

690

and vile intrigue are learning to hate the Prussian yoke and the Nazi name as nothing has ever been hated so fiercely and so widely among men before. And all the time, masters of the sea and air, the British Empire—nay, in a certain sense, the whole English-speaking world—will be on his track, bearing with them the swords of justice.

The other day, President Roosevelt gave his opponent in the late Presidential Election a letter of introduction to me, and in it he wrote out a verse, in his own handwriting, from Longfellow, which he said, "applies to you people as it does to us". Here is the verse:

> . . . Sail on, O Ship of State!
> Sail on, O Union, strong and great!
> Humanity with all its fears,
> With all the hopes of future years,
> Is hanging breathless on thy fate!

What is the answer that I shall give, in your name, to this great man, the thrice-chosen head of a nation of 130 millions? Here is the answer which I will give to President Roosevelt: Put your confidence in us. Give us your faith and your blessing, and, under Providence, all will be well.

We shall not fail or falter; we shall not weaken or tire. Neither the sudden shock of battle, nor the long-drawn trials of vigilance and exertion will wear us down. Give us the tools, and we will finish the job.

## A NEW MAGNA CARTA
### A STATEMENT TO THE HOUSE OF COMMONS ON THE PASSING OF THE UNITED STATES "LEASE-AND-LEND" BILL
### 12 MARCH, 1941

The Lease-Lend Bill became law yesterday, when it received the signature of the President. I am sure the House would wish me to express on their behalf, and on behalf of the nation, our deep and respectful appreciation of this monument of generous and far-seeing statesmanship.

The most powerful democracy has, in effect, declared in solemn

Statute that they will devote their overwhelming industrial and financial strength to ensuring the defeat of Nazism in order that nations, great and small, may live in security, tolerance and freedom. By so doing, the government and people of the United States have in fact written a new Magna Carta, which not only has regard to the rights and laws upon which a healthy and advancing civilization can alone be erected, but also proclaims by precept and example the duty of free men and free nations, wherever they may be, to share the responsibility and burden of enforcing them.

In the name of His Majesty's Government and speaking, I am sure, for Parliament and for the whole country, and indeed, in the name of all freedom-loving peoples, I offer to the United States our gratitude for her inspiring act of faith.

## "UNTIL VICTORY IS WON"

### FROM A SPEECH TO A CONFERENCE OF DOMINION HIGH COMMISSIONERS AND ALLIED COUNTRIES' MINISTERS AT ST. JAMES'S PALACE, LONDON, 12 JUNE, 1941

What tragedies, what horrors, what crimes have Hitler and all that Hitler stands for brought upon Europe and the world! The ruins of Warsaw, of Rotterdam, of Belgrade are monuments which will long recall to future generations the outrage of the unopposed air-bombing applied with calculated scientific cruelty to helpless populations. Here in London and throughout the cities of our island, and in Ireland, there may also be seen the marks of devastation. They are being repaid, and presently they will be more than repaid.

But far worse than these visible injuries is the misery of the conquered peoples. We see them hounded, terrorized, exploited. Their manhood by the million is forced to work under conditions indistinguishable in many cases from actual slavery. Their goods and chattels are pillaged, or filched for worthless money. Their homes, their daily life are pried into and spied upon by the all-pervading system of secret political police which, having reduced the Germans themselves to abject docility, now stalk the streets and byways of a dozen lands. Their religious faiths are affronted, persecuted, or oppressed in the interests of a fantastic paganism devised to perpetuate the worship and sustain the tyranny of one abominable creature. Their traditions, their culture, their laws, their institutions, social and political alike, are suppressed by force or undermined by subtle, coldly planned intrigue.

The prisons of the Continent no longer suffice. The concentration camps are overcrowded. Every dawn the German volleys crack. Czechs, Poles, Dutchmen, Norwegians, Yugoslavs and Greeks, Frenchmen, Belgians, Luxembourgers, make the great sacrifice for faith and country. A vile race of quislings—to use the new word which will carry the scorn of mankind down the centuries—is hired to fawn upon the conqueror, to collaborate in his designs, and to enforce his rule upon their fellow-countrymen, while grovelling low themselves. Such is the plight of once glorious Europe, and such are the atrocities against which we are in arms.

It is upon this foundation that Hitler, with his tattered lackey Mussolini at his tail and Admiral Darlan frisking by his side, pretends to build out of hatred, appetite, and racial assertion a new order for Europe. Never did so mocking a fantasy obsess the mind of mortal man. We cannot tell what the course of this fell war will be as it spreads remorseless through ever-wider regions. We know it will be hard, we expect it will be long; we cannot predict or measure its episodes or its tribulations. But one thing is certain, one thing is sure, one thing stands out stark and undeniable, massive and unassailable, for all the world to see.

It will not be by German hands that the structure of Europe will be rebuilt or the union of the European family achieved. In every country into which the German armies and the Nazi police have broken there has sprung up from the soil a hatred of the German name and a contempt for the Nazi creed which the passage of hundreds of years will not efface from human memory. We cannot yet see how deliverance will come, or when it will come, but nothing is more certain than that every trace of Hitler's footsteps, every stain of his infected and corroding fingers will be sponged and purged and, if need be, blasted from the surface of the earth.

Hitler may turn and trample this way and that through tortured Europe. He may spread his course far and wide, and carry his curse with him: he may break into Africa or into Asia. But it is here, in this island fortress, that he will have to reckon in the end. We shall strive to resist by land and sea. We shall be on his track wherever he goes. Our air power will continue to teach the German homeland that war is not all loot and triumph.

We shall aid and stir the people of every conquered country to resistance and revolt. We shall break up and derange every effort which Hitler makes to systematize and consolidate his subjugation. He will find no peace, no rest, no halting-place, no parley. And if, driven to desperate hazards, he attempts the invasion of the British Isles, as well he may, we shall not flinch from the supreme trial. With the help of God, of which we must all feel daily conscious, we shall continue steadfast in faith and duty till our task is done.

This, then, is the message which we send forth today to all the States and nations bond or free, to all the men in all the lands who care for freedom's cause, to our allies and well-wishers in Europe, to our American friends and helpers drawing ever closer in their might across the ocean: this is the message—Lift up your hearts. All will come right. Out of the depths of sorrow and sacrifice will be born again the glory of mankind.

## "THE FOURTH CLIMACTERIC"
### FROM A BROADCAST ADDRESS ON THE GERMAN INVASION OF RUSSIA, 22 JUNE, 1941

At four o'clock this morning Hitler attacked and invaded Russia. All his usual formalities of perfidy were observed with scrupulous technique. A non-aggression treaty had been solemnly signed and was in force between the two countries. No complaint had been made by Germany of its non-fulfilment. Under its cloak of false confidence, the German armies drew up in immense strength along a line which stretches from the White Sea to the Black Sea; and their air fleets and armoured divisions slowly and methodically took their stations. Then, suddenly, without declaration of war, without even an ultimatum, German bombs rained down from the air upon the Russian cities, the German troops violated the frontiers; and an hour later the German Ambassador, who till the night before was lavishing his assurances of friendship, almost of alliance, upon the Russians, called upon the Russian Foreign Minister to tell him that a state of war existed between Germany and Russia.

Thus was repeated on a far larger scale the same kind of outrage against every form of signed compact and international faith which we have witnessed in Norway, Denmark, Holland and Belgium, and which Hitler's accomplice and jackal Mussolini so faithfully imitated in the case of Greece.

All this was no surprise to me. In fact I gave clear and precise warnings to Stalin of what was coming. I gave him warning as I have given warning to others before. I can only hope that this warning did not fall unheeded. All we know at present is that the Russian people are defending their native soil and that their leaders have called upon them to resist to the utmost.

Hitler is a monster of wickedness, insatiable in his lust for blood and plunder. Not content with having all Europe under his heel, or else terrorized into various forms of abject submission, he must now carry his work of butchery and desolation among the vast multitudes of Russia and of Asia. The terrible military machine, which we and the rest of the civilized world so foolishly, so supinely, so insensately allowed the Nazi gangsters to build up year by year from almost nothing, cannot stand idle lest it rust or fall to pieces. It must be in continual motion, grinding up human lives and trampling down the homes and the rights of hundreds of millions of men. Moreover it must be fed, not only with flesh but with oil.

So now this bloodthirsty guttersnipe must launch his mechanized armies upon new fields of slaughter, pillage and devastation. Poor as are the Russian peasants, workmen and soldiers, he must steal from them their daily bread; he must devour their harvests; he must rob them of the oil which drives their ploughs; and thus produce a famine without example in human history. And even the carnage and ruin which his victory, should he gain it—he has not gained it yet—will bring upon the Russian people, will itself be only a stepping-stone to the attempt to plunge the four or five hundred millions who live in China, and the three hundred and fifty millions who live in India, into that bottomless pit of human degradation over which the diabolic emblem of the Swastika flaunts itself. It is not too much to say here this summer evening that the lives and happiness of a thousand million additional people are now menaced with brutal Nazi violence. That is enough to make us hold our breath.

The Nazi regime is indistinguishable from the worst features of

Communism. It is devoid of all theme and principle except appetite and racial domination. It excels all forms of human wickedness in the efficiency of its cruelty and ferocious aggression. No one has been a more consistent opponent of Communism than I have for the last twenty-five years. I will unsay no word that I have spoken about it. But all this fades away before the spectacle which is now unfolding. The past with its crimes, its follies and its tragedies, flashes away. I see the Russian soldiers standing on the threshold of their native land, guarding the fields which their fathers have tilled from time immemorial. I see them guarding their homes where mothers and wives pray—ah yes, for there are times when all pray —for the safety of their loved ones, the return of the breadwinner, of their champion, of their protector. I see the ten thousand villages of Russia, where the means of existence was wrung so hardly from the soil, but where there are still primordial human joys, where maidens laugh and children play. I see advancing upon all this in hideous onslaught the Nazi war machine, with its clanking, heel-clicking, dandified Prussian officers, its crafty expert agents fresh from the cowing and tying-down of a dozen countries. I see also the dull, drilled, docile, brutish masses of the Hun soldiery plodding on like a swarm of crawling locusts. I see the German bombers and fighters in the sky, still smarting from many a British whipping, delighted to find what they believe is an easier and a safer prey.

This is no time to moralize on the follies of countries and governments which have allowed themselves to be struck down one by one, when by united action they could have saved themselves and saved the world from this catastrophe. But when I spoke a few minutes ago of Hitler's blood-lust and the hateful appetites which have impelled or lured him on his Russian adventure, I said there was one deeper motive behind his outrage. He wishes to destroy the Russian power because he hopes that if he succeeds in this, he will be able to bring back the main strength of his army and air force from the East and hurl it upon this island, which he knows he must conquer or suffer the penalty of his crimes. His invasion of Russia is no more than a prelude to an attempted invasion of the British Isles. He hopes, no doubt, that all this may be accomplished before the winter comes, and that he can overwhelm Great Britain before the fleet and air power of the United States may intervene.

He hopes that he may once again repeat, upon a greater scale than ever before, that process of destroying his enemies one by one, by which he has so long thrived and prospered, and that then the scene will be clear for the final act, without which all his conquests would be in vain—namely, the subjugation of the Western Hemisphere to his will and to his system.

## "PREPARATION—LIBERATION—ASSAULT"

### FROM THE SPEECH TO THE CANADIAN SENATE AND HOUSE OF COMMONS AT OTTAWA, BROADCAST TO THE WORLD, 30 DECEMBER, 1941

The Canadian Army now stationed in England has chafed not to find itself in contact with the enemy. But I am here to tell you that it has stood and still stands in the key position to strike at the invader should he land upon our shores. In a few months, when the invasion season returns, the Canadian Army may be engaged in one of the most frightful battles the world has ever seen, but on the other hand their presence may help to deter the enemy from attempting to fight such a battle on British soil. Although the long routine of training and preparation is undoubtedly trying to men who left prosperous farms and businesses, or other responsible civil work, inspired by an eager and ardent desire to fight the enemy, although this is trying to high-mettled temperaments, the value of the service rendered is unquestionable, and I am sure that the peculiar kind of self-sacrifice involved will be cheerfully or at least patiently endured.

We did not make this war, we did not seek it. We did all we could to avoid it. We did too much to avoid it. We went so far at times in trying to avoid it as to be almost destroyed by it when it broke upon us. But that dangerous corner has been turned, and with every month and every year that passes we shall confront the evil-doers with weapons as plentiful, as sharp, and as destructive as those with which they have sought to establish their hateful domination.

I should like to point out to you that we have not at any time asked for any mitigation in the fury or malice of the enemy. The peoples of the British Empire may love peace. They do not seek the lands or wealth of any country, but they are a tough and hardy lot. We have not journeyed all this way across the centuries, across the oceans, across the mountains, across the prairies, because we are made of sugar candy.

Look at the Londoners, the Cockneys; look at what they have stood up to. Grim and gay with their cry "We can take it", and their war-time mood of "What is good enough for anybody is good enough for us". We have not asked that the rules of the game should be modified. We shall never descend to the German and Japanese level, but if anybody likes to play rough we can play rough too. Hitler and his Nazi gang have sown the wind; let them reap the whirlwind. Neither the length of the struggle nor any form of severity which it may assume shall make us weary or shall make us quit.

There shall be no halting, or half measures, there shall be no compromise, or parley. These gangs of bandits have sought to darken the light of the world; have sought to stand between the common people of all the lands and their march forward into their inheritance. They shall themselves be cast into the pit of death and shame, and only when the earth has been cleansed and purged of their crimes and their villainy shall we turn from the task which they have forced upon us, a task which we were reluctant to undertake, but which we shall now most faithfully and punctiliously discharge. According to my sense of proportion, this is no time to speak of the hopes of the future, or the broader world which lies beyond our struggles and our victory. We have to win that world for our children. We have to win it by our sacrifices. We have not won it yet. The crisis is upon us. The power of the enemy is immense. If we were in any way to underrate the strength, the resources or the ruthless savagery of that enemy, we should jeopardize, not only our lives, for they will be offered freely, but the cause of human freedom and progress to which we have vowed ourselves and all we have. We cannot for a moment afford to relax. On the contrary we must drive ourselves forward with unrelenting zeal. In this strange, terrible world war there is a place for everyone, man and woman, old and young, hale and halt; service in a thousand forms is open. There is no room now for the dilettante, the weakling, for the shirker, or the sluggard. The mine, the factory, the dockyard, the salt sea waves, the fields to till, the home, the hospital, the chair of the scientist, the pulpit of the preacher—from the highest to the humblest tasks, all are of equal honour; all have their part to play. The enemies ranged against us, coalesced and combined against us, have asked for total war. Let us make sure they get it.

That grand old minstrel, Harry Lauder—Sir Harry Lauder, I should say, and no honour was better deserved—had a song in the last war which began, "If we all look back on the history of the past, we can just tell where we are." Let us then look back. We plunged into this war all unprepared because we had pledged our word to stand by the side of Poland, which Hitler had feloniously invaded, and in spite of a gallant resistance had soon struck down. There followed those astonishing seven months which were called on this side of the Atlantic the "phoney" war. Suddenly the explosion of pent-up German strength and preparation burst upon Norway, Denmark, Holland, and Belgium. All these absolutely blameless neutrals, to most of whom Germany up to the last moment was giving every kind of guarantee and assurance, were overrun and trampled down. The hideous massacre of Rotterdam, where 30,000 people perished, showed the ferocious barbarism in which the German Air Force revels when, as in Warsaw and later Belgrade, it is able to bomb practically undefended cities.

On top of all this came the great French catastrophe. The French Army collapsed, and the French nation was dashed into utter and, as it has so far proved, irretrievable confusion. The French Government had at their own suggestion solemnly bound themselves with us not to make a separate peace. It was their duty and it was also their interest to go to North Africa, where they would have been at the head of the French Empire. In Africa, with our aid, they would have had overwhelming sea power. They would have had the recognition of the United States, and the use of all the gold they had lodged beyond the seas. If they had done this Italy might have been driven out of the war before the end of 1940, and France would have held her place as a nation in the counsels of the Allies and at the conference table of the victors. But their generals misled them. When I warned them that Britain would fight on alone whatever they did, their generals told their Prime Minister and his divided Cabinet, "In three weeks England will have her neck wrung like a chicken." Some chicken; some neck.

# THE END OF THE
# BEGINNING

\*

## THE OUTLOOK FOR 1942
### FROM A SPEECH TO THE CENTRAL COUNCIL OF THE
### CONSERVATIVE PARTY, AT CAXTON HALL, LONDON
### 26 MARCH, 1942

I AM PERPETUALLY asked to devote more time and attention to the rebuilding of the post-war world, and measures, some of them elaborate and all of them carefully thought out, have been taken to prepare by study and planning for that most important and longed-for period. But as you will, I am sure, agree, we must be, above all things, careful that nothing diverts or distracts our thoughts or our fullest energies from the task of national self-preservation and of inter-allied duty which will require the total concentration for an indefinite period of all that we can give.

I will not therefore enter on these subjects today, except to say that a few weeks ago one of our leading intellectuals, a great thinker —and as the father of our new President once said, one of the great difficulties about great thinkers is that they so often think wrong— asked in public whether I was working for the new England or the old. It is an easy question to answer, for you as well as for myself: we are working for both. The new England, or the new Britain, for we have our Welsh and Scottish friends represented—[a voice: "And Northern Ireland"]—and Northern Ireland which we never forget—the new Britain and the old Britain have always dwelt side by side in our land, and it is by the union and inter-play of the new impulses and the great traditions both working together that we have managed to solve peacefully, yet finally, problems which have ruined for ever the unity of many a famous State.

It is by this dual process that we have contrived to build up over generations that basis of life with its rights and tolerances, its individual freedom, its collective associations, and, above all, its infinite power of self-improvement and national progress, that decent way of life which the broad masses of our people share and for which they now show themselves prepared to fight, and if need be to die.

This is a very hard war. Its numerous and fearful problems reach down to the very foundations of human society. Its scope is world wide, and it involves all nations and every man, woman, and child in them. Strategy and economics are interwoven. Sea, land, and air are but a single service. The latest refinements of science are linked with the cruelties of the Stone Age. The workshop and the fighting line are one. All may fall, all will stand together. We must aid each other, we must stand by each other.

We must confront our perils and trials with that national unity which cannot be broken, and a national force which is inexhaustible. We must confront them with resilience and ingenuity which are fearless, and above all with that inflexible will-power to endure and yet to dare for which our island race has long been renowned. Thus, and thus alone, can we be worthy champions of that grand alliance of nearly thirty States ·and nations which without our resistance would never have come into being, but which now has only to march on together until tyranny is trampled down.

## PRIME MINISTER FOR TWO YEARS
### FROM A WORLD BROADCAST, 10 MAY, 1942

The tremendous period through which we have passed has certainly been full of anxieties and exertions; it has been marked by many misfortunes and disappointments. This time two years ago the Germans were beating down Holland and Belgium by unprovoked brutal, merciless invasion, and very soon there came upon us the total defeat of France and the fatal surrender at Bordeaux. Mussolini, the Italian miscalculator, thought he saw his chance of a cheap and easy triumph, and rich plunder for no fighting. He struck at the back of a dying France, and at what he believed was a doomed Britain. We were left alone—our quarter of a million Dunkirk troops saved, only disarmed; ourselves, as yet unarmed—to face the might of victorious Germany, to face also the carefully saved-up strength of an Italy which then still ranked as a first-class Power.

Here at home in this island, invasion was near; the Mediterranean was closed to us; the long route round the Cape, where General Smuts stands on guard, alone was open; our small, ill-equipped forces in Egypt and the Sudan seemed to await destruction. All the world, even our best friends, thought that our end had come. Accordingly, we prepared ourselves to conquer or to perish. We were united in that solemn, majestic hour; we were all equally resolved at least to go down fighting. We cast calculation to the winds; no wavering voice was heard; we hurled defiance at our foes; we faced our duty, and, by the mercy of God, we were preserved.

It fell to me in those days to express the sentiments and resolves of the British nation in that supreme crisis of its life. That was to me an honour far beyond any dreams or ambitions I had ever nursed, and it is one that cannot be taken away. For a whole year after the fall of France we stood alone, keeping the flag of freedom flying, and the hopes of the world alive. We conquered the Italian Empire, we destroyed or captured almost all Mussolini's African army; we liberated Abyssinia; we have so far successfully protected Palestine, Syria, Persia and Iraq from German designs. We have suffered grievous reverses in going to the aid of the heroic Greeks; we bore unflinching many a heavy blow abroad, and still more in our cities here at home; and all this time, cheered and helped by President Roosevelt and the United States, we stood alone, neither faltering nor flagging.

Where are we now? Can anyone doubt that if we are worthy of it, as we shall be, we have in our hands our own future? As in the last war, so in this, we are moving through many reverses and defeats to complete and final victory. We have only to endure and to persevere, to conquer. Now we are no longer unarmed; we are well armed. Now we are not alone; we have mighty allies, bound irrevocably by solemn faith and common interests to stand with us in the ranks of the United Nations. There can only be one end. When it will come, or how it will come, I cannot tell. But, when we survey the overwhelming resources which are at our disposal, once they are fully marshalled and developed—as they can be, as they will be—we may stride forward into the unknown with growing confidence.

During the time that we were all alone, we were steadily growing stronger. He would have been a bold man, however, who in those days would have put down in black and white exactly how we were going to win. But, as has happened before in our island history, by remaining steadfast and unyielding—stubborn, if you will—against a Continental tyrant, we reached the moment when that tyrant made a fatal blunder. Dictators, as well as democracies and parliamentary governments, make mistakes sometimes. Indeed, when the whole story is told, I believe it will be found that the Dictators, for all their preparations and prolonged scheming, have made greater mistakes than the Democracies they have assailed. Even Hitler makes mistakes sometimes. In June last, without the slightest provocation, and in breach of a pact of non-aggression, he invaded the lands of the Russian people. At that time he had the strongest army in the world, trained in war, flushed with incredible unbroken success, and equipped with limitless munitions and the most modern weapons. He had also secured for himself the advantages of surprise and treachery. Thus he drove the youth and manhood of the German nation forward into Russia.

The Russians, under their warrior chief, Stalin, sustained losses which no other country or government has ever borne in so short a time and lived. But they, like us, were resolved never to give in. They poured out their own blood upon their native soil. They kept their faces to the foe. From the very first day to the end of the year, and on till tonight, they fought with unflinching valour. And, from the very first day when they were attacked, when no one could tell how things would go, we made a brotherhood with them, and a solemn compact to destroy Nazidom and all its works. Then Hitler made his second grand blunder. He forgot about the winter. There is a winter, you know, in Russia. For a good many months the temperature is apt to fall very low. There is snow, there is frost, and all that. Hitler forgot about this Russian winter. He must have been very loosely educated. We all heard about it at school; but he forgot it. I have never made such a bad mistake as that. So winter came, and fell upon his ill-clad armies, and with the winter came the valiant Russian counter-attacks. No one can say with certainty how many millions of Germans have already perished in Russia and its snows. Certainly more have perished than were killed in the whole four and a quarter years of the last war. That is probably an understatement. So besotted is this man in his lust for blood and conquest, so blasting is the power he wields over the lives of Germans, that he even blurted out the other day that his armies would be better clothed and his locomotives better prepared for their second winter in Russia than they were for their first.

There was an admission about the length of the war that struck a chill into German hearts as cold as the icy winds of Russia. What will be the sufferings of the German manhood in this new blood-bath? What is there in front of Hitler now? Certain it is that the Russian armies are stronger than they were last year, that they have learnt by hard experience to fight the Germans in the field, that they are well-equipped, and that their constancy and courage are unquenched. That is what is in front of Hitler. What is he leaving behind him? He leaves behind him a Europe starving and in chains; a Europe in which his execution squads are busy in a dozen countries every day; a Europe which has learned to hate the Nazi name as no name has ever been hated in the recorded history of mankind; a Europe burning for revolt whenever the opportunity comes.

But this is not all he has left behind. We are on his tracks, and so is the great Republic of the United States. Already the Royal Air Force has set about it; the British, and presently the American, bombing offensive against Germany will be one of the principal features in this year's world war. Now is the time to use our increasingly superior air strength, to strike hard and continually at the home front in Germany, from which so much evil has leaked out upon the world, and which is the foundation of the whole enormous German invasion of Russia. Now, while the German armies will be bleeding and burning up their strength against the two-thousand-mile Russian line, and when the news of casualties by hundreds of thousands is streaming back to the German Reich, now is the time to bring home to the German people the wickedness of their rulers, by destroying under their very eyes the factories and seaports on which their war effort depends.

If we look back today over the course of the war as it has so far unfolded, we can see that it seems to divide itself into four very

Winston Churchill, Cambridge, 1948, after General Smuts had conferred on
him the honorary degree of Doctor of Letters

With Mrs. Churchill at Dover, 1946 (as Lord Warden of the Cinque Ports).
(*Below*) With her on his seventy-seventh birthday

Leader of the Conservative Party, 1951

On his eightieth birthday, Sir Winston arrives at Westminster Hall for a presentation ceremony

At 10 Downing Street, Queen Elizabeth as the Churchills' dinner guest in April, 1955

clearly defined chapters. The first ended with the over-running by the Nazis of Western Europe and with the fall of France. The second chapter, Britain alone, ended with Hitler's attack upon Russia. I will call the third chapter, which then began, "the Russian glory". May it long continue! The fourth chapter opened at Pearl Harbour, when the military party in Japan treacherously attacked the United States and Great Britain in the Far East. That is where we are now.

The aggression of Italy in 1940 had carried the war from Europe to Africa. The aggression of Japan has involved all Asia, including unconquerable China, and in one way or another has drawn in, or will draw in, the whole of the American continent. Thus the struggle has become world wide, and the fate of all states and nations and their future is at stake. This latest chapter—universal war—confronts us with many difficulties and immense complications. But is there any thoughtful sensible person who cannot see how vastly and decisively the awful balances have turned to the advantage of the cause of freedom? It is true that the Japanese, taking advantage of our preoccupations elsewhere, and of the fact that the United States had striven for so long to keep the peace, have seized more easily and more quickly than they expected their lands of booty and desire in. the East Indian Archipelago. Henceforward they will find resistance stiffening on all their widely-spread fronts. They can ill afford losses such as those they have sustained in the naval action of the Coral Sea; so far we have no detailed accounts, but it is obvious, if only from the lies the Japanese have felt compelled to tell about the sinking of a battleship of the *Warspite* class, that a most vigorous and successful battle has been fought by the United States and Australian naval forces.

The Japanese war-lords cannot be indifferent to the losses of aircraft inflicted upon them at so many points, and particularly off the northern coasts of Australia, and in their repulse at Colombo and Trincomalee. At the start the pent-up, saved-up resources of Japan were bound to prevail in the Far Eastern theatre; but the strength of the United States, expressed in units of modern war power, actual and potential, is alone many times greater than the power of Japan. And we also shall make our contribution to the final defeat and punishment of this ambitious and greedy nation. Time will, however, be needed before the true strengths on either side of the

705

Eastern war become manifest. I am not prone to make predictions, but I have no doubt tonight that British and American sea power will grip and hold the Japanese, and that overwhelming air power, covering vigorous military operations, will lay them low. This would come to pass, of course, very much sooner, should anything happen to Hitler in Europe.

Therefore tonight I give you a message of good cheer. You deserve it, and the facts endorse it. But be it good cheer or be it bad cheer will make no difference to us; we shall drive on to the end, and do our duty, win or die. God helping us, we can do no other.

## "KEEP RIGHT ON TO THE END"
### FROM A SPEECH IN THE USHER HALL, EDINBURGH, WHEN THE PRIME MINISTER RECEIVED THE FREEDOM OF THE CITY, 12 OCTOBER, 1942

Our enemies have been more talkative lately. Ribbentrop, Göring and Hitler have all been making speeches which are of interest because they reveal with considerable frankness their state of mind.

There is one note which rings through all these speeches; it can be clearly heard above their customary boastings and threats—the dull, low, whining note of fear. They are all speeches of men conscious of their guilt and conscious also of the law. How different from the tone of 1940 when France was struck down, when Western Europe was subjugated, when Mussolini hastened to stab us in the back, when Britain stood all alone, the sole champion in arms for the freedom and inheritance of mankind! How different are these plaintive speeches and expostulations from what we used to hear in those days!

Evidently something has happened in these two years to make these evildoers feel that aggression, war, bloodshed, the trampling down of the weak, may not be after all the whole story. There may be another side to the account. It is a long account, and it is becoming pretty clear that the day is coming when it will have to be settled. The most striking and curious part of Hitler's speech was his complaint that no one pays sufficient attention to his victories.

"Look at all the victories I have won," he exclaims in effect. "Look at all the countries I have invaded and struck down. Look at the thousands of kilometres that I have advanced into the lands of other people. Look at the booty I have gathered, and all the men I have killed and captured. Contrast these exploits with the performances of the Allies. Why are they not down-hearted and dismayed? How do they dare to keep up their spirits in the face of my great successes and their many misfortunes?"

I have not quoted his actual words. I have given their meaning and their sense. That is his complaint. That is the question which puzzles him and angers him. It strikes a chill into his marrow, because in his heart he knows that with all his tremendous victories and vast conquests his fortunes have declined, his prospects have darkened to an immeasurable degree in the last two years, while at the same time Britain, the United States, Russia, and China have moved forward through tribulation and sorrow, steadily forward, steadily onward, from strength to strength. He sees with chagrin and amazement that our defeats are but stepping-stones to victory, and that his victories are only the stepping-stones to ruin.

It was apparent to me that this bad man saw quite clearly the shadow of slowly and remorselessly approaching doom, and he railed at fortune for mocking him with the glitter of fleeting success. But, after all, the explanation is not so difficult.

When peaceful nations like the British and the Americans, very careless in peace time about their defences, carefree, unsuspecting nations, peoples who have never known defeat—improvident nations, I will say, feckless nations, nations who despise the military art and thought war so wicked that it could never happen again— when nations like these are set upon by highly organized, heavily armed conspirators, planning and calculating in secret for years on end, exalting war as the highest form of human effort, glorifying slaughter and aggression, prepared and trained to the last point science and discipline can carry them, is it not natural that the peaceful, unprepared, improvident peoples should suffer terribly and that the wicked, scheming aggressors should have their reign of savage exaltation?

Ah! But that is not the end of the story. It is only the first chapter. If the great, peaceful Democracies could survive the first few years of the aggressors' attack, another chapter had to be written. It is to that chapter we shall come in due time.

It will ever be the glory of this island and its Empire that we stood alone for one whole year of mortal peril, and gained the time for the good cause to arm, to organize and slowly bring the conjoined, united, irresistible forces of outraged civilization to bear upon the criminals. That is our greatest glory.

Surveying both sides of the account—the good and the bad, with equal composure and coolness—we must see that we have reached a stern and sombre moment in the war, one which calls in a high degree for firmness of spirit and constancy of soul.

The excitement and the emotion of those great days when we stood alone and unaided against what seemed overwhelming odds and, single-handed, saved the future of the world, are not present now. We are surrounded by a concourse of governments and nations, all of us bound together in solemn unbreakable alliance, bound together by ties not only of honour but of self-preservation. We are able to plan our slow but sure march onward. Deadly dangers still beset us. Weariness, complacency, or discord, squabbles over petty matters, would mar our prospects.

We must all drive ourselves to the utmost limit of our strength. We must preserve and refine our sense of proportion. We must strive to combine the virtues of wisdom and of daring. We must move forward together, united and inexorable.

Thus, with God's blessing, the hopes which are now justified, which we are now entitled to feel, will not fail or wither. The light is broadening on the track, and the light is brighter too. Among the qualities for which Scotland is renowned, steadfastness holds perhaps the highest place.

Be steadfast, then, that is the message which I bring to you, that is my invocation to the Scottish people, here in this ancient capital city, one of whose burgesses I now have the honour to be. Let me use the words of your famous minstrel [Sir Harry Lauder]—he is here today—words which have given comfort and renewed strength to many a burdened heart:

"Keep right on to the end of the road,
Keep right on to the end."

# "THE END OF THE BEGINNING"

## FROM A SPEECH AT THE LORD MAYOR'S DAY LUNCHEON AT THE MANSION HOUSE, LONDON, 10 NOVEMBER, 1942

At this time our thoughts turn towards France, groaning in bondage under the German heel. Many ask themselves the question: Is France finished? Is that long and famous history, adorned by so many manifestations of genius and valour, bearing with it so much that is precious to culture and civilization, and above all to the liberties of mankind—is all that now to sink for ever into the ocean of the past, or will France rise again and resume her rightful place in the structure of what may one day be again the family of Europe? I declare to you here, on this considerable occasion, even now when misguided or suborned Frenchmen are firing upon their rescuers, I declare to you my faith that France will rise again. While there are men like General de Gaulle and all those who follow him—and they are legion throughout France—and men like General Giraud, that gallant warrior whom no prison can hold, while there are men like those to stand forward in the name and in the cause of France, my confidence in the future of France is sure.

For ourselves we have no wish but to see France free and strong, with her Empire gathered round her and with Alsace-Lorraine restored. We covet no French possession; we have no acquisitive appetites or ambitions in North Africa or any other part of the world. We have not entered this war for profit or expansion, but only for honour and to do our duty in defending the right.

Let me, however, make this clear, in case there should be any mistake about it in any quarter. We mean to hold our own. I have not become the King's First Minister in order to preside over the liquidation of the British Empire. For that task, if ever it were prescribed, someone else would have to be found, and, under democracy, I suppose the nation would have to be consulted. I am proud to be a member of that vast commonwealth and society of nations and communities gathered in and around the ancient British monarchy, without which the good cause might well have perished from the face of the earth. Here we are, and here we stand, a veritable rock of salvation in this drifting world.

709

# ONWARDS TO VICTORY

★

## THE DESERT ARMY

A SPEECH TO THE MEN OF THE EIGHTH ARMY AT TRIPOLI
3 FEBRUARY, 1943

GENERAL MONTGOMERY and men of the Joint Headquarters of
the Eighth Army,

The last time I saw this army was in the closing days of August
on those sandy and rocky bluffs near Alamein and the Ruweisat
ridge, when it was apparent from all the signs that Rommel was
about to make his final thrust on Alexandria and Cairo. Then all
was to be won or lost. Now I come to you a long way from Alamein,
and I find this army and its famous commander with a record of
victory behind it which has undoubtedly played a decisive part in
altering the whole character of the war.

The fierce and well fought battle of Alamein, the blasting through
of the enemy's seaward flank, and the thunderbolt of the armoured
attack, irretrievably broke the army which Rommel had boasted
would conquer Egypt, and upon which the German and Italian
peoples had set their hopes. Thereafter and ever since, in these
remorseless three months, you have chased this hostile army and
driven it from pillar to post over a distance of more than 1,400
miles—in fact, as far as from London to Moscow. You have altered
the face of the war in a most remarkable way.

What it has meant in the skill and organization of movement and
manoeuvres, what it has meant in the tireless endurance and self-
denial of the troops and in the fearless leadership displayed in action,
can be appreciated only by those who were actually on the spot.
But I must tell you that the fame of the Desert Army has spread
throughout the world.

After the surrender of Tobruk, there was a dark period when
many people, not knowing us, not knowing the British and the
nations of the British Empire, were ready to take a disparaging

710

view. But now everywhere your work is spoken of with respect and admiration. When I was with the Chief of the Imperial General Staff at Casablanca and with the President of the United States, the arrival of the Desert Army in Tripoli was a new factor which influenced the course of our discussions and opened up hopeful vistas for the future. You are entitled to know these things, and to dwell upon them with that satisfaction which men in all modesty feel when a great work has been finally done. You have rendered a high service to your country and the common cause.

It must have been a tremendous experience driving forward day after day over this desert which it has taken me this morning more than six hours to fly at two hundred miles an hour. You were pursuing a broken enemy, dragging on behind you this ever-lengthening line of communications, carrying the whole art of desert warfare to perfection. In the words of the old hymn, you have "nightly pitched your moving tents a day's march nearer home". Yes, not only in the march of the army but in the progress of the war you have brought home nearer. I am here to thank you on behalf of His Majesty's Government of the British Isles and of all our friends the world over.

Hard struggles lie ahead. Rommel, the fugitive of Egypt, Cyrenaica, and Tripolitania, in a non-stop race of 1,400 miles, is now trying to present himself as the deliverer of Tunisia. Along the Eastern coast of Tunisia are large numbers of German and Italian troops, not yet equipped to their previous standard, but growing stronger. On the other side, another great operation, planned in conjunction with your advance, has carried the First British Army, our American comrades, and the French armies to within thirty or forty miles of Bizerta and Tunis. Therefrom a military situation arises which everyone can understand.

The days of your victories are by no means at an end, and with forces which march from different quarters we may hope to achieve the final destruction or expulsion from the shores of Africa of every armed German or Italian. You must have felt relief when, after those many a hundred miles of desert, you came once more into a green land with trees and grass, and I do not think you will lose that advantage. As you go forward on further missions that will fall to your lot, you will fight in countries which will present

711

undoubtedly serious tactical difficulties, but which none the less will not have that grim character of desert war which you have known how to endure and how to overcome.

Let me then assure you, soldiers and airmen, that your fellow-countrymen regard your joint work with admiration and gratitude, and that after the war when a man is asked what he did it will be quite sufficient for him to say, "I marched and fought with the Desert Army." And when history is written and all the facts are known, your feats will gleam and glow and will be a source of song and story long after we who are gathered here have passed away.

# THE SINEWS OF PEACE

★

A SPEECH TO WESTMINSTER COLLEGE, FULTON, MISSOURI, 5 MARCH, 1946

WE MUST never cease to proclaim in fearless tones the great principles of freedom and the rights of man which are the joint inheritance of the English-speaking world and which through Magna Carta, the Bill of Rights, the Habeas Corpus, trial by jury, and the English common law find their most famous expression in the American Declaration of Independence.

All this means that the people of any country have the right, and should have the power by constitutional action, by free unfettered elections, with secret ballot, to choose or change the character or form of government under which they dwell; that freedom of speech and thought should reign; that courts of justice, independent of the executive, unbiased by any party, should administer laws which have received the broad assent of large majorities or are consecrated by time and custom. Here are the title deeds of freedom which should lie in every cottage home. Here is the message of the

British and American peoples to mankind. Let us preach what we practise—let us practise what we preach.

Now I come to the crux of what I have travelled here to say. Neither the sure prevention of war, nor the continuous rise of world organization will be gained without what I have called the fraternal association of the English-speaking peoples. This means a special relationship between the British Commonwealth and Empire and the United States. This is no time for generalities, and I will venture to be precise. Fraternal association requires not only the growing friendship and mutual understanding between our two vast but kindred systems of society, but the continuance of the intimate relationship between our military advisers, leading to common study of potential dangers, the similarity of weapons and manuals of instructions, and to the interchange of officers and cadets at technical colleges. It should carry with it the continuance of the present facilities for mutual security by the joint use of all Naval and Air Force bases in the possession of either country all over the world. This would perhaps double the mobility of the American Navy and Air Force. It would greatly expand that of the British Empire Forces and it might well lead, if and as the world calms down, to important financial savings. Already we use together a large number of islands; more may well be entrusted to our joint care in the near future.

The United States has already a Permanent Defence Agreement with the Dominion of Canada, which is so devotedly attached to the British Commonwealth and Empire. This Agreement is more effective than many of those which have often been made under formal alliances. This principle should be extended to all British Commonwealths with full reciprocity. Thus, whatever happens, and thus only, shall we be secure ourselves and able to work together for the high and simple causes that are dear to us and bode no ill to any. Eventually there may come—I feel eventually there will come —the principle of common citizenship, but that we may be content to leave to destiny, whose outstretched arm many of us can already clearly see.

The safety of the world requires a new unity in Europe, from which no nation should be permanently outcast. It is from the quarrels of the strong parent races in Europe that the world wars we have witnessed, or which occurred in former times, have sprung. Twice in our own lifetime we have seen the United States, against their wishes and their traditions, against arguments, the force of which it is impossible not to comprehend, drawn by irresistible forces into these wars in time to secure the victory of the good cause, but only after frightful slaughter and devastation had occurred. Twice the United States has had to send several millions of its young men across the Atlantic to find the war; but now war can find any nation, wherever it may dwell between dusk and dawn. Surely we should work with conscious purpose for a grand pacification of Europe, within the structure of the United Nations and in accordance with its Charter. That I feel is an open cause of policy of very great importance.

In front of the iron curtain which lies across Europe are other causes for anxiety. In Italy the Communist Party is seriously hampered by having to support the Communist-trained Marshal Tito's claims to former Italian territory at the head of the Adriatic. Nevertheless the future of Italy hangs in the balance. Again one cannot imagine a regenerated Europe without a strong France. All my public life I have worked for a strong France and I never lost faith in her destiny, even in the darkest hours. I will not lose faith now. However, in a great number of countries, far from the Russian frontiers and throughout the world, Communist fifth columns are established and work in complete unity and absolute obedience to the directions they receive from the Communist centre. Except in the British Commonwealth and in the United States where Communism is in its infancy, the Communist parties or fifth columns constitute a growing challenge and peril to Christian civilization. These are sombre facts for anyone to have to recite on the morrow of a victory gained by so much splendid comradeship in arms and in the cause of freedom and democracy; but we should be most unwise not to face them squarely while time remains.

I repulse the idea that a new war is inevitable; still more that it is imminent. It is because I am sure that our fortunes are still in our own hands and that we hold the power to save the future, that I feel the duty to speak out now that I have the occasion and the opportunity to do so. I do not believe that Soviet Russia desires war. What they desire is the fruits of war and the indefinite expansion of their power and doctrines. But what we have to consider here today while time remains is the permanent prevention of war and the establishment of conditions of freedom and democracy as rapidly as possible in all countries. Our difficulties and dangers will not be removed by closing our eyes to them. They will not be removed by mere waiting to see what happens; nor will they be removed by a policy of appeasement. What is needed is a settlement, and the longer this is delayed, the more difficult it will be and the greater our dangers will become.

Last time I saw it all coming and cried aloud to my own fellow-countrymen and to the world, but no one paid any attention. Up till the year 1933 or even 1935, Germany might have been saved from the awful fate which has overtaken her and we might all have been spared the miseries Hitler let loose upon mankind. There never was a war in all history easier to prevent by timely action than the one which has just desolated such great areas of the globe. It could have been prevented in my belief without the firing of a single shot, and Germany might be powerful, prosperous and honoured today; but no one would listen and one by one we were all sucked into the awful whirlpool. We surely must not let that happen again. This can only be achieved by reaching now, in 1946, a good understanding on all points with Russia under the general authority of the United Nations Organization and by the maintenance of that good understanding through many peaceful years, by the world instrument, supported by the whole strength of the English-speaking world and all its connexions. There is the solution which I respectfully offer to you in this Address to which I have given the title "The Sinews of Peace".

Let no man underrate the abiding power of the British Empire and Commonwealth. Because you see the 46 millions in our island harassed about their food supply, of which they only grow one half, even in war-time, or because we have difficulty in restarting our industries and export trade after six years of passionate war effort, do not suppose that we shall not come through these dark years of privation as we have come through the glorious years of agony, or that half a century from now, you will not see 70 or 80 millions of Britons spread about the world and united in defence of our traditions, our way of life, and of the world causes which you and we espouse. If

715

the population of the English-speaking Commonwealths be added
to that of the United States with all that such co-operation implies
in the air, on the sea, all over the globe and in science and in industry,
and in moral force, there will be no quivering, precarious balance of
power to offer its temptation to ambition or adventure. On the
contrary, there will be an overwhelming assurance of security. If
we adhere faithfully to the Charter of the United Nations and walk
forward in sedate and sober strength seeking no one's land or treasure,
seeking to lay no arbitrary control upon the thoughts of men; if all
British moral and material forces and convictions are joined with
your own in fraternal association, the highroads of the future will
be clear, not only for us but for all, not only for our time, but for
a century to come.

## FROM A SPEECH TO
## THE GENERAL ASSEMBLY OF VIRGINIA
### 8 MARCH, 1946

It is upon the future rather than upon the past that I wish to rest
this morning. In these last years of my life there is a message of
which I conceive myself to be a bearer. It is a very simple message
which can be well understood by the people of both our countries.
It is that we should stand together. We should stand together in
malice to none, in greed for nothing but in defence of those causes
which we hold dear not only for our own benefit, but because we
believe they mean the honour and the happiness of long generations
of men. We ought, as I said to the Congress of the United States in
a dark hour in 1941, to walk together in majesty and peace. That I
am sure is the wish of the overwhelming majority of the 200 million
Britons and Americans who are spread about the globe. That this
is our destiny, or, as most of us would put it, the Will of God,
seems sure and certain. How it is to be expressed, in what way and
in what hour it is to be achieved, I cannot tell.

We must find the means and the method of working together
not only in times of war and mortal anguish but in times of peace
with all its bewilderments and clamour and clatter of tongues. It is
in the years of peace that wars are prevented and that those foundations are laid upon which the noble structures of the future can be

built. But peace will not be preserved without the virtues that make victory possible in war. Peace will not be preserved by pious sentiments expressed in terms of platitudes or by official grimaces and diplomatic correctitude, however desirable this may be from time to time. It will not be preserved by casting aside in dangerous years the panoply of warlike strength. There must be earnest thought. There must also be faithful perseverance and foresight. Greatheart must have his sword and armour to guard the pilgrims on their way. Above all, among the English-speaking peoples, there must be the union of hearts based upon conviction and common ideals. That is what I offer. That is what I seek.

## A SPEECH AT ZÜRICH UNIVERSITY
### 19 SEPTEMBER, 1946

I wish to speak to you today about the tragedy of Europe. This noble continent, comprising on the whole the fairest and the most cultivated regions of the earth, enjoying a temperate and equable climate, is the home of all the great parent races of the western world. It is the fountain of Christian faith and Christian ethics. It is the origin of most of the culture, arts, philosophy and science both of ancient and modern times. If Europe were once united in the sharing of its common inheritance, there would be no limit to the happiness, to the prosperity and glory which its three or four hundred million people would enjoy. Yet it is from Europe that have sprung that series of frightful nationalistic quarrels, originated by the Teutonic nations, which we have seen even in this twentieth century, and in our own lifetime, wreck the peace and mar the prospects of all mankind.

Yet all the while there is a remedy which, if it were generally and spontaneously adopted, would as if by a miracle transform the whole scene, and would in a few years make all Europe, or the greater part of it, as free and as happy as Switzerland is today. What is this sovereign remedy? It is to re-create the European Family, or as much of it as we can, and provide it with a structure under which it can dwell in peace, in safety and in freedom. We must build a kind of United States of Europe. In this way only will hundreds of millions of toilers be able to regain the simple joys and hopes which make life worth living. The process is simple. All that is needed is the resolve of hundreds of millions of men and women to do right instead of wrong and gain as their reward blessing instead of cursing.

And why should there not be a European group which could give a sense of enlarged patriotism and common citizenship to the distracted people of this turbulent and mighty continent, and why should it not take its rightful place with other great groupings in shaping the destinies of men? In order that this should be accomplished there must be an act of faith in which millions of families speaking many languages must consciously take part.

Our constant aim must be to build and fortify the strength of U.N.O. Under and within that world concept we must re-create the European family in a regional structure called, it may be, the United States of Europe. The first step is to form a Council of Europe. If at first all the States of Europe are not willing or able to join the Union, we must nevertheless proceed to assemble and combine those who will and those who can. The salvation of the common people of every race and of every land from war or servitude must be established on solid foundations and must be guarded by the readiness of all men and women to die rather than submit to tyranny. In all this urgent work, France and Germany must take the lead together. Great Britain, the British Commonwealth of Nations, mighty America, and I trust Soviet Russia—for then indeed all would be well—must be the friends and sponsors of the new Europe and must champion its right to live and shine.

# "UNITY, VIGILANCE AND FIDELITY"

## FROM A SPEECH ON FOREIGN AFFAIRS DELIVERED
## IN THE HOUSE OF COMMONS 11 MAY, 1953

I venture to read to the House again some words which I wrote eight years ago, 29 April, 1945, in a telegram I sent to Mr. Stalin:

"There is not much comfort," I said, "in looking into a future where you and the countries you dominate, plus the Communist Parties in many other States, are all drawn up on one side, and those who rally to the English-speaking nations and their associates or Dominions are on the other. It is quite obvious that their quarrel would tear the world to pieces, and that all of us leading men on either side who had anything to do with that would be shamed before history. Even embarking on a long period of suspicions, of abuse and counter-abuse, and of opposing policies would be a disaster hampering the great developments of world prosperity for the masses which are attainable only by our trinity. I hope there is no word or phrase in this outpouring of my heart to you which un-wittingly gives offence. If so, let me know. But do not, I beg you, my friend Stalin, underrate the divergencies which are opening about matters which you may think are small to us but which are symbolic of the way the English-speaking democracies look at life." I feel exactly the same about it today.

I must make it plain that, in spite of all the uncertainties and confusion in which world affairs are plunged, I believe that a conference on the highest level should take place between the leading Powers without long delay. This conference should not be overhung by a ponderous or rigid agenda, or led into mazes and jungles of technical details, zealously contested by hordes of experts and officials drawn up in vast, cumbrous array. The conference should be confined to the smallest number of Powers and persons possible. It should meet with a measure of informality and a still greater measure of privacy and seclusion. It might well be that no hard-faced agree-ments would be reached, but there might be a general feeling among those gathered together that they might do something better than tear the human race, including themselves, into bits.

If there is not at the summit of the nations the will to win the greatest prize and the greatest honour ever offered to mankind, doom-laden responsibility will fall upon those who now possess the power to decide. At the worst the participants in the meeting would have established more intimate contacts. At the best we might have a generation of peace.

I have now finished my survey of the world scene as I see it and as I feel about it today. I express my thanks to the House for the great consideration with which I have been treated. I hope I have contributed a few thoughts which may make for peace and help a gentler breeze to blow upon this weary earth. But there is one thing I have to say before I end, and without it all the hopes I have ventured to indulge would be utterly vain. Whatever differences of opinion may be between friends and allies about particular problems or the general scale of values and sense of proportion which we should adopt, there is one fact which stands out overwhelmingly in its simplicity and force. If it is made good every hope is pardonable. If it is not made good all hopes fall together.

This would be the most fatal moment for the free nations to relax their comradeship and preparations. To fail to maintain our defence effort up to the limit of our strength would be to paralyse every beneficial tendency towards peace both in Europe and in Asia. For us to become divided among ourselves because of divergencies of opinion or local interests, or to slacken our combined efforts, would be to end for ever such new hope as may have broken upon mankind and lead instead to their general ruin and enslavement. Unity, vigilance and fidelity are the only foundations upon which hope can live.